Praise for *Walter Fuller*

Winnington's highly readable and carefully researched biography rescues from historical neglect both an intelligent, creative, versatile, and appealing figure, the well-connected yet self-effacing Walter Fuller, and his no-less-remarkable sisters. It also sheds fascinating light on a surprising variety of networks – those of student politics, journalism, theatre, musical performance, peace activism, socialist campaigning, and radio broadcasting – on both sides of the Atlantic during the first three decades of the twentieth century.

Martin Ceadel, Professor of Politics, University of Oxford

Walter Fuller, though too little known today, left an indelible mark on the twentieth-century Atlantic world. We are fortunate indeed to have Peter Winnington's biography.

John Fabian Witt
Allen H. Duffy Class of 1960 Professor of Law, Yale Law School

WALTER FULLER

Other books by the same author:
Vast Alchemies (2000); reissued,
revised and expanded, with illustrations, as
Mervyn Peake's Vast Alchemies (2009).
The Voice of the Heart: the working of Mervyn Peake's imagination (2006)
Harriet Martineau, Miss J, and Ellen McKee (2019)

Books edited:
Mervyn Peake: the man and his art (2006)
Miracle Enough: papers on the works of Mervyn Peake (2013)
Kissing the Joy: the autobiography of Rosalinde Fuller OBE
A History of Music in the British Isles
(two volumes) by Laurence Bristow-Smith (2017)

Author information:
https://gpeterwinnington.com/

Walter Fuller

the man who had ideas

G. Peter Winnington

◆

The Letterworth Press

Published in Switzerland by the Letterworth Press
http://www.TheLetterworthPress.org

Printed by Lightning Source

© G. Peter Winnington 2014
The rights attributed in the Acknowledgements
constitute an extension of this copyright notice

Whilst every care has been taken to ensure the accuracy of the information in this book, the publisher cannot accept responsibility for any mistakes that may inadvertently have been included.
Similarly, every effort has been made to contact and acknowledge copyright holders of texts quoted and illustrative material.
If this has been unsuccessful, copyright owners are invited to contact the publisher directly.

ISBN 978-2-9700654-2-5 (hard cover)
978-2-9700654-3-2 (soft cover)

3 5 7 9 8 6 4

Contents

	Illustrations	ix
	Acknowledgements	xi
	Introduction	xvii
1	Editor	1
2	Peter Pan	29
3	Impresario	63
4	Peace Activist	105
5	Propagandist	137
6	Husband	181
7	Father	213
8	New Worlder	237
9	Rewrite Man	281
10	Radio Man	313
11	Epilogue	359
	Sources	381
	References	391
	Index	403

Illustrations

Walter Fuller as a medical student	2
Walter Fuller leads the Students' Representative Council. A cartoon by Hamilton Irving	7
Walter in his early thirties	30
John Ross, Mohammed Hussein, Gilgal, Walter, Weekes, and Patrick Geddes	47
Page 654 of the *Musical Times* for 1 October 1911	62
Dorothy, Rosalind and Cynthia by Alice Boughton	64
The Fuller Sisters by Durr Friedley	73
Walter watches from the wings as his sisters say goodbye to Maurice Browne, drawn by Dorothy	83
Two admirers with May flowers for the Fuller sisters: a story in three sketches by Dorothy	103
Jane Addams and Mary McDowell in 1917	106
US Delegates to the International Conference of Women at the Hague, 1915	106
The Wraggle-Taggle Gypsies, by Dorothy	134
Crystal Eastman, ca. 1913	138
The image of Jingo in the US newspapers	169
Crystal Eastman on 29 March 1916	182
Walter Fuller in 1916	183
An 'Allegorical sketch of Crystal as the Goddess of Peace' etc., by Dorothy	193
The young Max Eastman	198
The masthead of *Four Lights*	208
Walter holding Jeffrey	214
Advertisement for the People's Council	238
Walter in the 1920s	282
Walter listening to the wireless	314
Savoy Hill, the first home of the BBC	336

Illustrations

Three generations: Mr Fuller, Walter, and Jeffrey	346
Rosalind in the sea	360
Walter with Annis and Jeffrey in 1927	371
Riss in 1938	373

Further images relevant to this book,
and most of Walter Fuller's signed writings,
will be found on the dedicated page
of the publisher's website

http://www.TheLetterworthPress.org/WalterFuller/index.html

Acknowledgements

> For Carol Odell (1921–2013)
> who did her best to preserve
> the memory of the Fuller Sisters
> and their brother Walter

As this book is largely based on unpublished documents, it owes a great deal to the people who generously made them available to me. In particular, Carol Odell shared with me her transcriptions of many family letters in her possession. The words and drawings by her mother Dorothy Fuller are copyright her estate, represented by her executrix Jessica North. The words of Dorothy's sisters – Oriska (Riss) Ward, Rosalind(e) Fuller and Cynthia Dehn – are copyright their respective estates, represented by Conrad Dehn QC. The words of Walter Fuller and Crystal Eastman are copyright their grandchildren, represented by Anne Fuller and Rebecca Lesh (née Young). The words of Arthur Dakyns and the writings of his daughter Janine are copyright his son, Andrew Dakyns. The poem, 'Five Souls', and letter by W. N. (Trilby) Ewer are copyright Biddy Greene and Paddy Ewer. To each I address my sincere thanks for permission to quote.

I gratefully acknowledge the supply of pictures of Walter by Anne and Cordie Fuller, of Dorothy's drawings by Carol Odell, of Alice Boughton's photograph of the Fuller Sisters by one of Dorothy's daughters (who has declined to be named), and of Arnold Genthe's portrait of Crystal by the Library of Congress, and I thank them all for permitting me to reproduce them here.

Not in a lifetime could I have carried out this research without Google's search engine and the detailed finding aids to archived documents that libraries that have posted on the internet. (Britain lags behind both in preserving such documents and publishing indexes to them. More than once I was obliged to travel to England, or pay someone on the spot, simply to con-

Acknowledgements

sult an index or a list.) I am also grateful to the persons and institutions who have generously shared family histories, letters, and photographs by posting them on the net.

More specifically, I wish to thank the librarians and archivists who, time after time, patiently answered my questions, brought out dusty documents and copied them, or sent me microfilms. In the United States and Canada in particular, they have proved unfailingly helpful and willing to go out of their way to provide me with what I needed.* For help and (where applicable) permission to quote from documents in their possession, I wish to thank the following (ordered by institution):

The Naval Historical Branch of the Ministry of Defence in the Admiralty Library at Portsmouth, England.
Carol Bowers, reference manager at the American Heritage Center at Laramie, Wyoming;
Linnea M. Anderson, Interim Archivist, Social Welfare History Archives, Archives and Special Collections, Elmer L. Andersen Library, Minneapolis;
Carol Stewart, senior library assistant, Special Collections at the Andersonian Library of the University of Strathclyde, Glasgow;
John B. Straw, director of the Archives & Special Collections Research Center, Bracken Library, Ball State University, Indiana;
Alison Clemens, Archivist; June Can, reader and access services; and Adrienne Sharpe, access services assistant, at the Beinecke Rare Book & Manuscript Library, Yale University, New Haven, Connecticut;
Jeff Walden, archives researcher at the BBC Written Archives Centre, Reading;
Sarah Romkey, archivist of Rare Books and Special Collections University of British Columbia Library, Irving K. Barber Learning Centre, Vancouver;
Jo Elsworth, keeper of the University of Bristol Theatre Collection, and her assistant Rachel Hassall;

---

* One English library sent me a batch of photocopies so pale that at first I took them for blank paper. They refused to make a second attempt at copying them. 'The originals are in pencil,' they protested, as though copying machines could not be adjusted for contrast. Nor would they agree to a refund when I invoked the Sale of Goods Act, unreadable copies being clearly not 'fit for purpose'. That said, I should mention the kind librarian in Portsmouth who used his mobile phone to photograph documents that he was otherwise unable to copy.

Acknowledgements

customer services at the British Library;
Ben Gocker, Librarian for the Brooklyn Collection at Brooklyn Public Library, New York;
Frank Bowles, Superintendent, Manuscripts Reading Room, and Sarah Gresswell in the Manuscripts Department, Cambridge University Library;
Leslie Calmes, archivist at the Center for Creative Photography, University of Arizona at Tucson;
Alan King, Historical Collections Librarian, Central Library, Portsmouth;
Jane Muskett, Archivist at Chetham's Library, Manchester;
Kenneth Baxter, archives assistant at the University of Dundee, Scotland;
Chris Densmore, archivist of the William Isaac Hull Papers, Friends Historical Library of Swarthmore College, Pennsylvania;
Tony Lees and his colleagues at the Greater Manchester County Record Office for access to the archives of the Co-operative Holidays Association (CHA) and to copies of *Comradeship*;
Danielle Sigler, associate director, Jean Cannon and Natalie Zelt, interns, at the Harry Ransom Center of the University of Texas at Austin;
Lesley Schoenfeld, access services coordinator, Special Collections, Harvard Law School Library, Cambridge, Massachusetts;
the staff at the Harvard Theatre Collection in the Houghton Library of Harvard University, Cambridge, Massachusetts;
Carol A. Leadenham, assistant archivist for reference at the Hoover Institution Archives, Stanford, California;
James Peters, University Archivist, and the staff of the Document Supply Unit at the John Rylands University Library in Manchester;
Béatrice Bourgeois of the inter-library loan service at the University Library, Lausanne, Switzerland;
Florence Hayes at Library and Archives Canada;
Courtney Pruitt, Customer Service Section of the Library of Congress, Washington DC;
the director and research staff at the Lilly Library of the University of Indiana at Bloomington;
Sue Donnelly, archivist, and Silvia Gallotti, archives assistant, at the archives and rare books library of London School of Economics and Political Science;
Renu Barrett and Sheila Turcon, archivists, and Adele Petrovic, secretary for Research Collections in the William Ready Division of Archives and Research Collections, McMaster University Library, Hamilton, Canada;

Acknowledgements

Kristen Turner, special projects archivist at the Seeley G. Mudd Manuscript Library, Princeton, New Jersey;
Simon J. Roberts, secretary of the National Liberal Club, London;
Olive Geddes, senior curator in the manuscripts division of the National Library of Scotland in Edinburgh;
the premium document supply service at New York Public Library;
the Manuscripts Department, University of North Carolina Library, Chapel Hill, North Carolina;
Emily Lockhart, assistant archivist, Oberlin College Archives, Oberlin, Ohio;
Sarah Hartwell, reading room supervisor at the Rauner Special Collections Library at Dartmouth College, Hanover, New Hampshire;
Mark Pomeroy, Archivist at the Royal Academy of Art, London;
Dr Peter Horton, reference librarian, and Christopher Bornet, deputy librarian (archives) at the Royal College of Music, London;
Sarah Haylett, Heritage Services at the Royal National Institute of Blind People (RNIB);
Geoffrey M. Danisher, Interlibrary Loan Librarian, Sarah Lawrence College Library, Bronxville, New York;
Lynda Leahy at the Schlesinger Library, Cambridge, Massachusetts;
Carolyn Troup at the Geddes collection, Strathclyde University Archives, Scotland;
Wendy E. Chmielewski, George R. Cooley Curator, and her staff at the Swarthmore College Peace Collection, Swarthmore, Pennsylvania;
Jill Hughes at the Taylor Institution Library, Oxford;
Judith Vera, Territory Manager, Thompson Henry Limited;
Special Collections at University College London;
Prof. Steven Probst, and Judy Miller, Special Collections Librarian, Valparaiso University, Indiana;
Peta Webb, assistant librarian, at the Vaughan Williams Memorial Library, the English Folk Dance and Song Society;
Ian C. Jackson, the librarian of the Woodbrooke Quaker Study Centre, Birmingham, England;

Of the individuals whose help has been invaluable, foremost is Amy Aronson, a professor of Journalism and Media Studies at Fordham University, who is preparing a study of Crystal Eastman. She has been most generous with her time and in sharing information with me. My thanks also to the following people who helped me with information (on the topic indicated in

Acknowledgements

parentheses): Prof. Richard J. Aldrich (GCHQ); Prof. Harriet Alonso (the People's Council); C. J. Bearman (Cecil Sharp's diaries); David Briggs (Rosamond Impey and the Hankinsons); Sather Bruguière (Rosalind); Sam Brylawski (Victor gramophone recordings); Norma Bulman (research assistance); Prof. Peter Bunnell (Rosalind); Prof. Martin Ceadel (Norman Angell); Hugh Cobb (Vaughan Williams); Blanche Cook (Crystal Eastman); Ian Crutchley (Rosamond Impey): Tony Currie (*Radio Times*); Andrew Dakyns (Arthur Dakyns); Conrad Dehn (his mother Cynthia); Jim Enyearts (Francis Bruguière); Susan Figg (Hamilton Irving); Alain Frogley (Vaughan Williams); Cordie Fuller (her father Jeffrey; also feedback on a draft of this book); Darren Giddings (*Radio Times*); Josh Gosciak (Claude McKay); Robin Greer (*Readers' Review*); Cynthia Hall (genealogy); Prof. Miranda Hickman (Stanley Nott); Hilary Holt (the Dehns); Prof. Chris Hopkins (Caradoc Evans); John Impey (Rosamond Impey); Alison Ironside (Rosamond Impey); Peter Jones (Rosamond Impey); Jane Keefer (Folk Music Index); Elise Kirk (music at the White House); Prof. Sylvia Law (Crystal Eastman); Scott Ledbetter (illustration); Prof. Anne McCauley (Lance Sieveking); Aintzane Legarreta Mentxaka (Kate O'Brien); Michael Morrison (John Barrymore); Adam Nott (his father Stanley Nott); Mairin Odle (research assistance); the Hon. Laura Ponsonby (Hubert Parry and Arthur Ponsonby); Prof. Jem Poster (Edward Thomas); Sue Powell (Stalbridge); Robin Rausch ('Five Souls'); Alan Ruston (Fred Hankinson); Prof. Jurg Schwyter (BBC English); Dr Robert Snape (CHA and NHRU); Karen Stoneman (Fuller genealogy); Prof. Paul Taylor (Stanley Nott); Hugo Vickers (Rosalind); Prof. Samuel Walker (ACLU); Eibhear Walshe (Kate O'Brien); Jan Ward (Leonard Stokes); David Williams (Jingo); Monica Wilson (her mother Cynthia); Prof. John Witt (ACLU); Lindy Woodhead (Harry Selfridge); Prof. Gregory Woods (Crocombe). My apologies to anyone I may have inadvertently omitted.

I thank the friends who read this book (or parts of it) at various stages in its development and patiently commented on it: Laurence Bristow-Smith (who pointed out my Gallicisms), Tanya Gardiner-Scott, Gerard Neill, and Professor Agnieszka Soltysik. Any defects the reader may find in the finished work are entirely my responsibility, not theirs.

I gratefully acknowledge a subsidy from the Société Académique Vaudoise for travel expenses and the purchase of books not available in Swiss libraries.

Introduction

One cannot place one's hand on what Walter Fuller did; but one cherishes deeply all that he was; and one knows that deeds and achievements scatter like dust, whilst such a life leaves a permanent trace on every person it has touched.[1] *New Republic*

Walter Fuller's life went largely unrecorded; his name is unknown today. Yet what he did helped shape the world we live in. So this biography attempts to tell the story of his life, gathering up some of that long-dispersed dust, recording his deeds and achievements, and tracing some of the people he touched, in order to cherish anew all that he was.

His first achievement came at the end of his university studies: in 1904, he convened the first national assembly of British student councils, a stepping-stone on the road to the National Union of Students. In 1911, after editing periodicals in London for several years, he took three of his sisters to sing folksongs in New York, launching the revival that was to transform popular music in the twentieth century. When the Great War broke out in Europe, Americans looked on aghast. Numerous peace groups sought to prevent their country from joining the conflict. Walter supported them by introducing anti-war songs for his sisters to sing – the modern protest song – and by conceiving in 1916 a large anti-war exhibition that was shown in New York and other cities around the Union. In so doing, he pioneered in the art of propaganda. He edited small periodicals that denounced the suppression of civil rights and the appalling treatment of conscientious objectors.

After the war was over, he made New York's *Freeman* 'the best written and most brilliantly edited of the weeklies of protest,' characterized by its 'wit and vigor and lucidity.'[2] Then he returned to England, where he was recruited in the mid-1920s by the fledgling BBC for his ideas about the potential of broadcasting. There he developed the concept of the *corporate image*, which has had a lasting impact on how the BBC is perceived through-

Introduction

out the world. After a brief stint directing the London (2LO) and Daventry (5XX) stations, he was chosen to edit the BBC's flagship publication, *Radio Times,* to which he gave a form that lasted fifty years.

These achievements went generally unrecognized, largely because Walter maintained a low profile throughout his life. His obituary in *The Times* makes little mention of his years in the United States. Instead, it underlines how

> Walter Fuller belonged to the days of anonymous journalism. Few men can have handled more of the writings of others and, in his editorial capacity, have exercised more influence upon the ideas that the public receive, and yet have remained personally so little known. People who themselves were engaged in creative work of all sorts – writing, painting, designing, education, and all such forms of endeavour – knew him and respected the keen interest and comprehension that he possessed for all their spheres of activity, but he himself never published a book, and his own name hardly ever appeared in print.[3]

And when his name did appear in print, he seems to have told almost no one, so that his work colleagues and even his family remained unaware of his writing. While researching this book, I identified him as 'John Wessex', the author of *A Masque of the Seasons* (1911), and tracked down letters and articles that he contributed to periodicals. They proved too numerous for an appendix, so they are posted separately on the website that accompanies this book, http://www.TheLetterworthPress.org/WalterFuller/index.html.

Seeking what Walter Fuller wrote or edited has resulted in some surprises. One closely kept secret concerns the periodical, *Four Lights,* which was issued during 1917 by the New York branch of the Woman's Peace Party. Until now it has been celebrated as a exceptional magazine written and edited entirely by women. I have come to the iconoclastic conclusion that it was actually edited – and largely written – by Walter Fuller.

Besides modesty, Walter had another reason for not trumpeting his name. Throughout WWI, when he was living in the United States, he was a peace activist. From the moment that country entered the war, his activities were branded as sedition or treason; he risked a heavy fine and long years in prison. Yet he discreetly imported from Britain something that Americans have come to prize very highly: the concept of *civil liberties.* Ever since then, it has been – along with the older notion of *civil rights* – the most important principle for the protection of US citizens. It is upheld by the American Civil Liberties Union, which Walter's wife Crystal Eastman created with Roger Baldwin. The need for it today is as great as ever.

Introduction

The sub-title of this book – 'the man who had ideas' – suggests another reason why Walter's name has remained unknown. Ideas carry no signature; once they are passed on, the identity of their originator is lost. Walter was 'always brimming with ideas, pulling them forth like newborn rabbits from his hat,' and he shared them liberally.[4] 'I suffer from ideas,' he complained.[5] One of his sisters noticed that his forehead even seemed to bulge with them. And he invariably had them well in advance of his time.

Walter got on well with people, and they found him kind, loyal, tender, generous (to a fault), and witty. For Llewellyn Powys, 'he had a heart of pure gold.'[6] (Has any other editor ever been qualified like this by one of his authors?) He was good at bringing people together. He introduced Van Wyck Brooks to Lewis Mumford, and the resulting literary friendship spanned four decades. He introduced the photographer Francis Bruguière to Lance Sieveking, the script editor and writer of the unique high modernist radio play, *Kaleidoscope* (1928), and they collaborated on avant garde art works.

Walter's personal qualities – and his ideas – captivated Crystal Eastman, a leading pacifist-feminist-socialist lawyer of the day in America – she co-authored the Equal Rights Amendment, for example. Her colourful reputation has overshadowed Walter's. When the history books mention him, he is identified simply as her second husband, a poet, or an artist. Although he sometimes penned a little ditty to entertain his sisters,* he was by no means a poet. Nor did he draw or paint – but he had the soul and creative imagination of an artist. Along with *altruism*, the words that characterize his life are *imagination* and *enthusiasm*. This biography brings him out of the shadows.

Walter's life was intimately linked with the lives of his four younger sisters. He was their confidant, counsellor, coach, and critic, and for several years, during which he directed their singing in the United States, he was financially responsible for them. His philosophy contributed to their outlook on life, and the fifty-year stage career of his third sister, Rosalind, was one of its fruits. So in this account their stories are intermingled with his.

Telling these stories brings in a great many other people; a profusion of famous and not so famous figures – artists, writers, poets, actors, editors, and

---

* Crossing the Atlantic in January 1913 with three of his sisters, Walter added a verse to John Masefield's famous poem, 'Cargoes':
>Great German liners, ploughing the Atlantic,
>Caring less than nothing for the rough sea rollers;
>With a cargo of millionaires, stewards,
>Emigrants, European riff-raff, and four sick Fullers.

Introduction

musicians – flit across the pages. Rest assured, though: if a person receives more than passing notice, you can be certain that they will return later in the book, revealing unfamiliar (and sometimes previously unrecorded) aspects of their lives. President Woodrow Wilson makes several personal appearances, along with his wife and daughters. The Right Honourable the Earl Russell never plays a leading part in the story, yet he manages to look in (as plain Bertrand Russell) in almost every chapter. Among the less famous names there is Jessie Holliday, whose portraits of leading socialists hang in the National Portrait Gallery in London, and her friend Kathleen Wheeler, the English sculptress who portrayed famous people and famous horses with equal skill. Here you will find more about them than in any other book. You will also discover that for many years the most respectable Sir Norman Angell, winner of the 1932 Nobel Peace Prize, enjoyed sex with Walter's sister Rosalind and denied it – 'cross my heart' – in his autobiography. Scott Fitzgerald had an affair with her during his engagement to Zelda; in fact, she inspired him with the story that financed his wedding. Here too you will learn how John Barrymore, playing Hamlet on Broadway, communicated to Ophelia that he wanted to make love with her after the show. And on it goes: Virginia Woolf mis-spells a person's name; T. S. Eliot gets stuck in the mud; Charlie Chaplin plays charades; and Cecil Sharp discovers three 'ludicrously lovely' girls – Walter's sisters, of course – who can sing folksongs better than anyone else.

All these people link up in hitherto unsuspected ways. For instance, in 1918 Bertrand Russell encouraged Rosalind to practise free love.* Soon afterwards she was enjoying sex with the man who twelve years later fathered two children by Russell's wife Dora, precipitating their scandalous divorce. At the heart of this fascinating network of interconnected relationships, we find Walter and his sisters.

The many books, letters, archival documents and manuscripts† that I consulted are listed at the end of the book. Additional information is placed at the foot of the page, to be read or not, as you please.

Mauborget, March 2014

---

* She adopted it as her way of life: 'free love is better than marriage,' she told *The Times* in 1968.[7]

† Unpublished documents have been left largely as written, rather than editorially improved. In quotations, the original British or American spelling has been retained, so both forms will be found. (Walter sometimes used US spellings in his letters to Crystal.)

1

Editor

My dreams – my grandest possessions – which I would not exchange to be the King's physician.[1]   Walter Fuller

He always seemed to me to stand out against the crowd ... as a creature of fine perceptions and sensibility – attuned, as I think he must always have been, to a magic world remote from the world as it is. This quality in him made him, to my mind, appear delightfully wistful and uneasy – as if it were surprised – as a stranger thrown among a crowd of meaningless and savage barbarians. He found, eventually, a place for himself in the Universe, but it was only by dint of keen intelligence and a strong sense of humour. Beneath an agreeable softness of manner and address, there lay, I know, a firm independence of mind, which jibbed at any attempt to guide or coerce it.[2]   Arthur Dakyns

HE HAD RARE EDITORIAL GIFTS![3]
Norman Thomas

Walter Fuller as a medical student at Owens College, Manchester [4]

WALTER GLADSTONE* FULLER was born in Portsmouth, England, where his father (and his grandfather before him) had a draper's shop in Commercial Road – and a social conscience. For the convenience of his fellow citizens, grandfather Fuller had proposed a road extension and built a small covered market behind his shop. Walter's father added a meeting room – immediately dubbed Fuller's Hall – above the market to provide working men's families with free entertainment on Sunday afternoons.†

Organizing these 'Pleasant Sunday Afternoons for the People' took up much of Mr Fuller's spare time. He arranged talks, invited missionaries to give illustrated lectures and local musicians to perform, and encouraged children to recite poems. He himself gave readings from Dickens, who was born a few hundred yards up their street. (Dickens became one of Walter's favourite writers, the one he would read if he were sick in bed, or in need of consolation. Allusions to Dickens' novels and comparisons with his characters are hallmarks by which we can identify Walter's unsigned writings.) Fuller's Hall also served as a meeting-place for the local community.‡ In October 1893, for instance, during a dispute between the shipbuilders in the Royal Dockyard and their employers at the Admiralty, the Reverend Robert Dolling of St Agatha's Mission in Landport addressed the assembled workmen in the Hall. Afterwards Mr Fuller led a delegation of workmen to London where the conflict was amicably settled.[6]

Walter's mother Elizabeth was the daughter of a shipyard carpenter with social pretensions: he always carried his lunch in a neat paper parcel, not a bright red cloth like the other men.[7] His children were forbidden to play in the street like other children and their shoes were always polished. Elizabeth became an apprentice in the draper's shop and Mr Fuller fell for her, for she was very pretty. They married on 28 June 1880, and little Walter was born on 3 April 1881. On 28 September two years later, he was joined by Oriska

---

*   He owed his middle name to his father's admiration for the Liberal Prime Minister who, at the time of Walter's birth, had recently been elected to his second term of office.

†   This kind of entertainment originated in 1866 when the National Sunday League defied the Lord's Day Act of 1761 (which prohibited public amusement or debate on a Sunday) by instituting 'Sunday Evenings for the People' with music 'of an unobjectionable nature' and educative lectures on a variety of subjects.

‡   After the Fullers moved away, the Hall took on a new life as a cinema. The entry remained unchanged: a grand stairway lined with statues leading to a glass-roofed conservatory where the Fuller children played on rainy days. Later it became a boxing hall, then a grain store, and finally disappeared under the bombs of WWII.[5]

Violet, with whom he bonded closely. 'I don't know what mother's magic secret can have been that has bound us so close together all our lives,' he wrote to her when he was twenty-eight. 'We are a sort of spiritual Siamese twins, you & I.'[7] After a six-year gap, Walter and Riss (as Oriska was always called) were joined first by Dorothy Daisy (4 December 1889), then Rosalind Ivy (16 February 1892) and finally Cynthia Rose (21 October 1896). Thus Walter was fifteen-and-a-half when his youngest sister was born. All the girls had their mother's beauty, each in her own way: Riss was fair-haired, with violet eyes; Dorothy had straight dark hair and startlingly blue eyes: Rosalind had dark eyes and irrepressibly curly dark hair; and the blonde and blue-eyed Cynthia was spoiled by them all. They worshipped their big brother who was, by turns, their confidant, counsellor, coach, and critic. But most of all, he adored his mother, and she him.[8]

Whereas Walter and Riss attended the local grammar school, the younger girls were taught by a succession of governesses. All the children learned to play the piano, and each girl studied another instrument as well. From an early age Riss was taught the harp, Dorothy the violin, and Rosalind the cello. Like their mother, who sang them folksongs and lullabies when they were small, they would entertain each other with music in the evenings. Their father had them perform in Fuller's Hall, of course. Riss played her harp, Dorothy, who developed a rich, strong mezzo-soprano voice, sang ballads and recited poems while Rosalind mimed the action. Unlike Dorothy, who was quite at ease on the stage, Rosalind suffered from self-consciousness: 'If I was called upon to sing a duet with her, I was so nervous that saliva would fill my mouth, and I would have to stop and swallow.'[9] So, as she confessed many years later, she 'hated and feared the whole business.'[10] Emotions produced powerful physical responses in Rosalind; even the anticipation of some joyous event could give her a bilious attack.

Performance of a different kind was expected of Walter, who grew up with the sensitivity of his mother and the social conscience of his father. As the only boy in the family and the eldest by far, he was the focus of all his parents' hopes and ambitions. At eighteen he was tall and slim (his chest measured only thirty inches), rather short-sighted, and he tended to walk with a stoop. Someone remarked (as he bitterly recorded in his diary) that he looked like 'a pale young curate.'[11] He wanted to be a doctor, rather than a clergyman or a Navy paymaster, as suggested by his parents. They took some persuading. In the end, though, with the financial assistance of a maternal uncle, he went up to Owens College, Manchester, in the autumn of 1899 to study medicine.

It was a long way from Portsmouth, but at that time Manchester rivalled London as the intellectual centre of England – 'What Manchester thinks today, London will think tomorrow' was a catch-phrase. Walter enjoyed living up there, made a number of good friends and developed a lifelong love of all things Lancastrian. Alongside his medical studies, he was active in the social life of the College. He joined the Debating Society but, being terribly shy, it took him almost eighteen months to summon up the courage to speak. When finally he rose to his feet, he was 'astonished to find a great calm pervading my mind.'[12] Things were different after that. In his third and fourth years, he served as secretary of the Society. He also read papers to the Literary Circle, acted in plays put on by the Student Union, represented the students on the refectory committee, and served on the Ancoats Settlement committee.* In 1902 he was elected Junior Secretary of the Owens College Union.

That year, Riss won the Whitcombe-Portsmouth scholarship to study the harp at the Royal College of Music, with accommodation in Alexandra House, the student residence attached to the College. The younger sisters remained at home with neither Walter, whom they adored, nor Riss, who had mothered them, for company. In mid-1903 Rosalind and Cynthia went down with diphtheria. Their doctor blamed the drains in Commercial Road and Mrs Fuller hurried them out to a friend's cottage made from a disused tram-car in the middle of a chalk pit near Portsdown Hill. During the long days of sickness, she sang to them; as they gradually recovered, she taught them singing games that she had learned from her mother.

Mistrusting the Portsmouth town drains, the Fullers decided to move out into the country. That autumn they found a double-fronted brick house a stone's throw from Portchester Castle; from there Mr Fuller could be driven to and from the station in a pony trap by the gardener. Walter disliked the house at once, scorning its bourgeois croquet lawn, laurel bushes, and stone urns at the front door. Luckily, rolling countryside lay behind it. Telling his sisters to ignore the formal garden, with its 'blue and white flowers planted in regimented rows by some unimaginative gardener,' he enjoined them to appreciate 'the beauty of Portsdown Hill running like a wave behind you.'[13] When he came home on vacation, he took them for long walks, and picking

---

* Ancoats was the area of Manchester where the poorest labourers lived among cotton mills, foundries and glass factories. Various institutions, principally the Methodist church and the Salvation Army, ran hospitals there, a workhouse for men and a night shelter for women. Manchester students assisted with fundraising and voluntary work.

Walter Fuller

wild flowers soon became one of their favourite occupations. He also directed their attention to the ruins of the nearby Castle, telling them to look it up in their history books and pretend they lived in it.

Walter was also reading widely. During his first year, he learned from an article on 'Life as a Surgeon on a P&O liner' that the surgeon, 'being the one with the most leisure, is in charge of the ship's library.' 'I should rather like that, I fancy,' he reflected in his diary.[14] As well as novels, he read cultural and political books and periodicals. Even in the midst of exams, he found time to look at *Punch* or the *Tatler* and the illustrated weeklies, along with a range of daily newspapers. He read the *New Liberal Review* from its launch in January 1901. 'Its politics are strongly Roseberyan* and therefore I agree with all heartiness with its views,' he noted.[15] He subscribed to '100 Best Pictures' when it came out in weekly instalments. At sixpence an issue, it was expensive for him; after a few weeks he arranged to share the pictures with his best friend, Bill Hankinson, who was studying pharmacy. On this varied diet he grew into a new Walter. As the family moved into the new house, he directed his father to take a liberal newspaper instead of the *Daily Mail*, and his mother to throw out her favourite prints and replace them with reproductions of Turner and Constable.

Walter was also on the committee of the *Owens College Union Magazine*† – and 'only those who have worked with him have any idea of the amount of work he has done for it.'[16] Published every month by the Union during the university terms, it contained a mixture of serious and humorous articles, photographs (and sometimes cartoons) of staff and students, and reports on the various social and sporting events. In his final year, 1903–04, Walter wrote the editorial pages.

In the autumn of 1902, he was elected to the medical school's Students' Representative Council (SRC), the body that gave students a voice in matters affecting their interests and a channel of communication with the

---

*   The reference is to the 5th Earl of Rosebery, who succeeded Gladstone as Prime Minister in 1894. He supported the Boer War and opposed Home Rule for Ireland. Walter's views soon evolved away from both these positions.

†   Launched in 1868 as the *Owens College Magazine* to 'stimulate social intercourse amongst past and present students of the College, and increase their interest in and foster the spirit of goodwill and loyalty towards their Alma Mater,' it became the *Owens College Union Magazine* in 1894, then *Manchester University Magazine* when Owens College became Manchester University in 1904, and finally the *Serpent* (1917–56). It was one the first student magazines in Britain and one of the most successful, setting the tone for such publications right up to the WWII. Some contributors are still remembered; George Gissing and Anthony Burgess both wrote for it when they were students.

university authorities. At that time, medicine was the only department at Owens College to have an SRC, but the desire was there for all the students to be represented by this means. While Edinburgh university had pioneered by setting up its Council in 1880, English universities lagged far behind: so far only Birmingham and Liverpool had SRCs. During 1901 the subject was hotly debated at Owens and a petition was prepared and printed – but not circulated for signature. 'Nothing more was done until last December [1902] when the question was brought up by Mr Fuller,' reported the *Magazine*. 'About the same time, the Women's Union had some correspondence on the matter with the Union; and in February last a small but representative meeting was summoned, through the enthusiasm of Mr Fuller, to discuss the question.' With the sanction and approval of the College authorities, a temporary Executive Committee was formed; it worked hard and fast to draw up a Constitution. By the beginning of the next academic year – which happened to be the first of the renamed Victoria University of Manchester – the project was ready.

Walter leads the Students' Representative Council.
A cartoon by Hamilton Irving, from *Owens College Union Magazine* No 87 (June 1903)

At the AGM of the Union in October 1903, 'thanks especially to Mr Fuller, who prepared the original draft [and] to Mr Dehn, whose assistance has been invaluable upon legal and formal points,' each chapter of the Constitution was proposed, discussed, and approved.[17] 'The Vice-Chancellor then called upon Mr Fuller to move the adoption of the Constitution' and it was accepted unanimously. 'Before the meeting broke up Mr Fuller moved a hearty vote of thanks to the Vice-Chancellor for the interest he had shown during the whole period of the formation of the SRC. . . . This was seconded by Mr Dehn in an effective little speech, and was carried with much enthusiasm.'[18] Thus Manchester became the third English university to give its students formal representation, 'a red letter day in the history of our student life.'[19] The *Magazine* printed a photograph of Walter and brief biography. He was Senior Secretary of the Union, and when the elections to the University SRC were held, he became its first President.

Student life at Manchester included a Christmas soirée organized by the Union. For the 1903 vintage, Walter invited Riss to come up from London and play the harp, if they could rent one; failing that, he asked her to play the 'Chopin polonaise in A flat' (Opus 53), a virtuoso piece that she was studying, loftily assuring her that 'M/c people of course know it well from Busoni's rendering.'* He also brushed aside her request for a fee: 'Why, the Union lose every year on the soirée as it is and everyone is expected to give their services' for free.[20] The following issue of the *Magazine* reported all kinds of entertainment at the soirée, including Bill Hankinson's sister Hilda playing the piano, but does not mention any musical performance by Riss.

Walter may have been only half-unconsciously discouraging, for he was extremely possessive when it came to Riss; the idea of her coming up to Manchester made him feel 'quite cross.' 'It will be something dreadful, I know. I shall hate to leave you at Herne Hill,' where she was to stay with friends, 'and I shall have to. I had rather not take you anywhere – since we shall be unable to go alone together.'[21] Unwilling to share Riss with anyone, he disliked the fact that other men found her most attractive. At Herne Hill she met a student named Dawson and Walter blithely invited him to visit the family in Portsmouth. Riss and Dawson fell in love and talked of getting married, much to the disapproval of her father: 'He is only twenty-one and you but twenty, and I am certain it would be better for both of you to think nothing whatever of love,' pronounced Mr Fuller.

---

* The concert pianist Ferruccio Busoni (1866–1924) is best known today for his transcriptions for the piano of Bach's organ music. At a concert Walter attended in 1901, Busoni played this polonaise as an encore.

Dawson will need to be single-minded and single-purposed to make his way in the profession. You too will probably be some years at College and make a name for yourself, whereas if you are engaged and married in a year or so, all the cost and anxieties of the past few years will be lost, and all your abilities as a harpist prevented from being of service to the world.[22]

This attitude was typical of Mr Fuller's generation, for whom a married woman could do nothing but keep house for her husband. He asked Riss not to mention this veto to Walter until his spring exams were over – 'it will only bother him.' When Walter did hear of it, he agreed with his father and insisted that Riss 'cut' Dawson entirely. She took months to recover from the break. To take her mind off it, she began to correspond, as a friend, with another of Walter's fellow students, Basil Ward.

Ward was the son of a Glossop clergyman. Many of the family were artistically inclined: his eldest brother was a landscape painter and he had an uncle who painted figures and landscapes. He himself was a keen amateur actor; in December the *Magazine* joked that 'Mr Stanley Heathcote and Mr B. V. Ward, the well-known members of the Dramatic Society, are intending to present Sheridan's comedies, *The Critic* and *St. Patrick's Day*, at a well-known London theatre during the forthcoming winter season.'[23] In company, on the other hand, Ward said little. In fact, his conversation was often limited to an enigmatic 'Mmsk' and Walter's sisters found him rather dull. The story goes that on his first visit to the Fullers at Portchester, their three-wheeled dog-cart, being inherently unstable, tipped over as it turned into their gateway and deposited him, fortunately unhurt, at the feet of his waiting hosts. 'Mmsk,' he said.

Up in Manchester, Walter embarked on an ambitious project. At his instigation, the SRC invited student representatives from all the universities of England and Wales to attend the first Inter-Universities Students' Congress. The new SRCs and Unions all responded favourably and some forty delegates, representing ten Universities in England and Wales, assembled over 30 June–2 July 1904. It was a momentous occasion, the first step on the road that led to the National Union of Students, marked by congratulatory telegrams from the Prince of Wales and Joseph Chamberlain (the immensely popular Colonial Secretary who was much interested in educational reform). Walter was elected to preside the Congress. The *Magazine* quipped: 'They say that it is the intention of Alake of Abeokuta on the occasion of his forthcoming visit to Manchester to confer the honour of Krotara M'Wanga (the Order of the Golden Cloak) upon the President of the SRC.'[24]

Mr Fuller's concern for Walter's nerves during his exams was well founded. He hated exams. It was not that he lacked ability and he certainly enjoyed the more theoretical side of medicine (therapeutics being his favourite subject); it was the practical side that defeated him, for he sympathized too deeply with the sick to be able to treat them dispassionately. So he agreed with his examiners when they failed him in July: 'I am not a safe man to let loose on a trustful public,' he confessed to Riss.[25] On the other hand, thanks to the *Magazine*, he had discovered his true calling. Years later, a BBC colleague declared, 'He was a born editor with a welcome for every promising idea, and he put his personality into any paper he handled.'[26] Walter's fellow students recognized this ability. One of the decisions of the Students' Congress was to establish a national inter-university magazine under his editorship, with an editorial board of big names.* That sugared the pill when he returned home to report that he had failed his finals.

Walter spent the autumn of 1904 up at Manchester, preparing the new journal. In addition to soliciting contributions, there was everything to arrange, from its design to its distribution (as far as India and Australia). The Manchester bookshop-cum-publisher Sherrat & Hughes (who printed the *Magazine*, so Walter was used to working with them) agreed to publish it, and in November they paid Walter his first salary – a cheque for £10. Having cashed it for 'a five-pound note and some gold and silver' he at once spent four shillings on a hundred daffodil bulbs which he sent home, rejoicing that they would be 'filling the garden with beauty' the following April, 'when all England will be reading the first copy of my *University Review*!' It is typical of Walter that he anticipated the pleasure the flowers would give his family without considering the labour of planting them. Telling Riss of what he had done, he enclosed some books of folksongs for her – 'may they make you happy. You'll find they contain the very essence of fresh air.'[27] He was always encouraging her to investigate folksongs.

Thanks to his mother, Walter's interest in folksong and dance began in childhood, as it did for his sisters. It was fuelled by the re-discovery of them that was taking place at the time. The Folklore Society had been created in 1878, with Laurence Gomme and his wife Alice as founder members. She published a two-volume collection of *Children's Singing Games,* with beautiful illustrations by Winifred Smith, in 1894. (A volume with Dorothy

---

* The list of board members was not published, but it included Sir William Ramsay, who won the Nobel Prize for chemistry in 1904, and Sir Thomas Barclay, one of the artisans of the Entente Cordiale who was knighted in the birthday honours of 1904. He was nominated for the Nobel Peace Prize in 1905, 1906, 1907, 1908, 1910, 1913, 1914, 1923, 1925, and 1928, but never won it.

Fuller's illustrations, entitled *Old Fashioned Singing Games,* was published just ninety years later.) At this distance in time, it is not possible to know what books Walter sent to Riss; one of them may have been Cecil Sharp's first series of *Folk Songs from Somerset,* which had just been published.*

At the beginning of 1905, the administration of the *University Review* was transferred to Sherrat & Hughes' office in London. Walter moved there too, meeting up with some of his Manchester friends. He was to see a great deal of two of them over the following years. The first was another medical student, Hamilton Irving, who was four years older than Walter. He had a gift for drawing and during his studies he contributed monthly caricatures of professors and fellow students, including Walter, to both the *Manchester Medical Students' Gazette* and the *Owens College Union Magazine.* Before leaving Manchester he had a selection of these drawings privately published as a slim volume of *University Sketches* (1904). He had a high sense of his own worth, letting it be understood that he expected to inherit a large estate in Scotland, although his father was but a Huddersfield doctor. Trained as a surgeon, he was aiming to set up a private practice in the fashionable part of London.

The other friend, Curt Dehn, was the law student three years younger than Walter who had advised on the Constitution of the SRC at Owens. His family had come over from Hamburg in 1886 and settled in Manchester, exporting cotton goods to East Africa.† They continued to speak German in the home and had Continental manners that the English found quaintly formal. The *Magazine* printed a limerick:‡

> There is also a lawyer called D – n,
> Who I'm sure never runs for his train;
> For he's too good and proper
> To e'er come a cropper,
> This dignified lawyer called D – n.[28]

Curt worked as a solicitor in London. The story goes that before his first visit

---

* 1904 was a significant year for folksong research: the ailing Folksong Society was revived by Lucy Broadwood along with Cecil Sharp and Ralph Vaughan Williams, who started to go around the countryside, particularly the south west of England, collecting songs.

† In the late nineteenth century, Manchester was home to a large expatriate German community which contributed enormously to the city's cultural life.

‡ There was also a limerick about 'An important young person called F—r.' As the only rhyme the poet could find was 'Buller', he remained mute 'On the good points of capable F—r.'

to the Fuller family, Riss, who had already met him in Manchester, warned her little sisters to behave themselves and keep out of his way, as Curt did not like children. Curious to see such a man, they hid behind the summer house to watch his arrival. On this occasion the pony trap safely negotiated the gateway and Curt strode towards his hostess, who awaited him at the front door. Catching his foot in a croquet hoop on the lawn he fell full length before her. This was irresistible; the three girls rushed out with peals of laughter. Curt saw only Cynthia with her blue eyes and blonde hair; there and then he decided that he would marry her. She was about eight at the time.

Early in 1905 Walter took his sisters to a see new show called *Peter Pan*, launched at the Duke of York's Theatre the Christmas before. It was all the rage; everyone was whistling the theme tune. Hearing the famous words, 'I want always to be a little boy, and to have fun,' Walter recognized himself in Peter Pan. Four years earlier, as his twentieth birthday approached, he had recorded in his diary, 'just think of it, twenty, twenty. Oh how I covet – how I gloat over – and cherish – the happy irresponsible years of my teens.'[29] His fantasy world was ever present: 'If all my dreams are realized there shall be no limit to what we will do,' he crowed to Riss. 'There shall be no people like we two in all the land. None so active – none so good – none so happy – none so loved by all as you and I. We will be King and Queen.'[30] On his birthday in 1905, he told her (for he continued to write regularly to Riss, even though they were now both in London), 'I've been feeling awfully "Peter Panish" today. Dreadful. . . . To be 24 is simply too dreadful. I sigh for the Never Never Never Land. Can nothing stop these relentless years?'[31] For a while, 'feeling awfully "Peter Panish" . . . dreadful' was a refrain in his letters.

Riss will have understood perfectly what he meant, for the Neverland was nothing new to the Fullers. As children they too had their fantasy world which they called the Paper Kingdom. It was peopled with figures cut from magazines and newspapers and stuck onto cardboard, so that they stood up. The figures had to match for size and appearance, and were grouped into families that lived in newspaper houses. Reading periodicals took on a whole new dimension – and so did meeting new people. The habit of wondering, 'Would (s)he fit into the Paper Kingdom?' remained with them into adulthood.

Walter also read with a pair of scissors to hand, ready to cut out an article. His letters to family and friends invariably enclosed clippings, marked 'Please return'. (He laughed at himself for this, saying that when he travelled 'his luggage consisted of one small bag and a couple of trunks of newspaper-cuttings.')[32] This habit was reflected in his editorial practice. He would appropriate a submission, revise it substantially, and give it a life in the world by printing it. For this he took no credit.

In a sense, this is what Peter Pan does. He takes boys who have fallen out of their prams and remain unclaimed by parents or nannies and gives them a colourful life, full of adventure, in Neverland. The sharing is important: Peter would have a lonely existence without the Lost Boys. It was this that made Walter an editor rather than, say, a novelist. To create anything new requires imagination, and that he had in ample supply. For a novel or a play, the writer imagines the story and then, usually in solitude, brings it to life on the page. Editing a periodical, on the other hand, requires collaboration. The editor imagines what the contents might be and recruits others to share his dream with him; he masterminds a joint creation.

Walter always encouraged his sisters to dream and imagine what they might become: artists, musicians, politicians – the choice was theirs. To realize their dream, first they had to imagine it, and believe in it, and then take steps to realize it. Leonardo da Vinci imagined all kinds of flying machines, the helicopter and the parachute, but had not means to realize them. The Wright brothers acted upon their dream and achieved flight exactly 375 days before the first performance of *Peter Pan*, the play in which flying is possible if you think the right thoughts.

Much of Walter's behaviour, his adolescent idealism and infectious enthusiasm, his demand that his sisters cultivate their imaginations, his relationships with his parents and friends, both men and women, and his unreliability in money matters are best understood by seeing the Peter Pan in him. It made him an enchanting personality, able to infuse others with his visionary ideas, but sometimes an infuriating one, unworldly, unwilling to face facts. In this he was very much a product of the 1890s, when parents sought to preserve the image of the innocence of childhood that their mid-Victorian parents had instilled in them. Twenty years later, we find Walter exhorting his wife to keep their two young children 'both innocent and gentle.'[33]

In April 1905, Riss completed her studies at the Royal College of Music (and modestly blushed at the prospect of putting the letters ARCM after her name). Exceptionally she was allowed to continue studying the harp, the piano and singing at the College for a further year. However she had to relinquish her room at Alexandra House, so after a summer holiday she went to 'keep house for Walter' in a new flat he had taken at 9 Purcell Mansion, Queens Club Gardens, West Kensington. 'I'm just longing for it,' she told

Basil Ward. 'More cakes, more tarts, more beetrooty faces and flour-tipped noses!'[34] Hardly had she arrived, however, when Cynthia caught scarlet fever. Riss hurried home to keep house while her mother nursed Cynthia. To escape the infection, Dorothy and Rosalind (now aged sixteen and fourteen) were despatched to stay with Walter in London.

He asked a friend called Wendy to keep them company. Given her name, it was inevitable that he should invent a game in which his sisters became two of the Lost Boys, Tootles and Curley, from *Peter Pan*.* When Cynthia recovered, she joined them for a holiday, bringing her dog Laddie. She became Liza, the little maid in the Darling family; Riss took over as Wendy, and Laddie was Nana of course. The flat was renamed the Little House. Walter's friends were enrolled too: Hamilton Irving was Captain Hook, and Curt Dehn was Smee. A new friend, Kathleen Wheeler, became Tiger Lily. Soon there were ten Neverlanders in all and for the rest of their lives they regularly referred to each other, and to themselves, by their Peter Pan names. The only one to keep his own name was Walter himself. He was so obviously Peter Pan that no change was necessary.

Kathleen Wheeler (1884–1977) was a talented sculpture student at the Slade School of Art. About this time she made two busts of Cynthia which were much admired by Curt; his son still has one of them. He would come round of an evening and ask Cynthia what she would like to do. Her reply was invariably, 'Go for a ride in a hansom cab over the bridges of London.' She far preferred the old cabs and buses with their different coloured horses to the red London General omnibuses that were starting to invade the streets.

Throughout this time, Walter was working away at the *University Review* (hereafter simply the *UR*). It must have involved a great deal of correspondence, for contributions to a new periodical do not walk in off the street. What is more, each issue contained up to fifty pages of news from universities and colleges in Britain, the United States and the Continent, plus features on colonial universities like Calcutta and Melbourne (making it a treasure trove of facts and figures for researchers today). Subtitled 'a magazine of

---

* They went to another performance of *Peter Pan* on 22 February 1906 and collected an illustrated postcard signed by 'Curley', to which they added their own Neverland signatures, including Walter's 'Peter Pan'. Curly was played by an actress who feminized the boy's name by adding the 'e'. When Rosalind became an actress, she too added an 'e' to her name.

academic and general interest', it was the first national (and international) platform for discussion of every aspect of academe: its aims, practice, and administration, and its relationship with religion, patriotism, and the army. It debated university reform, access to higher education for women and working men, and the training of teachers, clergymen, solicitors, and architects. It embraced the teaching of disciplines ranging from the traditional – the pronunciation of classical Greek – to the innovative, like Russian, technology and sociology, as well as relationships between disciplines – English history and English literature, for instance. Then there were essays on a wide variety of cultural topics, from painting to gypsies (by Scott Macfie): some were reprinted and sold separately; others became chapters of books. The contributors ranged from distinguished professors – including Ramsay Muir, who had initiated student representation in England – to recent graduates, often friends of Walter's, for whom it was a first (and sometimes only) publication. Under his direction the *UR* was no doubt more serious and high-brow than the Student Congress had anticipated.

Two atypical contributions deserve separate mention. The issue for February 1906 included 'A Confession in Doggerel' by Lady Victoria Welby (signed only 'VW'). Her pioneering reflections on meaning paralleled the development of semiotics – she corresponded with Pierce for eight years – and she debated her ideas with Bertrand Russell and Patrick Geddes. Around 1910 she also corresponded with the young C. K. Ogden, and her theories greatly influenced the direction of his thought, although he tended to downplay their impact. Then, at the end of 1907 and the beginning of 1908, Walter printed four short stories, in English translation, by Anatole France, who was awarded the Nobel Prize for Literature in 1921. This seems to have been the first appearance of his works in English.

The first number of the *UR* (cover-dated May) came out in April 1905, as planned, with a glittering line-up of contributors.* It ran to 128 well-filled,

---

* An 'introductory note' on the university movement was provided by the Right Honourable James Bryce, who had just been made Chief Secretary for Ireland (a post he was not to hold for long, for in 1907 he was appointed British Ambassador to the United States). Three articles came from the University of Birmingham: its principal, Sir Oliver Lodge, offered 'questions for discussion'; the professor of English literature, Churton Collins, wrote on the education of the citizen; and the professor of Latin and Greek, E. A. Sonnenschein, investigated Shakespeare and Stoicism. The Sir Alfred Jones Professor of Tropical Medicine at the University of Liverpool, Major Ronald Ross, reflected on 'malaria and a moral' and the Langworthy Professor of Physics at the University of Manchester, Arthur Schuster, raised the much-debated question of university examinations.

carefully edited, and nicely printed pages – no small achievement for a debutant editor. From the list of contents, it might have seemed that the *UR* was going to voice only the views of the establishment, but the second issue, cover-dated June, contained a piece by J. A. Hobson (1858–1940), the economist who is now recognized as a pioneer of the welfare state. He had been ousted from academe for his unpopular theory of under-consumption. Turning to journalism, he covered the Second Boer War for the *Manchester Guardian* and came out strongly against it. This led to Hobson's iconoclastic view that, far from being a high-minded enterprise, British empire was simply the product of capitalism's continual need for new markets in which to make profits. For him imperialism was both unnecessary and immoral, and his 1902 book on the subject inspired thinkers like Bukharin, Trotsky and – fifty years later – Hannah Arendt (*The Origins of Totalitarianism*). Lenin drew heavily on it for his *Imperialism, the Highest Stage of Capitalism* (1916).

As Walter corresponded with his contributors and edited their writing, he widened his general knowledge and formed his own opinions. In particular he developed views on military preparedness and pacifism. In the issue for April 1906 Sir William Ramsay wrote on 'Patriotism in the Universities', expressing his 'firm conviction that the way to avoid war is to be well prepared.' It was therefore 'the duty of every young man of education to bear his share in insuring his country against future misfortune' by including military training in his university studies.[35] This prompted Walter to solicit dissenting views and give space to them. In the issue for August, John W. Graham, the Principal of Dalton Hall, Manchester, wrote:

> Doubtless we shall have an army for long years to come; only by slow and very complicated changes, passing through several stages, can militarism become a thing of the past; and so long as we have officers they must be trained; but do not allow such teaching . . . to spoil a university. There can be no claim that this teaching has anything to do with a liberal education.[36]

In the same issue H. S. Perris, MA, maintained,

> We have a right to look to the universities for a training, not in the Brutalities, but in the Humanities, not in the use of firearms, and the senseless routine of military 'Drill', but in the forwarding of high ideals of justice, law and international order. We do not want our Universities to become recruiting grounds for Jingoes and physical force men, but for peace and moral force men.[37]

Ten years later, these were very much Walter's views as he campaigned against the policy of preparedness in the United States.

A major topic in the *UR* during 1905–06 was the question of halls of residence. At the beginning of the twentieth century, purpose-built student accommodation was almost unknown in Britain. Whereas 'Columbia University alone had dormitories for 1000 students, there were, except in the two ancient universities [i.e., Oxford and Cambridge], only eleven halls for men, with 470 places, and fourteen halls for women, with 729 places.'[38] Consequently the second resolution passed at the 1904 Student Congress in Manchester called for the establishment of halls of residence. An Inter-Universities Halls of Residence Committee was formed and reports submitted to the congresses of 1905 and 1906.* They were largely inspired by the situation in Scotland which, thanks to Patrick Geddes, was far ahead of England. In 1887 he had founded University Hall, Edinburgh; 'by 1905 it was the largest hall of residence in the country and contained nearly one-third of the total number of men in residence in such halls in all Great Britain.'[40] From the mid-1890s onwards, Geddes had been campaigning for a similar hall in London, and Walter proposed that, alongside general articles on the topic, the pages of the *UR* might be used to support 'the movement for starting a University Hall of Residence at More's Garden.'[41] This was exactly what Geddes wanted and he made a first contribution to the *UR* in July 1906 with 'University Studies and University Residence.' Thus he and Walter became acquainted, first by letter and then in person, for Geddes (although the professor of Botany at Dundee) spent a good deal of time in London, supervising the More's Garden project. He made a deep impression on Walter, who embraced his ideas with enthusiasm and applied them for the rest of his life. (In 1920 Lewis Mumford told Geddes that Walter had been 'Boswellizing' him 'in sputters of enthusiastic anecdote.')[42] Geddes responded by encouraging Walter's editing.

The achievements of Sir Patrick Geddes – he was knighted shortly before he died in 1932 – include the discovery of chlorophyll, the founding of sociology in Britain, and the development of modern town planning. His thought can be situated at the intersection of the sciences that gave rise to ecology, for he was the first to stress the need to view man and nature, town and country, as a single inter-related system. With his boundless energy and interest in an equally boundless range of subjects, he influenced and inspired a great many people. In these respects Walter resembled him, on a lesser scale. On the other hand, Geddes was not an easy man to work with. When passing on his ideas and projects to others, he assumed that they shared his inspiration,

---

* Walter was proud to address the 1906 conference in Edinburgh, 'speaking for and representing the students of the English and Welsh universities.'[39]

but he provided them with neither sufficient direction nor financial support, which led to mutual disappointment.

Under King Edward VII, a public holiday was introduced in June to replace the immensely popular celebration of Queen Victoria's coronation. Many towns around Britain chose to mark the occasion with entertainment in the form of a pageant. In Portsmouth, planning began with a public meeting the autumn of 1906, which Walter's father attended. He saw the educational value of a pageant: instead of dry dates, 'it would place before the children living representatives of the men and women who lived in far off days, and remind them of the great inheritance they had succeeded to. . . . Mr Fuller asked the meeting to approve the proposal and above all to be enthusiastic about the matter.' A Colonel Gunner 'thought they should look at the matter from a more business-like point of view' but at Mr Fuller's insistence, for money 'was sure to be found,' a planning committee was formed.[43] In the end Mr Fuller was appointed joint honorary treasurer of the event and he devoted much time and energy to organizing it.

The pageant was held within the walls of Portchester Castle and depicted highlights from its history: the building of a fort by the Romans, the founding of the Priory in 1133, the departure of Henry V for Agincourt in August 1415, the visit of Elizabeth I in 1588, and so forth. Each scene involved at least a hundred volunteers from local villages. These episodes were followed by a grand spectacle involving 'Boadicea and her attendant retinue of pages and maids of honour, followed by Europe, Asia, Africa, and America, . . . England, Ireland, Scotland, and Wales, each bearing emblazoned shields and wearing costumes appropriate to the countries,' to the accompaniment of the full band of the Royal Artillery.[44]

All the Fuller family and their friends participated; Cynthia, in a long white dress and leading Laddie on a gold leash, was a child in the court of Edward I; Rosalind was dressed as a page in velvet doublet and hose; and Dorothy was a May queen, her long brown hair wreathed in flowers. She sang 'Early One Morning' accompanied by Riss in medieval costume playing on a small Irish harp that she had acquired. Walter, Hamilton Irving (called 'Captain' by everyone) and Curt Dehn appeared as bishops in long robes and high mitres. In the end, despite bad weather, the pageant made a modest profit of £36 3s 10d, thanks to the 800 visitors who came by special train and boat. A similar event on the Isle of Wight made a loss of £700, notwithstanding royal patronage. Enthusiasm had carried the day.

While his father was preparing the pageant, Walter was preparing to edit two new periodicals, one for the National Home Reading Union (founded 1889) and the other for the Co-operative Holidays Association (1893). As its name implies, the first encouraged the reading and discussion of books in the home. The second provided accommodation in good places for hiking, not only in the Peak District and the Lakes but also a chalet in the Swiss Alps and a log house in the Black Forest. It offered free holidays to poor families from industrial towns and, before WWI, to children from German cities as well.* Both were created by J. B. Paton (1830–1911), the social crusader – 'one of the outstanding Christian leaders in Britain at the turn of the century'[45] – and a friend of Patrick Geddes. It was no doubt Geddes who put forward Walter's name to edit their publications.

At a meeting in May 1903, the Co-operative Holidays Association (CHA) proposed to draw up a list of suggested reading for members – 'the open air course' – and to seek Professor Geddes's advice on the 'list of requirements and recommended books'. In practice, it was the National Home Reading Union (NHRU) that fielded the request and in June 1905 the CHA decided to produce a magazine 'with an attractive cover' containing lists of recommended books and articles on them. It would be sent to members of both associations: by virtue of a new arrangement, every member of the CHA was automatically a member of the NHRU. A year later the project was reconsidered and a sub-committee appointed to pursue it. Meeting in June 1907, they 'read correspondence received from the NHRU secretary and Mr W. G. Fuller' and proposed a fourteen-page magazine, to be published by Sherrat & Hughes, to appear in September and November 1907, and January, March and May 1908. The management of it was to be 'in the hands of W. G. Fuller with the advice of a small editorial committee.'[46] They reserved the sum of £100 for publishing it. No mention was made of any remuneration for the editor.

The first issue of the magazine, *Comradeship*, came out in October 1907. In the words of the General Secretary of the CHA, it aimed 'to draw all our members into a guild of readers, either in the sociable ways of a reading circle, or as individual readers in the quiet of their own firesides. Our ideal is to see a good-sized reading circle formed in every town, city and village in which one or more CHA members live.'[47] But this idea did not catch on; the annual report for 1911 regretted that 'the expectation that CHA circles

---

* Inspired by nineteenth-century romantics like Arnold, Ruskin and Morris, the Co-operative Holidays Association (now the Countrywide Holidays Association) lies at the origin of the Youth Hostel Association and the Family Holidays Association.

would spring up in districts where members live in large numbers has . . . not been realized.' On the other hand, 'the magazine of the Association with its five numbers a year seems to find acceptance with our large body of members.' There were over 13,700 of them in 1911.[48]

Unlike a magazine for ramblers today, *Comradeship* contained challenging reading. The first year's 'open air course' included *Chapters in Modern Botany* (1893) by Professor Geddes, and *Comradeship* printed five long commented summaries (called 'reviews') of it by Ernest E. Unwin.* Also in the first volume were five equally long essays on 'Citizenship' by J. A. Hobson and two on 'Shakspere [*sic*] and his dramatic art' by J.J. Wright, who had written a number of books, including one on reading called *So Many Books! So Little Time! What to do?* for the NHRU in 1891. The programme (and therefore the associated articles) for 1909 comprised *The Life of the Fields* by Richard Jefferies, G. F. Scott Elliot's *Nature Studies*, and *The Natural History of Selborne* for the 'open air course', plus (under the heading 'Poverty and the State') 'The Break-Up of the Poor Law' published by the Fabian Society, 'No Poor Law or New Poor Law' (a pamphlet by the students of Toynbee Hall), and *Some Social and Political Pioneers of the Nineteenth Century* by Ramsden Balmforth. The socialist leanings are evident. What role Walter played in the selection of titles is not known, but it would seem that he and his little editorial committee had a good deal of freedom in choosing their commentators. Walter certainly recruited writers whose work he had published elsewhere.

A recent book on Ruskin and the construction of cultural tourism in pre-war Britain devotes several pages to *Comradeship*. The authors see in it 'an overwhelming focus on Ruskin' which 'owed much to the agenda of the NHRU' and 'also helped to define a dominant ethos for the core membership of the CHA.'[49] In the two pages they devote to listing all the 'most direct and literal references to Ruskin in the pre-First World War issues,' only the last three items fall outside the period during which Walter was the editor.[50] So the 'focus on Ruskin' probably owed something to his sympathy with Ruskin's thought and his ability to line up contributors who were similarly inspired. (He was certainly familiar with Ruskin's writings, as we shall see.)

The *Readers' Review* was dreamed up by a Mr Cawthorne, the chief librar-

---

* Ernest Unwin (1881–1944) was a Quaker who gained his MSc in 1908; from 1912 he taught at Leighton Park, a Quaker school. A conscientious objector during WWI, he emigrated to Australia in 1923 to become headmaster of the Friends' School in Hobart. It would be interesting to know if he and Walter remained in contact, for he was a pioneer in educational broadcasting.

ian of Stepney public libraries, who believed that the 'vast *clientèle*' of the nation's libraries needed a periodical recommending the best books on a wide range of subjects. He sounded out members of the Library Association in the summer of 1903. News of his idea reached the NHRU, and in the summer of 1906, 'they sent their representative, Mr W. J. [*sic*] Fuller' to consult Mr Cawthorne 'on the question of establishing a closer relationship between Public Libraries and the National Home-Reading Union.' Walter 'enthusiastically took up the idea, and convinced the National Home-Reading Union that the *Readers' Review* was *the missing link* required to connect that agency with the great Public Library system throughout the land.'[51]

After a dummy issue had been circulated to libraries around the country, Walter attended the general meeting of the Library Association on 18 September 1907, alongside Dr J. B. Paton, the honorary secretary of the NHRU. Walter's description of the project and his answers to the librarians' questions overcame their doubts and the proposal was adopted. Thus he became the editor of the *Readers' Review – a monthly guide to books and reading* (hereafter the *RR*), backed by a board (whose role seems to have been purely nominal) representing the Library Association and the NHRU. The first issue appeared in February 1908, with contributions by Sir John Cockburn, who had been agent-general for Australia ('Books about our Colonies'); W. E. A. Axon of the *Manchester Guardian* ('Whittier, Poet and reformer'); the novelist Frank T. Bullen ('The Literature of the Sea'); H. H. Turner, Savilian Professor of Astronomy at Oxford, ('Books about Astronomy'); and the first of a long-running series called 'Books and Bookmen' by Thomas Seccombe, who had worked for twenty years on the *Dictionary of National Biography* as an assistant to Leslie Stephen (Virginia Woolf's father). Contributors like these do not volunteer; each and every one of them needed to be identified and recruited, and Walter became a prolific writer of letters.

Despite initial confidence that the *RR* would be financially viable, it almost never broke even. The problem was that individual libraries were free to take up or ignore the periodical, as they wished, and participating libraries were responsible for securing local advertising to pay for the venture. As they had no incentive to do so, cash was in short supply right from the start. (With national advertisements it might have been viable.) After the first issue came out, Walter was obliged to borrow from the printers – Sherrat & Hughes – to pay William Axon a modest honorarium.[52] One wonders whether he received anything himself. By June, the circulation of the periodical was just short of 20,000 copies a month,[53] but a year later it was still making a loss. Having solicited another article ('Manchester in Literature') from Axon at a rate of a guinea a page (750 words), Walter found he could pay only half the promised sum three months after the article came out.[54]

By the spring of 1908, Walter was editing three periodicals, of which two were distributed internationally (for the NHRU had branches in Australia and New Zealand). Although he would invite contributors to one of them to write for the others – for instance, J. A. Hobson wrote at length on citizenship in both *Comradeship* and the *UR* – there was relatively little overlap in the end.* Writing to Geddes in January 1908, for instance, he accepted an article on 'City & University' at the same time as soliciting 'a short article of not more than 2000 words on the story of the growth of cities' for the *RR* (proposed honorarium two guineas); a short review (not more than 200 words) of *The Memoirs of a Surrey Labourer*, also for the *RR*; and three short seasonal articles on Botany (and Nature Study generally) for *Comradeship* (for which he offered five guineas), to appear in the issues for February, April, and June 1908. Walter was quite clear as to what was wanted: 'We should like the review to be in two parts – the first telling the contents and general scope of the book – the second its contribution to the literature of the subject and the special claims of the book upon the attention of the Library reader.'[55] Geddes, however, had bigger fish to fry and contributed to neither periodical.

On the home front, Christmas 1907 saw the usual family gathering at Portchester, where the Fullers were joined by Basil Ward. Another guest was a new friend, Stanley Nott, who had been apprenticed to a draper in Bournemouth and had hated it (like H. G. Wells in Windsor and Southsea, and Caradoc Evans in Carmarthen and Cardiff). As soon as he could free himself from his articles, he got a job on a farm, preferring outdoor life to the claustrophobia of the shop. For his twenty-first birthday on 10 January 1908 – he was half way between Riss and Dorothy in age – Nott's mother gave him a nicely bound 'writings album' or autograph book, to which Dorothy, Rosalind and Cynthia each contributed a drawing and their parents an elevating sentiment, as was the custom at the time. Mr Fuller quoted from the Scottish classical scholar and poet, John Stuart Blackie: 'Difficulties are the true test of greatness – cowards shrink from them, fools bungle them, wise men conquer them.'[56]

He was acutely aware of impending disaster. Without weighing the possi-

---

* In all, Walter drew on more than 250 contributors, many of them prominent figures of the day, and among them many with a social conscience. Indexes to the contents of the *UR* and the *RR* under Walter's editorship can be found on this book's website.

ble consequences, he had underwritten or guaranteed the experiments of a Mr Oborne (or Obourne) to develop what Cynthia remembered as 'some new sort of gas for motor boats.'[57] The venture failed and bankrupted Mr Fuller.* First went the governess and domestic staff, then the shop, and finally the house and furniture, although it later transpired that Curt Dehn, who served as the family's legal adviser on this occasion – as for the rest of their lives – had bought their favourite pieces of furniture and put them into storage for them. That spring the Fuller family were left with nothing but Rosalind's cello and the clothes they stood up in. Cynthia was sent to stay with an aunt in Portsmouth, leaving Laddie in the conservatory behind the closed shop, fed each day by an ex-shop-assistant. Dorothy was sent to a relative somewhere in Dorset. Riss, Rosalind and their parents came to stay in Walter's flat in Purcell Mansion. Mrs Fuller was almost constantly breathless with asthma, and Mr Fuller had sick attacks.

For the girls, however, London in the early summer of 1908 was a most exciting place: even the Chelsea Historical Pageant, held in Old Ranelagh Gardens at the end of June, was quite eclipsed by the activities of the Women's Suffrage Movement. In January, a handful of suffragettes had chained themselves to the railings of number 10 Downing Street, and the WSPU had introduced its stone-throwing campaign. Soon Dorothy came up from Dorset, and Rosalind reported to Cynthia:

> I have a great piece of news to tell you: Riss and I are *Suffragettes*. I suppose you heard about the great demonstration of women in Hyde Park on June 21st? Well, on the Saturday a girl by the name of Jessie Holliday came to spend the night with us, as she was walking in the procession on Sunday. In the evening we had great discussions with Captain [i.e., Hamilton Irving] and Mullins [not identified] and Father, who as you doubtless guess are against it! Jessie H is such a queer girl, and I don't agree with her in all things. She is a Suffragette (for which Hurrah!), she is a vegetarian, a great believer in Bernard Shaw, a non-sugar, and she really thinks that in time people will not eat at all. She is also an artist.†

---

* I have not managed to trace this Mr Oborne, who was still dunning Mr Fuller for money in 1916. A Tom Oborn, who seems to have lived a blameless life, served as joint honorary treasurer with Mr Fuller on the Portchester pageant; perhaps it was a relative of his.

† Jessie Holliday was born into a Quaker family in 1884. She studied at the Royal Academy Schools from 1903 to Christmas 1906, when she left of her own accord, having decided to make portraits of leading Suffragettes (e.g. Lady Constance Bulwer-Lytton) and Socialists. By the end of 1909 she had portrayed George Bernard Shaw (printed in

Walter Fuller

While we were talking of Suffragettes, Riss said how sympathetic she was with them, and so Jessie H said, 'Will you come with me tomorrow and swell the numbers?' Riss very willingly agreed to, and as I am in favour of getting the vote, I asked if I might go as well, and she said 'Come by all means,' so I got my wish. Dorothy, who does not like Suffragettes, said she would rather see the procession, so it was agreed that Dorothy, Captain, Mullins and Father should come and see us march. [The next time she wrote she added that Walter was there too.]

When Sunday morning arrived, Jessie H, Riss (with collar) and I went to Trafalgar Square where we saw crowds of banners and people. Riss was given a banner to carry and she wore a band over her shoulder with 'Votes for Women' on it. I had a little piece of ribbon with *the colours* on it. Perhaps I had better tell you what they are in case you want to wear them in your hat or have a tie of them; they are *Purple, Green and White*.* Presently the bands began to play and away we marched. The words on the banner were: *Righteousness exalteth the Nation*.[58]

It was a historic occasion. While the *Daily Chronicle* estimated the crowd at 300,000, the *Times* thought there might have been as many as 500,000 people there, most of them women, brought in by train from all over Britain.

That summer the Fullers saw a good deal of Jessie Holliday, who had been introduced to them by Kathleen Wheeler (Tiger Lily). She was a talented portraitist, six months younger than Riss. While studying at the Royal Academy Schools she had exhibited a portrait of Kathleen Wheeler in 1905, and in 1907 her picture, 'The Reader', was accepted by the RA. In August, when she was preparing a cover illustration for the *Music Student*, Walter and Cynthia took her to the British Museum; later drawings, of which she was very proud, appeared in *Punch*. At the end of September she attended the Fabian Summer School, for she was a fervent socialist.

It must have been very cramped in Walter's two-bedroom flat, even though his sisters went off and stayed with friends whenever they could, and Walter camped for a while in – or above – the offices of the NHRU at 12 York Buildings. It was a desperate time for him, for he was supporting the entire

every edition of Archibald Henderson's biography of Shaw since the first in 1911); Christabel Pankhurst (daughter of the celebrated Suffragette); and both the Webbs, Beatrice and Sidney (later Lady and Baron Passfield). The drawings of the last three now hang in the National Portrait Gallery. Jessie suffered from an eating disorder. It was to be her downfall, as we shall see.

* The Suffragettes' colours were chosen earlier that year by Mrs Pethick-Lawrence to represent *dignity, hope*, and *purity*, respectively.

family on his income of £200 a year. Riss, it is true, earned something with her harp recitals (at Eton College in December 1907, for instance[59]) but they were only occasional and brought in little more than pocket money. In August, staying with farming friends down in Stalbridge, she sent her family a box of eggs – but failed to wrap them adequately. Walter regretfully reported '3 killed, 5 wounded, and 6 escaped uninjured' (adding playfully, 'these figures are correct; Father's are from the *Daily Mail*'). To this he appended a parody of Blake that went,

> Little egg, who sent thee?
> Dost thou know who sent thee,
> Wrapped thee up and put thee in
> One by one this box of tin,
> Gave thee clothing of delight –
> *Daily Mail*s all crisp and bright?
> Gave thee such a gentle bed
> So as not to break the head?
> Dost thou know sent thee?[60]

His levity belied the gravity of the situation. Mr Fuller, who was 53 in July that year, had high hopes of finding work in London. 'I cannot believe that I shall not get a job in this great city,' he told his wife as he advertised in the *Drapers' Record* and answered advertisements in the *Daily Telegraph*, *Christian World* and *Daily News*.[61] But Walter thought otherwise; in fact he had 'not least expectation of his being able to get a post,' and he arbitrarily set the sixth of September as the deadline: if Mr Fuller had no job by then, some other solution had to be found.

In a long letter to Riss, he weighed up their prospects. 'We should have a dismal time in London even if we can combine incomes & collect £400 a year. *Which we can't*.' It would cost much less to live in the country, and their father might possibly manage a village grocery store, for instance. Failing that, they could live 'in some little "sun-gilt white-washed cottage" in the Blackmore Vale' and 'Father could go about the county in a little pony trap selling odds & ends of drapery to the cottagers' and farmers' wives.' Walter could contribute £2 a week. As 'cake maker, flower gardener, music teacher, organist in the village church and composer' Riss 'could bring in anything between £25 and £2000 a year. Well, say £50.' On that they could manage. As an afterthought, he added:

> And couldn't you compose a symphony on *The Return of the Native*? . . . The music would come singing itself into your head some early morning as you lay in your white bed with the air of Blackmore Vale blowing through your

open window. And think of the research you could do in folk music and folklore among the Dorset peasantry.[62]*

These suggestions were not entirely unfounded. In the early years of the century, Riss had been in contact with the music publisher Feldman & Co (of The Strand, London), who had made an offer for a composition of hers, but apparently nothing had come of it in the end.

As for himself, he would take a room somewhere in Bloomsbury, 'which with breakfast would cost about 20 shillings, leaving me with another 20 shillings to spend only on myself – I should be passing rich.' Just think, he concluded, 'of the adventure of the country scheme. Why there's been nothing to equal it since the Pilgrim Fathers set out for America.'[63]

At once, Riss and Rosalind set about looking. By 6 September they had found a long, low, thatched cottage with a small garden and a large orchard in a tiny hamlet called Hartgrove Hill, four miles southwest of Shaftesbury, in the depths of Hardy's Wessex, where they could live just as Walter had envisaged. It was tiny: only a living-room, a red-tiled kitchen and three small bedrooms. Water had to be carried from a well some distance away; there was no bathroom and the lavatory was a shed in the garden. 'You could sit there,' recalled Rosalind, 'with the door wide open looking over the countryside, a pattern of green fields and darker hedges, and in the distance the hilly town of Shaftesbury.'[64] And the rent was only two shillings and sixpence a week (£6.50 a year).

Walter responded to the news with a rhapsodic letter to Riss, foreseeing happy days ahead in the Neverland of Hardy's Wessex,

> beginning with an overture by an orchestra of birds and ending at midnight with the great chorus of the stars. When I come down, you and I must go out and explore the neighbourhood – we'll search out some Roman remains maybe. . . . But what is more than this we will look for and see – yes, in broad daylight – the ghosts of those old warriors – and we will walk with them – yes and talk with them – for we have *imagination* – and to have that is better than to have wealth or knowledge or skill. . . .
>
> And find out all the good places in the garden where daffodils will grow so that next March we may have regiments of them.[65]

Riss, Rosalind, and Mr Fuller, who had come down to inspect Laurel Cottage, as it was called, moved in at once, borrowing mattresses from a

---

* At this time, only Henry and Robert Hammond had collected Dorset folksongs, between 1905 and 1908.

neighbouring farmhouse, and bedding, kitchen pans and crockery from the local vicar. Rosalind reported to Curt:

> Last Saturday evening, while Father, Riss and I were discussing where each piece of furniture was going, who should come walking up the little red path – but – Mother, Walter and Cynthy! Oh, it was more like the last scene in *Peter Pan,* when – but as Wendy wisely says in the play, 'over which we will draw the veil.'
>
> The tree tops look lonely without the 'Little House' but everyone must now come to Mrs Darling's house and we shall have to put screens round the beds, on 'at home' days – it will be lovely to see you again! Fancy, it is months, actually *months* since we've seen you.
>
> Mother and Cynthy went to Stalbridge (for about a week) today, as the beds haven't all come – only two as yet, and also the men haven't finished doing the house.[66]

It was in fact late November before they received the furniture that Curt had saved for them, but that at least left time for workmen to make some repairs and freshen up the paintwork. Subsisting largely on cabbages from the garden and apples from the orchard, they shared out the tasks. Rosalind volunteered to fetch the water. She had always loved the story of Jesus and the Woman at the Well, and knew the painting by Ingres, called 'The Source', of a naked girl (not unlike herself, she thought) with a pitcher of water on one shoulder. So she secretly nourished the hope of meeting Jesus one morning.[67] While Riss made curtains and bedcovers from a bolt of material retrieved from the back of the empty draper's shop, Mr Fuller began to dig the ungrateful soil of the garden. Although it soon began to feel like home, Mrs Fuller fought back tears. 'You can't live on a view,' she protested.[68]

2

Peter Pan

WENDY (*knowing she ought not to probe but driven to it by something within*) What are your exact feelings for me, Peter?
PETER (*in the classroom*) Those of a devoted son, Wendy.
WENDY (*turning away*) I thought so.
PETER You are so puzzling. Tiger Lily is just the same; there is something or other she wants to be to me, but she says it is not my mother.
WENDY (*with spirit*) No, indeed it isn't.
PETER Then what is it?
WENDY It isn't for a lady to tell.
   (TINK, *who has doubtless been eavesdropping, tinkles a laugh of scorn.*)
PETER (*badgered*) I suppose she means that she wants to be my mother.
   (TINK's *comment is 'You silly ass.'*)
WENDY (*who has picked up some of the fairy words*) I almost agree with her![1]

              J. M. Barrie

Walter in his early thirties

For a bankrupt, the only form of social welfare at that time was the workhouse, generally chosen as a last resort because of the social stigma it carried. In 1862, when Mr Fuller was a boy of six, his mother died and his father placed his baby sister in a workhouse for a few months, until he found a second wife. Never again! Much to the consternation of Curt Dehn, Walter swore to support his family so long as his father had no work. It was a fateful decision, for he quickly ran out of money and borrowed to keep afloat. He carried debts for the rest of his life.

He had never been good with money. As a student, he regularly overspent, despite resolutions to economize that he recorded in his diary. He was not extravagant; he wore the same clothes as long as they held together, and had his shoes repaired only when holes appeared in the soles. His pleasures were a steady drain on his weekly budget – a concert here or a play performance there, a new periodical or a copy of *Strand* magazine to read on the train – but they were a trickle compared with his thoughtless generosity. One week he spent a third of his budget on a birthday present for a fellow student, leaving himself with just a ha'penny for the weekend's meals. (On this occasion, Bill Hankinson saved the day by getting himself and Walter invited out to tea and supper on both Saturday and Sunday.) Generosity made him improvident. Like his father, he trusted that if money was needed, then money would be forthcoming. And sometimes it was. On one occasion, just when he wanted to pay for that week's instalment of '100 Best Pictures', he found a two-shilling postal order on the pavement. Into the front cover of his diary for 1899, he wrote (or copied): 'Every man has a duty of distribution as well as of accumulation laid upon him. God expects every man to have bestowed so much as well as laboured so much before his time comes.'[2] Giving was just as important as earning, but God, or chance, was never so generous with Walter as Walter was with other people.

To live more cheaply, he gave up his flat and (thanks to Professor Geddes) moved in October 1908 into the newly opened student hall of residence at 2–5 More's Garden, Chelsea. Here he found himself in an international community of admirers of Geddes and his philosophy.* They were headed by John Ross, the accountant who substituted for Geddes as warden of the hall, and Victor Branford, an ex-student of Geddes's and now his friend and colleague, who had just founded the Sociological Society. Branford was

---

* Residents that Walter mentions include E. V. Burns, from St Kitts in the West Indies; Lieutenant Broe Hansen, from Denmark, who became a regular visitor of the Fuller family; Mohammed Hussein, an assistant magistrate from Khartoum in the Soudan; Dr Lee MB, ChB, from Dublin, etc.[3]

already well known to Walter, for he contributed essays to the *UR* in September 1906 and March 1907. Walter promptly commissioned a series of eight articles for the *RR* on 'The Study of Society'.

More's Garden was the site of Geddes's ambitious project to preserve Crosby Hall (built behind Bishopsgate in or shortly after 1466) by reconstructing it as the centrepiece of a 'collegiate city' in Chelsea with the architectural cachet of Oxford and Cambridge. He envisaged links with the Battersea branch of the Worker's Educational Association on the other side of the river. However, after the original Hall had been dismantled, with each stone and beam carefully numbered, its new site became the object of controversy and competition. Gordon Selfridge apparently wanted to relocate it to the top of his department store, which was then under construction – a detail that would barely merit notice here were it not that Walter corresponded on friendly terms with Selfridge after WWI. A more serious competitor was Emilie Barrington who wanted to recreate Crosby Hall in the back garden of Leighton House, in Kensington. However, the fact that Crosby Hall had been leased to Sir Thomas More in 1523–24 argued in favour of the More's Garden site. In May 1908, Geddes's University and City Association of London won the day;* work began on the corner of Cheyne Walk and Danvers Street.

A junior architect working closely with Geddes on the project was Adrian Berrington. A talented artist with a penchant for drawing landscapes, he was five years younger than Walter and the two got on well. After mutual visits, their respective families became acquainted. Adrian's father was one of the designers of the Stanley Dock Tobacco Warehouse in Liverpool: at the time of its construction (1897–1901), it was the largest brick building in the world. In the autumn of 1908, Adrian's mother sent flowers for Cynthia to plant in the garden at Laurel Cottage,[4] and Rosalind was invited to the coming-out party of Berrington's sister Dorothea. (The similarity between the names *Emilie Barrington* and *Berrington* was not lost on Rosalind: when some poems of hers were published in 1917, she swapped over two vowels to create a pseudonym for herself: *Emilia Berrington*.)

Walter's best friend in London was always Curt. He stayed with Curt's

---

* Among the personalities on the board of the association, alongside Walter Crane, Mrs Humphrey Ward and H.G. Wells, was Laurence Gomme, London County Council's main defender of historic buildings; he was also honorary secretary, director and president of the Folklore Society. Walter got him to write on 'British Folklore, Folksongs, and Games' in the fourth issue of the *Readers' Review* for May 1908.

family in Moss Side, Manchester, on many occasions, and knew Curt's brothers, Fred,* Frank and Harold, as well as his cousins, Edward, Tom and Dickie. The seven boys were very close, for their respective fathers had married girls who were sisters. Tom studied at Balliol College, Oxford, and contributed a piece on 'Plato and the Twentieth Century' to the July 1907 issue of the *UR*. On his recommendation, Walter also printed an article on Maxim Gorki by a college friend of his, Arthur Dakyns.

As Arthur Dakyns came to loom rather large in the lives of the Fuller family, a proper introduction to him is called for here. Although he was two years younger than Walter, the Fullers always referred to him and addressed him as 'Dakyns', and I shall do so too, unless to distinguish him from his brother Henry, or his father, a schoolmaster at Clifton College who had tutored Alfred Lord Tennyson's sons. On graduating from Balliol, Dakyns was uncertain as to what profession to embrace. To help him decide, Walter provided him with introductions to prominent contributors to the *UR*.† They brought Dakyns short-term employment with the South London branch of the Workers' Educational Association in the spring of 1908, renewed in September that year, after Dakyns had taken a long summer holiday during which he travelled extensively.

Dakyns' best friend at this time was Bertrand Russell, who enjoyed debating philosophical questions with him but found him 'a very restive disciple, always going after the false gods of the Hegelians.'[5] They holidayed together several times and occasionally Russell stayed with the Dakyns family.‡ Other friends included the philosopher George Moore, and Crompton Llewelyn Davies, who was at Cambridge with Arthur Dakyns' brother Henry.§ Both Crompton and Henry were friends of the composer, Ralph Vaughan Williams (1872–1958). Dakyns also knew people in what became known as

---

* Fred was the father of Paul Dehn, poet and scriptwriter, known for the *Planet of the Apes* and some of the James Bond films.

† The first was Michael Sadler, who had contributed to the *UR* in July 1907. He was Professor of the History and Administration of Education at Manchester. When he joined the University, Walter printed a brief summary of his political career and a photograph of him in the *Magazine* for February 1904. Sadler sent Dakyns to Albert Mansbridge, the secretary of the Workers' Educational Association, another contributor to the *UR* (August 1905 and March 1908).

‡ Russell's wife Alys contributed an article to the *UR* on Bedford College for Women back in August 1905.

§ Davies was the uncle of the five boys who inspired Barrie's *Peter Pan*; he became their guardian after the deaths of their parents.

the Bloomsbury group, starting with Charles and Dora Sanger. Charles, a brilliant barrister, was a friend of both Bertrand Russell and Virginia Woolf, who dedicated *Orlando* to him. Dakyns' sister Frances knew Madge Vaughn, one of Virginia Woolf's closest friends. Thus it came about that, on 1 November 1908, Virginia wrote to Madge, 'I met a young man who admires you the other night – Arthur Daykins [*sic*].'[6]

That meeting probably took place as a result of Arthur's decision, in October 1908, to set up a Friday Club for talks on literature. It was a replica of the Friday Club for painting that Virginia Woolf's sister Vanessa had started in 1905. Some of the speakers at his Friday Club attended Vanessa's, and there was overlap in the membership too. In February 1910, for instance, Arthur reported to his father that 'there was a very good meeting of the Friday Club at the Bells' last Friday. . . . Fry read a v. good paper and there was a rather good discussion until 12 midnight.'* On his informal committee were: a Mr Evans, a sub-editor on the *Nation*;† Thomas Seccombe, an intimate of the Stephen/Woolf/Bell families who had been contributing to the *RR* on a monthly basis since the first issue in January 1908; Mary Sheepshanks who, as acting Principal of Morley College, had recently invited Virginia Woolf to start teaching there; later she edited the journal of the International Women's Suffrage Society, *Jus Suffragii*; Frank Sidgwick, who had just founded the publishing firm of Sidgwick & Jackson; a Miss Read, who was the secretary of the National Home-Reading Union; and Walter. He probably put forward some of these names. At any rate, Dakyns told his father that he would also 'invite G. M. Trevelyan to join when he returns to town and he is certain to as well.'[7] Trevelyan had contributed an article on 'English Life in the Seventeenth Century' to the *RR* only a couple of months earlier, August 1908.‡

The meetings of Arthur Dakyns' club seem to have passed unrecorded. I have found no mention of them in accounts of the activities of the Bloomsbury group; our sole source is Dakyns' letters to his father and his sister. It is furthermore almost impossible to distinguish them from meetings of Vanessa's club, which have themselves been eclipsed by the attention given

---

* This would be Roger Fry, of course, an old boy of Clifton College, where Arthur's father taught.

† This is possibly Caradoc Evans, who was a journalist in Fleet Street by 1906.

‡ Trevelyan (1838–1928) became the first president of the Youth Hostels Association, some of whose roots lie in the CHA. Their headquarters is called Trevelyan House in his honour.

to its exhibitions. In a letter dated 9 January 1909, for instance, Dakyns announced a meeting to be held on 29 January, chaired by Ralph Sawtrey, at which the poet Laurence Binyon (1869–1943) was to read a paper 'on some unknown Elizabethan painter. We have our meeting here next Friday and some members of the Friday club to dinner beforehand.' Binyon's topic suggests that it was a session of Vanessa's club, but Dakyns added, 'I have now finally arranged for the dinner to be at the Villa Villa in Gerard Street.' So he seems to have been involved in organizing both clubs. (Incidentally, he found Binyon's paper 'not at all interesting.') Later that year, he ventured to invite his father to a meeting – 'tea and pictures' – of the Friday Club at 22 Hyde Park Gate, the Stephens' house.[8] Given the venue, it may again have been Vanessa's club, discussing pictures rather than exhibiting them. In 1911 Dakyns chose to present *pantomime* as the topic for a meeting of his club. None of Walter's surviving letters mention attending the meetings. Well attested, on the other hand, are his evenings at the theatre in the company of Dakyns and the two Dehns, Curt and Tom. Not infrequently Dakyns would have to leave early, suffering from his weekly attack of asthma.

Dakyns records lunching with Walter on 9 October 1908 to meet Evans (of the *Nation*) and Max Hueffer (i.e., Ford Madox Ford, who had just launched the *English Review;* he wrote on 'German Letters and German Life' in the *RR* for September 1909) 'and various others' without specifying the purpose of the meeting. He was possibly looking for career openings. That winter his brother Henry was planning a round-the-world voyage with his wife Winifred, and they urged Arthur to go with them for the sake of his health. Their father supported the idea, offering to pay for Arthur's ticket and to cover all his expenses. In the hope of turning the trip to some account with journalism, Arthur and Walter met Evans again on 26 January 1909 – but nothing came of it. Henry and Winifred sailed without Arthur.

In the end, Dakyns plumped for law at Lincoln's Inn, and promptly regretted it. 'I have been having rather a nasty time with the law,' he told his father on 16 June. 'I think it was a great mistake to have gone into Chambers at once; but one couldn't tell. Anyhow, I shall have to go on with it now. I can't help thinking I might have done something else than go to the bar. Schoolmastering would certainly not have been more disagreeable.'* Dakyns

---

* He persevered and passed Roman Law (Class II) and Criminal Law & Practice (Class III) in March 1910. He gained a Class III pass in Constitutional Law and Legal History in May that year, and Class III in his Final Examination in April 1911. He was called to the Bar on 19 June 1912, but never practised as a lawyer.

seems to have found something of an elder brother in Walter, and joined him in the student hall at More's Garden. Walter was less keen. He did not invite Dakyns down to stay with his family before the spring of 1910, whereas Curt Dehn, Basil Ward, Hamilton Irving – still called 'Captain' – and various others from More's Garden were regular visitors, even when the Fuller home was the modest cottage on Hartgrove Hill.

At the time of the move to the cottage, Dorothy had been on holiday with Captain, and she returned very much in love with him. Riss complained that 'we don't get a look in as he and Dorothy are always out together.' Then, telling Curt about local superstitions, she let fall some news:

> The dear funny people here believe in witchcraft and it's many stories they will tell of old neighbour Nancy who is said to be bewitched and who seems to do the queerest things. By the way, this mad Nancy will be Captain's next door neighbour and his handmaiden when he takes possession of his country seat, of which I expect you have heard. It seems to me that Captain has great possessions.

So while the Fullers were coping with the realities of housing and feeding a family of six on £2 a week, Hamilton Irving was dreaming of inheriting an estate and filling Dorothy's head with his fantasies. After a few pages on everyday matters, Riss returned to him and Dorothy:

> they are beginning to talk of the future and of all the queer things they are going to do. They will study art together and singing and violin, and Dorothy is never to look at a cobweb nor a duster and there are to be hundreds of servants and two or three houses, with a piano in every room and we are to go and stay in turns . . . and you are too . . . and there are to be no conventions and no methods and meals are never to be regular. . . . These are some of the ramblings which overflow from Dorothy's pent up heart, after a walk with Captain. . . . Isn't it funny! Will they ever grow up, do you think?[9]

There was definitely a Wendy in Riss.

Now that the Fullers were living in the depths of rural Wessex, Walter was concerned for the education of his younger sisters and urged them to keep studying. Whilst they were happy to have seen the last of their governesses, he impressed upon them how lucky they were: girls who went to school were crammed with things they did not want to know, whereas they had only to ask how, why, when, or where, to learn whatever they wanted. (How Walter would have relished the internet!) So although his sisters never got far in algebra or geometry, for instance, he ensured that literature was part of their daily lives, bringing them books of poetry and novels. Nor was art neglected: he introduced them to a card game like Happy Families called National

Gallery. Rosalind remembered how even at the age of nine Cynthia could be heard asking, 'Have you got "Ulysses deriding Polyphemus"?' and she would reply 'No. Have you Carpaccio's "St George and the Dragon"?'[10]

Fired by Walter's philosophy, Rosalind decided that she would be a great 'cellist and 'spent hours practising in an icy-cold living room, with chilblains on my fingers and a burning ambition in my heart.' Curt gave her a small bust of Beethoven and a book of his piano sonatas. 'I delighted in trying to play them and when I had done my best I would press my lips against the carved cold mouth of the statue.... I also imagined that I looked like him and used to push my curly hair back from my forehead and press my lips out in profound thought.'[11]

Music was their passport into the local community, for by now they were all accomplished musicians; even before they left Portchester, Dorothy and Rosalind (aged fourteen and twelve) were playing in Fareham orchestra.[12] In October the girls performed at a concert in Stalbridge, playing solos, duets, trios and quartets. Captain recited 'The Village Concert' from *Social Sketches: In Verse* (1868) by Rose E. Thackeray, and Dorothy 'reduced the people to tears by singing "Sing me to sleep".'[13]*

Walter had another project for them. Hardly had he seen the new house and its orchard when he declared that it was the perfect setting for performing *A Midsummer Night's Dream*. During the winter they learned their lines and rehearsed, and in the spring of 1909 they put it on, under Walter's direction. Dorothy was a magnificent Titania, Rosalind played Oberon, and Cynthia was Puck. All their friends had parts too of course, with Captain as Bottom. Even Mr Fuller, whose lack of a job was making him feel very depressed, had a role. This raised his spirits and he threw himself into it with characteristic enthusiasm, persuading the local Vicar to join the cast as well. Mrs Fuller provided the lighting effects by turning up or down the wick of their large oil-lamp. It went so well that they decided to do it again for the local villagers. They came and sat on kitchen chairs and boxes and watched open-mouthed as these extraordinary new neighbours of theirs acted, sang and danced in the orchard. Walter assured his family afterwards that it was 'a truly magical and spellbinding performance.'

Although none of the Fullers could possibly have suspected it at the time, this was a significant moment for them all. Directing his sisters' musical and dramatic talents was to become Walter's principal activity during the next

---

* 'Sing me to sleep': probably by John Imrie (1846–1902), the Scottish poet who lived and worked in Toronto.

ten years – but it would take several financial and personal setbacks for it to become apparent to them that this was where their future lay.

By now, Captain, who was thirty-two in February 1909, was wanting to marry Dorothy, but as she had only just turned nineteen it was understood that they were to have a two-year engagement. For Christmas 1908 he took her to Switzerland – a favourite destination for his family as his father was in a curling team.* From there he wrote to Mr Fuller asking to marry that spring, on the grounds that Dorothy had 'changed greatly' since their engagement. 'She will never be more ready than she is now to come to me.' He went on, 'It is impossible for me to get down to the work I wish to pursue until I get married, . . . moreover I think it would be standing in Dorothy's way to prevent her.'[14] Having barely adjusted to the idea of the engagement, Dorothy's close-knit family reacted badly to this request. Her sisters wondered how she could possibly want to leave them, and resented Captain's intrusion into 'the fairyland of our lives.'[15] Six years earlier, when Riss was twenty, she had been told to 'think nothing whatever of love.' Now, however, things stood rather differently; it would mean one less mouth to feed, and Captain was determined. A July wedding was agreed upon.

Predictably, Walter was horrified at the prospect. 'What do you advise me to do about coming to this wretched wedding of Dorothy's?' he asked Riss.

I'd almost as soon go to her funeral. And for me not a moment of that day will be free from sadness and black anger. But I'll come if you think it best. I want to be a friend always with Dorothy, not only for her sake but for mine. Rather than lose her affection – it is no longer love of course – I would suffer myself to endure the ordeal of seeing her married. While I do not want to put myself up as a censor of morals and conduct I do feel that it is desirable for some member of our family to indicate that it has occurred to us that Dorothy is too young for marriage, and that Irving – in forcing the pace as he has done – has outraged our feelings in this matter. Everyone who has spoken to me of Dorothy's marriage has commented upon her childishness and it makes me sick. I see clearly that if I don't come home for the wedding ceremony I shall definitely break away from further relations with Dorothy – for many years at any rate. If I do attend I think it will be possible for me to see Dorothy occasionally. I can't see any peace or happiness ahead in either case so it doesn't seem to matter much whether I come home or not.

Do you, or does anybody at home want to give wedding presents? If so, just tell me what you're thinking of and I'll get it. Quite seriously (not to say

---

* The Scots introduced the Swiss to curling in 1885.

sadly) I'm saying this – won't Baby [i.e., Cynthia] or Rosalind or Father want to give the poor little soul something? Perhaps a book, or something silver and ornamental – or a picture? Why not give her one of our two busts of Cynthia?[16]

The ever practical Riss took charge of things, making it 'as festive a day as possible'. Walter relented to the extent of being present, but he was never reconciled to the marriage. And not without good reason, as it turned out.

As it was, Walter had other things on his mind that month. Having no common cause to defend or promote, the Inter-universities Congress of Students was gradually falling apart and it decided to discontinue publication of the *University Review* from June 1909, after issue number 45. This was a major blow, depriving Walter of his main source of income. Yet he was full of ideas. 'Let me tell you what I've been and done,' he crowed to Riss.

> You know I've had the idea for a long time that, when a new building is to be formally opened with pomp & circumstance, the men who have actually done the work – built the building, laid brick on brick – should have a share in the honour and glory. You know how things are managed nowadays in these matters, don't you – hence the present degradation of labour and the labouring man. Well, did you see that when the King went to open the new Museum buildings at South Kensington a few days ago, he received a deputation from the workmen & congratulated them on the splendid results of their labour. . . . Well, I do think that somebody should suggest that when the King goes to open [the Aston Webb building on 7 July at] the new University at Birmingham, he ought to honour some of the workmen as well. So this is what I've done: I've written to one of the Birmingham professors – whom I know quite well – Professor Muirhead by name – and asked whether he could see me on Saturday. There's a cheap excursion – 5/- [five shillings] return – to Birmingham on Saturday so I'll just run up to see if he says *yes*. You approve, don't you. I want to say to him that if he wants somebody to see the workmen and get them to ask Sir Oliver Lodge, the principal, to arrange for them to see the King, I'll just say that I'll go and see the men. 'Tis a very important idea, I think.[17]

I have found no record of the result of this venture.

He had other matters to pre-occupy him, as well. To all appearances, Walter was a confirmed bachelor. At nineteen, he had confided to his diary, 'All I trust is that I may always remain a bachelor,'[18] perhaps because he felt it his duty to look after his sisters, and certainly because of his affection for Riss. Loving any other girl would feel like betraying her, not to mention his mother. When we remember Peter Pan and Wendy, the probability of his marrying was not great. Yet he was clearly not immune to falling in love. In the spring of 1901, Bill Hankinson had introduced Walter to his sister Annie. She took a shine to him, and cancelled other arrangements in order to be at home during Walter's visit to the family in August. Returning to Manchester for the next academic year, he found himself 'getting a little foolish in this affair – just a little. I must be careful.'[19] But Annie had just been taken on as governess to Rudyard Kipling's children, and that autumn she accompanied the Kiplings to South Africa (where they regularly wintered).* There she met and married another man. For several years after that, Walter seems to have escaped romantic attachment.

Soon after Dorothy's wedding, however, he made a long confession to Riss. In August 1908, when 'everything of ours at Portsmouth and Portchester and Purcell Mansions was breaking up into smithereens,' he had felt an urgent need to flee to Neverland. 'I dived away into the blue – away where the wicked ceased from troubling and the weary were at rest' – and joined Bill Hankinson, another of his sisters, Hilda, and a Frederick (probably one of Bill's ten siblings†) for a week's holiday in Penmaen (or Penmain), south Wales. 'Blue sky – blue sea – sun and wind and stars! The wonder is that I didn't fall in love with the first girl I saw – and by the way I think as a matter of fact I did. – Well, that was the psychology of the situation.'[22]

The girl was Rosamond Impey, a friend of the Hankinsons. Born on 12 March 1889, she was eight years younger than Walter, and nine months older than Dorothy. She was a Quaker, a movement to which Walter had been introduced by Geddes (a Quaker himself) and with whose social philosophy he came to be increasingly sympathetic. On Walter's return to London, he and Rosamond began to correspond. On the pretext of debating Sunday School Reform, 'letters began to pass to and fro' from London to her home

---

* This tells us where Kipling found the name for his imaginary schoolboy translator of 'The Survival', Ode 22 in his imaginary Book V of Horace's *Odes*: 'I've got a new Fifth Booker whereof Hankinson Ma. is preparing the translation.'[20] 'Hankinson Major' also contributed a translation of 'Lollius'.[21]

† If this was Frederick Hankinson (and his family gives me every reason to believe it was), then Walter was with the Unitarian minister who visited nearly all the Suffragette leaders in their prison cells, reading to them the letters that they were forbidden to receive. The exception was Emmeline Pethick-Lawrence. By the time of her incarceration, in 1912, Frederick had been banned by the prison authorities, suspected of breaking prison regulations. His best friend, Frederick Pethick-Lawrence, wrote his obituary for *The Times*.

in Alvechurch, near Birmingham, and 'more often protests from Alvechurch to London.'[23] Ignoring the social implications, Walter called on her at home not long after, when he and Dakyns visited the newly established Quaker centre for adult education at Woodbrooke (the former home of George Cadbury, the chocolate manufacturer), only six-and-a-half miles from where the Impeys lived. Thereafter Rosamond made several visits to London, staying with friends. Walter would mention her in his letters to Riss, generally expressing more apprehension than pleasure: 'PS. Rosamond Impey arrives at Adelaide Road tomorrow. I'm only going to meet her at a Conversazione at the Chapel School. The Bonds will be there. Oh dear. Oh lor.'[24]

Rosamond spent more time in London during the summer of 1909, when Walter became involved (at her instigation, it would seem) in a series of amateur performances of Alice Buckton's medieval-style Mystery play, *Eager Heart*.* At the foot of a letter dated 31 August, Walter reported to Riss:

> There's just an inch left for me to tell you something of my doings these last few days. Saturday: *Eager Heart* in the afternoon (not acting myself) with Hilda [Hankinson], Rosamond and Hansen [the Dane in the hall at More's Garden] – afterwards to *Beethoven* (all four). Sunday I was here all day with [Curt Dehn], Captain & Dorothy & Price [not identified] for guests. Geddes very good. Monday in the afternoon Rosamond & I (failing to find Dorothy) had an hour's talk from Geddes. This morning Tuesday Rosamond returned home. This afternoon I acted in *Eager Heart* [for the] last time.[25]

'During all that time, and since then,' Rosamond and Walter were just good friends – outwardly at least. But as he told Riss,

> though no word – and hardly even a look – has passed between us, we have become – I have any rate – increasingly *distrait*, awkward and self-conscious.

---

* Published in 1904, *Eager Heart* is based on the legend that during Christmastime the holy family travels throughout the world and blesses it. It is set in the home of a woman called Eager Heart; having prepared to receive the Christ Child she welcomes instead a beggar, with his wife and child. All the other characters, blinded by their preconceptions, search for the Christ Child in fame, in good sense, in power, in love, in wisdom, and therefore miss His coming. For a few years, it enjoyed popularity in London as a Christmas play, performed in Lincoln's Inn Hall in December 1907 and again in 1908; in Passmore Edwards Settlement in 1909; in the Church House, Westminster, in 1911; and in a church hall, December 1912. Since then, it has been revived only very occasionally in England. On the other side of the Atlantic, however, its success has been durable, especially at those universities where Alice Buckton organized readings of it in 1911. In one college at least, it has been performed every year since then.

> It cannot continue thus for long. On December 4th Hilda tells me Rosamond is coming up to stay with her for a few days. I'm thinking of hiding away – 'Manchester' you know.

'Manchester' was Walter's default destination when he wanted to escape from a situation that was emotionally too intense for him, rather as 'Bunbury' was Algernon Moncrieff's excuse, in *The Importance of Being Ernest,* for avoiding unwelcome social obligations.

The problem was not so much Walter's feelings for Rosamond, but rather his possessive – and obsessive – love for his sister. 'I really think we *are* one another,' he confessed to her.

> That's how *I* feel anyway. As for either of us to think of loving anybody else – it is rank treachery. I cannot help being wildly jealous – in a real lover-like way exactly – of anybody who may be so audacious as to fall in love with you – and for my own part I cannot tell you of the sense of shame that comes upon me when I even think of loving any other girl than you. We were born engaged to one another, you and I – and it seems to me that for either of us to love anybody else will be like breaking off a twenty years engagement....
>
> And so now when I think of Rosamond Impey I feel not only that I am behaving like a scoundrel to you, but that you will never believe in me any more. I want always – not for any sentimental reasons but because without it I can never be happy in my heart – I want always for us to be able to end our letters to one another with mother's phrase, 'with all my love'. Yes – yes – yes, I know these are false difficulties that I am making – whatever happens to either of us, we shall always love one another just the same, that I know. But we must plan so as to keep ourselves always ready & free for this special feeling of deep affection. I mean – though I know it is true that we may love others without lessening our love for one another, yet we must see to it that our other love is not a rival to but an addition to our own long-standing love.
>
> And that is how I feel first of all with regard to Rosamond Impey. I would say so much as this – and I really and truly mean what I say – if you feel that you cannot think of me with Rosamond with just as much love and joy as you think of me now – why though I love her dearly (forgive me) yet will I willingly think of her no more and cleave to you with no less love. You understand. We do not ask our parents' consent in these things so much as one another's. You must commend Rosamond to me – ere I will commend her to you. You will know her now almost as well as I do – probably indeed better than I do.

Walter floundered and wrestled with his feelings like a fish out of water. The depth of his confusion is revealed by the religious echo of his closing words: 'It all depends on you – everything. Seriously do I say – quite seriously, "thy way, dear girl, not mine." Your help.'[26]

Riss's answer to his appeal has not survived; she no doubt encouraged Walter, for she liked Rosamond. At the same time the Wendy in her may well have been saying, beneath her breath, 'You ass!' At any rate, Walter continued to see Rosamond socially. Eventually she became a regular visitor to the Fuller family, but still he made no move. It would take a much more assertive woman – one that Barrie might have called 'less of a lady' – than Rosamond to break through Walter's block.[27]

It was perhaps because Walter felt guilty towards Riss that he arranged, in August 1909, for her – and Rosalind – to attend courses at Woodbrooke. Although Rosalind was only seventeen, below the minimal age, Walter managed to get her accepted. He knew some of the lecturers there and, according to her autobiography, written some fifty years later, 'one of the directors was interested in buying some shares' in the *University Review*. To persuade Riss to go, Walter wrote more emotionally than usual (and this is but one passage from a letter that runs to several pages):

> You will make me happy if you will but let me make some such sacrifice – Do please give me some chance of being a little bit of a hero to myself. Let me know of *something* good that I have done. I shall not brag about it – 'tis little enough in all conscience – but 'twill be something good to think about some day – and things good to think about are none too many – that I helped you to go to Woodbrooke. So then I would say to you from my heart – with my arms about you and with many kisses – 'Let me do this much for you. I am glad that it is difficult – I should be glad if it were more difficult. I cannot call it a sacrifice – that which I would do. I shall gain far more than it will cost me. I shall be happier – because you will be happy; richer – because you will be richer – and nearer to heaven and to God because I shall be nearer to you in love.'[28]

In the end, Riss accepted to go 'with mingled feelings – half in favour and half strongly against.' She told Basil Ward,

> I can't help feeling that it's most extravagant. At my age I ought to be earning rather than spending, and it troubles me. But Walter is so very anxious for me to go and I simply gave in to please him. When I love a person very much, I can refuse them nothing.[29]

It was indeed an extravagance. Walter must have borrowed again to finance his sisters' stay at Woodbrooke – and was relieved when Riss, after three weeks at the college, agreed that the experience was beyond monetary value.

Money was not his only problem: his mother was going to be without Riss's help in the house for five months. Walter's solution was to mobilize Riss once more:

> Can you build up mother's strength of mind and strength of body? Can you find a new house fit & worthy to be our new home? That is all you have to do – then I shall be no longer in doubt. The shock to mother of the first parting from you will be broken altogether and will escape her notice if she is carried away to London by Dorothy for a fortnight or three weeks – For the sake of all the happy memories you & I have in common – for the sake of our love – do not think for a moment of the money cost of going to Woodbrooke.[30]

As before, Riss came up trumps. Within three weeks she was writing to Basil Ward from Laurel Cottage,

> I've been out on the rampage again, and lo! at Sturminster Newton [some five miles to the southwest of Hartgrove Hill], there is a most sweet house. It's bigger than this, but something like it; with a thatched roof, oak beams and crooked walls; but besides these things, it has an oak staircase, a bathroom, water laid on; gas laid on; four bedrooms; and two big or three small living rooms, and oak corridors painted white! Now all these joys are to let and having seen them I was at once keen to have them for a real Home, and so off I dashed to the agent.

Being both competent and canny, Riss knew how to land a bargain. The estate agent, who had been living in the house, rent free, suggested £40,

> but of course the house is not worth that. . . . I told the agent that personally I would take it on a 99-year lease and pay £100 a year, if I could, but I said, 'My father is a practical man and he looks upon the beams as obstacles, so I don't think he will offer more than £25.' And so I went on, until I had got right round the agent and now he is mad, frantic – for us to get it.[31]

And get it they did, for £25 a year.

The American portrait photographer Alice Boughton visited the Fullers in the summer of 1912. In an article she contributed to *Harper's Bazaar*, she described how their home might look like a toy cottage, yet

> one is much surprised at the amount of space within. The house is of the rambling sort, where one goes on and on, sometimes down a few steps into a cheerful dining-room bright with old china, pewter, and brass and flowers – of course, flowers everywhere.[32]

As soon as he saw it, Walter fell in love with Bridge House – 'a dear, sweet place,' 'a little jewel'. It had many attractions for him: his mother would feel less isolated there and his father stood a better chance of finding work. Moreover, Thomas Hardy's Tess of the D'Urbervilles had walked down the road that passed in front of it. In fact, Hardy himself lived (albeit briefly) in a neighbouring house, Riverside, that had been owned and occupied by the Dorset dialect poet, Robert Young (1811–1908). The river itself was 'a little love song'.[33] The place had everything to recommend it, so the family prepared to move again. In mid-October Walter joined his father and Cynthia, whose thirteenth birthday fell on the twenty-first of that month, in supervising the removal.

Her mission accomplished, Riss set out for Woodbrooke at the end of September. Rosalind joined her there from London, accompanied by Walter, waved off from Waterloo station by Cynthia. Along with some fifty young adults of various nationalities, they followed courses in literature, logic, philosophy, and French (for the English speakers) in the mornings, with tennis and visiting in the afternoon, and social activities in the evenings. Riss and Rosalind were soon in demand for their musical skills, accompanying hymns on the piano and singing folksongs. Their daily life 'seems to me an ideal combination of feeling, thought, and action,' exclaimed Walter.[34] They had days off too. On 8 October, he commented, 'So today you have gone over to Alvechurch' where Rosamond's parents had a large house, built by her father in 1891, on a site covering eighteen acres. 'Indeed it is not without some pleasing prospects,' observed Walter, somewhat ambiguously.[35]

Mindful that Riss and Rosalind were studying hard, Walter enjoined Cynthia to keep up with her piano practice – she was learning '*Le Coeur de ma mie*' (1905) by Emile Jacques-Dalcroze – and to get her pieces by heart, so that 'when you are asked to play the piano, and have no music with you, you don't appear to be paralysed and helpless.'[36] At this period, he felt that she lacked initiative.

Ten days later, he detailed his own Sunday activities in a letter to Riss from More's Garden. I quote it at length, since it so informative.

> A word or two about my doings today so that you may come to know what kind of a life I'm leading nowadays. Well, to begin at the beginning, came Ross in his pyjamas into my room at 8 o'clock to tell me that it was time to get up if I wanted to be at the Battersea Adult School by 8.45. So up I got and had a hurried breakfast at 8.25 (cup of tea and some bread and butter – ordinary breakfast not being served till 9 o'clock on Sundays), a certain new resident here named O'Brien having breakfast with me. Just a word about this O'Brien [not identified]. He's an Australian, an MD and is engaged in research work at the Lister Institute of Preventive Medicine along on the Embankment here. And he's a splendid fellow. About 30 or 32 I should say, and as keen and as alive as a race horse. Geddes said to me of him, 'He's a

> man that will go far' – and he's ready and witty [and] good to look at. . . . I asked O'Brien to come and talk to the Battersea Adult School men on the Colour Question as it strikes an Australian – and he readily agreed – & so this morning he got up early – well 8 o'clock on Sundays is rather early – and came along with me. We got there in good time [and] exactly at 8.45 we had our hymn. O'Brien spoke very well and very simply – and had the sense to hand round some interesting postcards & views to illustrate his points. He is bitterly opposed to the entry of any Chinese or Japanese into Australia. The men were very much pleased with him – and we had a good discussion – then O'Brien left and we went on with our hymn and prayer and Bible reading – the special part about the latter was the lesson of 'sacrifice' – and after a more or less rambling discussion I wound the talk up with five minutes of the best & simplest little sermon I have ever given in my life. My point being that no sacrifice was worthy of the name which wasn't a personal giving of oneself – comparing the sacrifice of Florence Nightingale, of Sir Thomas More, and of the nameless thousands who have given the best of themselves to advance what they have thought to be the interest of true religion – in its widest sense – with those who like Carnegie simply write cheques. That is putting somewhat baldly the main point of what I said – but I know very well that I meant what I said and as a consequence what I said was good and true.

From this, it would seem that Walter felt that, by borrowing money to support his family and educate his sisters, he had not given the best of himself, since it involved no personal sacrifice. His letter continues:

> So we broke up – and came back over here . . . and so to the Current Events Club. There was a good muster this morning – I managed to get Pratt* to come and a new resident named Tripp (a son of a Unitarian minister in Leicester). We talked about the theory of government – how far was a majority justified in ruling a minority – and I spoke for a little while on the shooting of Ferrer – the Spanish educationist, you know – a horrible crime.†
> So to lunch . . . with Geddes for next door neighbour – and some good talk. Then after lunch – out to explore the foundations of Crosby Hall – they're putting it up in the grounds at the back of the place here – with Hansen, Ross & Geddes, & Pratt took photographs of the place and us.[37]

* J. E. Pratt, a civil engineer (BSc London), was staying in the hall of residence.

† Francisco Ferrer y Guardia (1859–1909), the originator of non-denominational, co-educational, private schools in Spain, was executed on 13 October after a fake trial. Shortly after, Pope Pius X presented the military prosecutor who had obtained Ferrer's death with a gold-handled sword engraved with his congratulations.

At the window are (*back row, from left to right*): John Ross, Mohammed Hussein and Gilgal; (*front row*): Walter, Weekes, and Patrick Geddes.

This letter tells us of Walter's developing social conscience and the role that religious belief played in his life. He adhered to no particular creed, coming as he did from a mixed background. His maternal grandfather was an atheist; for many years his paternal grandfather was a deacon in the Baptist Chapel in Portsmouth; his father was brought up a Baptist, but his mother was Church of England, so they compromised: Mr Fuller was a lay reader in their local church, whatever its denomination. Walter made his position clear in his letter to Riss the following Sunday. At the evening service in Sturminster Newton, he was sitting with his mother and Cynthia in the south transept,

> so that when the Apostles' creed came to be recited all the people round about us turned to the east. I could not bring myself to bow the knee to Baal – for so it is this turning to the eastward position and bowing at the mention of the name of Jesus – and so I kept still and faced away to the north. The people round about (including, I'm afraid, mother) seemed rather surprised – but it's no good, I'm a non-conformist all the way through and it's no use pretending to conform. I'm just a Christian and not a Churchman or a Unitarian or anything else.[38]

From here his position evolved; by 1 January 1915 (with WWI well under way) he felt able to write to his parents, 'The Quakers are the only Christians in these dark days, I believe – the Quakers and those like the Quakers, in whatever sect they may be.'[39]

Up at Woodbrooke, Riss and Rosalind found Quaker practices somewhat disconcerting at first. The day started with a prayer meeting at which they all sat in silence for twenty minutes, or until someone was moved to speak, pray, or propose a hymn. Rosalind would sit there dying for someone to break the silence 'for then I could swallow without it being heard'!⁴⁰

Another activity that was new to them was visiting the poor. Pairs of students were expected to 'take care' of a family. Rosalind and a Miss Doncaster were assigned a family of five in the slums of Selly Oak: 'the husband is out of work and they have no money' – a predicament all too familiar to the Fuller family. Walter responded to the news with one of his long missives, from which these are but extracts:

> So you're doing some real good work at last – 'tis the only work worth doing in life – *service*. The kings and knights and nobles of long ago knew that, thus the motto of the Prince of Wales is 'I serve' (*Ich dien*). . . . It isn't an aristocracy of blood we want, or an aristocracy of money, or an aristocracy of brains – *but an aristocracy of love*, of *service*. . . . Now about this family you are visiting in Hubert Road. Keep yourself from speaking of them as a 'case' or as 'my case'. Treat them all as living human beings who want a little help – not a group of creatures who want merely to be fed, clothed, and patronised. Treat them as people who can give *you* a little help too. . . .
>
> Believe me, dear girl o' mine, no act of Parliament will make stupid, dull people sensible. An angel from heaven can't make the man with a muck rake look up. An Act of Parliament can't by itself give people ideas, courage, initiative, cheerfulnesss, imagination, That's what it is – that's what is wanted more than anything else, by everybody from children in the schools to old age pensioners, from the King on his throne to the sandwich man in the gutter: imagination – IMAGINATION – IMAGINATION. If we can but have that, all other things will be added unto us – If we had imagination we shouldn't want Dreadnoughts.* It's imagination women want – and men too – not votes. – Not votes any more than books or guns or work. What imagination has this family of Plant? Very little, well give them some. Make their garden to blossom like the rose. Why has the new baby been called Kathleen? Hang a picture up on their wall. Give a Pink Book to the children.† Teach those children how to play 'London Bridge is falling down'. Suggest a party for the children on Hubert Road on St Hubert's Day. Find out all about St Hubert and let a pageant of his life be acted by the children at the party. Talk about these things to somebody. Go and see the schoolmaster of the neighbouring school. Wake people up any way.

---

* Battleships were called dreadnoughts in the early twentieth century, named after the first of them, the Royal Navy's *Dreadnought*, launched in 1904.

† He is probably referring to *The Pink Fairy Book* by Andrew Lang, 1897.

Peter Pan

At this point Walter deviated into discussing votes for women, a subject in which Rosalind was becoming ever more interested. During the following week she went, along with other Woodbrooke students and Rosamond Impey, to hear Christabel Pankhurst and Marion Wallace Dunlop – 'the woman who had had forcible feeding' – address a public meeting in Birmingham Town Hall, which strengthened her views on women's suffrage. Walter was concerned to curb her enthusiasm:

> Give the vote to women (and remember that means giving it to Auntie Nellie, and Auntie Jessie and Mrs Plant and Auntie May and Mrs Clifford, and all the rest of the women we know) and do you think *they* will make things any different? Hubert Road will be Hubert Road – though Christabel Pankhurst be Prime Minister and Victor Grayson Home Secretary.*

The letter continues:

> You are wondering what on earth (and in heaven) can the 'King of Love' mean to Mrs Plant, and what can she mean to the King of Love. A mockery, you say. But dear – do you not think, after your visit with those flowers that day, that that poor woman was nearer to believing that the king of Love was in truth her Good Shepherd? Else why were you there – why did you speak kindly to her – why did you show her and tell her that you loved her? Was it not Love that sent you to her – and so the King of Love her shepherd is, and that you went to her in her need and took nothing but love, was to her a proof that the goodness of the King of Love had not failed her utterly. But you say 'Love can't bring her anything.' Dear, it has brought her *you*. That is a very great deal. There are half a dozen people at least who would rather have you than £10,000. Then indeed has Love brought a very great deal to that poor woman.[41]

Following the family habit of sharing letters received, Walter enclosed

---

* Both Pankhurst and Grayson followed courses at Owens College, the latter from 1904, i.e., immediately following Walter's departure. Pankhurst was conspicuous as the only woman student of law and graduated first equal in 1906, but there is no record of Walter having met her – or Grayson either. Although enrolled in the neighbouring college that trained Unitarian ministers, Grayson founded (and chaired) the Owens College Socialist Society. Pankhurst was his vice-chairman. At the time when Walter was writing, Grayson was a highly controversial figure; the year before, it had looked as though he might wrest the leadership of the Labour Party from Ramsay MacDonald, but in January 1909 he failed to present the motion he had tabled at the national conference of the party in Portsmouth, having been abducted that very morning and abandoned in the neighbouring countryside. He subsequently disappeared from politics until after WWI, when he threatened to reveal corruption at No 10 Downing Street – and promptly disappeared again, for good.

notes from both his parents (marked 'please return') and returned to Riss ('with thanks') a letter from Rosamond Impey and one from a Mrs Braithwaite.* Also enclosed were: 'Particulars of an excursion [i.e. a reduced rate railway ticket] from London to Birmingham on November 20th – which will probably bring me up to see you on that day. Oh happy day'; a back number of the *Bournville Works Magazine* with 'photographs of a little pageant' performed by the children at their summer party. 'Please do you and Riss look into this – and bethink yourselves about it. Have a hand in the making & shaping of next year's summer party. Find out all about it – whose idea it was – who got it up – etc. – Praise everybody concerned. Tell them they're doing the real thing – making imagination.' Finally he enclosed 'a wee bit of silver for you' and three books 'which may be of help and value to you and Riss', one of them titled *Social Work*.† In all, more than a dozen enclosures. A typical letter from Walter.[42]

The musical talents of Riss and Rosalind were much in demand. Rosamond organized a concert for them in the nearby village of Barnt Green and had handbills printed to advertise it. 'I hope you've sent a nice lot of these bills along home to father,' commented Walter. 'It will make him feel sure at last that your harp learning hasn't been in vain.'[43] Having heard them perform at Woodbrooke, the staff of the college encouraged them to sing one evening at a local boys' club. On 30 November, Riss reported to Cynthia,

> Tonight I am going down to my boys' club with Mr Burrows and Rosalind, and by special request I am taking the Irish harp, so that we can sing to them. Mr Burrows says that since my songs last week, he has heard that a great many more are coming tonight. Isn't it splendid.

Although Riss had studied singing at the RCM, Dorothy had generally been the one to sing in public, for of the four sisters she had the best voice, while Riss and Rosalind played their respective instruments. Now, with Dorothy married off to Captain, Riss and Rosalind were performing together. Unlike other young ladies of the day, they sang not the conventional pieces that could be heard any evening in middle- and upper-class homes but folksongs – which went down well with their working-class audience. Their repertoire was already wide, for with Walter's encourage-

---

* She was probably the wife of William C. Braithwaite, an inspirational writer and historian of the Quaker movement, who was much involved with Woodbrooke.

† Probably the book by W. Edward Chadwick, which had just been published (in a series of Anglican church handbooks) by Longman & Green.

Peter Pan

ment, Riss had been adding to the store passed down by their mother by collecting them from local people as well as printed sources. 'By the way, don't you sing those Hebridean folksongs sometimes?' asked Walter in his long letter to Rosalind. 'If not – why not? They are very important!'[44]*

These performances by his sisters mark a turning-point in the history of the revival of folksong. For generations the singing of these songs had been one of the rituals of essentially rural communities, like the May pole and Morris dances, that expressed and maintained social cohesion.† They were passed down by example, the young learning from their elders by watching and listening before joining in; thus there was no real distinction between performer and audience. By the beginning of the twentieth century, the rise of urban communities had almost wiped out these rural traditions, but folk material was saved from extinction by ethnologists. Cecil Sharp's demonstration performances inspired Mary Neal, a social worker who (along with her best friend Emmeline Pethick-Lawrence) had founded a club for seamstresses working in the sweat shops of the London dress trade, to give her girls a sense of community by teaching them Morris dances from Sharp's notes. This was such a success that the following year, 1907, she brought in real Morris dancers to do the teaching. Thus her activity perpetuated the traditional role of folk song and dance in providing social cohesion. The Fuller sisters, on the other hand, were taking the next step, which was to transform popular music in the twentieth century: singing folksongs purely for public entertainment.

Meanwhile, Walter was also drawn into the social activities organized by Woodbrooke. In November 1909, a Mr Price,‡ who was involved with organizing the Woodbrooke students' visits to the poor, arranged for him to speak at a working men's club in the Selly Oak or Birmingham area. 'About last night,' he reported to Riss:

> Well, I really was rather good I think. There was a nice little meeting of about 50 or 80 people – including some five or six women – all 'working people' of course. I flung all my ideas at them pell mell at 10 Geddes-power –

---

* This was no casual remark; in 1908 Walter had printed an article in the *UR* on 'The Educative Influence of Folk Music' by H.C. MacIlwaine, who had co-authored *The Morris Book* (1907) with Cecil Sharp.

† Walter first witnessed Morris dancing when he was a student in Manchester, recording 'a most extraordinary sight in Stockport Road: some men belonging to the Foresters dancing a most surprising sort of jig.'[45]

‡ This may well be the Mr Price mentioned earlier – see p.41. Walter recommended him to Rosalind: 'He's a very fine fellow. Let him help you – and ask him to let you help him.'[46]

and they seemed thoroughly to enjoy it. I really think I have got hold of a very good scheme in this idealization of work in general and trade unions in particular. One man said I reminded him of Ruskin's ideals in *Unto this Last* [an 1860 essay on economy] and another of Bellamy's *Looking Backward* [the utopian novel of 1888], which books I'm glad to say I've never really read. It seems to me that if I were to give some time and thought to the preparation of a careful statement of the scheme which I very roughly outlined last night I should have a message to deliver – a gospel to preach – which would brighten things up considerably. I think I'll see about do[ing] this. I was very much bucked by the way those men took to it all last night – labour Pageants, Trade Dinners, Labour Halls, Trade Union Holidays, etc. I must tell you all about these things at Christmas. At the close of the meeting most of the audience came forward to shake hands with me – I was much touched – literally and metaphorically. There were two reporters for local papers scribbling away most of the time – so there's likely to be some sort of a report of what I said in the local press – I'll send along for you to see whatever they put in.* The questions and discussion at the end was great fun – I was very witty(!).[47]

When Riss and Rosalind returned home for the Christmas holidays, Cynthia joined them in entertaining their parents and friends with scenes from Shakespeare, *Eager Heart*, and other plays. Writing to Cynthia in preparation for these events, Rosalind mentioned that there was 'good news about Walter's Music Hall scheme' – but I know nothing more about this.

In January 1910 they returned to Woodbrooke – but not for long. That month their mother became very ill with asthma and Riss went home to look after her. Rosalind would have stayed on, but the college board thought her too young to remain without her big sister. So she regretfully returned home too, maintaining a flirtatious correspondence with a boy she had met at Woodbrooke, until her father put a stop to it.

It was a godsend that, with an ailing wife and three daughters to feed, Mr Fuller found a job at this point. For a brief while he had worked as a travelling salesman, selling scented sachets for women to wear in their corsets, but now he found an activity that suited him perfectly. He became a warden of the Young Helpers' League, which organized children as donors and collectors of funds for Dr Barnardo's homes for orphans. The job combined everything that he enjoyed: touring the county to give talks and make presenta-

---

*   I have not managed to trace any news items mentioning Walter's talk.

tions with lantern slides; letter-writing, sometimes from home and sometimes from head office in London; and, most important of all, being active in favour of the underprivileged. He was paid a pittance, but he happily dedicated himself to the cause for the rest of his life.

Walter remained the family's main breadwinner – in theory, at least: following the closure of the *University Review*, he was in dire straits. He even borrowed the price of a new overcoat from Stanley Nott's parents. In an attempt to cut down on costs, he left the hall at More's Garden early in 1910, leaving unpaid bills. After living in a cheap room in Garway Road, he moved into a flat at 11 Cheyne Row with Arthur Dakyns, who was paying two guineas a week for it (four times as much as the Fullers were paying for Bridge House). The next weekend, Whitsun, they went down to Sturminster Newton for Dakyns' second visit: 'such pleasant people and such a nice place,' he noted.[48] But by the end of the month, Walter couldn't stand Dakyns' company any longer, and moved out, leaving his friend hurt and puzzled. Walter seems to have returned to More's Garden at this point; he was certainly living there the following September, when he told Riss, 'I'm in debt all round – more than £100 to this University Hall.'[49]

He was trying very hard to revive the *University Review* by creating a public company to issue it. In this he was advised by Curt, who prepared a prospectus for potential investors. Receiving half a dozen copies of it from Curt, Dakyns senior indulged in 'his favourite activity of button-holing well-known people and forging further connections for himself and his family' (as Arthur Dakyns' daughter Janine put it many years later).[50] By 20 June, Walter could report to Riss that he had sold 1000 shares, but there still remained £1500 of arrears to pay off. If Walter, rather than the Inter-universities Congress of Students, was responsible for monies that the UR had left owing, it may mean that he had obtained advances to the tune of £2500, to be reimbursed out of future sales. As it was, he sold no more shares; the money was not to be found.

The finances of the *Readers' Review* were also in crisis. Walter sought advice from various people, including Michael Sadler, whom he visited at his home in Weybridge with Dakyns in tow.* They advised him to find a publisher to take it over. So during the summer Walter had several meetings with J. M. Dent, and the editor of the Everyman series, Ernest Rhys, but, after months of frustrating hesitation and postponed appointments, they declined. By that time, the NHRU had decided to cease publication with the

---

* Dakyns happily reported to his father that Sadler seemed very friendly towards him.[51]

Walter Fuller

thirtieth issue, for August/September 1910. With it went another source of income.

Walter may have been desperately short of money, but he was never short of ideas. That autumn he began approaching daily newspapers with a completely new project, a four-page weekend supplement. He planned to have 'perhaps two of the four pages given over pictures,' making 'a sort of ha'penny *Illustrated London News* of it.' In his mind it had the potential for something far more culturally ambitious:

> And oh the teeming ideas for the covers, for the pictures, for the contents – the competitions, the children's pages – the science, the satire of the Philistines and the Barbarians. The new writers, new artists I shall discover!
>
> Oh well, I am always feeling this way when there are new things to be done, but really though – with such people as Dent and the *Daily News*...[52]

He tried the *Daily News* first because the editor, A. G. Gardiner, had contributed to the *RR* in October 1909. 'And if Gardiner says *No* – I shall go to the *Daily Chronicle*, and if the *Daily Chronicle* says *No* – well, I don't know what I shall do – but I won't anticipate failure – as a matter of fact I believe the *Daily Mail* would jump at such a scheme – but I really couldn't work for the *Daily Mail*, especially during these coming years of war with Germany and afterwards.' In the end, though, they all said no. But he had sown a seed. In 1912, the *Westminster Gazette* turned its Saturday edition into a separate publication, the *Saturday Westminster*. It concentrated on the arts, with reviews, stories by new authors, and competitions that were so erudite that only the highest of highbrows could enter. It was another fifty years before the weekend supplement began to resemble what Walter envisaged.

Leaving aside Walter's prescience about the war with Germany, four years before it was declared, his comments about the *Daily Mail* are somewhat ironic in the light of subsequent events. Between 1905 and 1912 the production manager of the Paris-based Continental edition of that paper was Norman Angell (1872–1967), who was eight years older than Walter. At that very moment he was engaged in publishing a book that Walter was greatly to approve of. Titled *The Great Illusion: A Study of the Relation of Military Power in Nations to their Social and Economic Advantage*, it was Angell's attempt to prevent war in Europe by arguing that no one but the capitalists stood to gain from the conflict. In 1931 he was knighted and in 1933 he received the Nobel Peace Prize for his efforts. At this point, though, he was quite unknown to Walter, as to the world. Yet they were soon to become closely acquainted, and Angell was to become the confidant and lover of one of Walter's sisters.

Meanwhile, Walter was penniless. When in mid-September Riss asked him for £12 for the rent of Bridge House, he told her to promise to pay the following week: 'That will give me some time to get the money.' Where Walter was getting his loans from now is a mystery. He must have borrowed from everyone he knew, including Curt Dehn and Basil Ward. A few years later, when Walter was putting on an anti-war exhibition, Basil complained that 'it seems quite impossible to prevent Walter frittering away his sisters' money on foolish and extravagant schemes, instead of getting out of debt!'[53]

Poverty also blighted Walter's relationship with Rosamond. Her father was both successful and wealthy, being the joint owner of the Kalamazoo accounting system, which was launched in 1904 (and is still in use today). In the same letter to Riss, Walter mentioned marriage for the first time.

> That's a long way off, like Halley's comet – and then none of us – you, father, mother or I – have a proper equipment of clothes. All four of us shall have *three of everything* – down to our very bootlaces – before I marry poor old Rosamond.[54]

We can be sure that Walter was bitterly aware that only with a decent income could he possibly aspire to Rosamond's hand in marriage.

Arthur Dakyns was differently situated, having independent means. He had been down to Sturminster Newton with Walter several times since Easter that year and greatly enjoyed both the company of his sisters and the life they led in the country. Despite his asthma and a persistent cough, he could spend a long weekend with them and return to London feeling 'splendidly well and very sunburnt after long walks on the Dorset downs' or a whole day messing about on the river.[55] Down there he met Dorothy and Captain, Basil Ward, and Alfred Nott (whose farm was at Winterborne Whitechurch, ten miles from Sturminster Newton). In August he took a continental holiday, and on the terrace of a hotel in Bozen (Bolzano) he was astounded to discover Riss lunching in the company of the composer Ralph Vaughan Williams and a Miss Ilbert.* Back home, Dakyns used the chance acquaintance to keep up with the Vaughan Williamses for some time, but they did not cultivate his company.[56]

Of all the Fullers, it was Rosalind who especially attracted him. He got to

---

* I do not know how Riss came to spend a month with the Vaughan Williamses in the Austrian Tyrol – the holiday seems to have gone unrecorded by his biographers. She may have been introduced to him by the director of the RCM, Sir Hubert Parry, who always gave her moral support and recommendations.

see more of her in September when she stayed with Dorothy in London to follow a Pitman's secretarial course. Much to her surprise, he wrote

> to ask a rather important question – at least it seems important to me, but judging by my previous experience of you I don't expect you will think it worth while answering.
>
> The question is this: Will you be my wife? – I love you <u>very</u>, very much, ~~as you ought to know,~~ and I think we should have a really good time together.
>
> But (unless of course you refuse at once) I want you to think the matter well over and weigh the consequences. Marriage is always a great toss up and worse for the girl than for the man if it turns out badly – as it generally seems to.

He followed this unpromising start with a paragraph on the absurdities of the current divorce laws, assuring her that

> Of course you could always break off the engagement at any time. I suppose too it will have to be a long one as I haven't got enough money to marry on. In fact I am not earning anything which shows what a worthless sort of person I really am. . . .
>
> It is a despicable thing to be a 'rentier' and destroys all one's self-respect. It has destroyed mine long ago.

Wishing that she knew him better, he concluded,

> Would you come with me to a theatre on Thurs. night? I should like you to, ~~even for one,~~ even if you refuse to marry me, we might still remain friends, mightn't we? Ugh! Yrs ever Arthur L Dakyns.
>
> PS I hope reading this stupid letter won't make you <u>late</u> for Pitman's tomorrow morning.[57]

This proposal set a pattern for all his letters to Rosalind. He presumed to know her thoughts and feelings, and judged them negatively; he showed that he was aware that she did not particularly like him, and anticipated a negative response; he paid no compliments (or if he did, they were back-handed), and presented both himself and his letter in a unfavourable light. Yet he sought her love and approval. Given that this was a marriage proposal, it is astonishing that he did not even bother to send a fair copy to Rosalind. He posted it just as it came from his pen, blots, deletions and all, down to the 'Ugh!' on the same line as the salutation and signature. I believe its disarming spontaneity and complete lack of respect or good manners stemmed not from passion but from self-absorption. He had no idea of how he might appear to another person, or of how his words might affect them. Others' feelings were of no account.

Rosalind, who was now eighteen-and-a-half, declined to go out with him, but she did not turn him down out of hand, being unwilling to offend him. Although he must have had some personal charm that does not come over in his letters, it is hard to determine what this might have been. He was small and slight – in fact 'very skinny and a bit of a weed' – with a mouse-like squeaky voice.[58] Riss found him 'jerky and spasmodic and so impossible to love.' Rosalind was desirous of love but 'meant never to marry,' so his proposal merely reinforced her determination to seek 'free love'.[59] At this point, 'free love' was still a Platonic concept for her, acquired through reading Shelley's 'Epipsychidion'; she was completely ignorant of the facts of life.

On 1 December 1910, Dakyns glimpsed her in the company of Dorothy and Jessie Holliday at Crosby Hall, where there was Morris dancing. Being something of misogynist, he found there were too many Suffragettes there, including Christabel Pankhurst.[60] Indeed, the suffrage movement was making itself felt once again.* That November, Prime Minister Asquith broke his promise to include the Conciliation Bill in his programme, and the Suffragettes protested angrily outside Parliament. One of them died from injuries incurred at the hands of the police; so they broke the truce and resumed throwing stones. Rosalind herself was active, along with Jessie, although exactly what they did is now lost to us. At any rate, one evening she was escorted back to Dorothy's flat by two burly policemen. When she returned to Sturminster Newton for Christmas, Riss found her to be suffering from 'Suffrage madness', and guilty of 'many wicked, naughty things.'[61] Having learned from her sisters' experience, Rosalind did not tell her parents that Dakyns had proposed to her.

Knowing nothing of this, Walter continued to invite him, along with other friends, down to Bridge House. He also embarked on a fresh project: a performance of *Eager Heart* at Sturminster for Christmas, with Alice Buckton's personal approval. Then, in the new year, he began to write for himself. Following the fashion of the day, Geddes's philosophy and his foible for masques,† he composed *A Masque of the Seasons,* a medley of familiar passages of nature poetry from Shakespeare to Browning, with lines in the Dorset dialect by William Barnes, all set to music. Riss and Rosalind arranged the music and the dances, drawing on a dozen composers from Beethoven (of course) to Rachmaninoff, as well as traditional tunes. The

---

*   1910 was also the year of the first large suffrage parades in New York City.

†   Geddes wrote *The Masque of Learning* at about this time; another masque planned to mark the opening of Crosby Hall was cancelled because of Edward VII's death.

whole was held together by a verse commentary by Father Time, written by Walter. It was performed by the Fuller family (with Cynthia as Spring; Dorothy as Autumn Leaves, Riss playing the harp and Rosalind at the piano) and their friends; some fifty other parts were played by 'the young men and maidens of the village and the little children.'[62] From January onwards, Walter and his sisters were busy training them all in folkdance, deportment, and elocution. After four performances in the village hall early in May 1910, the local vicar presented Walter with the profits – income at last – but they were modest compared with his debts.

A Masque of the Seasons by 'John Wessex' was printed locally as a booklet. All the musical quotations are carefully identified, with precise directions, such as 'at the end of the 5th bar he speaks quietly and slowly'; often an alternative composition is proposed. Of particular interest are the illustrations by Adrian Berrington, Walter's architect friend from the Crosby Hall project. It was apparently his only published artwork before 1917–18 when, as a patient at Craiglockhart War Hospital (which specialized in treating shell-shocked officers during WWI), he designed the cover of its magazine, the *Hydra*. The periodical is now famous for containing poems by Wilfred Owen and Siegfried Sassoon. After the war, Berrington became Professor of Architecture at the University of Toronto, but like so many war veterans he died young, on 4 April 1923, aged only 36, during a visit to England.*

Walter's *Masque* had a short life. Following 'favourable press notices in *TP's Weekly*, the *Review of Reviews*, the *Daily News* and the *Times*,' it was performed as an end-of-term entertainment by the girls of Bournemouth High School. 'It was so well received that they are going to do it again' in the autumn.[63] It was revived at Christmas 1914 by the pupils of Casterbridge School, Dorchester, on which occasion the *Western Gazette* called it 'extremely pretty and effective', but identified 'John Wessex' as Walter's father.[64] The proceeds went to the Belgian Relief Fund. Then it disappeared entirely, along with the fashion for masques, wiped out by the war.

After this, Walter remained at home, desperately trying to think up schemes to soak up some of the sea of debt that his efforts to fund his family had plunged him into. He tried writing articles for various newspapers, without success. While he was usually witty and cheerful with his family, financial worries made him dry and humourless. Unable to bear him like this, Riss

---

* Adrian Berrington was a friend of Rachel Annand Taylor, the poet much admired by D. H. Lawrence. When Lawrence visited her in the autumn of 1910, she introduced him to Berrington, who loaned him his copy of Taylor's 1909 volume of verse, *Rose and Vine*.

took Rosalind up to London to search for work. As harpists were uncommon, her College was pleased to see her back and passed on to her enough work for the two girls to live on. Engaged to play in a private house (for a Lady Wilde), Riss asked – just for once – if it was solos on the orchestral harp, or old English folksongs to the accompaniment of a portable harp that were required. Lady Wilde chose the latter and so the two sisters sang together as they had done at Woodbrooke. It was their first professional recital, and a great success. Lady Wilde booked them for an At Home in the winter and also for the following summer. They followed this up with several other private engagements, and again they were invited to return in the autumn.

This prompted Riss to write to Cecil Sharp. 'I told him that we had been studying folksongs in Dorset, and that I had set many of them to the accompaniment of a small Irish harp, etc, etc.'[65] He invited them to tea at his house in Uxbridge. On hearing them, he asked them to perform at two of the lecture-demonstrations he was giving at Crystal Palace in the context of the Festival of Empire. There he showed them off as though he had invented them himself, and asked them to sing again at his Teachers' Summer School at Stratford-upon-Avon on 10 and 11 August.

On the recommendation of Sir Hubert Parry, the director of the Royal College of Music, Riss and Rosalind also auditioned with agents in London, first in the Steinway Hall, then the Aeolian. At the latter, they were complimented on their performance, but the modest Riss maintained that it was the Irish harp that had fascinated the agent. While they awaited his decision, the girls returned to Bridge House where Walter was organizing a performance of scenes from Edward German's comic opera, *Merrie England* (1902), to mark the coronation of George V at the end of June. They joined him teaching local amateurs the basics of Morris dancing and singing and speaking in public. But as the day of the performance approached, everything began to go wrong. First their aunt Jessie died and Mrs Fuller was too distraught to attend her sister's funeral; Mr Fuller was away in Scotland, on Young Helpers' business. Then Dorothy came home as expected, for she too was to perform in *Merrie England* along with Captain – but she came alone. Captain had taken a studio for himself, and she was going to divorce him for desertion. The marriage had lasted just two years.

It turned out that during his numerous absences, ostensibly to attend patients or conferences, Captain had been with other women. In fact, one of his mistresses had just borne him a daughter. (She was given away for adoption and has not been traced.) Fifteen years later, when the Royal College of Surgeons produced a volume of *Lives of the Fellows,* a Mrs Hamilton Irving, who was born in 1892, supplied the information that she and her husband had married on 9 September 1911 – that is, ten weeks after Captain abandoned Dorothy and fifteen months before their divorce was pronounced (and reported in the *News of the World*). In all likelihood she began living with him on that date, but they did not actually marry until 1915, by which time they had a daughter. (The child born in 1911 was not hers.) Their marriage certificate identifies Irving as a bachelor and not a divorcee, and the ceremony was performed not by licence or banns but in Scotland by sherriff's warrant, so it was thoroughly irregular. Thus Dorothy returned to the fold while her husband was shown to be a wolf; how appropriate that the Fullers had made him the Captain Hook of their Neverland. His own sister, who became a JP and was awarded an MBE for her defence of women's and children's rights, approved of him no more than the Fullers did. In fact she disowned him in the first line of her will. But in the spirit of *Peter Pan*, we'll give him the last word. In 1929, answering an enquiry from Owen's College about his student drawings, he wrote that he had already retired from 'the detested profession of medicine and surgery.'[66] He died in 1932, a few days after his fifty-fifth birthday.

Both Curt Dehn and Arthur Dakyns were expected at the Fullers' for that last weekend in June 1911; Hilda Hankinson was already there. Curt arrived on the Thursday but Dakyns was delayed by an attack of asthma. On his arrival, he received a telegram announcing that his father had died, so he hurried off to his family. The following day, he wired for Curt to come and join him, so in the end neither performed in *Merrie England*. As it was, the weather turned cold and wet; they all took refuge in the village pub and were happy to make it a short evening. 'Merry England' it was not. In her diary, Riss recorded that week as the saddest she had ever known. The only good news came from Mr Fuller, who announced on his return home that he had been made warden of the Young Helpers' League for all of Scotland, in addition to Hampshire, Dorset and the Isle of Wight.

Straight afterwards, Riss and Rosalind returned to London with Dorothy, camping in Captain's abandoned flat in Chancery Lane. Riss used his notepaper – 'it's so swagger!' – to send a long report of events to Basil Ward. With deadpan humour she informed him that although Walter was still at home, 'I think he will not be there much longer. Ros[amond] is going to stay there next week for a few days.'[67] Poor Walter, chased out of his own home by his girlfriend! He no doubt found it necessary to pay a visit to Manchester. Rosamond, by the way, brought her old bicycle for Cynthia, who was truly grateful for it.

In August, Riss and Rosalind took up Cecil Sharp's invitation and performed at the Stratford-upon-Avon Summer School of Folksong and Dance. The School was a response to the Board of Education's decision in 1909 to include folksongs and dances in the national curriculum. This was such a novelty that teachers needed separate training, and 1911 was the second year in which the School was held, under the direction of Cecil Sharp. Participants, over two hundred in all, came not only from Britain but also France, Holland, Canada and the United States. It was a serious business, with lessons, workshops and demonstrations in singing and dancing, including Morris dancing, punctuated by discussions on various aspects of teaching the folk traditions (debating, for example, whether folksongs should be performed with or without actions). By way of entertainment there was a masque, called 'The Merry Haymakers'; participants also had tickets for the seven Shakespeare plays in the Memorial Theatre. The Fuller sisters gave their demonstration on 11 August, and were loudly applauded. When *Musical Times* reported at length on the event, their performance was singled out for particular mention, accompanied by a photograph of them.[68]

After their return home, comments echoed on in their minds:
Americans who heard us sing at the Festival of Empire and again at Stratford assured us that the people in Canada and the States who have settled over there have never heard these old songs of the Motherland, and they almost begged us to try to arrange a visit as soon as possible.

Cecil Sharp has said the same thing, and he has told us that, if it were not for his work and his not very good health, he would certainly accept the many invitations he has had to go and make these songs known to the descendants of the old folk who first made and sang them.

Mr Walter Ford (joint Hon. Sec. of the English Folk Song Society) has told us the same thing – has told us that there is a distinct 'call' for the songs, from America.[69]

They shared these comments with Walter 'who, like the Athenians of old, dearly loves a new thing, and he took it up enthusiastically.'[70] To the dismay of Mr and Mrs Fuller, their children began to dream of the New World.

despite the intense heat, every one seemed to enjoy himself and to enter heartily into the holiday spirit of the place. The keenness and intelligence shown by the students and their regular attendance at the classes was quite remarkable. But this of course was to be expected; for only those in close sympathy with the movement, who had felt the beauty and realised the educational value of our national music, would voluntarily devote a week of their summer vacation to school work. No wonder, then, that the students were keen; so keen indeed that many expressed a wish to renew their studies at the earliest opportunity; and it is possible that a Session may be held in the winter holidays, probably in the first week after Christmas.

The large attendance and the success which the Summer School undoubtedly achieved shows that it satisfied a genuine need. The revival of the practice of folk-singing and dancing in the universities, schools, clubs, and settlements, and elsewhere, is proceeding apace; as fast indeed as the friends and pioneers of the movement could possibly or reasonably desire.

The need of the moment is not so much to arouse enthusiasm as to guide it into the right channel. And this is mainly a question of education; for the folk-movement is, primarily, an artistic one. Consequently, the immediate problem, upon which the promoters of the movement would do well to concentrate their attention, is how to provide school-teachers, scout-masters, and others with competent instruction and advice, so that the dances and songs of the people may be launched and disseminated in their best, purest and most traditional forms.

Two years ago the Board of Education very wisely recommended the introduction of folk-dances into the elementary and secondary schools. So far, however, they have done little or nothing to supply their teachers with the requisite technical knowledge. This, as is so often the case in this country, has been left to private effort. For two years or more, men and women teachers have been carefully trained in the mysteries of English folk-dancing at the Chelsea Physical Training Colleges, where periodical examinations are held and teachers' certificates granted to successful candidates. Some effort has, then, unofficially been made to satisfy the demand for professionally-trained teachers.

The Summer School, above described, is a further attempt to meet the necessities of the case. Stratford-upon-Avon, the home of Shakespeare, situate in the middle of England, readily accessible from all parts of the country, annually attracts a large number of visitors—we believe that 50,000 persons passed through the birth-house last year. Moreover, it is already the centre of a great national movement. For the last thirty-four years, the Governors of the Shakespeare Memorial Theatre—the only endowed theatre in England—by a yearly presentation of a series of his plays, the establishment of a Shakespearean library and picture gallery, and in various other ways, have striven to foster and encourage the study and love of Shakespeare.

Now in the works of Shakespeare the English people found, if not their first, certainly their most complete expression. To propagate, therefore, a knowledge and understanding of the Shakespearean drama is to nourish and quicken the spirit of nationalism, to stimulate the growth of a pure and wholesome patriotism. Shakespeare is called our greatest national poet because, in a higher degree than anyone else, he was the spokesman of our race—the mouthpiece, as it were, of the English folk, in the wider sense of that word. It is here that the link between the two movements, now associated with Stratford, is to be found.

For the folk-art of a country, whatever its artistic merits or demerits, is the sincere expression of a community, the embodiment, in terms of literature, dance, or song, of national ideals and aspirations. Indeed, in the nature of things, an intimate and abiding relationship must always exist between the conscious, intentioned works of the really great, individual artist, and the un-selfconscious output of the people from which he sprang. What, then, Shakespeare, the individual, achieved through the medium of dramatic art, the folk have, in a lesser degree, because within narrower limits, collectively expressed in their own primitive art.

Naturally, then, the Governors of the Memorial Theatre were among the first to sympathise with the pioneers of the revival of English folk-song and dance, and, latterly, to give them practical aid in the advancement of their cause.

THE MISSES FULLER SINGING FOLK-SONGS.

Hence it is that the small country town of Stratford-upon-Avon is now the centre of two educational schemes of the highest national significance, both moving on parallel lines toward the same goal. The first and the elder of these is already established, and, if the experiences of the last month may be taken as an augury, it will not be long before there will be erected by its side a National School of Folk-song and Dance, which, by giving cohesion to the various forces at work, by conserving tradition and upholding a high standard of performance, will rest upon a secure and enduring foundation.

It may interest many readers to know that classes for the study of Morris, Country and Sword-dancing, and Children's Singing Games, under Mr. Sharp, will be held this winter at the South-Western Polytechnic Institute, Manresa Road, Chelsea. Full particulars can be obtained from Miss Wilks, at the Institute.

A TALE OF OLD JAPAN.*

NEW CHORAL CANTATA.

This cantata for soli, chorus and orchestra is by Mr. Coleridge-Taylor, and has just been published. It is a setting of a poem by Alfred Noyes, and is in narrative form. The story relates how Yoichi Tenko, the painter, was the guardian of little O Kimi San, the orphan child of his brother. A student, Sawara, came

* Novello & Co.

3

Impresario

We hope to make a good deal of money, for we are told by many who know something of public taste in America that these songs will surely make a very strong appeal to American audiences. With my share of the profits, I shall first get out of debt, and then start again with a clean slate, and try to write something on it worth reading.[1]
Walter to Patrick Geddes, October 1911

There's been nothing to equal it since the Pilgrim Fathers set out for America.[2]
Walter to Riss, August 1908

Dorothy, Rosalind and Cynthia photographed by Alice Boughton

HERE WAS A PROJECT after Walter's heart! He had been schooling his sisters all his life. He had directed them in plays and concerts. Taking them over to America to make their fortunes by singing folksongs would be like Peter Pan saving lost boys and giving them new and adventurous lives in Neverland. He had been studying the subject of folksongs all that year, reading and re-reading Cecil Sharp's *English Folk Song: Some Conclusions* (1907) and Baring-Gould's work.* He and Riss had observed and recorded some of the folksongs of North Dorset. So he felt that 'here at last is a subject I can truly say I know something about.' He could direct his sisters and lecture on their songs with authority. And what is more, taking the songs over to America, where apparently all knowledge of them had been lost, was an equally Peter Panish thing to do. 'To make these songs known to the descendants in the New World of the old folk who first made and sang them seems to me to be a piece of sane and clean Imperialism well worth working for,' he exclaimed to Geddes.[3]

So he set about writing to every influential person he could think of – and he knew a great many, if only by letter – asking for recommendations and contacts in the New World. Thanks to a fellow student from Owens College, now on the teaching staff at McGill, 'a first-class agency in Toronto . . . put our names on its book and promises us a string of good engagements at good prices,' he told Geddes. 'Further, we shall give recitals on our own account. . . . Our plan is to start from Montreal and work through Ottawa to Toronto, and thence to go into the States – to Philadelphia, Boston and New York.'[4] By early October, they had already been invited to give a recital at the University of Pennsylvania, so they planned to sail from Bristol for Montreal on 1 November.

Walter decided that his sisters should wear Victorian dresses and they 'found three genuine period dresses – 1850 – in the village. As we were small,' wrote Rosalind, the youngest (at nineteen) and smallest of the three, 'they fitted us perfectly and we felt at home in them.'[5] They were almost grateful to Captain for abandoning Dorothy, who was twenty-two that December. She would be their lead singer. Riss, whose soft, breathy voice went so well with the harp, celebrated her twenty-eighth birthday in September. Cynthia, who turned sixteen in October, was of course too young to go. Walter was starting on a new career as an impresario, musical director and tour manager at the ripe old age of thirty and eight months.

---

* Sabine Baring-Gould (1834–1924) was a pioneer collector of the folksongs of southwest England. He published numerous volumes of them and advised Cecil Sharp in his research. He was also a hymn-writer, 'Onward, Christian Soldiers' being the best known.

Walter Fuller

For some reason, the Canadian scheme fell through, despite recommendations to the Minister of Agriculture and to the Strathcona Professor of Pathology at McGill. So they decided to make New York their primary destination. Equipped with three trunks, four suitcases, a small Irish harp, and a great deal of courage, they finally left from Southampton on 6 December 1911. An experienced traveller had suggested that they might perform to the saloon passengers during the crossing: 'a word to the Purser would probably ensure it.'[6] In the event, they hardly left their cabins, for it was one of the roughest crossings on record; Walter wished himself dead a hundred times over. They dined once – on the day they sailed – and only on the day they docked did Walter put in an appearance at breakfast. As in *Peter Pan and Wendy* (published on 11 October that year), reaching the land of their dreams was much more dangerous and uncomfortable than they had anticipated.

Once safely on terra firma, they went straight to the YMCA where they enquired about a reasonably-priced hotel. They were recommended the Hotel Aldine on 29th Street, which advertised its 'very moderate prices' in the local press. There they unpacked – and were struck by the enormity of the gamble they were taking. They had arrived ten days before Christmas; party organizers had booked their entertainers long before, and were expecting to hear traditional carols rather than unfamiliar folksongs. The troupe was quite unknown, inexperienced – and almost penniless. On the little money they had brought with them, they could afford two weeks in their hotel. They had no return tickets.

After that crossing, 'sink or swim' was a phrase they avoided. Walter encouraged himself with other metaphors when he sent his first impressions to Cynthia:

> Oh, the noise of New York! It's like London through a megaphone! Perhaps the roaring will drown our folksongs – maybe. But we will try and make them heard. We must be brave and fight hard, and remember David – how he got his smooth small stone – just like a folksong – straight into the brain of the ugly giant Goliath. Courage then for all of us. We will go forward with colours flying – and you, dear girl, keep the flag flying up there on the home front – we're always thinking of the dear place and its dear garrison.[7]

David and Goliath was a change from Peter Pan and Captain Hook, but the challenge was just as great.

They began to explore the 'great big ugly city, like London with all the churches, cathedrals and old buildings left out, and most of the warehouses and office buildings built on top of one another, instead of side by side. . . . There is more confusion of traffic, and much more mud in the streets,'

Impresario

despite the fact that 'the horse is almost extinct: a horse-drawn vehicle is quite an unusual sight in main streets like Broadway and Fifth Avenue.'⁸ On Fifth Avenue they found the Presbyterian Church, to whose incumbent they had an introduction. He was an Englishman, Dr John Henry Jowett, who had arrived there only a few months before.* He received them very kindly, giving them the names of New York society women in whose homes he thought the girls might offer to sing, and Walter began writing letters. Jowett also introduced them to his assistant, Dr Allen, who took them under his wing, advising them on where to shop and how to observe the conventions and manners of American society. He even invited them to spend Christmas with his own family.

Another of Walter's recommendations was to Professor Charles Farnsworth (1859–1947) at Columbia Teachers' College, who was interested in using folk songs and dances in the teaching of music. He promised to find them engagements and also introduced to them to a good friend of his, Luther Gulick (1865–1918).† Both men had suffered from frequent ill-health in their youth and were concerned with the physical health of young people. Having trained as a doctor, Gulick devoted his life to promoting sports and physical training for young people, becoming an early exponent of using folk dances in community recreation and physical training. He was also active in creating and developing the Boy Scout movement in America.

---

* Jowett (1864–1923) was one of the great preachers of the day. Visiting the United States in 1909, he preached twice in this church and so delighted the congregation that they immediately asked him to stay. Hearing of this, more than 1400 members of his home church in Birmingham signed a petition begging him not to leave. But the Fifth Avenue Church called him again, and then a third time. Finally Jowett concluded that this must be God's will and went to New York in 1911. At once, attendance on Sunday mornings shot up from 600 to 1500; queues for unclaimed seats extended half a block. Not having reserved a pew, the Fullers tried in vain to get in on Easter Sunday 1912; there wasn't even standing room at the door. It was a high-class congregation there too; one Sunday, a year later, the Fullers noticed President Wilson among them.

† From 1886 Gulick worked as head of physical education at the YMCA Training School in Springfield, Massachusetts. There he helped one of his students, James Naismith (who later became a teacher at the School), to develop a new indoor sport, basketball. Gulick was also the designer of the YMCA's triangle emblem, which represents the three sides of man, physical, spiritual and social. In 1903 he became director of physical education for the New York public school system, and founded the Public School Athletic League (a privately funded association that organizes sports activities for all New York's schoolchildren and students); then he became the first director of the Russell Sage Foundation's child hygiene department.

Together with Farnsworth and their respective wives, he had recently founded the Camp Fire Girls – a forerunner of the Girl Guide movement. Both men made the Fullers welcome in their homes.

Dr Jowett's recommendations and Walter's letters bore fruit. They were engaged to sing at a private party given by a Mrs Macaulay Parker. This was closely followed by a similar engagement from a Mrs Worthington, who was At Home every Monday afternoon. She was so pleased with their performance that she made their presence a regular feature of that season. Moreover, she thoughtfully suggested that they join the National Arts Club, which was already receiving female artists on an equal footing with men. The Club welcomed them to its elegant house (now a National Historic Landmark) on the south side of Gramercy Park, waiving the usual membership fee: they were its guests for as long as they remained in New York.* This made a much more congenial setting than their hotel for the Fullers to receive people, sit and read or write letters – pens, ink and paper were supplied. It also provided them with a postal address and Walter had visiting cards printed at once, for guests at the parties where they sang were asking for their cards. There too they met other artists, notably the portrait painter Douglas Volk (1856–1935), and the popular book and magazine illustrator, John Rae (1882–1963), always called Jack. They both became good friends who helped spread the word about this new group of folksingers.

Also spreading the word was the investigative journalist, Ida M. Tarbell (1857–1944), who had practically invented 'muck-raking journalism' with her articles on the nefarious activities of Standard Oil. Along with Lincoln Steffens and Ray Stannard Baker (whom the Fullers also got to meet a little later), she co-founded the *American Magazine* in June 1906; it ran for over fifty years. How they met Ida Tarbell I do not know, but she managed to get them a booking at the Metropolitan Club, familiarly known as 'The Millionaires' Club': even when it opened in 1894, the 'initiation fee' was $300 and the annual dues a further $100. Their audience was charmed.

This instant success amazed the girls, but it did not go to their heads. Riss wrote satirically to Basil Ward about their experience:

Dear – such a time as we are having never was before. We are tasting for the first time how it feels to be a lion! Quite casually we go to an At Home, or a Reception, and we come away long-haired lions! We sing our songs and

---

* After a couple of months, they moved to a quieter hotel, the Irving, that also overlooked Gramercy Square. As it was only a few doors from the National Arts Club, they usually ate lunch there.

when it is over such a clapping, and then 'pitter, patter, pitter, patter' over come all the ladies to talk and give us cards, and ask for cards, and then next day there is such a big post and all the ladies have written asking for terms! Last Friday we were invited to the At Home of a Madam Emma Thursby who is a most noted singer* (but we didn't know this when we met her) and there, just before we began to sing, 'pitter, patter, pitter, patter' over came a stout and beautiful lady all in a flutter of joy. She seized Rosalind and me by the hands and said, 'My dear girls, I've been just crazy to find you! I heard you sing at Stratford last summer, and I've been looking for you ever since.' I'm afraid the real lions, with the genuine long hair, were completely put in the shade.

There was a tremendous violinist there, with a chin to match his reputation, and he played regular fireworks on his beautiful fiddle – a fiddle that could have sung the sweetest things if only it had been given a melody. But the people like High Jinks, so he gave them that sort of thing.

And there was a pianist with big, dreamy eyes and hands (yes, dear, he really had them both) who played accompaniments for the Chin. And there was a Russian lady with a sneezing name and wonderful red hair and a beautiful dress, who stayed with Pachmann once, and talked of it all the time. She sat down and tickled the piano keys, and seemed to try to catch a very quick spider every now and then, and eventually succeeded in the common chord of C. 'It's what the people like,' she told me afterwards.

And two ladies had come to sing, one in a pink chiffon dress with costly white furs and hat (awful effect) and one in white lace with white boots and stockings and all. And their voices were like angels and their faces like pictures, but they sang Grand Opera in Italian and nobody cared.

Then, as friends of Madam Emma, we were asked to sing, and we sang 'Mowing the Barley' and 'Keys of Canterbury' and the minute after all the ladies were sitting in rows at our feet. The lady in white furs left right away, and refused to sing again. The lady in white lace asked us where she could get the 'cutie little songs'. The man with the dreamy eyes took my hand and held it in his two dreamy ones till I got pins and needles and had to wake him up. The Chin decided that I was 'one of him' because I was an ARCM and began talking to me of Adagios and diminished sevenths. And the Russian lady stroked my hair, and Rosalind's cheeks, till we both felt utterly stupid.⁹

Riss concluded, 'When they come and purr over us, we feel so silly because

---

* The height of Emma Thursby's international fame had been in the last quarter of the nineteenth century.

we know it's only us.' Rosalind took it in her stride too: 'We are quite used to singing to strangers now,' she wrote, 'and we don't swallow in the middle of sentences. We've become very successful so far with our engagements – everyone is charmed with these simple songs and has, of course, never heard anything so beautiful nor original.'[10]

Professor Farnsworth was as good as his word and arranged for them to perform to students of the Teachers College at Columbia University. The recital was scheduled to take place in the College chapel, but it was full long before they started, so they all moved to a big hall. 'The hall was packed to overflowing – people were standing in the gallery! We had a large harp and the small one, so Riss played solos.'[11] At the end they were recalled and recalled – never before had the University given singers such a rapturous reception.

Believing in the beneficent virtues of folksongs, Walter wanted his sisters to sing to the underprivileged as well as millionaires and academics. So while milking society hostesses, he sought to meet settlement workers. Farnsworth and Gulick introduced him to Elizabeth Burchenal (1875 or 76–1959). Even as a teenager she collected traditional folk songs and dances, riding out to remote mountain cabins in Indiana, where she was born, to hear the music. An instructor in physical education, she added folk dancing to the curriculum of the Teachers College in 1903 – years ahead of Cecil Sharp's initiatives. Becoming Executive Secretary of the Girls' Branch of Luther Gulick's Public School Athletic League, she promoted folk dancing so successfully that by 1907 she had 250 teachers training 7,219 girls in 128 schools. When she was appointed inspector of Athletics for the New York City Department of Education in 1909, she made folk dancing part of the physical education programme in public schools. There being no reference books in this field, she wrote *Folk Dance Tunes* (1908); *Folk Dance and Singing Games* followed in 1909. By 1913, she had 10,000 girls doing Maypole dances in the New York City. When the Fullers arrived, she was researching *Dances of the People,* which was published in 1913.*

---

*   Elizabeth Burchenal promoted folk dancing all her life. With the encouragement of Gulick, she founded in 1916 the American Folk Dance Society which in 1929 became the Division of Folk Dance and Music of the National Committee of Folk Arts of the United States, of which she was both director and national chairwoman. In 1943 she was the first person to be awarded an honorary doctorate for study and research in the field of Folk Arts, and in 1950, she received (rather appropriately) the Gulick Award, the highest honour in physical education in the United States. Elizabeth Burchenal authored fifteen books, for which her younger sister Emma wrote the piano arrangements.

Mrs Burchenal made them so welcome that her apartment became the girls' second home. They made friends of her daughters, particularly the youngest, known familiarly as Emkin, who was Cynthia's age, and they often danced folk dances together, learning fresh ones from each other. Mrs Burchenal put them in contact with Mollie Best, a story teller working in the settlements in the Bowery.* She shared some of her venues with the girls and arranged for them to sing to the poor and the disadvantaged. They also sang in hospitals. 'In one ward there was an Irish woman, dying, so we sang "Come Back to Erin", and she liked it *so* much she suddenly sat straight up in bed and frightened the doctors!'[12]

Soon they were very busy. Between recitals, there were callers who wished to meet them, interview them, photograph them, or paint their portraits. One man begged permission to photograph Rosalind sitting at his mother's spinning wheel; another wanted to 'capture her innocence' in a portrait before it faded. Riss, who was just a whisker more worldly-wise than her sisters or Walter, insisted that no one should go alone to sit for a portrait. They were not in America to catch husbands. For herself, she felt sure that on her return to England, Basil Ward would want to marry her. They had been writing to each other for eight years now and although he only wrote when she did, so that two months or more could elapse between letters, he now seemed worried that she might decide to remain in America, and needed reassuring that she would return. Dorothy, bruised by the failure of her marriage to Hamilton Irving and receiving maintenance payments from him, was more or less indifferent to male attention. Rosalind was not. She loved it, but had no intention of being ensnared. In her innocence, however, she was liable to discuss her philosophy of free love with anyone, and men might get the wrong idea. So the rule was made, and they stuck to it.

A young man who was smitten by them, individually and collectively, was Durr Friedley (1888–1938),† who had just started work as an assistant at

---

* I have found no biographical details of Mollie Best; a big, untidy woman with a loud voice but a beautiful smile and a heart of gold, she was in her mid-to-late-thirties. After WWI she wrote books signed Mary Agnes Best on *Rebel Saints* and *Thomas Paine*.

† Both at Harvard, where Friedley studied fine arts, and later in life, his name was spelled Freedley, but in records from the nineteen teens he was always Friedley. At the Metropolitan Museum of Art he progressed rapidly to Assistant Curator and then Acting Curator. In 1917, after the Curator was called up by his native Germany, Friedley was offered this post, but he left the Museum to paint camouflage on US warplanes. After the war he worked as a portrait painter and muralist. His best remembered work is the interior of the Memorial Chapel at the Seaman's Church Institute of Newport.

the Metropolitan Museum of Art. Having laboured long over drawing them, forever sharpening his pencils, he presented his work as a collective Valentine, and allowed them to use it in their advertisements. (See facing page.)

Walter was kept busy preparing and distributing handbills. They had brought from England a small supply of photographs of his sisters wearing their Victorian dresses, but many more copies were needed. Luckily, one of the most admired portrait photographers of the day, Alice Boughton (c.1867–1943), invited them to sit for her, and took some excellent pictures.* Like everyone they met, she was enchanted by them and visited them in Sturminster Newton the following summer. She contributed an article about the Fullers and their home to *Harper's Bazaar*.†

With the success of their singing, they seemed set to make their fortunes, as planned. There was, however, an obstacle: Walter's handling of money. As he found the business of banking cheques and making payments tiresome, an uncomfortable reminder of the debts he had left behind, he did not keep accounts, which made it hard to know how well, or how badly, they were doing.‡ They might receive $50 (£10) for an At Home recital, but was it enough to cover all their expenses – living in a hotel and eating out for every meal – and also pay for their return journey? Incidentals, like their laundry bill, ate up money at an alarming rate. Then there was his open-handed generosity. He would happily accept a payment of only $10 for his sisters' singing at an institute for the blind or an orphanage for coloured children; it went against his nature to profit from the poor and underprivileged. On the other hand he made sure that those who could afford it paid a reasonable fee so that his sisters lacked nothing – they were, after all, the ones doing the

---

* When her photographs were exhibited at Vassar in the autumn of 1914, a portrait of the Fuller Sisters was singled out for particular compliments by the reviewer.[13]

† It ends:
'Every hut has its garden and a friendly rustic gladly shares a nosegay. He tells you, when you admire his fruit and flowers, how 'this particular rose is not like other roses – this one keeps his petals for dyes – and Miss, when you puts 'im hin your buttonhole and goes ter Bournemouth, you can wear 'im hall dye, and 'e'll come hup fresh has hanything hif you puts 'im hin water when you comes back hin th' hevening!'

'The little singers seem just like this particular kind of rose – they may wilt a bit in the strenuous rush of our American metropolis, but with a very little care they become quite fresh again and give pleasure to many.'[14]

‡ He could be quite incompetent in simple practical matters. During a picnic with Professor Farnsworth, Rosalind found it 'such a funny sight to see Walter cooking a piece of bacon on a twig! He just can't do things like that!'

Impresario

work. He also sent money and presents back to his parents and Cynthia. For Rosalind's twentieth birthday, on 16 February, Walter bought a silver watch at Tiffany's, and had it engraved with her initials. Inside was written, 'To sweet and twenty from R. D. and W. New York 1912.' Towards the end of that month, he made a rough calculation:

    Board and lodging for 10 weeks at £10 = £100
    Sent home at various times £20
    Spent on ourselves – books etc £20
    Besides this, we have £20 in hand.

One wonders how much of the money in hand was owed to the printer of their handbills, to newspapers and magazines for advertisements, and to Tiffany's. They had yet to buy their tickets home.

    Having no budget, Walter made no allowance for misadventures. One morning, after feeling run down for a few days, he found himself too weak to get out of bed. His sisters thought of the only doctor they knew, met when they mingled with the audience after a recital at Cornell University Medical College. Riss telephoned him and he very kindly came at once. He prescribed some medicine and told Walter to stay in bed for a complete rest. He came back the next day, and twice the following day, for Walter's condition was not improving. He suspected blood poisoning, and thought it was associated with a large swelling that had suddenly appeared on Walter's leg. He arranged for Walter to be transferred to the New York Hospital and promised to operate on his leg himself. The girls were distraught with worry – and breathed not a word of all this to their parents.

They were extraordinarily fortunate in their doctor. Trained at Yale (1877) and Columbia (1887), Francis W. Murray (1855–1929) was one of New York's leading surgeons, Professor of Clinical Surgery at Cornell University Medical College and Surgeon to the New York Hospital. He had published articles on unusual infections and developed innovative treatments. Walter could not have been in better hands. After the operation on his leg, he remained in hospital for quite some time, gradually recovering his strength, for it had been a near thing. When his sisters enquired what all this was going to cost, Dr Murray waved their worries aside: he would not charge anything. There was only the hospital bill of $7 a day for them to pay. His generosity merely confirmed Walter in his belief that if money were needed, it would be forthcoming, whereas he should have learned (in the absence of insurance of any kind) to set aside funds for such contingencies.

While Walter was out of action, Riss took over as manager. She was used to discussing the concert programmes with him – for the sisters did not sing the same songs at every venue: they made a fresh selection to suit their audience. For At Homes they might sing a compilation they called 'The Seven Ages of Man' (consisting of a lullaby, children's songs, love songs (happy and tragic), songs of work and play, dramatic ballads, and ending with the Scottish Dirge); for a country club they composed 'A Garland of Country Song'; for the students of an agricultural college they sang of the seasons ('The Winter it is Passed') and the associated farming activities ('The Sheep Shearing Song'; 'Mowing the Barley'; 'The Merry Haymakers'; 'The Plough Boy'). They also introduced songs evoking the place where they were singing: in Philadelphia they sang

> When first in this country a stranger
> Curiosity caused me to roam,
> My search was for love and for danger,
> So I left my Philadelphia home.

'Local colour' always went down well with their audience. So the girls carried on without Walter, announcing their songs themselves, with 'a clear accent and correct pronunciation almost as pleasant as their singing'.[15] Riss found herself 'rushed off her feet' with all that he usually attended to – answering the telephone, making appointments, arranging interviews, following up requests for information, fixing dates for engagements and advertising them. Yet she still found time to lecture on folksongs herself.*

As he recovered, Walter wrote home nostalgically:

Oh, Mother, how often do we wish that we were all safe and quiet and peaceful at home – going to bed at ten o'clock – having a nice quiet breakfast in the kitchen with some of your marmalade to eat (marmalade is an unknown luxury in this savage land), and then a beautiful curry for dinner (they don't know what a curry is in America) and then a round-the-fire-tea at four-thirty (it's impossible to get tea in New York) and then at eight-thirty or nine, one of your simple little fish suppers, and so to our quiet beds, far, far away from the rush and roar of electric trams, and the motor-cars and the noise and tumult of a big city. Well, we will be back again soon I hope, when the primroses are beginning to fade, but we must make our own little pile of dollars first.[16]

To his father, he revealed that he planned to make some money on the side by importing harps from England, for Riss's little Irish harp was much admired by their audiences. 'We have sent an order to Morley's for three small harps – all orders – and we shall make £2 or £3 profit on selling each one. We usually make £10 for an engagement now. We are getting on famously.'[17]

As soon as he was well enough to do so, he accepted Dr Gulick's invitation to speak on folksongs to a select audience that included many of those who had visited him in hospital. (Mollie Best, for instance, brought him fresh-baked bread and country butter from a Long Island farm.) His sisters provided musical illustrations of the points he made. He was used to introducing their recitals with a few words about folksongs, but this was rapidly becoming superfluous: more and more people were coming to hear them for the second, or third time. It was time to seek a wider public.

In the last week of March, Walter travelled up to Boston where he had several introductions. In particular Durr Friedley had recommended them to the architect Ralph Adams Cram (1863–1942); he invited them to sing in his home where he was hosting a visit from the President of the Royal Institute of British Architects, Leonard Stokes. Cram found his inspiration in the great medieval churches of Europe, which resulted in his 'Collegiate Gothic' designs, of which the most famous is the University of Princeton. Predictably, he found 'all the inspiration of ancient architecture' in the sisters' folksongs, and recommended them to the best society of Boston.

---

* Her talk at a public school in Baltic Street was advertised in the *Daily Standard Union*, Brooklyn, 25 February 1912, p.9.

Walter also had an introduction from Ernest Rhys,* the editor of Dent's Everyman series, to Franklin B. Sanborn of Concord, Massachusetts. Sanborn (1831–1917) was the venerable biographer of Emerson, Thoreau, and Hawthorne. After hearing them perform, he sang their praises in a lengthy piece titled 'English folksongs revived' in the Springfield *Republican* (for which he was a correspondent from 1868 to 1914).

These contacts resulted in an invitation from the Principal of the New England Conservatory of Music to perform for its students and staff in their Jordan Hall, opened less than ten years before but already famous for its beauty and acoustics. No fee was offered, but Walter agreed to it – the publicity would be invaluable. His sisters were now fulfilling up to three engagements a day in New York; perhaps they could do the same in Boston.

At this point Walter decreed that from now on they should perform in crinolines, with hoops. When they joined him in Boston, they brought new dresses, made in linen with genuine old English patterns that Durr Friedley had helped them to choose. As Walter had anticipated, crinolines made the girls more graceful on stage – but complicated their lives. They had to re-learn how to move – not just themselves but their luggage too: a large trunk was required just for the dresses.

In Boston they did everything in style, staying in a more expensive hotel and arriving at Jordan Hall in a carriage-and-pair. The recital for the Conservatory was such a success that Walter decided to hire the Hall for a public performance. To his amazement, the manager agreed to let him have it without charge. All the profit would be theirs. So while they fulfilled various private engagements, such as the Lawn Club at Yale and afternoon At Homes, they prepared for their public debut. Walter sent out press releases and the girls addressed envelopes for circulars; Friedley, who had joined them in Boston, handed out prints of his Valentine for shops to put in their windows. They added new songs to their repertoire so that the matinée and evening programmes would not be the same.†

During this time, Riss received a letter from Jessie Holliday, the talented young portraitist. They had not seen her since the autumn of 1910 when

---

* Although Ernest Percival Rhys (1859–1946) knew practically every important literary figure in his lifetime, he was never too busy to be kind, encouraging, and supportive. Walter had met him when he was trying to find a publisher for the *Readers' Review*.

† One of the new songs was 'The Chesapeake and Shannon', about the 1813 naval engagement in which a British ship captured a US frigate. Not perhaps the most tactful choice, it went down well nonetheless.

Rosalind was staying with Dorothy in London. It turned out that she had crossed to America only three months before the Fullers to join her fiancé Ned – Edmund Trowbridge Dana III (1851–1931), a scion of the Dana dynasty* – whom she had met while attending a Fabian Society conference in North Wales. They were to be married on 15 June.

The Fullers enjoyed catching up on Jessie's news, meeting her future in-laws, and visiting Craigie House, where Longfellow had lived. They missed her wedding because they were back in England by then, but they read of it in the press – 'one of the most interesting Boston has ever known', an avant-garde event for which the bride wrote the ritual. It was held with 'no minister, no bridesmaids, ushers, or best man' in the garden of Craigie House.[18] By way of a honeymoon, the couple went to Chicago to fast, for Jessie had persuaded Ned to adopt her dietary theories. 'The poor young man has to be a vegetarian, as Jessie is one,' Rosalind told Cynthia. 'He eats only two meals a day, for he is striving to please her – and I suppose it is a very good sign when one party will let the other rule the stomach?'[19] After forty days on fruit juice and water – Ned managed seventeen days – Jessie returned to England 'for a rest.'[20] She returned in April 1913 (when Walter met her briefly in New York) and the following year gave birth to a son she called Shaw, after her great hero. (He later changed his name.) However, Jessie was too starved to breastfeed her baby, who was not the wonder child she had expected but a perfectly normal little boy. She became thoroughly depressed. On her third wedding anniversary, she went swimming in the sea and drowned. Ned rejected the coroner's finding of accidental death and in a widely publicized statement declared his conviction that it was suicide, 'a tremendously tragic but beautiful end.'†

The girls' recital in Jordan Hall was a triumph. They came away laden with flowers, and the press presented reviews like bouquets. With no small satisfaction, Walter remarked to his parents, 'It may be true that Bostonians have the reserve of the English, and the critical capacity of academics, but

---

* Ned was the grandson of the American poet Longfellow, and his uncle Richard Henry Dana, Jr., was the author of *Two Years before the Mast* (1840), which had just come out in a new edition.

† This open acknowledgement of her suicide cost Ned his job: the Dean of his Faculty at the University of Minnesota, where he was an assistant professor of philosophy, dismissed him for lacking 'the discretion necessary for a teacher. . . . The great majority of our community regard the days following such a bereavement as a time for silence, for reserve, for dignity. . . .Your actions have shocked the people of the community,' wrote the Dean.[21]

they also have the appreciation and sensitivity of true musicians!'[22] It was the beginning of celebrity for the Fullers – and funds for their return journey.

They had initially planned to return home in April. Walter had even made provisional reservations on the first east-west crossing of a new liner called the *Titanic*. In the event, they had not yet made enough money for it – and the ship never reached New York. With their success in Boston, fresh engagements came pouring in; time and again they postponed leaving. 'And when we cross we shall choose one of the more modest and less pretentious ships. Perhaps it is best after all that we are not coming in April when icebergs are about,' observed Walter.[23]

The sinking of the *Titanic* affected them personally, not merely because they had so nearly sailed on it, but because they knew people who lost relatives in the disaster. They spent many pleasant evenings with a new friend in Boston, Josiah Millet, whose brother Frank was one of the most well-known victims.* Mr Millet loved folk music and would accompany the girls on his guitar, surrounded by his wife and children in their fine old house. He was a pioneer in sonar, using sound waves under the sea to warn ships of dangers to navigation. Just after the turn of the century, he co-founded the Submarine Signal Co; by 1912 underwater warning bells had been installed around the coastlines of the United States, Canada, the British Isles, France, Portugal, Italy, Brazil, Chile, and China. It was a bitter irony that while this prevented countless ships from being wrecked, his system could not save the *Titanic* from a free-floating iceberg. That level of detection was a whole generation away. In the midst of his loss, he did his best, through the influential people he knew in Washington, to get the girls invited to sing for President Taft. However, his main contact, Major Archibald Butt, who was his brother's best friend and housemate, also went down with the *Titanic*.†

The girls had a busy time in New England, singing in private homes, schools and universities, starting off with Smith College and Amherst. The

---

* Francis Davis Millet (1846–1912), always called Frank, was an internationally recognized historical genre painter who helped found the School of the Museum of Fine Arts, Boston, and co-founded the US Commission of Fine Arts. He was also a tireless globetrotter and journalist who set up home in Broadway (Worcs), England. According to W. D. Howells, Millet painted 'the best likeness of Mark Twain that ever was done.'[24] In 1912 he was secretary of the American Academy in Rome. His was one of the few bodies recovered after the *Titanic* sank.

† Major Butt was military aide to President Taft, who loved him like a son or a brother. At a commemorative ceremony for Butt, held in Washington, DC, on 5 May 1912, Taft broke down and wept, unable to complete his eulogy. In 1913, a Butt-Millet Memorial Fountain was erected in the city.

morning after their recital in a large hall at Smith, some students came and sang their thanks beneath their bedroom window. But on arrival at Amherst, Walter collapsed with exhaustion. He had cut himself shaving and it had gone septic. After calling in a local doctor, who lanced and dressed the wound, the girls sent him back to Boston to rest. He was sufficiently recovered to join them at their next venue, a private house in Princeton, which he found 'more English than any town we have seen over here. The grass was green, the trees were green, there were hedges and gardens and even a soft drizzle of rain – so it was altogether completely English!'[25] At this recital they were introduced to the Governor of Massachusetts and his wife; the Dean of Princeton and various professors; the other famous muck-raking journalist, Ray Stannard Baker;* and to Woodrow Wilson's eldest daughter. All these contacts led to further engagements.

At this point, Walter decided that his sisters needed a rest too, and took them off for a three-day break at Atlantic City, 'a characteristic American jumble of Brighton and Blackpool,' as he put it. The sea air, rather than the kitsch and bright lights, refreshed them for the next series of recitals, which took them to New Jersey, Philadelphia, and Washington. In Washington they were befriended by Colonel Thompson† who asked them to sing at a reception he was organizing for the Japanese Ambassador. This resulted in an invitation to perform at a similar do in New York.

It also resulted in the much hoped for invitation to sing for President Taft. Unfortunately, they were already engaged on the proposed date and Walter would not hear of cancelling. The secretary of the White House came up with another date, 31 May. By now they had booked to sail home on 1 June; this would mean an overnight dash from Washington to the ship in New York harbour. It was too tight. Reluctantly, they had to decline; they just could not fit the White House in. But it left them determined to come back for another season.

---

* Following his active support of Woodrow Wilson during the 1912 presidential campaign, Ray Stannard Baker (1870–1946) became one of Wilson's friends. He served as his press secretary at the 1919 Paris Peace Conference and, after Wilson's death, was appointed Wilson's authorized biographer. For the final two volumes of his *Life* he was awarded the Pulitzer Prize for Biography in 1940. The Fullers got to know him 'very well'.[26]

† Robert Means Thompson (1849–1930) was in fact a naval officer. 'Colonel' was an honorary title earned during the Spanish-American war that he carried with pride. As chairman of a company supplying the metals for the US navy's ships, he had a great deal of influence in Washington. He knew everyone who was anyone.

Walter Fuller

Their last days in America were indeed hectic. Walter listed their engagements for Cynthia:

May 21 New York
    22 South Manchester, near Hartford, Connecticut
    24 Springfield, Massachusetts
    25 Williamstown, Massachusetts
    26 Farmington, Connecticut
    27 Cambridge, Massachusetts
    28 Plainfield, New Jersey
    29 New Brunswick, New Jersey
    30 Doylestown, Pennsylvania
    31 New York

It was a demanding timetable for them all. In South Manchester, Walter suddenly grew pale and faint. Recognizing the symptoms, the girls at once despatched him back to New York, where Dr Murray met him at the station and operated on another swelling. Thanks to these prompt actions, Walter was well enough to sail a week later.

Instead of singing in the White House on 31 May, the girls were invited to the studios of the Victor Gramophone Company.* Unfortunately, the recording was not put on sale because the equipment could not satisfactorily reproduce the sound of their voices combined with the harp, and it was not preserved either. So we shall never hear the singing of the Fuller Sisters.

They sailed home on the *St Paul*, having spent five and a half months in America. They had not made their fortunes, but the family (although not Walter) was out of debt and could afford to pay for Riss's wedding. She married Basil Ward on 17 July. There is no record of how Walter felt about it, but if his attitude towards Dorothy's wedding is anything to go by, compounded with his possessive love of Riss, he was surely depressed by the whole affair. Rosalind, who generally shared Walter's opinions, disliked weddings on principle. She saw in them the death of the bride's independence – 'as though something were broken' when the ring slipped onto her finger during the 'stupid ceremony.'[27]

The more conventional Riss had been thinking of little else for several months, buying 'half-a-dozen cutie little white nighties and one camisole

---

* Company records show that they sang: A Cradle Song; The Frog and The Mouse; Here Comes a Duke A-Riding; Leezie Lindsay; Mowing the Barley: Song of Youth; Lord Randal; I'm Seventeen Come Sunday; O No, John!; The Wraggle-Taggle Gipsies; and The Merry Haymakers. They also recorded for Columbia, at Christmas 1914; again no record was released.

and one cute little combie' for her bottom drawer during a white sale in New York. She felt sure that she would be very happy with Basil. 'He writes such funny letters – simple, unflowery epistles which don't tell a thing that he doesn't mean – but which show tremendous affection to me. He is just the kind of man I like,' she told her mother that spring. 'He doesn't like women as a rule, and doesn't say a lot of pretty things.'[28] It came as a great shock when he told her that he did not want to have children and would therefore not be consummating the marriage. Riss wanted children very much, but she hid her disappointment, from him and from her family. She opened her heart to Basil only seven years later, when she was waiting for him to return from serving as a WWI army doctor in Egypt. In a letter she made it clear that she wanted to be 'a real wife' to him when he came back. She never had a child. Basil was in all likelihood a closet homosexual, for whom marriage served as social camouflage.

Time and again, during that first tour, Walter tried to pin down what made his sisters' singing so popular. 'Of course, the harp is one of the secrets of our success, another is the dresses, another is that we are all one family – brother and sisters – another is the English speech and ways – another is our faces – expressions, complexions. So you see, the explanation of our success is a complex one – but the folksongs themselves are the basis of it all.'[29]

He was right. Awareness of a fast-disappearing folk culture was just impinging on the educated public in America, as it was in England. At first, the emphasis was on re-discovering the dances; the Fullers brought folksongs and ballads. With their old-fashioned dresses* and their unsophisticated air – Walter insisted that they should never wear make-up – they presented an image of purity, freshness and innocence, an olde worlde charm, that was popularly associated with a lost folk culture, and struck a chord in American hearts. *Harper's Weekly* summed it up in one sentence: 'They come to America at a time when everybody is seeking stress and marked sensation, and they bring an art of entire purity, gentle, historical significance and quaint, inviting charm.'[33] (Exceptionally, the article was not signed, which suggests that it was written by the editor, Norman Hapgood.)

As she accompanied her sisters' singing, Riss observed their sophisticated

---

* It was more than fifty years since crinolines had been fashionable in England and France, and to American eyes they were 'undeniably quaint and pleasing to the eye' (Felix Borowski).[30] 'The moment they appear,' wrote Arthur Guiterman in a long review, 'the crowd falls in love with them. They wear such attractive, old-fashioned clothes!'[31] For Franklin Sanborn, 'their hoop skirts "heighten the rurality of the music".'[32]

audience in Washington and concluded: 'there must be something very beautiful and subtle about our songs – for they often soften the hardest, unbend the stiffest, and make everybody lovable.'[34] The simple directness of traditional folksongs circumvents the defences we raise against being touched and arouses deep emotions. Introducing his sisters' recitals, Walter liked to quote from Andrew Lang: 'Folksongs are a voice from secret places, from silent people and from old times dear, and as such they stir us in a strangely intimate fashion.'[35]

Then there was the manner in which the Fuller sisters sang. Under Walter's direction, they avoided styles redolent of the drawing room, the musical hall, or the opera house. On the contrary,

> they maintained completely the straightforward objectiveness necessary to folk-music, never for a moment seeming to be superior to the songs or to be personalities in their own right. The important thing was to get the song sung, distinctly, simply, and joyously. Their dramatic gestures and dance steps seemed to be perfectly spontaneous and never studied. There was little or no variation in tempo or shading to correspond to changes in the emotional story. Nor was there any super-civilized attempt to smooth over misplaced accent. Their attitude was one of immense respect for the song, as a thing to be enjoyed, and no respect whatever for good taste or formal beauty as such. These are qualities of all art in the militant stage, but it is very difficult to persuade folksingers, trained in a sophisticated school, to observe them.[36]

Only Riss, of course, had any formal training, but Walter had definite ideas.

During the recitals, he would stand behind the audience and watch everything. Then he would give his sisters feedback as they practised each morning. As there was no amplification in those days, the voices of just three girls (and only Dorothy's had any power) had to fill anything from a drawing room to an auditorium for over a thousand people (as at Boston's Jordan Hall). Quality of production had to compensate for lack of volume, so he paid close attention to their enunciation. And it worked. Reviewers regularly wrote things like, 'Their voices are so unstagey, so unaffected, and their enunciation is so clear – why, you can hear every word!'[37] H.K. Motherwell said much the same:

> Their enunciation is so simple and perfect that not only is not a word of their program lost, the hearer forgets to try to listen and simply enjoys. In so singing the Misses Fuller give their songs an immense advantage over concert songs, which not once in a blue moon are so well enunciated and consequently lose, if not their meaning, certainly their intelligibility.'[38]

Walter watches from the wings as his sisters say goodbye to Maurice Browne after a run in his Little Theatre in Chicago; a sketch by Dorothy

Walter also studied his sisters' body language, scrutinizing each expression, every gesture, and told them how to act. Just as he encouraged them to mingle with the audience during the interval or after their performance,* receiving compliments and answering questions with simplicity and modesty, so too he insisted on unsophisticated behaviour in performance. As Riss re-tuned her harp for a song in a different key, she would tell the audience about the instrument. He had them acknowledge applause with a curtsey, and studied how they should respond to encores: 'When the applauding house joyously demands more, those bewitching girls laugh too, as though they enjoyed it all as much as anyone. They consult and hesitate, and Rosalind steps forward, smothering her laugh, and says, "Very well, we'll sing you another song, called, 'No, John, No!'" So there is another burst of applause and laughter.'[40] Motherwell was a perceptive critic: 'The Misses Fuller . . . seem to enjoy their singing immensely, relishing it with such a child-like pleasure that one is prejudiced in favour of the songs from the start. If their enjoyment is not always sincere but only a part of their art, then they are most excellent actresses.'[41] In short, Walter turned his sisters into thorough professionals, 'ruling them with a rod of iron,' as the theatre director, manager, and playwright Maurice Browne put it, 'directing their songs and mime with a skill past my yardsticks, adoring, adored.'[42]

Their spontaneity was genuine. At engagements for children, they would perform singing games. On one occasion, when they announced that they were going to sing 'London Bridge is Falling Down', a little boy jumped up and said he knew that one. They invited him onto the stage and he became part of the bridge that Rosalind danced beneath. She recalled how 'the part he liked best was where he and Dorothy marched me off to prison – he fairly shone with happy determination!'[43]

Professionalism is a state of mind acquired through discipline. Rosalind described how 'the most difficult thing' was to 'keep each song absolutely fresh' when singing it for the nth time. The mind is inclined to wander:

> Sometimes I am thinking, 'Does the audience like this song?' – 'What time is it?' – 'What encore shall we give?' – Of course this is terrible. It means that our expression is working mechanically and the people are not receiving the points and message of the song. So I am continually throwing myself into the song and thinking of the words and meaning – and so they keep fresh.

---

* The New York *Herald* was surprised by this: 'Originality seemed to be the keynote of the afternoon, for, during the intermission, the Misses Fuller went to the tea room and met their audience, or a greater part of it.'[39]

People like to know that we are enjoying them as much as they are, as we surely do when we are *in* that song.'⁴⁴

Rosalind enjoyed performing more than her sisters did – the reverse of how things had been when she was a little girl. Now it made her feel more real, and 'in love with the world!'

Back home, Walter started to plan a second tour. Once it was clear that Riss was going to get married and remain in England, Cynthia had been preparing to take her place. Envious of her sisters' adventures, she learned to play the harp well enough to accompany Dorothy and Rosalind, but at just seventeen she had neither Riss's musical training nor her experience. Other changes for the new season concerned their names. As Dorothy's divorce became final on 25 June 1914, she felt she was almost a Fuller again. They could truly call themselves 'the Misses Fuller' or, as they preferred from now on, 'the Fuller Sisters'.* Rosalind, who until then had been called by her first name, Ivy, decided that now she wanted to be Rosalind. Did she feel that it fitted better alongside *Dorothy* and *Cynthia*, both 'sweetly old-fashioned names' to American ears?⁴⁵ Or had she noticed that the word Americans most frequently associate with *ivy* is *poison*? At any rate, *Rosalind* was highly unusual at the time.†

On 8 January 1913, the refreshed troupe sailed from Southampton on the *Kaiserin Auguste Victoria*. The Burchenals, who had been the last to see them off, were the first to welcome them back and spread the news of their return. They hastened to have new photos taken by Alice Boughton – one of them opens this chapter – and began publicizing their availability. Soon engagements began to flow in, and Walter was enjoying himself immensely. Dorothy commented: 'Walter is busy running about like Boots and Brewer in Dickens' *Our Mutual Friend,* but with more purpose and better results!'⁴⁷ In Riss's view, 'the busier and more muddled he is, the happier he is, I think!'⁴⁸

Much to Walter's surprise and relief, Cynthia adapted very quickly to this new life, despite her lack of experience. Her harp had been slightly damaged during the crossing, but once it had been attended to she settled into playing in public with natural ease. Walter felt very proud of her, reporting to Riss that 'Dorothy and Rosalind are better than they were last year, and Cynthia

---

* I use the capitalized 'Sisters' when I refer to them as a musical group, and 'sisters' as individuals.

† In a sample of 78,755 girls born in the United States between 1891 and 1900, 5565 were called *Mary* and 40 were called *Ivy* – but there were no *Rosalinds* at all.⁴⁶

is very simple, graceful and self-sufficient . . . she's getting on splendidly.'[49] Soon her sisters were making Cynthia lead them onto the stage. 'I don't know why,' she told her parents,

> but just before I go on I always wish I was not there and I get sort of funkie, but directly I am on the stage and bowing to the audience I don't mind at all. It is just like a bather before he goes into the sea – he wishes he need not do it, but once he is splashing about in the salt water he loves it, and doesn't want to come out! Well, that's the way I feel for that moment just before I put my foot on the stage.[50]

Now that Rosalind was no longer the youngest of the trio, she felt more responsible, and assured Riss that she always listened carefully when Cynthia tuned the harp, 'though it's seldom now she tunes it badly.' Still, 'I look to everything and everybody now that you are not here, but I'm getting used to it!' Cynthia's voice not strong enough to sing a tune against the other two, as Riss could do, but everyone remarked on the prettiness of her golden hair and blue eyes and agreed that 'she looked like an angel harping away.'[51]

After the performance in Boston's Jordan Hall, Walter was well aware that they stood to make much more money by singing in theatres, rather than at schools, universities or private venues, although they needed all of these to establish their reputation. During their first tour, the Little Theatre movement had been launched in Chicago by an Englishman, Maurice Browne, and Walter had heard that 'it has a very good following.' Such was the success of Browne's venture that Little Theatres sprang up all over the country (and then in England), starting with the Toy Theatre in Boston and the Little Theatre in New York, both in 1912. This was just the venue for the Fuller Sisters. So Walter reserved this 'latest and best and most exclusive of New York theatres' for 14 February – 'a mighty expensive proposition,' as he admitted to his parents. It held only 300 people and to break even he calculated that they had to fill 100 seats. Although they filled the theatre and received glowing reviews, they made less money than Walter had anticipated, for he splashed out on leaflets and newspaper advertisements. The time had not yet come when the very name of the Fuller Sisters would suffice to fill a theatre.

Mid-February also brought mixed emotions when they learned of the death of Scott in the Antarctic. One of Walter's friends, G. C. Simpson, who had helped with the *Owens College Magazine* and visited Walter in his London flat, was the meteorologist on Scott's ill-fated expedition, one of those who brought back the sad news. (In 1920 he was appointed director of the Meteorological Office in London.)

Impresario

When accepting bookings, Walter now asked for costs in addition to their performance fee. This helped to make ends meet, but when they stayed overnight in the surrounding States, they retained their New York hotel rooms, so that bill had to be paid too. In the end, exasperated by Walter's late payments, their hotel asked them to move out. Luckily, a rich admirer who was leaving to visit England came to their rescue at just the right moment: during her absence she let the girls live in her studio above the National Arts Club, at no charge. Walter took a room just below. Another admirer paid for their annual subscription to the Club, and they resumed their habit of lunching there whenever they were in town.

By the month of March, they were working as hard as ever. Walter reported:

> On Friday we're to go to Chatham in New Jersey, and then to the Studio Club. On the 13th we sing at the Little Theatre again. It is a paid engagement, though the proceeds will go to raise money for a Settlement. The next day the girls are to sing three groups of songs at the St Regis Hotel in 5th Avenue (one of the swaggerest) in aid of the Crippled Children's Home. Our fee $25.* As soon as we have done our stunt, we hurry to Grand Central Station and take the train to Bridgeport, Connecticut, where we sing to the Contemporary Club, a fee of $75 and all expenses. We shall stay there the night, returning to New York next day. Then we set off for Hartford, Connecticut, where we are singing at a girls' school, fee $50 and all expenses. Back next morning to New York where that evening we are to sing after dinner to some very pleasant rich Jews, Benjamin by name, fee $50. On Friday 21, we set off for Northampton (Massachusetts) to sing to the professors and students of the Massachusetts Agricultural College, fee $50 and all expenses. We shall probably get another engagement at Smith College on the same day. On the Monday we return to New York to sing for a Mr Adams Brown in a private house, $75,† and on the following day, we go to Stamford, Connecticut, to sing for Mr Houghton [of the Houghton, Mifflin

---

* This benefit concert was arranged by Mary Breck (1874–1953), who later accompanied them on their tours. Of her I know only that her father had distinguished himself in the Civil War, both on the field and as the author of 120 letters reporting on events that were printed in the Rochester *Union and Advertiser*. Mary lived with her father in the same apartment building as the Burchenals, and had an elder brother George who suffered from tuberculosis.

† This would be William Adams Brown (1865–??) who held the Roosevelt Chair of Systematic Theology at the Union Theological Seminary in New York. He was active in founding and running settlements in the poorer quarters of the city.

& Co publishing house], fee $50 and expenses. The same evening we go to Springfield (Massachusetts) to sing for the graduates of Smith College, fee $75 and expenses. Back again to New York, where in the afternoon we sing for Mrs James Roosevelt, $75.* On the next day there is the possibility of a great adventure: we may go to Cleveland, Ohio, which is half-way to Chicago – if so, we shall have to leave New York on Friday the 28th, at midnight, sleep, breakfast and lunch en route and reach Cleveland Saturday at tea-time. Our fee will be $100 and expenses. From Cleveland we will go to Boston and stay about a month.

As this breathless list shows, the Fullers were starting to range farther afield; after the eastern seaboard, they now took on the mid-west. The journeys were much longer, tiring, and expensive; it was also harder for Walter to secure more than one venue per day, whereas by remaining in the same place, they could fulfil three. Yet it was the next step in establishing their reputation.

So they were very grateful to friends like Helen and Jack Rae,† who welcomed them for weekend breaks in their house some sixteen miles from Lovell (Maine), deep in the country with a view of Kezar lake and the mountains beyond. It was a wonderful place to relax, take walks, and eat home-cooked food. Helen was a vegetarian and in summer she prepared large and varied salads; in winter she served up homemade soup before a blazing log fire, and whatever the season there was her freshly-baked bread. In return, the sisters served as models for Jack; he would draw and paint them, and their figures – if not their faces – can often be found in his commercial work of the time.

April brought them to Boston, fully booked every day. Dorothy, writing to her parents late one night, offers a glimpse of Walter:

> I expect he is writing too, but presently, when the clock strikes twelve, he will start to find his bed, which lies somewhere under a pile of papers, press notices and newspaper cuttings! He was never so busy last year and his forehead swells visibly daily.[52]

The girls made several more friends. There was Mrs Burgess, a rich and lonely widow active in settlement work, who treated them like daughters;

---

*   James Roosevelt Roosevelt (1854–1927) was the older half-brother of President Franklin Roosevelt.

†   Rae illustrated (and sometimes wrote his own) children's books at the same time as providing artwork for popular American magazines like the *Woman's Home Companion*. (See the website for an example.) In all he illustrated some fifty books. Later in life he turned more to portraiture, depicting Albert Einstein and Card Sandburg, for instance.

Edward Filene, who instituted the famous Bargain Basement in his father's department store.* He had them sing in his shop, drove them around in his motorcar and lodged them at the Wayside Inn in Sudbury, Massachusetts, the site of Longfellow's *Tales of a Wayside Inn*; and Charles and Jeannette Peabody, who initially invited the sisters to sing for an audience of children.† Their four children adopted the Fuller girls as big sisters (although the eldest, Fifine, was taller at sixteen than any of them). And then there were the Athertons: Frederick Atherton (b.1865) was a prosperous businessman whose brother Percy was superintendant of the Music Department at Harvard and a composer of song music.‡ Percy invited the Fullers to sing at Harvard on several occasions – 'a fine feather in our cap,' as Walter put it.[53]

Frederick Atherton's wife Ellen seems to have spent as much time entertaining in a large house next door to the Russian Embassy in Washington as at their home in Boston. She asked the girls to perform at a reception in Washington; Mrs Woodrow Wilson heard the news and soon the Fuller Sisters received the coveted invitation to sing at the White House,§ where President Wilson had been installed since 4 March. For this occasion Walter decided that his sisters should have new dresses, so once they were back in New York, where they had two engagements each day, he provided their dressmaker with some material that he had found. (When it came to his sisters' clothes, Walter would 'come out strong,' as Cynthia put it, helping them choose everything from hats to shoes.) In Washington, they sang on the afternoon of 30 April for Mrs Atherton, who was receiving the ambassa-

---

* Edward A. Filene (1860–1937) was an astute businessman who believed in expanding the consumer's purchasing power as a way to sell more goods. So he bargained collectively with his shop staff, instituted profit-sharing, and supplemented salaries with a then-novel array of fringe benefits.

† The Peabodys' home was a centre of social and intellectual activity in Boston. Charles Peabody (1867–1939) was the director of the department of Archaeology at the Phillips Academy, Andover, and the first curator of the Robert S. Peabody Museum of Archaeology in Cambridge. A keen interest in music led to his collecting the first documented ragtime music from his workmen during his excavations in Coahoma County, Mississippi, in 1901–02.

‡ At Christmas 1913, a Chorale ('Hymn to New York') by Percy Lee Atherton (1871–1944) was given pride of place at the New Year's Eve Celebration at Madison Square Garden, performed by 5000 singers and a 100-piece band.

§ Music has always featured in the official entertainment at the White House, and in the nineteenth century folksongs were performed by American ballad singers, such as the Bakers and Hutchinsons. This seems to be the first recital by a foreign troupe.

dors of France and Holland, and then headed for the White House and their evening recital. Amazingly, it was only while they waited in an anteroom that they discussed what songs they should sing. They each wanted different ones, but they settled it in time to join the hundred or so guests in the East Room, the 'public audience room' of the White House.

Dorothy reported home:

We began our programme with the prologue of the Sword Dances. Then I sang the Irish Lullaby. Then Rosalind and I sang Here Comes A Duke A-Riding. Then we three sang My Man John, the Roman Soldiers, Mowing the Barley and O No John. Then I sang The Twa Sisters, Lord Randal, Leezie Lindsay and the Lyke Wake Dirge. Then we sang a few more that I can't remember now, and at the end, Brixham Town. They were very appreciative, Wilson especially liking the Roman Soldiers and the Lyke Wake Dirge. Mrs Wilson liked the Twa Sisters.[55]

It lasted about an hour, after which they were introduced to the President who had obviously enjoyed himself (and revealed a weakness for limericks) and his guests. Dorothy added that 'Walter, who was looking very nice and English in his evening dress, was introduced to everyone too, and had quite a long talk with Mrs Wilson who is very sweet and unaffected.'[56] Cynthia wrote:

Mrs Wilson called us all 'dear', and held our hands and made me sit next to her, and asked questions about Riss [whom she had met on the first tour], and then her daughter, Jessie – she has fair hair and wore a primrose-coloured evening dress with pearls around the top – she was perfectly sweet, and for some strange reason fell in love with me, would not leave go of my hand, and said how sweet I was, how she loved me, and would adore me for a sister, I was so cute and so on and so on! I felt quite overwhelmed with it all. Then we went into another room and had ices, then back again to see the dancing; wonderful tangos and dips, and then Rosalind, like a bold girl, went and danced with a young Army officer! It looked so out of place to see such a full skirt amongst such tight hobbles, but it amused the beholders greatly.[57]

Dorothy had thought to herself, "it is too formal here for one to learn a dance,' but here was Rosalind going through all the steps as cool as a cucumber!'[58]

Walter was well aware that Riss would have loved the occasion, so he wrote to her at length, concluding,

We had the broth of a time and Mrs Wilson asked so kindly after you, and what was your name now and where were you living and would you ever come to America again and said, 'She must bring her husband with her so that we can see whether he deserves her!'⁵⁹

In the event, Basil Ward's only foreign travel seems to have been during his wartime service in the Medical Corps.

On leaving the White House, the Fullers caught a night train for Cincinnati, where they gave two recitals, and then on to Chicago and its Little Theatre where Maurice Browne was awaiting them. Browne, who knew everyone – he was best friends with the poet Rupert Brooke and the novelist John Cowper Powys – had already been warned by Cecil Sharp of what to expect:

> They sing the old ballads better than anyone – *anyone* – whom I know; and I know every folksinger in Britain. Their voices . . . are natural, soft, true and exquisitely sweet. And always, clearly and without the slightest sense of strain, you can hear every word which each of them sings. . . . They are completely unaffected and unspoiled. On the stage they give the illusion of perfect spontaneity. And to cap everything they are – believe it or not – ludicrously lovely.⁶⁰

Browne could but agree. In *Recollections of Rupert Brooke*, he qualified a blue sky as being 'like Dorothy Fuller's eyes,'⁶¹ and in his autobiography he declared Rosalind to be 'the most bewitching creature I have known outside a fairy tale; and as in a fairy tale, there was something unearthly about her enchantment.'⁶²

The sisters sang for a week at the Chicago Little Theatre. Never had it been so full; despite extra seats, people had to be turned from the door. The success was enhanced by an article by the American composer and classical organist Eric DeLamarter:*

> The most fascinating recital of the season was given last evening at the Little theater in the Fine Arts building by the Misses Dorothy, Rosalind and Cynthia Fuller – a program of English, Scottish and Irish folk-song. They are to sing again this evening, tomorrow afternoon and tomorrow night. While it is not according to professional ethics to recommend such functions in this place, that tradition is broken here and now. For this is something the like of which Chicago has not heard since the memorable recitals given two seasons ago by Elsa von Wolzogen. These programs have the direct appeal, the depth of feeling peculiar to spontaneous art, and the surpassing loveliness of an emotion and an instinctive eloquence unspoiled

---

* From 1918 to 1933, Eric DeLamarter (1880–1953) served as assistant conductor of the Chicago Symphony Orchestra and then, from 1933 to 1936, as its associate conductor.

by the meddling of the scholiast. These young women sing with a charm that defies analysis.

Theirs is no pretentious art. They mirror faithfully the spirit of these mellow old tunes. Untrained in technical niceties though they be, their voices boast a purity, a healthiness of timbre refreshing to jaded ears, and their interpretations, which are not studied formulas of declamation, are almost primitive in fidelity to the medium.[63]

They could have stayed longer in Chicago, but Walter had accepted an irresistible offer from the enthusiastic Colonel Thompson in Washington: he was prepared to pay all their travel expenses, plus an extra $150, for the sisters to sing at a luncheon (and afterwards at a banquet at the New Willard Hotel) that he was organizing for representatives of Belgium, Britain, Australia and Canada, who had come to mark the centenary of the signing of the Treaty of Ghent.* So they made the long journey back to the capital where they also sang for Mrs Woodrow Wilson, her daughter and a party of friends, carrying magnificent flowers supplied by Mrs Wilson from the White House conservatory.

After this, it was time to fulfil their engagements in the mid-west and they set off on a thirty-six-hour train journey to St Louis, where they sang in a women's club. It seemed that everyone in the audience wanted to invite them to tea, and numerous were the requests for them to sing in private homes. They could have remained there for weeks, but they had agreed to return to the Little Theatre in Chicago, so Walter accepted only two engagements: one from the wife of Percy Chubb,† whom he had met in New York, and one

---

* On this occasion, the sisters sang 'High Germany,' which ends with
> O cursèd are the cruel wars that ever should arise
> And out of merrie England press many a lad likewise!
> They took my true love from me, likewise my brothers three
> And sent them to the cruel wars in High Germany.

It went down well. Addressing the guests, Wilson's Secretary of State, William Bryan, assured them that there would be no war during his term of office. 'When I say this, I am confident that I shall have no cause to change my view, for we know no cause today that cannot be settled better by reason than by war.... I believe that there will be no war so long as I live, and I hope that we have seen the last great war.'[64] He resigned his office in June 1915 in protest against Wilson's strong response to the sinking of the *Lusitania*, and died in 1925 immediately after the Scopes 'Monkey Trial', at which he had attacked Darwinism and evolution.

† Percival Chubb was born in England in 1860. Working as a civil servant in London he was a charter member of the Ethical Society (which was similar in philosophy to the Fabian Society but less politically active). He emigrated to America in 1889 and taught

Impresario

from Mrs La Follette, wife of Senator Robert La Follette, whom they had met in Boston. Cynthia described him as 'short, with masses of hair that stands up on the top of his head, a kind face, bright eyes and a very hearty laugh.'*

Having charmed the Chubbs and the La Follettes with their singing, they made their way back to Chicago via the University of Missouri, their farthest west so far. It was a joy to return to Maurice Browne's Little Theatre. They loved the venue, the audiences, the social life (for they were invited into many homes), and Maurice Browne himself along with his American wife, Ellen Van Volkenburg, known familiarly as Nellie Van. Browne had such a strong Oxford accent that on one occasion when he congratulated them on their performance, they heard something like 'Yardooneggod'. It was only as they were retiring to bed that evening that they realized he had said, 'You do one good.' Their audiences were obviously of the same opinion: they clapped and shouted and brought them back for encores again and again. As Walter told Riss, 'The people are just crazy over all the old favourites' – but the Fullers kept adding fresh songs to their repertoire.

To conclude their tour, they visited Boston again, stayed with the Raes – who announced that they had booked to cross to England on the same ship as the Fullers – and then returned to New York, with a few recitals along the way, to pack and say goodbye to the Burchenals. They left on 27 June 1913, on the *St Paul* again. This time the crossing was smoother and the girls – but not Walter – were beginning to get their sea legs. They even attended a concert in first class, and were invited to play and sing.

In England they stayed with Riss (who taught Cynthia some new tunes) and received the Raes and other friends from England and America at their home in Sturminster Newton. But it was a relatively short break, for Walter had decided to start the next tour at the beginning of October. To ensure that they could start earning money from the moment they arrived, Walter had retained the services of an agent, William Feakins, having been assured

in New York's Ethical Culture school. Moving to St Louis, he became the leader of the Ethical Society there in 1911.

*   In the House, Senator La Follette earned the ironical nickname 'fighting Bob' for his strong opposition to US participation in WWI. Accused of being unpatriotic, and threatened with expulsion, he valiantly maintained that international disputes should be resolved peacefully. He also denounced secret agreements between countries, for they meant that, by accepting to go to war, for instance, the people were agreeing to pacts with implications and clauses of which they were quite unaware.

that if he gave agents six month's notice, 'we could fill every day and night with engagements, in which we could all have the profits!'[65] By 18 July, Feakins had lined up some twenty engagements for them, between 1 November 1913 and 20 March 1914, in venues from New York to Sioux City, Ohio (450 miles west of Chicago). There were pros and cons to using agents: they held out for higher prices than Walter dared ask and insisted on expenses being covered; these benefits more than compensated for the commission they took. On the other hand, agents were used to exclusive arrangements, and would dispute Walter's right to accept another engagement in a town where they had secured one. Refusing impromptu invitations for which they had both time and energy left bad feelings all round.

The Fullers left for their third tour on 27 September on the *Minnehaha*. Recognized by passengers, they were asked to sing, but as it was 'awfully rough' they never felt quite up to it, and Walter remained in his cabin for almost the entire crossing. Only Rosalind summoned up the courage to play the piano at the Sunday service. They arrived on 6 October, welcomed by their faithful friends in New York, and installed themselves in a new hotel, the Belmont, which was conveniently just across the street from Grand Central Station. After a few days to recover, they plunged into an intense programme of local bookings followed by a series of venues in the mid-west, starting in Detroit, from which they returned to Boston, passing the Niagara Falls on Cynthia's birthday, 21 October. She was delighted to receive a signed birthday card from President Wilson.

While in Boston, where they renewed their friendships and rejoiced their audiences, they were again lodged at the Wayside Inn for a few days by Mr Filene. On this occasion he invited more than twenty young musicians and painters to come and meet them. Then it was back to New York where they performed six times at the Berkeley Theatre in mid-November. The audiences were not large, but friends and acquaintances (like Dr Allen, Mary Breck, Mrs Burchenal, and a reporter from the Chicago *Post*) were often present and requested encores.

Until now, they had always managed to fulfill their engagements, despite the fatigue of travelling – during which Dorothy would invariably be sick – and the occasional ailment. But on this tour the New England winter got the better of them and they all had recurrent colds. Early in December, they had to cancel some engagements. Ten days later they were well enough to perform at the Toy Theatre in Boston, with a programme that included Christmas carols. Walter reported:

We had splendid audiences in the afternoon and not so splendid ones in the evening – but the total proceeds will be for us, so we are not doing so badly, and shall soon be making money in fine style. We need to, too, for we have only just been paying our way up to the present. I'm pretty well tired of agents. Feakins is just a poor fool – he's not a rascal, thank goodness – he's just a muddler. Of course his illness has upset things a great deal – but ill or well he's just the same – he hasn't got the 'grace, grit and gumption' which Dr Paton* used to say a worthwhile man must have. But I'm working pretty independently of him now, and doing better in consequence – people like to deal with us direct.⁶⁶

They made $283 at the Toy Theatre, which 'has put us straight in the matter of clothes and debts – and we shall start the New Year with a clean slate,'⁶⁷ but it was at the cost of sore throats and a hoarse voice for Dorothy.

Mr Filene asked them to sing to staff and customers in his shop, and then rewarded them with seats at the Boston Opera Company's production of *Cavalleria Rusticana* in which Anna Pavlova danced. For Christmas the girls were the guests of the Peabodys in Cambridge, Massachusetts. As they had three teenage girls and a boy of seven, it was a family Christmas, with stockings hanging from the mantelpiece in the hall. They were also visited by Mr Millet and Percy Lee Atherton, who brought presents and a loving card. As there was not room for Walter as well at the Peabody's, they paid for him to stay at the Union Club in Boston, half-an-hour away. Although he joined them for Christmas Day, he spent a rather lonely Boxing Day in bed at the Club, nursing a bad cold with 'a pint of hot lemon water' and all the English papers and periodicals that the Club could provide.

The New Year brought a telegram from Norman Hapgood,† who had edited *Collier's* when it was a leading muck-raking magazine and had recently moved on to *Harper's Weekly*, asking them to sing at his home in New York the very next night, to entertain some distinguished guests. One of the girls was invited to dinner, in her Victorian dress; the other two were to arrive later with Walter. They hastened to New York. After the train jour-

---

* There are many candidates for this Dr Paton. The phrase was popularized by John Pugh, a railway worker turned minister who in the late nineteenth century advertised for 'men of Grace, Grit and Gumption' to serve as missionaries to the workmen of South Wales.

† Hapgood first met the Fuller Sisters at a recital organized by Luther Gulick. His brother Hutchins Hapgood, also a journalist, wrote an early review of their singing and later claimed to have 'enabled their tour to be successful. Indeed, Walter Fuller told me that it would have been very difficult for them to be recognized without my aid.'⁶⁸ Unfortunately, I have not been able to trace his review.

ney, Dorothy had a headache, and Cynthia was judged too young to go alone, so it fell to Rosalind to represent them at the meal. There she found a party of about thirty writers, artists, actors, and musicians, including Walter Damrosch, the conductor of the New York Symphony Orchestra. But the prize guests were Sir Johnston Forbes-Robertson and his wife Gertrude Elliot.* Forbes-Robertson had just completed a season (29 September–29 December 1913) in New York, acting in seven different plays, including *Hamlet*, his most famous role. The sisters were not overly impressed by this select company. Although Hapgood was kind to them, his wife's coldness made them feel uncomfortable. (The Hapgoods divorced in 1915.) Walter Damrosch condescended to Cynthia (as he was liable to do with concert audiences, especially young ones), calling her 'quite a little orchestra in herself.' 'If she had been an inch shorter, he would have patted her on the head!' was how Dorothy saw it. Sir Johnston was tired and tactless; only Gertrude Elliott behaved politely. So the Fullers were glad to get away and return to the warmth of Boston society, where they made the rounds of now familiar venues: private homes, clubs, schools and colleges. Still, they were gratified to find a full-page photograph of themselves and a flattering article in *Harper's Weekly* for 31 January, 1914.[69]

Back in Boston, they all suffered from the harsh winter, Dorothy with headaches and nose bleeds, Rosalind with bilious attacks, Cynthia and Walter with heavy colds. So they were pleased to accept another invitation from Mrs Atherton, whom they found 'very, very kind,' to sing at one of her receptions in Washington, where (not to be outdone) Mrs Franklin Roosevelt invited them the following afternoon. From there they travelled on to a new venue in Pittsburgh, where Walter had a surprise for them: a concert by the Russian violinist Mischa Elman. They all enjoyed it immensely, particularly Cynthia who had never heard a great violinist before.†

---

* Sir Johnston Forbes-Robertson (1853–1937) was considered the finest Hamlet of the nineteenth century – with his naturalness he made Sir Henry Irving look artificial – and one of the best actors of his time. For Americans, however, his greatest role was that of the Passer-By in *The Passing of the Third Floor Back* (1909). He was knighted in 1913 at the time of his farewell performance at the Drury Lane Theatre, London. He followed this by touring America for three seasons, while his actress wife, Gertrude Elliott, continued her twenty-year-long career with tours in New Zealand, Australia, and South Africa. Her last notable performance was as Gertrude in Leslie Howard's 1936 production of *Hamlet* at the Imperial Theatre in New York City.

† Throughout their tours, Walter always took opportunities to let his sisters see and hear great artists. With our easy access to audio-visual entertainment, it is easy to forget how, a hundred years ago, such occasions were rare treats.

Then they went on to Chicago and a warm welcome from Maurice Browne, whose Little Theatre they filled twice a day for two weeks. They were also much in demand for private recitals, and simply for themselves: 'Every hostess in the city wanted them;* they were the toast of Chicago,' he recorded.[70] But the weather turned really cold again in the middle of February. The wind blew straight across the lake and froze their faces, so they were grateful to be staying in a hotel that connected directly with the Little Theatre, enabling them to pass from their rooms to the stage without getting frostbite on the way.

At this point Dorothy provides another glimpse of Walter, busy with correspondence as usual: 'Imagine,' she wrote to Riss,

> you had a long telescope and could really see what we are doing at this moment. Turn your glass into Walter's bedroom first. You had better look carefully round the room before you decide he isn't there among all that paper of his. You see he has taken his coat off. I wonder if he will find it again before dinner. The pile you see on the right are letters he has written – he looks anxious, but very well, in other words he has a lot on his mind, but seems to enjoy it. Between his sortings out of different letters he makes jokes about us in his funny way – and if we *can* think of an extra good one about him we call it out from our room.[72]

After a Valentine's Day performance of love songs, which filled the theatre in spite of a heavy snowfall, they travelled to St Louis, where Walter's letterwriting had secured more engagements for them. In particular, they sang in support of Equal Suffrage and then went to hear a talk by the famous blind and deaf girl, Helen Keller (1880–1968). Greatly impressed, they went backstage to meet her afterwards, and she asked them to sing for her. She had developed such sensitivity in her hands and fingers that she could lip-read by feeling people's lips as they spoke, and 'listen' to music by feeling its vibrations through her hands. So with Walter looking on, she placed her hands on their lips and throats as they sang, saying, 'Beautiful! Beautiful!'

Back in Chicago for another run at the Little Theatre, they were delighted to meet up with Kathleen Wheeler – 'Tiger Lily' of the Peter Pan game in Walter's flat – whom they had not seen since that time. She had gone from strength to strength as a sculptress, specializing in life-size

---

* One of these hostesses was Fanny Butcher (1888–1987). In 1913 she began a lifetime career as a writer and literary critic for the Chicago *Tribune*. In her autobiography she mentions memorable people from this time, including 'Rupert Brooke, who was so beautiful that both girls and boys swooned at sight of him, as well as the Fuller sisters, three enchanting young English folk singers.'[71]

'portraits' of horses – that is, of specific horses, not just generic horses such as most artists produce. In 1910 she went out to Canada, where she lived on a ranch with her married sister. A sculpture called 'Out West' of two horses and a girl (actually her sister) that she produced there was exhibited at the Royal Academy in London. King George V so admired it that he ordered a cast in bronze which is apparently still in the royal collection.[73] In Canada she heard from Jessie Holliday that the Fullers were in America, so she arranged to meet them in Chicago in February. At once the Fullers began introducing her to chosen members of their circle. This included the sculptor Lorado Taft (1860–1936, a distant relative of the ex-President) who was well known for his pioneering support of women sculptors.*

Soon Tiger Lily found a studio nearby, in the artists' quarter. Among her first works that spring was a head of Dorothy 'because of her fine features,' and a small group portrait of the three sisters, complete with harp. She regularly attended their recitals in the Little Theatre, and they loved to see her among the audience. Although Walter had his 'doubts as to whether she will be able to earn her living here – or anywhere,' she remained in America for the rest of her life, celebrated for her equestrian statues and busts of prominent persons.†

The Fullers punctuated their stay in Chicago with journeys to venues as far west as Kansas City and as far north as Madison, Wisconsin, before returning east via Pittsburgh, reaching Philadelphia on 3 April, Walter's thirty-second birthday. By now they were all back in good health, but very tired, so they much appreciated rest and recuperation at Atlantic City during Easter week. Then they picked up their travels again, with New York as their base, Boston as farthest north, and Philadelphia as farthest south, with a brief foray to Pittsburgh once more. They renewed their contacts with friends: Mr Millet and Mrs Burgess; Mary Breck, who took them for a long drive through Central Park and Riverside; and Mollie Best, who had been touring her stories. While staying with the Fullers at the Raes', she

---

* During preparations for the World's Columbian Exposition of 1893, there was concern that the sculptural adornments on the Horticultural Building might not be finished in time. Taft asked if he might employ some of his female students to speed the work and was told, 'Hire anyone, even white rabbits if they'll do the work.' This resulted in the development of a group of talented sculptresses, popularly known as 'White Rabbits.'

† According to the Seattle *Times* of 19 October 1924, 'she has modeled twenty-eight of the most famous race horses the world has ever known.' When Queen Elizabeth II visited the United States thirty years later, one of the official presents she received was a sculpture of herself by Kathleen Wheeler.

announced that she was going to England in the summer, as was Durr Friedley; they would both visit Riss and the Fuller parents.

The girls were certainly refreshed by the end of April. The Springfield *Republican* reported:

> Their singing is as charming as could be, and gives the effect, probably delusive, of being wholly untutored; it is at any rate wholly spontaneous and carries the conviction that in an ideal state of society people in general would be able to sing like that – sweetly, daintily, prettily. . . . A word must be said too of their mellow southern English voices, equally delectable in the song and in the little spoken introductions which were quite informally made. . . . To hear the language sung and spoken as it was sung and spoken last night is in itself a rare privilege, and the beauty of the medium added to the spell which was worked by the humor, vivacity and dramatic feeling of the performers. . . . There were no false touches last night; everything was kept to the right scale of simplicity, colored only by roguish humor. It was a striking example of how far the most ordinary materials may be made to go if they be kept unspoiled.[74]

In Philadelphia their recital in a 500-seat theatre was sold out days before they arrived. 'And how the audience enjoyed the songs – once, one of the encores was encored! – they just *would not* stop clapping,' exclaimed Cynthia. Now receptions were held in *their* honour, such as one hosted by Mrs Otis Skinner, the wife of the popular American stage actor* who excelled in Shakespearean roles. They found these occasions more tiring than singing: while the guests ate the food they had to stand and shake hand after hand, answering the same questions time after time. It was the price of fame. At one private recital, a guest brought their hostess a present from Chicago: the small sculpture of the Fuller Sisters by Kathleen Wheeler!

They stayed for several days with Dr & Mrs Robert Tait McKenzie† who introduced them to the staff at Bryn Mawr, where they sang several times in the context of a May Day festival. They met ex-President Taft, who looked old and tired, and his wife told them how sorry she was that they had not managed to fit the White House into their schedule two years before. Mr Millet turned up at this point, and took them to hear the Polish pianist Paderewski, which particularly delighted Rosalind:

---

* Clarence Derwent, who was inspired by Rosalind to create the Derwent Awards for actors and actresses, found Otis Skinner 'one of the finest and most lovable personalities I have met in the American theatre.'[74]

† Robert Tait McKenzie (1867–1938) was a Canadian-born doctor, educator and sculptor, whom they had got to know during their first tour. His daughter Sandra adored Riss.

Riss, I heard Beethoven's piano concerto in E Flat Major, Opus 73, and Wagner's *Tristan and Isolde* Overture and Gluck for the first time! Can you imagine my delight? A new planet has swum into my ken. . . . Beethoven's music is like the working of nature – though *all* that music was wonderful. I could not help the tears coming to my eyes. . . . Some of the themes were so beautiful – too beautiful to be the work of an individual. It opened up to me a heaven where the music will not seem so far away – it seemed to give a glimpse of something beyond all this. Paderewski played your Chopin Polonaise –'galloping horses' I think was what *we* called it.[76]

Back in New York, they packed in more engagements, including one at which they dined with the Tiffany family* at Laurelton Hall and then sang to their eighty guests. By now they were very ready to return home. It had been a long tour. Even the harp was wearing out, with a cracked shoulder, and Walter developed an infected finger that Dr Murray lanced for him. Cynthia wrote, 'We feel something like the Lost Boys in the Never Never Land who began to forget what their home and Mother and Father looked like – so that Wendy cried out: "Oh! I can see it's time to go home!"'[77]

As usual, they spent their last evening at the Burchenals', but the following day, with everything packed and ready to go, they put in a final performance (free of charge) at the Colored Orphanage Home, in Smithtown. Waved off by the Raes, who came to New York especially see them, they endured another rough crossing and fell into the arms of their family.

Having made all the money on this tour that he had hoped to make on the first two, Walter went on a spending spree, buying diamond earrings for his mother, a gold watch for his father, and a baby grand piano for Riss. Since most of their instruments had gone in the bankruptcy of 1908, he added a new violin for Dorothy, a baby grand for Rosalind, and a silver watch and fountain pen for Cynthia (who played Rosalind's old cello). The girls had a large globe delivered to Bridge House as a surprise for Walter, along with subscriptions to his favourite periodicals. Thus equipped, they settled down to enjoy a well-earned holiday.

---

* Louis Comfort Tiffany (1848–1933), the artist and designer best known for his stained glass, built the 84-room Laurelton Hall in 1905 on a 600-acre estate on Long Island, New York, and filled it with objects that he had designed and collected. After his death, many of the artefacts were dispersed and the house caught fire in 1957. What remains of his collection has been assembled at the Morse Museum of American Art in Winter Park, Florida. It contains the chapel he designed for the 1893 Chicago World's Fair.

Impresario

The summer of 1914 being a turning point in world history, it is a good moment to evaluate the Fuller Sisters' impact on America during their tours. Walter maintained that they were 'doing splendid work – the world needs what we are giving it: simple, happy songs and cheerfulness.'[78]

They certainly helped to raise the awareness of folksongs in the United States. When they first sang in Chicago, Floyd Dell was a writer and literary critic for the Chicago *Evening Post*. Like many others, he found that 'the greatest music of the nineteenth century' would put him to sleep. But then he discovered that 'there was one kind of music in which I could take the deepest enjoyment. This revelation was afforded by the Fuller Sisters ... who sang old English ballads to the harp. I went happily mad over old English ballads, and the Fuller sisters, especially the enchanting Rosalind, whose voice never ceased to vibrate in my memory.'[79] Thousands of people shared his revelation (with regard both to folksongs and to Rosalind).

Their singing stimulated the collecting of half-forgotten songs. For instance, the Emporia *Gazette* reported on 28 September 1915 that

the Treble Clef Club is planning to give a program of Old English folksongs in costume. Such a program was given at the Normal last year by the Fuller Sisters, and proved to be one of the most popular numbers of the lecture course. Material for such a concert has been received by the Normal School of Music from Miss Mary Plumb [a friend of the Fullers], who recently presented the department with eight volumes of rare English folksongs.

They themselves contributed to this collecting. People spontaneously brought them old songs* and they added them to their repertoire, which reached well over 200 songs and ballads. Wherever they went, they trawled through old collections in libraries, becoming experts at identifying genuine works. After singing a group of Hebridean folksongs at the University of Wisconsin, Rosalind discussed them with Professor Dykema, its Professor of Music, and agreed with him that they lacked the familiar qualities of folksong, as though they had been freely edited.†

This expertise had a historic consequence for the preservation of folksong in the United States. In May 1915, Luther Gulick brought William Chauncey

---

* A Mr Barry of Boston brought them his own collection of Irish folksongs. 'We have not learnt them through yet, as we have not had time, but we have thoroughly tried them though. They have such queer tunes – still, the more we try, the more tuneful they seem.'

† Peter William Dykema (1873–1951) was Professor of Music at the University of Wisconsin at Madison, Wisconsin, from 1913 to 1924. They first met him when he was in charge of music at the Ethical Culture School in New York (1901 to 1913).

Langdon, who was the head of the Russell Sage Foundation's recreation department and worked extensively with 'community pageants', to one of the sisters' recitals. A few days later, Langdon caught them as they were changing trains at Grand Central Station and showed them some of the southern mountain ballads which Olive Dame Campbell had collected while she accompanied her husband on his Russell Sage Foundation-funded social survey in the Appalachians. The girls were fascinated. Langdon reported to Campbell, 'they were inclined to think [that these ballads] were purer and older, many of them, than their own Dorset and Somerset versions.'[80] Rosalind sent some of these ballads to Cecil Sharp, who had just arrived in America as dance advisor for a production of *A Midsummer Night's Dream*. As soon as he saw them, Sharp asked to meet Olive Dame Campbell, for until that moment he had believed that there was no such thing as American folk music. When they met in Lincoln, Massachusetts, she showed him some 200 songs that she had taken down. Immediately realizing their significance, Sharp began to plan an expedition to collect and record folksongs and dances in the Appalachian mountains. So Rosalind's prompt action triggered the research on which half of Cecil Sharp's reputation is founded. Walter reviewed the book that resulted from it, *English Folk Songs from the Southern Appalachians,* in the *Survey*.[81]

The Fuller Sisters' singing inspired composers from Percy Lee Atherton to Leo Sowerby (1895–1968), who was the organist of the Episcopalian Cathedral in Chicago for thirty-five years. His music was regularly performed in the 1920s and 30s, but has proved too traditional for modern taste. At the age of nineteen he attended one of the girls' recitals in the Chicago Little Theatre and was so moved that he came back to hear them whenever he could.[82] He discussed music with them and listened to their rehearsals. This led to his studying for a while with Percy Grainger (1882–1961), whose music drew inspiration from folksong, and resulted in one of Sowerby's earliest compositions, a work for small orchestra called 'Rhapsody on British Folk Tunes' (1915). He used other songs that he heard the girls sing in 'Three Folk Tunes from Somerset' (1916) and in his orchestral suite, 'Homage to England's Country Folk' (also 1916).* Also in 1916 he composed a brief orchestral piece, 'The Irish Washerwoman: Country Dance Tune.' The Sisters were an important influence on his development as a composer.

When Americans deplored the craze for rag-time, some maintained that

---

* He returned to one of these tunes, 'The Cuckoo', in an unpublished arrangement for cello and piano that dates from 1927.

Two admirers, each with three bunches of May flowers, come to see the Fuller Sisters off at Boston station. A story in three scenes, sketched by Dorothy, captioned 'All's Well that Ends Well.' The man on the right is the composer Percy Lee Atherton.

it could – or should – be replaced with folksongs, and cited the Fuller Sisters, 'at present on their second visit to this country,' as a model of what could be done.[83] Rosalind's conviction that Americans would 'carry on the tradition of singing folksongs long after we have left these shores' was of course perfectly correct, but only in the 1930s and 40s, with singers like Woody Guthrie* – who was born in the year that the Fuller Sisters launched their career – did it begin to pick up momentum. It peaked in the 1950s and 60s, becoming a mass movement.

---

* Guthrie was named after the newly elected President, Woodrow Wilson.

4

Peace Activist

I'm getting a raging, tearing, anti-war maniac, and wherever I go I sow some splendid anti-war seeds, which will spring up and bear fruit some day, I hope!
Walter to Riss, January 1915

So long as Christianity is the miserable pretence it is, so long shall we have fighting and killing.
Walter to his father, February 1915

If war is right, then Christianity is wrong, false, a lie.
If Christianity is right, then war is wrong, false, a lie.[1]
John Haynes Holmes

Above: Jane Addams and Mary McDowell demonstrating in 1917

Below: US Delegates on the *Noordam*, about to leave for the International Conference of Women at The Hague, 1915

AFTER TWO MONTHS' HOLIDAY during which they received visitors from the States (including Mollie Best and Mary Breck), Dorothy, Rosalind and Cynthia attended Cecil Sharp's Folk Dance Festival at Stratford-on-Avon to catch up on his latest findings. There they heard on 4 August that war had been declared.

In Sturminster Newton, the day before, 'there was practically a free fight for the morning papers' which arrived only at 10.30 (it being Bank Holiday Monday). As they were the sole source of news, the demand for them was such that ha'penny papers were selling for a penny. Mr Fuller bought the *Mail* and *The Times* – 'two papers but one in spirit and ideals,' commented Walter, bitterly. 'These hideous papers seem to be nursing the war spirit – gloating over it – fanning it – and yet half afraid at the big blaze they've helped to start. . . . If there is to be war for England I think we ought to go to America as soon as possible so as to make some money to help mother and father to live comfortably through the period of high prices.'[2]

Three days later, he was no longer so sure that a return to the States was the best course of action, or even if it was going to be possible. He asked Curt for his opinion, enquiring at the same time after his family. Curt's younger brother Frank had married a German girl. She was visiting friends and family when war was declared and was unable to return to England, where she had left her little son Stanley with Frank. Curt himself and his elder brother Fred, both born in Germany, were naturalized British subjects; now the country of their birth was at war with their country of adoption. Aware that they might have divided feelings, Walter trod carefully. After reading in *The Times* the diplomatic correspondence which had led up to the war, he told Curt, 'I do not come to the conclusion which *The Times* is happy in being so confident about – that this country could not avoid conflict with Germany. My conclusions are quite otherwise. Please bear with me if you think differently.'[3] In the event, the Dehns were thoroughly pro-British and served in the army.

Walter found the outbreak of war deeply disturbing. When he welcomed his sisters back home, they found that he could hardly speak, so powerfully was he affected. 'I have not felt such depression of spirits since the *Titanic* went down. Now a thousand *Titanics* seem to be sinking – and I feel myself drowning,' he told Curt.[4] Predictably, he wanted to get away from it all, and soon he was off on a walking tour with Bill Hankinson; six weeks later, he spent 'a few days wandering about in rural England, far from the madding crowd's ignoble strife' with Curt.[5]

He had long felt the futility of resolving international rivalry through war.

Walter Fuller

Less than a month after arriving in New York in 1911, he had written to the New York *Times*:

A Navy to Insure Peace!

To the Editor of the New York Times:

The recent efforts of certain prominent men to boom a 'peaceful navy' remind me of the story of Johnny Smithers. Said Johnny to his paternal relative one day:

'Papa, what is a peaceful navy?'

'A peaceful navy, my boy, is a navy that is large and powerful enough to keep peace,' answered Smithers senior.

'How can it keep peace, papa?'

'By intimidating or subduing other navies.'

'Should the United States have a peaceful navy?'

'Most certainly, Johnny.'

'Should Great Britain have a peaceful navy?'

Smithers Senior, hesitated. 'Er – er – say, Johnny, don't you want to go and play with your new aeroplane?'

'No, papa. Should Great Britain have a peaceful navy?'

'Well – yes, I suppose so.'

'Should every nation have a peaceful navy?'

'Look, Johnny, those boys are having lots of fun over there. Run along and play with them.'

'Guess I don't want to go out now, papa. Should every nation have a peaceful navy?'

'You're not old enough to understand these things, my boy,' said the elder philosopher. 'Don't bother me.'

'Well, papa – if another navy should attack our navy and we should subdue it, wouldn't that be keeping peace?'

'Yes.'

'And if the other navy was larger and powerfuller, and was to subdue ours, wouldn't that be keeping peace?'

Mr Smithers quite disapproved of encouraging inquisitiveness in children, so he sternly bade Johnny be silent.

The next day Johnny proudly announced to his father that he had kept peace with Jimmy Jones. 'How was that my son?' asked the parent, scrutinizing a dark crescent under the youngster's eye.

'Well,' said Johnny, 'I'm bigger and powerfuller than him, so I tried to intiminate him first, but he hit me and then I just subdid him.'[6]

W. F.

The parable came easily to Walter's pen, and metaphor was to play a major part in his personal campaign against war.

Like everyone, he pored over the newspapers. In September he read with eager interest the open letter to the press announcing the launch of the Union of Democratic Control (UDC), for its aims closely matched his convictions. Soon to become the most important of the anti-war organizations in Britain, it had three main objectives: parliamentary control over foreign policy (to put an end to secret agreements); the formation after the war of an organization to help prevent future conflicts (realized, somewhat ineffectively, in the League of Nations); and post-war peace terms that neither humiliated the defeated nation nor artificially rearranged frontiers in ways that might cause future wars. (Failure to observe these precautions were to cause many conflicts, including WWII.) The UDC was largely financed by the Quaker chocolate manufacturers George Cadbury and Arnold Rowntree, and supported by many well-known figures, some of whom were already known to Walter: J. A. Hobson, Bertrand Russell, Lady Margaret Sackville (the poet), and Mary Sheepshanks, for instance. In the course of the war, he got to know two of the founding members, Frederick Pethick-Lawrence and Norman Angell.

In the end, the Fullers stuck to the original plan of returning to America at the end of October: they already had more than twenty bookings, from Boston to Washington, starting on 4 November. Getting earlier ones was very difficult from the other side of the ocean, even though Walter engaged the services of an agent.* This left him free to stay for several weeks with Riss ('like old times indeed'), during which time he did much letter-writing to organize the visits to England – and to the Fuller home – of various American friends, including Mrs Burgess and Mr Peabody. He also made frequent trips up to London, where he stayed at Curt's flat, and went on shopping expeditions with his sisters. As usual he was particular that they should be properly equipped for their next tour, from shawls and dresses down to warm underwear. One day, just as he was going into the Constitutional Club to meet Curt, he was hailed by Mollie Best; she took him into a hotel across the road to meet Alice Hegan Rice, the American short-story-writer famous for the bestselling novel of 1901, *Mrs Wiggs of the Cabbage Patch*. After that, Curt joined them for lunch.

---

* This time it was the manager of the J.B. Pond Lyceum Bureau in New York. It represented many famous people, including Jerome K. Jerome, Helen Keller, and the son of Charles Dickens, Alfred Tennyson Dickens.

Walter Fuller

Thus, until the last ten days before leaving, he was more often than not away from Sturminster Newton. This absence relieved his parents: with the press insisting that every available man should enlist, they found Walter's refusal to volunteer embarrassingly unpatriotic, liable to bring social opprobrium upon himself and the family. Such men were treated as cowards. Girls sent them chicken feathers in the post. In the event, it was his friendship with Curt that caused trouble: a brick with a threatening message about what happened to people who consorted with the enemy was thrown through a window of Bridge House. 'With sympathy and anger that such a war should have been allowed to happen,' Dorothy and Rosalind preserved the family's reputation by helping to convert the local school into an emergency hospital.[7]

This time they were to sail from Liverpool, which they reached by train via London. Struggling through the crowds of soldiers on the platforms, they noticed with a shudder the contrast between the new recruits, 'Straight of limb, true of eye, steady and aglow' (Binyon) and those returning from France, weary and war-torn, not to mention the trainloads of walking wounded with crutches, slings and bloody bandages. At Liverpool, Bill Hankinson came to see them off with Manchester newspapers and news that Stanley Nott had joined up and Arthur Dakyns had already left for France.

The ship was full, additional passengers having been transferred from other liners at the last moment, so the girls were relieved when they found that they had an outside three-berth cabin to themselves. Walter, though, was thoroughly put out to learn that he would have to share, until he discovered that his cabin mate was Laurence Binyon, on his way to lecture in the United States. Not only did Walter remember Binyon's Friday Club lecture of January 1909, he had even read an elegy of his that had appeared in *The Times* on 21 September – 'For the Fallen' it was called. Today there can hardly be an English-speaking person in the world who does not (however vaguely) recognize its fourth stanza. Ever since Remembrance ceremonies were instituted throughout the Empire at the end of WWI, it has been intoned each year with awful solemnity.*

> They shall grow not old, as we that are left grow old,
> Age shall not weary them, nor the years condemn.
> At the going down of the sun and in the morning
> We will remember them.

To Binyon's face, Walter may have polite about the poem, but in truth he

---

*   In Canada they have it in French translation as well.

found this sentimental celebration of pointless slaughter rather surprising from the pen of a Quaker. He preferred a poem called 'Five Souls' that a journalist, William Norman Ewer (1885–1976; always known as Trilby*) had contributed to the *Nation* on 3 October:

First Soul

I was a peasant of the Polish plain;
I left my plough because the message ran:
Russia, in danger, needed every man
To save her from the Teuton; and was slain.
I gave my life for freedom – This I know
For those who bade me fight had told me so.

Second Soul

I was a Tyrolese, a mountaineer;
I gladly left my mountain home to fight
Against the brutal, treacherous Muscovite;
And died in Poland on a Cossack spear.
I gave my life for freedom – This I know
For those who bade me fight had told me so.

Third Soul

I worked in Lyons at my weaver's loom,
When suddenly the Prussian despot hurled
His felon blow at France and at the world;
Then I went forth to Belgium and my doom.
I gave my life for freedom – This I know
For those who bade me fight had told me so.

Fourth Soul

I owned a vineyard by the wooded Main,
Until the Fatherland, begirt by foes
Lusting her downfall, called me, and I rose
Swift to the call – and died in far Lorraine.
I gave my life for freedom – This I know
For those who bade me fight had told me so.

---

* Ewer's granddaughter informs me that the nickname originated in his youthful habit of going barefoot, like the heroine of George du Maurier's novel – nothing to do with any hat he may have worn, as has generally been assumed.

Walter Fuller

Fifth Soul
I worked in a great shipyard by the Clyde;
There came a sudden word of wars declared,
Of Belgium, peaceful, helpless, unprepared,
Asking our aid: I joined the ranks, and died.
I gave my life for freedom – This I know
For those who bade me fight had told me so.

In 1914, these lines were Ewer's sole claim to fame. Although they might not be such great poetry as Binyon's, the message – that all the fallen, irrespective of nationality, were the victims of indoctrination – and the irony, bordering on the cynical, of the refrain, were closer to the way Walter saw things.

The crossing was as rough as usual and Walter spent much of the time down in the cabin, reading and discussing poetry with Binyon. His sisters fared better, cheered by bunches of grapes sent along by Binyon and the kind attentions of Mollie Best, who was on the same ship. As there were so many people on board, lounge seats were at a premium, so they too spent much time in their cabin, reading, relaxing – and writing poetry: inspired by Binyon's presence, they each tried their hand at it.

Of all their friends, Mary Breck was the only one who met them as they disembarked on 10 November 1914. 'She is fiercely anti-German,' Walter told Riss, 'and expects a German invasion of America immediately following the defeat of the Allies.'[8] Her fears were not untypical. The American press was indulging in its customary scaremongering; by devoting many pages to war news, it gave readers the impression that it was all happening on their doorsteps. The main newspapers drew large crowds by pinning the latest telegrams from Europe to giant noticeboards outside their offices. 'It is the foremost subject in all people's minds – everyone is talking of it, not with any anti-German feeling but a good anti-war feeling. . . . There is no fear that America will join in,' Rosalind assured her parents.[9] Other people dismissed the war as a purely European problem – in someone else's backyard. A popular joking comment went: 'I'm neutral, I don't mind who beats Germany.' So the climate in the United States was very different from what they had left behind, and Walter observed it with passionate attention.

In England the war was up close and personal; those killed were husbands, brothers, cousins and friends; a torrent of the horrendously wounded flowed home through the railway stations. The guns of the Western Front could be heard from the south coast of England, and in December 1914 Scarborough, Whitby, and Hartlepool were shelled from the North Sea by German battle-cruisers. Later came the Zeppelins, dropping bombs on English towns and villages. With war not just on their doorsteps but entering their very homes, British women put their suffrage movement on hold and attended to the immediate need of replacing men in the national workforce.

America had a strong pacifist tradition with an international orientation. It had supported the first peace conference at The Hague in 1899; the second was convened in 1907 on the initiative of President Roosevelt. In 1910 the wealthy publisher Edward Ginn gave a million dollars (one third of his fortune) to set up the World Peace Foundation. Less than a year later, Carnegie – not to be outdone – coughed up ten million dollars to fund his Endowment for International Peace. By subsidizing America's many small peace societies, it influenced their policies. So when, on the outbreak of the war in Europe, the Endowment advocated non-intervention – not even mediation – in favour of building a peaceful world after Germany had been defeated, most of the smaller societies fell into step behind it. Only American feminists begged to disagree.

According to Jane Addams, the great American social pioneer, feminist and pacifist (who first came to public notice with a speech at a convention of National Peace Societies in 1904), the outbreak of war was greeted with widespread disbelief: for thousands of men and women, war was 'an archaic institution . . . a throw-back in the scientific sense.'[10] This reflected the theories of Charlotte Perkins Gilman who, in *The Man-Made World* (1911), maintained that women, being formed to carry children, were naturally inclined to peace, whereas men, whose bellicose tendencies showed their congenital inferiority to women, were responsible for all the social ills of the world. This is why American suffragists did not resort to the violent actions of their sisters in Britain. For them, the outbreak of war highlighted the failure of feminists to obtain their political rights: 'if women had had the vote in all the countries now at war, the conflict would have been prevented,' proclaimed Carrie Chapman Catt, President of the National American Woman's Suffrage Association.[11] Thus her Association, which had already submitted a woman's suffrage amendment to Congress, became a peace movement. On 29 August 1914, women's organizations in New York sent 1500 women (some sources say 2000) dressed in black down Fifth Avenue to the sound of muffled drums in protest against the inhumanity of war and to mark their sympathy with European women. The procession was led by Mrs Villard, the widow of the owner of the New York *Evening Post* and the *Nation*, carrying a large banner depicting the dove of peace. In retrospect, it was a powerful symbol 'of all the lives, hopes and possibilities that the world war would destroy,' as Jacqueline Van Voris puts it in her biography of Catt.[12]

Walter Fuller

That autumn, two European feminists whose ideas coincided with the Americans' crossed over to the United States. Rosika Schwimmer (1877–1948), an energetic Hungarian, who had been one of the organisers of the 1913 Budapest International Woman Suffrage Congress, met Carrie Catt at the board meeting of the International Woman Suffrage Alliance in London. (She called herself its 'International Press Secretary'.) On 9 July 1914 she got herself invited to breakfast with the Chancellor of the Exchequer at number 11 Downing Street; in his memoirs, Lloyd George confessed that she was the first person to warn him of the imminence of the war! After it was declared, America was just about the only place she could go; the borders to Hungary were closed, and as an enemy alien she was no longer welcome in Britain. Carrie Catt promised to arrange a US lecture tour for her and advanced the cost of her passage. She arrived on 6 September and Catt, who had her entries to the White House, arranged for her to meet President Wilson on 19 September – one month to the day after his declaration of American neutrality. Schwimmer brought him a petition, she said, from a million women in thirteen European countries, begging him to lead the world in calling for a cessation of hostilities and mediation between the belligerents by the neutral countries (Denmark, The Netherlands, Norway, Spain, Sweden, and Switzerland). The President listened to her politely, assured her of his interest – and did nothing. So Schwimmer set out on a lecture tour of the United States, inciting its citizens to demand that President Wilson call a conference of neutrals.

The other woman who came to lecture in the United States at this point was Emmeline Pethick-Lawrence (1867–1954), whom we have already noticed as the person who chose the colours for the English Suffragettes, and the best friend of Mary Neal. Although a close associate of Mrs Pankhurst, she had distanced herself from militant action. She too had met Catt in London that July. Her opinion that the war was 'the final demonstration of the unfitness of men to have the whole control of the human family in their hands' chimed perfectly with the views of American suffragists.[13] Both she and Rosika Schwimmer had been introduced to the feminist, pacifist lawyer, Crystal Eastman at the 1913 Woman Suffrage Congress. The founder of a Woman's Peace Party in New York, Eastman invited Mrs Pethick-Lawrence to come and lecture on women's rights as the key to international peace; she arrived in October 1914. From New York, Crystal Eastman sent her to meet Jane Addams in Chicago. Rosika Schwimmer was there too; from then on, Pethick-Lawrence and Schwimmer often shared the same platform. Representing as they did the two sides of the war – the Allies and the Central

Powers – their collaboration inspired the founding of countless fresh peace groups by women throughout the United States.

Walter followed all these developments through the newspapers. He judged George Bernard Shaw's 'Common Sense About the War' (printed in the New York *Times*[14]) to be the most 'enheartening demolition of the mass of canting humbug' to have appeared in the press since the outbreak of war, whereas back in England many people found it unpatriotic. 'Thanks to Shaw I feel I can go about among decent people of any nationality without having to pretend to be a martyred angel,' added Walter.[15]

Meanwhile his sisters' fourth tour made 'a very slow, poor start' because their agent had made so few bookings. Worse, he had not always provided the venues with a list of the songs they were to sing, which caused an embarrassing scene one day when they arrived at a prestigious private school. Conversely, when he booked them in at the no less prestigious Columbia Theatre in Washington,* he failed to warn them that they were expected to sing several new songs which they had added to their programme for this tour and rehearsed but not yet performed. It was only while they were changing for the concert that they saw the list and had a moment of panic. By now they were true professionals, though, and simply rose to the challenge.

> Soon it was time to go on and – we *were* surprised at the size of the audience! It almost filled the large theatre, and the gallery and boxes were filled too. It was quite thrilling. Well, we did *very* well – so brother Walter said afterwards, even with the newest songs. He had been at the back of the theatre, so it was real praise from him. He says we sing much better than last year – which is all very encouraging – especially after singing in such a large theatre.[16]

When they received some of the audience in the Stars' room afterwards, they were delighted – and relieved – to hear how their new songs were admired. They were indeed singing better than ever before; they had more confidence and were more relaxed. 'Even the critic, Walter, is sometimes left speechless, with no criticism to offer! If you knew what last year was like in this respect, you would understand what that means!'[17] As for the agent, Walter broke the contract at the end of the year, vowing to make all their future reservations himself. 'Agents are no good for ordinary people like ourselves,' he concluded.

Fewer engagements than usual left room for spontaneity. Learning that

---

* This was the old Columbia Theatre; the current one, which is on the National Register of Historic Places, was opened only in 1925.

there was to be a banquet in their Washington hotel for a convention of US architects, Walter proposed a recital for them. It was gratefully accepted and proved a tremendous success. The following day, the girls went off to the Library of Congress in search of more folksongs. While Rosalind and Cynthia copied out words and music from old collections, a curator showed Dorothy ballad broadsides illustrated with woodcuts. She found a carol that she thought they could add to their Christmas repertoire. They also found a singing game called 'Would You Know How Doth the Peasant?' which they added to their store.

The broadsides gave Dorothy an idea. Back in New York she began to draw illustrations, in a style imitating woodcuts, to some of the songs they sang. Walter was delighted with them and proposed that they should sell illustrated copies of their songs, just as ballad singers had done in the past. So while Dorothy made more drawings, Walter approached the celebrated De Vinne Press in East Village, one of the oldest in the country. They printed the broadsides for them in a style suited to the illustrations, with the title and texts in the American copy of William Morris's Troy Type – let's hope that Walter did not know that the Americans call it 'Satanick'! – and the score with square rather than round or oval notes. Over the space of a year, Dorothy illustrated ten songs in all, some with a single drawing, others with two or three; 'When I was a Young Girl' had no less than nine, one for each stanza. Beneath each was neatly hand lettered, 'Dorothy Fuller, Her Work'. The New York music publisher H. W. Gray, who represented Novello & Co in the United States, acted as distributor. When the series was complete they sold sets stapled into a sepia card cover titled 'English Folk Songs – The Fuller Sisters' in black and red.

Then it occurred to the girls that they could colour the pictures themselves, by hand, so they had the price of 'ten cents plain, and twenty-five cents colored' added to the foot of the broadsides. From mid-January 1915 onwards, whenever they had a spare moment, they would mix up some paint, spread broadsides around their hotel room and go round with brushes, each adding a different colour as they went. It was tedious work, but the broadsides sold well and brought in welcome extra money.

At their very first recital of the season in Montclair, New Jersey, Walter noticed how a hush came over the audience of six or seven hundred students when one of their songs expressed the wish that the war would soon be over. So he chose some anti-war songs for his sisters to sing as encores, but there were so many requests for old favourites that they were hard to fit in. However, during the following concerts, in schools, colleges and women's clubs, they managed to sing some, with encouraging results. So after listening to Dr. David Starr Jordan,* Chancellor of Stanford University and President of the World Peace Foundation from 1910 to 1914, preach a 'Sermon for Peace' in Washington, Walter proposed to the host institution, the Fairmont Seminary, that his sisters should sing some anti-war songs – free of charge, as a donation to peace, so to speak. They sang the four songs they knew, and 'Brixham Town', to an ecstatic audience. This brought a request from Dr Stephen Newman, the Principal of Howard, that they sing at his all-black university the following morning. Walter was delighted, of course, but having performed free of charge at Fairmont, he could hardly ask a fee from Howard. They could ill afford to sing for nothing – but the experience was priceless, for never before had they performed to an all-black audience, or witnessed so many signs of genuine feeling. 'It was so strange and such a new experience for us to see and meet so many coloured people. I felt as if I were looking through black glasses,' Rosalind told her parents.[18]

As they had so few anti-war songs in their repertoire, it occurred to Walter that they might set Trilby Ewer's 'Five Souls' to music and sing that, so he wrote off to the *Nation* and Ewer to request permission. This was the birth of the modern folksong as a vehicle for socio-political protest, particularly in favour of peace, that was to play so large a part in popular music in the decades to come, especially the 1960s.

He discussed the idea with his sisters and Rosalind took up the challenge of setting the poem. One evening, Cynthia reported home from the parlour of the Belmont Hotel: 'At the desk next to me, Rosalind is writing out some music for Walter. Dorothy is upstairs drawing – and Walter is in his room writing.'[19] Instead of seeking a traditional tune that fitted the lines of the 'Five Souls', Rosalind turned to the composer she loved best, Beethoven, and adapted the Allegretto from Symphony no. 7. At first she had difficulty with the ending, but early in January 1915 she told Riss, 'now I have put the last bars of the symphony at the end of the last Soul's verse, and it sounds fine.'

Before going to Chicago in January 1915, where they were booked for three weeks at the Little Theatre, they tested the song on a few friends. The first to hear it were the Peabodys in Boston over Christmas. They immediately sent the girls across the road to sing it again to Josephine Preston Peabody, the poet and dramatist. She 'wept in silence' to hear it. This must have been a tremendous moment for Walter: into his diary for 1901 he had

---

* 'He was an old, big, man with a very hoarse voice, but the thoughts he had were beautiful, just like Walter's,' noted Dorothy.

copied a poem – the only poem in that diary – called 'Forethought' by Josephine Preston Peabody. And here he was, a dozen years later, moving her with a poem of his choice set to music and performed by his sisters.

With this encouragement, they asked Maurice Browne and a few friends to listen to it after their first performance in Chicago. When they finished, Rosalind reported 'there was a holy silence, when the Little Theatre seemed almost oppressively full of thinking minds – and then it was "You *must* sing it after your recitals – everyone must hear it!"' After a first public test on 3 January at the Fine Arts Theatre, when Percival Chubb (who led the Ethical Society's pacific resistance to WWI) spoke on Peace, they did indeed add it to their programme, with great success. Apparently some people came to their recitals just to hear it at the end.

Dorothy described how they performed the 'Five Souls', as staged by Maurice Browne.

> During the intermission in the middle of our programme, Mr Browne tells the audience that after our folksongs we want to sing some verses about the war – and if anyone should care to stay to hear them, they will be welcome. At the end of the recital, after 'Brixton Town', the lights are turned on and there's a moment's interval during which anyone who wishes can leave – but no one ever does. Rosalind and I go off the platform, to the right, and she sits at a piano. The lights are turned off again, all except for the lamp on the stage table, at which Cynthia sits, with her head bowed. Then our voices are heard, first Rosalind's, then mine, singing those pathetic verses of the 'Five Souls.' There is complete silence in the audience afterwards – for they see the truth.[20]

Sometimes they reversed the order, Dorothy taking the first, third and fifth verses, and Rosalind the second and fourth.

Singing the song off-stage, as disembodied souls, so to speak, was clearly dramatic – and daring. It would require perfect enunciation for their audience to make out the words of a new and unfamiliar song. Musically, too, it was by no means an easy piece. In *Partisans and Poets: the political work of American poetry in the Great War,* Mark W. van Wienen observes that it 'placed high demands on its performers, as its main theme developed through insistent repetition and gradual modulation. Its opening musical phrase, which repeats the same note ten times consecutively, varying only the rhythm, demands particularly skillful execution.'[21]

It was quite by coincidence – but so appropriate – that they first sang the 'Five Souls' in Chicago, the city so closely associated with Jane Addams. Inspired by the work at Toynbee Hall in London, she had created there the first settlement house in the United States, Hull House, and made it a household name. Seeing how members of widely different ethnic groups could work together in harmony at Hull House, she became an ardent advocate of arbitration in place of conflict. 'She's a Quaker too, of Quaker stock,' Walter told his parents, 'so she is naturally taking the lead in anti-war campaigns.'

Early in January 1915, Carrie Catt invited Addams to co-organize a woman's peace convention, hosted by the newly formed Washington Peace Association and attended by over 3000 delegates, representing over a hundred women's suffrage and peace groups. It lasted two full days, with overflow meetings at which Jane Addams and Mrs Pethick-Lawrence each spoke twice. The result was the creation on 10 January 1915 of a national Woman's Peace Party (modelled on Crystal Eastman's New York party), with Jane Addams as President, and Rosika Schwimmer as International Secretary. Its eleven-point programme called for the neutral nations to convene in the interests of peace, for the limitation of armaments, and for opposition to militarism in America. Point five, 'The democratic control of foreign policies' and its concern to build a league of neutral nations to prevent future wars, reflect the influence of the Pethick-Lawrences and the Union of Democratic Control.

The Woman's Peace Party (WPP) made its headquarters in Chicago, in the same building as the American Peace Society and the Church Peace Union. With the Fullers making a hit with the 'Five Souls' in the Little Theatre, it was inevitable that they should be invited to sing at local rallies and meetings in favour of peace. 'At all these meetings,' wrote Dorothy, 'we are singing without a fee, because we want to give something to the cause which is fighting against this fearful war.'[22] Walter was delighted: 'We are getting more and more into Peace circles,' he reported to Riss. 'That "Five Souls" stirs people up tremendously – we shall probably get it published, distributed and broadcast.'[23] ('Broadcast' does not refer to radio; public wireless broadcasting was still ten years away. He means 'widely distributed.') Indeed, the WPP adopted the song as part of its propaganda. For Jane Addams 'it poignantly expressed what many of us felt in those first months of war.'[24]

However, the song was not published by Walter. When the 'Five Souls, as sung by the Fuller Sisters' and 'adapted to the allegretto from the 7th Symphony by Beethoven' was registered in March 1915 at the US Copyright Office, ownership of the arrangement was claimed by Frances Frothingham. She was a music teacher who wrote children's pieces, with numerous adaptations to her name. The 'Five Souls' was printed by Summy Co. of Chicago, her usual music publisher. A music specialist at the Library of Congress has suggested to me that 'it may be that Frothingham was simply a savvy business woman who capitalized on the Fuller Sisters' popularity with her own "arrangement" of the piece.'[25] Be that as it may, the Fullers realized too late that someone else (who was actually a member of the WPP) had cashed in on 'their' song. The WPP sold copies supplied by Summy Co. at 25 cents each, and Frances Frothingham pocketed the proceeds, along with the good repute that went along with them.

Consequently, incorrect information can be found in every history book that mentions the 'Five Souls'. Typical is *Rendez-vous with Death: American Poems of the Great War,* edited by Mark W. van Wienen. Its entry for Trilby Ewer states that his poem 'enjoyed its greatest popularity in the United States where it was introduced ... by Frances Frothingham. ... Published in this musical version for the WPP it was sung across the nation by the Fuller Sisters, an English quartet [*sic*].'[26] According to van Wienen, it was a staple of peace meetings for up to twenty years after the armistice.

A variation on the story appeared in Marie Louise Degen's *History of the Woman's Peace Party*:

> In the early spring of 1915 the [WPP] experimented with various propaganda techniques. Some of their methods were, to say the least, unusual. A poem entitled 'Five Souls,' which had appeared in the London *Nation*, appealed to them so much that they had it set to Beethoven music and employed three young English women to sing it on various stages throughout the country.[27]

Degen's book was published in 1939 and until now no one has questioned her account.

At the end of January, the Fuller Sisters left Chicago to continue their tour westwards. Their first major port of call was St Louis, where they gave a concert in the Ethical Church, and also sang in the context of a stirring lecture on peace by Frederick Pethick-Lawrence (shortly to become Treasurer of the UDC). This was probably Walter's first personal contact with either of the Pethick-Lawrences; it was by no means the last. A month later, Mr Lawrence sought out Walter in San Francisco, and arranged for the sisters to give a recital at a peace meeting there, so there is every likelihood that they corresponded, although no letters seem to have survived.

From St Louis the Fullers journeyed on to Sioux City and then Kansas City, with stops in smaller places along the way. Walter usually arranged for them to make the long stages by night train, travelling while they slept. This was efficient but tiring. When they arrived at a venue after an uneasy night's sleep, their hosts – from a peace society, a women's club, a school or a university – would want to show them round their town and institution. Then there would be interviews with the local press. All this allowed little time for the girls to collect their wits for a recital in the afternoon, followed by an evening concert, after which they often found themselves hurrying in the darkness to a midnight train for the next venue. It was a gruelling way of life, which took its toll. Dorothy, in particular, was prone to headaches, nose bleeds, and feeling faint just before performances. It also left precious little margin for misadventures. All the good of two free days in Kansas City, which enabled them to recuperate somewhat, was undone when the car taking them to the station as they left was involved in a collision. Shaken but unhurt, they just made it to their train for Emporia where, within hours of arriving, they sang to an delighted audience of a thousand people. 'And Walter made a splendid introductory speech which brought forth peals of laughter and hearty clapping.'[28] Enthusiastic receptions like these gave them the energy to carry on.

After performing in Denver and Boulder, they sang in the majestic Burns Theatre in Colorado Springs. 'The Misses Fuller are Real and Rare Artists' headlined the *Gazette Telegraph* the following day.

> Not once in a blue moon does one have the opportunity of enjoying the art of the Misses Fuller . . . the only ones presenting this particular art to the public today, in anything like its true form. . . . The ability to sing these simple songs of simple folk – not the technical ability; the interpretive – is the main thing. And this ability the Fuller Sisters possess in a very advanced degree.
>
> First of all, they sing their folk songs of the British Isles in a most simple manner. They make not a single concession to the 'artistic sense,' as it is commonly known. Their voices are good and pleasing: not fine. And this is fortunate, for were they possessed of extraordinarily good voices they could not, and probably would not, devote themselves to songs of this character. Their enunciation is almost perfect; seldom does one lose so much as a word. Their tones are given full emotional value. Last of all, the Misses Fuller seem to thoroughly enjoy singing their songs. So much do they relish it that one is inclined to let go all preconceived notions of the songs without a protest.
>
> The stage appearance of the sisters shows that they have not ignored the problems of the concert platform. They have approached them in the same thorough manner they have taken up the songs of generations gone by –

and with the same uncommon success. The silk brocade and hoop skirts look somewhat out of place, at first, but they harmonize with the songs. So perfectly in fact, that one scarcely notices the peculiarity of dress after a number or so. With the hoop skirts goes the grace of the period to which they belonged. The girls have assumed the manners with the most natural ease in the world. This, too, adds immeasurably to the interpretation of the songs. Not a gesture is forced, not one out of place; all come naturally with the singing. . . .

The Misses Fuller were free with encores and very accommodatingly gave request numbers. All of which won great respect and appreciation from a well-filled house.[29]

From Colorado Springs they continued through Ogden to Salt Lake City, where they came across a sight that surprised, pleased and at the same time almost embarrassed them: the main theatre draped with banners announcing a concert by THE FULLER SISTERS. In San Francisco, where they remained for ten whole days, they had time to make several visits to the Panama-Pacific Exposition (which ran from February to November 1915) and another small one. Later Walter declared, 'those two exhibitions in California are as much an expression of civilization as the war is a denial of it.' After singing in Los Angeles and 'a little seaside town' nearby called Santa Barbara, then San Diego, where they performed on Coronado beach, they began the return journey, through Phoenix, El Paso, Dallas, and San Antonio to New Orleans where they arrived on 2 April. Along the way, they sang anti-war songs and the 'Five Souls' whenever they could. Such was the impression they made that May Wright Sewall, the early suffragist, President of the International Congress of Women (1899) and chairwoman of its standing committee on peace and arbitration from 1914, begged them to return to the west coast at the end of their tour to sing for the cause of women and peace, instead of returning to England.

In New Orleans they found to their dismay that they had no engagements; the local agent said simply that there had been no interest. So, aided by 'a bright typist he found round the corner' and 'surrounded by papers, letters, maps, magazines, cuttings and photographs,' Walter spent his birthday, 3 April, writing letters to secure bookings during their return journey up the Eastern seaboard.[30] Given the state of their finances, he would accept no present from his sisters, not even a cufflink, but in the evening they went to the theatre and saw Pavlova dance with her Russian Ballet Company.

This pause in their hectic life, coinciding with his birthday, allowed Walter time to collect his thoughts. He had been wondering 'what we should do – what should *I* do – when we get home?' He had already told Riss a few days before that during their next break between tours,

> I should want to work for some Peace Society – or, say, the recently formed Union of Democratic Control. . . .
>
> I should like to spend as much time of the summer as possible in London. Do some anti-War work for the Quakers . . . and learn German at a Berlitz School. Yes, I want to be able to speak German, so that some day when the war is over I may be better equipped to play a part in healing some of the wounds – for there will be even worse wounds than physical wounds to heal.[31]

Here Walter put his finger on one of the consequences of war that was barely noticed at the time, because it was quite invisible. The minds of all those who fought and survived were permanently marked, presenting a variety of post-traumatic symptoms which doctors called 'shell shock' and could not alleviate. Those who escaped without physical injury were at the greatest risk, for they had nothing to show that drew sympathy or called for a cure.*

Riss reported that Basil was considering joining the Royal Army Medical Corps (RAMC), so Walter took the opportunity to write to him for his birthday, begging him not to join up. In particular he pointed out the contradiction between military and civil heroism and formulated for the first time the philosophy that was to underlie much of his anti-war propaganda. (We should remember that Walter failed his medical studies because he sympathized too closely with the patient.)

> It is difficult for me to see how a doctor can bring himself to patch up a sorely wounded man, so that right after a few weeks' convalescence he may be sent back to carry on the work of killing and maiming his fellow men. . . . Are there no sick women, and children, and older men at home who need your care? Is it not as patriotic a service to cure a civilian of typhoid, or pneumonia, or to ease the last days of an old woman, as to amputate the leg or arm of a wounded soldier? Basil, dear lad, don't consider it. Keep yourself out of it, and when the peace is made, and the period of reconciliation and reconstruction begins, . . . you will find life cleaner and sweeter and better worth living, because, . . . unlike most people, you will be innocent and undefiled by the evils of war.[32]

The phrase 'reconciliation and reconstruction' shows that Walter was

---

* *Survivor guilt* and the *survivor syndrome* were not recognized as medical conditions for another fifty years.

already aware of the Fellowship of Reconciliation. Yet the Fellowship had been in existence only four months, and its membership was tiny at this point, a few hundred perhaps; by the end of 1916 it was approaching 5000, and by 1917 it had grown to 7000.

The idea for the Fellowship came in July 1914 when an ecumenical conference in Switzerland hastily abandoned its proceedings to enable participants to return home before the borders closed. As they parted, Henry Hodgkin, an English Quaker who taught philosophy at Queens' College, Cambridge, and Friedrich Sigmund-Schultze, a former chaplain to the Kaiser, swore that they would not let the war come between them. Back in England, Hodgkin gathered a group of like-minded persons and formed the Fellowship of Reconciliation (FoR). Its basic principle was disarmingly simple, based on the gospel of St Luke (6: 27–31): 'Love your enemies. . . . If someone strikes you on one cheek, turn to him the other also.' This made the FoR a more radically pacifist organization than the UDC. It was particularly active in defending the rights of conscientious objectors.

Although no correspondence dating from this period has survived in the archives of the FoR, it is clear that Walter must have been in contact with its secretary: by the time the Fullers reached Washington, he was urging Riss to read about it for herself. 'Dear girl,' he wrote, 'the Fellowship of Reconciliation has for its Secretary Miss Lucy Gardner. Won't you send Miss Gardner a line saying you'd like to know about the Fellowship?' As for himself, his mind was made up.

> I want to dedicate myself heart and soul to fight against war – not the miserable humbug of the present so-called 'war to end war', but a thorough-going, uncompromising attack upon the whole pernicious system of militarism and navalism as well as in other countries. The cause is going to enlist the best men and women of our generation, and I want not only to rank myself among them, but to have my dear sisters alongside of me.[33]

From this moment onwards, Walter began to spend time away from his sisters as never before, leaving them to sing at a venue while he met up with peace activists or attended a peace meeting. This led to their first real scare in America. Preparing to go to bed in a private house where they had performed to guests, the girls realized with horror that the only other person in the house was their host, a man whose strange behaviour had already made them feel uneasy. Quickly they packed their bags and decamped. Luckily Walter was able to meet them at the station and see them to a hotel for the night. Thereafter, he ensured that they stayed with trustworthy friends when he was apart from them – as he was in mid-May, attending the 21st

Lake Mohonk Conference on International Arbitration.* There he heard Wilson's Secretary of War advocating military preparedness for the United States. So too did Norman Angell, who had just arrived in America for a lecture tour. He feared that unless the United States clarified its thoughts on foreign policy, it might simply blunder into war.

The Fullers concluded their tour at the end of May in Boston, where they were invited to the last concert of the season given by the Boston Symphony Orchestra conducted by Karl Muck, to whom they were introduced afterwards. They sang at no less than five peace meetings, including one at the Harvard Union, which was a rare honour. On this occasion the speaker was Professor Jay W. Hudson of the University of Missouri; he also addressed a meeting of the Massachusetts Peace Society in mid-June, which Walter probably attended.

They had planned to leave for England at this point, but following the sinking of the *Lusitania* by a U-boat, they (and their parents) reluctantly decided that it would be safer for them to remain in the United States for the summer. Not only would they be preserved from torpedoes; Walter would thus avoid the risk being called up and imprisoned if he refused to serve. In the event, he did indeed avoid the national registration of all able-bodied men for military service, which took place in July. Remaining in the United States also saved the cost of the journey, for what with all the travelling and performing for free in the cause of peace, they had barely made a profit on this tour. (If only the WPP had indeed 'employed' the Fuller Sisters to sing the 'Five Souls' throughout the country, as Degen believed.[34]) So they needed somewhere to stay. Luckily, good friends in New England came to their rescue: Mrs Burgess put them up first; then they stayed for three weeks with the Peabodys in their country house at Chocorua, up in New Hampshire; on 26 July they moved on to stay with Percy and Marion MacKaye in nearby Cornish. They had met the poet and dramatist Percy MacKaye (1875–1956), on a number of occasions – in Boston during their first tour, and at the National Arts Club during the second. The friendship burgeoned during this stay.

That summer, Cecil Sharp was visiting the United States and conducting a summer school in English folk dancing at a village (now a small town) called Eliot in Maine. The sisters went there at the end of the first week in July, joined in the folk dancing and sang him some of the new songs they had

---

* These meetings, which took place between 1895 and 1916, led to the creation of the Permanent Court of Arbitration in The Hague, Netherlands.

learned. Meanwhile Walter remained at the St Botolph Club in Boston, engaged in peace work.

While the Fullers were singing their way round the Union, the repercussions of the creation of the WPP were making themselves felt. On 8 February 1915 Robert La Follette, who was sympathetic to their cause, introduced a joint resolution in the Senate to authorize the President to 'convey to all neutral nations the desire of this government for an international conference for the purposes of promoting by cooperation and through its friendly offices the establishment of peace among the warring nations of Europe, and for other purposes.'[35] The collateral purposes included the limitation and nationalization of the manufacture of military equipment, the prohibition of the export of such equipment, the establishment of an international tribunal and the neutralization of certain waters and maritime trade routes. Such a progressive stance made Senator La Follette rather unpopular, but the pacifists showered him with congratulatory telegrams. It also encouraged the WPP to invite every public organization that recognized the desirability of international peace to a National Emergency Peace Conference in Chicago in early March. Out of this emerged a National Peace Federation, with some 40,000 affiliated members and Jane Addams as its chairperson.

At about the same time a group of women in The Netherlands called for an international conference of women at The Hague, and invited Jane Addams to chair it. She accepted, although she had few illusions as to how much they could advance the cause of peace:

> We do not think we can settle the war. We do not think that by raising our hands we can make the armies cease slaughter. We do think it is valuable to state a new point of view. We do think it is fitting that women should meet and take counsel to see what may be done.[36]

Shortly before sailing, Addams paid a much-publicized visit to Henry Ford, who had become an instant popular hero the year before when he announced that he would pay his factory workers $5 a day, more than twice the going rate for unskilled labour, and introduce three eight-hour shifts a day, instead of two nine-hour shifts. Interviewed by the New York *Times Magazine*, he was quoted as saying, 'I am opposed to war in every sense of the word.' To him was attributed Jane Addams' statement: 'To my mind, the word "murderer" should be embroidered in red letters across the breast of every soldier.' The image was current among pacifists in America. In January Rosalind had told Riss, 'They call it "defense of the country" – it is really organized murder. . . . This sudden sense of duty to one's country by killing or being killed is nonsense.'[40] As usual, her view closely reflected Walter's.

By mid-April, forty-two American women – and Emmeline Pethick-Lawrence – representing a wide range of women's clubs, trade unions and peace organizations, were on their way to The Hague. Their departure, accompanied by a handful of journalists and observers, including Louis P. Lochner,* the secretary of both the National Peace Federation and the Chicago Peace Society, was treated with derision by the press, especially as they had no official sanction or recognition whatsoever. They did however have President Wilson's good wishes, for he admired (with a fair degree of male condescension) women like Addams and sympathized with their hope for peace in the world.

Held between 28 April and 1 May 1915, the conference was attended by some 1500 women (some sources go as high as 2000, not all of them being delegates, of course) from twelve nations.† It led to the creation of an International Committee of Women for Permanent Peace which, four years later, became the Women's International League for Peace and Freedom (WILPF), still active today. It also resulted in a unique peace initiative that was important as a symbolic gesture: two groups of women were delegated to carry a request for the cessation of hostilities and immediate peace talks to the leaders of a dozen nations, plus the Pope, on behalf of the women of the world. The first, headed by Addams, visited the belligerent countries; the second, led by Schwimmer, visited those that had remained neutral. Their reception was polite but non-committal, and the initiative was given little coverage in the press. Nonetheless, several of the principles they were

---

* Although born in the United States, Lochner (1887–1975) was a German speaker. After The Hague conference he went to Germany to arrange Jane Addams' interview with German government officials. At her request, he presented to President Wilson on 2 June 1915 his observations on the situation in Germany and the meetings that the delegation of women had had there.

† Of the 180 British women who applied to attend, only twenty-four were granted passports, and when they presented themselves for the crossing to Holland, they were informed that there were no ferries. Only two, who had left a week earlier, made it to the conference. The *Noordam* carrying the American delegates was inexplicably held up in the Channel for four days. Today it is a commonplace for historians to imply, or even affirm, that the British government was deliberately obstructing the 'peacettes' (as the English newspapers mockingly called them). No one seems to have realized that, in the run up to the Gallipoli campaign which opened on 25 April, the British high command halted all sea traffic to Holland from 19 April as a ploy to make the Germans believe that the Allies were planning to land on the north coast of Germany. It was quite fortuitous that the lifting of this ban at the end of the disinformation operation allowed the American delegates to arrive just in time for the opening of the conference.

upholding showed up again in 1918 among President Wilson's 'Fourteen Points'.

Four days after Jane Addams returned to America on 5 July 1915, she was treated to a public welcome in Carnegie Hall, which was filled to its capacity of three thousand people. Walter Fuller was among them, and thrilled to hear her speak; thousands of others were turned away. He had been thinking hard about peace and what he might do for it. Early in May, Curt Dehn had grown tired of receiving 'diatribes' in which Walter vented his pent-up pacifist feelings. 'Stop for a moment,' wrote Curt, 'and indulge in ten seconds of clear thinking,' at the end of which he thought that Walter would realize that 'nobody had ever defended war as such – that nobody had even desired war.'[37] Walter responded by quoting from the lecture on war that Ruskin had delivered at the Royal Military Academy, Woolwich, in 1865:

> All the pure and noble arts of peace are founded on war. . . . There is no great art possible to a nation but that which is based on battle. . . . All great nations learned their truth of word, and strength of thought, in war; they were nourished in war, and wasted by peace; taught by war, and deceived by peace; trained by war, and betrayed by peace.[38]

He also looked through the library of the St Botolph Club, finding the lectures on 'Germany and England' that Professor J. A. Cramb had pronounced in February and March 1913 at Queen's College, London (where he had the chair of Modern History). Believing that, in the eyes of the Germans, 'The enemy of enemies is England: she bars the way to the realization of all that is highest in German life,' Cramb was convinced that war was inevitable.*
Walter checked out Kipling, an article by Lowes Dickinson† in the *Atlantic Monthly*, and 'such clear thinkers as Mr Roosevelt, Lord Roberts, Lord Grey, Admiral Mahan, Colonel Maude, and Prof. Spenser Wilkinson.' Naturally, he continued to see 'darkly' (as he put it to Curt), since he chose only those authors and passages that supported his view – which a good few historians would concur with today – that 'many many people in England, as in all other countries, did earnestly desire that this present war should come about.'[39] He finished his letter to Curt in Philadelphia where he had gone to see Professor William Isaac Hull, a Quaker pacifist who taught history at

---

*   Cramb was spared seeing his prediction come true, for he died in October 1913. His lectures were published, as *Germany and England,* the following year.

†   One of the few men to attend the women's conference at The Hague, Dickinson (1862–1932) was a founder of the internationalist pacifist movement called the Bryce Group, a member of the UDC, and the source of many ideas that led to the creation of the League of Nations.

Swarthmore College from 1892 until his death in 1939. Walter trusted his opinions, for Hull was a lifetime supporter of peace movements, the limitation of armaments, and international arbitration.

Alongside his reading, Walter made contact with the local Peace Societies and with the Boston branch of the WPP, which already had 2500 members. By 10 June, he had great news for Riss:

> I have been asked by the Peace Society here to be the director of their summer campaign! Can you beat it? I am going to put Peace on the map. I enclose a list of suggestions which I laid before a committee meeting yesterday. They enthusiastically adopted them all and told me to go ahead and do my best. They are going to give me $20 a week just to cover my expenses and then will pay for all travelling and out-of-pocket expenses besides. My main object is to educate public opinion over here as to the real meaning of militarism and navalism as we know it in Europe. Then, with a public with a strong peace sentiment behind him, Wilson will not only be able to withstand those influential public men who are demanding the immediate organization of a big army and navy for the United States but he will be strengthened in the demand he may be able to make when the Terms of Settlement are discussed for a *people's peace* in Europe – not a soldiers' peace or a diplomatists' peace which will merely lay the foundation for another big war as soon as the nations have recovered from their losses in this one. . . .
>
> Dearie, you can imagine, I expect, what a relief this is to me to have an opportunity to do something for peace . . . to do some good – as it seems to me – not merely for the people of *one* country – for 'above all nations is humanity.'[41]*

Unfortunately Walter's sheet of typewritten notes, annotated with the comments that he made as he presented his plan, is no longer with this letter. However, the *Peace Advocate* for July 1915 reported that on 27 June 10,000 people heard peace lectures on Boston Common. From a later letter, we know that he also planned 'an international concert on July 4 (Independence Day and a public holiday)' but

> it fell through owing to the shortness of time in which to organize it. The German-American Alliance promised to send a chorus of Germans to sing folk songs. So did the Norwegians to sing Norwegian songs – and Cecil Sharp's English dancers promised to come, but we couldn't get the Italians or the Greeks – of whom there are many in Boston.[42]

---

* The quotation is attributed to the English historian Goldwin Smith (1823–1910), for it is engraved on a stone bench that he presented in 1871 to Cornell University, where he had been professor of English and Constitutional History.

Walter Fuller

The next event he planned was a memorial day marking the first anniversary of the outbreak of the war, with special services in the churches on Sunday 1 August.

> The Episcopalians (corresponding to our Anglican church) and the Unitarians have agreed. Next week I'm to see the Catholics and the Jews and the smaller protestant denominations.
>
> Then I'm trying to organize a procession to the historic Boston Common made up of say 12 representatives of all the nationalities of the world – both the warring and the neutral – each carrying their national flag draped in black. The bands will play only the Beethoven and Chopin funeral marches. And the meeting on the Common will be addressed by some public man or woman. Ex-President Taft we are hoping for.[43]

This activity left Walter happy for the first time since the war started, but peacemaking, as he told Riss a fortnight later, was difficult work:

> I'm a bit discouraged by the strange, intangible opposition to an active, peace-making policy, which seems to possess everybody.* It all derives from the attitude of the President. He is keeping silent – and inactive† – and everybody who is anybody tries to copy him. Thus I have been seeing people during the last two weeks regarding a scheme for marking August 1st as the first anniversary of the war. Many have supported the idea but today a leading citizen – one of the great men of Boston – to whom I went with a letter of introduction from the Mayor (who, by the way, is in favour of the scheme) took the view that such a scheme, if carried out, might 'embarrass the President'. And he rang up the Mayor on the telephone and told him that this was his view, and at once the Mayor weakened and gave way. I'm afraid this is the death of the plan – but I'll see what can be done tomorrow to save it.[44]

In the end, Walter did manage to organize an event called 'the World's Peace Meeting' on the Common, with a local figure as the main speaker.

Four weeks later the entire Massachusetts State Militia was mobilized to prove its readiness for war, and the 8th Regiment of Infantry established a demonstration camp on Boston Common – 'Great Crowd Shown Glimpse of War' titled the *Boston Globe*.[45] 'If other nations use force to protect their rights,' observed General Cole, 'we've got to be prepared to protect ourselves

---

* In a letter dated 14 June 1915 to B.N. Langdon-Davies, Norman Angell called it 'neutralitis'.

† President Wilson's inactivity was only apparent. At this moment his trusted emissary, Colonel House, was in London discussing a secret agreement with Sir Edward Grey – just the kind of arrangement that Walter, reflecting the UDC, wished to see abolished.

in the same way.' Only six weeks earlier, Walter had confidently told Riss, 'You may rest assured that the USA will not go to war with Germany – for several reasons. The chief is that there is no army and a very much unprepared navy – so that there is little if anything that America could do.'[46] Now the tide had turned. The American press started to call for the re-inforcement of the army and the navy. The watchword was 'preparedness'.

Peace activists like Walter faced quite a challenge. It is one thing to argue for *peace*, a state that is universally understood and desired; it is quite another matter to combat *preparedness*. The Boy Scout movement was just ten years old and its motto, 'Be prepared', had already become a by-word. Telling Americans *not to be prepared* seemed to fly in the face of reason. It was like recommending the behaviour of the five foolish virgins (Matthew 25: 1–13). While the peace movement was scratching its collective head, support came from an unexpected quarter. Henry Ford, whose anti-militarism was becoming known, was quoted by the Detroit *Free Press* as saying, 'I will do everything in my power to prevent murderous, wasteful war in America and in the whole world; I will devote my life to fight this spirit . . . of militarism.'[47] Ford added his belief that 'preparation for war can only end in war.'* Now *there* was a slogan, and his words were reprinted in practically every American newspaper.

Ford loved favourable attention from the press. Interviewed a second time by the same Detroit journalist early in September, he was more specific as to what he was prepared to contribute to the peace effort. It took people's breath away: one million dollars for a peace campaign in the United States and the world, some of the money to go as a prize for an anti-war history and some to fund factories throughout the world to build tractors – this was not quite swords into ploughshares, but he called tractors 'implements of peaceful labour' – plus unspecified funding for other 'practical suggestions'. Ford's office was inundated with suggestions and requests for interviews at the rate of 600 a day, with the result that he would see no one.

While Walter was considering how to oppose America's military build-up, his sisters were staying with Percy and Marion MacKaye at Cornish, New Hampshire.† Although Walter had met Percy MacKaye occasionally over the previous three years, it was only in Boston in mid-June (when they sat up

---

*   This view allowed Ford to change his mind completely over the following months. In the end he gave total support to the war, even proposing to President Wilson that his car factories should make munitions.

†   The village remains an artists' colony to this day. It's where J. D. Salinger hid himself away for more than fifty years.

talking half the night) that he realized that MacKaye was a dreamer after his own heart: he fervently believed that vast pageants, in which thousands of people participated, could actually substitute for war. In such a pageant, as in war, the dull round of daily life becomes infused with meaning, 'transfigured by order, discipline, organization, imbued with a majestic unity of design: the enacting of a national drama, *in which the people themselves participate.*' His wife Marion was an active supporter of the WPP in New York, so in August, stimulated by discussion with Walter and his sisters, Percy wrote to Crystal Eastman suggesting that the New York branch of the WPP, of which she was the President, should stage such a pageant 'to lure the imaginations of men away from war to peace.'[48]

Marion recorded in her diary for 30 July 1915:

The darling Fuller sisters from Dorset, England, are staying with us. They came about two days ago and have given us such a world of pleasure with their treasure of old English ballads sung so dramatically, poetically, and bewitchingly.

The other night, Rob Barrett came down and we all sat up till about two in the morning, singing, telling tales, and dancing folk dances – and today – that is what I'm getting at – they sang to a quantity of guests on the terrace in front of the house. The people sat on benches and chairs at the south end, and the dear Misses Dorothy, Rosalind and Cynthia, in their quaint early Victorian costumes, had the northern hills for a background. They sang their captivating lays to Cynthia's accompaniment on a beautiful little Irish harp, and people simply didn't want to go home. The last to go were the daughters of Woodrow Wilson.[49]

President Wilson and his daughters were indeed taking their summer vacation in Cornish that year, renting the same large house as in 1913 and '14. Wilson's wife had died on the day Britain declared war, 4 August 1914, and his eldest daughter Margaret was substituting as First Lady. She was musical and sang well, so she was delighted to hear the Fullers. Her middle sister Jessie, who had much admired Cynthia at the White House recital, was now married to Francis Sayre, a professor of law and government official. The youngest daughter, Eleanor, had married Wilson's Secretary of the Treasury, William Gibbs McAdoo. That summer they all participated actively in the social life at Cornish. Sayre and MacKaye played tennis together nearly every afternoon; sometimes Dorothy and Rosalind joined them for doubles.

It was on the day the girls arrived at the MacKayes' house that Robert Barrett (1871–1969) dropped by. Tall and charismatic, he was like a character out of a boys' adventure story. Independently wealthy, he spent his life exploring remote corners of the world.* In Cornish, where he returned every now and then to the comfort of an Indian wigwam on a hilltop (or a nearby cave), he had met and married Katharine Ellis, the author of a series of novels for teenagers about 'the Wide-Awake Girls'. As a concession to matrimony, he replaced the wigwam with a Japanese pagoda-like house (known later to locals as the Glass House, but also as the Paper House, because of the inner dividing screens). Invited there the following afternoon, the Fuller sisters sat on cushions on the floor and ate with their fingers off wooden platters. Soon they were all firm friends, and the girls renamed the Barretts 'Gypsy Davy' and 'Lady Ba', after the characters in the 'Wraggle-Taggle Gypsies.'† Ten years later, after yet another expedition onto the roof of the world, the Barretts compiled *The Himalayan Letters of Gypsy Davy and Lady Ba* and asked Dorothy to draw decorations and a dustwrapper for it.

For Walter's sisters, Cornish was a paradise of friendliness and art, with paintings, sculptures, and poems being created all around them. Percy MacKaye would read his poems aloud; disliking interruption he would even make the maid wait for him to finish before allowing her to serve dinner. Rose Nichols, the landscape gardener and pacifist (and niece of Augustus Saint-Gaudens, who was largely responsible for creating the Cornish colony), whom they had already met in Washington, lived with her mother next door to the Wilsons. The girls stayed with them for a couple of days to give the MacKayes a break. They visited the sculptor Herbert Adams and the painter William Howard Hart. Maxfield Parrish (1870–1966), the most popular American painter of the first half of the twentieth century – his 'Daybreak' was on every livingroom wall – dropped by each morning with his sketchpad. Echoes of the three sisters can be found in a number of his

---

* He explored: the Canadian Rockies of British Columbia, where he lived with the Indians (1892); Norway, where he studied the water table (1897); and Russia, where he travelled from Moscow to Semipalatinsk, in East Kazakhstan (1902). The following year he made a parallel trip from the mouth of the Volga river, on the Caspian Sea, to Tien Shan, which is just over the eastern border of Kyrgyzstan, in the ancient Buddhist kingdom of Aksu (Xinjiang province, China). Then he led the Barrett (Huntington) Expedition of 1905–06 through the Himalayas, where he made numerous measurements with a photo-theodolite. These expeditions were reported in the *Bulletin* of the American Geographical Society, of which Barrett was a founding member.

† Geoffrey Martin, who wrote a three-page obituary of Robert Barrett in the *Professional Geographer*, did not know where the nicknames came from, noting simply that 'Barrett found the appellation "gypsy" appropriate.'[50] N.B. The 'Gypsy Davy' recorded in 1940 by American folksinger Woody Guthrie was an Americanized version of the English ballad.

The Wraggle-Taggle Gypsies, O!

Copyright, 1915, by The H. W. Gray Co. Dorothy Fuller Harthorn

There were three gyp-sies a - come to my door, And down-stairs ran this a - la - dy, O!

One sang high and the oth-er sang low, And the oth-er sang bon-ny, bon-ny Bis-cay, O!

2] Then she pulled off her silk finished gown
And put on hose of leather, O!
The ragged, ragged rags about our door —
She's gone with the wraggle-taggle gypsies, O!

3] It was late last night when my lord came home,
Enquiring for his a-lady, O!
The servants said, on every hand:
She's gone with the wraggle-taggle gypsies, O!

4] The Lord:
Come, saddle to me my milk-white steed,
And go and fetch my pony, O!
That I may ride and seek my bride,
Who is gone with the wraggle-taggle gypsies, O!

5] Then he rode high, and he rode low,
He rode through wood and copses too,
Until he came to an open field,
And there he espied his a-lady, O!

6] The Lord:
What makes you leave your house and land?
What makes you leave your money, O?
What makes you leave your new wedded lord,
To go with the wraggle-taggle gypsies, O?

7] The Lady:
O what care I for my house and land?
What care I for my money, O?
What care I for my new wedded lord?
I'm off with the wraggle-taggle gypsies, O!

8] The Lord:
Last night you slept on a goose-feather bed,
With the sheet turned down so bravely, O!
But to-night you'll sleep in a cold open field,
Along with the wraggle-taggle gypsies, O!

9] The Lady:
O what care I for a goose-feather bed,
With the sheet turned down so bravely, O!
For to-night I shall sleep in a cold open field,
Along with the wraggle-taggle gypsies, O!

This English Folk Song, printed at The De Vinne Press, and issued to the public by The H. W. Gray Company,
in the City of New York, sole agents for Novello & Co., Limited, at the price of
ten cents plain, and twenty-five cents colored.

Broadside No. 4

paintings from this time.* He invited them to give a recital in his studio – the first of several they gave in Cornish that summer, financed by the generous Robert Barrett.

Another visitor to the MacKayes that summer was Norman Angell. He had crossed the Atlantic in the hope that the Carnegie Endowment, which had supplied no less than $36,000 to reprint and disseminate *The Great Illusion* in cheap editions, would provide funds for him to lecture in the United States and support the UDC. He was, after all, a high profile author; as Jane Addams put it, 'There seemed to have been a somewhat general reading of . . . Norman Angell's *Great Illusion*' in American universities during the period leading up to the outbreak of the war.[51] This had led to the creation of dozens of 'polity clubs' for the promotion of his ideas. But once the war broke out, the Endowment stopped supporting anti-war propaganda, and ceased to fund European-based activities. So Angell turned to the World Peace Foundation in Boston, where he spent much time in late May and June, meeting people (like Mr Filene) already well known to Walter. If he and Walter had not already become acquainted at the Mohonk conference, they certainly got together in Boston. While Walter's sisters were preparing to go and stay with the MacKayes, he told them, 'They are going to have a peace meeting when you're there. . . . They tried to get Norman Angell but he can't come till the 18th August.'[52] So Angell's visit did not overlap with the sisters' stay. Arvia MacKaye, who was aged thirteen at the time, remembered him as

> a small tightly-knit man with a large head and brow, reserved and a little dry but with an extraordinarily keen mind and a warm kindly nature. He and my father spent much time together in talks concerning world events and my father's book, *A Substitute for War*, for which he wrote the Preface. At odd intervals, I had the opportunity to model a bust of him, which was a very rewarding event for me.[53]

Walter joined his sisters in Cornish only for the last weekend of their stay.

He found them tanned and fit whereas they found him pale and citified; he looked well, however, 'with no signs of being worried or tired.'[54] To his mother he confirmed that he was 'well and happy. I am doing what little I can for peace – quietly, secretly, without strain or worry, mostly by seeing people and talking with them.'[55] By this time he seems indeed to have

---

* Several years later, when Maxfield Parrish was commissioned to paint a large mural depicting music or musicians for the Eastman School of Music in Rochester, he expressed his regret that the Fuller sisters were not there to sit for him.

met everyone who was anyone in the peace movement from Boston to Washington. It was a source of great satisfaction to him, for he hoped to unite them in some great action. Still, he seems to have felt that he needed a break, for he took some ten days' holiday in mid-September, joining his sisters when they moved on to stay with Helen and Jack Rae. For once, he wore easy clothes, went on long walks, picked blackberries with Cynthia, and played tennis and pingpong. He was even heard dreamily picking out 'Meet Me by Moonlight Alone' with one finger on the piano. There was no holiday from the newspapers, though. Dorothy reported to her mother,

> Helen allowed Walter to cut out clippings all over the sittingroom floor, to his heart's content. She would bustle into the room when Walter was nearly up to his waist in paper and dig him out, and throw armfuls of paper into the fire-place, till he got buried to the waist again. Helen can't understand his strong feeling for cuttings, but treats him like a spoilt child on holiday.[56]

Among the newspapers that Walter read so assiduously was the *Manchester Guardian*. In a survey of new verse, a three-line epigram from Rabindranath Tagore's *Stray Birds* (1916), caught his eye:

> They hated and killed, and men praised them.
> But God in shame hastens to hide its memory
> under the green grass.[57]

Shortly afterwards, while Dorothy was seeking more folksongs in the Boston Public Library, she came across a very old tune that just fitted it. At once the sisters added 'The Green Grass' to their repertoire – new words set to a traditional melody as anti-war protest.

Brown as a berry and physically refreshed, Walter returned to Boston and then to other east coast cities, making bookings for their autumn season and meeting with peace activists. Between 11 and 14 September he had attended a peace conference organized by Philadelphia Quakers at a mountain resort called Pocono. There he met 'a young woman of about 40, I suppose,' as he told Riss, a couple of weeks later. 'Not so long ago I should have thought that to be a hoary old age; probably she is on the sunny side of 40.'[58] She was in fact thirty-four, just forty-five days younger than Walter. Her name was Crystal Eastman, the living embodiment of everything that he had encouraged his sisters to aspire to, and she changed Walter's life.

5

Propagandist

The conscious and intelligent manipulation of the organized habits and opinions of the masses is an important element in democratic society. Those who manipulate this unseen mechanism of society constitute an invisible government which is the true ruling power of our country.

We are governed, our minds are molded, our tastes formed, our ideas suggested, largely by men we have never heard of. . . .

In almost every act of our daily lives, whether in the sphere of politics or business, in our social conduct or our ethical thinking, we are dominated by the relatively small number of persons . . . who understand the mental processes and social patterns of the masses. It is they who pull the wires which control the public mind, who harness old social forces and contrive new ways to bind and guide the world. . . .

The mechanism by which ideas are disseminated on a large scale is propaganda, in the broad sense of an organized effort to spread a particular belief or doctrine. . . . Yet whether, in any instance, propaganda is good or bad depends upon the merit of the cause urged, and the correctness of the information published.[1]   Edward L. Bernays, *Propaganda* (1928)

Crystal Eastman, ca. 1913

CRYSTAL EASTMAN – she always preferred to be known by her maiden name – was one of the most colourful figures of the American feminist movement. The press loved her: she was pretty, provocatively outspoken, and daring. Although trained as a lawyer, she got herself appointed, in December 1914, as the head of the sales department of a large garage – a position never before held by a woman – and immediately took on fifty-two saleswomen to work on an equal footing with the male employees. This made wonderful copy. So did her advice to fellow suffragists. Campaigning for women's rights in Wisconsin, she told them, 'when you are in need of financial help, go out and ask for it. Either they will help you because they are interested in the cause, or they will give you something to get rid of you, or they will hand you something because they like your looks.'[2] Like practically everything she said, this was reported in all the papers.

In appearance, Crystal was nothing like the stereotype blue-stocking suffragette of the popular imagination. Somewhat to its surprise, the *Oregonian* found itself writing, 'She is young, pleasing in appearance, dresses well and has attractive curves.'[3] In the spring of 1913, the suffragists planned a march on Washington by thousands of women. At once, the press began to treat it as a beauty contest:

> Mrs Crystal Eastman Benedict of Wisconsin; Mrs Huntington Wilson, wife of the assistant secretary of state; Miss Gladys Rinkley, and Miss Inez Milholland, the four reigning beauties of the 'votes for women' propaganda, have entered the lists. Mrs Benedict, according to the western contingent, is the best-looking woman in the suffrage movement. She is tall, dark and vivacious.[4]

Crystal was the only daughter of Congregationalist ministers. When ill-health obliged her father to reduce his activity, her mother (one of the first women to be ordained as a minister in the United States) took over his duties, and they worked as a team. The family of Mark Twain's wife lived just across the street from their church, so it happened that 'my mother, with Mr Beecher, officiated at the lonely funeral of Mark Twain's beloved daughter Suzie, in 1896. My father offered the prayer at the burial of Mark Twain's wife. And when Mark Twain himself died, it was again my father, reading a manuscript that my mother had written for him, who officiated at the funeral.'[5]

Crystal had three brothers, the eldest of whom, Morgan, died of scarlet fever at the age of seven. He was 'saintly-beautiful and of such sweet-tempered poise and precocious sensibility and swift intelligence' that the loss deeply marked the family.[6] Crystal had the illness at the same time and survived, although her health was permanently impaired. She also had many of Morgan's qualities: 'She poured magnetic streams of generous love around her all the time,' wrote her brother Max, two years her junior, 'and she loved me with especial warmth.' He loved her back with a passion that was notably similar to Walter's feelings for Riss. As a boy, Max used to 'burst into a cold sweat at the thought that some day I would have to propose to a strange girl. . . . As a result of this emotion, I maintained stoutly for some years that I was going to marry my sister.'[7]

Crystal's feelings were similar, but not incestuous. In 1902, she confided to her diary that the man she married would need to have Max's qualities: 'I don't believe there is a feeling in the world too refined and imagined for him to appreciate,' for 'the highest compliment you can pay a man [is] to say that he has the fineness of feeling and sympathy of a woman.'[8] It is instructive to place this beside what Walter learned one evening when he was nineteen. Dining with friends, he was introduced to a Miss Black, who promptly offered to read his hand. 'Whether palmistry is merely a specious sort of flattery or not, I do not know,' he remarked in his diary,

> but if there is anything 'in it' then I am assuredly a most superior individual. I have high ideals – Miss Black said – ah, God knows I have. I have a love for the beautiful, am sensitive, have a delicate touch – a fact Miss Black amplified by saying I should make a good surgeon! – am analytical, she said, and I am also religious![9]

Walter had all the fineness of feeling, sympathy, and imagination that Crystal hoped to find in her partner.

She grew up in Glenora, a tiny community on the western shore of Seneca Lake in New York State. She was fiercely independent and naturally inclined to believe in the equality of men and women. When she adopted a man's costume for bathing in the lake, arguing that since men were not obliged to swim in skirts and stockings, she should not be either, her parents could only bow to her logic and look the other way. The neighbours were shocked. She did not ride side saddle either, another source of social opprobrium. Yet it stood her in good stead. For the 1913 demonstration, the organizers decided that 'heralding the approach of the riding and marching suffragette cohorts, four feminine Paul Reveres will gallop in relays into Washington on 3 March with news of the progress of their sisters.' Crystal was one of these 'expert horsewomen', all dressed in white, who delighted both the press and the public.[10]

In one respect she was quite unlike Max. He freely admitted that he 'had never been driven by the urge, amounting to a neurosis in many males, to be the money-earner of the family. Indeed I had often thought how sensible it would be to find a wife who could support me and enable me to write with no motive but the writing.'[11] In a world where job opportunities for women of her calibre were rare, Crystal had that urge to be a money-earner. She studied sociology at Columbia for a year and then moved to law at New York. On graduation she was hired by Paul Kellogg to examine industrial accidents – and the inadequate compensation of the victims – as part of the Pittsburgh Survey for the Russell Sage Foundation. Out of this came her ground-breaking book on *Work-Accidents and the Law* (1910). Every newspaper noticed when she became the only woman appointed to sit on the Employer's Liability Commission in New York. While on the Commission, she participated in drafting America's first workers' compensation act. However, she never practised law, for at that time male lawyers refused to work with women. So her main activity became the cause of women's rights, which she approached as a socialist.

As Crystal's feminism recognized the reproductive function of women and the power of her own libido, she had nothing against marriage – as long as it meant equality. In 1911, she married a Milwaukee insurance salesman named Wallace Benedict. 'A common interest in work accidents brought them together,' but his Epicurean philosophy of life was far removed from 'the world of devotional humanitarianism in which Crystal had grown up.' 'Pleasure for him had little to do with attaining ideals,' observed Max.[12] Two years later, the couple went on a European tour during which Crystal attended (as mentioned in the previous chapter) the conference of the International Woman Suffrage Alliance in Budapest. The marriage broke down after this; Crystal returned to New York alone, and threw herself into the suffrage movement, helping to found the National Woman's Party. But 1914 was not a good year for her health. In the space of six months, she was seriously ill four times, and hospitalized twice. This no doubt signalled the onset of the nephritis that ultimately killed her. A painful, progressive disease of the kidneys, it was not fully identified at the time and consequently there was no treatment for it.

After WWI broke out in Europe, the American suffrage movement split. Whereas some women continued to give priority to obtaining the right to vote, believing that war might be averted if women had a voice in matters of international policy, Crystal gave priority to maintaining peace, fearing that if the United States entered the war, all the social reforms she had fought for might be lost. So she was one of the founding members of the American League to Limit Armaments, led by Louis Lochner, which was formed at the instigation of Oswald Garrison Villard* in New York on 18 December 1914. In January 1915, it was renamed the American League for the Limitation of Armament. It called on President Woodrow Wilson to advance the cause of a world federation or league of nations.

Crystal's brother Max did his PhD at Columbia, where one of his professors was the future President Wilson.† A socialist, he became the editor of the leading left-wing monthly, the *Masses*. He was a feminist too. *The History of Woman Suffrage* reveals the kind of energy that he put into his activities:

> From 1910 to 1917, the Men's League for Woman Suffrage was an influential factor in the movement in New York. It was believed to be the first of the kind and the idea was said to have originated with Max Eastman, a young

---

* Oswald Garrison Villard (1872–1949), whose mother led the women's protest in August 1914, had inherited the New York *Evening Post* and the *Nation* on the death of his father in 1900. He supported women's suffrage, trade union law reform, and equal rights for black Americans. (He and his mother were founding members of the National Association for the Advancement of Colored People.) He believed that the United States should stay at home and not go to war abroad (especially not in Latin-America). For him, preparedness meant readiness to take the lead in proposing international disarmament and calling for a peace conference.

† In his autobiography, Max tells how his reputation as a suffragist led to a memorable evening with Woodrow Wilson. At a banquet in 1911, the two men were placed side by side 'and conversed almost without interruption for two or three hours.'
> [Wilson's] first remark to me at the table was:
> 'They tell me you are interested in woman suffrage. I am badly in need of instruction about that. I have a feeling that these women are avoiding their duties rather than demanding their rights, but it is only a feeling. I really would be grateful if you would teach me what I ought to know about the whole question.'
> As Woodrow Wilson was the first President to come out for a constitutional amendment and make woman suffrage an issue in national politics, I like to think I did some important teaching during those hours.

Max had been invited to the banquet as a humorous speaker, whereas Wilson was known rarely to laugh. Noticing that, when the time came for speeches, Wilson and Max 'were in a smilingly friendly mood', the organizer took Max aside and offered him 'a dollar a minute in addition to my fee as long as I would keep Wilson laughing.'
> When I got up to speak, I saw Mr Clancy pull out his watch and set it down significantly on the table. I began my speech by telling Wilson about this little arrangement and saying that, if he didn't enjoy hearing me talk, I was sure he would enjoy watching Mr Clancy lose money. It made a grand beginning, and throughout the speech, whenever Wilson chuckled, I had only to glance towards Mr Clancy to turn the chuckle into a laugh in which everybody joined. I earned $40 that night in addition to my fee.[15]

When in later years Max had occasion to address President Wilson in person on matters of great moment, he was probably given more generous attention than would otherwise have been accorded to him, thanks to pleasant memories of that evening.

professor in Columbia University, but in a sketch of the league by him in the *Trend* in 1913 he said that in 1909, when he went to consult Oswald Garrison Villard, editor of the New York *Evening Post*, he found that Mr Villard had received a letter from Dr Anna Howard Shaw, president of the National American Woman Suffrage Association, asking him to organize such a league; that he had conferred with Rabbi Stephen S. Wise and they had 'agreed to share the ignominy' if someone would undertake the organizing. This was done by Mr Eastman, who, armed with letters of introduction from Mr Villard, succeeded in getting the names of twelve men of civic influence. Using these names he sent out several thousand letters to such men over the State and finally obtained twenty-five members. . . .

In 1910 the league took part in the first big suffrage parade and no act of men during the whole history of woman suffrage required more courage than that of the 87 who marched up Fifth Avenue on that occasion, jeered by the crowds that lined the sidewalks.[13]

Max married within a few months of Crystal but, as with her marriage, it did not last, so her joking suggestion that after they had both experimented with marriage they might end up living together, just as they had as students at Columbia, was more or less fulfilled. In 1915, their respective homes in Greenwich Village were but a few doors apart, and they regularly took their meals together. In his biography of Max, William O'Neill calls Crystal 'the best of a great generation of women, combining feminism, socialism, and pacifism with common sense and charm. She could not be spared, least of all by Max, who took advice from no one else.'[14]

This was the exceptional woman that Walter met in September 1915. He described her to Riss:

> She is a very striking, attractive person – rather like a younger and smarter Miss Best. She is very American – in the New York sense of the word – no respecter of persons – no sentimentality – no Europeanized refinements. She's rather a smart dresser – though she's a little daring in the matter of colours. She's a fierce Suffragette, and whenever she isn't working for the Peace Party she is speaking at street corners for suffrage, I'm told. Well, after one of the meetings at Pocono, I was talking with her, and urging my old idea about the need for Pacifists to go out in the highways and hedges, and educate the people there, talk[ing] in a language that is familiar to them, and one which they can understand. Thus, for instance, I said, why not use the cinematograph? By the way, this idea is specially urgent over here just now, because half the theatres in New York – moving picture-theatres and the other kind – are all about war, and most of them rather glorifying it – and all

preaching the lesson that America must aim to be armed to the teeth, so as to be prepared to fight whoever wins in Europe, in case the victor there should become drunk with victory and attack America! (Can the human mind conceive of any greater nonsense than that, I ask you, my dear?) And yet there they are, these evil preachers of panic, getting away with their awful bluff (as Miss Best would say).

Mrs Benedict said: 'Gee, that's just what I've been saying. What do you think would make a good subject for a moving picture?'

'Well,' said I, ready for the challenge, 'I've been thinking that the "Five Souls" would make a fine theme to hang a great story on (and, of course, thanks to the girls, everybody over here knows the "Five Souls").'

'Yes,' said Mrs B, 'so it would – but I've been thinking of Ray Stannard Baker's article in the *American Magazine** about the German invasion of America – wouldn't that make a good plot?'

'Rather!' I said, seeing possibilities by the million.

We talked a little while about it, and arranged to return to New York together the next morning. On our way to town we talked over the plan, and began to see such vast opportunities that we arranged to collaborate in the writing of a scenario (as moving-picture plots are called).

I then went back to Boston – spent the week there† – saw the girls – helped them off to Cornish again, and last Saturday returned to New York. I came for a three-fold purpose:

1. To get busy on the moving-picture scheme with Mrs B.
2. To go on to Philadelphia to meet Professor Hull about a Christian protest against the war.
3. And to lay before a special meeting a scheme for an Exhibition of Peace and War.[15]

On the other hand, Walter made no mention of 'Mrs Benedict' (whom I shall call Crystal from now on) or the scenario when he wrote to his father a few days later:

I have come down to New York for a few days to meet the leaders of the

---

* Baker's 'article' (which had appeared in January 1915) was an early science-fiction story entitled, 'The Last Phase of the Great War: the German invasion of America – AD 1915–1916 – from the *History of the Twentieth Century* by Simeon Hardcastle, New York, AD 2014.' It was a response to an article in *Harper's Weekly,* entitled, 'Are We Ready?' which offered a lurid description of Madison Square after a German air raid.

† During that week in Boston, Walter wrote a letter to the editor of the Boston *Herald* deploring the 'crush Germany' attitude and suing for peace. Dated 12 September, it was published on 19 September 1915. It is reproduced on the website.

various Peace Societies in New York tomorrow afternoon and submit to them a plan which I have been working at during the past few weeks for a big Exhibition of Peace and War – a graphic survey in popular style of the whole case against war and armaments and militarism and navalism. If the scheme is accepted the Exhibition will take place in New York some time during December and then go through the country, spending a week at all the principal cities. The great fight that is now on in this country is between the militarists and the pacifists. The former want a big increase in army and navy – the latter want disarmament. I belong to the latter party with all my heart and soul – and am grateful to think that I can serve them in some way.

Then I am to meet two Quaker friends on Friday next. One of them is a Professor of International Law at a university in Philadelphia and discuss with them a plan for an organized effort on the part of the Protestant churches of America of all denominations to support the Pope in his efforts for peace.[16]

Whatever came of this second plan, Walter seems not to have been involved in it, for he did not refer to it again. On the other hand, it reflects his conviction that the Christian churches could, if they chose, halt the war.

This war will be won by those who stop it. If the bankers stop the war, we shall all be in the pockets of the financiers; if the diplomats and politicians stop the war, we shall have more 'diplomatic' arrangements of the map of Europe, which will ensure another big war in 30 or 40 years time; if the soldiers fight the war out, to a decisive finish, we shall have a military dictatorship – under the Prussians if Germany wins, or under the Tory reactionary militarists in England, or France or Russia, if the Allies win. Then who can stop the war? Women? Can they? Well, not by themselves they cannot, though they have had a mighty good try. What other force is left? Religion. Yes. The churches might stop the war. This is the hour of destiny for Christianity, and for the Churches; if it passes and nothing is done, then all is over with Jesus Christ and his Church as a vital force in men's lives. Only the spirit of love can stop this war.[17]

Walter was remarkably clear-sighted in his predictions. The diplomats and politicians decided the future of Europe at the Paris Peace Conference of 1919. Twenty years later, still smarting from the humiliation she had suffered in Paris, Germany went to war again. Hitler underlined this by making General Pétain sign the French surrender in the self-same railway carriage in which the Germans had signed the 1918 Armistice. As for the church, the great decline in religious observance dates from WWI; it was hastened by WWII.

Walter Fuller

These thoughts prompted Walter to acknowledge his sympathy for the Quaker way of life. Seeming to forget that Riss had been to Woodbrooke, he encouraged her to seek out information on the Friends for herself and confided, 'I am myself practically a Quaker now. I think when I come home I shall join the Society.'[18] This would have pleased Rosamond Impey. By a curious coincidence, she married a Harold Briggs in the Friends Meeting House at Longbridge on 10 October that year.* Her marriage will have relieved Walter of any lingering sense of obligation towards her.

The ambitious exhibition that Walter was proposing was to mobilize much of his energy over the next nine months, for it took far longer to implement than he had anticipated. He told Riss about it in some detail:

> Scheme for an Exhibition of Peace and War
>
> A Human Welfare Show. A graphic – dramatic – artistic indictment of war. A Protest of Civil Life against Militarism, Armaments and Diplomacy. How would it be done? Well, a great hall would be taken for a week or 10 days in New York, and at the end of that period the whole hallful of stuff would go on to Boston – thence to Philadelphia – Chicago etc – all big cities.
>
> What would it consist of? Well, the case for War would be attacked from *every* angle.
>
> *Art*
> Paintings and photographs of paintings would be collected from all sources showing war as it is.
> Statues – Modern works showing suffering in war contrasted with old statues showing war heroes.
> Drama – Plays like *War Brides*; *The Trojan Women* [already being staged in cities throughout the United States by the WPP] and a specially written anti-war Masque would be performed each day.
> Music – Here we would get the leading singers and musicians to perform.
>
> Fritz Kreisler (Austrian), Harold Bauer (German), Schuman Heink (German), John McCormack (English), and many others of all nationalities have all publicly expressed their opposition to this war, and their desire for it to stop at once, on any terms. We would get them to give their services, in a great international concert, at the Exhibition one day. Then there

---

* Walter surely learned of Rosamond's marriage from Riss, who remained in regular contact with both Rosamond and Hilda Hankinson. In January 1915, Rosalind wrote to Riss begging her to stop Harold's brother, Lionel Briggs, from joining up. 'Make Hilda see there is no glory in it – tell her that a soldier is a slayer of men.' He did volunteer, and he and Hilda were married shortly after. He survived the war, but died within ten years.

would be an International Orchestra – men and women of all nations to play music together throughout the day.
Science
The effect of war on Science – especially on medicine – would be shown. How men of all nations, united, were learning to conquer disease – now they are separated – also the American public would be shown the facts of war from the medical side. How strong and healthy men are mangled and broken – and patched-up in hospitals. You must know, dear, that much that is now familiar to you over there, in Europe, as to the meaning of war, is yet unknown to the great mass of the American public. The newspapers here still give too much of war's exciting 'heroic' sporting side.

Then there would be a *Historical Section* – showing truths about old wars – how they arose – what ended them, the nature of the different peaces. Thus we could show how impossible it is to *crush* a nation – failing in The Netherlands, England; failing in Ireland, Germany; failing in France, Russia, Finland, etc.

Then *Geography*
There would be plenty of large-scale maps of all the world – especially maps *without frontiers* – showing the world all green – with rivers and mountains, as God made it.

Then there would be a hall set aside for religious meetings – for silent continuous prayer for this war to cease. The Roman Catholics might have a special chapel of their own.

There would be another room for debates – lectures – discussions – classes.

There would be many, many sociological graphics of the Georgian type* – such as pictures of leaders like Hindenburg and the Crown Prince and Roosevelt (who naturally is yelling for war over here) and Winston Churchill and men of that ilk. Compared with photos of Marconi, Edison, Madame Curie, Jane Addams, John Thomas, Dr Patin, and all the kindly gentle souls who have blessed the world.

Then there would be a great plea for the *Folk* of the world. The quiet peaceful, unknown peasant, artisan class of all nations who never want war – we would show their arts and crafts – their songs, dances and drama.

---

* Walter is referring to the economic philosophy of Henry George (1839–1897), who held that people own what they create, but that things found in nature, most importantly land, belong equally to all. It inspired the Single Tax political theory, which was widely promoted in the first half of the twentieth century.

Then we would show the perfect Athlete – so that the human body may be seen as something too beautiful, too noble to be destroyed by machinery for any purpose whatsoever, whether for revenge or some national policy, or for dividends. This we could show by having gymnastic displays of free Danish and Swedish gymnastics. Then we would have statistics and facts about war in general, and then war in particular – its cost in lives and money, and figures showing what could have been done for human welfare by such a vast expenditure.

Then another idea would be to have a big wooden statue of the God of War set up in a little side room, round the walls of which we would fix pictures of his victims – French, German and English – little faces of men killed, taken from illustrated papers like the *London News* and French and German papers of that kind.

Then, on the last day of the Exhibition in each city, we would have the monstrous God taken out and burned by the mob in some public place – and we would get guns and uniforms to be thrown into the flames along with it. This should be made a fiery cross[?] to sweep through the country – a free people destroying the idol of war.

Then there would be other things shown. The efforts made to preserve bird life – to save the trees – compared with the toleration, even admiration, of this institution of war.

Then there would be a terrific indictment of *Secret Diplomacy* – photos of the men who 'represent' nations in the different capitals.

Another section would be a statement of the women's case against war – pictures – statistics – models – graphics of all kinds.

There would be another section set apart with chairs and tables, with a library of books on peace and war – with foreign magazines and newspapers for everybody to read freely.

Another section would show the efforts for peace which are now being made in all the warring countries.

Another would be an indictment of Censorship – showing the power it gives to the war-party – against the better instincts of democracy.

Another section would show modern journalism and the war – lies it makes -the prejudice it creates between peoples of different countries.

We would also have a chamber of horrors, to which only adults would be admitted, showing some actual war horrors.

The object of the whole Exhibition would be educational – to help the people to right-thinking, by giving them the truth, the whole truth, and nothing but the truth.

In planning this extraordinary show, Walter drew on exhibitions he had visited in Britain and the United States, including the 1912 Baby Saving Show in Philadelphia, but the idea of making war itself the theme of a preventative exhibition was completely novel. It frightened some people, who refused to have anything to do with it. What is striking is the wide variety of approaches that Walter envisaged, calling on the graphic, visual and plastic arts (in symbolic as well as literal forms), music and drama, and many sciences, even the as-yet undefined science of ecology. (It was another fifty years before anyone concerned themselves with the effect of war on wildlife and vegetation.) Central to his project was his aim to address the emotions quite as much as the rational mind, and to make the effects of war *personal* by showing the faces of otherwise anonymous victims. In the hundred years since then, all of these things have been done, in various combinations, in the memorials raised after the conflicts were over. Rarely, if ever, are they used for the *prevention* of war, and never, to my knowledge, have they all been combined in a single show such as Walter envisaged.*

He went on with his account to Riss:

Well now, these ideas and some others have been filling my mind lately so that at the [Pocono] Peace Conference I asked my friend – a Quaker – Hollingsworth Wood – a lawyer by profession† – also Secretary of the American League to Limit Armaments – I asked him to arrange a private meeting of representatives of different Peace Societies before whom I might bring this Exhibition Scheme. He promised to do so – and on Wednesday afternoon last (Sept. 22), at the offices of the Church Peace Union, the leaders of seven of the principal Peace Societies in New York listened, for about an hour, while I described this Scheme of an Exhibition.

Well – they received it enthusiastically. After about an hour's discussion I was asked to put the whole plan down in black and white. It is to be printed and signed by all the Peace Societies and then submitted to Mr Ford (the maker of the motor-car) with a request for a grant of money with

---

* A book called *Krieg dem Kriege* (i.e. *War against War*) – the identical title seems to be pure coincidence – published in Germany in 1924 by Ernst Friedrich (1894–1967) is infinitely more famous and still in print, but it cannot compare with Walter's exhibition; it consists 'only' of horrific photographs of the victims of war, a form of sensationalism in the name of peace that would have disgusted Walter. Friedrich also displayed the photographs in the windows of an anti-war museum that he opened in Berlin. It can be visited today, in the suburb called Wedding (how ironic).

† Hollingsworth Wood (1873–1956) was 'a big-chested, kind, strong-hearted' New York lawyer and, as a friend of Luther Gulick, a great supporter of the Campfire Girls.[19]

which to finance the undertaking, for he has promised unlimited funds for a real live peace idea.

And you should have heard the enthusiastic things which were said about the scheme – and the schemer.

Well, since then I have been pegging away at it – and with Mrs Benedict at the German Invasion play. So it's been a pretty busy week. The German Invasion play is going to be simply wonderful! You know there has arisen here a wonderful new producer of moving pictures – a man named Griffith. His masterpiece is called *The Birth of a Nation* – if it ever comes to England, as it surely will some day soon, you must go and see it at all costs.* It's worth a special run up to London – yes, indeed. Simply wonderful. And so full of new ideas and methods. Incredibly beautiful, and altogether convincing.

Well, Mrs Benedict and Ray Stannard Baker (you remember him at Amherst – Molly Best's friend) and I hope to lay this play of ours before Griffiths – of course there may be a fortune of money in it for all concerned – but I'm not letting myself think of that. The idea of the play is like that of the article – of course America keeps its head and good humouredly receives the invaders, and finally laughs them out of the country. We have enriched the story with many new characters and developments, and now it is nearly finished. It does really seem to me to be awfully good! I'll tell you in my next letter of any further progress, and when the thing is typewritten I'll send you a copy.[20]†

The very length of this letter reveals the tremendous upsurge of inspiration and fresh sense of purpose that meeting Crystal awakened in Walter.

He had just spent the first of many weekends in a converted cider mill at 70 Mount Airy Road, Croton-on-Hudson, that Max Eastman had bought as a holiday home. There were four small rooms, one of which was the bathroom, so Max had a study in the barn next door. Although Walter described Max as 'a very quiet reserved shy young man,' there were always many visitors at the house. They would gather on the verandah, which commanded a glorious view over woodland to the Hudson River, or on the home-made tennis court just below. Walter added that

Amos Pinchot‡ – who took you into dinner at Norman Hapgood's, Rosalind

---

* D. W. Griffith (1875–1948) was a pioneering American film director, and the epic *Birth of a Nation* is his best known film.

† Unfortunately, no copy of this script seems to have survived.

‡ Amos Pinchot (1873–1944) was a wealthy lawyer who supported a wide variety of progressive causes. A close friend of both Crystal and Max, he served as their financial

– was there on Friday night. (He wished to be remembered to all of you.) I got on very well with Mrs Benedict – building up that non-resistance moving picture. It's really awfully good. If only we can get it placed properly it might make a stir.[21]

That week, he and 'Mrs Benedict' spent two mornings together on the scenario.

Their creative effort will have been focalized by advance publicity for a film that was in favour of equipping America with strong armed forces to repel invasion by a foreign army: *The Battle Cry of Peace* – now unfortunately lost, having been banned during the war.* It premiered in New York on 15 September. Having seen it, Walter penned a long and highly ironical letter about it to the editor of the *Evening Post*.† Rosalind found his letter 'splendid'[23] and Dorothy told him that it was 'the best you have ever written.'[24]

When his sisters joined him in New York on 5 October, he had much to tell them, new friends to introduce – and a full programme for them. On the sixth they lunched with Crystal and Hiram K. Motherwell, the journalist and drama critic who had been praising their recitals ever since the first tour. That evening they all went to a Peace Concert. The following day Walter lunched with Percy Mackaye and in the afternoon his sisters sang at a Community meeting, at which Senator Taft was present. He and Walter had a long talk afterwards.

The eighth of October was equally well filled. All four Fullers lunched with Crystal's secretary, Ruth Pickering, and were joined afterwards by Marion and Percy MacKaye, with Arvia in tow. To reach the Friends' Meeting House, where the girls were to sing, they all crammed into a taxi, Arvia carrying the flowers. On arrival they found Jack and Helen Rae waiting for them, with Douglas Volk, and then Max Eastman and Norman Angell turned up as well. The concert of songs contrasting war and peace, suffering and happiness, had been advertised in that day's New York *Times*.

adviser and provided much of the money for the *Masses*. In 1919, he married Crystal's secretary, Ruth Pickering. Their daughter Mary, who married a high-ranking CIA official, was having an affair with President J. F. Kennedy at the time of his assassination; soon after that, she too was shot dead as she walked in the street near her home.

* To achieve a high degree of realism in its 'motion-picture play', 'the Vitagraph Company destroyed $30,000 worth of frame, brick and stone buildings,' using 'real cannon and real shells of the largest calibre. When you see building after building toppled over on the screen at the Metropolitan Opera House, you see pictures of real devastation wrought in deadly earnest and the effect is marvelous.'[22]

† Walter's letter was published on 11 October 1915. It is reproduced on the website. The *Post* was the paper that resisted most strongly the line of the super-patriots.

It was packed out and a great success; they sang encore after encore. However, coming straight after their leisurely holiday, it was a bit intense for the girls; Dorothy, in particular, needed peace and quiet to collect herself before a performance, and disliked being with crowds of people at such moments.

They were due to spend the last ten days of October in Detroit and then return to Chicago for two weeks. Feeling that new songs were needed to maintain the variety of their programme, Dorothy paid another visit to the New York Public Library. There she found, as well as peace and quiet, a dozen new folksongs to add to their repertoire. But would they be enough? At this point the Fullers decided to end their recital with some folk dances, which required a fourth person. By chance, it turned out that one of the girls they had met at Cecil Sharp's summer school at Eliot, Constance Binney, was the daughter of their printer, Mr Gray. As a young teenager, she was so stage-struck that her parents took her out of Westover and sent her to a convent school in Paris. She returned as determined as ever to become an actress, so they consented to her joining the Fullers to make up the foursome for folk dances. She was just eighteen.*

At this point Walter took his sisters by surprise: he announced that he was not coming with them to Chicago, but would remain in New York to work on his exhibition project. They were stunned, but Walter's decisions were not subject to debate. Then Maurice Browne decided that his theatre had become too small for them. 'To their grief and ours, for they were happier singing on our miniature stage than anywhere,' he recalled,

> we had to take the Fine Arts Theatre for them; otherwise our little place would have been wrecked. They packed the Fine Arts too; they could have packed the Manhattan Opera House.
>
> The stoutest objection to this transfer came from the girls' brother, Walter. . . . 'You'll make more money in the Fine Arts,' I kept urging. 'But you'll make less,' he groaned.[25]

Neither wanted to do the other down.

---

* The following January, Constance made her debut as an actress by appearing with her sister Faire at the Gaiety Theatre in *Erstwhile Susan*, which was filmed in 1918. Thereafter she had a six-year career on the stage and in silent films with Realart (Paramount), which earned her a star on the Hollywood Walk of Fame, at 6301 Hollywood Blvd. A curious postscript: in 1941 Leonard Cheshire, the famous RAF bomber pilot who was awarded the VC during WWII, met and married her in Canada. It was her first marriage and he was twenty-one years her junior – born two years after she joined the Fullers. Like many war-time marriages, it did not last long. Constance died only in November 1989.

The sisters rehearsed the dances thoroughly with Constance before leaving for Detroit, and when they got to Chicago, found that Maurice Browne had designed a perfect set for them at the Fine Arts. It was another triumph. 'The girls are in splendid form and spirits,' Browne reported to Walter. 'The dances went distinctly well, and some of the new songs are superb.' Then he confessed, 'I get a sort of lump in my throat at seeing them anywhere but in the Little Theatre.'[26]

During this run, the girls exchanged almost daily letters and telegrams with Walter, and his instructions were forever in their minds. 'We are practising the new songs this morning, with a sharp look-out for "words",' Dorothy assured him, adding, 'it seems awfully strange without you.'[27]

'I wish you were here to criticize,' wrote Rosalind. 'We miss you very much – but I try to remember not to strain and other rules of my singing-master.'[28]

He missed them too. 'To think that it should have come to this – you three dear things in Chicago, me in New York, and Riss in Berkswell! My god, what are we at?'[29]

He was also painfully aware that his parents would feel that he was neglecting his duty as chaperone and guardian of his sisters, so neither he nor they let on in their letters home that they were alone in Chicago, and Walter told Riss only well after the event. Cynthia had just turned nineteen, Rosalind was twenty-three, and Dorothy would be twenty-six in December – still in need of his protection (by the standards of the day) – but as seasoned travellers and professional performers, they managed very well without him.

In New York, he was certainly busy. First he completed a detailed description of his exhibition and had it typed.* A hundred copies were made and distributed to representatives of the movements supporting his project (which included the Woman's Peace Party, the New York Peace Society, the Church Peace Union, the League for the Limitation of Armament, and the Inter-Collegiate Anti-Militarist League) and also to influential persons who might be willing to serve on the organizing committee, particularly those who knew Henry Ford and could recommend the exhibition to him. On a typical day, he met with Norman Angell in the morning, lunched with Bishop Greer,† met with professors from Columbia in the afternoon, and dined with Louis Lochner.[30]

---

* On Crystal's recommendation, he engaged a typist who worked for him every morning from 9.30 to 12.30, for $8 a week.

† David Hummell Greer (1844–1919) was the bishop of the New York diocese of the American Episcopalian church.

Max and Crystal took a copy of his project to Thomas Mott Osborne, the prison reformer who was warden at Sing Sing. They introduced Walter to Gerald Stanley Lee, the author of *Inspired Millionaires* (1908) and the best-selling study, *Crowds: A Moving Picture of Democracy* (1913). They also introduced him to Norman Wilkinson ('the man who designs Granville Barker's productions, you know') and to Winold Reiss, 'a fine big quiet good-humoured fellow' who had just launched the *Modern Art Collector*; he later became famous for his portraits of American Indians.

> Norman Wilkinson is a good type of Englishman – very very anti-war – anti-government – with views very similar to mine. We talked over the Exhibition scheme – and these two men are both keen about it and want to help. Norman Wilkinson wants to do the theatrical part – the staging of plays etc. – and Reiss the colour scheme of the exterior part – the Exhibition itself. Isn't that splendid? Of course these two are at the head of their respective lines. Also Thomas Mott Osborne has joined the Executive Committee and promises to help interest Ford – and also Mrs Norman Hapgood wants to help on the theatrical side, getting up the right kind of plays etc.[31]

This interest and support greatly encouraged Walter; such a 'splendid Anglo-German-American combination' embodied the spirit of his exhibition. 'We're going to demonstrate the fact that we can't get on without one another – indeed that we love one another, and we don't care a hang for political nationality.'

His sisters served the cause of peace, too. Interviewed by the press on the subject of folksongs, they maintained that 'the pacifist is not a new human being. There are any number of old English and Scottish songs which prove that the humble people have always been against war.'[32] While they were in Chicago, the Arts Theatre was the venue of a large peace meeting organized by Louis Lochner at which Jane Addams spoke and the girls sang. On the last day of their run, they lunched with Maurice Browne and Jane Addams.

For all his work on the exhibition, Walter still believed that 'the war can't outlast the winter.' Consequently he was refusing bookings for recitals after March, in the hope that they would then be able to return to England.

> There'll be much fine splendid glorious work to be done and I think we're likely to be useful. Anyway, there will be the Exhibition to think of and I hope that if you're free in April you'll be able to raise your voices there. The earliest that the Exhibition can open is March 1st. Then, if the war has stopped, we might start a similar Exhibition scheme in England.[33]

He was also spending all the time he could with Crystal. We have no record of their feelings for each other at this point, but on the back of a postcard postmarked 8 November, Walter jotted down quotations from Keats ('The moving waters at their priestlike task / Of pure ablution round earth's human shores' from 'Bright Star'), Binyon ('O world, be nobler, for her sake'), and Kipling's 'Recessional' –

> For heathen heart that puts her trust
> In reeking tube and iron shard–
> All valiant dust that builds on dust,
> And guarding, calls not Thee to guard – *

They suggest how his feelings for Crystal were intimately related to his rejection of war.[35]

He was certainly working with her on more than just the film scenario. When after months of apparent indecision, President Wilson began hinting that he was now in favour of preparedness, increasing the size of the army and the navy, Crystal mobilized the New York branch of the WPP to mount the biggest parade yet in New York: on 24 October 44,000 suffragettes marched through the streets. Among them was Mrs Burchenal with her daughters Betty and Emchen. And Walter watched. It was followed by a two-week long WPP forum in New York at which the women planned policies 'to counteract the wave of jingoism.' Crystal made a rousing speech, employing an extended metaphor that was surely developed in collaboration with Walter, for rhetoric like this had not previously featured in her speeches:

> Most of the world is at war. Our rights are bound to be trampled here and there. It is a dangerous time for us, and every morning we face a new crisis. A fire as big as that with only the ocean between us is bound to scorch us. It is only by keeping cool, by playing the hose on our roofs all the time, and stowing all inflammables and combustibles out of sight that we can keep from catching fire.
>
> To start in just now on a great program of military and naval expansion, to spend millions on submarines and battleships, to increase the standing army, to start military training camps, to talk, think and act 'preparation for war' is, psychologically speaking, like pouring kerosene on the roof when there is a fire across the street and the wind is blowing our way. Sparks are bound to fall. If they fall on a cool wet roof, there is a chance of their going out. If they fall on a dry roof, 'prepared' with kerosene, what chance is there?[36]

At this meeting, she also proposed that the Party should call for a public

---

* Like Binyon's 'Ode to the Fallen', Kipling's 'Recessional' is quoted in Anzac Day ceremonies in Australia and New Zealand.

investigation into the state of their national defences; it was adopted as the WPP's national policy at its next annual convention.

In mid-November, Walter surprised his sisters by turning up in Detroit, where they were performing at the Pontiac High School. There he saw them dance with Constance Binney for the first time,* and on his return to New York, wrote: 'I thought the dancing fine – it just wants the touch of the master hand (i.e. mine) to make it perfect!'[38] However, he had not come to Detroit for this, but to ask Henry Ford's support for his project. The WPP had found a way to circumvent Ford's guard dog, Liebold, and arranged a meeting at which its representatives could plead their various causes. Although Walter came away without funds, others were successful: Mrs Ford gave $10,000 to the WPP for a telegram campaign, instructing ten thousand women's organizations, large and small, throughout the nation, to ask President Wilson to mediate between the warring parties.† This resulted in the White House receiving 12,000 telegrams, a massive demonstration of American women's wishes on this point.

Two days later, Ford arrived in New York, where he again met with WPP leaders. They put another idea to him: that a delegation of ordinary American citizens should sail to Europe and organize a peace conference there.‡ Ford, remembering the women's expedition to the conference at The Hague, jumped at the proposal. He already had an appointment with President Wilson on 24 November, at which he had intended to express his support for the WPP's program, but now he could tell the President that he was taking action himself. By midnight that day he had secured the first- and second-class space on the *Oscar II,* which was preparing to sail for Europe. The Ford Peace Ship was launched.

The WPP tried to increase the pressure on Wilson by holding a large demonstration in Washington on 26 November with Rosika Schwimmer as their main speaker. Henry Ford succeeded her on the platform and, carried away by the occasion, proclaimed that he would find a way to 'get the boys

---

* According to the Chicago *Daily Journal*, Constance was the best dancer of the four, with Cynthia a close second.[37]

† In *Peace and Bread*, Jane Addams gives slightly different figures: 'She sent us a contribution of $5,000.00 which she afterwards increased to $8,000.00' (p.18). She was writing from memory, ten years after the event. My figures are from contemporary documents in the archives of the WPP.

‡ Dorothy's daughter, Carol Odell, believed that this idea originated with Walter, but I have found no evidence to support her theory. Rosika Schwimmer is thought to have come up with the suggestion.

out of the trenches by Christmas.' This was patently not possible, of course, so it was received with derision by the press, but it gave Ford's project the kind of publicity that he loved.

When Walter's sisters returned to New York (after a recital at a convention of 3000 teachers, where they shared the platform with ex-President Taft), they were met by Crystal, who announced her intention of sailing on the Peace Ship. In the event, she did not go, for she had other business that would brook no delay. Nor, for that matter, did Jane Addams; she was hospitalized shortly before the ship sailed on 4 December. But Louis Lochner and the Eastmans' good friend Inez Milholland were on board and, among the journalists (who equalled in number the 'fantastic pilgrims', as the pacifist women were called by the press), there was Lella Faye Secor, whom we shall be meeting later.

As expected, Wilson presented Congress with his National Defense Bill on 7 December 1915. For Walter, this made it all the more urgent to mount his exhibition. He told Riss:

> Of course it seems to me as though democracy is at stake. If the United States is militarized, then indeed is freedom dead – and then indeed is humanity doomed to an unending series of wars. . . . Many leaders of opinion believe that this Exhibition will be a valuable means of public education as to the truth about war and foreign policies. You see, nobody reads pamphlets nowadays – very few people read serious books – the orator and the public meeting are not the powerful moulders of public opinion that they once were. The new power is the Press – and the photo – whether reproduced in the illustrated papers – or in the Cinematograph theatre. Therefore we are going to use this last new weapon – the photo, the picture. This Exhibition is going to do it.[39]

It's worth taking a closer look at what Walter is saying here. First there is the notion of democracy. Like an increasing number of people, he had come to realize that, once elected, the representatives of the people tend to serve ends that reflect neither the will nor the wishes of their electors. While private individuals may sacrifice their lives to keep their word or uphold a principle, persons in power will rarely do this. The process of election washes the morality out of them, allowing them to go back on their electoral promises with a clear conscience.* Wilson was to provide a fine example of

---

* In an article for the Brooklyn *Daily Eagle* in June 1924, Walter bemoaned this failing in Ramsay MacDonald, one of the founders of the Union of Democratic Control who had a passion for 'open covenants openly arrived at' – yet once he became Prime Minister this ideal evaporated.

this over the coming year. From the outbreak of the war he had listened with sympathy to the advocates of peace, and made statements like, 'As long as I am President, this country will not go into that war,' but he took no step to mediate between the adversaries.[40] Although he was desperate to lead, he delayed because he wanted to be sure of success and act as the sole mediator, coming like a kind of messiah to save a world at war, and messiahs do not make mistakes. Re-elected at the end of 1916 – even by those who were otherwise opposed to him – because he seemed to stand for peace, he threw the United States into the war within six months. And just as Walter feared, democracy, in the form of individual freedom of action, speech, and opinion, was the first casualty on the home front.

Preparation for war, as Walter said, raised questions about 'public education as to the truth about war and foreign policies.' Wilson was well aware that large numbers of Americans were not in favour of their country going to war, so in April 1917 he instituted a powerful government propaganda machine, the Committee on Public Information (CPI, also known as the Creel Committee), to make the American people *want* war. The CPI used every medium available at the time to achieve this end: the written word with its daily *Bulletin* (distributed to newspapers, post offices, government offices, and military bases); images in posters, photographs and films; the spoken word (with 'Four-Minute Men': volunteers who spoke about the war for no more than four minutes at a time at social events and gatherings); military displays and exhibitions. It even organized concerts; at one, the Irish-American tenor John McCormack sang before an audience representing Irish-American organizations.

It is striking to realize that, eighteen months before the CPI was dreamed up, Walter was planning to use (or already using, for his sisters had been singing the 'Five Souls' since January 1915) all of these means and more to broadcast his message of peace and reach the public who did not read newspapers, pamphlets or books. He had proposed and the WPP implemented a scheme similar to the 'Four-Minute men' whereby WPP volunteers spoke for five minutes in cinemas every half hour from early afternoon until the end of the evening. The CPI was clearly copying his ideas. Two of the six persons who comprised the Creel Committee were the journalists Ray Stannard Baker and Ida Tarbell (hence it was dubbed 'a roll call of muckrakers'). As we have just seen, Baker in particular was familiar with Walter's plans for an exhibition right from the start. So his propaganda to prevent war provided the CPI with a blueprint to do just the opposite. Even his averred aim of educating the public was echoed by the man in charge of the

CPI, George Creel, who maintained that 'our effort was educational and informative throughout.'[41]

But all this is to anticipate events. Throughout November and December 1915, Walter was seeking distinguished and influential persons for the committee of his exhibition. By the time he petitioned Ford for funding, about thirty had agreed ('and we're hoping to get Edison to be chairman'). A new recruit was Robert Edmond Jones, the stage designer of Percy MacKaye's pageants. He became a good friend of the Fullers, who knew him as Bobby.*

Thanks to Crystal and Max, Walter and his sisters enjoyed a whole new social life. At parties in Max's Washington Square apartment they discovered the Bohemian lifestyle of Greenwich Village and savoured relaxed discussions of new books and ideas with all kinds of people. It was also a two-way exchange, for Walter introduced some of the Fullers' friends to the Eastmans: Mollie Best, Mary Breck, Percy MacKaye – and Douglas Volk, who began to provide drawings for the *Masses*.

In this new life of Walter's there was little room for letterwriting. Feeling guilty for 'neglecting' his duty towards his sisters, he wrote rarely to his parents and, as Crystal became increasingly important to him, less and less often to Riss. Soon even Dorothy was complaining of his failure to write

> not only home but to friends and people here who nearly go out of their minds when letters are not answered. Of course, if he was not such a critical, foreheady brother, I am quite sure that at the ripe age of 26 I should be able to answer them myself – but gracious! everyone knows how critical he is in that line, so I daren't.[42]

He may have been as critical as ever, but he was changing, as his sisters noticed.

Their Christmas letters home, and to Riss, provide us with unaccustomed views of Walter: their strait-laced, sober-sided brother was beginning to loosen up, and they could not guess why. Cynthia told her mother that

> Walter and I had lunch down at the grill today – and now he's in my room (for company), perfectly happy in a large armchair drawn up by the bed, which he has nearly covered with newspapers – and is carefully looking down each page, with a large pair of scissors in his hand, waiting to pounce on anything mentioning Peace or War. He is well, dearie, and seems much happier than of old – he doesn't get so angry or worried. I think that is a sure sign of good health, don't you?[43]

---

* Robert (Bobby) Jones (1887–1954) went on to produce many plays at the Greenwich Village Playhouse, design and direct a large number of O'Neill's plays, and work on Broadway productions.

Walter Fuller

To Riss, she wrote how

> On Monday last, we four went to hear Norman Angell lecture at the Lyceum Theatre – which was crowded – boxes and all. It was a splendid, sane talk, and Walter, who was by my side, kept forgetting himself, and shouting out 'Hear Hear!' in a very English voice. Afterwards we all went off to the Astor where we had a very swagger and interesting lunch party of peace-thinking people. Oh, a Mrs Benedict – Walter's peace friend – was also one of the party. We all went down-town to this studio, and tripped through 'Gathering Peascods'. It was the funniest sight to see Walter alone 'setting' and 'siding', enough to make one hold one's side with laughter! . . . We all had a jolly time – and Walter loved it, and wants to dance more. I can't think what's coming over him. He even asked the other day how to do the one-step! and when some dance-music, such as Chin Chin is played, he can hardly keep his feet and shoulders still!!![44]

Dorothy wrote home in confidence:

> He is (and you must never let him see this) a much stronger man than he was before. Whether it is having these big plans to think about, and write about, and talk about, I don't know – but certainly it was not sufficient work for him to be doing things with us – writing programmes, carrying the harp, and being only the brother of the Misses Fuller. . . . His forehead is just full of ideas, and I know they must, at least some of them, bear fruit.[45]

And to Riss she said simply, 'He is a man with a Purpose.'

He was indeed. But as the year closed, his plans were stymied. Although the New York branch of the WPP received a thousand dollars from Henry Ford,[46] it refused to support the exhibition. Greatly disappointed, Walter spent a day in bed with a headache, while his sisters practised a new song, the poem 'Reconciliation' by Lady Margaret Sackville, which he had recently set to music. The following day he was out all afternoon with Stanley Lee, who had become a good friend of his. That evening Crystal telephoned, asking Walter to hasten to Washington, 'on business.' He left early the next morning, and his sisters spent a lonely New Year's Eve in their hotel.

In an attempt to prevent Wilson's National Defense Bill from going through, the American League for the Limitation of Armament convened a national conference of all the anti-war groups on 21 December 1915 and united them in a national 'Anti-preparedness Committee'. (The following April it was renamed – since 'anti-preparedness' was such a poor concept to defend – the American Union Against Militarism (AUAM), which is what I shall call it from now on.) It rapidly became the largest and most influential peace group in the country, with branches in all the major cities. Amongst its leaders were Crystal and Max, Charles Hallinan* (who became their Washington lobbyist), John Haynes Holmes (a Unitarian minister in New York City; a prominent and active pacifist), David Starr Jordan (Chancellor of Stanford University), Paul Kellogg (editor of the *Survey* periodical), Louis Lochner, and Hollingsworth Wood. Following a meeting at the end of December, Walter was brought in as its PR man, providing 'his distinctly expert services at the moderate rate of $150 a month' (according to the minutes of the committee meeting of 31 January 1916). Being the only non-American at the heart of the AUAM, he also contributed a valuable international perspective to its policies and actions.

The term 'PR man' was not actually used; it had yet to be invented. Nor did the AUAM call Walter a 'propagandist'; that too had yet to gain currency. But a propagandist he was. In 1915 only a handful of people worked in public relations. One of them – possibly the earliest professional manipulator of public opinion (another new concept) – was Ivy Ledbetter Lee. He had helped the railway companies rebuild their reputation after Ray Stannard Baker revealed their scandalous business practices in 1904. Then, following the denunciation of Standard Oil by Ida Tarbell and the violent suppression of the 1914 coal mining strike in Colorado (known as the 'Ludlow Massacre'), John D. Rockefeller Jr entrusted Ivy Lee with the task of restoring the image of his family and their oil company. Unfortunately, Lee attempted a cover-up operation, maintaining that the fifty-three strikers who had died were victims of an overturned stove, when in fact they had been shot, executed by the Rockefellers' private militia. This earned him the nickname 'Poison Ivy'. To restore his own public image, Lee would later affirm that 'the essential evil of propaganda is failure to disclose the source of information' – a much-quoted statement that sidesteps the real issue. It would be more true to say that 'the essential evil of propaganda is the *hidden interest* of the source of information.'

Whereas Lee's work had been largely retrospective, cover-ups to alter public perception of past events and thereby the present image of the compa-

---

* Described by Max as 'a keen-minded, genial Irishman' from the Middle West, Charles Thomas Hallinan (1880–1971) had worked as an editorial writer for the Chicago *Evening Post*. Floyd Dell remembered how he 'devoted immense care to learning how to say forbidden things in innocent and unimpeachable ways.'[47] In 1914, he moved on to become the publicity manager of the Press Bureau of the National American Woman's Suffrage Association. Later he served on the board of the *Liberator* and became 'a dear friend' of Crystal and Walter.[48] He is unanimously remembered for his kindness.

nies and people involved, Walter was seeking to change the public's perception of the present situation in order to influence its future attitude and behaviour. Ten years later, Bernays called this 'the conscious and intelligent manipulation of the organized habits and opinions of the masses,' which he saw as 'an important element in democratic society.'[49] It was the shape of all future propaganda.

As a matter of fact, it had already taken this shape in Britain, although Walter could not possibly have known it. In September 1914, the government set up a War Propaganda Bureau (WPB; also known as Wellington House), directed by Charles Masterman, a writer and Liberal MP. To maintain public morale by giving the impression that Britain was in control of the war, Masterman recruited twenty-five authors to write propaganda books and pamphlets for him, on the basis of suitably doctored information that he supplied. (They were all sworn to secrecy, with the result that the activities of the WPB became public knowledge only in the mid-1930s.) Aware that the public might not believe government-issued brochures, Masterman arranged for these works to come out through the authors' usual publishers, reassuring names like Hodder & Stoughton, T. Fisher Unwin, Macmillan, Methuen, John Murray, Nelson's, and Oxford University Press.* Thus the British public (unlike the Germans or the Americans) received 'official British propaganda . . . through unofficial sources.'[50] Novelist John Buchan wrote of *The Battle of Jutland* and *The Battle of the Somme*. In 1917 he was made head (with an annual salary of £1,000) of a new branch of the WPB, the Department of Information. Unlike his US counterpart Bernays, Buchan believed that 'the main aim of propaganda was to impart accurate information and to explain British policy.'[51]

Inspired only by his ideas for the promotion of peace and determined to tell what he perceived to be 'the truth, the whole truth, and nothing but the truth' about the realities of war to the American people, Walter the PR virgin set to work at once, aiming at the highest level. At the end of 1915, following the sinking of two Japanese ships in the Mediterranean, there was speculation as to whether Japan would enter the war too. Japan soon made it

---

* In all, 1160 publications were issued. They included: *To Arms!* by Sir Arthur Conan Doyle; *Barbarism in Berlin* by G. K. Chesterton; *The New Army* by Rudyard Kipling; *The Two Maps of Europe* by Hilaire Belloc; *Liberty, A Statement of the British Case* and *War Scenes on the Western Front* by Arnold Bennett; *Gallipoli and the Old Front Line* by John Masefield; *A Sheaf* and *Another Sheaf* by John Galsworthy; *England's Effort* and *Towards the Goal* by Mary Humphrey Ward; and *When Blood is Their Argument* by Ford Madox Ford.

clear that her response would depend on the reaction of the Allies, and she sent three cruisers across the Pacific to guard the Panama Canal. America acknowledged their presence with a radio message.* The minutes of the AUAM meeting on 3 January 1916 record that 'Mr Hallinan submitted a suggestion from Mr Walter Fuller that the second wireless message from America to Japan should be a strong word from President Wilson of international goodwill and friendship between the two countries.'

While the AUAM was meeting in Washington, Walter was at the home of the mother of Oswald Garrison Villard, addressing a small assembly of people on 'Preparedness and its Relation to Women' while his sisters performed their anti-war songs. Two days later, there was an enormous peace meeting in Carnegie Hall, at which Helen Keller spoke (through her sign interpreter) on 'The Working Man and Militarism' and the sisters sang three of their peace songs. 'Now dear,' wrote Cynthia to their mother, 'that hall is immense – holds thousands – so picture us singing there. But we did, and nearly all heard.'[52] The Hall seats three thousand people whose clothing absorbs sound quite dramatically. To state that nearly everyone heard them, without electrical amplification, indeed any amplification beyond the human lungs and larynx, suggests a remarkable performance.

Immediately afterwards the girls left for Boston, where they had a series of bookings and an intense social life, meeting Alfred Noyes, Robert Frost, and John Masefield (in the United States for a lecture tour). In the meantime Walter went to Washington, where the AUAM had its headquarters, with Crystal. She was attending the first annual convention of the WPP, at which she argued that the whole preparedness campaign was a lie and that the millions who were dying in Europe proved that it was a lie, a position she would probably not have worded so strongly were it not for her discussions with Walter. Another of his ideas was debated for the first time: it was suggested that, in view of the cosmopolitan nature of the population of America, the WPP should seek the cooperation of all foreign-born citizens in its peace programme. Also at that meeting, at the suggestion of Mrs Villard, the WPP revised its Constitution to include the aim of enjoining the nations of the world 'to respect the sacredness of human life.' This was probably the first time that any association had voiced such an aim. The meeting ended with a plea addressed to the Senate and the House committee for a peace conference of neutral nations, which they felt would surely take place if the United States agreed to participate.

---

* Radio contact with Japan had been established six months previously.

At this point, the AUAM decided to mount Walter's exhibition, albeit on a reduced scale, without the participation of people like Wilkinson or Reiss, making seven points about preparedness and militarism:

What we have and what is wanted.
Who wants it?
The cost of it.
How does it work?
Against whom?
Does it prevent war?
What is the alternative? (See the website for more details)

At the same time, the AUAM took up to a challenge that President Wilson had thrown out, telling his opponents to hire their own halls and set their case before the public, by embarking on a nationwide 'Truth about Preparedness' campaign, organized by Crystal and supported with posters and cartoons by Walter. It opened with the mass meeting in Carnegie Hall mentioned on the previous page and moved on to Pittsburgh, Cincinnati, Chicago, Des Moines, Minneapolis, Kansas City and Detroit.

By mid-January, a graphic artist had prepared, on the basis of Walter's ideas, 'a series of cartoons to be sent out in mat form to the papers over the country.' It included images of

'Mexico as Hearst sees it' versus 'Mexico as the plain man sees it.'

A bird's eye view of the Canadian frontier, dotted on our side with forts named after the timid civilians who have fallen for the preparedness program, like Fort Lyan Abbott, Fort Seth Low, Fort Talcott Williams, Fort A. Lawrence Lowell.

Six or seven wounded and exhausted soldiers, shaking hands after the war; Uncle Sam, heavily armed, comes up saying 'Now, I'm ready for you.'[53]

There were also plain text inserts for the newspapers, asking, 'If armies are raised only for defence, why is England now in Turkey, France in Greece, Germany in Egypt, and Russia in Persia?' or listing Garrison's Continentals under appropriate names like 'Bethlehem Infantry', 'Midvale Steel Battalion', and 'Homestead Guards'.

At the end of January, Walter's services were retained for another month and an additional $100 was allocated to equip him with an office and stenographer so that he could take charge of supplying the AUAM with window cards, lantern slides and other graphic material for local peace societies. These were widely distributed from April onwards. The Massachusetts Peace Society, for instance, placed a large stereopticon in the back of a car, with gas cylinders to 'fire' it, and offered it for use at public meetings throughout the State. The stereopticon – a double magic lantern that could superpose two images to create a three-dimensional effect or make one image dissolve into another – projected images onto a screen set up a distance away. In the days when country people had never yet been to a cinema, an outdoor show like this must have been a great attraction. A report in *La Follette's Magazine* for August 1916 describes some of the lantern slides:

> First we see a map of the world with the countries at war shaded black. It makes clear at a glance how very small is the part of the world ablaze. Then comes the Militarist's Ladder of Progress – on the lowest rung the caveman's bludgeon; the topmost, a can of chlorine gas. In quick succession come Zeppelins, gas masks, samples of trenches – one with French soldiers living like rabbits in burrows during a bombardment.
>
> A little girl is shown bidding her soldier-father goodbye. She asks him, 'Daddy, are you going to kill some other little girl's father?'
>
> There are other leave-takings – men are seen marching away, leaving an old mother, an agonized young wife and a little child. . . .
>
> Raemaekers' cartoon* is shown of dead men dangling on barbed wire like scarecrows in a storm. . . . A train of slowly moving baggage cars with the blood of wounded soldiers oozing from beneath the doors and dripping, dripping.
>
> A picture of the three Apostles of Preparedness: Power, Panic and Profits. Power is a helmeted militarist, lusty for conquest. Panic a timid soul, a victim of manufactured fear. Profits, a fat-jowled capitalist obsessed with greed. Then a chart of the price of the shares of Bethlehem steel, 42 before the war, 600 fourteen months later.[54]

This is typical of the propaganda that Walter was producing. It will be noted that some of the images made powerful appeals to people as *parents* by taking the child's view of war. One of his most poignant posters depicts soldiers advancing on enemy lines, captioned 'Here go good fathers to kill other good fathers.'

In January 1916 Walter arranged with Mary Breck, whom he had got to know and appreciate for her level-headed organization of charitable events, to accompany his sisters in his place on a tour of the southern and south-western States. It went very well. The Greensboro *Daily News* reported that their recital at Chapel Hill was 'absolutely unique': 'Their

---

* The WPB employed the refugee Dutch artist Louis Raemaekers (1869–1956) to illustrate a pamphlet on *Alleged German Outrages*. He produced some of the most powerful propaganda drawings to come out of Europe during WWI, depicting supposed German war crimes – and Walter borrowed them when he could, using them to denounce all war.

Walter Fuller

subjects demanded perfection of execution: the Fuller sisters attained it.'[55] This allowed Walter to remain in Washington and concentrate on coming up with ideas for the AUAM.

In the middle of February, however, he returned to New York for a few days to help Crystal. In response to the projection in movie theatres of a three-minute silent film of Theodore Roosevelt defending preparedness, he and Crystal arranged for Paramount Pictures to film peace supporters (including Crystal and Amos Pinchot of the AUAM) speaking on 'Shall we Prepare?' in the offices of the WPP in New York. Included in a newsreel about preparedness, the footage was shown across the United States. They organized parades of private automobiles through the streets of the city, decorated with peace flags and slogans like 'Preparedness means War'. Walter had become the PR man of the WPP as well as the AUAM, the two most influential peace groups in the country.

When the WPP headquarters in Chicago was offered free advertising space at the Panama Pacific Medal Winners Exposition at the Coliseum, Chicago, the office secretary sent telegrams to Walter at both the Hotel Belmont in New York and the Munsey Building in Washington, where he had his AUAM office, asking for publicity material. It was needed for the beginning of March but, as Walter explained a few days later, the material was not yet ready. Unable to get production accelerated, he sent her

> the copy which we used for some lantern slides here the other day. I am sorry I have been unable to send this to you before but as we had loaned the slides to some people here for use at a meeting, I have only just been able to have this typewritten copy made.
>
> I have asked Mr Hallinan (our Editorial Director) whether he could let me send you any of the original cartoons he has, but I am sorry to say that these are all in use just now and he cannot promise to send them to you for some days.[56]

The lantern slides were paired drawings, with contrasting text beneath them along the lines of

> The Naval Board demands $300,000,000 for new ships but . . .
>> Wm H. Taft says that recommendations of naval officers should be taken with caution.
>
> The War College says we need 1,500,000 soldiers and $500,000,000, but . . .
>> Lord Salisbury said, 'Don't listen to military experts; they would fortify Mars against the Moon.'
>
> All the preparedness programs lead to compulsory military service, but have you heard that . . .

2,000,000 British workmen have just declared compulsory military service contrary to the spirit of British democracy? How about American democracy?

The last one was humorous, in the form of a roadsign sandwiched between two texts:

To any Congressman, Washington, D.C.

THE ROAD TO WAR IS
PAVED WITH PREPAREDNESS.
GO SLOW.

(Signed) Any American Citizen

Walter's first response to the WPP's request for material had been a startling telegram: 'COST OF TRANSPORTING ARMORED DINOSAUR TO CHICAGO TWO DOLLARS'.[57] The symbol that he had dreamed up for both his exhibition and the anti-preparedness campaign was a fifteen-foot long *papier mâché* model of a stegosaurus, nicknamed Jingo (after the popular term for chauvinistic patriots, widely used in the United States in 1916).* A plaque on its base read, 'This is Jingo, the armored dinosaur: All Armor Plate and No Brains. This animal believed in Huge Armament – He is now Extinct.' Once it was announced that Jingo was available for display, the demand from peace groups around the country was such that three copies were made and widely displayed. In mid-March, for instance, one resided for a week in the window of the Wilmington Gas Co., under the auspices of the Delaware Peace Society.

Of the stegosaurus Walter wrote:

Here was an animal unable to do even a little intelligent thinking. Its brain cavity in proportion to the size of its body was more diminutive than that of any other vertebrate. Like the militarist, therefore, it was unable to conceive of any intelligent foreign policy. Moreover, its vision was limited. Its eyes were small and could look only in a sidewise direction. It could not look ahead.

It is also considered likely that the dinosaur had no funny bone.

It is thought by those who have studied these creatures that at one time there were at least fourteen different species of armored dinosaurs roaming about the face of the earth. This fact has a peculiar significance, as there are just that number of patriotic societies in this country now urging dinosaurian preparedness upon us. Increasing bulk and development of the

---

* J. A. Hobson, an early contributor to Walter's *University Review* and now an active member of the UDC, published a book in 1901 titled *The Psychology of Jingoism*.

armor caused the dinosaur to lose celerity of movement; he became a sluggish, slow-moving creature of low mentality. Whereas his contemporaries in the animal kingdom, whose minds did not run so much on 'preparedness,' kept their wits about them and decided upon some workable plan by which to live and let live, with the result that modern man and the armored dinosaur now meet one another only in museums.[58]

Appropriately, Jingo paid a visit to the Smithsonian at the end of March, 'attracting considerable attention on account of its original style.'[59] Reactions were varied. 'Pacifists of the type who participate in such a silly spectacle have neither brains nor armor,' wrote the Seattle *Daily Times*.[60]

Pursuing its Truth about Preparedness campaign, the AUAM held mass meetings during the second week of April in a dozen major cities across the United States. To advertise them, Jingo was paraded through the streets on a horse-drawn cart (and in the mid-west on the back of a truck sponsored by the Ford Motor Co), gaining more press coverage than the meetings themselves. One Buffalo newspaper, for instance, 'putting Jingo's picture on its first page along with its daily war alarms, endeavored to take the curse off this indiscretion by attacking the truckload as not only unpatriotic but impious. The Almighty created the dinosaur, it said, and put his ponderous shell on him, and who are we to say that the Almighty erred?'[61] Praising 'the genius who conceived the warping of this goliath from his place in the museums', the *Survey* devoted a whole page to the press response to Jingo.[62] Public awareness of the symbol may be judged by the number of cartoons alluding to it. (See website for examples.)

Literal-minded supporters of preparedness took delight in ridiculing Jingo, but they missed the true significance of the model. Amateur though he was in manipulating public opinion, Walter had intuitively arrived at the two basic principles of propaganda many years before they were formulated in any book: *people's minds are most easily changed by addressing their emotions,* rather than by reasoned argument, and *the best trigger lies not in the literal but in the symbolic message conveyed.* The CPI is credited with inventing this approach during the years of American participation in WWI, and the image most commonly associated with it is the poster depicting German planes flying round a battered Statue of Liberty. Rationally, it was ridiculous: German planes could not possibly have reached New York. Even German battleships lacked the coal capacity to cross the Atlantic. But the *image* was deeply disturbing. With symbols detached from reality like this, it is the emotion that counts, not the facts.

The mastermind behind the CPI was Edward L. Bernays, who might have

Propagandist

The syndicated picture of Jingo that was reproduced in almost every US newspaper

stepped out of the pages of a novel by George Orwell. Born in Vienna in 1891 – so he was ten years younger than Walter – he came to America with not just the theories of Sigmund Freud but his very bloodline: his mother was Freud's sister, Anna, and his father was brother to Freud's wife Martha Bernays. He is considered to have been the first to use the unconscious to manipulate public opinion, or what he superciliously called 'the masses'. He believed that ordinary citizens, being subject to the urgings of the unconscious and to libidinal impulses, were not competent to vote wisely, so it was necessary to control and regiment them without their being aware of it. He called this the 'engineering of consent.' He was therefore just the person Wilson needed to persuade Americans to want war with Germany. Without the benefit of Bernays' intimate knowledge of Freud and the working of the unconscious, Walter anticipated his approach by at least eighteen months. The big difference between them was financial: Walter worked on a shoestring, whereas Bernays had an almost unlimited budget.

During this time, Crystal had been busy on personal matters: at the end of February, she filed a divorce suit against Wallace Benedict for infidelity. As a matter of principle, she asked for no alimony, which she called 'a relic of the old, old days when women were considered like children and had to be supported by men' – but the money would have been welcome.[63] The suit was uncontested and by the end of April Crystal was a free woman again.

The opening of the exhibition on 6 April, in an empty store in Brooklyn, was announced by Jingo. 'A pre-historical argument against preparedness was wheeled through the streets yesterday,' headlined the press. At strategic points, he was 'attacked by sabre-toothed tigers,' personified by pacifists such as Hollingsworth Wood and Norman Thomas.[64] An eight-foot high figure of Uncle Sam wearing a gas mask and carrying all the latest weapons was also paraded through the streets. The message at his feet read: 'All dressed up and no place to go.' This set the tone for the whole show, demolishing the ideals of the militarists 'by means of keen caricatures, bullets of ridicule and darts of sarcasm.'[65] Walter attributed the idea to Charles Dickens. 'When he wanted to reform the midwife situation in England, Dickens created the figure of Sarah Gamp; when he wanted to improve the boys' schools, he created the cheap schoolmasters of Yorkshire in *Nicholas Nickleby*,' he told reporters. This humour did not go down well in some quarters. Mabel Hyde Kittredge (later President of the national WPP) resigned from the New York party in protest. Following complaints in the press that the figure of Uncle Sam held the United States up to ridicule,* a Kings County grand jury visited the exhibition – but no prosecutions were made. Walter responded by adding a second figure: Uncle Sam dressed like a gentleman, draped with the Stars and Stripes; a placard proclaimed him 'the world's greatest mediator'.†

---

* A letter in the New York *Times*, signed A.B.P., ended: 'I vehemently insist that this "War against War" exhibit should be suppressed. Its doctrines are false, its influence insidious, and its purpose questionable, if not treasonable.'[66]

† Pictures of these figures and other features of the exhibition can be found on this book's website.

Compared to Walter's original scheme, the exhibition was disappointingly modest. It proved too costly to make mechanical models with soldiers popping up through maps of France and Germany to illustrate the increasing size of standing armies, for instance, so the displays were largely static, with lifesize figures enacting symbolic scenes, backed by panels with arguments in words and images. One of them depicted a large pair of weighing scales, with 'Submarines are for Protection | Dreadnoughts are for Aggression' written across the beam. In one pan there was a battleship; in the other, eighteen submarines. Down the stem ran the explanatory text: 'We can get 18 submarines for one dreadnought.' Another showed men and women, ordinary citizens from both sides of the conflict, almost crushed by enormous burdens on their backs: the weight of taxation caused by war.

The two Uncle Sams stood at the entry to the show, which was decorated with banners bearing the words 'War against War' in twenty-five different languages. Further in was 'an immense relief map, eight feet long and four feet wide, showing the world as it is. Immediately above it, a map of the world as the nervous patriot sees it. The United States has shrunk to the size of an island, while Japan has assumed the proportions of a continent.'[67] There was a film (silent, of course) showing movie footage and static images of warfare, interspersed with frames with a text commentary. Rather disturbingly, a chuckling figure of Satan stood by, watching the screen. At the end, there was a 'bridge of sighs' crossed by haggard groups of women and children, their faces marked by the horrors they had witnessed, all too accurate an anticipation of post-war Europe.

There were regular lunch-time lectures, usually given by committee members of the AUAM or WPP. They included Oswald Garrison Villard, Rabbi Stephen S. Wise, Dr John Haynes Holmes, and Morris Hillquit, a leading socialist; Norman Angell was a guest speaker. There were also theme days, including a Physicians' Day, a Political Day, and a Mothers' and Suffrage Day, emphasizing the relevance of the exhibition's theme to individual lives.

During the first three weeks, it drew at least 5000 visitors a day, so it was extended to mid-May. Then the WPP moved it to the ground floor of an office block at 208 5th Avenue, where it was viewed at a rate of 8000 a day. Rather conveniently, the site was opposite the reviewing stand of a massive preparedness parade that passed right in front of the building on 13 May 1916. This brought 11,000 visitors in a single day and over 50,000 pieces of literature were distributed.

On that occasion, Walter was determined to 'steal the thunder' of the preparedness parade. He had an immense banner hung up above the entry to the exhibition, reading:

> There are only 100,000 of you.
> You are not the only patriots.
> 200,000 farmers, 500,000 mine workers and
> organized labor of America are opposed to what
> you and Wall St. are marching for.
> Are you sure you are right?[68]

He also had original ideas for distributing flyers:

> Early in the day fifty young women dressed in white, calling themselves the 'Real Patriots,' circulated among the crowds giving out handbills asking militarists to 'think it over.' They carried palm leaf fans and wore placards bearing mottos considered appropriate to the occasion. In addition, some of them distributed literature printed in red and blue on white paper, presenting arguments and catch phrases against armament.
>
> One was entitled: 'Who Starts the Cannon Balls Rolling?' Another was headed: 'What Are We Afraid Of?' A third presented to the eye the well known 'The Voice With the Smile Wins.' A fourth said 'Keep Cool,' and the palm leaf fans were intended to convey that injunction.[69]

These leaflets in eye-catching colour – see the book's website for facsimiles – were much admired by other branches of the WPP, and they were distributed widely; the AUAM also used them. They contributed to the New York WPP's growing reputation for being 'particularly energetic and imaginative' and 'highly inventive in its methods' of propaganda.[70] An undated document in the archives of the New York WPP confirms that 'the keynote of its activities were its "dramatic, daring stunts".'[71]

While the exhibition was nominally under the aegis of the AUAM, it was in effect organized by the New York WPP, whose secretary did her best to bring in private donations to cover the cost, more than $2000. Walter's expenses were defrayed by the AUAM and he continued to receive $50 a month – paid anything up to six weeks late, however, for funds were in short supply. At a meeting on 8 May, hope was expressed that, 'with Mr Fuller's help, we can soon develop some popular money-raising scheme which will see us through the year.' So the payment of his salary depended partly on his own efforts to bring in donations.

By now the AUAM had added Norman Angell to their list of 'consultants'. At the end of February, Charles Hallinan arranged a 'Dutch Treat' dinner for a number of Congressmen to meet him, and in April Paul Kellogg presented the AUAM with the draft of a letter to President Wilson, which he had drawn up with Norman Angell, Walter, and three others. It urged him to announce a definite international policy and suggested the manner of its application to Germany, should diplomatic relations be severed. The letter was referred for revision to a committee consisting of Hallinan, Kellogg and Walter. Shortly afterwards, the President agreed to meet them in May. On this occasion they concentrated on the compulsory draft. Wilson told them that he was asking only for a large body of trained men, not a standing army. The AUAM delegates refused the distinction: the former, they said, would lead to the latter. Wilson continued to maintain that 'If you say, "We shall not have any war," you have got to have the force to make that "shall" bite. . . . In the last analysis, the peace of society is obtained by force.'[72] He would not admit that he was on a path that would inevitably lead to war.

In the meantime, the Fuller Sisters' tour with Mary Breck proved more tiring than previous ones, for she booked them into less comfortable hotels than Walter would have chosen, and roused them before dawn for day-long train journeys, rather than take the night trains as he did. By the first week of April, the girls were quite worn out, and Cynthia caught measles. Dorothy nursed her through the worst in a quarantined hotel room, and then Walter sent her to Atlantic City with Mary to recuperate while Dorothy and Rosalind fulfilled their engagements with a piano accompanist. But a week later Rosalind collapsed just as she was about to go on stage. Walter cancelled the following recitals and sent her and Dorothy to Atlantic City too. Consequently they missed the launch of the War-against-War Exhibition in New York.*

As soon as his sisters had rested and could fulfil their engagements once again, Walter got them to sing at the exhibition. Thoroughly refreshed, they were performing better than ever. A reviewer praised their

> finest sense of balance and proportion. . . . They do not merely interpret – they embody the songs they sing. No smallest shade of humor or pathos goes unperceived or unportrayed. The art of the Fuller Sisters is so perfect that we take it very much for granted. It never occurs to us to wonder whether Cynthia had to practice long hours before she could play the harp as she plays it now. We think of her as born to do just this rare and luminous

---

* By this time, they had imitators. A Mrs Marjory Kennedy-Fraser and her daughter Patuffa had collected folksongs in the Hebrides. They performed them at the Aeolian Hall in March 1916, each accompanying the other on the piano. For several of the songs the daughter also played a small Celtic harp. They prefaced the performance 'with a short talk explaining the origin [of the songs] and the manner in which they were heard and written down.'[73]

thing.... We feel that Rosalind tosses away one mood and irradiates another as much for her own delight as ours, and that Dorothy has only to follow the prompting of the moment to command our emotions as she will.

Apparently it is the most natural thing in the world that they should carry their beautifully enunciated phrases along an unbroken stream of melody in the traditional way. The floating forward of these young voices is something that one cannot forget.... One comes away with certain things which can never be lost – a quickened appreciation of the round, golden beauty of English words... and the perception that the finest spontaneity springs from an inexhaustible reserve fund of graciousness.[74]

They were at the height of their fame – stopped in the street for autographs or simply for a fan to express delight and admiration.

But now it was Walter's turn to break down. While he may have been feeling a sense of anti-climax after striving for nine months to mount his exhibition, he had other, more conflictual problems. Following the sinking of a French liner by German submarines on 24 April, his parents had written that they did not want their children to risk a trans-Atlantic crossing, but Walter had been counting on his sisters returning to England to free him up for his peace work. He had made no bookings for them beyond the end of April. How were they to live, if they remained? Doctors' bills, cancelled concerts, and the unscheduled break at Atlantic City had consumed their meagre reserves. Nor was this all. He blamed himself for not going with them on their tour to the south and the mid-western states, during which they had had bad colds and got run down. He had been brought up to look after them and he felt guilty for neglecting his duty. Consequently he had not told his parents about Cynthia's illness or Rosalind's collapse. Nor, for that matter, had he said anything about Crystal. He had even stopped writing to Riss, because he felt that his growing love for Crystal betrayed his devotion to her. To cap it all, Basil had given up his medical practice to join the RAMC, 'bringing the war into the family,' as Walter put it. Torn between duty and desire, unable to speak to anyone about it all, and having no place to run away to, he bottled up his emotions. The result was severe headaches and then prostration. One morning at the end of April, he just lay in bed with his eyes closed and refused even a cup of tea. His sisters called the hotel doctor who prescribed rest. The next day they called another; he diagnosed a nervous breakdown and gave Walter a sedative.

The following day he woke feeling much better and immediately sent a telegram to Crystal, saying that he could not see her. His sisters found this strange, but he explained that it meant that she would have to take over supervising the exhibition for a few days. Then he began writing to Riss:

> Dear girl – dearest sister. It's a hard saying – but you'll find it in Mark's Gospel in the third chapter – when Jesus – so loving – so tender, said 'Who is my mother or my brethren?' These strange evil times in which we are now living make the meaning of Jesus in asking such a question vividly clear.

Riss will have been puzzled, to say the least of it, but he was trying to tell her that he was redefining his relationship with her. 'Dear girl,' he continued,

> you must think of me as a new man. This war has changed the whole world for me – I see opportunities for action everywhere. I hear calls for service all the time. Indeed, dear, my peculiar gifts are finding an outlet – whereby I am becoming a really useful – even perhaps important member of the group with which I am working. I have felt – I still do feel, it is impossible to make the whole situation clear and intelligible to you over there, with 3000 miles of ocean and the Censor between, and both of us so differently situated in such different environments. But then I know that if you were over here you would be with me – urging me on in the course I am taking, just as earnestly as do these dear girls here. First of all; you must know that I really am wanted at last – my ideas are listened to – discussed – adopted – and carried out in some form or other – and as a result our society, 'The American Union Against Militarism' is today, though only four months old – the most vigorous – most active – most progressive – of all the peace societies. . . .

At this point his sisters intervened: he should be resting, not writing! So he finished in haste:

> The girls say that this much letter must go – they say 'anything is better than nothing.' But, dear, I hate to do it – only it must be just a beginning. I'll get something off in the next mail which will be worthwhile. Dearest, I love you. I need you. I think of you, plan for you, work for you – as much now – as more than ever. Walter.[75]

Of all the visitors who called to enquire after Walter's health, Norman Angell was the most understanding and supportive, listening and talking calmly and positively. He had started to spend more and more time with the Fullers, acting like a second big brother to the girls. He went for walks in the park with them and 'took us to see *Justice* the other evening and we all talked until past twelve at night, discussing the law, the church and the war,' reported Rosalind in a letter to Riss. 'It ended by NA calling me an iconoclast which, since I have looked it up in the dictionary, I think to be a little wrong, for I would build up new idols or images for those I destroy.'[76]

As she listened to Walter debating whether he should give up his peace work and return to managing his sisters' tours, Rosalind took stock of the situation. It was clear that things could not continue as before, when 'we had all the work and Walter was really simply our guardian and friend – well, that he is now, and will always be – I hope – but he is too clever for that – he really has genius for this other sort of work.'[77] As Cynthia put it,

> The Peace people he is working with just marvel at the original brilliant ideas which flow from Walter's lips – whenever they want a new kind of notepaper, or advertisement, they go to Walter, and out comes 'this' and 'that', like a hen laying golden eggs. He seems so very happy, and says he feels there's a call for him to do this work, and that it will lead to what will be his life's work. He is meeting so many literary men, authors, and newspaper men, that like him, and admire his work. You should see him, dear, in his new suit – it's a grey-green-blue of the fashionable cut – and then, can you believe it – he has a tie of the same shade! And he is so proud of it, and glad we noticed it.[78]

Rosalind could see that 'he is better where he is, doing work, real work that is the joy of life.' This led her to think hard about the future, in terms that he would have commended. They each had their own lives to live and the right to pursue happiness in their own way. It was ridiculous to imagine Walter still managing their careers at the age, say, of fifty-six, instead of following his own course, just because his parents thought he should. 'As far as I'm concerned I hope to continue singing for at least forty years!' she exclaimed. As for retiring and marrying, as Riss had done, 'Never! While I have my life, I have ability to make my fortune, I believe, and by believing we can move mountains of doubt – is it not so? . . . I will always have the ability to finish my life as I hope to live it: with courage.'[79] With thoughts like these, she laid the foundations for a independent career that would last not forty but sixty-six more years.

After staying for just a few days with Helen and Jack Rae (who had named their son, born earlier in the year, after Walter), Walter bounced back into action, having chosen neither his propaganda work nor tour management, but endeavouring to keep both going at the same time. He remained, as Cynthia put it, 'the same Fullerian, hopeful put-off he has always been these 31 or 32 (is it?) years.' Down to Washington he hurried on AUAM business, and then met up with his sisters in Philadelphia, where they were joined by Crystal. She and Walter took the girls out to Croton, where they had a good time – except that Walter and Crystal spent the whole afternoon talking on the verandah, ignoring everyone else.

On 18 May, Walter brought representatives of six neutral nations to a mass meeting around the exhibition, calling for their governments to organize a conference of neutral nations. On this occasion, his sisters sang the 'Five Souls'. It proved to be the last performance of their tour. On 5 May 1916 the German government had promised not to sink any more ships without allowing time for the passengers and crew to get into lifeboats. Soon afterwards, Norman Angell decided to return to England and offered to escort the girls if they chose to return with him. They seized the opportunity and after a mad scramble to obtain tickets and passports, they left on 20 May. Walter was free to devote all his time to peace work – and Crystal.

Having waved off his sisters, 'the loneliest man in America' took the train to Chicago, where he arranged with the headquarters of the WPP for his exhibition to be shown there until 1 July, and launched a fund-raising campaign in the mid-west for the AUAM.[80] In addition, he had plans for Memorial Day. Originally a ritual of remembrance and reconciliation after the Civil War, Memorial Day had become an occasion to honour the dead (like All Saints Day in Europe), but since it always fell on a Monday, the long weekend also become an excuse for family trips, gatherings, and popular events like the Indianapolis 500 automobile race (which was initiated in 1911). Walter hoped to turn it into a day of mourning for all those who, whatever their nationality, had been killed in the current war. After WWI, a step was indeed taken in this direction: Memorial Day was officially extended to honour all American victims of war.

Soon he wired the AUAM that Cincinnati, St Louis and Chicago were enthusiastic about this scheme, and on 29 May he reported that he had organized a committee in St Louis which guaranteed $500 toward the Union's funds. Then he hastened back to New York for a meeting of AUAM members at a private house on 1 June. 'Mr Walter G. Fuller, who produced the War against War exhibit, now being shown at 208 5th Avenue, will describe two brilliant plans for the summer in which our help is needed; one, a great, good-natured cross-country adventure against militarism, the other a far-reaching step towards internationalism.' I have been unable to discover any further information about these projects.

That day, the National Defense Act was announced; it raised the size of the standing army to 175,000 men and the National Guard to 450,000, a fourfold increase. It also created what is now known as the Reserve Officer Training Corps (ROTC) and empowered the President to place obligatory orders with manufacturers capable of producing war materials. The anti-preparedness campaign had pitched David against Goliath, and Goliath was winning.

However, Chicago and St Louis both agreed to show Walter's exhibition when the up-coming political conventions were held there. It was wanted by Detroit and possibly Buffalo; later by Boston and Philadelphia. Not having been designed to be taken apart and re-mounted elsewhere, it had to be reduced in size for transport to these cities. For wider distribution to local peace societies, women's clubs, schools, and so on, the panels and cartoons were lithographed and printed on thin poster paper. By mid-July, 500 sets of fifty panels were available for sale at a mere $8 each. It was hoped that they would bring in useful funds during the summer. It was also planned to have individual panels and cartoons reproduced in periodicals like *Christian Work, Survey, Independent,* and the *Advocate of Peace* (issued by the American Peace Society).

Over the next few months the exhibition was shown in over a dozen major cities across the Union and an unknown number of lesser sites. The October issue of the *Advocate* reported, for instance, that the posters 'have been used effectively in many 'peace booths' at state fairs during the summer, and on other occasions of the display of peace propaganda. It is reported that on the island of Nantucket this exhibit was displayed on the front of the Methodist Church during the week of August 7.'[81] In December, the Orlando section of the Peace Society expressed the hope that 'the "War against War" exhibit of posters and placards may soon be procured, to extend propaganda work where the volunteer workers are themselves unable to go.'[82] However, after America declared war on Germany in the spring of 1917, the exhibition panels and posters disappeared entirely, as did Jingo, deliberately erased from the record and forgotten.* All such opposition had become treason. In the end, both the exhibition and Jingo proved as ephemeral as the Fuller Sisters' concerts, now known only though contemporary newspaper reports. So Walter's innovative approach to promoting peace and denouncing war in ways that could be seen and heard, instead of merely read about, became an unrecorded milestone in the history of propaganda.

In mid-June, Walter spent a weekend with Crystal and Max at Croton. Other guests included Ruth Pickering, Hiram K. Motherwell and his wife, and Boardman Robinson.† He was a new contributor of highly political

---

* A photograph of Jingo, misleadingly dubbed 'a World War I mascot', featured in the Smithsonian's blog on 16 November 2009.

† Dorothy described Robinson (1876–1952) as a big tall man, with 'fluffy red hair – and red eyebrows.' He had recently returned from Eastern Europe where, with the journalist John Reed (1887–1920), he had seen at first hand the effects of WWI on countries such as Russia, Serbia, Macedonia and Greece. He illustrated Reed's account of their journey, *The War in Eastern Europe* (1916).

cartoons to the *Masses*; later they caused it to be prosecuted under the Espionage Act. There was also 'a young man named Griffin Barry [who is] going out on Saturday next to Russia as an attaché to the American Embassy in Petrograd – a very good fellow.'⁸³ He crops up again in the lives of the Fullers and their friends, as we shall see.*

Returning to New York with Crystal by the Monday morning train, Walter had a meeting with Norman Hapgood to put forward his Memorial Day project; 'he was very much pleased' by it. As Crystal was planning to spend the summer campaigning in favour of Wilson in the upcoming presidential election, Walter took the opportunity to ask Hapgood if he might join in too: 'I've got some good ideas which ought to be worked off. I think they'd help Wilson a whole lot.' But it turned out that 'my nationality is against me' – being British precluded all participation.⁸⁴ So he went to meet the secretary of the Federation of Anglican Churches of North America where he outlined his plan for Memorial Day once again. The secretary was very sympathetic and promised his support.† That day Walter lunched with Boardman Robinson, Lincoln Steffens (Mary Agnes Best's friend) and Ray Stannard Baker. In the evening he called on the Burchenals and dined with the Brecks. It was a full and busy life.

Crystal was no less busy. In June and early July she used the AUAM's Inter-American Peace Committee to resolve a crisis in the long-running border war between the United States and Mexico. By organizing private mediation and a publicity campaign in Mexico (funded largely by the AUAM), she was personally responsible for averting a war. It was a major triumph for the AUAM, and certainly her greatest. It confirmed her belief that 'the *people* acting directly – not through their governments or diplomats or armies – can stop all wars if enough of them will act together and act quickly.'⁸⁵ It was a belief shared by Walter, but not by diplomats, nor by politicians and the governments they formed.

---

* Griffin Barry, born 1884, was an occasional journalist with aspirations (never fulfilled) to be a writer. After a mission with Herbert Hoover's Commission for Relief in Belgium in 1915, he signed up for a similar job in Russia, providing the kind of services provided by the Red Cross to German and Austrian civilians whom the Russians had interned as enemy aliens.

† According to a letter from Cynthia to Rosalind dated 11 August, Walter organized a masque in Detroit, but I have found no record of it. Percy MacKaye's 'Sanctuary: a Bird Masque' was perfomed on Memorial Day in several places, so this is perhaps a misunderstanding on her part.

6

Husband

What I am opposed to is not the *feeling* of the pacifists, but their *stupidity*. My heart is with them, but my mind has a contempt for them. I want peace, but I know how to get it, and they do not.[1]   President Woodrow Wilson

If after three years of the most fearful fighting the world has ever seen, the people of the world may not talk peace, what in God's name can they talk about?[2]
Bulletin of the People's Council / *Four Lights*

There is no law of God or man which requires a nation to avenge a bad act by a worse one.[3]   Dr. David Starr Jordan

Crystal Eastman photographed by Arnold Genthe
on 29 March 1916, when she divorced Wallace Benedict

Walter Fuller in 1916

BACK IN ENGLAND, Walter's sisters' holiday proved something of an emotional roller-coaster. It all started shortly before they left New York with the arrival of a letter for Rosalind from Arthur Dakyns. 'I am not going to begin to apologise for writing,' he wrote, 'although I expect you will think it absurd to hear from someone whom you haven't seen or heard of for more than four or five years.' Indeed, Dakyns had given no sign of life since the day in 1911 when he had dropped everything on learning of the death of his father, although the Fullers had heard occasional news of him through Curt Dehn and Bill Hankinson. First he had travelled the world, going as far as New Zealand. Then, in September 1914, he had joined the RAMC as a water-carrier behind the lines of the Queen's Volunteer Rifles in France and Belgium. In October 1915 he transferred to the Army Service Corps, but

> after two months of the most dreary and tiresome existence, and plagued by continual saluting, and repeated attacks of asthma (which I never got at the front) I went before a medical board and was compelled (there was no compulsion) to relinquish my commission on grounds of ill-health. Since then I have been living all too comfortably in London trying to finish a book on philosophy, which I shall never finish, learning Russian, and working at a boys' labour exchange in Poplar.

'When I got back from the front last October,' he added,

> I found that most of the people I formerly knew were either extreme pacifists or conscientious objectors. What has surprised me is to find that there are so many men in the country – many thousands in fact – willing to suffer ignominy and severe punishment for an ideal – a point of view – in which they quite sincerely and firmly believe, without belonging to any anti-war denominational sect.[4]

Dismissing the pacifist ideal as a mere 'point of view' was hardly likely to endear him to the Fullers.

Their homecoming was stressful enough as it was. England was far different from the country they had left behind in the autumn of 1914. Conscription having been introduced in January 1916, every able-bodied man was in uniform. (Had Walter come over, he would have been called up.) The streets and railway stations were thronged with soldiers, hotel rooms were hard to find, and the sisters were confronted with the unfamiliar sight of women doing jobs that had previously been the preserve of men, working as porters and ticket collectors, and even driving vehicles. As Dakyns had intimated, there was widespread resistance to conscription, and various organizations were active in supporting conscientious objectors (dismissively referred to as 'conchies' by the press). Just a week after they arrived, Bertrand Russell was tried and fined £100 for writing a No-Conscription Fellowship leaflet.

Home was not the same place either. Their parents had given up Bridge House in Sturminster Newton and were boarding in Bournemouth while they looked for somewhere else to live. Like all the other resorts along the south coast, Bournemouth was a sorry sight, filled with the wounded; those who could still walk pushed their comrades in wheelchairs, while others hobbled about on crutches. Their numbers increased daily. On the first day of the battle of the Somme, launched on 1 July 1916, 22,000 were killed and another 40,000 wounded by nine o'clock in the morning. Over the next five months, over one million British soldiers were killed or wounded in that battle alone.

Curt came down from London and proposed to Cynthia, but they agreed to keep it secret for the moment. He also brought the news that his brother Harold had been killed on the Somme on 8 July. Six weeks later, he was astounded to learn that in fact Harold was only wounded – 'severely but not dangerously' – and a prisoner in Germany.[5] Mixed with the joy of his return to life was the fear of how the Germans might treat a German-born soldier who had been fighting for the British: would they consider him a traitor? With a heavy heart, Curt left for officers' training camp.

Arthur Dakyns also hastened to Bournemouth as soon as he heard from Rosalind that she was back in England. Announcing his visit, he wrote, 'Curt says you have changed a great deal – meaning, I can only suppose, for the worse!'[6] It had been his intention to stay for at least a week, but he was quite put out to find that the Fullers were expecting Norman Angell, so he left almost at once. From London, he wrote relentlessly to Rosalind, continuing to protest his love for her at the same time as belittling her in a manner that she found deeply disturbing. He sent her philosophy books (Bacon, Plato, and Webb's *History of Philosophy*) as preparation for her reading of the first chapter of his 'book that will never be written' about Bacon. 'I should like your opinion of it,' he told her, 'because you are, as you say, "very intelligent" in certain peculiar ways.'[7] When she allowed a few days to pass before she answered, he complained: 'I first thought that you were going to allow another interval of five – or possibly, this time, of ten – years to elapse before writing again.'[8] A week later, he was exclaiming, 'What good letters you write, although of course there is little one can agree with in them!' He put a few words in Russian, adding: 'but then, you don't know any Russian.'[9] Occasionally, he would reveal the true problem, only to shift the blame onto her, as when he wrote: 'you see I am non-plussed and angry with my own failure and folly – as much as with what I really feel to be your blindness.'[10]

This treatment left her hurt and confused, wondering what on earth she had done to deserve it. 'My mind, my soul, is like a little boat tossing on deep ploughed-up feeling,' she told Cynthia. 'I am suspicious of myself – sometimes my reason seems to stand apart and watches this tumult going on in my mind and body, and then I must strain to clutch her cold hand – for it is cold – but what relief it brings to a fevered mind!'[11] Dakyns had told her that 'the great thing is to keep well and happy & never to feel morbid or depressed. Nothing else matters' – but he made her feel depressed, for which she took aspirins, which annoyed him.[12] Of course she continued to address him as 'Dakyns' (rather than 'Arthur'). That also annoyed him. He ended one of his letters by crossing out his surname in his signature. She was his whipping girl, a substitute for self-hatred and self-punishment.

Nonetheless, Rosalind went up to London to stay with Dakyns and his sister, taking the opportunity to look out more songs at the British Library. Dakyns introduced her to his boss in the Ministry of Labour; she proved to be the Mary Neal who had pioneered Morris dancing in the early years of the century. She was delighted to learn how the Fullers were singing folksongs in the United States and provided them with some more. Hearing of this, Dorothy exclaimed to Rosalind, 'what a wonderful dreamlike time you have been having!'[13] Little did she realize that with Dakyns it was more like a nightmare.

Down in Bournemouth, Dorothy and Cynthia stumbled on the just the house for their parents to rent. Alum Cottage, close to the top of a ravine called the Chine running down through the cliffs, was free for immediate occupation. The owner offered to redecorate it for them at his own expense, and the rent was only £60 a year for a seventeen-year lease. They signed at once. Everyone lent a hand in preparing the house – Dorothy supplied furniture that had been in storage since she parted from Irving – and early in August they moved in. Then Curt came along on weekend leave and told them that they could not afford it. They remained there all the same.

Luckily Norman Angell came and stayed nearby for a few days. During the crossing, he had endeared himself to the girls with his calm and quiet attentiveness. Now he went for coast walks with them and introduced them to sailing (always a passion of his) which they enjoyed with nervous excitement. (Cynthia was just learning to swim that summer.) His cheerful good humour soothed Rosalind's bruised soul and she took the opportunity to unburden herself to him about her toxic relationship with Dakyns. Rather than give direct advice, Angell began to invent a story in which she could recognize all the characters, starting with Dakyns and herself, and gain a fresh perspective on them.

Then a letter from Walter arrived for Riss. 'You know I suffer from ideas,' he reminded her.

> The disease has been pretty acute with me lately – and here is an idea that has been keeping me awake at nights when I should be dreaming, and has set me dreaming in the day time when I should be awake. This idea is something special – something if spoken aloud at night to the stars would make them dance in their courses. And there's more in the idea than meets the eye. 'Tis something about which I'm already convinced – something on which I have set my heart: . . . that you should return to America with the girls when they come in September. That you should come over for just a short time – returning home in time to spend Christmas with Mother. If you can come I can promise you your first class boat fare both ways – and all expenses paid over here during your stay – and £100 over and above for yourself. My idea is that you should take part in some public concerts in Boston, New York and Philadelphia – and possibly Chicago – that I am planning. There's a special place for you to fill – something that you can easily do, and something that will prove a strong attraction to the public – of course in Boston and generally throughout the East the opportunity of seeing and hearing the Four Fuller Sisters would ensure packed houses – all the time – everywhere.

He ended with 'I'm longing, longing to see you – and be with you again – Don't disappoint me – will you?'[14]

What he did not mention was that his situation had unexpectedly and radically changed. He had planned to stay at Centre Lovell with Jack and Helen Rae (and their little son Walter) during July, and return to New York in August when the temperature in the city became more bearable. But, much to the annoyance of Mary Breck, who was helping him organize the next season of recitals, Walter hurried back to New York after only a few days. 'You remember,' she complained, 'one great reason you gave for going up with the Raes was that it would save you about $10!' His trip to New York 'upset the scheme by breaking into July and [his] bank account' at the same time. Worse, he returned to stay with the Raes in August. So while she was in the city where it was still 'as hot as a crater,' he was 'picnicking, feeding, tramping, etc.' in the cool of the country.[15] Envy fuelled her annoyance.

The cause of his sudden dash to New York was news from Crystal: she had told him that she was pregnant. We can but imagine the emotion of their meeting. Late in July she accompanied him back to Centre Lovell. On

11 August, Cynthia reported from Bournemouth to Rosalind in London that, according to a letter just received from Walter, Jack Rae had set up a tent for him beside Kezar lake and Crystal was staying at a hotel on the other side. 'A very strange thing – eh??'[16] From there, Crystal travelled to Colorado Springs for the WPP's national conference on 10, 11 and 12 August. After that, she and Walter paid a visit to Glenora where Crystal introduced Walter to her father. And they arranged to get married.

At this point, Walter's feelings were very mixed. Although he was in love with Crystal, he still felt as though he were betraying his love for Riss. Worse, he had got Crystal pregnant without so much as being engaged to her, never mind married. With his strict principles, a wedding was required, as soon as possible, although marriage had never been part of his life plan; he no doubt felt dismay at being forced into it. He was also painfully aware that in the eyes of his parents he had been neglecting his duty towards his sisters. So, mingled with an unfamiliar sense of pride at having sired a child, there was also a good deal of shame. After all, he had been his sisters' moral guide for as long as he could remember. What kind of model was he now?

His most immediate need was to have Riss come out to America to meet and approve of the woman he was going to marry. The 'special place' that he had told her of was at his side and in his heart. But the only way to finance her visit was for Riss to become the Fuller Sisters' harpist once again. So Walter persuaded himself that they could make a fortune by performing as a singing and dancing quartet in the vaudeville theatres,* the New York equivalent to London's musical halls, and he found two agents who showed interest in the idea. After a run in New York, the Sisters could revisit all the venues of their first tour where Riss had been such a success. The more he thought about it, the more realistic a plan it seemed.

His dream fell apart when Basil announced that on no account would he consent to Riss making the trip to America. For Mary Breck's organization of the next tour, it was back to square one – and she was apoplectic. How could she possibly make bookings when Walter changed plans as fast as he moved place? If Walter had been thinking rationally at this point, he would have accepted Mary Breck's proposal to open the next season with four weeks of recitals arranged by an agent – guaranteed income – followed by their own commission-free bookings for the rest of the tour. As before, she

---

* Vaudeville performances generally featured about a dozen individual, unrelated acts: acrobats, comedians, magicians, singers, trained animals, jugglers, and dancers.

would travel with the girls and they would cover her costs. However, Walter was always ruled by his heart rather than his head, and more so at this point than at any other. He stubbornly persisted with the vaudeville idea. As the agents he approached would make no bookings without an audition, he begged his sisters to come over as soon as they could. There was another reason for his impatience, of course: he could not make his confession by letter. He had to see them in person to unburden himself – but how was he to pay for their crossing? He had almost no money at all.

Walter had been living off his sisters' singing, supplemented with a little from the AUAM. Now both sources had dried up: the AUAM had exhausted its funds on the Mexican crisis – in fact, it was talking of disbanding* – and his sisters had not sung since mid-May. So he turned to his friends. Robert Barrett, generous as ever, paid for the girls' tickets, and Jeannette Peabody sent $100 ('all I can spare at present'), adding tartly that the girls needed to start making money *now*.[17] That, of course, was what they were coming to do. Little did they realize, though, how much Walter needed them. Arriving in New York harbour on 7 October 1916, they were astonished to see him climb out of the pilot boat: he had come to greet them on board the *Saint Louis*, an extravagance he could ill afford.

For all Walter's feelings of mingled shame and pride, his sisters found him looking very well, for he had put on several pounds.† They were also stunned to learn that he and Crystal were married. The ceremony had been conducted very discreetly by Crystal's father at Croton four weeks before, on 11 September. The witnesses were Charles Hallinan and Anna Crockett (whom I have not traced). In July 1917, when Rosalind was desperately talking of marrying Dakyns to put an end to his persecution of her, Walter suggested to her that 'The marriage could be just like Crystal's and mine – a bare legal contract with the personal & private agreement and understanding to live together – to give the marriage a chance – for three years.'[18]

As yet, Crystal and Walter had told no one that they were married. His sisters were among the very first to learn of it. Only a month after they arrived did Crystal inform her work colleagues. On 6 November, Margaret Lane, the secretary of the New York WPP, wrote to Albert deSilver, 'It is

---

* Sales of printed copies of the exhibition panels brought in only $210 during September, and that was a good month.

† Some men put on weight when their partner is pregnant. Known as the couvade syndrome, it appears to be more common in relationships where the female is the dominant partner.

good news about Crystal. She is such a wonder that she deserves all the happiness there is.'[19] On the fourteenth, Crystal added a PS by hand to a typed business letter to Jane Addams: 'You know Walter Fuller and I were married? We both send our love.'[20] The same day, the New York *Times* announced that 'friends of Crystal Eastman learned yesterday that she and Walter Fuller are married, although they were reluctant to reveal the date and the place where the ceremony was performed.'[21] Thanks to Crystal's public notoriety, the system of syndicated news, and the wireless telegraph, the news spread like wildfire. Every local rag in the Union ran the story, with slight variations. Beneath a photo captioned 'Mrs Crystal Fuller', the Fort Wayne *Daily News* reported: 'Friends of Miss Crystal Eastman, who even before she divorced Wallace J. Benedict, an insurance man, last winter, insisted upon retaining her maiden name, were greatly surprised today to learn that she has again become a bride, now being married to Walter Fuller, although she still calls herself Crystal Eastman.'[22]

'New Venture Made' headlined the *Oregonian*. 'Radical woman undaunted by one unhappy marriage: No. 2 is taken secretly. Suffragist who refused alimony and who keeps maiden name now is bride of Englishman. . . . When and where the pair were married remains a mystery among the radical society of Washington Square.' After a few lines about Crystal's life and work, it concluded, ironically enough: 'she has been for several years a preacher of the doctrine of birth control,'[23] a highly contentious topic at the time.*

We can guess that the reason for being so discreet about the date of their wedding was to avoid future embarrassment: when Crystal's child was born, no one would be able to count back the months and realize that she had been pregnant when they married. There was another reason for discretion: at that time an American woman who married a foreigner (irrespective of their place of residence) immediately acquired the nationality of her spouse and lost her American citizenship. This happened to Inez Milholland, who was a good friend of both Max and Crystal.† Visiting England to observe the struggle for women's rights at first hand and participate in the Pankhursts'

---

* Doctors were prosecuted for giving advice on contraception, even to married women.

† Educated at Vassar, Inez Milholland was admitted to the New York bar in 1912, specializing in criminal law in favour of the poor. She was one of the women who led the 1913 suffragette march into Washington, riding a white horse and wearing a white cape. (See the website for a photograph.) A pacifist, she sailed on Ford's Peace Ship at the end of 1915. In October 1916, she collapsed while giving a public lecture in Los Angeles and died of pernicious anaemia on 25 November, aged only 31.

campaign, she met and married Eugen Boissevain.* To enable her to get her passport back, Boissevain renounced his British nationality and they took up residence in the States.

On the marriage certificate delivered by the clerk for Croton-on-Hudson, there is no mention of Walter's nationality. As a result of this omission, Crystal retained her American citizenship. It probably saved her from being arrested during the Red Scare of 1919 and even, at the end of that year, from being expelled, along with Walter, when America deported to Russia – regardless of their country of origin – 248 assorted anarchists, socialists, pacifists and radicals.

Once the news of their marriage was out, Walter and Crystal could openly live together. To accommodate Walter's sisters as well, they took a three-bedroomed apartment at 102 Washington Square. As soon as the girls arrived, Crystal tactfully asked Dorothy to help choose the colours for the paintwork and wallpaper. Durr Friedley and Bobby Jones† also gave freely of their advice. When the flat was ready, the girls took turns to be the one who slept out in a nearby hotel.

At last Walter felt he could be more open with Riss. 'Now we are all together again, we're the four happiest people in New York,' he told her.

> Every day we have important consultations together, and make important decisions about this and that, and the other thing, and we all get on together better than ever before. They are more experienced – more balanced – than before. I, too, like to think I have changed for the better. I am more tolerant – better humoured – more experienced, too. We have several hopeful schemes – money-makers all, I think – and the girls are with me – one and all together in hoping and working for their achievement.
>
> Dear, how I wish you could have come over with the girls – I have been wanting you over here all through the year. I have wanted you to see, and know, and give me your judgment on Crystal Eastman – a strange, wonderful, dazzling creature whose path crossed mine for the first time just a year ago. How often have I wondered, 'What would Riss think of her?' and here we are now – with thousands of miles of salt sea between us, and no chance

---

* As we shall see, Eugen Boissevain (1880–1949) became one of Max's best friends. Floyd Dell described him as 'an adventurous man of business, [who] was in private life a playboy with incredible energy, romantic zest, and imagination.'[24]

† Bobby's career was just taking off: he had been invited to design the decor and costumes of *Till Eulenspiegel* for the Ballet Russe – the only American ever to design for them. This production toured the United States and revolutionized modern ballet. Of course, they all went to a performance and were thrilled by Nijinsky.

of a sight of you, or a sound of you, for six months. Oh, what am I to say or do?

Can I describe her? Crystal – she's indescribable. In conventional language, I'm very much in love with her. In some things we are alike: both natural-born Radicals for instance – in some things we are as unalike as chalk and cheese – for instance, I'm a Christian – she isn't (no, no – she's not a Jewess – she simply hasn't got a conventional religious sense – and you know I have one pretty well strongly developed). In some things we agree, in some things we disagree pretty strongly. Physically – she's as tall as I am – and is sturdy and strong – a much finer woman than I am a man! In age she's two months younger than me. She earns her living as secretary of the American Union Against Militarism (£60 a month).* She is also Chairman of the Woman's Peace Party of New York. By profession she is a lawyer – being an LLB of the New York University, and an MA of Vassar College. But these political and academic distinctions do not weigh heavily upon her. She lives them down pretty well, and is, in all respects, none the worse for them. Her Mother died about three or four years ago – her father is a Congregational Minister in a small town – up-State New York – her brother Max Eastman is a well-known socialist and Editor of the *Masses* – a monthly socialist magazine. That is about all to say about her – except that she was married about five years ago to a man named Benedict whom she divorced for desertion in April. I think most people agree that she is really very good-looking, and she is most certainly a very active, keen, intelligent mind. Well dear, despite our manifest glaring differences we get on very well together, she and I. She enjoys my fancy, my wit and humour and suggestiveness, and I her courage, strength of mind and purpose, and her activity.

We know no one in England with whom I can compare her – she is so typically American. During the past year – especially since January – we have seen a lot of one another, she and I. When I was up in Maine with the Raes she came to Centre Lovell for a few days, and later I visited her father's home where she was staying during the summer. I'm trying to give you a very true and faithful conception of her – not a highly-coloured picture – just a simple photograph. Do I think you'd like her? Yes, I do – but oh, how I wish you were here to see and speak for yourself. I'm too old – too tired of

---

* As we have seen, this source had more or less dried up, but she still had a salary from the New York WPP and a certain amount from the *Masses*. According to Max, this amounted to ninety dollars a week – plenty to live on.[25]

Husband

An 'Allegorical sketch of Crystal as the Goddess of Peace, as an arranger of a room, and as a Lawyer' by Dorothy (from a letter home)

the game – to indulge in any ravings about the beloved – I can imagine a lively, restless, unsettled working partnership between Crystal Eastman and me. I think we should help one another – for she has many important and necessary qualities that I do not possess – and I think, in some ways, I can be of help to her. In a modern, middle-aged way I think we are in love with each other. What will happen next? Who can tell?

Dear – I'm tired and sleepy – dearest goodnight.

Your loving Walter[26]

He avoided the word 'marriage' and funked mentioning the pregnancy, although he prepared the way with 'What will happen next?' Moreover, neither he nor his sisters had yet breathed a word of all this to their parents. When he wrote to his mother in mid-October, Walter mentioned Crystal for the first time, admitting that he had seen a lot of her over the past year. 'This summer I visited her father . . . so I think I know her pretty well. . . . I don't want to make another mistake, such as I made a few years ago with Rosamond Impey.'[27] Once this letter was written, the girls were free to mention his 'engagement' to Crystal (a term he had not used) and tell their parents what they thought. 'This is a good step on Walter's part, I think,' wrote Dorothy early in November, 'for never has he seemed more at peace in his mind, or happier – and never have I seen him looking so well and strong.'[28]

However, their parents were not pleased with the news and, as Walter had anticipated, accused him of neglecting his duty. His sisters wrote back that he was looking after them as well as ever, reporting that they found Crystal 'honest, clever, frank and simple – and practical.' She did not defer to Walter, and they admired her as 'someone who doesn't do everything he tells them to (like his sisters)!'[29] 'The more we see of Crystal,' added Cynthia a few weeks later, 'the fonder we grow of her, and her influence over Walter is doing him a lot of good. She understands all his moods and the continual flow of ideas. So, darling, I don't think he is making a mistake. We can't think of anyone we would rather have him love.'[30] Their parents remained unconvinced. It was all too sudden for them.

It was not easy for Crystal either. She clearly adored her impecunious Walter whose wit made her laugh – and 'Crystal loved to laugh,' recalled Roger Baldwin.[31] Together with his love, he gave her 'ingenious, warm, and witty help in promoting the AUAM,' and, as Max observed, provided 'that companionship in idealism for which, with pleasure-bent Bennie as a husband, she had been starving.'[32] Had it been just the two of them, they could probably have scraped along on their limited resources, as newly-weds so often do. But Crystal was providing board and lodging for three penniless sisters-in-law as well, who were surprised when she insisted that there should be no more singing for free. No one had told them how things really stood. A month later, however, the hotel presented a bill for $140, and they discovered to their horror that Walter had only $9 in his bank account. The next morning, Dorothy spent a mere twenty cents on her breakfast, which they always took at a restaurant close by, rather than at the apartment.

The fact is, Walter's hopeful scheme for making money in the vaudeville theatres came to nothing. It was not for want of planning. He had thought up a new programme of country songs and dances with new words and actions that required Constance Binney (for lack of Riss) for the dances, but he was unable to obtain any kind of firm commitment from the agents he approached. Twice he made appointments for his sisters to demonstrate their skills to the great Arthur Hopkins, and twice they were cancelled. Then, at a few hours' notice, Hopkins called for an audition in the Palace Theatre in New York, which from 1913 to 1932 was the premier vaudeville house in the United States. They hurried along and danced and sang for him in the noise and dust raised by workmen preparing the stage for a new show. After days without news, Walter went round to enquire, and was informed by an assistant that they had made a favourable impression. He continued to wait, and to visit, but never heard anything more. The reason, they learned later, was that the Palace would only take on artistes who had a following, and as vaudeville artistes the Fuller Sisters were unknown.

In other circles, they were celebrated. For Farmer's Day, 21 October 1916, President Woodrow Wilson invited some 3000 guests to his summer residence, Shadow Lawn, and asked the Sisters to come and sing for them. Afterwards, while they were having tea with the Wilson family, Cynthia revealed that it was her twentieth birthday. On their return to New York, she received a personally signed card from the President. This performance could have been a great advertisement for the Fuller Sisters, but Walter had not alerted the press beforehand, so it was mentioned in only a few papers. Mary Breck was furious at the lost opportunity and after a fierce argument with Walter she abandoned them to their fate.

Although the girls had a few engagements at their now familiar venues, mostly colleges, and occasional ones at private parties and peace rallies, they were not earning their keep. They approached Mr Pick, an agent they had already worked for (but whom Walter did not like); after blowing hot and cold, he agreed to put them on at the 300-seat Punch and Judy theatre at 155 W. 49th Street. Under Walter's critical eye, they went over every detail of their programme – words, tone, movements, gestures, entries and exits. Bobby Jones provided his expertise. Only a couple of weeks earlier the girls had been admiring his sets and costumes for the Ballet Russe. Now he was advising them on the cut of their dresses, shopping with them for ribbons and trimmings, and arranging the stage backdrop and props. He even came to the theatre on the morning of their opening, 27 November, to check the lighting. And all of this free of charge. Filled with confidence, they opened to a packed audience – meaning that it consisted largely of their friends and admirers. By the following Sunday morning, attendance had dwindled as low as four (and only children at that), and they realized that Pick was not advertising the show at all. He admitted that no tickets had been sold for the coming week. Crystal and a lawyer friend of hers advised them to break the contract. Although Pick dropped them from the Punch and Judy programme, they could not possibly pay the compensation he demanded for breach of contract, so they promised him a commission on the series of recitals they planned to make in Chicago – but they no longer trusted him.

This setback was exacerbated by the unsolicited advice they were receiving from Arthur Dakyns. From his vantage point in London, he assured them that they were mistaken in trying to launch in New York. They should try the provinces first – or even England. Moreover, he 'would willingly stand the risk, up to a certain amount' if they returned to England to try out the public there. 'Think over this proposal among yourselves and don't dismiss it as you usually dismiss my suggestions,' he concluded. In the same letter to Cynthia he recalled how he and Walter had 'quarrelled' in the Cheyne Row flat in 1910, 'and he hasn't forgiven me, I think.' He ended by adding that Rosalind 'is hopeless in letter-writing as in everything else. . . . Tell her that I shall not trouble her with any further letters in the New Year.'[33]

They were desperate for money. The girls set about repairing the breach with Mary Breck; Walter hastened to Philadelphia where he knew he could count on Quaker friends for support. Almost at once he had a booking for them at the Baldwin School for girls at Bryn Mawr, and an invitation for them to spend Christmas with Robert Tait McKenzie and his family, whom they had not seen since he left for England in 1915 and joined the RAMC.*

While his sisters were in Pennsylvania, Walter conjured up a busy programme of recitals for them in the New York area during the last week of 1916 and the first week in January. This was to be followed by a tour in the mid-west with Mary Breck, starting on 9 January, and then a three-week run at the Fine Arts Theatre in Chicago during February. Their new programme featured medieval songs, so the girls wanted medieval-style dresses to go with them. As they could not afford the services of their usual dressmaker, they settled down to make them themselves. They also helped Walter and Crystal paint banners for a massive international peace gathering that Walter organized for New Year's Eve. So it was a busy time for them all.

In the midst of this, there took place a conjunction, not of celestial bodies but human ones, that was to have long-term consequences. Rosalind made love with Crystal's brother, Max. She was just coming up to her twenty-fifth birthday and, for all her sensual nature, her experience of men so far had been limited to a few chaste kisses and discreet fondling. But over the past few months she had started to discover a side of life that all her education had hidden from her. During the summer, her physical restraint had infuri-

---

* Like his childhood friend James Naismith, McKenzie believed in the benefit of sports for young people, so he was happy to advise on the physical training programme for new recruits to the British Army. Then he worked in orthopedics, designing artificial limbs for the wounded. He also spent much time helping plastic surgeon Dr William L. Clark remodel the hands and faces of disfigured soldiers. When the girls stayed at his home, they were shocked to discover, alongside sculptures and paintings, photographs of horrific war wounds.

ated Dakyns, who could not take responsibility for his emotions and blamed her for his own feelings: 'I think what you have in mind,' he wrote,
> is that by not writing to me first, by never making any attempt to see me until I almost force myself on you, and by just taking my kisses without kissing me in return, you will be able to shift all the responsibility of my feelings towards you onto my shoulders.

He went on to predict how he was likely to behave as a result:
> One thing is certain; if you ever do come back from America next year you will find me a very different creature to the one which you invited to Bournemouth three months ago. You will find a poor wretch, half frantic with longing and desire and nervous depression and wholly unlovable.
>
> Well, I suppose that makes you smile, but if you really think it sounds absurd, read any book on the psychology of sex and see what are the mental effects on a man of unsuccessful courtship and how they are the exact reverse of those of successful courtship.[34]

Knowing Rosalind's enquiring mind, we can suppose that she took him up on this and started to read about the psychology of sex. She certainly read a good deal of philosophy at his suggestion, in particular Nietzsche, and this led to discussing morality in her correspondence with Dakyns. He was appalled to discover that she was ready for what she called 'complete union' with a man, and he responded vehemently. 'While I believe, as I have told you often enough, that the act of sex and everything leading up to it, is perfectly harmless and natural and even beautiful *when* there is love between a boy and a girl, it is, on the other hand, *beastly* – something *degrading* and cold as ice – when there is nothing in the minds of the two people except *lust*.'[35] Since he understood that 'you want of me just what many, but busy, selfish men want of a woman, well,' he generously conceded, 'I will give it to you.' Being on the other side of the Atlantic, however, he could not fulfil his offer and cursed the fate that kept them so far apart (adding that it was of course her fault).

That summer, Rosalind had shared her thoughts on the sexual emancipation of women with Curt Dehn, and he had dismissed her as 'a worthless sort of person,' which she well knew was not true.[36] Norman Angell, on the other hand, listened to her theories without judging her. Throughout that autumn, she corresponded with him, expressing the 'tormenting self-questioning' that she experienced as a result of Dakyns' ambivalent behaviour.[37] By way of answer, Angell continued his invented story about Langdon (himself), Ethel (Rosalind) and Dalton (Dakyns; later replaced by another fictional character, Etherington), in which he explored the psychology of the

The young Max Eastman

protagonists and wrote frankly about human sexuality. This was a real eye-opener. When Angell warned Rosalind about sexually transmitted diseases, she responded with incredulity: 'It can't be true of all men – not those I meet.'³⁸ Each chapter of the unfolding story spurred her to tell Angell more about Dakyns and her feelings, and Angell would incorporate the information in the next instalment. This intimate correspondence continued for about eighteen months, an evolving *roman-à-clef* that revealed Angell's own feelings for Rosalind, and she responded by sending him her *amitié amoureuse* (loving friendship – Angell was fluent in French, having lived and worked in Geneva and Paris). By Christmas 1916, Ethel (disguised as a man) was on a sexually charged camping trip with Langdon.

Now Rosalind was living with Walter and Crystal. She had stayed with Dorothy and Hamilton Irving during their marriage, but in England she had experienced nothing like Crystal's open acceptance of her sexuality.

Finally, there was Max Eastman. A tall, handsome, loose-limbed man, he was more liable to drape himself elegantly over a sofa than to sit upright in a chair. He had married Ida Rauh in 1911 and realized at once that he had made a mistake. By the end of 1916, they were living part and he was savouring his new-found freedom.* His flat being close to 102 Washington Square, he would sometimes drop by for the simple pleasure of seeing the Fuller girls' pretty faces. 'They were lovely in three different ways and brimming with melody like birds in a bush, and their tours were quite an event in the history of song.'[39] Rosalind was his favourite, though.

> I could not help thinking how neat it would be if I divorced Ida and fell in love with Rosalind. Indeed I did fall in love with Rosalind whenever she stepped forth from the trio to sing 'She's gone with the wraggle-taggle gypsies, oh!' That song made me want to go and take her in my arms and carry her to the extreme rim of the universe. . . . But I did not try to express it to her.[40]

According to him, Crystal was aware that Rosalind 'was just on the edge of opening like a tulip into thirsty bloom,'[41] but it was in all innocence that one afternoon she asked Rosalind to step round to Max's flat to see if he would like to come for supper that evening. Max was in bed, recovering from 'flu. And without further ado, Rosalind slipped out of her clothes and into his bed.

For each of them it was a pivotal event in their lives. Shortly afterwards, Max recorded in a notebook that 'my life began in January 1917.'[42] Thirty years later, they both wrote rapturously of that moment when a 'jewel of inconstant, intermittent, irresponsible, and yet indestructible love was born.' In his autobiography, Max wrote that

> Rosalind was of great moment to me because her joy in life is unwounded with fear and compunction. I needed to be reassured that my avid thirst of experience, and my belief in the freedom to have it, were not abnormal and base. I needed to find flowerlike beauty and exquisite fineness of stem and of spirit in a friend who shared my thirst and went all the way with me in my belief. It was as though God sent a young angel direct to my bedside to explain how the saints had misunderstood Him. [The angel] was only my sister-in-law; she had walked only two blocks to get there; and the message she

---

* Max and Ida separated permanently, and their divorce was pronounced in 1922.

brought was most casual. Her eyes, however, were incredibly blue, and their lashes were like petals of an aster; her cheeks glowed brightly against a dark fur, and her lips and teeth as she spoke shone red and white like the halves of a fresh winter apple. My heart was beating violently before she reached my bedside, and she was trembling when she touched my brow. . . . Our love has been like a mountain brook that trickles a little way glistening from its source, and then disappears under the earth and under a leafy and luxuriant forest, but after a while emerges in the valley and flows with increasing volume, still glistening joyfully, all the way to the sea.[43]

When he showed Rosalind a proof of this passage, she wrote back:

Happy, happy thought of Crystal's to send me to bid you come to dinner – I remember how I trembled with excitement when I walked from the door to your bed. I remember the walk along to your house – but I cannot remember the walk back. I think I floated on a vivid stream of joy. I remember singing as I got tidied for dinner. I wanted to sing loud above the noise of New York – it was a song like the skylark that tumbles out a never-ending stream of gay turbulent sound – and from then until now and on into the future that song will be in me – the song of you.[44]

In her own autobiography, written when she was in her sixties and seventies, she declared: 'he had lighted a flame in me that could never be put out.'[45] It was a flame that needed feeding, and they would make love whenever they met, right up until Max's death in 1968. That was not enough, though, for Rosalind; she was to have many, many partners in her lifetime.

Had Walter known of this liaison, he would have been horrified. Unlike Max, who freely admitted that, from his own experience, 'of all Freud's plain and fancy inventions, the concept of an "incest barrier" was one of the most easily verifiable,'[46] Walter would not have recognized a sexual component in his relationship with his sisters. Yet when he kissed them, it was full on the mouth. Since he had almost completely repressed his sexuality, it took a bold woman like Crystal to awaken it. Her lack of inhibition no doubt inspired the iconoclast Rosalind to leap the barrier. Having sex with her brother-in-law was displacement; many years later, she made love with Walter's son and commented, 'It was like having Walter.'[47]

Before Rosalind and her sisters left for their tour, she and Max managed to sneak in a few more trysts without anyone noticing. But when they started to write to each other, Rosalind's refusal to let her sisters see Max's letters made them suspicious. Dorothy expressed her concern to Walter, but his mind was elsewhere at the time, for his child had just been born and Crystal was very ill. So the matter was dropped.

Having settled his sisters' immediate future, Walter concentrated on peace work. He had been active on numerous fronts throughout the autumn. To start with, there must have been a great many informal meetings with like-minded friends that went unrecorded, as well as animated discussions round the supper table with the Eastmans and their many friends. On 25 and 26 October, he was alongside Crystal at a conference (hosted by the Church Peace Union) in Taylor Chapel, New York, attended by some seventy-five persons in a private capacity from twenty of the main peace societies, including John Haynes Holmes (Moral Resistance League); Manley Hudson* (Missouri Peace Society; International Polity Clubs); Paul Kellogg (AUAM); Louis Lochner (as General secretary of the Neutral Conference for Continuous Mediation); Lella Faye Secor (of the Executive Committee of the American Neutral Conference Committee) and Rebecca Shelly (as Secretary of the same); plus Lilian D. Wald and Hollingsworth Wood, both of the AUAM. A committee of nine was appointed to continue the work of the conference, as the Associated Movements for the Establishment of World Justice through World Organization. At the first meeting of this committee, ten resolutions were adopted, ranging from the revival of the Court of Arbitral Justice, which was to be completed and established as an International Court of Justice, to the institution of physical education rather than military training in elementary and secondary schools.

Walter was also constantly seeding both the AUAM and the WPP with his novel ideas and approaches. He had long felt that immigrants who still had ties with their country of origin, especially those from the Central Powers, could be counted on to support the peace movement. For them, war against Germany would mean fighting against parents, brothers, sisters, or cousins – which Jane Addams called 'exquisite torture'[49] and Theodore Roosevelt heartlessly dismissed as 'nonsense and criminal nonsense to boot,' adding, 'We can have no fifty-fifty allegiance in this country.'[50] Walter was one of the initiators of a Conference of Oppressed or Dependent Nationalities which was held in the context of the WPP Annual Convention in Washington on 10 and 11 December 1916. It enabled representatives of more than a dozen European countries to voice their concerns. It also led to the creation of an ephemeral League of Small and Subject Nations.

* Manley O. Hudson (1894–1960), who was a great admirer of the Fuller Sisters, became a member of the Permanent Court of Arbitration and a judge of the Permanent Court of International Justice from 1936 to 1946; he was twice nominated for the Nobel Peace Prize. Of the other committee members, we should note that Paul Kellogg was a devoted friend and supporter of Crystal.[48]

He was on the American Neutral Conference Committee that tried to bring Bertrand Russell over to lecture in the United States. In the event, Russell was refused a visa, so he wrote a letter to Woodrow Wilson. Knowing that it would not pass the censors, he arranged for a girl to smuggle it across to America where the Committee presented it to the President on 23 December and ensured it was published in the press.

As the war clouds gathered, Walter felt the need to demonstrate popular resistance to war. Meeting on 5 January 1917, the joint conference of American Peace Societies recommended to the executive committee of the AUAM a scheme that he had thought up. His idea was to send tens of thousands of registered voters, irrespective of their political opinion or allegiance, postcards printed with a text rejecting war with Germany and demanding that US citizens be consulted by referendum before war could be declared. An accompanying letter invited electors who agreed with the text to sign the cards and send them to their senator. Immediately dubbed 'the postcard referendum', the proposal was carried unanimously.

The idea was not entirely new. Over the previous decade or so, small groups in Britain and America had sometimes consulted their members by postcard. Walter's proposal was on a far larger scale and dealt with far more important issues. The first mailing was to 100,000 registered electors in five congressional districts in different parts of the country. The returned cards revealed strong majorities in favour of an advisory referendum and against going to war. On 10 February, Charles Hallinan recommended to an emergency meeting of the executive committee* that the postcard referendum be extended by a further 100,000 electors. The Cincinnati branch of the WPP helped by handing out cards to the people who came to see the War-against-War Exhibition which they displayed during March.

At the same meeting, Paul Kellogg presented 'a suggestion in writing from Mr Walter Fuller with regard to the possibility of putting into practice in the present emergency the economic non-intercourse doctrine of Norman Angell.'[51] This was referred to a sub-committee. Four days later, at a regular meeting, a letter was read in support of Walter's suggestion. Then, following an encouraging report on the results of the postcard referendum, it was agreed to send him a letter of thanks for giving the Committee 'the unique and very valuable idea' of consulting people by this means.

Soon after this, the New York branch of the WPP managed to unite the

---

* Norman Thomas (1884–1968), who was soon to employ Walter as an editor, was present at this meeting by special invitation.

city's various peace societies in an Emergency Peace Federation. At a joint conference over 22–23 February, the proposed slogan, 'No war without a referendum' failed to obtain a majority. Instead it was agreed to send a delegation, that included Jane Addams, Lillian Wald, Emily Greene Balch, Paul Kellogg, Amos Pinchot, and William Hull (the professor of history at Swarthmore who, like Max, had been one of Wilson's students), to meet with the President. He received them on 28 February and several of the points they made echoed Walter's ideas. In particular Jane Addams emphasized the anxiety and distress of German and Austrian émigrés in the United States. Max Eastman presented a statement on behalf of the AUAM. No official record was made of the President's response, but the delegates came away with divided feelings as to his desire to find a peaceful solution to the conflict. They followed up this meeting with a letter to the President on 8 March 1917.

In the course of the previous autumn, the girls mentioned more than once in their letters home that Crystal was encouraging Walter to do more writing. We should remember that their relationship began when they collaborated on a film script. What happened to it is not known, but in the spring of 1916 the screenwriter C. Gardner Sullivan outlined a scenario that matched their aims and intentions. It became Thomas Ince's spectacular film, *Civilization*, launched to rave reviews in September 1916. According to one reviewer it achieved just what Walter would have wished:

> After seeing *Civilization* one can truthfully say that had Henry Ford produced a film like this one that Ince directed, and sent it broadcast throughout the civilized world as an argument against war, he would have accomplished more for universal peace than did his famous 'peace expedition.' He would have reached the great mass of people who have but a faint recollection of the horrors of war, and would have showed them the pain and the suffering and the sorrow that war brings with it. Had such a picture as *Civilization* been shown to the people of Europe before the war started there would have been no war.[52]

The following year – after America had declared war on Germany – the CPI banned the film.

On 4 October, the New York WPP sponsored a special showing of *Civilization* in a New York cinema. The AUAM took the opportunity to send panels from Walter's exhibition (which was touring various states, including Ohio and Minnesota, at this time) to Thomas Ince, with the suggestion that he might use some of them in connection with advertising the film.

Crystal proved persuasive: Walter contributed an article about war to the January issue of the *Masses* and one on folksong to the *Survey* for 20 January 1917.[53] (Both are posted on this book's website.) His contribution to the *Masses,* 'The Lady with the Lamp', is a chilling denunciation of war. Faithful to his conviction that people are more likely to reject armed conflict if the victims are given names and faces, he invited the reader to

> Suppose that all the male members of the royal families of the warring nations, and all the Premiers and Presidents and Cabinets, and all the Army Councils and Commanders in Chief and their staffs, and the Editors of all the leading journals, and the Presidents of all the big Banks, were compelled to go up to the front line trenches – and stay there.... Undoubtedly some of them would be killed outright – perhaps Asquith and King Albert and Count Zeppelin and the Editors of the *Outlook* and the *Fatherland* and *Punch*. The rest of them would be more or less badly wounded.[54]

He went on to confront the reader with horrific descriptions of dying soldiers borrowed from Ellen la Motte's book, *The Backwash of War,* which had been published a few months previously. Working as a nurse in army hospitals close to the front in Belgium, la Motte recorded what she saw with unflinching lucidity and frankness. Walter's article drew attention to her book and it was reprinted several times. Then Max promoted it in the *Liberator* (which took over from the *Masses* in 1917), but since it courageously faced up to the reality of war, *The Backwash of War* was banned as soon as the United States joined the conflict. It was not republished until 1934.

When Crystal encouraged Walter to write, he no doubt told her that he was happier editing than writing. From early January 1917, she provided him with a 'fully equipped' office at 32 Union Square.[55] This was not the address of the WPP headquarters, but it was where Max had his private office* from January 1918 onwards.[56] There was also a secretary to whom Walter dictated his letters, including those addressed to his sisters, but – he assured them – their letters to him remained strictly personal and were read by no one else. And what was he editing? It happens that, on 27 January 1917, the New York branch of the WPP launched a fortnightly periodical, *Four Lights,* written and edited by a handful of its members. Subtitled 'An Adventure in Internationalism,' it aimed 'to voice the young, uncompromising woman's peace movement in America, whose aims are daring and immediate – to stop the war in Europe, to federate the nations for organized peace . . . and to guard

---

* The *Liberator* letterhead carried an address on W. 13th Street, so it may well be that Max took over Walter's office when he no longer had a use for it.

democracy from the subtle dangers of militarism.'[57] *Four Lights* rapidly gained a reputation for being 'remarkably clever' (Starr Jordan), 'a journal of truth and sense in a time when many have gone mad' (Carolus P. Harry) and 'better than anything that has come to my desk for some time' (Scott Nearing). Others considered it 'a foolish, dangerous, unthinking, un-American and disreputable paper' that 'ought not to be tolerated in any self-respecting community' (Charles M. Sheafe, Jnr).[58] In short, it had an impact out of all proportion to its modest four pages per issue. I believe that the person behind it was Walter Fuller.

Although his name appears nowhere in the pages of *Four Lights,* the stamp of his handiwork is writ large on every one of them. First of all, a periodical does not come into existence by spontaneous generation. It takes someone to imagine it, design it, decide on its periodicity, and so on. Each issue bore the names of two or three different women as editors; some of them barely knew the others; few participated more than once. None ever subsequently claimed credit for editing it – or even writing for it. If only to provide continuity of style and layout, someone – and preferably someone accustomed to editing and to seeing a periodical through the press – was needed to oversee it through twenty consecutive issues. Although the thirty or forty women whose names appear in *Four Lights* were well educated and some of them had been published before, few had any experience of editing, and none is remembered for the quality of her prose or verse, her ironic humour, or her outspokenness. Yet *Four Lights* is treasured for just these qualities by historians of periodicals (and not just those produced by women). For Van Wienen, 'Despite its modest format, the magazine deserves comparison with better-known avant-garde literary magazines such as *Blast, Others,* and *Seven Arts* that had similarly brief runs.'[59]

Years later, Norman Thomas recalled Walter's ability to transform other people's writing:

> He could take an article which contained valuable ideas, expressed in a stilted, wooden or colourless style, and make that article a LIVING THING. It used to be amusing to see how many writers complacently assumed that the article, after this treatment, was their own, unchanged.[60]

The person behind *Four Lights* conjured into existence better writing than ever before or since in the lives of the respective contributors, including Madeleine Doty's only published short story.

Four Lights contained many short unsigned items with witty and ironical titles. In the words of Erika Kuhlmann,

> the *Four Lights*' editors adopted a strategy of reprinting news items from the

daily press and then topping the story with a mocking headline. Editors Joy Young and Anne Herendeen reprinted a news item about the Red Cross: 'The American Red Cross is the big brother of the army and the navy.' The title to this snippet read, in bold letters, 'WE THOUGHT IT WAS A GIRL.' Young's and Herendeen's sense of irony undoubtedly came from their reading of numerous Red Cross recruitment and propaganda posters, which featured women nurses eagerly signing up to join the war effort. By speaking of the organization in male terms, the daily paper overlooked female domination of the Red Cross. *Four Lights*' title suggested that women's work went unrealized by the press and that the Red Cross recruitment posters fooled women into expecting recognition for their work.[61]

Ironical titles and the denunciation of sexism – and racism and militarism on other pages – featured in every issue, so they cannot be attributed to any particular pair or trio of named editors. On the other hand, brief news items with titles that were variously found to be witty, sardonic, ironical, or flippant, are a hallmark of Walter's editing.

These short summaries of news items or snippets from a wide range of newspapers constituted on average half of each issue of *Four Lights*. Some readers joked that it provided them with an international clipping service. Issue number four was all news items; there were no signed pieces at all, except for a policy statement on the last page – '*Four Lights* believes war to be the stupidest of all old-fashioned illusions' – followed by the names of the three editors. A typical item told how

> a student at the College of Liberal Arts, Syracuse University, was taken from his room in Sims Hall, one of the dormitories, May 18, by a mob of students, who declared he had committed an unpatriotic act when he burned a paper napkin on which was printed an American flag. He was thrown into an automobile, driven to the outskirts of the city and then pummelled until insensible. He was left at the hospital without explanation.[62]

This was headed, SAVE SOILED NAPKINS. *Webster* tells us that between 1910 and 1920 women's sanitary towels were usually called *sanitary napkins*, or simply *napkins*, so the punning title was particularly apposite in a periodical supposedly written and edited entirely by women.

These unsigned items were often linked, explicitly or implicitly. Contrasting titles include 'Preparing for Peace' versus 'Preparing for War' and 'Red Bloods' versus 'Molly-Coddles' ('Which are you?'). Sometimes the irony arose simply from their position on the page:

> The June 2 issue offered a number of news fragments [that] the editors reprinted alongside each other. Below the headline, 'Little Words of Love'

(also an ironic title), the editors printed President Wilson's conversation with Representative Thomas Heflin (D-Alabama): 'There is no hate in our hearts for the German people.' The editors then described a number of German workers whose US employers had discharged them because of their ethnicity. The next item, under the title, 'Still More War Horrors,' described Lord Beresford's reaction at London's Savoy Hotel when he discovered he had been eating off plates made in Germany. He and a number of guests hurled their dinnerware to the floor.[63]

By this means, *Four Lights* pointed out the fallacy of Wilson's words. The truth was printed (with bitter insight) in issue six, dated 7 April and therefore written only days before America declared war on Germany: 'If we've got to fight Germany, we've got to hate Germany. Hate as well as ammunition has to be manufactured in preparation for war.' The statement was not signed.

The pages of *Four Lights* reflect salient features of Walter's exhibition: maps, cartoons, and contrasting tabular data. One piece, printed in the first issue and signed by Edna Kenton, took up one of his favourite ideas: we are prisoners of the belief that borders 'can separate the nations of Earth' when in reality 'boundary lines are as imaginary as the equatorial line.' Each issue repeats ideas from the exhibition. The slogan on the front of the first issue – 'to guard democracy from the subtle dangers of militarism' – echoes Walter's words to Riss: 'democracy is at stake. If the United States is militarized, then indeed is freedom dead.'[64]

The centre spread of most issues featured a piece of artwork, often cartoons borrowed from other publications, including the *Masses*. Two or three of them were specially drawn and the commissioning letters reveal how the editor had a precise idea of what he wanted.* To Boardman Robinson, one of the main contributors to the *Masses*, he wrote that he wanted to make the issue dated 28 July 'a mourning number', as it would come out close to 4 August 1917, 'the anniversary of the declaration of war.'

> I am anxious to have a frieze in silhouette, very black, running straight across the top of the inside pages. This frieze should be a procession of mourning figures – widows with little children dragging at their skirts, bent

---

* A few letters survive in the archives of the WPP. They are all singularly anonymous, not to say anonymized; they do not read like letters written by women to other women. Unlike most WPP correspondence, the carbon copies were not made on headed notepaper, and the name of the signatory is missing. None have an office code, such as the initials of the writer and the typist, at the foot. A few announce that they were 'dictated and not read', meaning that the typist signed the letter on behalf of the writer.

Walter Fuller

The masthead of *Four Lights*

old people and crippled soldiers. Some of the figures might represent by their costumes some of the different nationalities that are engaged in the war, but all of them to be very gloomy and broken with grief.⁶⁵

The idea of mourning this anniversary of the outbreak of WWI in Europe – not the entry of the United States into the war – was one of Walter's first suggestions as a peace activist, and the procession of women and children echoes the closing tableau of his exhibition. For a fee of $25, Robinson came up with a memorable drawing which was printed immediately above the names of the belligerent countries, listed in the order of their participation in the war.†

For all its proclaimed internationalism, *Four Lights* had a decidedly British slant. Beside British newspapers and parliamentary reports, it quoted from British rather than American authors in a ratio of something like five to one. Issue five quotes from: Bertrand Russell's Letter to President Wilson (mentioned above); H. G. Wells; George Bernard Shaw; Thomas Hardy; R. C. Hale and Richard le Gallienne – and also, just once, Mark Twain. In issue fifteen (dated 11 August) we find Rudyard Kipling, H. G. Wells, George Bernard Shaw, Frederick C. Howe – and excerpts from an article by George Naismith. It recommends Norman Angell's 'Aiding the Enemy's Diplomacy' and Brailsford's 'War on Steel and Gold.'

All these signs point to Walter as the mastermind – at the least – behind *Four Lights*. Its title alludes to Antonio Pigafeta's account of Magellan's *First*

---

* The frieze is reproduced in Mark Van Wienen's *Partisans and Poets: the political work of American poetry in the Great War*. He devotes eleven pages to *Four Lights*.

Voyage Round the World (1519–22), in which we learn that Magellan showed four lights 'when he wished the other ships to set full sail and follow in his wake.' This was quoted on the masthead of the periodical, alongside a drawing of a galleon in full sail, showing four lights from her stern. According to the WPP, the editors had made internationalism their goal and '*Four Lights* is their announcement that they have set full sail.'[66] In concept and execution it was about as Walterish a venture as can be imagined, on a par with sailing with his sisters to sing folksongs in the New World.

In July, the WPP was honoured with a visit from a representative of the Department of Justice. He came to find out how many of the editors of *Four Lights* were German. Margaret Lane, the WPP's office manager, resented the assumption that 'outspoken lovers of Liberty and Peace' could not be found among Americans. She rustled up brief biographical notices of twenty-eight contributors and printed them on a sheet loosely inserted into the next issue of *Four Lights*.* Half of them were potential Daughters of the American Revolution. Undeterred, issue seventeen thumbed its nose at government interference: it offered to 'lend Mr Burleson a hand' by printing quotations from the *Arbeiter Zeitung* (Vienna); *Vorwärts* (Berlin); *National-Zeitung* (probably from Munich rather than Basel); *Az Est* and *Magyar Orizag* (Budapest); the *Hamburger Fremdenblatt*; and the *Frankfurter Zeitung*. (Not exactly daily reading for DARs.) Issue nineteen even proposed to 'lend Mr Burleson to the Kaiser.'

The radical stance and irreverent, ironical humour of *Four Lights* undermined the reputation of both the New York WPP and Crystal herself, for everyone assumed that *Four Lights* reflected her opinions.† In the event, she neither accepted nor denied this. She and Walter no doubt discussed its contents, but its tone was definitely Walter's, not hers.

Two pieces in the 'Sister Susie number'‡ of 14 July upset many people by

---

* This document is my sole source of contemporary information about some of the contributors.

† Critics continue to make this assumption today. *Portraits of American Women* (1998) blithely affirms that 'Crystal Eastman was directly responsible for its tone, and it was the official paper of the organization over which she presided.'[67] The *Encyclopedia of Women Social Reformers* (2001) even states that 'During the war, Eastman wrote regular articles for the WPP newsletter *Four Lights*'[68] – yet her name appears not once in its pages.

‡ In England, 'Sister Susie's Sewing Shirts' was a popular 1914 tongue-twisting song about soldiers who would rather wear thistles than Sister Susie's shirts. It is another example of the British perspective of the periodical.

criticizing the women who served the war effort. The first, by Katharine Anthony,* pointed out that, before the war, women wage-earners were already leading a precarious existence.

> Now, the danger has been suddenly intensified by the peculiarly infantile form of patriotism of those who have been dubbed 'Sister Susies' in England and who threaten to dump their unskill and inexperience on the disturbed labor market of this country.
>
> Innocent of economics, societies of well-to-do women – 'militias of mercy' and the like – are distributing wool and urging women to knit and sew for the soldiers. In spite of the common report that the sailors use the knitted garments for cleaning guns and swabbing decks; in spite of the statement of a British officer who openly advised the guardsmen for the good of their feet to refuse to wear home-knit socks; in spite of the fact that the government has ordered three and a half million pairs of socks; – the knitting goes merrily on.[69]

She concluded that 'women should think twice before launching projects which must finally result in throwing other women out of work.'

The second piece, by Katharine Anthony's partner Elisabeth Irwin (founder of the Little Red House School in 1921), dealt with national efforts to regulate food supplies and prevent shortages. She started out by dividing American women into 'those who accept their position beside the garbage cans as they have always accepted what God and man has put upon them to endure' and 'those who fail to see the crux of the food situation in the gospel of the clean plate.' After these strong words, she went on to attack Herbert Hoover's Food Administration for suggesting that women were wasting food, when in reality 'bushels of peas and rows of lettuce are being plowed under because their price is too low to satisfy the food speculators.' She reported that when a Mrs Rogers protested that women were not responsible for this wholesale waste of food, Herbert Hoover had complained that 'this woman's attitude is one that we simply cannot stand for.' With these words, observed Ms Irwin, he revealed 'the cloven hoof of the military dictator.' His 'naughty little temper,' she continued, 'is bound to be encountered by any of his co-operators except the most docile plate-lickers and unremitting garbage-guarders.'[70]

This language deeply offended women like Jane Addams who collaborated with the Food Administration. The number and value of donations to

---

* Like Crystal, Katharine – sometimes spelled Katherine – Susan Anthony (1877–1965) was a member of the feminist New York-based Heterodoxy Club.

the New York WPP began to dwindle. Lack of funds and disagreement among the contributors – Florence Guertin Tuttle wanted to supply articles that would fill several consecutive issues – caused *Four Lights* to be suspended after the issue for 20 October 1917. By this time Walter was busy with other projects. Is it a coincidence that the masthead image of the sailing ship was absent from the last two issues?

Of course Walter sent a copy of his folksong article to his sisters. They were having a very successful tour with Mary. At the University of North Dakota they delivered 'a program of unmingled joys, a feast to the eyes, to the ear, and to the soul. . . . Their voices are sweet, clear and of delicate natural beauty. . . . They sing so spontaneously that one feels they are enjoying it as much as their hearers, and that is saying a great deal.'[71] In the course of their travels, they met Crystal's eldest brother Anstice, who now called himself Peter. He sent her a loving message: 'If Walter Fuller is half as nice as his sisters, don't reform him!'[72] Then they returned to Chicago where the War-against-War Exhibition was running.

There they gave a series of concerts arranged by Mr Pick. Walter told them, should they need legal advice in their dealings with him, to consult a pacifist lawyer that he was acquainted with. They did so, devoting the best part of two mornings to discussions with him, and in the end the contract with Pick was amicably concluded. The lawyer was Clarence Darrow, a man of wit and deep humanity who was to become one of the most famous criminal defence lawyers in America.* Not one of his clients was executed. He has gone down in history as the defender of John T. Scopes in the notorious 'Monkey Trial' of 1925, the subject of numerous books and films.

In Chicago, the girls saw a good deal of Kathleen Wheeler. She designed a poster for them, made a bust of Rosalind and also a now well-known one of Clarence Darrow. (Was this in lieu of payment for his services to the Sisters?)

Their Chicago recitals were a triumph, thanks in part to Walter's advice. 'Oh, Walter,' exclaimed Rosalind in a letter, 'how the actions you suggested for Clerk Tammas and all the other songs – how they are liked. They really do help the songs enormously!'[73] The medieval songs were a great success too, helped by the new dresses. Rosalind pointed out to Walter that

---

* Clarence Darrow (1857–1938) gave Rosalind a signed copy of his first book, *A Persian Pearl and Other Essays* (1902). It contains essays on Omar Khayyam's *Rubaiyat*, Walt Whitman, Robert Burns, realism in literature and art, and the importance of facing up to past mistakes without fear or shame – advice which Rosalind seems to have taken.

you can use your whole body to express the song and not only arms and head as in the crinolines. I remember how actions you suggested that looked very good when done in dressing gowns were unconvincing in crinolines. . . . There is no doubt that people love a change of costumes . . . it makes people take notice – because many people use their eyes more than their imaginations.'[75]

By the end of February they had made enough money to send £20 back home to their parents, although they still had debts left over from the disastrous start of the season in the autumn.

That day, a glowing review by Glenn Aumont appeared in the *Kalamazoo Gazette*. Although 'ordinary terminology does not seem to suffice' to express 'an experience where the impression lies deeply within us, and we do not choose to tell of it in words,' he noted how the Fuller girls' performance had improved over the years. He also described the carefully calculated by-play (thanks again to Walter) that increased the impact of their recitals:

Could anything be more enjoyable than the (seeming) indecision, the whispered conferences, and the admirable attitude of listening to each other? It is all so authentic, so unprepared that one comes away quite convinced that here, at last, is something that expresses personalities that refuse to be governed by anything that has gone before.[74]

After Chicago, they moved on to Pittsburgh and Philadelphia. In Pittsburgh, where the girls sang to an almost full hall of 2000 people, their paths crossed Cecil Sharp's. He had arrived in America on 7 March to raise funds for his research by lecturing and teaching folk dancing. The sisters took the opportunity to invite him and Maude Karpeles to dine with them. Sharp noted in his diary, 'dined with Fuller sisters' – without further comment.[76]

A week later, Walter suddenly stopped writing to them.

7

Father

> Though I've become a terrible letter writer,
> I'm still a good thinker.[1]
> Walter Fuller

> When you have to make a speech these days, it is very hard to decide what it is safe to say. When anybody tries to stop the war, he gets arrested for disturbing the peace.
> When anybody questions whether we are fighting a war for liberty, he gets knocked on the head and deprived of his own liberty in order to prove to him that we are.[2]
> Max Eastman

Walter holding Jeffrey

CRYSTAL WAS EXPECTING for mid-to-late April 1917. At a WPP committee meeting on 14 March, an indignant participant insisted that she should call herself 'Mrs Somebody.' At home, Mr Somebody's conscience was troubling him. Receiving a letter from Riss, he told her,

> I cannot open it until I have written to you – written to you just a word of love. How I do love you – how I do long to see you – to be with you – to live with you. These long silences of mine mean nothing as to any wavering of my love for you. You know that, don't you? You do not doubt me? I am heartsick at this long separation....
>
> Never think for a moment that I am not in daily – yes, in daily – spiritual communion with you.[3]

Crystal, meanwhile, was feeling thoroughly unwell. By 12 March, her doctor was adamant that because of high blood pressure she was to do absolutely nothing more until the child was born. Four days later she had convulsions, which suggests eclampsia. She was rushed to a hospital at 3 Riverside Drive and in the course of an operation on 19 March was delivered of a 'very puny, weak child.'[4] At first the doctors feared for her life, and she remained critically ill for several days. Consequently all Walter's attention was for her and he told his sisters nothing of the baby. Nor did he send any news to Riss or his parents. Gradually the condition of both mother and child, named Jeffrey Sterling Fuller,* improved. As soon as they were well enough to leave hospital, Walter took them up to the little house in Croton to benefit from the country air.† They decided to remain there until the end of the summer, sub-letting their apartment in Washington Square.

On 30 March, Dorothy was apparently still unaware of the child's gender for she wrote to Walter asking, 'But how about the poor little baby? Is it still alive?'[5] She learned it had been 'slightly injured' during the operation and 'prematurely born', with the result that it was 'a little paralysed down one side of its face.... I know Walter is very disappointed, though he won't say so,' she wrote when she broke the news to Riss early in April. 'And he is a little ashamed of it, I believe.' Crystal, on the other hand, was 'pathetically fond of it.' One reason for continuing to refer to Jeffrey as 'it' may be found in Dorothy's next comment: 'I won't write any more about the newcomer, until we are sure that he is going to live on this earth.' She was protecting

---

* Walter no doubt wished to endow his son with the admirable qualities that 'sterling' denotes. He later styled himself Jeffrey Eastman Fuller.

† I do not know if this was Max's house, or their own. In *Love and Revolution* (p.65), he mentions that Walter and Crystal bought a house close to his, without indicating a date.

herself, trying not to become too attached to her nephew in case he did not survive. When she visited Crystal in hospital – the only one of Walter's sisters allowed to do so – the baby looked up and smiled at her, and she 'fell in love with him on the spot.'[6] 'I *do* hope it will get alright and live – because Walter is so fond of children – and it is a boy – and coming from Walter and Crystal *he* [her emphasis] certainly ought to be a genius!'[7]

Out of respect for her brother, Riss did not pass on the news to her parents, so they learned of the birth of their first grandchild only through a telegram that Dorothy sent them on 20 April. Clearly, Walter was embarrassed to report the birth of a child when he had barely admitted to being married to Crystal and was still protesting, 'I dearly, dearly love you best of all' to his mother and 'you are always the nearest and dearest to me' to Riss. Thus both he and his sisters continued for months to refer to Jeffrey as 'Crystal's baby'. The Fuller parents cabled Crystal their congratulations, and she was very touched. 'Walter said she cried for joy.'[8] Her own mother being dead, it meant a lot to her to feel that she had the support of Walter's mother.

During these early months of 1917, a series of events and influences combined to push President Wilson into declaring war on Germany, much to the consternation of all those (of both parties) who had voted for him in the belief that the slogan 'He kept us out of war' would continue to hold true.* Somewhat half-heartedly he encouraged the warring parties to accept 'peace without victory'. The Entente rejected Germany's proposal for peace talks and demanded the return of all occupied territories. The Zimmermann telegram revealed that if America entered the war, Germany wanted Mexico to open a second front in an attempt to recover its lost territory in Texas, New Mexico, and Arizona. The final blow came when Germany announced that it would resume unrestricted submarine warfare in the Atlantic, and confirmed it by sinking three US ships on the same day. When the 65th Congress opened on 2 April 1917, President Wilson asked for a declaration of war, arguing that the United States needed to 'safeguard the rights of mankind' and 'make the world safe for democracy.'†

No one knows what percentage of the American population was opposed

---

*   The slogan was in fact a creation of Wilson's campaign managers, and he had tried to call it back.

†   In the June issue of the *Masses*, Max courageously affirmed: 'It is not a war for democracy,' even though he was well aware that other people had already gone to prison for expressing such 'an unpleasant truth about one's country.'

to going to war. The postcard referendum in February suggested that it was very high. Charles Hallinan reported from Washington:

> From Toledo alone, 614 returns have indicated 507 people against the war, 107 in favour of it. Congressman Tavenner of Illinois reports returns from his district fifteen to one against war; and Congressman Bailey of Pennsylvania, who had 6000 referendum cards distributed in his district, declares sentiment against hostilities 'overwhelming'.[9]

According to Oswald Garrison Villard, two separate polls were taken of Congress in March and 'both confirmed the fact that, if there could have been a secret ballot, a large majority would have voted against our going to war.'[10] Senator La Follette declared that 'if the people had a chance to vote, they would register their opposition ten to one.' Countering President Wilson's claim that the German Government had gone to war without 'the previous knowledge or approval' of the German people, Senator Vardaman maintained that it could be 'no less reprehensible for the President of the United States and Congress to involve their constituents in war without their consent.'[11] But Wilson had already intimidated the opposition. The Senate approved the declaration on 4 April by a vote of 82 to 6, and on 6 April the House of Representatives passed the resolution with 373 votes for and 50 against. The President signed the declaration of war on 6 April 1917.

This re-opened the split that had divided all those who campaigned for women's rights and peace since 1914. Now the question had become: was it patriotic to oppose war? Even in March, as a result of the Threats against the President Act which Congress passed on 14 February, the WPP in Cincinnati had wondered, as they prepared to open the War-against-War Exhibition, whether it might be misconstrued as antagonistic towards the President. By April the pacifists' dilemma was starkly clear: should they maintain their opposition to war and risk prosecution and imprisonment, or abandon their principles? For the Emergency Peace Commission of Massachusetts the choice was simple: 'since war has been declared the purpose of the commission is at an end, and its members will take up other work of national usefulness.'[12] Large numbers of suffragists, of whom the most prominent was Carrie Chapman Catt, the honorary vice-chairman of the New York WPP, decided likewise to suspend their activities and become Sister Susies – knitting socks and scarves, rolling bandages, and making up parcels of supplies like soap and cigarettes for the soldiers. Catt resigned from the WPP.

Others, especially the Quakers, held firm to their principles. In January 1917, the Alice Paul who had upstaged and embarrassed President Wilson by organizing the huge suffrage parade in Washington, just before his 1913 inauguration, now launched a silent protest outside the White House. A group of women held up signs that quoted slogans from the President's own speeches, rousing statements like 'Liberty is the fundamental demand of the human spirit,' to which they added, 'How long must women wait for liberty?' In April 1917, some changed their slogans to 'Democracy begins at home' and 'Kaiser Wilson'. This was too much for men passing by. They assaulted the women, both verbally and physically, and the police did nothing to stop them. On the contrary, as the scuffles continued, two of the protesting women (but none of the aggressive men) were arrested for 'obstructing the traffic', although they had carefully remained on the pavement. They were carrying a banner quoting from Wilson's speech to Congress: 'We shall fight for the things which we have always carried nearest our hearts: for democracy, for the right of those who submit to authority to have a voice in their own governments.' The charges against the women were soon dropped, but three days later, twelve more were arrested on the same pretext and sentenced to serve three days in jail or to pay a $25 fine. They chose jail. On 14 July sixteen women were arrested and this time they were sentenced to sixty days in jail or a $25 fine. Again, the women chose jail. However, after they had served three days in the Occoquan Workhouse in Virginia (now the Lorton Correctional Complex), Wilson pardoned them. Soon after, 218 suffragists were arrested; ninety-seven, including Alice Paul and Hazel Hunkins (who was to play an important role in the Fullers' lives after the war), were given six months in prison. There they went on hunger strike to protest against their illegal incarceration; with the full sanction of President Wilson they were force-fed. This brutal treatment outraged a portion of the American public who saw the women as martyrs. By the end of November, they had all been released, except for Alice Paul, who had been re-arrested on 20 October and sentenced to seven months in prison.

Even within the AUAM there was division. Oswald Garrison Villard tells of a memorable committee meeting:

> In the midst of a discussion of what our policy should be, Rabbi Stephen S. Wise said that he felt the time had come for a re-orientation of the pacifist point of view and that he wished to read us extracts from a sermon he intended to deliver the next Sunday. It bowled us over for it was a complete yielding on every point, an acceptance of the war as high-minded and all for the best – a complete reversal of everything he had stood for. He asked us to state our frank opinion one after the other, and got what he asked for. Crystal Eastman, Walter Fuller, Lilian D. Wald, Amos Pinchot, Agnes Leach, L. Hollingsworth Wood, Mary W. Ovington, Norman Thomas, I

and others told him exactly what we thought. Never have I heard such plain, straightforward language; never have I seen a man so flayed to his face.[13]

A few weeks later, Wise delivered his sermon, but after the war he admitted that he had been wrong and swore that he would not have anything to do with another war to free humanity. In the autobiographical memoir that he published at the end of the 1930s, Villard wondered what the Rabbi's position would be 'if that war should be the one to save the Jews from Hitler.'[14] In the event, Wise became an outspoken critic of Hitler's regime.

Although Crystal was 'crazy to get back on the job'[15] (as she wrote to Amos Pinchot not long after Jeffrey was born), it was two months or so before she was able to resume her activities in the WPP and the AUAM. Moreover she never regained the high level of energy that she had previously enjoyed. At meetings, decisions were often taken on the basis of letters received from her, rather than in her presence. When she resumed work, Jeffrey remained at Croton in the care of a nanny. Crystal was so weak after his birth that she did not breastfeed him and is reputed rarely to have changed a diaper,[16] so she did not form a strong bond with him, which she regretted later. Walter does not seem to have taken this opportunity to be a hands-on parent either. In his letters to his sisters he mentioned Jeffrey only to report that he was gaining weight normally. Nor, for that matter, did he mention Crystal. It is striking that, in a family who were constantly expressing their love for each other, none of his letters ends with 'Crystal sends her love' or any message of that kind. Her illness diminished her presence in both her professional and her family life.

During her absence, Crystal missed a major meeting on 4 and 5 April 1917 in the offices of the Church Peace Union in the Ginn Building on 5th Avenue.* The meeting was attended by representatives of anti-war groups of all persuasions who agreed, in their joint concluding statement, to work 'for the defense of American ideals and for an early and lasting peace.'

She was in time, however, to participate in a more radical transformation of the American peace movement. Since the beginning of April, Walter had been on a committee representing the three main peace movements – the AUAM, and the New York and Chicago branches of the Emergency Peace Federation – organizing the First American Conference for Democracy and Terms of Peace. It was chaired by Louis Lochner. Other members included

---

* The building was named after the prosperous publisher, Edward Ginn, who had set up the World Peace Foundation in 1910. It was known familiarly as 'Treason's Twilight Zone' after the graffito that some fanatic patriot had painted on its facade.

Walter Fuller

Emily Balch, Morris Hillquit,* Rebecca Shelly, Norman Thomas, and Harry Dana – Jessie Holliday's brother-in-law.† Hollingsworth Wood, representing the New York Society of Friends, was also a signatory to the call for a conference. Its aim was 'to clarify public opinion on the issues arising out of America's participation in the war; to devise means for safeguarding American liberty and democracy; and to formulate the demands of forward-looking Americans as to the terms of the coming peace.' A preparatory meeting was held on 2 May 1917 in the Hotel Astor in New York City.

At once an ideological split became apparent. The majority of participants were in favour of the peace proposals that the Bolsheviks had made following the Russian Revolution.‡ They were the best that anyone had yet come up with; even President Wilson was thrown on the defensive by them, having nothing better to offer. A minority, led by Lillian Wald of the AUAM, preferred a more moderate, home-grown approach; they walked out of the meeting. Officially, then, the AUAM was not associated with the events that followed, but individual members, Crystal and Walter included, took an active part in them. They called for a two-day Conference for Democracy and Terms of Peace on 30 and 31 May in Madison Square Garden, 'to discuss how best we can aid our government in bringing to ourselves and the world a speedy, righteous and enduring peace.'17

This Conference was attended by an estimated 20,000 people, one third of whom were women. Because the local authorities feared violence, either on the part of the participants, whom they viewed as dangerous revolutionaries, or from the nationalist opposition, exceptional security precautions were taken. More than 400 armed policemen were mobilized; '100 were kept at the Fourth Avenue entrance ready to charge through the interior in flying wedge formation at a moment's notice.' Police cars equipped with searchlights patrolled the neighbouring streets, and two fire engines were at the

---

* A leading lawyer, one of the founders of the Socialist Party of America, Morris Hillquit (1869–1933) gave Crystal her first job in his New York office in 1907, when it was unheard of for women to become lawyers.

† Although the writer and peace activist Henry (usually called Harry) Wadsworth Longfellow Dana (1881–1950) had been teaching comparative literature at Columbia since 1912, the University dismissed him in the summer of 1917 because he opposed America's participation in the war. He became a major defender of civil liberties and in particular the rights of conscientious objectors.

‡ It should be remembered that the United States was the first country to recognize and welcome the new regime in Russia, on 22 March 1917, just one week after the Revolution.

ready, 'with lines of hose ready to run out.'[18] Inside the hall, there were three hundred policemen in plain clothes as well as numerous government agents; they tried to look invisible when Rabbi Magnes – who delivered the keynote address – invited them onto the platform beside him and offered to provide them with stenographic services. In the end, the Conference proceeded peacefully, with speeches by leading figures representing the socialists, liberals, civil libertarians, trade unionists, and religious pacifists, including Professor William Hull (to mention just one speaker with whom Walter was closely associated). The climax of the meeting came on the second day when Rebecca Shelly called for the establishment of a People's Council of America for Democracy and Terms of Peace,* with a national convention in the Midwest on 1 September, and the publication of a national *Bulletin*. These proposals were massively applauded.

The spirit of the People's Council was positive and profoundly patriotic, demanding that 'American democracy, American ideals, [and] American peace be preserved inviolate.'[19] It upheld the right to a free press, freedom of speech and assembly, and protested against the violation of homes and offices without a search warrant. It demanded that private mail should not be tampered with, denounced the newly introduced conscription laws as unconstitutional, and demanded exemption for all conscientious objectors.† Secret diplomacy was to be abolished, replaced by democratic control of foreign policy, with public debate of alliances and treaties. It aimed to bring the war to a rapid conclusion 'through negotiation in harmony with the principles outlined by the President of the United States and by revolutionary Russia, with no forcible annexation of territory, no punitive indemnities, and free development for all nationalities;' to defend freedom of assembly and of speech (including the press); to bring about the repeal of the Conscription Act; and to defend the rights of labour during wartime, insisting that 'where women take the place of men they [should] receive men's wages.'[21] It was a programme that won widespread approval.

Over the next few weeks, plans for this People's Council were drawn up by its leaders, who were Rebecca Shelly (Financial Secretary), Lella Faye Secor (Organizing Secretary), Crystal, Morris Hillquit, Louis Lochner (Executive Secretary), Harry Dana, Rabbi Judah Magnes (the first Chairman), and

---

*   The term 'People's Council' attempted to render the Russian word *soviet*.

†   Conscription violated the longstanding right of America's young men to decide whether or not to give their lives in the service of their country. As Oswald Garrison Villard put it, 'It meant the strangling of the most precious thing in the world, the conscience of the individual.'[20]

Emily Balch.* They set up committees to appoint a treasurer and fix salaries; publish their *Bulletin*; contact a visiting Russian delegation; send a message to French and Italian socialists; conduct their legal defence; appear before the Joint House and Senate, and so on. The programme of the People's Council was ambitious, with nationwide councils of workers on the Russian model: local councils, state councils, and a national committee with one delegate from each state and from each of the numerous national organizations of workers. A National Council of Workers would serve as a watchdog, observing the federal government and confronting it whenever it departed from principles which the average citizen upheld. Topmost of these were free speech, a free press, and the freedom of assembly – what we would call basic human rights.

From the moment America entered the war, Congress began to restrict these rights and criminalize all those who defended them, confirming the ever-present fear in the American people that their federal government represents the greatest potential threat to individual freedom. Today, these rights are divided into civil *rights* and civil *liberties*. Civil rights are granted by the federal government to ensure equal treatment of citizens. Civil liberties, on the other hand, are claimed by the citizens to protect them from the government; they set limits on its power to interfere with their lives. The situation in 1917 was that

> such liberties were only to be protected for those citizens who had demonstrated, both by their attitudes and their behaviour, that they were prepared to utilize those freedoms in positive and constructive ways. The decision as to whether a citizen deserved to have his civil liberties formally protected was to be made by those responsible elements within the society that were knowledgable in the proper use of personal freedom. Liberty, in short, was a condition conferred by the community at its discretion, usually only to 'good people' who had earned their prerogatives. Blacks, Indians, Orientals, aliens – particularly those from Eastern Europe – women, or people espousing radical and destructive economic and political theories, clearly were not ready for the full utilization of their constitutional liberties.[22]

In short, the only persons whose civil liberties were assured were white Anglo-Saxon men. Even they could lose them if, by their behaviour, they revealed a lack of moral character or failed to fulfil their social responsibilities. Clearly, conscientious objectors and draft dodgers (or 'slackers' as they

---

* This order is based on the frequency of their attendance at meetings in June and July 1917 for which minutes have survived. There were eighteen other occasional participants, including Max.

were called) failed on both these counts; so did those who encouraged or supported them. They were not 'good people' and thus forfeited their rights. The same principles applied to the freedom of speech and opinion. Statements 'deemed contrary to the public welfare' might be punished, even when those statements could be shown to be true.[23]

Because the question of civil liberties had not exercised the American public to any extent since the 1798 Sedition Act – in fact, the term was introduced only in mid-1917, thanks to Walter Fuller – no fresh statutes had been passed for over a hundred years. And since statute law did not formally restrict civil liberties, there was no case law to draw upon. Local courts were left to judge on a case-by-case basis. 'This meant that the criterion by which a citizen got civil liberties could legitimately include the attitude of the judge towards the person.'[24] When 'good people' are the arbiters of civil liberties, a sufficient degree of moral indignation can turn a law-abiding citizen into a lyncher. That year, whipping, tarring-and-feathering, or hanging, or all three together, of innocent citizens (who happened to be unpopular) became so common as to be worth no more than a line or two in the newspapers. If the perpetrators were brought before a judge (which was rare), they were invariably allowed to walk free. The law condoned mob justice.[25]

On 19 April 1917, a man known as 'Shiloh' was arrested for distributing an 'ultra-pacifist' pamphlet during a 'Wake up America' parade in New York. Brought at once before a magistrate called Wylie, he was sentenced to six months in prison. According to the press, Wylie told Shiloh that 'the crowd would have given him his deserts if it had lynched him.' The Emergency Peace Federation immediately announced that it would appeal on Shiloh's behalf. At this, Chief Magistrate McAdoo pointed out that 'Magistrate Wylie is a new man on the bench and it must be taken into consideration that he is merely a human American' [sic]. Although McAdoo was not acquainted with the contents of the pamphlet, he approved the six-month sentence. Magistrate Wylie – is that pronounced 'wily' or 'why lie'? – later claimed that he said, 'if the people watching the parade had read the pamphlet they probably would have mobbed the man distributing it.'[26] The Secretary of the Emergency Peace Federation, Lella Faye Secor, declared that this was further evidence of a need for a ruling on the right of free speech. (The 1920 Lusk Report on 'Revolutionary Radicalism' in America dismissed the Emergency Peace Federation as 'traitorous and dangerous, not alone to the United States, but to world civilisation.')

Instead of a ruling, there came the Espionage Act, introduced within days of the declaration of war and promulgated on 15 June. Making the world 'safe for democracy' turned out to involve the denial of democracy at home, for the Act severely limited freedom of expression. In particular, any 'attempt to cause insubordination, disloyalty, mutiny, or refusal of duty, in the military or naval forces of the United States, or [to] obstruct the recruiting or enlistment service of the United States' could 'be punished by a fine of not more than $10,000 or imprisonment for not more than twenty years or both.' Further, the act declared it unlawful for any person in time of war to publish any information that the President, *in his judgment,* declared to be 'of such character that it is or might be useful to the enemy.' Thus the United States embarked on the most severe repression of its citizens by its own government in its history. A Minnesota man was arrested for sneering that no soldier ever saw the socks that women were knitting for them. Max Eastman's friend Fred Boyd was beaten up by fellow diners in Rector's restaurant in New York City because he had failed to stand up when the national anthem was played.[27] In Chicago, another man who failed to stand was arrested for 'disorderly conduct' and fined fifty dollars.*

As *Four Lights* had foreseen, hate was cultivated for anything German or associated with Germany. Schools stopped teaching German, periodicals in German were harrassed until they ceased publication, German books were burned, and music by German composers, even Beethoven, was no longer played. Any person with a Germanic name was suspected of harbouring treasonous sympathies. The celebrated Swiss conductor of the Boston Symphony Orchestra, Karl Muck, whom the Fullers had met and dined with on several occasions, had unfortunately been born in Germany. When America entered the war, he offered to resign his post. This was rejected as unnecessary, but then an ex-governor of Maryland proposed to lead a mob to prevent him from conducting a concert in Baltimore, since that would insult America and its flag. A newspaper drummed up a campaign against him; Muck was interned and finally deported. The rest of this book could be filled with similar – and far more bloody – stories.

In this climate of repression, the groups that Crystal and Walter worked for played a historic role in defending conscientious objectors (hereafter COs). As with other civil rights, there were no operational norms or prece-

---

* Another case, out of hundreds: in October 1917, a Russian immigrant declined to purchase a Liberty Bond from a street vendor. He was dragged before a Night Court. In the absence of an interpreter – which he needed – he was informed by the magistrate that he should have been lynched 'right then and there.' He was sentenced, right then and there, to six months in prison. Despite the efforts of the Bureau of Legal Advice, the magistrate, Francis Mancusco, was never sanctioned for his words, or his decision.

dents relating to conscription or the legal status of a man who refused to be drafted. Pragmatically leaving aside the question of the constitutionality of conscription, the joint meeting in April of the WPP and the Emergency Peace Foundation resolved to organize 'a legal defense and legal advice bureau for the benefit of conscientious objectors.' It became the Bureau of Legal Advice. A similar group was formed within the AUAM. Roger Baldwin (who had been brought into the AUAM to replace Crystal during her prolonged maternity leave),* Crystal, Norman Thomas and several other radical AUAM supporters set up a Bureau of Conscientious Objectors. However, this caused dissention within the AUAM. Some committee members, including Paul Kellogg, felt that support for COs was at variance with the aims of the AUAM. In a statement dated 14 June, Crystal agreed that it would be politic to distinguish it from their campaign for peace. At her suggestion the Bureau of Conscientious Objectors was renamed the Civil Liberties Bureau of the AUAM. It aimed to lobby for the repeal of legislation penalizing conscientious objection, to recruit lawyers to assist COs, and encourage COs to make their beliefs known by registering with the local authorities. This step was important enough to merit an article and editorial comment in the New York *Times* of 3 July 1917. The Civil Liberties Bureau, it affirmed, 'has obtained the services, without pay, of a large number of lawyers throughout the country, who will render legal aid to the organization. Among the lawyers named are several who are members of the so-called People's Council of America, which is agitating for a world peace.'[28]

But the internal contradiction remained. On 1 October 1917, again at the instigation of Crystal, the Civil Liberties Bureau became an independent and separate organization, the National Civil Liberties Bureau. The following month the AUAM changed its name to the American Union for Democratic Peace (another of Crystal's suggestions), but its heyday was over. Of the committee at this point,† only two were still on board when it was dissolved on 1 February 1922.

As for the National Civil Liberties Bureau, its director was Roger Baldwin.

---

* Like Crystal, Roger Nash Baldwin (1884–1981), a militant social worker from St Louis, had enormous energy and a superhuman capacity for hard work. He instantly became a major driving force within the movement. Luckily, he and Crystal generally saw eye to eye.

† Committee members included Jane Addams, Emily Balch, Max Eastman, Charles Hallinan, John Haynes Holmes, David Starr Jordan, Norman Thomas, Oswald Garrison Villard, and Hollingsworth Wood. The latter was the first to leave, resigning to go and work for Senator la Follette in Washington.

Hollingsworth Wood served as chairman and Norman Thomas, vice-chairman.* Shortly afterwards, the Bureau of Legal Advice was put under its direction, thus uniting the efforts of the WPP, the Emergency Peace Federation, and the AUAM. When Paul Kellogg joined this larger entity in 1920, it was renamed the American Civil Liberties Union (ACLU); it is still active and performing valuable services today.†

What was Walter's role in all this? Although he is rarely mentioned in the archives I have consulted, he was as active as ever in the background. He supplied Crystal with a steady flow of ideas, and her actions and proposals were the fruit of discussion with him. To start with, he closely followed the development in England of groups that opposed conscription and offered advice and protection to COs. So when in May 1917 the WPP was lobbying in Washington for exemption from conscription for COs, I suspect that he was the source of their argument that 'England has suffered much embarrassment in the imprisonment of three thousand such men who could not fail to receive much popular admiration.' He was in all probability the main contributor to the report on recent British legislation recognizing political (as opposed to conscientious) objectors to war that the AUAM submitted to a government committee that same month. Similarly, when the newly formed National Civil Liberties Bureau issued a statement of its aims, it quoted at length from a speech that Lord Parmoor had recently made in the House of Lords. This speech was not reported in American newspapers; only someone who read the British press and closely followed the defence of COs in England can have supplied them with it. Most importantly, as John Fabian Witt, a Professor at Yale Law School, puts it.

> The name of the new Civil Liberties Bureau emerged out of the same transatlantic internationalism from which the AUAM had arisen.‡ Though the term 'civil liberty' had long been central to Anglo-American law and political theory, eighteenth- and nineteenth-century lawyers and political writers only sparingly and erratically employed its disaggregated form, the plural 'civil liberties.' The phrase had been popularized just a year earlier by the British National Council for Civil Liberties.... With the establishment of

---

* Other committee members included Helen Phelps Stokes (treasurer), Walter R. Nelles, Albert deSilver, Edmund C. Evans, John Haynes Holmes, Agnes Brown Leach, and Amos Pinchot.

† The founding committee members were (in alphabetical order) Jane Addams, Roger Baldwin, Clarence Darrow (as its defence lawyer), John Dewey, Crystal, Elizabeth Gurley Flynn, Paul Kellogg, Abraham Muste, Upton Sinclair, and Norman Thomas.

‡ As we have seen, this international component was supplied by Walter Fuller.

Father

the Civil Liberties Bureau, the AUAM adopted the National Council's coinage as its own. Roger Baldwin, the recent addition to the AUAM staff who headed-up the new Civil Liberties Bureau, would later recall that the Bureau's name represented 'the first time that the phrase "civil liberties" had been so used in the United States.'[29]

Through Crystal, then, Walter was responsible for introducing into the United States the concept which has become so important for the defence of its own citizens: 'civil liberties'.

The *Evening Post* for 8 June carried another of his letters. It was short and simple, quoting a news item from the British press. After learning that the last of her three sons had been killed on the Western Front, an English mother exclaimed, 'I wish the Lord would have me.' Later she was found dead. The inquest concluded: 'Death from natural causes.' Walter left readers to draw their own conclusions.

He was full of ideas for propaganda, but what he actually produced is hard to uncover, for the conceiver of advertisements, slogans and handbills is rarely identified. In just one case, however, we have a signed work. The No Conscription League, newly organized by the notorious anarchists Emma Goldman and Alexander Berkman, had announced a mass protest in Madison Square for 23 June 1917, and the New York *Sun* sent a reporter to cover the event. As the first No Conscription League rally had drawn about 8000 people and ended in fights, the authorities were on the alert. On that day, however, Berkman was 'unavoidably detained in the Tombs', and Emma Goldman was awaiting trial under the newly passed Espionage Act. So the police, state marshals and mobilized guardsmen were outnumbered only by 'representatives of the leisure class' enjoying 'a pleasant Saturday afternoon.' At a loss for copy, the *Sun* reporter described 'a lurid leaflet titled "My Country"' which a young lady called Pauline Angell* was selling. 'It purports to be printed in the interests of the Red Cross [which was attempting to raise $50m], but has the President's war message so printed in ink of varying degrees of blackness that a human skull stares from it. (The editors are Walter Fuller and Pauline Angell.)'[31] So here was yet another medium for Walter: propaganda images created with printed words and letters.

---

*   A graduate of Vassar, Pauline Knickerbocker Angell (no relation to Norman), a friend of both Crystal and Walter, an active suffragette and a member of the AUAM and the New York WPP, was one of the many 'editors' of the *Four Lights*. She was also one of those fifty girls dressed in white who distributed 'Keep Cool' leaflets during the Preparedness parade in May 1916. When Jingo was sent to Chicago a few weeks later, the Springfield *Daily News* punned that she was its guardian angel.[30]

As an Englishman in the United States, he was not eligible for conscription, but he was required by the Department of Labor to make a 'Declaration of Intention'. On 17 May, he swore before a court in New York that

> It is my bona fide intention to renounce for ever all allegiance and fidelity to any foreign prince, potentate, state, or sovereignty, and particularly to George V, King of Great Britain and Ireland, of whom I am now a subject. . . . I am not an anarchist; I am not a polygamist nor a believer in the practice of polygamy; and it is my intention in good faith to become a citizen of the United States of America and to permanently reside therein: SO HELP ME GOD.[32]

This was closely followed by a 'Notice of Enrollment Under Military Law'. 'Pursuant to the provisions of the Military Law of the State of New York,' Walter was informed that he was 'duly enrolled as liable to service in the Militia of the State.' From 25 June, he carried a certificate of enrolment to show on request to any person of authority. Such persons were not just policemen. A number of quasi-vigilante bodies were empowered to stop any man who looked as though he might be eligible for conscription and require him to demonstrate that he was not a 'slacker'. In Manhattan and the Bronx, 11,652 'suspects' were apprehended over a three-day period. Three hundred of them were forcibly drafted and at least 1,500 were turned over to their local draft boards as 'delinquents'.[33]

In the midst of this extraordinary climate of violence and repression, Rosalind dumbfounded Walter by walking into his office on 14 May, saying that she wanted to go back to England to see Arthur Dakyns. Although he had written to Riss, back in February, that he was 'determined to break off all relation' with Rosalind, Dakyns had continued to harrass her.[34] He had been particularly scathing of late and she experienced his words 'like the lash of a whip' that 'curled stingingly' round her heart.[35] She fell into the trap that awaits all victims of sustained violence, whether verbal or physical: she protested to her abuser that she loved him. This merely exacerbated his possessiveness and he began demanding that she return to England. Walter did his best to calm her over a long and lingering lunch together. In view of her emotional state, he sent her to see a psychoanalyst he knew, a Dr Parker. Then he took her out to Croton to rest overnight. Although he stressed the risks attendant on a two-way crossing of the war-torn Atlantic, and argued that her life was far too precious to throw away on a whim like this, Rosalind still wanted to leave. Others braved the mines and torpedoes; so could she.

Dakyns was confident that his brother Henry – who worked for the Booth Shipping Line – could get Rosalind a passage home, even though women passengers were not being accepted so that as many soldiers as possible could be sent to Europe. On Dakyns' instructions, she called on Henry, who happened to be in New York at that moment. Ten days later, she reported to Dakyns:

> I tried to get permission to return to England for a few months, returning here in the autumn to fulfill our contracts for next season but the consul would not agree to such a scheme – it was absolutely impossible. . . . Henry was splendid – I don't know what I should have done without him those hectic days. His good temper, kindness and humour kept me from enlarging my sorrow to so great a strength that it would have overpowered me – I feel I am entangled in a plot that is too intricate for me – besides I cannot see clearly – no one has told me what I as yet only imagine is the case. I am lonely – and very very sad.[36]*

Although she rejoined her sisters after a couple of days, she continued to seek ways to go home and pacify Dakyns.

For Walter, the risk was that, if Rosalind did manage to cross to England, she might not be allowed – either by Dakyns or the passport office – to return to America, and without that assurance, he could not guarantee that the Fuller Sisters would fulfill their next season's engagements. As it was, a lady who had booked them for the whole of June fell ill. Immediately, the staunch Mary Breck began to travel around Connecticut in search of fresh venues, and arranged for them to perform at charity concerts, sharing the proceeds with the Red Cross. Walter would have preferred them to sing in aid of 'innocent sufferers' like orphans, rather than war victims, but they had little choice. However, their songs were no longer in tune with the times, for with the entry of the United States into the war attitudes were rapidly changing. Men in their audience began to protest against the 'Five Souls'; one man asked to hear 'The Star-Spangled Banner' instead. Others even began to question whether it was patriotic to attend concerts at all. Musical fashion was changing too. Since the beginning of the year a new kind of music called jazz, with unfamiliar rhythms and harsh sounds more in keeping with the spirit and sound of warfare, had begun to sweep across the country.

As the girls' bookings – and thus their income – declined, they increasingly relied on friends to put them up. At the end of their tour, one very

---

* The depth of her distress may be gauged by her poem 'Sorrow', printed a few months later in the *Masses*. It is reproduced on this book's website.

good friend, the widow of the composer Edward MacDowell (1860–1908), offered to accommodate them in the colony for artists that she had founded in memory of her husband. It consisted of one-room-studios isolated in pine woods near Peterborough, New Hampshire, where the artists could work by day. Overnight they were accommodated in a central house, their midday meals being brought out to them in the studios.* The Fuller sisters spent almost two months there and made good use of their time. Cynthia painted and, through her contacts with other painters at the Colony, was exhibited in a New York gallery. Rosalind wrote poetry. Two sonnets were printed in that year's *Poetry Review*; another poem appeared in the *Masses* the following October. Dorothy made illustrations to accompany children's singing games, and sent them off to Houghton Mifflin. They – and later other publishers – liked them but ultimately declined to publish them, even with an introduction by Norman Angell. In the end, Dorothy's daughter Carol brought them out in 1983 as *The Children's Book of Old Fashioned Singing Games*.

Arthur Dakyns continued to demand Rosalind's return. She and Walter wrote to each other almost daily, and sometimes more than once a day. He listened to her outpourings and sent reasonable, patient, and loving advice, encouraging her to set aside her answers to Dakyns for a day or two, and to re-read and reword them before sending them off, but he was at a loss to understand the dynamic between them. Early in July, she passed on to him a letter from Dakyns in which he proposed that all three girls, not just Rosalind, should return to England at once. He offered to pay for their tickets, 'first class, *both ways*' – for he promised to do everything in his power to secure their return passage in October. If this proved impossible, he added that he would not only defray the cost of the broken contracts but also 'the loss of a good season in America.' Having made this generous offer, he ordered Rosalind to

> show this letter to Dorothy and Cynthia, talk it over with them, and send me a cablegram worded either 'All three coming' – 'coming alone' – or 'not coming'. If I don't get a cable from you by the end of this month (June), or I get a cable saying 'not coming' or words to that effect, then I shall *know* that you really don't care for me sufficiently to want to make an effort to see me again. I shall take your decision as a sign – a sign that your letters are empty words and your friendship for me worthless.[37]

---

* The MacDowell Colony still exists. Max Eastman's third wife, Yvette, went there in the early 1990s to start writing her memoir, *Dearest Wilding*. In 1997 the Colony received the National Medal of Arts – the highest award given by the United States to artists or patrons of the arts – for 'nurturing and inspiring many of this century's finest artists.'

Father

On Friday 6 July, Walter wrote back:
> Rosalind – dear – I've just read your letter through for a second time – and Arthur's letter too (thank you for sending it). I am amazed – amazed by Arthur's letter, not only by its tone, but also by his words and his style. His nerves are on edge – what he says is all so raw and crude – it seems to me. He talks about crossing the Atlantic as most people talk of ferrying over to Jersey City. You are right when you say, 'What is the good of a sense of humour on one side only?' There's as much humour in Dakyns' note as there was in Austria's ultimatum to Serbia. In fact, that's just what Dakyns' letter is – an ultimatum.[38]

Three days later, Walter was again writing to Rosalind when a cable arrived for her:
> Strongly urge you return. Cancel August engagements. Love Dakyns[39]

Two days after that there came another:
> Everything depends on your return with or without others. Cabling fares on hearing. Dakyns

This time Walter took matters into his own hands and cabled back,
> Rosalind anxious to come but please await next mail before cabling money.[40]

Then he wrote to Rosalind again, spelling out their financial situation:
> If you must go – and if neither of you can wait until March 1918 – *then go in September.* Why? Well, by that time you may have made a little money to pay off debts and to set Dorothy and Cynthia going until October. We owe *Musical America* $143 [for advertisements] and the printers $158, and that is about all – certainly not more than $20 besides – making a total of $321. . . .
>
> For myself I shall try to get a job on the *Evening Post* or to write a book. As it is, I owe Crystal $125 and I can't go on letting her support me and the baby & nurse & cook. But I have kept my troubles pretty much to myself in all this correspondence because I want you to feel yourself to be, as you are indeed, an entirely free agent. If you *must* go by the very next boat – war or no war – debts or no debts – why of course you must – and I won't stop you – or try to stop you – but it would seem to be taking such wild, irresponsible action as to deserve the name of neurotic.[41]

'Neurotic' was a term that Dr Parker had used. In her own mind, though, Rosalind was resolute: Dakyns 'cannot and will not insist on my staying in England – I am not his servant but one as free as he to lead my own life and do my own work.'[42]

With Rosalind's permission, Walter wrote a long letter to Dakyns which was acknowledged on 9 August. 'I was delighted to receive last Tuesday an envelope with the once familiar handwriting thereon,' wrote Dakyns. 'Not having heard from any of you for nearly two months I was still more glad to get your letter.' The mail may have been slow, but letters and cables had been getting through. He was clearly not aware that Rosalind had shown Walter their correspondence. 'By the way,' he continued, 'this was your business letter, not the letter of "the prisoner's friend" which is not yet to hand & which will be exceedingly interesting.'[43]

In his eight-page response, Dakyns laid before Walter his plans for the future lives of Rosalind and her sisters. He listed reasons why all three should return to England at once, including 'the fact that neither Dorothy nor Cynthia appear to be really keen on another season.' (Considering that he claimed not to have heard from them for two nearly months, he seems singularly well informed about their present feelings.) As it was, 'this American touring business' was bad for the girls: 'nobody of that age could stand the flattery and attention without having their heads turned. . . . This is especially so in the case of Rosalind who writes in a vain, self-conscious and affected way.' Finally,

> If Rosalind wants me in her life, she must return *now*. . . . I am not prepared to wait until next year. . . . The fact that she has neither returned not written shows that her feelings are a sham. For the moment her choice is a perfectly simple one – either America or me. . . . I am more than willing to pay any fair compensation for loss of profits due to giving up America for the time being. If you are too proud to take or borrow the money from me then all I can say is you are very foolish. The money is not mine by virtue of my own labour but by virtue – or rather vice – of inheritance. . . .
>
> Now what I want you to do is this: book, if you have not already done so, berths for your three sisters on the next home-going liner. Then at the same time cable me if they want any immediate cash and let me know by letter how much you think that you & they have lost by abandoning next season's engagements. I will fulfil my side of the bargain.

As for what the three girls should do for the rest of the war, he proposed that

1) Rosalind should agree to live with me in London – going through some form of marriage – real or pretence – to keep the respectable hypocrites and busybodies quiet & get some work to do. . . .

2) Cynthia should live with us and see the best that London can offer in the way of artists and nice people. It is a splendid opportunity for her, while [Curt] Dehn is away in India. Between you and me, admirable as our friend Dehn is in many ways, I don't honestly think that he is the husband for Cynthia. He simply is not good enough for her by a long chalk, either politically, socially, artistically, or morally. And personally I would sooner see him

marry Rosalind, with whom he has been far more intimate than with Cynthia or any of the others.

Here is a great opportunity for both R & C to make new friends among the nicest & most progressive sorts of people!

As for Dorothy, I think that with a little judicious introducing she could find a very good market for her art. I have plans for her too but I can't go into them now.[44]

Who, one wonders, were 'the nicest & most progressive sorts of people' that Dakyns had in mind? This letter was written from Bosham where Dakyns was spending ten days with the as-yet-unknown poet, T. S. Eliot, and his wife.*

By the time Arthur's letter arrived, Rosalind had accepted that she could not obtain a pass to visit England, and had calmed down. She went out one evening with a young soldier called John Nightingale and stayed out so late that Dorothy panicked and called the police. Manley Hudson paid them a visit. He was on a walking tour and took them up a nearby mountain, where he read to them from the latest book by Bertrand Russell. Then the girls heard from Norman Angell, who had just returned to the United States; he proposed to take them sailing for a couple of weeks on Lake Champlain (which connects Vermont, New York State, and Quebec). Walter approved the idea – he even suggested that Crystal might join them in September – and in great excitement the girls left the colony to join Angell at La Motte. There they found that he had thoughtfully prepared everything for them: a two-berth sailing boat and two tents, along with very practical dungarees to wear. When they set up camp at a suitable mooringplace, two of the sisters slept on the boat, Angell slept in one tent and the third sister slept in the other. Only Rosalind will have recognized that this played out an episode in Angell's *roman-à-clef* in which 'Ethel', disguised as a man, had gone camping with 'Langdon'. Predictably, when it was her turn to sleep on land, she 'would wait until it was dark and then, creeping into Angell's tent, would stay there until the sun was outlining the hills, returning to [her] bed like a contented cat.'[46] Dorothy and Cynthia were quite unaware of these activities, although when they joined Rosalind and Angell for breakfast they were surprised to find them already up and drinking coffee together most companionably. Angell held them spellbound with stories of his adventurous life, for as a teenager he had gone out West instead of studying at university – but

---

* On 1 July Eliot reported to his mother that he had played tennis yesterday with 'a man named Dakyns, a friend of ours.'[45]

of his estranged wife, he breathed not a word. His marriage remained secret until after his death.*

He and the girls had a wonderful time, swimming in the lake, fishing, and cooking their catch. He taught them to tie knots, read the chart and sail the boat, as well as all manner of camping skills they had never had a chance to practise before. They had long discussions about their immediate future and, with Angell's help (and Walter's encouragement), decided to take up Dakyns' offer and return to England together rather than risk another tour in wartime. It was a wise decision: during the following winter and for the next two years, there was little demand for concerts or plays, bringing hardship to the entertainment profession in America. Together they composed a carefully worded telegram, asking Dakyns to provide the promised funds. Before they could send it, a letter arrived from him to Cynthia in which he wrote that he no longer wanted Rosalind to come back. Since he had changed his mind so often before, they went ahead and sent off their cable.

A week later, Walter asked Angell by telegram to join him in New York for a few days. The girls were nervous about remaining on their own, but Angell left them his revolver for protection, and they managed very well. Then came another telegram with the news that Dakyns had agreed to send the money – and that Crystal was asking Dorothy to come and look after Jeffrey for two weeks while she and Walter attended an important meeting in Minneapolis. Dorothy left at once and was just in time to see Crystal off from Croton on 30 August. She found Jeffrey looking well and happy, but saw little of him, for his nurse brought him downstairs only at four in the afternoon. So she spent her time reading and writing letters.

Crystal had been very busy, organizing a large peace meeting for women only, especially mothers. This had been in preparation for a long time: Pauline Angell was proposing a mothers' protest back in April that year, and in June the secretary of the New York WPP reported that she was receiving 'pitiful appeals from women all over the country' for their voices to be heard.[47] So on 29 August the branch sponsored a mass meeting for women 'to demand a concrete statement of America's peace terms' from the Wilson administration. Crystal planned that it should be 'unique among peace meetings, with only mothers speaking and only women in the audience' so that women would feel free to attend and speak up.[48] She even asked that the

---

* Another secret was that, during this summer, Angell was supplying Woodrow Wilson's political advisers with arguments *in favour of* US participation in WWI. A year later, he was recruited by the CPI to persuade pacifists and isolationists that the war had to won before any progress could be made towards a world organization for peace.

reporters and police officers assigned to cover it should all be women too. In the event, it was 'a tame affair'[49] because President Wilson published his response to the Pope's peace proposals on the day before the meeting took place, quite taking the wind out of their sails.

To Dorothy's surprise, Walter returned on 3 September, a week earlier than planned. During the days that followed, he was often deep in consultation with friends, both at Croton and in New York. Max was there too, with his new girlfriend, Florence Deshon, an upcoming silent movie actress. Then Rosalind and Cynthia arrived from Lake Champlain, and the sisters settled down to discuss their future with Walter. He thought that after a visit to England they should try their luck in Canada, but the girls preferred not to sign any further contracts before they were safely back home. So they set about finding berths. Walter contacted his friend Dudley Field Malone, a lawyer and politician who had been made Collector of the Port of New York by President Wilson as a reward for his help during the 1913 presidential campaign.* He suggested that the girls should seek passage on a troopship, some of which were taking on a few passengers, and they were accepted on the French liner *Espagne*, leaving for Bordeaux on 15 September 1917.

They needed British passports and, because they were crossing to France, French visas as well. The British Consul refused to deliver passports without a good reason for their journey. That their parents were waiting for them counted for nothing. Then Rosalind served her trump card: her fiancé, Arthur Dakyns, a government official, was demanding her return. The Consul demanded proof, and the girls hurried back to the New York flat to search for his letters. Rosalind unearthed one of his telegrams demanding her return. That did the trick, although it was a while before the officials agreed to hand over passports for all three girls. After that they went to the French Consulate, where the officials threw up their hands with Gallic eloquence and declared that they could not possibly issue visas in time. Back the girls went to the apartment and this time they consulted Mary Breck. She suggested calling in Norman Angell, who was in town. The following morning he took them round to the French Consulate before it was even open; his name and fluent French worked miracles. The Consul himself

---

* Since then, Malone had become an advocate of women's suffrage. In 1917, he resigned his position as Third Assistant Secretary of State in protest at Wilson's failure to address the issue of women's rights. That September, he was preparing to defend the 'silent sentinel' suffragettes. In 1918, he successfully appealed their convictions. He later became famous for his role in the 1925 'Monkey Trial' when he joined Clarence Darrow in defending John T. Scopes.

Walter Fuller

came out to greet them and their passports were stamped in no time at all. It only remained to pay for the tickets. The money from Dakyns arrived at the very last moment, just as their trunks were being loaded onto the ship.

Returning to 102 Washington Square for the last time, they found Crystal in great distress: Walter had collapsed and been taken to see a doctor. The following day, feeling frail and looking decidedly unwell, he followed the doctor's orders and did not to come to the dockside to see his sisters off. They made their adieux at Grand Central Station, and Crystal took him out to Croton. In their place, Norman Angell and Mary Breck came to watch the Fuller Sisters step aboard the *Espagne*, and wave them off, leaving their American career behind them for ever.

For Walter it was the end of more than that. His guardianship of his sisters had been central to his life ever since he was a boy. He had brought them over to Neverland – or rather, the New World – to make their fortunes and now they were going home penniless, their tickets paid for by another man. His venture had failed. Worse, he was not going with them. From now on, he would be cut off from them by the Atlantic, unless he were to return to England and face imprisonment as a conscientious objector. As it was, unplanned parenthood and an equally unplanned marriage retained him in the United States, a land where he was starting to feel decidedly unwelcome. He could almost hear Wendy calling, 'It's time to go home!' No wonder he collapsed.

8

New Worlder

'Censorship' is a word to be avoided. It is offensive to Americans, and likewise misleading.[1]   George Creel

Opposition to the war declared by constituted authority becomes treason.[2] Samuel Gompers

It may often be that a man or woman has greater foresight than the masses of the people. And it may be that in the history of things, he who seems wrong today may be right tomorrow.[3]   Judge Mayer sentencing Roger Baldwin

PEACE

Will Repeal the Conscription Laws,
Lower the Cost of Living,
Save Endangered Labor Standards.

The People's Council of America

Demands Immediate General Peace Based on the Russian Formula,

No Forcible Annexations
No Punitive Indemnities
Free Development for All Nationalities

WE ASK YOU TO JOIN THIS GREAT MOVEMENT

Thirty Councils formed in Chicago, Atlanta, Salt Lake City, Philadelphia, San Francisco, St. Louis, Detroit, Seattle, and forty other local Councils under way.

Three hundred and seventy-eight local organizations directly affiliated.

Conferences on Democracy and Terms of Peace held in New York, Chicago, Los Angeles and Philadelphia. One million two hundred thousand Americans represented.

Any American citizen may join as an individual or as a member of a local People's Council.

Any organization—labor, farmers, women, single-taxers, Socialists, church groups, peace bodies—having fifty or more members may join on the basis of one representative for each 1,000 or fraction.

No organization shall have more than three delegates.

THIS IS OUR PROGRAMME

Concrete statement of America's war aims.

Early general peace based on no forcible annexations, no punitive indemnities and free development for all nationalities.

International organization for world peace.

Repeal of conscription laws.

Democratic foreign policy and referendum vote on questions of war and peace.

Freedom of speech, of the press, right of peaceful assembly and the right to petition the Government.

Safeguarding of labor standards.

Taxation of wealth to pay for the war.

Reduction of the high cost of living.

Is This Programme Worth While?
THEN HELP TO PAY FOR IT.

WE NEED $50,000

before September 1st, 1917.

YOU MUST PAY FOR PEACE. The People's Council has no endowment—no wealthy men back of it. We must depend on YOU—the people. We need your money—you need our power—the organized power of a great body of people. In no other organization can your strength count so much.

SEND YOUR MONEY NOW—ALL YOU CAN SPARE—AND THEN ADD SOMETHING BY PERSONAL SACRIFICE.

The Organization Committee
PEOPLE'S COUNCIL OF AMERICA
for Democracy and Peace,
2 WEST 13TH STREET, NEW YORK CITY.

SEPARATION FROM HIS SISTERS was not the only matter weighing on Walter's mind in the September of 1917. The People's Council, launched in a wave of enthusiasm in Madison Square Garden at the end of May, had run into deep trouble. At first it had flourished, receiving generous donations in cash and in kind. The Emergency Peace Federation disbanded and merged with the Council, donating all its office equipment, mailing lists and 'machinery of propaganda' (but also a deficit of almost $3000). By the end of June, no less than 284 organizations had affiliated with it, representing one-and-a-half million workers, many of them from trade unions with a socialist anti-war stance. Soon afterwards, the newly formed Workmen's Council, with 430,000 members, affiliated with it too. In all, the People's Council represented close on two million working men (when the total population of the United States was about 103 million).

Its leaders included Louis Lochner, Rebecca Shelly, and Lella Fay Secor, whom Max described as 'a slim milky-skinned golden-red-haired girl with hard force but a smile like a Correggio madonna.'[5] Other familiar faces were Hollingsworth Wood, Norman Thomas, Max and Crystal. At a meeting in July, Walter (who was present by invitation) was elected to head the editorial committee and produce the Council's *Bulletin*. During the first year (August 1917 to the issue for September/October 1918), twenty-four numbers appeared; the second year saw only eight issues, ending with a double issue for July and August 1919. It bore no mention of the editorial team, nor even of where it was printed. Although a perfectly legal publication, it was subject to 'petty annoyances' on the part of those opposed to it, so it chose to remain discreet (like Walter himself).

Looking like a miniature newspaper with four columns, the early *Bulletin* printed all the minutes and reports of the People's Council, plus articles and open letters to the New York *Times* by its most voluble members, notably Scott Nearing, a prominent socialist academic. The first issue reproduced a page from the *Bulletin* for 15 March 1917 of the People's Council in Petrograd, followed by the Great Charter of the British National Council of Workmen and Soldiers that had been printed not long before in the *Daily Herald* (which the British government would not allow to be sent abroad, so Walter had a private source for this). A later issue reproduced Lord Lansdowne's letter to the *Daily Telegraph* of 29 November 1917, in which he called for a negotiated peace with Germany. President Wilson is reputed to have been impressed by this letter.

But the US government was not impressed by the People's Council, nor was the English-born leader of the American Federation of Labor, Samuel

Gompers (1850–1924).* He had promised the government his Union's full support, including complete compliance with the orders of the War Labor Board and a no-strike policy. Although the latter was contrary to his oft-quoted challenge, 'Show me the country that has no strikes and I'll show you the country in which there is no liberty,' he cast his principles aside for what he believed to be the best interests of American workers in wartime. In return, the government supported a pro-war labour organization that Gompers created specifically to attract workers away from the People's Council, the American Alliance for Labour and Democracy. President Wilson himself supplied funds for its salaries, the rent of its office and the cost of its publicity. At the same time, the CPI swung into action, undermining the public image of the People's Council. George Creel decreed that it was 'made up of traitors and fools, and we are fighting it to the death.' To ensure its demise, he personally instructed a friend in Minneapolis to

> have patriotic societies and civic organizations pass resolutions condemning the People's Council as pro-German and disloyal. . . . Get a good committee together to . . . see all the newspapers and see to it that they get the point of view and action that I am giving you.

He closed with: 'Tear this letter up.'[6] The Lusk Report merely rubber-stamped his opinion of the Council.

After successful rallies in major cities like Chicago, Los Angeles, San Francisco, and Philadelphia during July, in August the Council suddenly found itself disparaged by the press and branded 'pro-German'. Denounced as 'an organization that ought to be suppressed by the government,'[7] it was accused of seeking 'to embarrass the government of the United States in its conduct of the war by urging peace on all occasions.'[8] On 11 August, the New York *Times* called it a 'German peace party,'[9] although a week later it admitted, in a report on one of the Council's public meetings, that 'not a word was spoken at which offence could be taken.'[10] Even Rabbi Stephen Wise bitterly attacked the People's Council, calling its members, many of whom had been his friends, 'betrayers of the peoples of the Earth' and 'unpaid servants of Kaiserism.'[11] The New York *Tribune* affirmed that the People's Council maintained an 'elaborate propaganda headquarters.'[12] In all probability, its propaganda machine comprised two people: Walter Fuller and his secretary.

Meetings organized by the Council, particularly in the mid-West, were broken up by vigilantes while the local authorities turned a blind eye – or

---

* Kathleen Wheeler made a bust of the unprepossessing Gompers. A thousand replicas were produced and distributed to AFL affiliates around the country.

even lent their support. Max Eastman narrowly escaped a 'necktie-party' in Fargo, North Dakota, after his talk was interrupted by soldiers who had been given the evening off for just that purpose.[13] Thanks to George Creel, the long-planned national constituent assembly of the People's Council in Minneapolis, from 1 to 6 September, was compromised. Walter was scheduled to lead a discussion on the *Bulletin* on the fourth day. But Gompers rented all the available halls in Minneapolis for the American Alliance for Labour and Democracy. The governor of Minnesota declared that traitors had no right to freedom of speech and forbade any meeting of the People's Council in any town in all the State. So they shifted the venue to Hudson, Wisconsin. Several of the organizers, including Louis Lochner, were sitting in a hotel lobby there when an excited group of men burst in and asked them to sign a petition against the meeting. Naturally they declined. '"Get a rope," someone shouted. "Get the tar and feathers," said another.'[14] Luckily, the County Attorney happened to be on hand and he persuaded the hot-heads not to commit violence. The trembling organizers were put on a train by a mob estimated at one thousand, and told never to return.[15]

Next they envisaged Milwaukee, or even Washington, but the authorities in both places notified their refusal to host the convention. In the end, while some of the special trains for delegates were already en route for Minneapolis, the organizers re-located the meeting to Chicago, where Mayor Thompson promised them the use of West Side Auditorium. Despite all these changes, 400 delegates made it to the opening at 10 a.m. on 1 September. They appointed Crystal to draw up the order of business and began to draft a constitution defining their objectives in terms that closely anticipated Wilson's Fourteen Points, adding their intention to defend their constitutional rights to free speech, a free press, peaceful assemblage, and the right to petition the government. While Mayor Thompson was out of town, the Governor of Illinois sent in the police to disperse the delegates. Some of them were detained without charge. Although they were later released, their papers were seized. There were no convictions because the People's Council had committed no crime, broken no laws, and made no seditious statements. They were simply being intimidated.

The next day being a Sunday, the delegates met in a factory outside town. Then the Mayor informed them that he had ordered the police to protect them, so they returned to the city to meet in a Jewish Social Hall. Whereupon the Governor called out the militia. The delegates worked quickly, completed their constitution and dispersed. When the Seventh Illinois Infantry stormed the hall, they found only a private wedding in progress. According to the newspapers, Louis Lochner 'hastened back to New York to confer with Max Eastman, Mary Ware Dennett, Walter Fuller, Frank Stevens, and Elisabeth Freeman' (1876–1942; the convention administrator). This unaccustomed mention of Walter in the press reveals that, although he was not on any of the executive committees of the People's Council, his ideas and advice were valued by its leaders. However, the evidence suggests that he resigned his editorship of the *Bulletin* at this point, and that the post-convention number of the paper was produced by a new team. In October, the executive committee resolved that the *Bulletin* would be a newspaper strictly for the People's Council, which may imply criticism of the pieces from Russia and England that Walter had printed.

The front page of *Four Lights* for 8 September 1917 carried the words 'In Memoriam – Democracy' in place of the usual image of a galleon. It quoted Ada Chase Dudley, from the Rochester Branch of the People's Council, on the sense of dismay and disorientation that the delegates experienced:

> We came out of the Chicago Auditorium after witnessing with our own eyes the first concrete proof that Free Speech is dead in America, and for several minutes nobody made a move to go anywhere. . . . We felt as if we had been turned absolutely homeless into a strange world; we felt as if we had lost something which we had been born possessing. And we had lost something. We had lost our country.[16]

This explains why a downcast Walter returned to Dorothy in Croton much sooner than expected. Crystal remained away a few days longer because on 3 September she was leading a meeting of the American Liberty League. (This is not to be confused with the fascist organization with the same name in the 1930s; this one was affiliated with the People's Council, organized by and for women.) Judging it expedient to leave Chicago, the women met in a hotel at Lake Geneva, Wisconsin, and resolved to picket the celebration of conscription day in Washington on 4 September with a display of banners. (I do not know whether Crystal participated in this protest; Walter told Dorothy that she was visiting her father at Glenora, which would be a logical pausing point on her way back to Croton from Lake Geneva.)

The People's Council had planned to raise funds during its constituent assembly; the disruptions prevented this, and it found itself saddled with a debt that, on 1 October, amounted to $11,500. Although it managed to reduce this to $4,900 by the end of 1917, it had to curtail its activities for lack of funding – and dwindling membership. The pacifists were the first to leave as it became more socialist in orientation. Vilified by the press and consequently by the majority of Americans, harassed by local, state, and federal authorities, sabotaged by the post office (which delayed issues of the *Bulletin* by up to four months), the People's Council fizzled out by the end of 1918. The Lusk Report denounced individual members quite as much as the People's Council itself, qualifying them as 'crafty' and accusing them of plotting to overthrow the US government. To protect themselves, several people, including Lella Fay Secor, left the country; others, like Rebecca Shelly, changed their names. Walter escaped mention.

The officially-inspired persecution of the People's Council was but the first stage in a drive to suppress all radical activity in the peace and labour movements. The second stage involved the international union called the Industrial Workers of the World (IWW, widely known as 'Wobblies'), which was opposed to participation in the war. Out of self-preservation, it ceased all agitation after April 1917, simply advising its members, when applying for exemption from the draft, to mark their papers 'IWW, opposed to war'. Incensed, the government turned public opinion against them. In August 1917, the Wobblies' most outspoken opponent of war, Frank Little, was lynched in Butte, Montana; his murderers went unpunished. Then on 5 September, federal agents made simultaneous raids on forty-eight IWW meeting halls across the country, arresting some 300 leaders and confiscating papers (which were burned) under the Espionage Act. Of the persons arrested, ninety-three were sentenced to serve an aggregate of 800 years in jail and fined a total of $2,500,000.[17]

A good many of these 'federal agents' were in fact members of the American Protective League, a private organization of self-appointed vigilantes, formed to help the Bureau of Investigation (the forerunner of the FBI). On payment of one dollar, members received an official-looking card attesting that they were agents of the 'Secret Service Division' (later changed to 'Auxiliary to the US Department of Justice', which was equally misleading). Having neither training nor restraint, they took advantage of these raids to ransack the offices they raided, smashing equipment and furniture. Some of them, claiming to be agents of the Justice Department, broke up meetings of the AUAM earlier in the summer. When the AUAM sent a fully documented report on these incidents to President Wilson, the Justice Department denied that federal agents had had any part in them. It took no steps to prevent further misrepresentation or acts of gratuitous violence by members of the American Protective League.

These voluntary 'auxiliaries to the US Department of Justice,' who numbered 100,000 at the end of June 1917 and peaked at 250,000, also

engaged in a variety of investigations, probing the loyalty of citizens [and] the status of conscientious objectors, and monitoring, in thousands of cases, suspicious activities reported by people throughout the country in response to appeals for vigilance in detecting spies and persons guilty of sabotage.[18]
Their activities were disastrous for the rights of innocent citizens.

In dozens of cities, government agents and their volunteer auxiliaries raided theatres, hotels, restaurants, train and bus depots, factories, union halls, offices, and even private homes, herding thousands of young men into overcrowded detention centres to check their draft cards.[19]

In New York City alone, over 20,000 men were arrested in September 1918.

This, then, was the new world that Walter's sisters were leaving behind. In a manner worthy of a totalitarian regime, Wilson's America was trampling on everything that Crystal and Walter believed in, suppressing the rights of its citizens in order to fight a war to 'safeguard the rights of mankind.' Gone was freedom of thought and opinion. Expressing a desire for peace was an act of sedition, and displeasing the government a federal crime.

The sentences passed were incredible in their severity. In New York three men and one young girl were sentenced by a US judge to 285 years in jail for circulating legal handbills criticizing our intervention in Russia, which, the court held, obstructed the draft. For saying in an angry moment that he hoped 'the government would go to hell,' a citizen of Lansing, Michigan, received twenty years in jail and was fined $10,000.[20]

Eugene Debs, the leader of the Socialist Party of America (SPA), was tried for obstructing recruitment. The prosecuting attorney called him 'the palpitating pulse of the sedition crusade' and the judge compared him to 'an old ewe.'[21] Aged sixty-two and internationally famous, he was sentenced to ten years in prison and deprived of his right to vote *for life*. This did not prevent him from standing as the SPA's candidate in the 1920 presidential election. On this occasion he garnered more than 915,000 votes – more than in 1912, when his share had been 6%. He was released by presidential decree on Christmas Day, 1921, but he was never pardoned.

The Espionage Act severely curtailed freedom of speech in the written as well as the spoken word, no matter how small the publication. The primary decision as to what should be denied distribution by mail was left to individual post office employees and, lest they should be found negligent after the event, they were zealous in sniffing out sedition and treason. The first publication to suffer from this treatment was *Four Lights*. All 5500 copies of the 'special atrocity number' of 2 June 1917 were blocked by the New York post office, nine days *before* the Act came into force. No notice was served on the

WPP. When the office manager, Margaret Lane, enquired why the issue had not been distributed, no explanation was offered. In this particular case, one can sympathize with the post office. Not only did this issue contain the items titled 'Little Words of Love' and 'Still More Horrors' already quoted, it offered provocative 'Thoughts for Bandage Rollers,' one of which ('On Murder' by Ada Chase Dudley) took up Walter's favourite theme of making war personal:

> Mother, think straight: are you a slacker? Suppose Congress were to decree – as it could – that, after training, only mothers of sons of conscript age should be transported to France and into the bloody war trenches. Suppose the saving of America's honor and the maintenance of the freedom of the seas were given into the keeping of mothers only. There is nothing in human experience you would not bear for your child; yet you would not commit murder for him. Will you allow him to do so without a protest?[22]

This could easily be construed as an 'attempt to cause insubordination, disloyalty, mutiny, or refusal of duty' in soldiers and 'obstruct the recruiting or enlistment service of the United States.'

By the time the WPP realized that the post office was going to retain the issue indefinitely, the Espionage Act was in force. Crystal sent a friendly letter (whose irony suggests that it came from Walter's pen rather than hers) to George Creel, introducing Margaret Lane, who planned to visit him in person, and mentioning 'some trouble' that she felt he could 'straighten out' for them. She concluded, 'I can assure you that it is a great comfort to us liberal-minded folks to know, if there must be censorship, that a man of your proved devotion to the essential principles of liberty is in charge of it.'[23] Creel spoke to the Solicitor General of the Post Office and wrote back that there was nothing he could do. Margaret Lane took up the correspondence, and there ensued an increasingly acrimonious exchange of letters, for a second issue *Four Lights,* number twelve for 30 June, was also impounded by the post office, even though the staff of the WPP were affixing the stamps themselves and using third-class mail, at the suggestion of Creel himself, so as not to abuse what he called the 'privilege' of second-class mail. In the end, the case of the *Four Lights,* along with a dozen or so other periodicals that had been suppressed by the postal authorities, was presented by Fannie May Witherspoon, of the Bureau of Legal First Aid, before Judge Herron in Washington. There was no prosecution, and issue twelve was finally distributed, but issue ten was lost for ever, along with the postage already paid. The cost was small compared with what they risked, as Max soon discovered.

On 5 July 1917, the postmaster of New York City decided that the August number of the *Masses* was not mailable. Four cartoons and four passages of text were considered liable to 'cause insubordination' in the armed forces and obstruct recruitment. Max responded on two fronts.

First he wrote to President Wilson, protesting that he 'had been studious not to publish anything unmailable under the law' and recalling the Anglo-American tradition of intellectual freedom that he knew the President valued.[24] According to Ray Stannard Baker, Wilson went to his Postmaster General, Albert S. Burleson, saying, 'Now Burleson, they are well-intentioned people. Let them blow off steam!' But Burleson had the whip handle and he was not going to let go. 'If you don't want the Espionage Act enforced, I can resign. Congress has passed the law and has said I am to enforce it. We are going to war, and these men are discouraging enlistment.' In the face of this excessive reaction, Wilson caved in. 'Well, go ahead and do your duty,' he is reputed to have answered.[25] Exceptionally, Wilson made Max's letter 'the occasion for a declaration on this subject which he gave to the press, and which was front-page news throughout the country.'[26] He also wrote privately to Max in September:

> I think that a time of war must be regarded as wholly exceptional and that it is legitimate to regard things which would in ordinary circumstances be innocent as very dangerous to the public welfare, but the line is manifestly exceedingly hard to draw and I cannot say that I have any confidence that I know how to draw it.[27]

For a President, it was a singularly indecisive letter, but a kind one, signed 'cordially and sincerely yours.'

Max also appealed against the decision. The contributors of the offending items in the August *Masses* appeared before the esteemed liberal Judge Learned Hand on 21 July 1917. He supported the defendants, ruling that the authorities' interpretation of the Espionage Act was not valid,* but – and this was the catch – 'if the magazine *had* violated the law, the proper procedure was to indict the editors.'[28] Max and his contributors were duly indicted and tried in April 1918. They faced up to twenty years in prison and a fine of up to $10,000 each. After three nail-biting days of deliberation, the jurors failed to agree and the case was dropped. The government appealed and a second trial was held in September 1918. By then John Reed ('a great, husky, untamed youth of immense energies and infantine countenance'[29]) had returned from Russia where he had been reporting on the Revolution; he was arrested on his arrival and placed among the accused. This time eight of

---

* Judge Learned Hand also considered that the wording of the Act was so vague as to threaten the American tradition of freedom itself.

the twelve jurors voted for acquittal and the defendants finally walked free on 5 October 1918. Max admitted that he owed much to the skill of his lawyers, Morris Hillquit and Dudley Field Malone.

All this, however, killed the *Masses*. When they tried to mail the issue for September 1917, they found that they had lost the right to distribute the periodical by post because the August issue had not been mailed. Max appealed against this, and lost, although the judge agreed that 'the act of the postmaster general in revoking [their] mailing privilege on the ground of an omission for which the postmaster himself was responsible seemed to him "a rather poor joke".'[30] (In a letter of protest to President Wilson, Upton Sinclair called this procedure 'disgraceful.'[31]) They published an October issue, in which Max printed a poem by Rosalind (as Emilia Berrington; see website), and one more issue dated November–December. They were sold only on newsstands, and at a loss. With a heavy heart, Max closed the editorial office and sold off the furniture. It was the end of a great venture in progressive publishing and innovative art, and the end of a steady source of income for both Max and Crystal: according to him, she had been receiving something like ninety dollars a week from it.[32]

It was at this point that Norman Thomas (1884–1968) invited Walter to work with him on a new periodical. He was a new friend of Walter's, for only in 1917 had Thomas begun to participate in the activities of associations like the AUAM. Three years younger than Walter, he came from a humble background; his studies at Princeton had been paid for by an uncle who had married into money. Some years after graduating, he decided to become a clergyman, and was appointed pastor of the East Harlem Presbyterian Church, where he ran a mission for immigrants. He also preached against American participation in the war, drawing down on himself the disapproval of the leaders of his church; so he resigned. At the same time, he began leaning towards socialism, which played an important part in American politics during the first quarter of the century. In 1917, the Socialist Party of America had two Representatives, dozens of state legislators, more than a hundred mayors, and countless lesser officials. When Morris Hillquit, who was one of thinkers of the SPA and secretary of the International Socialist Party, ran for Mayor of New York in the summer of 1917 on an anti-war and anti-conscription platform,* Thomas sent his good wishes. Hillquit invited Thomas to

---

* Even though the SPA was in decline (from a high of around 200,000 members to about 77,000 by this time), Hillquit got 22% of the vote in New York. It was by no means the highest socialist score in the local elections of 1917: in conservative Ohio, the SPA got 44% in Dayton and 34.8% in Toledo.

join his campaign, which he did, becoming a member of the SPA. In 1926 he took over the leadership of the Party from Eugene Debs, and ran as its presidential candidate in no less than six consecutive elections.

He also became the secretary of the American branch of the Fellowship of Reconciliation. Formed in the autumn of 1915, it had started with an exclusively pacifist stance. Over the next two years, as social workers joined its ranks, it came to view war as but one of many evil consequences of the contemporary spiritual poverty, and concluded that American society itself needed to be reconstructed on the principles of Christian love. Many people that Crystal and Walter knew and worked with, including members of the AUAM like Emily Greene Balch, and Jane Addams of the WPP, joined the FoR. Several prominent FoR members, including Norman Thomas, were involved in organizing the People's Council.

Late in 1917, Thomas decided to launch a periodical for the FoR, with himself as editor and Walter as editorial secretary. The board included Edward Evans, John Haynes Holmes (minister of the Unitarian church on Park Avenue; also of the AUAM), Rufus M. Jones,* and Oswald Garrison Villard. Called *The New World,* it was published by the Fellowship's own Press, whose treasurer was the ubiquitous Hollingsworth Wood. Walter shared in planning and designing the periodical, running a quotation from G.K. Chesterton – 'the characteristic demand of Christianity is for a new world' – as a banner across the top of the front cover. However, it turned out that another periodical was using that title, so they renamed it *The World Tomorrow* from May 1918. The first issue appeared in January 1918 and it ran until 1934, the leading voice of liberal Christian social activism in America. While Thomas chose the articles, Walter prepared them for publication. He also corresponded with members of the board, and with contributors. One person that he kept in contact with was Manley Hudson, both by post and in personal meetings, although Hudson does not seem to have published anything in the *World Tomorrow*.

In each issue, there were columns of short items, including one titled 'By the Way' and signed (at first) 'The Tramp' (an echo of Chaplin's film?), then 'The Road-Mender'. I believe that Walter wrote them. To start with, it is the editor's job to fill out the space remaining after the main articles have been

---

* Rufus Jones (1863–1948) was a leader of the American FoR. A regular visitor to England, he was offered – and regretfully turned down – the post of principal of Woodbrooke, which Riss and Rosalind had attended in 1910. He was at the origin of the American Friends Service Committee, which oversaw the feeding of more than a million German children per day when their country collapsed after the war.

placed. Then a 'road-mender' (with a hyphen) is a memorable figure in Dickens' *Tale of Two Cities*. Items in this column were drawn almost exclusively from English sources. In March 1918, one item opened with the words, 'it is quite as well to keep our eyes on England just now.' In July there was a quotation from Dickens and references to some of Walter's favourite books at the time, including *The Backwash of War* by Ellen la Motte and *Under Fire* by Henri Barbusse. Walter also resorted to the classic journalist's ploy of printing letters that he himself had written; in February 1919, for instance, there's one from Croton-on-Hudson signed 'F.G.W.' Although the evidence for Walter's authorship is only circumstantial, it is compelling. When he left for an extended visit to England in the spring of 1919, the signature at the foot of 'By the Way' changed from 'The Road-Mender' to 'The Apprentice.'

Norman Thomas much appreciated Walter's personal and professional qualities. Ten years later, he recalled

> Walter Fuller's personal charm and the joy it was to work with him. . . . He had an extraordinary fertility of ideas & an even more extraordinary generosity in sharing them without seeking personal credit. . . . I look back with keen delight to the years of our close association.[33]

He promoted Walter from editorial secretary to associate editor by the end of 1918.

As a monthly publication containing only twenty-four pages, the *World Tomorrow* cannot have required all of Walter's time. It would appear that towards the end of 1917 and during 1918 he also worked for the New York *Evening Post*, although I have been unable to uncover any details of this, for lack of extant records. At this time the *Post* was gaining an ill-founded reputation for harbouring pro-German sympathies, especially after it published (in January 1918) the secret treaties between the Allies and the Czar that had been discovered in the Russian Foreign Office after the October revolution.* This caused its circulation to decline and Villard sold the paper at the end of 1918. As Walter's opinions were very much in harmony with Villard's, his employment there is unlikely to have outlived Villard's ownership.

At the same time, Walter was helping Max and Crystal to start a new periodical of their own. After the demise of the *Masses*, they found themselves with nowhere to print the exclusive articles that John Reed was sending them from Russia. So they courageously set up *The Liberator*. A political,

---

* Although Villard reprinted these documents as a ten-cent pamphlet and sent free copies to every US politician, as well as to the White House, President Wilson always maintained that he knew nothing of them before he arrived at the Paris Peace Conference in January 1919.

artistic and literary monthly, it drew on the same writers and artists as the *Masses*. But it was not a collective; Crystal and Max were its joint owners, Crystal having raised $30,000 (heaven knows how or where) to launch it. According to Max, she 'really ran the magazine', leaving him more time for his own writing, as he preferred.[34] This is possibly why she did not associate Walter more closely with it: she wanted sole command. The first issue of the *Liberator* appeared in March 1918, and immediately sold twice as many copies as the *Masses*; at its peak, the circulation reached 60,000. It answered a need, and was good: H. L. Mencken exclaimed to Max, 'you produce the best magazine in America – not now and then, but steadily every month.'[35]

Beside these nascent periodicals and the *Masses* trial in April, several events held Walter and Crystal's attention in the early months of 1918. On 9 January, President Wilson finally announced that he supported the women's suffrage amendment and the following day it was approved by the House of Representatives. In England the House of Lords accepted a similar bill in February, but in the United States the Senate put off debating the amendment until October, when it failed by just two votes. Also in February, Crystal organized a convention of the New York City branch of the WPP at which it was decided to make it the WPP of the whole State, with Crystal in the chair. In March, the Circuit Court of Appeals in Washington DC decided that all the arrests, trials, and punishments of Alice Paul's 'silent sentinels' demonstrating in front of the White House had been unconstitutional – but the arrest of protesters resumed in August.

By that time, Walter was staying up in Croton to avoid the heat of the city, while Crystal was spending several weeks with her father at Glenora. Exceptionally, some of Walter's letters to her have survived; they provide unique insight into their relationship, as well as a picture of Walter the proud parent. Written just as the ideas came into his head, his letters are long and loving. The first is dated Monday evening, 12 August 1918, and included news of Jeffrey, whose nanny had taken him to school that day for 'the measuring ceremony':

> Annie says that Jeffrey behaved like a Lennie and was much admired by all parties. He was awarded a little card bearing the following information:
> Name: Jeffery [*sic*] Fuller
> Age: 1 yr 5 mo
> Weight: 27 lbs
> Height: 32 ins
> You should weigh: 24½ lbs

> He was just going to bed when I got home this evening. I had a little talk with him but he did not seem unduly puffed up by the possession of that extra 2½ lbs. I think he looked rather more beautiful than ever somehow.

'Unduly puffed up' is typical of Walter's ironic and very English humour, at which Americans were liable to take offence, finding it flippant. Luckily, Crystal enjoyed it.

Two days later, he reported,

> Jeffrey's a dear. This morning he tottered 14 distinct and separate steps across the room. His plan now is – when he wants to cross the room – to stand up, take three or four steps – fall down – crawl a yard or two – stand up again and walk the rest. He seems to stand the heat very well. He goes off to sleep very soon after going to bed and sleeps all through the night and his appetite is as good as ever. . . .
>
> It's too hot to take any photos of Jeffrey. . . . I tried to take a photo just before lunch today – out on the porch – but the boards were actually too hot for him to stand on.

He also had news for Crystal about the Civil Liberties Bureau:

> Norman [Thomas] asked me to go with him to the weekly lunch. We were there from 1.30 till 4 o'clock. Several important matters were settled about which you'll be hearing fully from Roger Baldwin soon, I guess. One is a decision to put up a fight against the Post Office on the matter of the non-mailability of certain of the Bureau's pamphlets. Another is the resignation of the present director in view of the coming draft of men of his age. A committee of the officers is to meet tomorrow to decide what action to take as a consequence of this resignation.

That summer, a new Selective Service Act came into force, and Roger Baldwin became eligible for the draft. He planned to register as a conscientious objector, and correctly anticipated that he would be imprisoned. (In the event, his incarceration was exceptionally short and painless.) As he did not want this to reflect badly on the NCLB, he resigned as its director, and Albert deSilver (born in 1888) replaced him. deSilver was a wealthy New York lawyer who had been a supporter of the *Masses* (and whose wife was active in the WPP). Although conservative in political and economic outlook, he profoundly believed in the need for freedom of speech and opinion. After taking over from Baldwin, he dedicated the rest of his life and all his fortune to defending radicals of every shade, even using his own war bonds to post bail for defendants in free speech cases. He died in a railway accident in 1924, aged only thirty-six.

Walter continued: 'By the way, am I right in guessing at a love affair between Roger Baldwin and Madeleine Doty? I think I am not mistaken. She was at the lunch.' He guessed rightly: they married a year later, when Baldwin was released from jail.

Beside Baldwin and deSilver, Rabbi Judah Magnes attended the meeting. He was very much against American participation in the war and, as we have seen, was (initially at least) a leader of the People's Council as well as the NCLB. In 1906 he had helped found the American Jewish Committee, and from 1908 to 1922 he presided over the Jewish community in New York, which was the largest in the world. In 1918 he played a key role, along with Albert Einstein and Chaim Weizmann, in founding the Hebrew University of Jerusalem;* he was its first Chancellor (1925) and then its President (1935–48).†

Also present at the meeting was 'Miss Stokes' – this must be Helen Phelps Stokes (the artist and daughter of the merchant, banker, publicist, philanthropist, and multi-millionaire Anson Phelps Stokes) who was on the board of the NCLB.‡ Along with her was Walter Nelles, a lawyer who followed his friend Roger Baldwin into the NCLB and became the ACLU's chief counsel. He was one of Max's legal advisers at the *Masses* trial. Later he wrote a biography of deSilver. His wife Helen was on the directing committee of the NCLB.

The other two persons at the lunch were Hollingsworth Wood and Manley Hudson. Quite by chance, Walter had written to Manley Hudson only a week before, asking, 'Where are you now? I wish we could get in touch with one another.' Hudson wrote back on 12 August that he had 'been in Washington most of the time and it now seems that I shall be all fall.' So their chance meeting in New York that day was most welcome.

---

* Some coincidences: Patrick Geddes, whom Walter so admired, was invited to design the new Hebrew University and to plan the enlargement of Jerusalem. The first President of Israel, Chaim Weizmann, arrived at Owens College, Manchester, in 1904, just before Walter left, and worked there as a research chemist.

† Having settled in Mandate Palestine immediately after WWI, Magnes sought for the rest of his life to create a binational community there, correctly anticipating that, 'with the permission of the Arabs we will be able to receive hundreds of thousands of persecuted Jews in Arab lands.... Without the permission of the Arabs even the four hundred thousand [Jews] that now are in Palestine will remain in danger, in spite of the temporary protection of British bayonets.'[36]

‡ Helen Phelps Stokes was the sister-in-law of the more celebrated (but married) socialist Rose Pastor Stokes. She had been tried shortly before under the Espionage Act and sentenced to ten years in jail. At this point, her sentence was suspended while she appealed; the case against her was ultimately dismissed in 1921.

From left to right: Eugene Debs, Max Eastman, and Rose Pastor Stokes.

This informal meeting of the NCLB was one of the last before it fell foul of the Justice Department. Ever since the inception of the Bureau, Baldwin had made strenuous efforts to assure the government that they were doing nothing illegal and not, in particular, hampering conscription, only providing legal advice for those who refused to be drafted. But Military Intelligence began to investigate the NCLB in the spring of 1918 and on 30 August the Justice Department swooped and seized its records. In the end, though, the NCLB was never prosecuted.

In his letters to Crystal, Walter tells of the other people he met, starting with his sisters' fan Edward Filene, of Boston, whom he bumped into twice in the same day.* In 1911, Filene had played a pivotal role in passing America's first Workmen's Compensation law, so 'he brightened up at the mention of [Crystal's] name, every time.'

On Sunday, Walter reported:

a little after twelve noon – Voices and calls for me (I being upstairs writing home to my mother – yes, really). I come downstairs and find Margaret & Dan Lane and Polly Angell & her brother, all very much excited because 50 dollars had just changed hands across the road. The talk was all about the glorious view, and what good friends [Margaret Lane's son] David and Jeffrey would be, and when should Walter Nelles come up to put everything in apple-pie order.

---

* Another coincidence: at one time, the propagandist Edward Bernays worked for Filene's store. He tells how the family got their name. It was originally Katz. Arriving in the United States in the 1840s, William Katz gave his name as 'Feline' (playing on 'cats' of course) but it was mis-recorded as 'Filene', and he had to live with it. It doesn't do to joke with US immigration officers. They can give you a bad name.

Walter Fuller

> They had walked over from Hartsdale to Irvington, and were going to walk a good part of the way back. I gave them some bread & butter & cheese and an onion or two (washed down with unlimited water) for lunch – They stayed only half an hour. . . .
>
> Aunt Mary and I had a very pleasant two or three hours with Mike and Sallie on Saturday evening. . . .
>
> One evening last week – one of the hot evenings – Louise and Gregory came down here and talked to one another for an hour or so – an awful lot of nonsense about the war & Russia & the future.

This tells us about the growing community of like-minded spirits in Croton. Margaret Lane was the executive secretary of the New York WPP and Polly (i.e. Pauline) Angell was the girl who had been selling the death's head flyer in aid of the Red Cross. Aunt Mary was Crystal's aunt; from a New York library, Walter borrowed books for her by Anatole France (whose stories he had published in the *University Review*) and Stacy Aumonier. I have not identified Mike or Sallie, but Louise is certainly John Reed's wife, Louise Bryant, who had witnessed the October Revolution with him.* She had worked as an assistant on the *Masses*. At Max's instigation, Reed had bought a house up at Croton (the one that Mabel Dodge had rented before leasing Finney Farm). So too had Dr Gregory Stragnell, New York's first psychoanalyst and associate editor of the *Journal of Nervous and Mental Disease*. A patient of his was the Russian filmmaker, Sergei Eisenstein. Another was Max Eastman. Stragnell was one of Walter's regular tennis partners at Croton.

By the summer of 1918, Boardman Robinson, Floyd Dell,† and Dudley Field Malone with his partner Doris Stevens had also bought houses up at

---

* Louise Bryant's *Six Red Months in Russia* came out in 1918, a year before John Reed's *Ten Days that Shook the World,* because his notes were confiscated on his return to the United States and returned to him only in November 1918, thanks to the intervention of Morris Hillquit. Warren Beatty's 1981 film *Reds* tells the story of Louise and John's time in Russia and his death there. He is the only Westerner to lie in the Kremlin Wall necropolis.

† Floyd Dell was one of the co-accused in the *Masses* trials – and a regular contributor to the *Liberator*. A year or so after he married, he visited Croton on his wife's birthday. As they walked up Mt Airy Road, they met John Reed and some others walking down. 'Jack [i.e. Reed] embraced us and said, "This is the Mount Airy Soviet, and we have decided that you two are to live here in Croton. And this is the house you are to live in." We were led to a little house in a tiny yard; the artist and his wife who owned it were going away, and it was for sale. . . . This, I felt, was our home. I had a ten-dollar bill in my pocket. I said, "We will buy the house."' It took several successful novels to pay for it, although half the asking price, $3000, was covered by a mortgage.[38]

Croton, and they often dropped round to see each other. The cartoonist Boardman Robinson was now a contributing editor of the *Liberator*. He was Walter's most frequent tennis partner on Sunday afternoons. When they were not playing against each other, they played doubles against Gregory and Louise. His mother was very deaf, and Walter joked to Crystal, 'When Boardman yelled down her ear trumpet, I felt sure you'd hear him up there in Glenora.'

He closed his first letter with:

Dear, I do love you – I'm longing to see you again – I'm sure this holiday is doing you a lot of good. I'm glad I've been to Glenora – I can picture you easily going here and there and up & down – Will you be going over to Dundee? Do you remember when we went over there shopping – buying vegetables – shoes etc – and again when we went to the movies?

All's going on very well here – Annie is very friendly and happy – Geneva is here most of the time apparently. No sign of Max anywhere. The August *World Tomorrow* is going through the mails all right, and is making a great hit. Harold Hatch [who was on the editorial board] wrote to Norman this morning that he's prouder of being connected with the *World Tomorrow* than ever. Good night dearest – Gee I wish you were here tonight – but don't hurry back – have a good time. W.[39]

The following day brought news of both Max and the movies: 1918 was the year that his girlfriend Florence Deshon made good, playing leading parts in nine films, three of them (*Love Watches, One Thousand Dollars,* and *The Girl and the Graft*) being released in July alone.

This evening Aunt Mary & I (having accepted Max & Florence's invitation) are going with them to supper at Ossining and then to see the great Deshon in the Motion Pictures! Annie & Geneva & Naomi & Bartlett & Margaret King have gone over to see the picture this afternoon. Just now I heard Billy Robinson yelling out to somebody on the road, 'Are you going over to Ossining to see Mrs Eastman in the movies?'

Max was on the 5.03 last night & he brought Boardman & me up from Harmon [the local railway station, 2½ miles away] in his car. He looks awfully well and happy and is full of praise for Nantucket and every hour of the time he spent there. Florence is a deep brown color and so is Max. . . .

Dear, I'm too hot & uncomfortable to write any more now. I'll go and play with Jeffrey for a while – & will write to you tomorrow – I think I'm going to stay in town tomorrow night –

                Yours altogether

                      Walter[40]

He continued the following morning, Thursday:

> Dearest – my dearest – everybody's dearest you are, but you are mine – and I am yours – first and best of all – I'm putting this into the open envelope as a sort of postscript – I'll write again tonight. I'm going to stay in town tonight – to talk things over with Norman – I came into town this morning on the 8.16 from Harmon – Max brought Florence & me down to the station in the car – she gossiped to me all the way in! But she's a dear thing and sometimes she looked awfully sweet in the movie last night. I'll tell you about that later. Aren't we getting one another's letters – I'm writing nearly every day – I mail them as soon as I get to town in the morning – I've had two letters here from you – that's all. All's well at home. Jeffrey looks so different – so big and so beautiful in a new & more striking way – when he stands up on his feet and starts to walk. I think he's going to be the wonder child of the century. Dearest I *do* love you – love you dearly – I have such hopes & dreams for a glorious happy future.

The one cloud hanging over their lives was lack of money, as these letters show. 'At about lunch time' on the previous Friday, 9 August,

> I called in at Meyrowitz's and got my new glasses – price 8 dollars. In reply to my groan the man said, 'prices of lenses had gone up owing to the war.' I left the place feeling very much depressed – Walked up 5th Avenue a block or two meaning to have my lunch at that place where you & I and Max had dinner the other evening – that momentous evening. I walked gaily in – as gaily as was consistent with an 8 dollar hole in my pocket,

and that was where he found Edward Filene. The following Tuesday, 13 August, he had a visit from the telephone company. The employee

> waved a lot of bills at me with your name & my name, and *Liberator* writing paper, and '102 Waverly Place' all mixed up, some yellow & some white & some pink, the whole proving to his satisfaction that we owe him $16.38. . . . So I asked him to write down the amount and I would let him have it at the end of the week. So will you please pay it – and I'll go halves with you, and will give you my eight dollars when you return.[41]

These remarks, like his admission in his letter to Rosalind the previous summer that he owed Crystal $125, show that each paid their share of joint expenses. When necessary, they subsidized each other.

His letter from Friday afternoon, 16 August 1918, is the last in this series.

> Dearest – just a line before I dash off to catch the home train – hope there's a letter waiting for me there in the little house on the hill – a letter from you – Are you still in Glenora I wonder? I am going to spend the weekend at home of course – returning to town on Monday. . . .

Norman [Thomas] & Gilbert [Beaver, President of the Fellowship Press] are both keen about making me assistant editor at $50 a week and promise to put it through quickly. They both swear to heaven that I'm an essential industry and no one else would do. That's nice, isn't it?

I've going to write you a love letter tomorrow – Jove, how I do love you my darling. Am I – do you – really feel me tugging at your dear heart – me & Jeffrey? – Well I guess that's what we are doing – and you at mine and his.

Walter[42]

The promised love letter has not survived, possibly because Crystal kept it with her for a time; she treasured his love letters. She and Walter each had a fusional relationship with their nearest sibling. Consequently they expected equal intensity in their marriage, and could not achieve it. That left them feeling unsure of each other and lonely whenever they were apart. So letters like these were the food of love for them both.

Here's another, written on *Liberator* headed notepaper, which probably dates from this period. It may have been written when Walter was expecting Crystal to return to New York from Glenora.

Dearest,

As I was walking along from the French Restaurant up to my office – I thought to myself – I'd like to leave some flowers to smile at Crystal all day on her desk – and for them to have Crystal smile, like the sunshine, on them. But I have no money so I could do no other than come up here & just leave a loving message to greet you – instead of flowers – and, bless you, I *know for certain* that you'll be more happy to have this letter – this message from me – than any other that the postman will bring you this morning. Let's phone today —

Walter[43]

Walter's comment that the August issue of the *World Tomorrow* was going through the mail all right shows that he knew full well how close to the wind it was sailing. As if the Espionage Act were not enough, Congress had passed in May 1918 an amendment called the Sedition Act which went further in defining all the various forms of sedition, making it illegal, for example, to

utter, print, write, or publish any disloyal, profane, scurrilous, or abusive language about the form of government of the United States, or the Constitution of the United States, or the military or naval forces of the United States, or the flag . . . or the uniform of the Army or Navy of the United States, or any language intended to bring the form of government . . . or the Constitution . . . or the military or naval forces . . . or the flag . . . of the United States into contempt, scorn, contumely, or disrepute.[43]

The penalties were the same as for the Espionage Act, namely a fine of not more than $10,000 or imprisonment for not more than twenty years, or both. In these conditions it took courage to express one's opinions.

Walter's fears were well founded. Staff at the New York post office had already alerted Military Intelligence, who replied ominously: 'We feel that [the *World Tomorrow*], particularly the editor thereof, Reverend Norman Thomas, is only a shade removed from questionable public utterances as compared with Roger N. Baldwin . . . now under investigation by the Department of Justice, and should be glad to keep this subject under continued observation.'[44] In October, the Road-Mender apologized to readers for the late delivery of the September issue. The question of its mailability had been referred to the Solicitor General of the Post Office. The objectionable article, by Norman Thomas, questioned the American intervention in Russia. He confronted Postmaster General Albert Burleson in Washington, and was told, 'You're worse than Gene Debs. If I had my way I'd not only kill your magazine but send you to prison for life.'[45]

Luckily, the Secretary of the Fellowship Press was J. Nevin Sayre, whose brother Francis had married President Wilson's middle daughter Jessie. He went to the White House and asked to see the President. Wilson invited him in for dinner. Over the meal, Nevin told Wilson of his connection with the *World Tomorrow* and its troubles. According to Fleischman, the President listened silently until Sayre was finished and then said, 'Let me see it,' whereupon he looked over the article. Then he told Sayre, 'Well, I don't think this is seditious and I'll tell the Post Office and Justice departments so. . . . But you go and tell Norman Thomas that an English historian once said, "There is such a thing as an indecent display of private opinions in public."'[46] The next day, he ordered Burleson to release the *World Tomorrow*. It was one of only two instances in which Wilson overruled the Postmaster General.

As the *World Tomorrow* continued to print 'indecent' private opinions, it was banned several times by the post office, but each time it was let off. In his biography of Thomas, Raymond Gregory tells of the occasion when

> the well known and well respected Rev. John Haynes Holmes, in an article entitled 'The Search – a Parable', sought to discover where Hatred resided. He searched for Hatred in many places, in the trenches, in the military hospitals, and at Army headquarters, but all in vain for it did not reside in any of those places. He ultimately discovered Hatred residing in a beautiful garden, frequented by an elderly man and woman and a clergyman. Apparently, post office authorities considered Haynes' contention that Hatred dwelled among elderly and religious noncombatants, but not in the minds of the country's military, to be subversive.[47]

New Worlder

Escaping prosecution through the personal intervention of the President did not change the attitude of the *World Tomorrow* towards his policies. By the autumn of 1919 it was criticizing the terms of the Treaty of Versailles, which imposed crippling reparations and territorial concessions on Germany. Thomas and his contributors rightly saw them as seeds for a future war.

Walter's mention of a telephone bill for 102 Waverly Place in his letters to Crystal reveals that he and Crystal were now living on the corner of Washington Square, close to where Max and Florence were renting a house with their friends. Max describes the arrangement in his autobiography:

> Crystal was a great one for thinking up new schemes for the happier, and more economical, living of life. . . . She wanted to save money and have fun. And one of her schemes for that winter of 1918–19 had been to gather a few congenial friends, rent a house in Greenwich Village, hire a housekeeping cook, and live somewhat – though carefully not too much – like a family. She found the house on Washington Place, just east of Sheridan Square. It stood in a little row of red brick houses, all on the same level, with five steps going up to a white doorway with a brass knocker. . . . Ours was a venerable house with slim white pillars in front, and all the beautiful old doors and woodwork left untouched. It cost us $179.17 a month. . . .
>
> Besides the comely and convenient house, Crystal collected a delightful halfway family to live in it. . . . Ruth Pickering took the big front room on the first floor. She subsequently married Amos Pinchot. . . . Eugen Boissevain [widower of Inez Milholland] . . . took the second floor. . . . I lived above him on the top floor in two rooms with slanty ceilings, and Florence, although still ostensibly living with her mother on Ninth Street, stayed most of the time in those rooms.
>
> By an odd evolvement, Crystal . . . lived some way down the street and she and her husband only took their dinners with us. We ate those dinners in a large room in the basement. . . .
>
> Crystal would sit at one end of the table. . . . Her husband Walter Fuller sat at the opposite end, a rather small man in rimless glasses, who looked at first glance like an 'organizational' bank clerk, but turned out to be brimming with irreverently humane irony and wit. . . .
>
> I sat at Crystal's right, and Florence next to me, Ruth and Eugen on the other side – Eugen always full of laughter and Ruth emitting a soft cool radiance because she was loved and in love. We were, on the whole, as happy as Crystal predicted – as economical too, though we each paid extra for guests and guests had a way of getting in pretty often.[48]

There was no room for children in Max's domestic paradise. We must assume that at mealtimes Jeffrey remained with his nanny at 102 Waverly Place.

That autumn saw the end of the war. America's brief participation in it brought immense financial benefits at the cost of only 126,000 men, whereas the European countries were ruined, and suffered millions of casualties.

The eighteen months or so following the return of Walter's sisters to England were not particularly happy ones for them. They had spent almost every hour of the past six years in each other's company and under Walter's management, bonded as siblings and by their common purpose. Suddenly, that purpose had evaporated along with their manager. It took a while to come to terms with this – and redefine themselves as individuals, each with a separate life and purpose.

The homeward crossing was very rough at first and then punctuated by submarine alerts; once their ship fired on a suspected target. However, they were cheered to discover a friend of the Eastmans on board, Griffin Barry, on his way to France to work for the Red Cross. He was good company, and the girls enjoyed the stories he told of Russia, where he had spent a year with John Reed. Had Walter known, he might have been pleased to think that Barry was keeping an eye on his sisters, but in truth it was like having a wolf guard the sheepfold, for Barry slept with anyone, and everyone, he could.

They arrived at Southampton with just £2 in their pockets, so they did not cash the cheque that Norman Angell had given to Rosalind for emergencies. After the joyful reunion with their parents, they tried to find work, only to realize that they were qualified in nothing but singing folksongs. They managed to land a few engagements, mostly at the Winter Gardens in Bournemouth and occasionally in private houses, but folksongs were not considered noisy enough for venues like Army camps. Worse, they met with none of the rapturous reception that they had enjoyed in America. In England, they were nonentities. It was most discouraging.

Cynthia tested as a retoucher with a local photographer, but proved unsatisfactory because she had no prior experience. While following lessons in art at a local school, she took occasional jobs, working for the post office at Christmas, for instance, but little else. She showed a number of people, including Roger Fry, the paintings she had done at the MacDowell colony, but they failed to impress. She became depressed and fell ill with a condition that required an operation on her leg. Only when Curt was demobbed and offered to pay for her to study art at the Slade did she begin to cheer up again. She married him in June 1919.

Dorothy tried to place her illustrated book of singing games. Although publishers were complimentary, they explained that there was no market for children's books at present, neither in England nor America (where Norman Angell sounded out the publishers for her, also seeking to place a proposed *Fuller Sisters' Anthology of Folk Songs*). She did some illustrating for magazines and calendars through a commercial art agency, but it paid little. In the end, she and Riss worked as clerks for the RAF, for which the only requirements were good handwriting and intelligence (in that order). Dorothy gave it up as soon as the war ended. Riss stuck it a year longer, for Basil was released by the RAMC only at Christmas 1919.

In the autumn of their return to England, the girls bumped into Stanley Nott on leave in London. After living in Tasmania, New Zealand, Australia and Canada, working on sheep stations and farms, he had been on a small island off the coast of British Columbia when the war broke out. He at once joined the Canadian Overseas Expeditionary Force, and had been on active service ever since. Now he became a regular visitor to Alum Cottage. As he preferred to stay with the Fullers rather than return home when he had leave, his mother would come to Bournemouth to see him. He and Dorothy became close and after he was invalided out of the Army she spent a few days with him and his parents – but she was shocked when she heard a local shopkeeper refer to her as Stanley's fiancée. It was not like that at all. Stanley had no doubt nourished some hopes but they were dashed when Dorothy fell for a freshly demobbed surveyor, Jack Odell, whose parents lived just across the road from Alum Cottage. Stanley left for America at the end of March and Dorothy married Jack in November 1919.

Rosalind, on the other hand, aspired to independence and a career. She had hardly hugged her parents before she was off to London, determined to go on the stage or act in films. Performing folksongs had made her intensely happy 'and I must go on doing this kind of work – for in it I live, and out of it I only exist,' she told Cynthia. 'Somehow on the stage I seem to lose my old self, and become some other; it is most strange. I love the responsibility of having a whole audience there in my hand – an instrument on which I can play!'[49] For a short while she lived with Arthur Dakyns, who alone had come to welcome the girls off the boat. He expected her to marry him, but she soon set him right as to that. He could have all the sex he wanted, but marriage was out of the question. For fifteen months – that is until the end of 1918 – they led a cat-and-dog life, with clashes, reconciliations, attempts to live together, and tempestuous ruptures. She supported herself by working at the Labour Exchange in Waltham Green, 'a prisoner to the clock and the government,' as she put it in a letter to Norman Angell.⁵⁰ Throughout this time she kept up her correspondence with him, and he sent her further instalments of his *roman-à-clef* about her life. Out of discretion, she received his letters through his secretary, Marjorie Manus, rather than at her parents' house or, worse, Dakyns'.*

When Rosalind lived in rented lodgings, the evenings were her own. She would go round London's theatres, meeting everyone she could, begging for a part, no matter how small. Sometimes she landed non-speaking roles. Once she was a corpse. She interviewed with the Gaumont Film Company, but nothing came of that. She also spent much time in her room reading plays, learning parts and rehearsing them by herself in front of a cheval glass. She took Dalcroze dancing lessons. At one point, she moved back in with Dakyns, and he rewarded her by paying for drama lessons from the sister of Lillah McCarthy.† But she landed no work as an actress.‡

Dakyns' promise to help the sisters find work was as empty as his other schemes, like his aim of introducing them to 'the nicest & most progressive sorts of people.'⁵¹ True, he did introduce Rosalind to T. S. Eliot, whom he saw often enough,§ but she seems to have found Vivien Eliot, 'his sad wife, a strange, frustrated ballet dancer,' more memorable than the poet.⁵³ That autumn Vivien complained to her diary that Dakyns was 'dragging his feet over arranging a dance'⁵⁴ – probably because his relationship with Rosalind was so unpredictable that he could not make plans involving her.

On the other hand, Rosalind never forgot an evening with Dakyns' old friend Bertrand Russell in December 1917. She took the opportunity to voice her opinions on female emancipation and sexual independence. They coincided with Bertrand Russell's views on marriage and morality – after all, his

---

* Marjorie Manus also worked for B. N. Langdon-Davies of the Union of Democratic Control and the National Council for Civil Liberties; she introduced Rosalind to him.

† Lillah McCarthy was George Bernard Shaw's favourite actress, married to Harley Granville-Barker.

‡ This answers the speculation by Hugo Vickers, in his biography of *Elizabeth, the Queen Mother* (2005), that Rosalind might have been the actress Miss Fuller who on 23 October 1918 relieved the twenty-three-year-old Prince Albert – the future King George VI – of his virginity. In a personal communication to me, Vickers admitted that it had been 'just a hunch' and he had 'absolutely no evidence whatsoever that Miss Fuller was Rosalind.' Had it been her, we can be sure that she would have performed her loyal duty with great pleasure – and recorded it in her explicit autobiography.

§ In September 1917, just before the Fullers returned, Eliot had paid Arthur and his sister an extended visit. 'They have a large house with a good library. I shall go home in a day or two, not to abuse their hospitality too long,' he told his mother.⁵²

own father, Viscount Amberley, had been an atheist and had consented to his wife's affair with their children's tutor, and Russell himself had had an affair with Vivien Eliot. When Rosalind asked what he recommended for her relationship with Dakyns, he advised her not to marry him but to lead the life of her own choice, hard though that might be at times. She was very grateful for his encouragement. The following February, when he appeared at Bow Street for making statements 'intended and likely to prejudice His Majesty's relations with the United States,' she was in court to provide moral support, and admired how his words 'flew about the dark court like meteors.'[55] She sent him comforting messages during his six-month sentence – which is more than can be said of Dakyns. In June, he told Russell that he had heard that Russell was 'not finding [prison] so bad after all' and wrote cheerfully of his own holiday plan to spend a fortnight in a wooden shed he had acquired just above Hampton Court.[56]

At the very end of 1918, Rosalind finally found work on the stage, although it was not quite the stage she had envisaged. She saw an advertisement to the effect that girls were wanted for a show called '*Folies Bergère*' in Paris. She went to the address indicated and was interviewed by Albert de Courville who, as a director of theatrical reviews in England, was acting as agent for Paris.* To her surprise, he simply looked her up and down, asked her to take her hat off and said, 'You'll do.' She signed a contract to start in January at 400 francs a week.†

Today it may seem incredible that neither she nor her parents, to whom she excitedly announced her glad news, quite realized what kind of show was put on at the *Folies Bergère*. Luckily, Norman Angell returned to London in December and he will have told her – but not her parents. That month, Rosalind regularly spent the night with him in his flat in King's Bench Walk. 'After talking and making love he would tuck me up on his divan in the sittingroom, with a sort of protective sadness. He was afraid for me and my freedom-behaviour. "Do take care of yourself," he would say.'[57] He was leaving for Paris on 27 December to cover the Peace Conference. She left the following day, and they agreed to spend New Year's Eve together. Rosalind could not have had a better guide and guardian in Paris.

* It was only in the 1930s that de Courville started to make the films for which he is remembered today.

† Rosalind was not the first Fuller to perform at the *Folies Bergère*. One of its most famous turn-of-the-century artistes was the American Marie Louise Fuller, known as 'La Loïe'. She is depicted in many artworks of the period, including a famous poster by Jules Cherét (1897). In 1902, she helped Isadora Duncan launch her European career.

Walter Fuller

In the event, however, she seems to have spent little time with him, for he was often busy meeting and debating with far more important people. On her arrival, Rosalind was met off the train by Manley Hudson, who was there with the US Peace Commission. In fact, everyone who was anyone was in Paris for the Conference, so she encountered many other people whom she had known in the United States or who were friends of Walter's. They would take turns to meet her at the stage door and invite her to join them and their friends for a late supper in a café on the Left Bank.* Thus she was introduced to Ella Winter and Lincoln Steffens, John Dos Passos, and Walter Lippmann. She met John Nightingale, her one-night stand from the summer of 1917, now a captain on President Wilson's staff. There was also Griffin Barry, working as a stringer for United Press. Dos Passos described him as 'a small rosy-faced man who knew everything and everybody . . . the insider incarnate. There was hardly anybody he hadn't been to bed with. . . . He was the future Greenwich Village encapsulated.'⁵⁸

Bertrand Russell's theories of sexual morality suited Rosalind, but they met their match in Griffin Barry. At the end of the 1920s, Russell was married to Dora Black (of whom more in a few pages) and by mutual agreement they both had occasional lovers on the side. In 1928, Dora went on a lecture tour in the United States where she had an affair with Griffin Barry. The following year she met him again, this time in France, and returned home pregnant. Although hurt, Russell agreed to accept the child as though she were his own daughter. Unfortunately, Dora had a second child by Barry, a boy, in March 1932.† By then, things had changed for Russell: his elder brother had died and he had become the third Earl Russell. For all his progressive thinking, he wanted the boy who inherited his title to be his own flesh and blood. He had a mistress forty years his junior who could bear him a son. He sued for divorce. Until the abdication of King Edward VIII and his marriage to a newly divorced American woman, the Russell case was the greatest social scandal of the 1930s.

Conscientious objectors were not treated well in the United States. Congruent with the notion that only 'good citizens' had rights, they were disqualified for life from voting. If they did work of national importance they were assured that they would be permitted to vote again a year after the

---

*   One of the journalist Lewis Gannett's 'oddest memories' was of doing just this in the company of Norman Angell and Manley Hudson.⁵⁸

†   In her autobiography, Dora's daughter Harriet titled the chapter in which her brother was conceived, 'Two looks like carelessness.'

war was over. Many were prepared to work but some refused to accept orders from the army they had not joined. Despite instructions to the contrary from the War Department, the military persisted in treating these COs as though they were mutinous soldiers. At camps like Leavenworth and prisons like Alcatraz, attempts were made to break their spirit through solitary confinement and a diet of bread and water. The most resistant of them were stripped and made to stand for nine hours a day in chilly cells, with their wrists handcuffed to bars above head height. They had no toilet facilities and slept on the soiled floor of their cells with but a dirty blanket to cover them. Two members of 'a little known religious sect' whose church 'forbade the wearing of military garb' died in prison of pneumonia as a result of this treatment.[59] Norman Thomas's brother Ewan was a conscientious objector of singular courage and determination. He 'voluntarily gave up congenial work and unflinchingly accepted confinement in one of these chambers of torture in order to make his protest against the coercion of his comrades.'[60] (One of them was Howard Moore who, before the war, had been 'awarded a medal and $500 by the Carnegie Hero Fund Commission for the gallant rescue of a woman at the risk of his own life.'[61])

The *World Tomorrow* was one of the rare publications that dared report this appalling treatment – which continued after the war was over – despite the risk that it ran of falling foul of the obdurate Burleson. It brought up the topic in every issue from September 1918 onwards, which must have exacerbated the authorities' antipathy towards it. The issue for January 1919 overstepped the mark. The post office refused to mail it because of an unsigned article titled 'Behind Prison Walls' which declared that

> The time for soft words on these continuing atrocities has passed. The War Department conceivably can make a case for its course in confining men who refused to be conscripted during the war. But to shut them up in a prison where they are continually subject to the very military order against which they are protesting is an absurd cruelty. . . . The torture of indefinite solitary imprisonment is nothing less than the revival of the cruelties of the Inquisition.
>
> To continue the imprisonment of these men or of any political prisoners when the emergency of the war is long past is to impair our right to appear at the international peace table as a champion of humanity against militarism. Therefore, we join our voice with those who throughout the length and breadth of the land are demanding an amnesty for all political prisoners not as an act of grace but as an act of simple justice – an amnesty – a release – not merely for the men condemned but for the very soul of America.

> Meanwhile ... comes a scandalous report from the Leavenworth Federal Penitentiary. ... It appears that in this Federal prison, a few days ago ... at least twenty-five men were put in solitary cells, cruelly manacled and, in addition to this, terribly beaten. One of the victims lay unconscious twenty hours. Some fourteen others were also sufficiently injured to require hospital treatment even when judged by the humane standards that obtain at such an institution.
>
> These serious charges call for a public investigation and immediate and thoroughgoing reform of our whole Federal prison system. Our country is already disgraced as the home of lynchings; are we to add to our infamy an easy tolerance of dark atrocities in our prisons?[62]

Today, dark atrocities are still committed in US prisons. The need for the American Civil Liberties Union is as great as ever.

Although it is not known what part Walter played in penning these lines, he will certainly have edited them for print. The irony and many of the turns of phrase, like 'throughout the length and breadth of the land' (one of his favourites) and the subtitle, 'A Blot on the 'Scutcheon', sound more English than American. He may even have been its author. At any rate, this piece contains a suggestion that recalls his *Liberator* article, in which he imagined sending princes and prominent figures to the front. Here it is proposed that psychiatrists be appointed to investigate the effects of this gratuitous cruelty on the minds of the COs. They should 'don prison uniform; hear ... the ominous clanging of their cell doors; submit to an indeterminate sentence of solitary confinement; be forbidden to read or write, and live the while on bread and water. ... We warrant that they would give us a report unusually well worth reading.'[63] The article does not propose to have them stripped or beaten; it shuns violence. Although the January issue was never released by the post office, the *World Tomorrow* escaped prosecution once again.

With the end of the war came greater freedom to travel, and Walter badly wanted to go to England and see his mother and his sisters. So he arranged a long leave of absence from his various activities. Crystal made similar arrangements, so that they could go together.

At the end of February 1919, she organized a Woman's Freedom Congress, with sessions on education and industry, the family and government, in the context of the annual convention of the New York WPP (now the Women's International League for Peace). The topics covered in the first session – modern education for girls, professional opportunities for women, the social and economic struggle of black women, labour legislation for women, and women and trade unions – point to the widening scope of Crystal's actions on behalf of women. The third session was more directly political, stressing the need for laws defending the woman's rights of citizenship, irrespective of her husband's country of origin. Crystal closed her opening statement with a rousing slogan: 'We will not wait for the social revolution to bring us the freedom we should have won in the nineteenth century.'[64] Financially, however, the conference was a disaster; it left a deficit of over two thousand dollars.

Immediately after the congress, Crystal resigned as President and left for England with Walter and Jeffrey. They arrived at Alum Cottage, Bournemouth, on 14 April 1919. It was a joyful reunion, for Walter had not been home for five years. But it was not a happy one. For some mothers it is not easy to accept the girl who has supplanted them in their son's heart. Mrs Fuller being devoted to Walter, and he to her, Crystal was bound to get a cool reception, and she resented it. The Fuller parents had reserved rooms for Walter and Crystal just down the road, but they did not like them and came back to Alum Cottage saying they wanted to stay there. Mrs Fuller was none too pleased by this idea. That evening Crystal went out by herself, leaving Dorothy to put Jeffrey to bed.

The following morning, Crystal tried to talk with her mother-in-law, but it ended with both women in tears and Crystal rushing out of the house. She was retrieved from the Chine some hours later by Mr Fuller. Things were calmer that afternoon as they all went out for a picnic. But the following day, Crystal announced that she was going away for two weeks and Walter went with her, leaving Jeffrey in Dorothy's charge. The atmosphere became even more tense when Riss discovered that Walter had never paid for the piano that he had given her, five years before. Some of Walter's creditors must have caught up with him, now that he was back in England.

The following weeks were punctuated by much coming and going. Being used to having a nanny for Jeffrey, Walter and Crystal would go off for a couple of days' walking or visiting – sometimes remaining away longer than announced – leaving him in the care of the Fullers (usually Dorothy). They seemed quite unaware of the strain that this placed on the family. Jeffrey, now just twenty-five months old, was understandably very unhappy at all these changes; he slept badly and cried a great deal, throwing tantrums when taken into shops. When Walter and Crystal returned, he refused to look at them. They resolved to place him in a residential 'school' in London.

This freed up Crystal to attend the Second International Congress of Women in Zurich, Switzerland (12–17 May). From there she went on to

Hungary, the site of her 1913 introduction to the international women's suffrage movement. Hungary had just experienced a popular revolution and was now a soviet republic. As an American socialist, she was given the privilege of addressing the Central Council, bringing greetings from American workmen. When this was reported in the US press, questions were asked about her right to travel. The State Department placed severe restrictions on the issue of passports, and socialists were not given them to attend political conferences in Europe. Crystal had got round this obstacle by travelling on a British passport in the name of Catherine Fuller. (Catherine was her first name.) She returned to England in time to attend the first convention of the British Labour Party on 27 June 1919. What Walter did during these weeks, I do not know, except that he was present at Cynthia's wedding in Manchester on 4 June. I think he was job-hunting.

He and Crystal probably supplied the unsigned texts that were printed in the 12 June issue of *Four Lights* – the first and only issue since October 1917. One reported on the resolutions of the Zurich conference; another quoted from addresses delivered by French and German women at a public meeting at Zurich University in the context of the conference. The only signed piece in that issue was by Jessie Wallace Hugan, reprinted from the *World Tomorrow*.

For July and August, Crystal and Walter rented number 22 Downshire Hill, on the edge of Hampstead Heath. To leave them free of their movements, Jeffrey remained in his 'school'. But now Walter and Crystal found themselves at loggerheads. Crystal was not happy in England. Although there were times when she enjoyed herself, as when they spent a weekend in a cottage with Cynthia and Curt, nothing drew her to the country; she liked neither the climate nor the way the people behaved. Both were too cold for her. She preferred America, where the seasons were more pronounced and the people more demonstrative, and wanted to go back there. Walter preferred England and wanted to find a job and stay. This difference of (largely cultural) sensibility remained something they could not resolve.

In mid-August, they visited Lella Faye Secor, who had settled in Cambridge with her husband Philip Florence, and hosted them in London a week later. While in Cambridge, they met Dora Black, 'a slender, vivacious dark-eyed' student who was shortly to became Bertrand Russell's secretary and then his wife. (Seven years later, Crystal interviewed her for *Equal Rights*.)[65] They met others in Cambridge too, among them C.K. Ogden. Walter wrote to him warmly soon afterwards: 'My dear Ogden, forgive my silence in Scotland – I had a very crowded time up there.' (It was his third wedding anniversary.) He, and presumably Crystal too, had been attending the Trades Union Congress in Glasgow.*

He passed on to Ogden 'a pleasant enough note' he had received from Gordon Selfridge, the owner of the department store in London, about 'the unfriendly attitude' towards America that Walter seems to have discerned in England.† He asked Ogden to follow up Selfridge's invitation and set up a meeting with him: 'any time that suits you both will suit me.' And he ended, enigmatically, 'Will try to finish Barlow business [not identified] here by Monday morning.'[66] After the meeting with Selfridge, Walter wrote to Ogden, 'I want very much to see you again – let's have a quiet chat *entre nous* next time.' In a postscript he added, 'there's a lot of good stuff in this week's issue of the *Magazine* – Congratulations.'[67]

It is highly probable that Walter had already been in contact with Ogden for some time. The first extant letter, quoted above, suggests an ongoing correspondence. During the war, the *Cambridge Magazine*, which Ogden had started while still an undergraduate at Cambridge in 1912, became a major organ of international comment on politics and the war. More than half of each week's issue was given over to extracts from up to one hundred foreign newspapers, under the direction of Mrs Buxton, whose husband was a prominent member of the Union of Democratic Control. Since official censorship prevented the British public from gaining direct knowledge of opposing views about the war, these extracts provided them with much needed perspective, and the magazine sold widely. As it was classed as a student paper, it escaped censorship – just.

It would be most surprising if Walter, being such a reader of periodicals, even very small ones, and addicted to press clippings, had not encountered the *Cambridge Magazine* in the early years of the war. If he had not, then a letter from a Mrs F. W. Ladd, dated 18 February 1917 and addressed to the Secretary of the New York branch of the WPP, will have brought it to his attention. She was seeking contributors of extracts from the foreign press and asked the WPP to forward her letter to anyone who might be interested.

---

* Walter provided the December issue of the *Liberator* with a three-page report on it. From the address in Cheadle Hulme, Manchester, at the head of this letter, I believe that Walter was staying with his old friend Bill Hankinson, by then a dispensing chemist.

† Anti-American feeling was a tender topic with Selfridge. It is not known how Walter came to correspond with him. In the spring of 1913, Mrs Selfridge met the Fullers after attending one of their recitals. She was often in the United States – her daughter Rosalie was at school in New York – and she played the harp. After she died of the flu in 1918, Walter may have sent a letter of condolence to her husband.

Walter Fuller

It is hard to imagine Walter turning down the opportunity to become a contributor. However, none of the *Cambridge Magazine*'s wartime correspondence has been preserved, so there is no way of proving that he supplied it with extracts. That said, the *Cambridge Magazine* was in all probability the source of the brief quotations from an ever-widening number of foreign periodicals that appeared in *Four Lights*. Walter certainly knew about the *Cambridge Magazine* by the time he was editing the *World Tomorrow*, for he mentioned it more than once in his column, 'By the Way'.

Being in Cambridge, Walter had to meet Ogden, if only because he applauded his Foreign Press Survey. And there was every reason why he should like him too, for Ogden was a Lancastrian, a pacifist, and a feminist. Did Walter realize that Ogden's financial situation resembled his own? As the *Cambridge Magazine* sold for only one penny, Ogden was constantly short of funds. In 1914 he had issued an 'appeal for immediate financial support'; among the signatories to it was his friend Bertrand Russell.

Walter remained in contact with Ogden after his return to America that autumn, sending him by bearer a letter of introduction to a young Jamaican 'poet of some distinction over here, Claude McKay,' who had started to contribute to the *Liberator*.* After McKay visited Ogden in 1920, the *Cambridge Magazine* printed some of his poems. As previous contributors had included Siegfried Sassoon, John Masefield, Thomas Hardy, George Bernard Shaw, and Arnold Bennett, it was a major coup for McKay, and contributed largely to his reputation.

In his book on McKay, *The Shadowed Country,* Josh Gosciak claims that Walter 'was confident that McKay would enjoy [Ogden's] company, as well as learn a bit about "deir [sic] solemn sacred beauty".' He maintains that in introducing McKay, Walter 'planted the seed of intrigue [sic] that would have lasting significance for postcolonial expression.'[68] He goes on:

> Fuller briefed the young poet on the rigors of his apprenticeship. It would be a unique experience, akin to the voyage in the eighteenth-century by the navigator Equiano, but on uncharted linguistic waters. Ogden, Fuller warned, was one of the brilliant contemporary minds in England, a member of a quirky group of talented Cambridge intellectuals infamous for all-night brainstorming sessions that usually included two other conspirators in revolt, I. A. Richards and James Wood.[69]

---

* Max and Crystal could hardly give their periodical the same title as the famous anti-slavery publication launched in 1831 by William Lloyd Garrison – grandfather of Oswald Garrison Villard – without a coloured contributor. In return, McKay worshipped Crystal, declaring she was the most beautiful white woman he had ever met.

New Worlder

I can only quote Gosciak on this, for I have not seen any document that contains these statements.*

Walter also made contact with many of those who had defended British conscientious objectors during the war, particularly B. N. Langdon-Davies, of the Union of Democratic Control and the National Council for Civil Liberties (hereafter NCCL). He was no doubt looking for a job. He also had an idea to put forward. Given the similar aims of the English NCCL and the American NCLB (soon to be the ACLU), Walter proposed that they should jointly organize a conference in New York on the postwar restoration of civil liberties, after which pairs of delegates from the two countries could tour the United States, sharing the same lecture platforms. It was an idea that he had suggested to Albert deSilver of the NCLB and now he put it to Langdon-Davies. He liked the idea and suggested potential participants, including Norman Angell and Bertrand Russell; neither of them was ultimately able to attend, although both wrote letters of support.

Organizing the conference was laborious because it took anything up to two months to exchange letters between the NCCL and the NCLB. On 30 June, Langdon-Davies told deSilver, 'I am seeing Walter Fuller and Miss Eastman again shortly. My idea would be . . . to send Fuller over with all the details so as to fix things up.'[70] However, that did not fit with Walter's plans and he remained in England until the beginning of October, returning to New York just two weeks before the conference opened. Instead, he wrote a long, frank letter telling deSilver about the English delegates who had definitely agreed to attend. First he referred deSilver to *Who's Who* (when relevant) and then gave his personal opinion, never imagining for a moment that his words would be filed away and ultimately made public. As usual, what one man says of another tells us quite as much about the speaker as it does about the person described, and Walter's letter shows that he now saw his fellow-countrymen through Americanized eyes. He also reveals his likes and dislikes in other men.

---

* None of the archives that Gosciak lists in his book happens to possess this particular document. He evaded the question when I asked where he found it and he has not responded to my request for a copy of it. In *The Shadowed Country,* Gosciak cheerfully introduces Walter as 'an English poet and the lover of Crystal Eastman' who studied at Cambridge with Ogden and published a volume of poems titled *A Game of Love* in 1904. Asked where he found *this* information, Gosciak answered that the book is in the catalogue of Cambridge University Library. True, its catalogue does list a book with this title by a Walter Fuller, but it is classed as fiction, not poetry. And nothing identifies its author as 'our' Walter Fuller. So I treat everything that Gosciak writes with circumspection.

On Frederick Pethick-Lawrence, Walter wrote, 'I have been meeting him several times lately – he strikes me as being very much disgruntled about everything in general – this may be particularly because he's a disappointed Wilsonian." C. G. Ammon, honorary secretary of the NCCL was

> a member of the London County Council and organizing secretary of the Civil Service Union. . . . I have met him several times and he has always struck me as a pleasant, genial man – a better mixer than most Englishmen. . . . In confidence I might express the hope that his visit to America will lead him to abandon the fashion . . . of waxing the ends of his moustache. The sight of a whole nation of clean-shaven men will perhaps suggest to him the desirability of cutting off those long needle-like pointers which stick out due east and west above the corners of his mouth.[71]

On Holford Knight, best remembered as the man who in 1919 almost single-handedly achieved equal rights for women to study and practice the law in England: 'He is a lively, witty fellow – not more than 40 to 45 years old – but I find him – as indeed I find nearly all Englishmen – very definitely egocentric.' Of Gilbert Cannan, the prolific writer who had been active with the National Council Against Conscription (and who had stolen J. M. Barrie's wife while working as his secretary; his dog Luath was the inspiration for Nana in *Peter Pan*), we learn that

> He has a typical Cambridge manner and speech. Is quite a dandy in the English style – wears white spats for instance and has a pretty taste in ties. They say he's a good speaker and quite a brilliant man. . . . He is certainly very likeable. His mood is that of Pethick-Lawrence – very gloomy and rebellious.'[72]

Walter was probably aware that Cannan was a Mancunian – always a recommendation in his eyes – but he may not have known that he had had a breakdown during the war. At this point in 1919 his marriage had just fallen apart because he was having an affair with Gwen Wilson; unfortunately she married Henry Mond while Cannan was lecturing in America following the conference. After living with Gwen and Henry in a notorious *ménage à trois*, Cannan had another breakdown in 1923 and spent the rest of his life – thirty-two years – in Holloway Sanatorium.

Walter considered Langdon-Davies to be

> the whole show at the Civil Liberties Council here. . . . Was organizer of the Norman Angell League and visited America and lectured extensively under the auspices of the Carnegie Endowment – I suppose at the invitation of Mr Secretary Keppel now of the War Office! He's a very keen worker – gets things done – knows everybody. A Welshman by birth, therefore not quite

so noticeably English as some of the others – Cannan for instance and Pethick-Lawrence – but is fully possessed of the English quality of egoism.[73]

Walter continued that he was very fond of J. A. Hobson, whom he knew from the days of the *University Review*. He had served on the executive council of the Union of Democratic Control during the war. Walter described him as

a quiet, witty, dry-humoured, slightly cynical old man – or perhaps I should say elderly man. . . . He is really the bright particular star of the whole company. Norman Thomas will appreciate Hobson as the anonymous author of that series of satirical sketches of England in 1920 which came out in the London *Nation* and was afterwards published in book form under the title of *1920*. Hobson is a delicate, frail-looking man – entirely lacking in aggressive qualities of any kind. Altogether most likeable, not to say lovable.[74]

Predictably, he enclosed with these remarks some press cuttings that he thought might interest deSilver, with the request that he pass them on to Norman Thomas, 'with my love.'

Over the following months, Walter continued to facilitate the conference, providing 'invaluable help' with publicity;[75] Langdon-Davies assured deSilver, 'I am in close touch with Walter Fuller and always consult him when I am in doubt.'[76] He often worked with Marjorie Manus, telling her to write 'long, bright and sisterly letters' to deSilver.[77] He also put delegates in contact with agents he knew from the tours with his sisters so that they could finance their stay in America by giving lectures.

When the conference took place over 24–25 October 1919, titled 'The Anglo-American Tradition of Liberty,' it was accompanied by a long list of statements of support from luminaries across Britain. They included Arnold Bennett, Annie Besant, Lord Buckmaster, Lowes Dickinson, Laurence Housman, Arthur Henderson, Jerome K. Jerome, George Lansbury, John Masefield, Arthur Ponsonby, Bertrand Russell, Olive Schreiner, C. P. Scott, George Bernard Shaw, Robert Smillie, C. P. Trevelyan, and Josiah Wedgwood. One wonders how many of them Walter had corresponded with. He was certainly in contact with George Lansbury, owner of the *Daily Herald*, and C. P. Scott, editor of the *Manchester Guardian* (whose son had married J. A. Hobson's daughter), for he had applied to each of them for a post on their staff. Lansbury wrote back:

Dear Fuller,

We have had a talk about your letter, and very reluctantly we are obliged to say no.

The simple reason is that on our Editorial side we are rather crowded at the present moment, and the number of people who have applied to come on board is very large indeed. . . .

I can only hope that you will have better luck in some other direction where you wish to put your work.

With best of good wishes,

G. Lansbury[78]

The 'we' in this letter probably includes the foreign editor of the *Herald*, Trilby Ewer. Both he and his wife Monica agreed to read papers at the Tradition of Liberty conference. Monica had been a member of the Executive Committee of the NCCL. She was drama and film critic for the *Daily Herald* and later became one of the best known writers of light romantic fiction of her generation. Several of her novels were filmed; she also wrote dialogue for films in the 1930s. At the conference her paper was on the right to travel and communicate.

At this point, the Fullers' connection with Ewer, which had begun in 1914 when Walter chose to add the 'Five Souls' to his sisters' repertoire and Rosalind set it to music, took a curious turn. Rosalind met Ewer in Paris, where he was covering the Peace Conference. 'One night when Griffin was seeing me back to my room,' she writes in her autobiography, 'we met W. N. Ewer on the Metro. . . . Griffin introduced me and somehow it was Ewer and I who left the train together and from that night a long romantic friendship began.' Instead of going to bed, they wandered the streets until dawn, when they joined the street cleaners in their shelter, grouped round a brazier 'like figures in a Daumier drawing.' After that, they met frequently, often at night, and explored Paris together. 'Once we breakfasted near the Eiffel Tower, then, going to the top, Ewer wrote me a poem, "Today I was the Eiffel Tower".'[79] When he returned to London, he continued to send her poems and letters.

Rosalind,

You have changed me from a dull misanthrope glooming at the world, to a horribly cheerful person. I have been shaken out of my unemotional self for the first time in my life. My love for you is not just physical; there is that of course and I'm not ashamed of it. But I want my love for you to be something different from the others'. I feel they just love the beauty of you and your joy and liveliness; they have a picture of you as the *bacchante* of the *boulevards*, but my picture is of a small silent figure standing on the steps of Sacré Coeur playing quiet melodies on the grey roofs of the city.

Love,

Ewer[80]

For all his reference to physical love, Ewer is practically the only man of whom Rosalind writes, 'We never made love.'

After completing her contract at the *Folies Bergère*, Rosalind took a holiday with Dos Passos and Griffin Barry. But 'we didn't get very far because two into three won't go, without one over. So I returned to Paris.'[81] Then, at the invitation of Dorothy Donnelly,* she joined a troupe entertaining the army of occupation at Koblenz. There she had an affair with a Texan captain, taking 'lovely horse-rides with him in the tall pine forests, in and out of shafts of light and deep shadows. I rode on his orderly's horse that was very class-conscious and insisted on walking a few paces behind his, so that romantic, intimate conversation was impossible.' Once, disguised as an airman, she was secretly given her first flight in an aeroplane: 'as the crotch of my flying suit came way below my knees, I looked like a small penguin.'[82]

She returned to England in July 1919, determined to become an actress in America, where Dorothy Donnelly had promised to help her. Arthur Dakyns, who had been having his own adventures with T. S. Eliot in a boat that went aground in soft mud in a falling tide,[83] took her for a holiday. But she knew that her future did not lie with him. In mid-February, he had sent her a suicide note by telegram: 'Unless you are home by Tuesday you will never see me again.' Abandoning her professional obligations in Paris, she hastened to England, arriving after the deadline to find him safe and well. Now she told him of her plan to go to New York, and he generously offered to pay for her crossing *on condition that*, as soon as she arrived, she would go to a psychoanalyst and be treated at Dakyns' expense. He was sure that there must be something wrong with her: she did not behave like a 'normal woman'. Rosalind, who had realized that it was he who needed psychological help, was happy to accept; anything that enabled her to know herself better was welcome. It would also help her to 'understand many of the play characters that I was sure I should soon be portraying.'[84]

Before leaving on 30 August 1919, she spent time with her family, including Walter and Crystal. Unlike the Fullers, Crystal encouraged her dream of becoming an actress and offered to help her with contacts.[85] Rosalind enjoyed a few days on the Norfolk Broads, 'basking in the sanity of Norman Angell.'[85] She also met Trilby Ewer, who entrusted her with letters to post in New York. There was one for deSilver which failed to arrive.

* The daughter of the manager of the Grand Opera House in New York, Dorothy Donnelly (1880–1928) was a stage actress, playwright, producer, librettist, and lyricist. She collaborated with composer Sigmund Romberg on a number of musicals, including – most memorably – *The Student Prince*.

It is noteworthy that Ewer asked Rosalind to post letters for him. He was surely not saving on postage, but rather evading the censor. For Ewer had things to hide. Not for nothing was the paper he delivered to the October conference entitled 'International Espionage'. At that very moment, the Directorate of Intelligence (Home Office) was investigating the *Daily Herald*. Its Special Report No 12, dated 25 November 1919, reveals that during the war Ewer, as a conscientious objector, 'undertook work of national importance on the land, where he failed to get on terms with the dumb animals under his charge – he is reported to have been tossed by a bull and bitten by a pedigree pig.'[87] This inability to establish a working relationship with farm animals was clearly suspicious; on the other side of the Atlantic it would doubtless be classed as 'interference with food production.' So the Home Office watched him. After protracted investigation, they came to the conclusion that, from the time of his visit to New York in 1919 until 1929, Ewer ran a Russian intelligence network in London. So Rosalind appears to have served, quite unwittingly, as a courier for a budding communist spy ring.*

Carrying these letters, she enjoyed the company of Felix Frankfurter (then aged thirty-six) on board the *Rotterdam*. 'I had met him many times in Paris during the Peace Conference. At that time he was a professor of administrative law at Harvard, and later became a Justice of the Supreme Court in America. He often invited me into the first class to dine with him.' She told him of her ambitions and 'he was encouraging and wise, bringing a sense of reality to my dreams.'[90] She does not mention that Frankfurter helped found the ACLU in 1920.

When Ewer went over for the conference, he met Rosalind in New York, and continued to send her loving letters and poems. His admiration was no doubt sincere, but he was also using her. In her autobiography, Rosalind does not mention any other small services she may have performed for him,

---

* Questioned by the security service in the early 1950s, Ewer maintained that his network, which provided 'employment for agents and a clearing house for soviet money destined for agents throughout Western Europe, served merely to inform the Russians on the capabilities of Britain's intelligence and counter-intelligence services.'[88] A 2003 article by Victor Madeira suggests that, by keeping subversive movements in Britain informed as to the level of official interest in them and forewarning them of any intended police action, Ewer damaged efforts to counter the 'reds' in Britain in the 1920s. In a response published four years later, Callahan and Morgan dismiss this notion of damage. What seems clear is that Ewer's activities arose out of what in retrospect can be called (at worst) mis-placed idealism. He broke with communism at the end of the 1920s, and became 'a virulent and outspoken anti-communist.'[89] This almost exactly parallels the evolution of Max Eastman's views – as of countless other 'reds' of the time.

for they would have had no significance for her at the time. Ironically, it was the reverse of the usual situation, for Rosalind relished the power she held over men.

It was difficult for her to break into the theatre world in New York, despite the help of friends. She was introduced to many famous faces, but the most memorable of her early encounters began at a party in a hotel where she knew almost no one. Suddenly, across the sea of 'chattering mouths and tinkling glasses,' she became conscious of 'a gay, challenging face' looking at her. 'He was fair and looked like one of the attendants of the gods in allegorical paintings' – only he was rather too small for the part.[91] They talked briefly, left the hotel, and took one of New York's horse-drawn hansom cabs that were already so out-dated as to be back in fashion as a novelty. Clip-clopping along Fifth Avenue and down Riverside Drive behind a horse that they nicknamed Pegasus, they explored each other's bodies beneath an old and rather smelly blanket.*

Over the next few weeks, they 'made love everywhere, in theatre boxes, country fields, under the sun, moon and stars.' On one occasion they experimented with Spanish fly, 'to see what devastating effects it would have' but Rosalind had no need of artificial stimulants; nor did he; nor for that matter did any man in her hands.[93] For while Arthur Dakyns had shown her what a man wanted of a woman in purely physical terms, she had also learned something more subtle: a man needs to be flattered; in particular he wants reassurance as to his manhood. So when a lover brought out his reproductive equipment, an 'Ooh!' from her and evident signs of anticipated pleasure would have him swelling with pride in a moment. We must remember that Rosalind was not just an actress; she was a very good actress (as Broadway was soon to discover). And she knew her Blake: 'In a wife I would desire / What in whores is always found / The lineaments of Gratified desire.'†

The young man – he was four-and-a-half years younger than Rosalind; the same age as Cynthia – was called Scott. Like Walter, he had left university without a degree, and he had dreams of making a fortune as a writer. In fact Scribner's, the New York publisher, had accepted his first novel on 16 September, and it was to be published the following year. His relationship

---

* Fifty years later, Rosalind told Edmund Wilson that she remembered 'the horsey smell of the rug.'[92]

† When I edited Rosalind's autobiography for publication, I titled it *Kissing the Joy: the Autobiography of Rosalinde Fuller* OBE (Letterworth Press ebook, 2016), for her motto was Blake's couplet: 'He who kisses the joy as it flies / Lives in Eternity's sunrise.'

with Rosalind inspired him with a story, and he began to write about a seventeen-year-old intellectual, Henry Tarbox, who chances to meet an aspiring young actress called Marcia Meadow. 'Life reached in, seized him, handled him, stretched him, and unrolled him like a piece of Irish lace on a Saturday-afternoon bargain-counter.'[94] (This metaphor is all the more striking when we remember that he was having an affair with an English draper's daughter.) Marcia is known for her shimmy – the way she shakes her shoulders on the stage. Improbably, she and Henry get married and by the end of the story they have switched roles: Henry is a celebrated acrobat with an 'amazing and original shoulder swing' and she is famous as a writer, having penned 'a distinct contribution to American dialect literature.'[95] There's a nice irony here, for when Scott met Rosalind she quite unknown; fifty years later, by which time she was writing her own monodramas, she was made an MBE for a lifetime of services to the theatre.

Scott called his story 'Nest Feathers' and on 28 October he sent it to the Paul Reynolds Revere literary agency asking to be accepted as a client. Harold Ober took him on and renamed the story 'Head and Shoulders' – 'referring doubtless to the fact that Mrs Tarbox supplies the literary and mental qualities, while the supple and agile shoulders of her husband contribute their share to the family fortunes.'[96] He sold it to the *Saturday Evening Post* for $400, an exceptionally high price for the time.

So it was with bulging pockets that Scott left New York to see his ex-fiancée in Alabama, Zelda, whom he had not mentioned to Rosalind. Zelda had broken off their engagement because Scott had no money to get married on. 'Head and Shoulders' caused such a sensation when it was published on 21 February 1920 that by the end of the month Scott's agent had sold the movie rights to it for a staggering $2500. Then his novel *This Side of Paradise* was published by Scribner's on 26 March and became an instant best seller, catapulting Scott Fitzgerald to a level of celebrity from which he never really recovered. He and Zelda married a week later. Unfortunately, she had not Rosalind's skill with men. She tended to mock her husband. Ten years later we find Scott seeking reassurance from Ernest Hemingway, having been told by Zelda that his penis was not big enough. An evening with Rosalind would have set him up again.

Scott Fitzgerald never forgot the time he spent with Rosalind – how could he? It was 'his first serious love affair.'[97] Between September and December 1919, he enjoyed the most intensely creative period of his life, writing or rewriting no less than nine short stories. The new confidence that she gave him overflowed into his fiction. He introduced determined young heroines

New Worlder

and wrote about young love for the first time, making his stories highly popular in the glossy magazines. It may not be chance that they contain more allusions to English writers, philosophers, and institutions than his other fiction. Writing of 'Head and Shoulders' to Max Perkins in June 1920, Fitzgerald confessed, 'I just brought in the chorus girl by way of contrast. Before I'd finished she almost stole the story.'[99] Fitzgerald is notorious for transposing other people and their experiences into his fiction, and Rosalind is no exception.* In her autobiography she notes that she could see 'bits' of herself in his later fiction, 'dressed up in other situations.'[99] In several stories she was turned into a call girl. James Mellow, who was the first to reveal her affair with Scott Fitzgerald, has shown that Rosalind's presence in his fiction is more extensive than this. That first evening ride together up Fifth Avenue in the hansom cab features briefly in 'Myra Meets His Family' which Scott wrote straight after 'Head and Shoulders'. Rosalind is probably 'the Venus of the hansom cab' in 'The Lees of Happiness'. Variations on the cab ride can be found in both *The Great Gatsby* and *Tender is the Night*.[100]

In June 1919, during Walter and Crystal's time in England,
> Congress reported the Nineteenth Amendment to the states for ratification. Wisconsin, where [Crystal] Eastman had worked so valiantly and unsuccessfully just a few years earlier, was not only pro-suffrage, but sought the honor of being the first state to ratify. . . . Simultaneously, Illinois was engaged in an effort to capture this honor. . . . It was then discovered that the Illinois ratification resolution had misworded the Amendment, and Wisconsin became the first state to ratify.[101]

Crystal's efforts were rewarded at last.

Rather than return to the United States, however, she would have preferred to extend her absence with a visit to Russia, but Max asked her to hasten home to prepare the next issue of the *Liberator*. This would free him to go and see Florence Deshon in Hollywood, where she had a contract with Samuel Goldwyn. So Walter, Crystal and Jeffrey returned to New York on 20 October 1919. The ship's manifest gives their US address as 1185, 20th (or possibly 26th) Street, New York, amended by hand to Hotel Earle, intending to remain 'for life'. The Hotel Earle (now the Washington Square Hotel) is at 103 Waverly Place, just opposite their flat at 102 Waverly Place. The most

---

* As *This Side of Paradise* was in the hands of the publisher before Scott Fitzgerald met Rosalind, the first name of the New York debutante in the book, Rosalind Connage, must derive from Zelda's sister.

probable explanation for this is that they had sub-let their flat during their absence and planned to live in the hotel across the road until it was vacated. For them both, it was back to the routine of editing periodicals. But while Crystal was happy to return to America, Walter was dreaming of England. Before leaving, he told his parents that he hoped to come back the following spring.

9

Rewrite Man

He possessed the kind of goodness that it is difficult for an American businessman to appreciate, the goodness of a clod of earth out of which a plant of clover is growing, the goodness of a basket of last year's pippins, the goodness of a soft-crusted cottage-loaf baked in a village oven.[1]   Llewellyn Powys

> The *Freeman* . . . was one of the important and influential journals of this century. Its 4,992 large double-column pages . . . must surely constitute one of the most massive monuments of journalistic excellence ever produced in so short a period.[2]   Tom Tanselle

> It was a civilizing influence . . . an antidote to American provincialism and cultural isolationism. . . . Virtually every important writer here and abroad contributed to it.[3]   Will Lissner

Walter in the 1920s

WALTER AND CRYSTAL returned to New York on the eve of some of the darkest days in the history of civil liberties. Just twelve months after the end of the war against Germany, the US Attorney General, A. Mitchell Palmer, was waging another war against an enemy that he imagined was plotting to overthrow the American government. In league with the head of the Bureau of Investigation's newly created General Intelligence Division, J. Edgar Hoover – who was equally paranoid – he celebrated the second anniversary of the October Revolution, 7 November 1919, by arresting 10,000 suspected communists and anarchists throughout the United States. No evidence of the dreaded revolution was ever uncovered. Thinking more like dictators than democrats, Palmer and Hoover concluded that they had not searched diligently enough and made a further 6,000 arrests in January 1920. Countless other people, including Crystal, were placed under surveillance. Many of those arrested were held without trial for a long time. In a cruel and gratuitous gesture, 556 of them were deported to other countries.

The Palmer raids put an end to the kind of political action that Crystal thrived on. As it was, during her absence, the New York WPP had split into three entities: a New York branch of the Women's International League for Peace and Freedom, a Woman's Peace Society, and a Women's Peace Union. So when she took up her campaign for equal rights for women, which she called 'a fight worth fighting even if it takes ten years,' it was through the National Woman's Party. She was one of the four authors of the Equal Rights Amendment (ERA) which aims to remove all discrimination between men and women. Introduced in Congress in 1923, it was re-introduced in every session for the next forty-nine years. Because of the country's federal structure, the ERA has to be separately ratified by each State of the Union. After almost a hundred years, this has still not happened. However, in 1964 the word 'sex' was added to the list of excluded grounds for discrimination in the Civil Rights Act, thus achieving a significant part of the aim of the ERA.

All Crystal's activities were hampered by her health. In January 1920 she made a brief lecture tour, but on her return Max reported to Florence Deshon that she was terribly ill with 'measles, acute bronchitis, a slight pneumonia, influenza – in that order.' He added, 'Crystal is barely walking around the room, and even when she is well she seems to have lost all her zeal for action. I am afraid I can never leave the *Liberator* in her hands. I don't think she wants to do it.'[4] As she began to recover, she joined the Lucy Stone League, seeking to make it legal for women to retain their maiden name after marriage – 'give their hearts and keep their names' as she put it.

Walter Fuller

For Walter, on the other hand, the end of 1919 brought a job offer that caused him to postpone all thought of returning to England, although he still 'yearned for his native land,' as Crystal knew all too well.[5] He was headhunted by Albert Jay Nock and Francis Neilson to edit a new intellectual journal of opinion and literature in the tradition of the *Nation*, the *New Republic* and the *Dial*. It was called the *Freeman* and like a comet in a starry sky it was brighter than them all, and more ephemeral, lasting only four years. Walter worked as its managing editor for the first twenty-six months of its existence, and established its reputation for quality and wit.

It was actually Nock, who prided himself as a talent spotter, who chose Walter. 'I can smell out ability as quickly and unerringly as a high-bred pointer can smell out a partridge,' he boasted.[6] For Francis Neilson,

> it was a stroke of genius on [Nock's] part to find Walter Fuller, the finest rewrite man I have met in all my long experience. He had a cultural background that was rare, and I have known some of the best English writers of my day. I was familiar with many of those who gathered around Alfred Orage when he published *The New Age,* and Orage was my literary god for this work.[7]

This praise comes from an Englishman who emigrated to the United States at the age of eighteen, worked as a labourer, became an actor and stage manager, and returned to London in 1900 to reorganize and manage the Royal Opera at Covent Garden Theatre, where he put on the largest productions anywhere in Europe. After only four seasons, though, he moved on to politics, became a Liberal MP and from 1912 to 1915 presided over the United Committee for the Taxation of Land Values. But the Liberal party was in decline, and the outbreak of WWI was a crushing blow to it. Neilson responded with a book, *How Diplomats Make War,* in which he denounced the machinations of the war-mongers. No publisher in England would touch it. Nock, who shared his single tax policy,* arranged for it to be brought out anonymously in America in 1915 by B. W. Huebsch (the young publisher who had dared issue James Joyce's *Portrait of the Artist*).

At this point, Neilson gave up both his political career and his British nationality, and returned to America. In 1916 he published an anti-war novel, *A Strong Man's House*, about a munitions manufacturer who pays the price of believing that the way to prevent war is to prepare for it. It was quite successful and Walter may have read it. Indeed they may have met at this point, as

---

* Walter was familiar with Henry George's single tax philosophy: see the plan for his Exhibition in September 1915 (p.147).

Neilson became a regular speaker at WPP meetings. At any rate, he married a Chicago heiress and soon he was using her money to pay Albert Jay Nock's salary as an editor on the *Nation* (in addition to putting $30,000 a year into the magazine). When, in mid-1919, Oswald Garrison Villard refused to endorse the proposed single tax, Neilson withdrew his support, and Nock persuaded Mrs Neilson to fund a new weekly magazine, the *Freeman*. The publisher was Ben Huebsch and the editorial team included Suzanne La Follette and Van Wyck Brooks. For Nock, Walter was one of the 'three super-excellent editorial minds on the staff.'[8]

Suzanne La Follette (also known as 'Clara') was the niece of Senator La Follette. She followed Nock from the *Nation*, where she had been getting $180 a month, so the *Freeman* offered her $200; Walter was paid $300. According to Sharon Presley, Nock told a friend in 1926, 'I think she is just as good an editor as I am and even a shade better.' Having penned a daring book on feminism and liberty, *Concerning Women* (1926), she founded the *New Freeman* in 1930, but ran out of funding after only fifteen months. In 1950, she started a third and equally shortlived *Freeman* before founding the *National Review* in 1955; she worked as its managing editor until her retirement in 1959.

Van Wyck Brooks was a brilliant Harvard graduate, five years younger than Walter, who had made two long visits to England before the war. By the end of his distinguished career as an essayist, biographer and historian of American literature and culture, he had collected a dozen honorary doctorates. He received the first of his literary prizes and awards from the *Dial* in 1923 (the year after T. S. Eliot), largely for his writing in the *Freeman*. Walter introduced him to Lewis Mumford, thereby launching a literary friendship that was to last four decades.

Mumford was only twenty-five in 1920 and not a university graduate, tuberculosis having forced him to interrupt his studies. During his enforced rest, he read widely, and he approached Walter in the hope of getting to write book reviews in the new periodical. Soon they discovered that they shared an admiration for Patrick Geddes, whom Mumford had been corresponding with for some time. Telling Geddes that Walter was 'now one of the editors of a new weekly,' Mumford added: 'I have spent hours in his company, and you were the only topic of conversation; Fuller Boswellizing you in sputters of enthusiastic anecdote.'[9] Soon after meeting Walter and then Brooks, Mumford left for London to edit the newly founded *Sociological Review* for Victor Branford. Thanks to his time at More's Garden, Walter was uniquely equipped to prepare him for life among the Geddes fans in London.

He also warned Mumford of the contrasting sensibilities of the British and the Americans, particularly the Briton's relative shyness and reticence, that were liable to cause misunderstanding. He begged Mumford to repeat to himself each night before he went to sleep, 'The English don't mean to be rude; the English don't mean to be rude.'[10] Mumford found this good advice and greatly enjoyed his stay in London.* He soon came to feel, nonetheless, that his future life and career belonged in New York. His tenure as editor of the *Sociological Review* lasted only six months, but it contributed to making him America's foremost philosopher of the city in the twentieth century.

Back in New York, he renewed his friendship with Walter, finding him always brimming with ideas, pulling them forth like newborn rabbits from his hat, or darting after them in the air with birdlike eagerness. Though he wrote nothing [which is not true, as we shall see], he helped to establish in the *Freeman* the air of urbane catholicity that saved it from becoming what it at first threatened to be, an organ that recognized only one enemy, the political state, and held fast to only one remedy for all human ailments, the Single Tax.[11]

There is a heartening warmth in Mumford's evocations of Walter. One of his favourite memories of this time is of Walter 'bursting into the Old Chelsea tea room, expressing beatification and apologies in words that ran together like drops of mercury.'[12] Van Wyck Brooks also remembered him with grateful affection. Thirty years later, reminding Mumford how Walter brought them together over lunch, Brooks exclaimed, 'heaven bless his soul!'[13]

By the autumn of 1921, Walter, Brooks and Mumford were 'as thick as – as a band of brothers' (to borrow one of Walter's phrases from the *Freeman*).[14] 'One animated and memorable night stands out,' recalls Mumford, who was newly married and living just round the corner from the *Freeman* offices. 'Brooks and Fuller dined with us to discuss in detail plans we three had already sketched for publishing a new series of books, modeled on the French *Cahiers de la Quinzaine*.'[15] 'Fuller, who could always be relied on for Latin quotations and Roman history, proposed to call these books Scipian Pamphlets, to contrast the bold departures and frontal attacks of the great

---

* Walter was doubtless familiar with G.K. Chesterton's opinion, expressed in his biography of *Charles Dickens* (1906): 'America will always affect an Englishman as being soft in the wrong place and hard in the wrong place; coarse exactly where all civilized men are delicate, delicate exactly where all grown-up men are coarse' (Chapter 6). Mumford may even have known it himself: he had early immersed himself in Dickens's novels and enjoyed Chesterton's poetry. He did not discover Emerson's view of the British, as expressed in 'English Traits', until much later.

Scipio with the evasive, retreating tactics of Fabius and Britain's latter-day Fabians.'[16] Although nothing came of this particular project, it contained the seed that grew into the Literary Guild and the five volumes of the *American Caravan* (1927–36) that Brooks and Mumford helped to edit.

Walter began work on the *Freeman* on 2 February 1920. Although his name was dropped from the masthead of the *World Tomorrow* in March, he remained on its editorial board. A year later, January 1921, by which time Nevin Sayre had taken over the editorship from Norman Thomas, he reappeared as a 'contributing editor' and this lasted until December 1922. All told, his relationship with the *World Tomorrow* lasted five full years.

Launched on 17 March 1920 by its team of colourful characters, the *Freeman* was generously welcomed by the liberal *Nation* as another liberal weekly. Nock hastened to write a corrective editorial: the *Freeman*, he insisted, was not liberal but *radical*, but instead of defining what he meant (for the terms *liberal* and *radical* were often used interchangeably) he sent readers to the dictionary. Twenty years later he expressed his thoughts more clearly: 'we struck straight through to the root of whatever subject we discussed.'[17] In other words, its radicalism was not political but philosophical. 'For the *Freeman*, the truly valuable things in life were outside the political realm.'[18] This coincided with – and quite possibly reflected – Walter's way of thinking.

The *Freeman* was in fact a remarkably open periodical in which the contributors, who had widely differing political views (Suzanne la Follette was anarchist and Brooks socialist, for instance), were allowed to express their opinions without constraint. It was to this tolerance of conflicting conviction and taste that it owed its particular savour. Neither Nock nor Neilson dictated an editorial stance; the topics for treatment were proposed by the individual contributors and discussed at a weekly meeting. 'If ever there was another co-operative effort performed by a literary staff, free to exercise initiative and resource equal to that of the *Freeman*, I never heard of it,' wrote Neilson in his 'Story of *The Freeman*'.[19] For Charles H. Hamilton, 'More than any other periodical of its time and as much as any since, it was concerned with freedom: the preservation and extension of individual freedom in all its variegated forms.'[20] It questioned the efficacy of political action and warned against the exploitation of the individual by the state, championing the civil liberties that Walter and Crystal had defended ever since Wilson went to war.

In format, structure and general appearance, the *Freeman* was modelled on the eighteenth-century *Spectator*, with two columns of print on quarto pages, and British spelling. This old-fashioned and thoroughly unfashionable presentation has never been explained. I suspect that Walter had some say in it. The annotations that he made in a bound volume of the *World Tomorrow* for 1919 show that he was familiar with the technical aspects of copy-fitting and page design. From here it is but a step to studying the solutions adopted by famous periodicals of the past. As for the spelling, we have only to consider that the *Freeman* had an ex-English owner and an English managing editor.* Americans found its rejection of their native spelling particularly shocking, since for many people it stood as a symbol of their country's social, political and cultural independence from England. This, then, was another feature that made the *Freeman* unique, eccentric, even (as some people said at the time) a *freak*. The *New Republic* (quoting Shelley's 'Ode to the West Wind') called it 'tameless and swift and proud.'[22] It was obviously just right for Walter.

Each issue ran to twenty-four well-filled pages. First came single paragraphs of Current Comment, unsigned but written by the editorial staff. This was followed by editorials, called Topics of the Day, of a page or more in length, also unsigned and written by staff. The Middle Articles were longer and covered a wide range of social and artistic topics; they were signed by an equally wide range of contributors. Then came a couple of pages of Letters to the Editors, often polemical or informative little essays in themselves. The Miscellany section of short, light-hearted pieces on current manners was signed 'Journeyman', often written by Nock, with individual paragraphs contributed by members of staff. The Reviews of three or four books, running to a page or a page-and-a-half each, were signed; the Shorter Notices, on the other hand, were not. And the final item in every issue was the Reviewer's Notebook, an essay on the past, present and future of American literature in the form of literary criticism or a review by Van Wyck Brooks (except for the last few months of publication, when Nock took over). Interspersed between these fixed points were one or more additional rubrics: Theatre, Music, Art, and Letters from Abroad. It also printed original works as well: poems, excerpts from forthcoming books (biographies, memoirs) and occa-

---

* Will Lissner quite disregards this, seeing the periodical as essentially American: What *The Freeman* demonstrated was that the English do not have a monopoly of the ability to turn out memorable reviews.... It was almost wholly an American enterprise and it showed that American writers and critics, given adequate support, could turn out a review that would stand comparison with the best English product. But it also proved that Americans, by and large, were not cultivated enough to provide an adequate readership for so serious an effort.[21]

sionally a short story. Always on the alert for new talent, the *Freeman* discovered Newton Arvin while he was yet an undergraduate, and developed writers like John Dos Passos, Constance Rourke, and Edwin Muir. The latter started contributing after H. L. Mencken, who had seen Muir's *New Age* articles, recommended his first book, *We Moderns* (published by Knopf in 1920), to Brooks.*

In all, over two hundred British and American writers, and a handful from the Continent, contributed to the 208 issues of the *Freeman*. One wonders to what extent Walter was responsible for the presence in its columns of Norman Angell and Laurence Housman, Bertrand Russell and Arthur Symons. It seems very likely that he was behind the brief contributions by Amos Pinchot in the very first issue and by Ruth Pickering on 2 June 1920, the articles by Trilby Ewer during the second six months of publication, and the articles and many single paragraphs by Charles Hallinan from the second year onwards. Only Walter would have sought a piece about Quaker food relief in Austria† from Mollie Best (writing as Mary Agnes Best, 8 December 1920) or a book review from Maurice Browne (20 April 1921). The half-dozen contributions by the sociologist C. Delisle Burns (who had written for the *Reader's Review*) spanned just those issues that Walter edited, suggesting that Walter was seeking him out. And who but Walter would have championed Gilbert Cannan? Although his writing is largely forgotten today, his 'Letters from a Distance' were much admired at the time and made a selling point in advertisements for the *Freeman*. Although it never had more than 7000 subscribers, it was eagerly read by all those who discovered it, including editors of other periodicals and lively minds as far away as England, where Ramsay MacDonald waited impatiently for each issue.[23]

A British contributor who much appreciated Walter was Llewellyn Powys, the youngest of the Powys brothers, three of whom are remembered for their writing. He was living in New York, where he met and married Alys Gregory six months after she became managing editor of the *Dial* in February 1924. (Her secretary had already married Lewis Mumford.) Powys contributed fourteen essays to the *Freeman*, two of them on writers close to Walter's heart: Thomas Hardy (on 22 March 1922) and 'William Barnes, the Dorset Poet' in July 1922.

---

* On the income from two articles a month for the *Freeman* and a weekly one for *New Age*, Willa and Edwin Muir eked out a shoestring existence in Prague. His *Freeman* articles were reprinted by Huebsch in 1924 in a volume titled *Latitudes*.

† Quaker food relief in post-war Europe lasted four years. In June 1921, their kitchens fed more than a million children each day in Germany alone.

Walter Fuller

In *The Verdict of Bridlegoose*, Powys recalled how, when he visited the editorial offices of the *Freeman*,

> I would often go direct to the room of this Dorset man in whose company I felt completely at my ease. Mr Walter Fuller had a heart of pure gold. In any New York office other than the *Freeman* he would have appeared out of place. . . . As one talked to him and heard him declaim against the crude noises of MacDougal Street, or the latest iniquity that had been perpetrated by some unscrupulous money-magnate, one realized in a moment how impossible it was for him to learn to dance to the American tune, and this in spite of the fact that he had won for his partner so splendid, so triumphant an amazon* as Crystal Eastman. As he stood fumbling with the papers on his desk, he would remind me of a barn-door owl who had been betrayed into forsaking the ivy-mantled tower of Sturminster Newton, and, having crossed the Atlantic with soft, downy flight, finds itself on the top of an iron-ribbed skyscraper, surrounded by flocks of over-sized American robins infuriated at the presence of so homely an apparition.[24]

This is beautifully apt. It took a Powys to express it.

Walter even found space in the *Freeman* for Arthur Dakyns. Having managed to obtain three months' leave-of-absence from the Ministry of Labour, Dakyns arrived in New York in mid-June 1920 to see and hear for himself how Rosalind was getting on. Her career was just taking off. Early in 1920, director-lyricist John Murray Anderson 'discovered' her and engaged her as the lead singer in an original musical revue called 'What's In a Name?' Rosalind must have savoured the title. While in Paris she had been advised by a numerologist to add a letter to her name: as 'Rosalind Fuller' she would never succeed on the stage. So, from her arrival in America, she adopted 'Rosalinde Fuller' as her stage name. And it worked. What *is* in a name, indeed? (I'll continue to call her 'Rosalind', nonetheless.)

According to a report in the New York *Tribune*, when she told her family the glad news that she had work, they turned up their noses. Perhaps they thought that something by the creator of the 'Greenwich Village Follies' would be on the same lines as those Paris *folies* that they had learned of.† But

---

* At this time, the term *amazon* was widely used approvingly of the new type of woman who had the self-confidence of a man while remaining perfectly feminine.

† In the 1921 season of the Greenwich Follies, Rosalind launched a new song, 'Three o'Clock in the Morning', as a duet with Richard Bold. Recorded *without the words* by Paul Whiteman and his orchestra the following year, it sold over three-and-a-half million disks.[26] Rosalind just missed being a top-selling 'pop-star' of the twenties.

Walter – and no doubt Crystal too – attended a performance and reported on it favourably to his parents. They sent 'Rosalinde' their congratulations.[25] The press loved the show, finding it 'filled with freshness and charm, much of which is due to a newcomer, Rosalinde Fuller.' She 'really sings and looks charming,' said the *Evening Telegram*. 'She also acts with great sincerity.' At Walter's instigation perhaps, Walter Pritchard Eaton wrote in the fifth issue of the *Freeman* on the 'so-called new stagecraft.'

> In musical comedy we are so far removed from reality that the public is willing to accept symbol for the bald statement and to seek beauty in other than conventional terms. It was a shrewd realization of this that enabled . . . John Murray Anderson to mount a musical entertainment at the Maxine Elliott Theatre without any scenery whatever, in the conventional sense – nothing but curtains, gauzes, towering screens, a tapestry, and the play of light. [In it] much . . . is crude, incompletely realized, even downright ugly. But there is enough which is successful and beautiful in a new, almost a disturbing way, to make the production notable. . . . For such a moment as [when Rosalind sings], for so unique and lovely a sensation, one would gladly sit through the inanities of far more inane musical entertainments than 'What's in a name?'[27]

The show ran from 19 March to 26 June 1920. Dakyns arrived on 19 June. Walter took him straight off the ship to the Saturday evening performance. Afterwards Dakyns went round to Rosalind's dressing room – as the *prima donna*, she had one to herself – and she consented to lunch with him the following Wednesday. He reported to his sister that he had found her performance 'excellent'.

The next day, Walter took Dakyns out to Croton where Crystal and Jeffrey were already installed for the summer; Walter went out there each weekend. Dakyns met 'some very interesting people' including Dudley Field Malone, 'who was until recently in Wilson's cabinet, and various other radicals and artists who live about.'[28] Dakyns was sufficiently impressed by him to attend the July meeting of the US Labor Party in Chicago at which Malone was designated the party's candidate for Governor of New York. Exceptionally, the *Freeman* opened its columns to Malone on 28 July so that he could report on the struggle that had marked the convention. It followed this up on 4 August with an account by Dakyns, printed as a letter to the editors. He gleefully told his sister that he had been paid two cents a word for it. 'I can get as much work as I like on the *Freeman*,' he boasted.[29] In the event, the only other writing of his that the *Freeman* printed was a review of Mary Beard's *Short History of the American Labor Movement* (1920) in the next week's issue (11 August). Perhaps Walter found him some other form of employment.*

During this visit, Rosalind made it clear to Dakyns that their relationship was over. As promised, she had seen a psychoanalyst – the Dr Parker that she had seen two years before, and already consulted by Walter (at Crystal's instigation, apparently) – and had learned more about herself. But, she recalled, 'I wasn't really worried about myself; I had no problem, only the one that Dakyns imagined. . . . Having nothing left with which to entertain [the analyst] . . . I stopped going. Anyway I needed the money to live on.'[31]

On his return to England, Dakyns signed off with a characteristic comment: 'Poor Ros, I see your problem. To be loved by one's enemy is ever so much more difficult and disagreeable than loving one's enemy. Still, there it is.'[32] Two years later he announced his engagement to a Welsh girl. They married in 1924, but she refused to consummate the marriage. After eight years, Dakyns realized that he disliked her intensely. It was surely no coincidence that in the same month he 'spent a *very* nice weekend with Curt and Cynthia, and on the Sunday I took Cynthia, Rosalind and a *very* nice American whom she lives with to supper and to *Le Soir de Rafle*.'[33] At any rate, he and his wife separated in October 1932; nullity proceedings were instituted early in the following year. Dakyns remarried in December 1933, exactly two weeks after his divorce was made absolute. He had two children by his second wife; the first was named Jane Rosalind. Always called Janine, she became a highly respected academic. Six years before her untimely death in 1994, she made notes on her father's relationship with the Fullers that have formed the backbone of this account of it. Dakyns died of a cerebral haemorrhage in March 1941, aged fifty-seven.

Rosalind met her 'American boyfriend' in mid-1920, shortly before Dakyns' visit. He was Francis Bruguière, the official photographer of the New York Theater Guild from 1919 to 1927. Born on 16 October 1879, he was twelve years her senior – eighteen months older than Walter; married but separated from his wife. When Rosalind was sent to him for publicity photographs for 'What's in a Name?' she found 'a sensitive-looking man with greying hair, deep-set, bright brown eyes and dark strong eyebrows.' As she sat under the studio lights, dressed as a bride, he observed enigmatically, 'Well, I suppose they'll want nothing in the face but beauty; you'd better

---

* Dakyns was at any rate grateful to Walter. He told Cynthia, 'I remember the delightful hours I spent with him in New York, where I saw him nearly every day and where, by his many introductions and society, he made my visit thoroughly enjoyable and interesting.'[30]

show all your teeth' and disappeared beneath a black cloth to look 'straight into her heart' through the lens of his camera. She was 'very much taken and intrigued by him.'[34]

One of four sons of a prosperous Californian banking family, Bruguière was talented in music and painting. This led him to photography, which he studied in New York with Frank Eugene and Alfred Stieglitz, who accepted him as a Fellow of the Photo-Secession. Bruguière then returned to San Francisco, where he set up a studio, recording images of the city after the earthquake and fire in a pictorialist style; some of them were reproduced in a book called *San Francisco* in 1918. He co-curated the photographic exhibition at the 1915 Panama-Pacific Exposition in San Francisco that Walter and his sisters had enjoyed so much. Meanwhile he was researching all kinds of things: multiple-exposure, solarization (years ahead of Man Ray), original processes, abstracts, photograms, and the colour response of commercial black-and-white film. Until his one-man show at the Art Centre of New York in 1927, he showed this work only to friends, and on request. One of the few people who knew of what he was doing was the great portrait photographer Imogen Cunningham, who made the prints of Edward Curtis's studies of North American Indians. She moved to San Francisco in 1917, and in 1918 worked with Bruguière in his studio. Their collaboration was very brief, however, because that was the year he moved back to New York. The decline of the family fortune meant that he needed an income.

Setting up a studio at 16 West 49th Street, he began photographing for *Vanity Fair, Vogue,* and *Harper's Bazaar*. Soon New York stage designers (particularly Norman Bel Geddes, Robert Edmond Jones, and Lee Simonson) were celebrating him as the man who could provide theatre managers with a realistic preview, based on their paintings and models, of the sets they were proposing, and also record the actual production with a fidelity never previously attained. Bruguière's secret was to 'compensate for the differences between the vision of the human eye and the vision of the lens, plate and paper' by taking account of 'the speed at which the different colours travel.' In practice, he would observe the lighting of a stage set, set up his camera for a long exposure and then instruct the technician to 'shut off the blue light at the count of five, the green at ten, the yellow at twenty, and the red at thirty,' for instance.[35] By this means he produced prints that corresponded to the way the human eye perceived the colours in a set. For all his technical skill, however, Bruguière's concern was with the ability of the image to communicate feeling and emotion. This he researched until the day he died in 1945, by which time he was deep into the philosophy and psychology of art, and painting rather than taking photographs. His most frequent model was Rosalind.

In combining great skill in a medium of communication with indifference to social recognition, Bruguière was much like Walter. He was a charming man, loved by all and nicknamed 'The Prince'. He soon became 'the main part' of Rosalind's love-life. 'Other lovers were only shadows that floated across it,' she wrote.[36] As Bruguière's wife would not consent to a divorce, he and Rosalind agreed on an open relationship. That suited them both and it lasted for the rest of his life.

In his role as managing editor of the *Freeman*, Walter revised all the contributions before they were printed, polishing the style and adjusting the tone, imparting the periodical's stamp of urbanity (and British spelling) to them all, producing 'a paper that was generally known as the best written in the country.'[37] He also 'wrote nearly all of the headings for the *Freeman* during his editorship. They often gave a sardonic flip to things, not inherent in the pieces themselves, and helped to make the magazine's reputation for wit.'[38] On one occasion, however, this did not meet with the contributor's approval. Long afterwards, Van Wyck Brooks still remembered with painful clarity

> a certain afternoon when Edmund Wilson on the phone shook my nerves, scolding me for altering the title of his review of some poems of Yeats, an enormity for which I personally was scarcely to blame. There had been a misunderstanding and the change had been made in my absence [for Brooks came in only two or three days a week], though I have no doubt that Wilson was rightly indignant. But in thirty years I have not forgotten the demoralizing onset of that nervously furious presence at the end of the wire.[39]

The only contribution by Wilson under Walter's editorship was in volume 5, dated 29 March 1922. The review is entitled 'The Poetry of Mr W. B. Yeats' – nothing exceptional, but no doubt Edmund Wilson had proposed something more original.

Wilson's complaint was an exception. As on this occasion, people tend to voice their feelings only when things go wrong, and say nothing when all is well; so the unanimous praise of Walter's erstwhile colleagues is remarkable. They all express how happy they were to place their writing in his hands. In 1946, Neilson recalled,

> I have seen Walter Fuller take an article containing one or two good ideas and reshape it so that its writer would swell with pride when he saw it in print. The toil and patience he devoted to slipshod manuscripts were worthy of the highest commendation. . . .

>Walter Fuller had instructions from me to use the material I sent in as he thought best. Nock was present when Fuller asked me several pertinent questions about how far he was empowered to rewrite the notes, the editorials, the miscellany, and the special articles contributed by the staff. Nock agreed with my suggestion that Fuller should consult him when important changes were necessary, but for all the usual procedure of editorial correction, he was to be held responsible. There was never any trouble about this matter.[40]

By the time he wrote this, Neilson's memories of his collaboration with Nock were jaundiced, but of Walter's qualities there was no dispute and he quoted with approval Nock's account of the complete trust he had in Walter:

>I feel free to speak thus frankly of the paper's quality because I had far less to do with forming or maintaining it than people think I had. . . . I did a good deal of writing for the paper at one time or another, but the managing editor treated my copy like anyone else's; it was in no way sacrosanct.[41]

All these sources indicate that Walter was editor quite as much as managing editor, just as Crystal told Cynthia:

>Walter is having the time of his life. He is really the whole thing at the *Freeman* – editor and managing editor. He does everything except write the paper. He works all the time, hardly has a moment to look at me and Jeffrey, but he loves his work so much and is so happy and confident and well that I can't complain.[42]

Because so many of the pieces in the *Freeman* were unsigned, no readers and none of his colleagues knew how often Walter contributed to its pages. Even Francis Neilson admitted that, from his interviews with Walter in London after the *Freeman* had ceased publication,

>I was forced to the conclusion that I did not know half the story of the *Freeman* and its editor. Fuller would tell me something, and then after taking in the surprised expression on my face, he would say, in his timid way, 'Didn't you know that?'[43]

Fortunately both Huebsch and Mrs Neilson kept copies of the *Freeman* with the name of the author written in beside each item. From these, Tom Tanselle compiled an index to the 'Unsigned and Initialed Contributions to *The Freeman*'. This reveals that Walter made eighty-seven separate unsigned contributions; two as FGW; and a further twenty in the form of letters to the editor under twenty different pseudonyms.

There are many reasons why periodicals print letters written by staff under assumed names, the first being simply the need to set the ball rolling: unless there are a few letters – the more controversial the better, of course –

readers are not inclined to write in. Under the cover of anonymity, Walter took the opportunity to congratulate his own periodical on printing Gorky's reminiscences of Tolstoy. As 'T.F.' he exclaimed, 'What a debt we owe you of the *Freeman* for giving this searching analysis of a great soul!'[44] He also set the cat among the pigeons when he complained about the poor quality of the persons sent over from America to unveil statues of Abraham Lincoln in England. 'Why may not we send one of our real men . . . such a man as Andy Furuseth, or Max Eastman or 'Gene Debs – let out as a "trusty" for the occasion.'[45] This added fuel to the controversy on the function of the writer in revolutionary times that Van Wyck Brooks and Max were conducting through the columns of the *Freeman* and the *Liberator* respectively.*

As in *Four Lights* and the *World Tomorrow,* Walter shared his lifelong habit of collecting snippets from newspapers: roughly half of all his contributions, single paragraphs and letters combined, quote or derive from items in the British press – or from the *Congressional Record,* in which he found numerous instances of political chicanery and hypocrisy. A letter that he titled 'The Vanishing of Dialect' and signed 'George Brangwyn' shows his concern for the English language. Decrying the determination of teachers and school inspectors in England to root out local accents, he brought the good news that scholars were getting together to preserve English dialects.[46]

A great advantage of having staff supply these letters is that they can be inserted at the last minute to fill out a column. The same applies, of course, to the short unsigned paragraphs that characterized many pages of the *Freeman* (as they had in *Four Lights* and the *World Tomorrow*). Quite often Walter's piece was the last in a series, no doubt tailored to fit the space available, but equally often his contributions appeared as 'Current Comment' on the front page. On more than one occasion, he contributed both the first and the last short items in an issue.

Common to nearly all Walter's contributions, single paragraphs and pseudonymous letters alike, is the pithy summing up of a contemporary situation, attitude, or policy with an anecdote, a quotation, or a witty comment of his own. Writing as 'T. R.' he assured readers who were frightened by the prospect of 'the dictatorship of the proletariat' that it had already arrived. 'A good friend of mine,' he confided, 'was lamenting to me the other day that he and his wife were earnestly desirous of having a child,' but they did not dare to do so because they knew that their cook would leave at once, and the jani-

---

* See the *Freeman*, 20 May 1920, pp.214–15; the *Liberator*, June 1921, pp.5–7; the *Freeman*, 20 June 1921, pp.382–83; the *Liberator*, August 1921, pp.7–9; and the *Freeman*, 31 August 1921, pp.598–99.

tor "won't stand for children in our apartment house." Could a dictatorship go further than that, I ask you?'[47]

On the delicate question of food shortages at a time of great social inequality, he supplied a conversation between a country gentleman and a notorious poacher:

"Morning, squire.'

"Morning, Jarvis.'

'Out early, squire.'

'Yes, I'm getting an appetite for my breakfast.' Then with a suspicious look at the poacher, the squire asked, 'What are you doing, Jarvis?'

'Getting a breakfast for my appetite, squire.'[48]

Military expenditure was a subject that Walter tackled several times. He quoted Lord Northcliffe in *The Times*:

'We know we are confronted with a Mesopotamian war on a considerable scale in which 100,000 British Indian troops are engaged. Order will eventually be restored, but only at considerable sacrifice of life, which will upset the budget still more.'

Walter commented: 'Yes, that's the worst of all this killing; it does upset the budget.'[49] Contrasting British government spending on military equipment and expeditions with the comparatively paltry sums spent on education, he concluded:

Perhaps, after all, there is a method in the general preference of all governments for military rather than educational expenditures, for what is the use, our rulers may well ask, of spending money to develop a child's brains when at the same time you are spending so much to blow them out.[50]

He denounced the cost – and the absurdity – of governments spying on innocent citizens. 'James Mordaunt' told 'a true story' of how a worthy gentleman called Mr A came to the United States and lectured from Maine to California on the 'moral aims of the war'. (Perhaps we can identify 'Mr A' as Norman Angell?) One night he fell into conversation with 'a chatty person' in his hotel.

Certain unmistakeable signs made Mr A suspect that the affable stranger was what is euphemistically called 'a Government agent'. So he promptly challenged the spy who at once confessed his occupation and said that his orders were to follow Mr A about everywhere and listen to all his speeches.

'But,' he added genially, 'after hearing you two or three times I knew you were alright and so I never go to any of your meetings now.'

'If that is the case,' asked Mr A, 'why are you still following me right out here in California?'

'Well,' said the spy in no way abashed, 'the truth is that I've never had such a good time in all my life seeing this wonderful country . . . and living like the Prince of Wales in all the best hotels.'

Walter's comment: 'As good citizens and tax-payers, we can only rejoice that the people who spend our money so lavishly for our safety and welfare are made so happy by it.'[51]

The aberrations of British imperialism, from Ireland to India, came in for stinging criticism. On the Amritsar massacre Walter observed that 'machine guns caused those five hundred Indians to know a more blessed peace than even the *pax britannica.*'[52] He quoted the *Daily Telegraph* on the inhospitable attitude of the Arabs:

It is clear enough that we are not particularly welcome and no substantial number of inhabitants appreciates our efforts to bestow upon them the blessings of a higher culture and complex civilization. The best we can do for them now is to make them capable of defending themselves and transfer our powers to some fairly stable native administration, if one can be found.

And observed: 'Now isn't that delicious – and so prettily put.'[53]

He was unsparing of politicians. In October 1921 he wrote:

We rejoice to learn that President Harding has had his finger-prints taken. We hope this excellent idea will spread, and that all our public officials will be put on record in this way. It will give us joy to think that the finger-prints of every Congressman are safely on file in the halls of Justice, all ready for use when the time comes.[54]

He proposed sending 'the honorary members of our various war-boards' to Romania. 'Their departure would not leave us inconsolable and we believe that they would soon feel quite at home, for Mr Grasty assures us that that country is "the profiteer's paradise" and is blessed with a "money aristocracy".'[55]

Walter liked to compare politicians to characters in Dickens' novels. 'It is a hard fate, but not undeserved, that gives the American presidency to Chadband after eight dispiriting years of Pecksniff,' for instance.[56] His favourite sources were *Bleak House*, *David Copperfield,* and *Great Expectations*. One of his pseudonyms was 'Philip Perrep', cribbed from the full name of Pip, who narrates *Great Expectations.*

There is every sign that Walter much enjoyed his work at the *Freeman*; at no other time do we find so many instances and mentions of his humour. He supplied his colleagues with anecdotes for their contributions, and was largely responsible for the small printed parody of the *Freeman* (called *The Freeman Jr*) which, on the occasion of the first anniversary dinner for the

Rewrite Man

staff in March 1921, lay on their plates like a menu. The list of fare included an editorial headed 'Where Can a Young Man Go?' (Harold Stearns had written one called 'What Can a Young Man Do?'); middle articles titled 'Ptomaine Street' by Sinclair Lewis Mumford, and 'Autocracy of Service' by Warren Gamaliel Harding; a letter headed 'A Home Brew' by H. L. Mencken; a poem, 'Artichokes and Amethysts' by Amy L., and a review of *The Gentle Art of Making Puns* by B. W. Huebsch. The editorial proclaimed: 'Today this paper waits with its back to the soil* for the time when everybody will have abundance and leisure to do the same.'[57]

Walter's two years and two months on the *Freeman* are summed up by this reminiscence in *New Republic* recalling

> all he had done to make the *Freeman*, in the first two years of its existence, a paper with a flavour and an individuality. He himself wrote scarcely at all; but that only made him the better editor, for he threw himself into the work of his contributors with a double zeal, tempering their sharpness, combing out their matted thoughts, removing the edges of boorishness, adding a whimsical turn of humor to the most matter-of-fact work, until suddenly – lo! it has the stamp of the *Freeman*; the humor, the grace, the urbanity that it claimed for its own. Mr Nock himself set the tone for the paper; it was Walter Fuller's role, in the formative period, to catch the essence of Mr Nock better than anyone else could do, and to stand as a buffer between Mr Nock and the less practiced contributors, until they, too, had become animated with it. . . .
>
> English by birth, a Mancunian by education, he was at home in neither England nor America: when here he remembered the bright red cottages, the neat hedges and the lush parks of England; when in England he remembered the openness of American manners and the informal ease of American friendships: in each country, he had a little too much of the opposite one's qualities not to be a little 'out of it'. A valuable part of the *Freeman* died, for me, when Walter Fuller left it in 1922 to return to England; a man like Fuller, so cordial, so enthusiastic, so tender and loyal, had a value to the paper out of all proportion to the calculable work that he did; and such people – there are none too many of them – have a similar value in the world.[58]

The notice is unsigned, but in all probability its author was Lewis Mumford.

---

* 'The soil' was a catchword at the time for the agricultural roots of American culture, as in 'The soil took its revenge on the Yankee mind, as the Yankee mind abandoned the soil' (Van Wyck Brooks).

Walter Fuller

Mumford had reason to be grateful to Walter, for he successfully mediated between him and Nock. What with Mumford's interest in sociology, his critical writing for the *Freeman* inevitably contained sociological terms. For Nock, sociology did not exist, there being economics on the one hand and art on the other, so he took exception to what he called 'neologisms' in Mumford's contributions. It took all of Walter's tact and experience to reconcile the two. Eventually, Nock came to admire Mumford's abilities and encouraged him to write a history of American civilization. He was capable of it, but did not rise to the challenge. He stuck to cities.

On the other hand, a challenge that he did take up was concocted together with Walter. In June 1921, they suggested to Patrick Geddes that he might come over to America for a series of public conferences, from California to New York. 'Should you consider seriously this proposal, Fuller and I will gather together an invitation committee and secure a financial guarantee,' wrote Mumford, adding: 'Fuller said that, although he would beg money for no other cause, not even for that of the paper with which he is associated, he would do it for you: so deeply does he feel his debt; and I of course echo his sentiments.' Furthermore, Mumford promised to meet Geddes in California and to 'personally conduct the whole trip!'[59] In the event, Geddes did not come over until the middle of 1923, by which time Walter had been back in England for a year, so he was not involved in the tour. He did, on the other hand, put Geddes in contact with Norman Thomas, as co-director of the League for Industrial Democracy. This ensured that Geddes gave many talks and left a lasting impression. Mumford fulfilled his promise and accompanied Geddes on his tour – much to his regret. Within hours of arriving, Geddes expressed the hope that Mumford would take the place of the son that he had lost in the war, a role that he could not possibly fulfil. Even though he had been warned often enough of how intolerably Geddes could behave, Mumford found his guest quite impossible, and their relationship was never the same again. It was a pattern experienced by almost all who tried to work with Geddes. Walter was fortunate to have escaped it.

In the midst of his editing, Walter found time to play a leading part in the founding of a new student association that aimed to coordinate the activities of discussion clubs in American colleges. At Christmas 1920, he joined a group of students representing the universities of Barnard, Harvard, Princeton, Radcliffe, Swarthmore and Yale to form the organizing committee for a national association of liberal students. One wonders how Walter landed amongst these young men and women, although of course it will have reminded him of his own efforts to unite British students twenty years before. The link may have been one of their leaders, Robert W. Dunn, who had served for two years (1916–18) as the President of the Collegiate Anti-Militarism League, and was an active member of the ACLU from its inception.

On the initiative of this committee, the Intercollegiate Liberal League was formed in April 1921 at the Harvard Union. Speakers at the founding meeting included President Eliot of Harvard University; Dean Briggs, the President of Radcliffe; H. N. MacCracken, the President of Vassar, and John Haynes Holmes. According to the *Harvard Crimson*,

> Of the other speakers at the dinner on Saturday night, Mr Walter G. Fuller, Associate Editor of the *Freeman*, who was one of the most instrumental men in organizing the Convention, made a plea for such 'extra-mural' activities as liberal clubs. He also pointed out to the Convention the splendid opening that might be before the liberal league in the international field.

The other speakers that evening were Walter Lippmann (of the *New Republic*), Francis Neilson, and Charlotte Perkins Gilman. The following day saw further speeches by a member of the Executive Committee of the Cambridge University Liberal Club, followed by a black speaker, A. G. Dill (editor of the *Crisis*) on 'Liberalism and the Negro,' and by Roger Baldwin of the ACLU.

From today's perspective, it seems like a gathering of pillars of society. Yet the National Security League (which Walter had satirized in a brief piece in the *Freeman*[60]) assumed that the new organization was the successor to the Intercollegiate Socialist League, formed in 1905 by Jack London, Upton Sinclair and Graham Stokes to promote awareness of socialism and social problems among American students.* At once, it denounced the Liberal League as an 'attempt to implant [the Socialists'] Utopian theories in the immature minds of the young men and young women in the colleges and universities of America.'[61] Although an institution of this kind inevitably attracts some left-wing members and possibly an extremist or two, the

---

* Helen Phelps Stokes (see pages 252 and 253) hosted the 1910 convention of the Intercollegiate Socialist League – some 125 persons, including Ida Rauh (i.e., Max Eastman's first wife), Morris Hillquit and Upton Sinclair – in her studio. She was not expecting so many people. 'When the meeting was called to order, nearly everybody was standing up. "Let us sit on the floor," called out Upton Sinclair. "You set the example," Mr Hillquit called back, thinking the author was in fun. Mr Sinclair did sit down on the floor, whereupon everybody followed his example and was comfortable.'[62] At this meeting, Crystal spoke on 'Socialism and Labor Legislation.'

Liberal League was never affiliated with the Socialist Party, nor were its members ever expected to be committed socialists; it took in a much wider view of the world.*

The President of the new association, John Rothschild, protested at the assimilation, but the damage was done; the League was henceforth branded as 'socialist' and as a result it features in every list of 'anti-American activities'. For his help in setting up the League, Walter is mentioned in Chapter 3 of R. M. Whitney's *Reds in America* (1924). The fear of 'the Reds stalking our college women' (to borrow the title of an article by Vice-President Coolidge) was dismissed by the *Freeman*: 'It appears to us that socialism, syndicalism, bolshevism and general non-conformity in American universities and colleges is a cloud no larger than a man's hand.'[63]

Denunciation by the National Security League did not prevent the Liberal League from expanding rapidly; it may even have helped. The following year, it merged with the National Student Committee for the Limitation of Armaments, and began to issue *The New Student*, which for some six years was the most influential student periodical in the country. When it joined the League for Industrial Democracy in 1928 as 'The Student League for Industrial Democracy', the journal was discontinued.

Early in 1920, the owner of Walter and Crystal's apartment block decided to demolish the building. During their search for somewhere new to live, 'it just seemed to happen' (as Crystal put it in an article for *Cosmopolitan*) that

> we moved into two places instead of one. I took a small flat for myself and the children [in fact there was only Jeffrey at this point] toward the edge of town where there are playgrounds and green spaces. My husband took a room in a clean rooming house within easy walking distance of his office. The two cost a bit less than we had had to pay for a place large enough to hold us in reasonable comfort, all together.[65]

This initiated an arrangement that was to prevail for the rest of their lives. Crystal titled her article 'Marriage under Two Roofs' and described it in some detail, referring to Walter as 'John'.

> John's clothes and strictly personal possessions went to the room. Mine and the children's and our furniture, pictures and joint accumulations went to

---

* The charter of the Intercollegiate Liberal League declared that it would 'espouse no creed or principle other than that of complete freedom of assembly and discussion in the colleges.' It aimed 'to bring about a fair and open-minded consideration of social, industrial, political, and international questions by groups of college students, [and] to create among college men and women an intelligent interest in the problems of the day.'

> the flat. Technically, he lives at one place and I at the other. But of course he keeps a change of clothes and all the essentials for night and morning comfort at my house, as might a favourite and frequent guest.
>
> Every morning, like lovers, we telephone to exchange the day's greetings and make plans for the evening. Two or three times a week we dine together at my house and John stays all night. If we are to dine at a friend's house, we usually arrange to meet there and at the end of the evening my husband may come home with me and he may not, according to our mood. If we are going to a theater, I meet him in town for dinner, and after the show there are again always two possibilities – going home together like married lovers or parting on the street corner and going off in the night alone to our separate beds. And because neither course is inexorably forced upon us, either one is a bit of a lark. It is wonderful sometimes to be alone in the night and just know that someone loves you. In other moods, you must have that lover in your arms. Marriage under two roofs makes room for moods.[66]

According to Crystal, it also brought an end to the arguments about how to bring up children.

> If the two parents come from an almost identical background, or if one has had a miserable childhood which he is glad to forget, there may be no difficulty at all. It is when, as in our case, both parents can claim a happy childhood but under totally different auspices, that their joint efforts to raise a family come so often to grief. I think my husband and I have quarrelled with more anguish and bitternesss over our children than over all other matters put together. But we quarrel no longer.[67]

In her article, Crystal paints a rosy picture of this solution.

> Now that we live under two roofs there are no storms, no quarrels, no tears. Our differences of opinion are not passionate and unbearable. They have an almost rational quality. Criticisms and suggestions are made with the gentleness and reserve that is common between friends. They are received with the open-minded forbearance of one who can be sure of the critic's early departure.[68]

This suggests that the critical partner was Walter, and that Crystal was glad not to have him in the house, so that she had no need to accommodate his divergent opinion. Although she admitted that 'most women tend to own and manage their husbands too much, and I am not free from that vice,' she could see only advantages in having the last word on the education of their children.[69] She disregarded the effect that the eviction of their father might have on them.

With this arrangement, Crystal recreated the dynamic that pertained in her parents' union. After the death of her brother Morgan, her father lost his vigour and faded out into what Max described as a 'frail, hollow, weakly-gesturing, half-whispering ghost of a minister.'[70] Mrs Eastman responded by taking over from her husband not only as a pastor but also as the head of the family. Having had such a model, Crystal would pose a challenge to any man, and she was aware of it. But it did not prevent her from easing Walter out, leaving her to rule the roost.

We do not know what Walter thought of this. Living in a small rented room may sound rather bleak and comfortless compared with a shared family flat, but it was what he had been doing all his adult life. Even when he accommodated his sisters in comfortable hotels during their tours, he would take a modest room nearby. Crystal tried to imagine what he thought:

> I wish I could set forth as freely and frankly my husband's feeling about this new scheme of life as I can my own. But he is not the sort of man who talks easily about himself. He is what the psychoanalysts call an 'introvert'. I know from a hundred signs that he likes it, but I can only guess why.

She did her best to understand:

> Much of John's depression and irritability which used to be so baffling to me in the old days was due, I am sure, to his having no escape from me, no place where I did not come, no retreat from my influence. Now he has one. Often when we lived under the same roof he must have said to himself, 'I love her but I can't stand her. She is too much for me.' Now I know he never feels that.[71]

She appreciated Walter's need for 'Manchester' – somewhere to retreat to – but she did not realize that it was not to be taken personally. Walter would have needed 'Manchester' on occasion, whoever he was with.

For all Crystal's celebration of its advantages, living under separate roofs put a strain on their relationship. The 'crucial test' was the matter of fidelity.

> Crudely put, the challenge is: 'If my husband sleeps under a separate roof, how do I know that he is always alone?' or again: 'If I don't go home every night, how do I know that some other man is not there in my place?' In a literal and exact sense you don't know. That is the answer.
>
> But after all, marriage, like business, is founded on trust.[72]

Crystal could have had few worries on that score, for there is no evidence that Walter ever allowed his affections to stray, even though (as Rosalind put it) 'many women fell under his charm and hoped to marry him.' According to her, 'he just wasn't interested in physical sex.' She added, 'I remember a psychoanalyst who had once treated him [that would be Dr Parker], telling me that Walter "didn't really exist below the waist".[73] He and Rosalind, so similar in some ways, were poles apart in their sex drive.

Marriage is not just about sex; it is about communicating with each other, and Walter was not good at that, as Crystal implies by calling him an introvert. He lived surrounded by unanswered letters from his parents, sisters and friends. When Crystal went to Provincetown for a few days in August 1920, she complained to Walter by telegram that she had received

> No letter from you since Friday. I am desolate if I have done anything bad. Please forgive me and wire at once. Also write care [of] C. W. Crooker. Jeff and I safely established here. Both send devoted love to you, Crystal.[74]

She needed reassuring, to hear Walter say (if only in writing) that he still loved her, and when he failed to do so, she would fear that the fault was hers. She distrusted her ability to retain his love. In this she again took after her mother. In Max's account of his parents, he describes Mrs Eastman's frequent 'mood of contrition' in which she would doubt that she was worthy of her husband's love. A letter that she wrote on one occasion, when she had travelled with their son ahead of her husband, almost exactly parallels Crystal's telegram, word for word. It ends, 'I hope you like me.'[75]

The practice of living under two roofs was assumed to be only temporary at first. In the middle of 1920, Crystal decided to buy a share in a new row of cooperative houses on MacDougal Street, even though she would have to sub-let half the house. At this point, she told Cynthia that it meant that 'Walter will have something like a home'[76] and in November she affirmed that 'we shall really be living like a family again.'[77] But Walter seems not to have lived at 80 MacDougal Street at any point. Yet it was a pleasant part of New York. As Mumford put it, 'These were the halcyon days of Greenwich Village, when artists and writers had not yet been displaced by tourists, sightseers, hangers-on, opulent arrivistes, and bedraggled hippies.'[78] Margaret Lane with her husband and little son David (born six months after Jeffrey) lived next door in number 78, so the two boys played together in the yard at the back. As their parents had hoped, they remained lifelong friends.

At about this time Max moved into a flat in St Luke's Place, only six or seven minutes' walk away, sharing it with Eugen Boissevain. Max and Crystal remained deeply involved in each other's daily life. When he returned from Hollywood after visiting Florence Deshon at the end of 1919, it was Crystal who sent her a telegram on 25 December, saying, 'We are having a jolly Croton Christmas but it needs you to make it complete. Love from everybody on the hill, Crystal, Walter, Dudley, Doris, Max, Eugen, Margaret, Dan, Fred, and Marie.' In Hollywood Max became good friends with Charlie Chaplin.* So did Florence. As soon as Max left, she started an affair with him and in order to work with him she broke her contract with Sam Meyer. But in August she cabled Max that she urgently needed to return to New York. Crystal answered: 'Wire your arrival. Will expect you Thursday or Friday. Love C.'[80] She arrived in a parlous state. The Eastmans' 'gynecological friend and general practitioner for most of Greenwich Village,' Dr. Harry Lorber, soon discovered the cause. 'Florence has been pregnant for three months and the foetus is dead,' he told Max. 'You came just in time.'[81] An immediate operation saved her life.

Charlie Chaplin arrived a few days later and stayed in a hotel nearby. As Max had shared Chaplin's Hollywood habit of getting together with friends and playing charades and other dramatic games almost every evening, the entertainment continued at Max's when Chaplin visited him. Rosalind was invited one evening and she left us a memorable account of the occasion.

I arrived a little late and found his flat buzzing with talk and laughter. Charades were being discussed and drinks passed round. [Prohibition had started in January 1920.] Standing in one active little knot of people was a small man with a neat, narrow body, dark blue eyes and a mop of thick hair. It was Charlie Chaplin. Max took me aside and told me that he and Charlie had both decided on their teams before I arrived and that I was to be in Charlie's. Suddenly a pause came into the general conversation, as it does in the theatre just before the curtain rises. We were to begin and Charlie led his group out of the room. Our word was to be *champagne* and I soon found that this wasn't just a guessing game, but an elaborately worked out drama.

Charlie helped us choose our costumes from the clothes and drapes that Max had put on the beds and we practically rehearsed each section of the word before going in. The final scene embodying the whole word *champagne* was supposed to be a wild party, an orgy. I lay on the sofa, voluptuous and wanton, while the others danced drunkenly round me. Suddenly Charlie, with a quick, clean pirouette, emptied his pockets over me, scattering cents and nickels in wild abandon.

The charade ended and we all went over to the rival team to find out if they had guessed the word. I looked around for Charlie. He was on his

---

* 'Chaplin and Eastman were fascinated with one another. Each saw the other as a "real man," a man of action. Chaplin saw himself as only a player, someone who pretended, who hid anything that might prove offensive to the public, while Eastman spoke his mind fearlessly, exposing himself to physical assaults and criminal prosecutions. Eastman saw himself as only a writer, a poor pencil pusher and dreamer, while Chaplin was a man of power and success.'[79]

hands and knees picking up the coins, carefully putting them back in his pocket. I was amazed to see the richest man in the room [in fact the most highly paid man in the world] concerned with the smallest coins.[82]

Chaplin stayed only a short while. In October, Florence followed him back to Hollywood but now he was cool and impersonal with her and offered no work. She returned to New York having made only one film in Hollywood (*The Roof Tree*, released 25 December 1921), and was equally cool and impersonal with Max. She tried to go back on the stage, but found no work there either. On the evening of 4 February 1922, in the flat that Max had found for her – it belonged to Dudley Field Malone and Doris Stevens, who were away on their honeymoon – she went to bed leaving a gas tap on. Alerted by the smell, a neighbour intervened and rushed her to hospital. Max was summoned and as she lay unconscious the doctors transfused some of his blood in an attempt to save her. In vain.

Max was devastated, 'possessed by an irrational, almost insane desire to go to the funeral parlour where she lay and be near her. My sister took me in hand like a mother and restrained me. She even persuaded me not to go to the funeral. I lay still in my room as though paralyzed until it was over.'[83] Within a few weeks, he left for Europe and Russia.

Ever since the revolutions of March and then November 1917, Max had wanted to see the country run by its people. In his mind, the glowing accounts brought back by John Reed and Lincoln Steffens ('I have seen the future, and it works') outweighed the negative reports by others. He had to go and see for himself and – let it be said – for Crystal too. He had been preparing to leave for some time, putting the *Liberator* in the hands of faithful contributors, although he had little confidence in their ability to maintain the success of the periodical. His misgivings were well founded; as arranged in his contingency plan, it was handed over to the Workers' party before the year was out. In 1924, it merged with other periodicals to become the *Communist Monthly*. Disposing of the *Liberator* brought no profit for Max or Crystal: what money it had was appropriated and lost on Wall Street by their accountant. He was replaced by their office manager, Margaret Lane.

Nineteen-twenty-one was a busy year in the lives of Walter and Crystal. At the National Woman's Party's annual convention in February, the Party split over the basic principles that it should defend. After feverishly heated debate, it accepted (by 170 votes to 98) an amendment proposed by Crystal to the majority report and defined its future aim as 'the removal of all legal disabilities for women.'

Shortly afterwards, Walter and Crystal hosted several visits from Clare Sheridan (1885–1970). An English sculptress known for her busts of famous men, Sheridan had just returned from Moscow with the heads of Lenin, Trotsky, and other Soviet leaders in her luggage. In her American diary, she describes a visit to the Fullers. 'I liked them. I liked her particularly. She is good looking, and extremely decorative. She sails into a room with her head high and the face of a triumphant Victory.'[84] One weekend in May, Sheridan went up to Croton with them and found it 'a sort of Colony' inhabited by 'work-worn journalists, artists and Bohemians generally.'[85] There she was entertained by 'Walter Fuller's little sister, who sang old English folksongs to us, and sang them gracefully without any self-consciousness.'[86]

> All the children were good (by a strange coincidence there was not a girl-child among them!) and all the people were happy. One or two mothers asked me (and I looked at them twice to see if they were serious) when in my opinion conditions in Russia would be sufficiently adjusted to enable them to take their children there for education.[87]

Clearly, she had not opened their eyes to the realities of life in Russia. Whatever she might have said was unlikely to affect Max's decision.

By the summer of 1921, Crystal was pregnant again, expecting for February 1922. Despite appearances, she was not up to child-bearing. On her doctor's advice she took to her bed in November and gave birth to a daughter on 12 December 1921, two months early. They called her Annis Diana – the first being the name of Crystal's mother. Where the *Diana* came from, I do not know; my personal hypothesis is that Walter saw something of the Roman goddess Diana in Crystal. She was very weak after the birth and remained in hospital for three weeks.

The medical expenses blighted the Fullers' finances. With two young children on her hands, Crystal needed help in the home and was earning nothing. She had expected her 'little pieces' to be lapped up by editors for $50 each, but between April 1921 (her last contribution to the *Liberator*) and December 1923 (when 'Marriage under Two Roofs' appeared in *Cosmopolitan*), she published no articles at all. Yet she defined herself as someone who paid her own way – living under two roofs forced the issue – and she *hated* having to depend on Walter's salary. When she told Cynthia that New York was so expensive that 'no one man can be expected to keep a family going,' she was proclaiming her own need for independence. By March 1922 she was desperate, 'in a terrible hole what with babies and hospitals and all.'

So after ten months of domesticity varied by illness I am out on the war path.

I must have money and I don't care much how I get it. All ways are hard I believe. This time I am trying to do it in some way that won't interfere too drastically with the business of being a mother. Some business. Isn't it?'[88]

An Amazon – or Diana – on the war path is a fearsome force of nature, and Crystal's desperation was exacerbated by her impatience with her slow recovery from the birth of Annis. The recent death of Florence Deshon no doubt contributed to making her very hard to live with, and Walter felt the need for 'Manchester'.

He had spent more than ten years in America and still did not feel at home there. London was calling, and he was longing to see his parents and his sisters again.[89] Without warning Crystal, he left the *Freeman* and sailed for England on 4 April 1922 – the day after his forty-first birthday – to seek work in England. An eternal optimist, he hoped to earn more in his home country, although he knew full well that 'you ought not to give up a certainty for an uncertainty, a not-bad state of things for a worse,' as he once wrote to Riss.[90] Living under two roofs made it all too easy to flit.

Within weeks of his departure from New York, Rosalind was chosen for a leading role in a Broadway production. She had been steadily making a name for herself, rejecting singing parts in favour of straight acting. This included turning down a two-year contract to appear in a musical comedy alongside the famous Marx Brothers. Her breakthrough came when Arthur Hopkins (who had given the Fuller Sisters the runaround six years before) and the great John Barrymore (1882–1942) decided to put on *Hamlet*. To everyone's astonishment, from among the experienced candidates who queued at the stage door and all the way down the block, they chose an unknown actress from the Greenwich Follies, a mere *folksinger*, to play Ophelia. The critic Alexander Woollcott, whose acerbic wit was notorious, scoffed that they might as well engage a *fencer* to play Laertes.

It was clearly Rosalind's interpretation of the mad scene at her audition that won her the part. Not withstanding the 'great black open mouth' of the dark and empty auditorium, she had the confidence to own the stage and move about freely. 'I had an idea and a feeling for the part. This was what Barrymore was looking for,' she writes.[91] In fact, Barrymore commented to his wife that day, 'She is a strange, unprepossessing little English woman but has a detached rather zany quality – which Margaret says might be developed.' (Unknown to Rosalind, Barrymore's voice coach, Margaret Carrington, was helping with the casting.) He went on, 'she sings infinitely better than she speaks. . . . She is *very* English and has a queer lack of vitality

– or humanity – but something very effective might be gotten there perhaps – particularly in the mad scenes.'[93] Blanche Yurka, who was cast as Gertrude (although she was five years younger than Barrymore), found 'Rosalind Fuller's Tanagra-like figure was lovely for the mad little Ophelia.'[94]

As soon as Rosalind was chosen, Barrymore took her for voice production lessons from Mrs Carrington at her country house in Connecticut.*

> My voice was rather high-pitched for speaking so she lowered it with some very simple exercises that she had devised. Barrymore's voice was limited in range, so while he was running up and down musical scales on the lawn, I would be moaning and groaning in low tones in the bushes.[95]

Robert Edmond Jones – the Bobby Jones who had been so kind to the Fuller sisters back in 1916 – designed the set for this production. He had just returned from a trip to Europe where he had been struck by the work of the German Expressionist Leopold Jessner (1878–1945). Although no one in America noticed at the time, he leaned heavily on Jessner for his inspiration.

This production proved to be the most famous *Hamlet* of all time, a clear break with previous generations, and Barrymore was hailed as the greatest American Hamlet; some even went so far as to say the greatest ever. It was a thoroughly modern interpretation, for Arthur Hopkins and Bobby Jones were both were deeply interested in Freud and contemporary psychology.

> By 1922, the Oedipus Complex and suppressed desires were common currency in American society. Many observers would note the 'incestuous' handling of the Queen's closet scene, yet it was apparent to others that the use of modern psychology extended even further, to the interpretation of Ophelia and to an overall view of the play.[96]

One of the 'extra ladies' in the court scenes was the daughter of the psychiatrist Smith Ely Jelliffe, and 'she recalled that her father had advised Hopkins on "how Ophelia should sing her mad song".'[97] Rosalind's memories of her interpretation may well be influenced by this, for she writes: 'To me her madness should be a breakthrough to freedom from the repressions of her normal life. I was very young, enthusiastic and unafraid. My interest in Freud and my experience with the psychoanalyst would surely come to my aid.'[98] This shift towards a 'psychological *Hamlet*' was reflected by

> landmark restorations to the traditional acting text. Since the time of Garrick it had been customary to eliminate the play's many sexual refer-

---

* Rosalind described Margaret Huston Carrington (1877–1942) as 'a very clever woman who had been an opera singer and was now married to a millionaire.'[92] Carrington had many famous students, whom she tutored for free. After the death of her husband in 1931, she married Robert Edmond Jones.

ences. . . . By the early 1920s, however, American society no longer deemed it necessary or even appropriate to Bowdlerize the Bard. Some observers saw the production's sexuality as pure sensationalism, but to others it was very much in tune with a new and welcome tendency to view Shakespeare's characters as psychological, fully-rounded human beings rather than the poetic idealized figures of Victorian and Edwardian tradition.[99]

Barrymore is reported to have told Hopkins that he wanted Hamlet 'to be so male that when I come out on the stage they can hear my balls clank.'[100] Rosalind confirms this with a telling detail: 'He never wore a jockstrap under his Hamlet tights and made no attempt to hide the erection that he so often had when he was acting.'[101] As for Ophelia, Rosalind's cheerful acceptance and enthusiastic expression of her own sexuality undoubtedly enriched her performance. The result, for the critic Stark Young, was 'a hint of that last betrayal that insanity brings, indecency.'[102]

The off-stage relationship that developed between Rosalind and John Barrymore undoubtedly contributed to the sexual tension of the scenes they played. Actors' parts often overflow into their private lives. 'Cynthia always says that bits of my theatre characters still cling to me, like cobwebs, when I am off stage,' remarks Rosalind.[103] And no young woman was indifferent to John Barrymore; he was the heart-throb of the day. So Rosalind could hardly fail to be moved when, 'looking into his face in the nunnery scene, I could see his love for Ophelia shining in his eyes, against the hard words he was saying.'[104] In his autobiography, Maurice Browne reveals what Barrymore once told him: 'at every performance he would leave his dressing-room to watch [Rosalind] from the wings during the "mad scene". "Her singing of the songs," he said, "would have melted the heart of God."'[105] So it comes as no surprise to learn that

> There would often be a knock on my door after the performance and my dresser would hand me a small tie-on label marked 'Mr Barrymore'. It came from one of the many oxygen cylinders he always had in his room to use when he felt tired. This meant he wanted to see me, a sort of secret code. Hurrying to his room I would see in the mirror the Hamlet I had known in Elsinore wiping off his make-up and saying, 'Rosalind, I need life and those damned oxygen robots can only give me air.' Then folded together on his sofa with his still-warm tights and tunics hanging against the wall amidst the smell of powder and grease paint we would lose ourselves in a sort of mirage of love . . . and I would watch his beautiful face hanging over me in the falsely lighted room.[106]

As Rosalind's choice of words makes clear, this was Ophelia making love with Hamlet quite as much as it was John Barrymore making love with Rosalind Fuller (and vice versa of course). At the end of the tour that followed their second season, Barrymore gave her a replica of the locket he had worn as Hamlet. Inside was a slip of paper on which he had typed the beginning of Hamlet's letter to Ophelia:

> Doubt thou the stars are fire;
> Doubt that the sun doth move;
> Doubt truth to be a liar;
> But never doubt I love.[107]

10

Radio Man

Don't worry about harsh words. Have I said any? If I have they certainly can be forgotten now. I knew you had to run away. That you couldn't even send me a line to say so and say you were sorry will for ever be incomprehensible to me. But then four-fifths of you is a closed book to me and four-fifths of me is a closed book to you – and yet we love each other a great deal. Don't we?[1]   Crystal to Walter, summer 1922

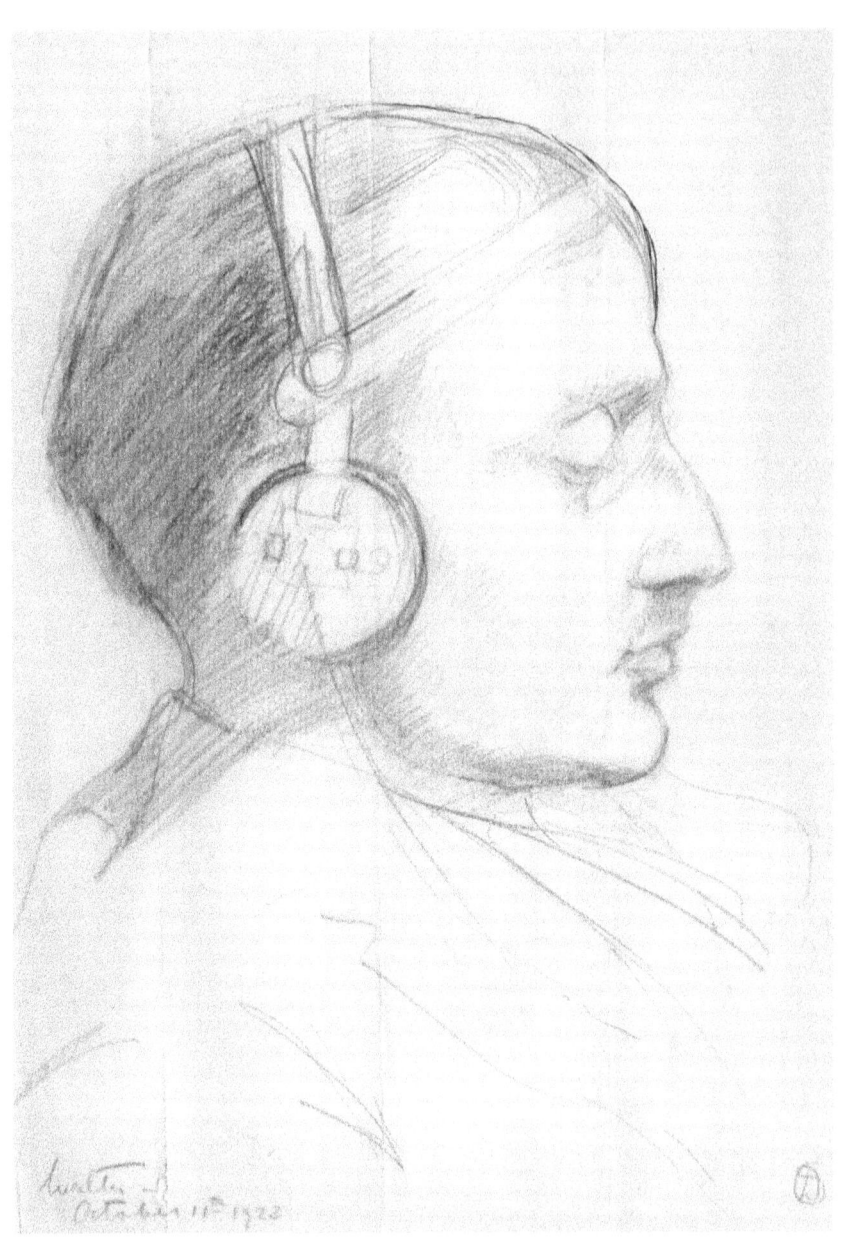

Walter listening to the wireless:
a pencil portrait by Dorothy, dated 11 October 1923

WALTER ARRIVED BACK in England on Sunday 9 April 1922, and went straight to see his parents in Bournemouth. There he received a letter from Crystal, dated 14 April: 'I am so lonely it makes a little sick feeling in my solar plexus,' she told him. 'I am not made of stern enough stuff to live alone. I hope you will come back here.' And she offered hope of a new job in New York:

> Paul Kellogg is hinting about the possibility of a job for you *here* on the *Survey Graphic*!* It sounds a really beautiful job, starting at $4500 and moving towards $5000. You'd have the chance to edit all the MSS, but also be make-up and art editor – and general inspirator.
>
> Later – I must have got so sleepy I couldn't hold the pen: I've never worked so hard since the Truth about Preparedness campaign, and I'm ready to drop into bed at 7.30 p.m. . . .
>
> Your cable has come with the money – and the warning that the *Freeman* is about to close! The money was welcome, dear, but what a mystery-maker you are!²

As the *Freeman* never attracted enough subscribers to make a profit, it was forever hovering on the brink of closing down. Walter's departure also came at a difficult moment: Van Wyck Brooks had arranged to take six months leave of absence to write his book on Henry James, and 'Nock began to show signs of wear and tear. He was frequently under the weather, and members of the staff were seriously disturbed at his condition,' recalled Neilson. 'How we succeeded in turning the third year without a breakdown was a mystery to me, for in the midst of our trouble, Walter Fuller decided to return to England' and he was 'the essential cog in the wheel of the machine. . . . What we were to do without him seemed to me to be an insuperable difficulty.'³ Henry Kellock replaced Walter, and Suzanne La Follette took over many of Nock's editorial tasks. The *Freeman* tottered on for another eighteen months.

Crystal suggested that Walter 'should consider Paul Kellogg's offer on the *Survey Graphic* very seriously, in view of the probable debacle of the *Freeman*.' She thought he 'could work with Paul' –

> he is sensitive and humorous. And, God be praised, that money will just pay our debts, and pay for necessary work on the house. It can't go towards living expenses. I can't think that your cable means all is over at the *Freeman*. Surely they would not let you off with only two weeks' salary – after all the good things they have said about your work?

---

* The Survey was retitled the *Survey Graphic* after the war.

But, if my worst guess is true, Paul's job might even do. They have the money to run the *Survey Graphic* for three years – just as long as you like a job to last! With you on it, I think the magazine could be wonderful. And it already has a real circulation, so it would be a chance to work on something growing. I'll say for Paul, too, what obviously can't be said of your *Freeman* bosses – he is honourable and straight in his dealing.

Of course Paul's letter to you may be exceedingly vague and tentative, and you may never get the offer – I suppose there *are* lots of people looking to that job. My purpose in this letter is to urge you to look favorably on the offer if you get it. You see, darling, I am still a very dependent wife. I've rented the apartment in New York to save the day!

I don't want to stop without telling you I am very happy and very well. My fatigue at night is healthy, and I sleep hard.

Forgive this miserable letter. I can do much better after I've heard from you.

Love
Crystal

P.S. I know they will regret it if they let you go. Nine-tenths of the praise one hears of the *Freeman* is for its good English – its fine writing. And everybody knows that's your mark. I suppose your letter will tell me all about everything. But it may not! I love you, anyway.[4]

It is not known if Kellogg made his offer; nor has Walter's answer to Crystal survived. At any rate, he remained in England, meeting up with friends, old and new.

One of the first was Alfred Nott – it may be that Dorothy put them in contact. Since March 1919, Nott had been round the world, visiting America, Japan, China, Malaya, Burma, India, Egypt and Italy. Then he spent almost a year in Vienna, where he managed to make some money, and as long again with a Quaker relief mission in the Ukraine. On his return to England, he was delighted to learn that Walter had just come back too. They met up at the Café Royal and had 'one of those rare talks that go to the heart like wine.' After that they 'spent some days together walking along the streets, strolling through the parks,' Walter showing 'all the exile's delight at being once more in London.'

'This is what I want now,' he said, taking in Piccadilly with a gesture, 'the richness, the quietness of London. Strangely enough in New York with all its rush I never felt that anything unexpected might happen. In London I always feel that round the corner an adventure is waiting. I may never meet it but I have a sense of expectation. And yet I feel relaxed, as though an enormous pressure has been removed.'

For all his Peter Panish delight, Walter 'had a dozen schemes for bringing England up to date on American lines, chief of which was to give every hotel and boarding house central heating and hot and cold water in the rooms.'[5] In the end, though, it mattered little which side of the Atlantic had the greener grass or warmer rooms; Walter was happier in London than in New York.

For Nott, Walter 'made things live. He made you see them from a new point of view.' 'He was able to arouse people from apathy – to wake them into life.' Moreover, he

> had a great deal of charm – not the superficial charm of manners, though he had that too – but the true charm, which is a sign of high development, that magic key which unlocks the hearts of men and women. . . . Fuller had this, and with it a brilliant mind; and he had wit and a rare sense of humour.
>
> His comments on people and things were richly amusing. 'We 'ad thought of going to Wales,' said the wife of a rich hat manufacturer to him in the early days of motoring. 'but we thought the 'ills would be too much for the car.'
>
> 'Yes,' answered Fuller, 'perhaps it is better to endure the ills we have than to drive to those we know not of.'[6]

Nott's pleasure in Walter's company was shared by two new friends: Frazier Hunt and Sinclair Lewis. How Walter came to meet them I do not know, but it was clearly very soon after his arrival in England for by 4 May he was heading for the hills of Scotland with them, by car.

Frazier Hunt was a journalist who had reported on the Paris Peace Conference and made a name for himself by smuggling the first copy of the Treaty of Versailles back to New York. In 1922 he embarked on a stay in Europe for the Hearst group of magazines. After a month in Ireland, he arrived in London in March, instructed by Hearst to make contact with Sinclair Lewis and try to secure his next novel for *Cosmopolitan*. Already well known for *Main Street* and noticed by the *Freeman* as a promising writer, Lewis was just finishing *Babbitt* when Hunt met him and for the next ten weeks the two were inseparable, for they 'mixed like scotch and soda.'[7] Hunt had brought from America an enormous Studebaker touring car in which he would 'gallop time and again from the southern coast of England to the mountains and lakes of Scotland.' He vividly remembered 'one long and rather leisurely trip' to Glasgow that he and Sinclair Lewis took with their respective wives. 'Gentle and beloved Walter Fuller accompanied us as our guide and peace-maker.'[8]

Given their thirst for alcohol, Hunt and Lewis seem unlikely companions for Walter, who almost never drank. They kept a tally of the names of the pubs they passed – 'the Red Lion won over the White Horse by a score of nineteen to seventeen' – and 'we pulled up at far too many of these inviting havens. . . . Late each afternoon,' recalls Hunt,

> we would choose an attractive, old-fashioned inn, and settle down for the evening. After supper, Red [i.e. Sinclair Lewis] and I would find a quiet seat in the taproom and buy mugs of ale for the village squire, the doctor, the butcher, and whoever else would sit and discuss affairs with us.[9]

It sounds as though it fell to Walter to keep their wives company in the meantime. At any rate he made a good impression on one of his companions: 'Immediately upon his return, Sinclair Lewis wrote a letter of introduction to Hugh Walpole for his new best friend, Walter Fuller, "one of the most charming people I know".'[10] He was suggesting that Walpole might help Walter find work in an editorial capacity. But no work in any capacity came his way. It was a bad moment to be looking for a job, all the demobbed soldiers having satisfied the market. So he set up in business for himself.

Three names appear on the letterhead of the Transatlantic Literary Agency: Walter G. Fuller; Charles Thomas Hallinan; and Stanley C. Nott. Hallinan had been a friend – the only one at Walter's wedding – since the early days of the AUAM. He had served on the board of the *Liberator,* and contributed to the *Freeman*. Hal (as he was usually called) had met Hazel Hunkins, the feminist and peace activist, on her release from the Occoquan Workhouse along with the other 'silent sentinels' who had picketed the White House. In 1920 he followed her to England where she was to research the English co-operative movement for the American Railway Brotherhood. They set up home together in London, and he joined Associated Press, ultimately becoming the financial editor of United Press International, while Hazel started writing a column for the Chicago *Tribune* under the pseudonym Ann Whittingham. She served as Secretary and then President of the Six Point Group, the British feminist organization. She was also involved in various other clubs and organizations, including the Americans for Democratic Action, the Anglo-American Families Association, and the Vassar Club of London. By the time Walter arrived, she and Hal had two children; two more followed; the eldest became the novelist Nancy Hallinan. They lived at 28 Redcliffe Square, and both Walter and Nott began to lodge with them on 1 June 1922.* Here, on Sunday afternoons, 'journalists would foregather, mostly Americans – Frazier Hunt of Hearst's, Hiram K. Moderwell

---

* The mysterious Ret Marut, better known as B. Traven, author of *The Treasure of the Sierra Madre* (1935), also stayed with the Hallinans in 1923.

of the Chicago *Daily News* and his wife Anne Herendeen, Griffin Barry the freelance, Norman Matson [not yet partnering Susan Glaspell] over from Vienna, Norman Ewer from the *Daily Herald,* and so on.'[11]

For the Transatlantic Literary Agency Walter rented an office at 44 Great Russell Street, W.C.1, just opposite the British Museum. He had *'Dum spiro spero'* (i.e. 'While I breathe, I hope') painted below the name plate, 'both to encourage ourselves in the venture and our clients in their long climb up the stairs,' as Nott puts it.[12] After that, they needed letterpaper. Walter had designed for the WPP, but he could not get the heading right for himself. In the end, he called on a new friend, Stanley Morison, who had been imprisoned during the war as a conscientious objector. Since then he had been working as a design supervisor, first at the Pelican Press and now at the Cloister Press, where he co-founded the Fleuron Society, which had a profound influence on type and book design in the twentieth century.* Walter and Stanley Nott went round to St Stephen's House, Westminster, where Morison quickly designed a simple, classic letterhead for them.

As its name suggests, the aim of the Agency was to place the writing of Britons in America, starting with the *Freeman,* for which Walter served as a talent scout for as long as it lasted. He also represented the *World Tomorrow*. His friendship with Frazier Hunt no doubt provided his clients with entry to the Hearst range of publications.† It was all very well in theory, but such an enterprise depends on recruiting promising writers. As Walter soon discovered, the articles and stories that his advertisements drew in were mostly second-rate and almost impossible to place. Furthermore, even a big name like Bertrand Russell would get no more than $100 for an article in the New York *Times*.[13] If the Agency retained 15% of that, it meant a mere £3. Money was far more likely to flow out than in. Nott reports:

> We debated whether we should charge a reading fee. The general idea was that reputable agencies did not make a charge. As we wished to be thought reputable, we decided there should be no fee for reading, though Fuller put in a great deal of time revising MSS gratis simply because he was interested in the writers.[15]

True to character, Walter also spent hours composing letters that would make rejection palatable to aspiring authors.

* Today, Morison is best known for designing the Times New Roman font for *The Times*. It was first used in 1932 and became commercially available in 1934.

† On Hunt's departure for America in January 1925, Walter arranged for him to be given 'a shelf-ful of authors' autographed copies' as a farewell present.[14] This confirms that he was in contact with many writers – without, unfortunately, revealing their names.

Walter Fuller

As no records have survived, it is not possible to say how many clients the Agency had. The few surviving letters that Walter exchanged with C. K. Ogden and Bertrand Russell reveal that he sought to place books and articles for them – with occasional success – and also for Dr H. G. Baynes, the translator of C. G. Jung. On 1 December 1922, T. S. Eliot reported that he had received a translation of a story by Pirandello from the Agency.[16] Clearly, Walter was seeking for commissions from established writers. He approached members of the 1917 Club (founded in the year of the Russian Revolution); it was the primary haunt of Fabians, radical Liberals, and the Bloomsbury set. Rosalind was a member, and so was Claude McKay, introduced by C. K. Ogden. But profitable clients were few.

Michael Farbman called at the Agency. He had been a member of the National Council for Civil Liberties during the war and had written on *The Russian Revolution and the War* (1917) and *Russia and the Struggle for Peace* (1918). Now he had just returned from a visit to Russia, bringing a lengthy interview with Lenin. Written on 27 October 1922, it was first published in *Pravda*[17] and extracts appeared in the *Observer* and the *Manchester Guardian*. Did Walter help place his next books, *Bolchevism in Retreat* (published by Collins in 1923) and *After Lenin: the New Phase in Russia* (Parsons, 1924)? At any rate, Farbman will have brought fresh news from Russia where Max was now living and loving.

According to Alfred Nott, who recorded his memories of the Agency ten years later, they received visits from Kate O'Brien (1897–1974), the future novelist and playwright. At this juncture, she had just returned from a stay in Spain and was working as a secretary in London, writing in her spare time. She must have shown some of it to Walter and it would be nice to think that she profited from his advice, for she sprang to fame in 1926 when her first play, *Distinguished Villa*, was staged by amateurs at the Aldwych Theatre. She wrote it very quickly for a bet, which suggests that by then she was confident that she could pull it off. *Distinguished Villa* met with such success that within weeks it was transferred to the Haymarket with a professional cast.

Other visitors included the playwright and actress Dorothy Massingham (1889–1933), and Hugh Miller (1889–1976), the film actor whose career began with *Bonnie Prince Charlie* (1923; now lost), and ended with *Lawrence of Arabia* (1962), on which he worked as a dialogue coach and was rewarded with the part of the RAMC colonel. Alec Waugh (1898–1981) came round and introduced Walter to his brother Evelyn (1903–1966), who at this point had published only reviews and short stories in Oxford university journals, and to their father, Arthur, the managing director of Chapman & Hall.

'When I went up the stairs of Chapman & Hall's to Arthur Waugh's private office' recalled Nott, 'I felt to the full the glamour that is associated with a publishing house in the hearts and minds of those who have never worked for one.'[18]*

Meanwhile, Crystal was doing her best to help:

> Walter dear – our friend Paul Kennedy [not identified] proposes this: if you will write and tell him something of your organization, what authors you have etc, and he is satisfied with you – and that it is a good concern, he will make a 50–50 agreement with you. That is, he will place all things in England through your agency, and you will agree to place all things in America through *his* agency – each going 50–50 in commissions! He would like to make the arrangement exclusive, on both sides, for a trial period of six months.
>
> It seems it would be a good thing. You see he has sold 4 successful plays – handles all of Ibanez – and has sold the movie rights for *The Four Horsemen*. The next move for you is to write him a grand type-written letter, stating your business, and making it sound as important as possible.
>
> I guess the truth is you haven't much business yet – or you would have an agency of your own in America.
>
> Oh, how I wish you would tell me something!
>
> Crystal[19]

There is no evidence to suggest that anything came of this proposal. Walter probably did not have enough clients to make a balanced exchange.

True to character, Walter kept putting off writing to Crystal in the hope of having better news, and then felt guilty about it. And also true to character, Crystal took his silence as a sign that perhaps he no longer loved her. Feeling lonely and frustrated, she cabled him and followed it up with a letter:

> I'm going to answer my favourite of all your letters. In it you say: 'Anyway this maddening 3000 miles apart relationship can't go on for ever. What are we to do? What is your plan? What do you want me to do? What do you want to do? What do you think we ought to do?'
>
> And later comes that most precious bit commencing: 'In this city of a thousand Vera Zordous [not identified] – I never see the likes of you.'
>
> And, at the end, comes 'Oh dear, oh dear! Walter.'
>
> My cable was in answer to that letter. For now something has broken

---

* By the time he wrote this, Nott had become a publisher himself.

down in me – the sense of injury has faded out at last, and I think we can come together – in spirit at least – and be happy again – even without the old Atlantic between us.

That is – if you still love me as much as you did when you wrote that letter.

I haven't heard from you for two weeks now, and, of course, it *might* be because you don't love me any more – but I guess it's because 'the miracle' hasn't happened yet, or because you are hurt at my long silence. . . .

You will go on expecting miracles – but I'm not going to. I am going to love you very much – sustain you as well as I can with letters and hopeful thoughts and *go to work*. If, later, things are going well with you – we'll come. But not now, when we would be a burden around your neck.

This is a hard decision for me to make. I want to come – all that is romantic in me pleads for it. To borrow money (where I don't know!) and *come*, to take a chance on our future together – that would be the romantic thing to do. But I'm only one-third romantic, as you know. The practical two-thirds sees the future too clearly. Poverty and struggle and debt – that's what it would be. I am too determined that the next time we live together, we shall be *happy*. Happiness with you and me means a decent income. Let's try and remember that.

But if you have a year in which to make your London dreams come true, they might indeed come true, then how happy my coming would be.

So I am starting out now to find a job – feminist editing and writing, if possible – but something that will support us three. Whatever money you can send will be tremendously welcome. (I think I can make a living – but we must begin to pay back my debt to Dad.* So send me whatever you can, won't you?) And, if the big chance comes – I'll come whenever it seems financially safe – or anywhere near safe.

In one letter you suggest that I could get a correspondent job over there – and I suppose I could. If you had a sure income, big enough for us to live on, then it would be great for me to begin work in London. But we mustn't both be trying.

I'm doing my best with my play. Pemberton is reading it now. I've read it aloud two or three times now, and I'm inclined to think a good lively show could be made of it.†

---

* Crystal must have borrowed from her father to buy the house in MacDougal Street.

† I know nothing more of this project. I presume that Pemberton was a literary agent.

Well, dear, send me a sincere human letter that will brace up my courage for this plunge into the great striving world again. Will you? And couldn't you tell me *something* about your daily life? I long to come and be part of it.

I wish you could see our baby. She is simply adorable. Max says her feet are worth going miles to see. And her smile: she smiles all the time. I love taking care of her. Oh, how I wish I had taken care of Jeff when he was a baby. I'd understand him better.

Love to you – and joy – and success

Crystal[20]

Within a few days, she wrote again:

Last Monday I wrote to you with great strength and confidence that I was going to settle down here and go to work. But I am so unhappy in that decision that I think I must be wrong. I feel as though I *must* see you pretty soon, if only for a few hours' conversation. So I have been thinking that perhaps I could rent out my two houses for a year, and run away to Germany or Austria, or one of those places where it is still phenomenally cheap to live. I really don't like the idea of settling down to a lonely, hard-working life in New York without you.

If I *do* that, then could you scrape up enough to keep us in London for a week? And to get us to and from the ship wherever we land?

You know, I am different, in some ways, Walter. To begin with, I am well – stronger than you have ever known me, I think. That would make our life together less difficult. Don't you think so? Just now in the last three weeks, I have found a perfect little colored girl to look after the children. Shall I hang on to her – and wait for you to come back? Or shall I bring her?

If we went to Berlin, you see, we could meet in London, on the way – we would be so much nearer. Do you think you could manage $5 a month towards our support? If you could, I am sure we could live on what I will have from the rent of the houses. Then we could pay off all the debts to a happier day. Is that what you would like to do? Then – if at any time you were making enough money, we could pull up stakes and come to London. I am finding out all about the details of cost of living, and schools, in Berlin – right away – though of course I must rent the houses first, and find, *somewhere,* the money for our passages.

Charles [Hallinan] says you are having a marvellous time – should you rather live that way – free and irresponsible? I suppose if that's really what you want – you wouldn't be happy with me – even in London.

But I don't think we ought to conclude without trying. Do you?

And I keep remembering that vast glorious double bed in our

Hampstead Heath house in London. Do you think we could find another house with a bed like that?

Goodbye, darling – do write me a letter with your feet on the ground – or near it – and say that you think the Berlin idea is brilliant.

Crystal

Walter must have encouraged her to come over, adding that his parents invited her to stay at Alum Cottage or somewhere nearby. Crystal answered:

Dearest – your letters are so sweet, and I am coming just as fast as I can. Don't cable me any more. Every cable would take us to a show in London. And I am so eager for a life with a bit of a margin. . . .

Walter dear, please don't get me in on any Bournemouth plans. I'm going straight to London – [to] find a place to lay our heads, find a school for Jeffrey, find a nurse for Annis – and then start on my articles. I am crazy for work and cities and shows. I'm through with the country, and the futile domestic life. I've had six months of it now.

Anyhow, with a baby, I can't make any stops anywhere. So please be firm with your family. It's sweet of them to suggest it – but I *won't go!* We can go visiting on weekends – after I'm settled.

I think I will get off at Plymouth – and then you simply can't help it – you can meet me there. Of course it would be wonderful to have help with the baby.

Let's go to a hotel for a while anyhow. I'm crazy to be on my way – but such a mountain of work yet.

Love
Crystal[21]

By August, she had

no doubt we can live on the rent money [from her two houses] with a little help from you – in one of those cheap foreign countries – Italy, Germany and Austria. Then we can see each other once in a while – & perhaps I can help a little too. But I'm not going to do anything that would take me away from this little charmer of ours. You don't want me to, do you?'[22]

She followed this up on 9 September with a letter to Cynthia, who had had a daughter in June 1920:

Cynthia darling

I'm coming to London!

Will you forgive me for not writing to you all this long summer, and let me be your best best friend – next to Rosalind? That's what I want to be. I want to come and help you fight the fight back to youth, and joy, and activity again.

Oh – and I want to talk to you, and see your beautiful Monica – and plan our lives and everything.

Could you be on the look-out for a good nurse and general worker for me – and a school for Jeff – all day school with lunch – very free and modern? These I must have. And I hope to find a way of living where I won't have to keep house. I *hate* planning meals, and I don't want to do it for at least a year. But I do want to live with my children.

I'll have $100 a month from my house in New York, and I expect to get a contract for at least one feminist article a month at $100. That's what we'll live on. If Walter can contribute something, that will go for fun. I'm not depending on his business prospects for bread-and-butter – or a roof. I know too little about them.

Best love to you

Crystal[23]

She was right not to depend on Walter; he could hardly keep himself in bread-and-butter: Hazel Hunkins Hallinan's records show that he was always behind with his rent. Yet – or perhaps *because* of this – he managed to take a holiday in France that summer.

Crystal arrived (at Tilbury, in the end) on 7 October 1922. The actor Miles Malleson* kindly loaned them his flat for a while so they were able to enjoy their reunion in privacy. Walter had got to know Malleson when (according to Nott) he came round to the Agency

> to talk about some plays he wanted to get produced in America. Fuller arranged for a reading of the plays at Malleson's flat in Mecklenburgh Square, and got Frazier Hunt, Hi Moderwell and one or two other important American journalists to be present. One of the plays was *The Fanatics*, which afterwards made a lot of money in England.[24]

To free Crystal up for writing articles and talking with the editors of periodicals that might take them, Walter took Jeffrey and Annis to stay with Riss.

Both Riss and Dorothy would have happily looked after their brother's children on a long-term basis, but neither Basil Ward nor Jack Odell would agree to it. To save money, Crystal and the children moved to Berlin – only to realize that she had to be in London if she was to be published. So Walter rented a house for them: 6 Upper Park Road, just half-a-mile from the edge

---

* Actor, playwright and scriptwriter Miles Malleson (1888–1969) was amicably divorcing his first wife, Constance (Colette) Annesley, who had left him for Bertrand Russell. He married a medical student, Joan Billson, in June 1923. On qualifying she specialized in family planning and became a prominent advocate of legalizing abortion. See p.350.

of Hampstead Heath. After Crystal moved in with Jeffrey and Annis, Walter retained his room at the Hallinan's. It was still marriage under two roofs, only without the Atlantic between them.

Even with a literary agent for husband, Crystal found her writing hard to place, for she was forthright and outspoken, while British feminists now favoured a more understated approach. Of the eight articles that she published in 1923, five were uncontroversial pieces in Lady Rhondda's *Time & Tide*; the others were in American publications: *Equal Rights, New Republic,* and *Cosmopolitan*. In 1924, she placed only four pieces, two in *Time & Tide* (in January and March), one in *Equal Rights* (also March) and the last – a letter to the editor of the *Nation* – in November, by which time she was back in the United States. So she was far from making the $100 a month she had been counting on. The debts began to pile up again.

The Agency was not paying its way, either. Yet it was doubtless with reference to this period as a literary agent that *The Times* wrote of Walter, 'Few men can have handled more of the writings of others.'[25] Editors like him are the midwives of literature. Just as some of us owe our survival to the timely intervention of an anonymous midwife, so it can be with works of literature.

Charles Hallinan left the Agency before the end of 1922; in October 1923, Alfred Nott left too, hoping to make his fortune in America. (In his place, a friend of Kate O'Brien's, a Mrs Stephens from the *Daily Herald,* came in to help with the office work.) Walter must have given Nott some letters of introduction, for on his immigration papers he indicated that he was going to stay with Dudley Field Malone in New York City. Three months later he was back with an idea. In Vienna he had seen tinsel prints which he thought he could market in the United States. So when he returned to New York in the autumn of 1924, it was with two trunks of prints. These he sold well enough to buy a half share in the Sunwise Turn Bookshop at 2 East 31st Street, in midtown Manhattan. There he fell under the spell of the Russian spiritual teacher George Gurdjieff (1866 or 1872–1949), who was making a brief visit in the company of A. R. Orage.* Subsequently Nott spent time in France at Gurdjieff's Institute for the Harmonious Development of Man. He helped to publish and distribute Gurdjieff's first book, *The Herald of Coming Good*. In the 1950s, he wrote three books about Gurdjieff, Orage, and Ouspensky.

---

* In 1924, Orage (1873–1934) sold *The New Age* – which had established him as a major literary editor and critic – to join Gurdjieff's community at the Prieuré des Basses Loges in Fontainebleau-Avon. In 1927 he married Jessie Richards Dwight who owned the other half of the Sunwise Turn.

Then Walter had a stroke of luck. He found a regular job as managing editor of the *Weekly Westminster,* which Ramsay Muir took over in November 1923. If Walter had had a role model when he was a student, Muir (1872–1941) would have been the perfect candidate. During his studies at University College, Liverpool, Muir edited the student magazine and used it to promote the idea of student representation. He then transferred to Balliol College, Oxford, where he gained firsts in Greats and Modern History; on the strength of these he returned to Liverpool as a lecturer. Then he was made Professor of History at Manchester (1906–13). It was in this capacity that he contributed to Walter's *University Review.* But now he had resigned his Chair of Modern History to devote all his time to politics. Having written *Liberalism and Industry* (1920) and helped to establish the Liberal Summer School in 1921, which for the next two decades provided the Liberal Party with many of its ideas, he became MP for Rochdale, and secured himself a platform in the press.

For thirty years, the *Westminster Gazette* had been the voice of Liberalism that potentates and politicians the world over (including the Kaiser) considered key reading to understand the British political scene. It was the only London paper that sold on its leader, written by the great J. A. Spender. It collapsed in 1921 when its owner decided to bring it out in the morning rather than the evening and Spender took the opportunity to retire. The *Saturday Westminster* had been issued separately since 1912. Its literary editor, Naomi Royde-Smith, published first-class reviews, poetry and short stories. From 18 February 1922 to 2 June 1923, its music critic was Aldous Huxley. Graham Greene's first poem was printed in its columns and 'The Garden Party' first appeared there in 1922.* It was a literary version of the weekend paper that Walter had imagined back in 1910. Acquired by Ramsay Muir and re-titled the *Weekly Westminster,* the new paper launched on 17 November 1923 with a now famous review by Humbert Wolfe of Eliot's 'Waste Land'.

It was a distinguished team that Walter joined: beside Muir himself and Naomi Royde-Smith, it included Herbert Farjeon, Philip Guedalla, H. M. Tomlinson, and Humbert Wolfe. (J. A. Spender was on the board.) They were soon joined by Maurice Gorham (1902–1975), who remembered that 'Tomlinson, Farjeon and Fuller lavished kindness unmixed with any condescension on a young beginner in a profession about which they knew so much.'[26] He found Walter 'a remarkable man to work with; a journalist of

---

* Katherine Mansfield spent the last months of her life at Gurdjieff's Institute for the Harmonious Development, dying there in January 1923, too soon for Nott to meet her.

Walter Fuller

wide experience, both here and in America, a radical by temperament, a man of imagination and sympathy as well as immense personal charm.'[27] Soon he 'worshipped Walter Fuller and enjoyed immensely working under him for two years.'[28]

Another greenhorn on the *Weekly Westminster* was Mary Hope Allen (1898–2001), the future radio producer and writer. She started as secretary to Naomi Royde-Smith, who divined her abilities – 'there may be a journalist lurking within you' – and invited her to write theatre reviews. She made friends of many of the contributors, including Edith and Sacheverell Sitwell, and Rose Macaulay. Soon she was a critic for the *Manchester Guardian* too and by dint of much reading acquired a thorough knowledge of British theatre. Three years later Walter invited both Allen and Gorham to join him at the BBC, where they had long and distinguished careers.

I cannot tell if Walter ever wrote unsigned articles for the *Weekly Westminster*, for there are no records to check in. As for his contacts with its contributors, the only trace I have found, apart from an urgent note to C. K. Ogden asking for 'short notices of those books you took the other day,' is a single letter dated 30 April to S. S. Koteliansky, who had previously visited the Agency:

Dear Koteliansky,

I simply can't tell you how sorry I am that Muir has turned down the wonderful diary. I have just had another talk with him about it and I can't shake his decision. He says that the effect of the thing as a story is cumulative and that one does not get a full sense of the drama and the tragedy of it if one reads only 5000 words. I am returning the typescript herewith but with your permission I should like to speak first to the Editor of the *Westminster Gazette* about it – and then to the Editor (Stuart Hodgson) of the *Daily News*. Will you give me a call on the phone and say what you would like me to do – and when we can meet for another chat?

Yours ever,

Walter Fuller[29]

The diary in question must have been *Dostoevsky Portrayed by his Wife; the Diary and Reminiscences of Mme Dostoevsky*, which was published by Routledge in 1926, translated and edited by S. S. Koteliansky. No doubt Kot (as everyone called him) was hoping to place a pre-publication extract in the *Weekly Westminster*. While sending a rejection letter, Walter offered help.

Under Walter's management, the *Westminster* printed stories by Liam O'Flaherty and Dorothy Richardson ('Truth' on 5 January 1924, and 'Death' on 9 February 1924), along with memorable critical essays. For instance,

Humbert Wolfe reviewed D.H. Lawrence's *England my England* (23 February 1924) and *The Boy in the Bush* ('Mr Lawrence in the wilderness', 27 September 1924). The work of Joseph Conrad was defended by Edward Garnett in 'The World of Books' (10 October 1925). These are historic assessments of historic books.

While editing the *Weekly Westminster*, Walter also started to write for the Brooklyn *Daily Eagle*, as its 'special correspondent in London'. Back in 1912, he had advertised his sisters' singing in its pages, and the *Eagle* had reported favorably on his War-against-War exhibition. Perhaps he had an editor friend there, met while working on the *Freeman*. These articles brought in a few dollars which he passed on to Crystal.

I have traced fifteen contributions, published between April 1924 and May 1925. They are very competent pieces of political commentary, reporting on key moments and key policies in Stanley Baldwin's and Ramsay MacDonald's governments, plus one (after the government made married women responsible for their own debts and misdemeanours) on how the 'Husbands of Britain Hope to Escape Culpability for [their] Wives' Infractions of the Law.' They show that Walter followed contemporary politics very closely and even – if we are to take him at his word – sat in the visitors' gallery of the House of Commons to hear the Chancellor of the Exchequer, Philip Snowden, read his budget speech on 1 May 1924. The tone is often ironical (which may have puzzled his American readers) and occasionally light-hearted, but always perceptive and even prescient as regards the long-term effects of contemporary policies.

Did Rosalind know that her brother was writing for a New York paper? I rather think not, for she would surely have mentioned it in her autobiography. In fact, no one seems to have known except Crystal. (I confess that I stumbled on his articles only by chance.)

In mid-1923, Rosalind made her first visit home since 1919. Having played Hamlet for 101 nights (beating Edwin Booth's record of 100 nights in the 1864/5 season at the Winter Garden Theatre), Barrymore ordered a two-month break. Rosalind took the opportunity to stay with each member of the family in turn and celebrate with all her old friends, including Trilby Ewer, Griffin Barry, and of course Norman Angell (but not Dakyns; he was in Ireland at the time). She found Cynthia suffering from an infection in her hip. To cure it, she was spending a whole year in bed with a weight on her leg. (Apparently this, and the condition that had required a leg operation in 1918, was a form of tuberculosis.) By the time Rosalind left, she felt confident that

Cynthia 'would soon take up her painting again and not be submerged by life.' Her return to America was marked by a rare letter from Walter, congratulating her on her success: 'I think you have grown in mental and spiritual stature and have something more to offer than love and knowledge. Wisdom and understanding have come to you; and now life can have no bitterness or despair.'[30] It meant a lot to her.

During Rosalind's month-long visit, Crystal attended the 9th Congress of the International Woman Suffrage Alliance, 12–19 May in Rome. On her way back, she took a break at Antibes, on the Côte d'Azur, to pen a thoughtful report on it for *New Republic*, underlining the progress made since the 1913 Congress in Budapest.[31] Antibes was cheap, and it afforded her peace and quiet for writing, particularly as she had left her children with one of her sisters-in-law or with Hazel Hunkins Hallinan. Hazel was a very good friend to Crystal; she took care of Jeffrey and Annis so often that she came to look upon them almost as children of her own.

By mid-1924, Crystal had decided return to the United States, taking Jeffrey and Annis with her. Since financial independence from her partner was a pillar of her personal identity, and she could not make enough in London, she *had* to seek work elsewhere. Before leaving on 21 June, she paid a last visit to Walter's parents in Bournemouth. While she was there, Max arrived at Folkestone, bringing with him a book on Russia, the draft of his biography of Trotsky, and a Russian wife, Eliena Krylenko. Max had met Eliena at the Genoa Conference in 1922, where she was present as private secretary to Maxim Litvinov, the Soviet government's roaming ambassador. Their relationship developed during Max's stay in Moscow. Although she was not a Party member, her brother had been commander-in-chief of the all-Russian army and Trotsky had made him the Commissar of Justice (equivalent to Attorney General in American terms). When Max decided to go back home, he found that his American passport had expired and, given his reputation as a red-hot socialist, not to mention two years in Russia, he would be refused entry to any European country. Litvinov obligingly provided him with travel papers as a member of the Russian delegation to the Inter-Allied Conference on Reparations in London (June–July 1924). Eliena was permitted to accompany Litvinov, but the Party made it a condition that she would agree to spy for them, which she did not want to do. Litvinov told her to sign and forget it, which she did, making it impossible for her ever to return home. Then they learned that she could remain in the West only if she was married to Max. Cornered, Max agreed, insisting that it was only a marriage of convenience. It lasted the rest of her life, thirty years.

(The parallels with Walter's marriage to Crystal are evident.) Getting Max into England was equally problematic. He was obliged to wait on the cross-Channel ferry until the Home Office consented to allow him ashore. He was granted a visa for two weeks, later extended to six.

Naturally he and Eliena stayed at 6 Upper Park Road. After seeing off Crystal, they began a round of social engagements arranged by Walter. In Cambridge they met C. K. Ogden and Lytton Strachey; in London John Strachey;* and, at a launch party for *The Week-End Book,* Francis and Vera Meynell. Walter seems to have met the Meynells when he was running his literary Agency: Nott remembered Francis as 'a romantic glamorous figure' and Vera as 'a girl whose beauty and poise brought to my mind the Egyptian queen Nefertiti in the British Museum.'[32] As he was working, Walter did not accompany Max and Eliena on weekdays, so he missed out on their visit to H. G. Wells, who had warned them that he had lots of questions to ask about Russia.† On the other hand, he joined them on the weekend when they motored, in Frazier Hunt's touring car, down to Oxford where they were the guests of John Masefield.

When Max's visa expired, he and Eliena set off for the south of France. After trying Saint-Jean-de-Luz, Max cabled Walter: 'Please telegraph poste restante Antibes what you or Ogden know about rooms, pensions there.' Walter contacted Ogden at once, confessing that he really knew nothing. 'I can't even remember the name of the place where Crystal stayed.'[34] With their help or without it, Max found a room in a villa in Juan-Les-Pins, an unspoiled little village between Nice and Cannes where

> there were no sports shops, no apartment houses, no crowds on the beach, nothing in this little corner of the coast to disturb a poet, a novelist, a political philosopher – whatever I might turn out to be – and yet much to attract a person who loved to dive and swim.[35]

Two years later, a hotel – Le Provençal – was opened, and Juan-les-Pins changed for ever.

After Crystal left, Walter missed her very much, and wrote to her on 1

---

* In Cook's *Crystal Eastman on Women and Revolution,* there's a photograph of Crystal with Leonard Woolf; so she and Walter were 'in' with the Bloomsbury set.

† Max recorded that Wells asked not one of the promised questions. This is all the more surprising when we remember that Walter Lowe, the father of Litvinov's English wife, Ivy Lowe, was one of Wells's close friends. Max observed that this 'revealed a self-absorption that surprised me in a man who knew so much about so many things outside himself. I should not say "surprised me", for I am continually wondering how people who never listen manage to know so much as they do.'[33]

Walter Fuller

July. Having told her how he longed for news of her safe arrival, he went on: 'These are lovely days in England – sunshine heat, and clear blue days & night till even Max and Eleana [*sic*] are enchanted.' Crystal heard the same about the weather from other people, and dubbing it the best summer since 1066 she lamented, 'and I had to be away!' Then Walter sent her a day-by-day account of his doings, just as she loved to receive:

I spent the weekend at Frazier's cottage and had a lovely time. . . . On Saturday afternoon I went with father to see his garden village where some of the Barnardo orphans live. We got away at 5 o'clock – in time for him to go to Dorothy's & for me to catch the 6.30 from Baker St for Frazier's. I got there in time for dinner and a game of croquet – afterwards Frazier read me long chunks of his novel which I greatly enjoyed and which I was able to praise with real sincerity. I think he has written the answer to *Main Street* – anyway, if it isn't a complete answer it can, and will I believe, be taken as such, and I think it will be a best seller for that reason. He has put into the book some of his most vivid memories of his life as a country editor in a little Illinois town, and his descriptions of the people and their lives and characters are really delightful, and sometimes very moving.* He reads it all very well.

On Sunday for lunch a well-known English journalist & his young wife came – Sir John Forster Frazier† – a Scotsman to speak truly – a very warm, hearty fellow. A Tory, one of Northcliffe's men but very likeable. After lunch Bessie Beatty‡ and her friend Miss I. A. R. Wylie,§ the novelist, arrived. Miss Wylie lives on Downshire Hill and seems to want to be friendly. I think you'd like her. Beatty is going to Paris this week and then at the end of the month for a motor ride with Miss Wylie in the Pyrenees.

---

*   Frazier's novel would be *Sycamore Bend: population 1300* which was published by Harcourt Brace in 1925. It was not a success: readers found it as slow-paced as the small-town life it depicted.

†   Frazer (1868–1936) was a travel writer, best known for having cycled round the world.

‡   From the way he writes, it would seem that both he and Crystal already knew the intrepid American journalist Bessie Beatty (1886–1947); that would not be surprising for she was a strong supporter of women's suffrage who had visited Russia in 1917 with John Reed and Louise Bryant, interviewing Trotsky in October 1917. She returned to Russia in 1921 and interviewed Lenin, Trotsky (again), and Mikhail Kalinin. At this point she was a freelance foreign correspondent who wrote for *Good Housekeeping, New Republic* and the *Ladies Home Journal.* In the 1940s she hosted a popular radio show.

§   Ida Alexa Ross Wylie (aka Ida *Alena* Ross Wylie; 1885–1959) was an Anglo-Australian novelist.

We had a jolly supper and then they all went off. I stayed the night at Frazier's and went into town with him on an early train the next morning.[36]

He continued with a practical matter, money:

I've paid the rates today		= £12-6-0
ditto	typewriter money	= £1-0-0
ditto	Jones Bros	= £1-0-0
Total		= £14-6-0

Yesterday I went to see your Banker friend & he gave me £5 10s 2d.

I've had another check from Brooklyn [for an *Eagle* article] for 10 dollars – so I think I'll send this one & the other that came last week along to you since it seems the most sensible way to do with dollars. By the way I've had to buy myself, today, a new pair of boots, my brown ones need repairing so badly. I've got a very comfortable pair of black ones for 29/6 [£1.47½p] and quite nice they look – so that's alright.

Then he began to write about their children. While Crystal used her first name Catherine on her British passport, Annis travelled as 'Janet Audrey Fuller' on her trans-Atlantic crossings. In this letter Walter refers to her by a pet name, 'the gobuga':

How is the gobuga looking? and do people over there appreciate her beauty and loveliness and general uniqueness? And how's Jeff getting along? Do keep them both innocent and gentle, won't you – like the dear babes they are and as we love to have them.

And he closed his letter with his 'love and arms around you, darling.'[37]

Crystal arrived in New York on 30 June 1924 with no regrets about her eighteen-month stay in England: 'I wouldn't have missed it for anything,' she told Cynthia, 'and I love the country much more than I thought I did. But it is certainly a place where you have to work hard. I think I'll stay in America until the children grow up.' Swearing not to go travelling again, she added, 'How's that for a promise? Will I keep it?'[38]

I believe that Walter sublet their house in Upper Park Road at this point, for after Crystal left he found it was 'getting messier and messier – I'm afraid I'm kinder [*sic*] losing my taste for it.'[39] (Is it the house itself or untidiness that he is losing the taste for? It may be both, for of course an untidy house quickly loses its appeal. After a lifetime of living in furnished accommodation, Walter knew little of dusting and cleaning.) As the Hallinans had a third child that year – Timothy, who also became a writer – they had no free space in their flat. So Walter took this opportunity to join the National Liberal Club, where he could sleep and enjoy all the perquisites of club life. He was elected a Town Member on 29 September 1924, proposed by Alfred

J. Bonwick MP* and seconded by H. Colin Edgell. By now Walter had a reputation in Liberal circles: Crystal reported on 4 November that 'Helen Auger wrote to Katharine Anthony† that you were getting so popular with the Liberals that she expected to see you in Parliament soon.'⁴⁰

Rosalind and Ruth Pickering-Pinchot met Crystal off the boat, and she was sorry that Rosalind was too busy to come out to Croton. She told Cynthia that she thought Rosalind 'the finest girl in the world – I'd like to see her every day.' That made her think of Walter: 'I am getting mighty homesick for Walter. I wish you'd write and tell me about him.'⁴¹ She was hoping to get a job in New York, but she had in all probability been blacklisted (thanks to the Lusk Report), for no regular work could she find. So she spent the summer at Croton, where both Jeffrey and Annis looked 'so beautiful and healthy and happy.'⁴²

In September she was finally taken on as the Secretary of the Women for Congress Campaign Committee of the National Woman's Party. Rosalind was a committee member too.‡ During the week, Crystal lived in New York but found it hard 'to be alone in a hotel room,' as she exclaimed to Walter, 'with you in London & the children sixty miles away – and then try to write. The loneliest kind of work!!' This made her realize how much he must have suffered when she took the children away. 'Never again! Let's stick together – rich or poor – England or America.' With this thought in mind, she resolved to rejoin him in London. But first she had to earn enough money for the crossing.

For three weeks I tried to raise money for this Campaign, with no results. What I did was to raise enough money to pay my salary and then quit. . . . I am too old and tired and disillusioned to work up other people for causes.

So she embarked on 'one final desperate effort to be a writer! Wish me luck, dear. This is what you have been at me to do for years.'

By 4 November, she was 'wildly homesick for you, darling.' And the chil-

---

* Bonwick (1883–1949) had been the Liberal MP for Chippenham. Although he lost the seat to the Conservative Victor Cazalet in the 1924 general election, he remained a Liberal Whip that year. He seems to have been involved in publishing (the *Nation*) and printing, being a member of the Committee of Enquiry into Government Printing Establishments, 1923–27.

† Katharine Susan Anthony, who had contributed to *Four Lights*, was now becoming known as a writer.

‡ Did Rosalind notice, one wonders, that in August 1924 students launched their 'Women for Congress' campaign by flying the NWP colours from a private yacht on Lake Champlain?

dren were missing Walter too. She enclosed a letter for him from Jeff and encouraged him to write back. 'If he could get a letter from you once a week when I got mine it would make him very happy.'⁴³ (This implies that Walter was managing to write a weekly letter to Crystal.)

When she wrote on 14 December 1924, she had (ironically enough) just finished re-writing 'Living under Two Roofs' for *Cosmopolitan* – 'all but the final typing. If they take it, I will have just enough (with the $30 you are sending) to pay my debts and get us home.' It is significant that London was now 'home' for her.⁴⁴ She sailed at Christmas 1924. Her resolution not to go travelling again had held for just six months.

After little more than a year at the *Westminster*, Walter was headhunted by the newly formed BBC. Public broadcasting was in its infancy, the invention of the amplifying vacuum tube around 1920 having made it possible to transmit recognizable speech and music, instead of just Morse code. Early radio stations discovered that live music went over the airwaves much better than gramophone records, but it was expensive to maintain a live orchestra (like the twelve-man group on the Manchester station, 2ZY), so the six major manufacturers-cum-broadcasters decided to pool their resources in a co-operative called the British Broadcasting Company Ltd. Thanks to an exclusive arrangement with the General Post Office, it was funded by selling receiving licences to the public, plus a royalty on the sale of authorized wireless receiving sets. Formed in October 1922, it began experimental broadcasting the following month.

Walter seems to have been noticed for being 'the first to treat broadcast programmes as the subject of regular artistic criticism.'⁴⁵ His young colleague, Maurice Gorham, observed that

> he had a constant interest in every new idea, and this new fact of broadcasting attracted him. Even in those early days he saw something of its possibilities for information and enlightenment; possibilities that had already dawned on some of the pioneers, notably the man who was then the mainspring of the BBC and who was in many ways the antithesis of Walter Fuller – the terrifying Mr Reith.⁴⁶

These 'possibilities for information and enlightenment' – which Gorham himself 'did not fully realize until years later, long after Walter Fuller was dead'⁴⁷ – suggest that Walter's ideas coincided with the visionary spirit that was already inspiring the BBC. For John Reith – later 1st Baron Reith, KT, GCVO, GBE, CB, TD, PC (1889–1971) – the wireless was to be an instrument for 'social well-being,'⁴⁸ and he aimed 'to give a conscious social purpose to

Savoy Hill, the first home of the BBC.
Walter's office was on the top floor, with the wide cornice.

It was an old building, with 'customs as quaint as the cries of Old London. "Any mice, please?" was the weekly wail of the Pied Piper of Savoy Hill – sometimes a pale-faced boy, sometimes a melancholy-looking man – who peregrinated the offices in search of the "small deer" of wainscottings and corridors.'[54]

the exploitation of this medium.'⁴⁹ Consequently, 'all kinds of petty discomforts – overcrowded rooms, long hours, arbitrary or tactless treatment – were overlooked in the general sense of adventure, progress and public service. You felt it a privilege to be "in" at the birth of such a mighty experiment.'⁵⁰

It was not, however, Reith who recruited Walter. It was Gladstone Murray,* the BBC's publicity director, in charge of publications and information. After a distinguished career as a wing commander in the Royal Flying Corps (during which he was selected to fly over a German airfield and drop a note to inform the Germans that their air ace, Baron von Richthofen – 'the Red Baron' – had been shot down), he went into publicity, working for a radio communications company at the same time as acting as the aeronautical correspondent of the *Daily Express*. When he joined the BBC, he remained in close contact with Fleet Street and that was probably how he got to meet Walter and hear his ideas, for (so far as I know) Walter never wrote about radio programmes. He and Walter became good friends. According to Maurice Gorham, Murry sheltered Walter 'from many buffets, for a man of his ardent temperament, with his sincere belief in the power of radio for good, was harassed at every turn by the intrigues and petty tyrannies of Savoy Hill.'⁵¹

It was Admiral Carpendale, the Controller, who hired and fired in the early years of the BBC. Almost as intimidating as Reith himself, he 'went about the building as if he was still on his quarterdeck.'⁵² (He was not alone in continuing to use his war-time rank. The early BBC was riddled with Captains and Majors.) He enjoyed destabilizing job applicants by barking, 'And what did you do in the war?' (How did Walter field this question, I wonder. Was he aware that John Reith had spent the last two years of the war in the United States, supervising armament contracts for the British forces?) By the time of Maurice Gorham's interview in 1927, Carpendale's question had changed slightly: 'You're a journalist. I don't want to know anything about that. Fuller and Murray understand all that sort of thing. What I want to find out is *what sort of fellow you are.* . . . What did you do in the General Strike?'⁵³

Walter certainly treated Reith with great respect. Gorham recalled that Walter Fuller stood in obvious awe of him, and I felt that anybody who could

---

* By a happy coincidence, Murray also owed his first name to the Grand Old Man of British Liberalism, although his parents (unlike Walter's) went the whole hog, christening him William Ewart Gladstone Murray (1893–1970).

frighten Fuller could certainly frighten me. When he ensconced me in the office that I shared with him, Fuller said to me:

'And if Mr Reith comes in — '

'But how shall I know which is Mr Reith?'

'Don't worry; you'll know him. If anybody opens that door and his head touches the lintel, that'll be Mr Reith. Then the great thing to remember is . . . you stand up and say "Sir".'

It happened quite soon, and when Fuller was out of the office. The door opened and there stood an unmistakable Mr Reith. His head touched the lintel, and I stood up, but I did not say 'Sir'.[55]

Gorham was not used to saying 'sir' to anybody. In 1933, when he was promoted to Editor of *Radio Times,* he felt that, since Reith 'had been sporting enough to give me the job in spite of my not calling him "sir", I could be sporting enough to call him "sir" now that I had got it. So I did.'[56]

When Walter began to work for the BBC, he spent his mornings on the *Weekly Westminster* in Cursitor Street (off Chancery Lane) and his afternoons at Savoy Hill, where he started as an adviser on programmes. During the first years of broadcasting, each of the BBC's transmitters put out a different programme, with the result that while listeners in one part of the country might have been enjoying a live concert, others were being treated to a talk. When a new high-power transmitter was built at Daventry, 'simultaneous broadcasting' became possible, all the stations sending out the same programme at the same time. In May 1925 a 'programme policy board' (PPB) was instituted, tasked with selecting these nationwide programmes. It was a small body, nominally only a chairman and six others, one of whom was Walter, but the Minutes usually report eight to ten persons present; a further ten to fifteen received copies of the Minutes for information.* The PPB met exactly four weeks and five days before the corresponding issue of *Radio Times* came out, this being the time required make the necessary arrangements, write the timetable of broadcasts, set the type, proof it, print it, and distribute it.

At its first meeting, on 26 May, the PPB decided to broadcast the speeches made at a *Time & Tide* dinner by Lord Hewitt, Lady Rhondda, Rebecca West and others. At that time it was not unusual for the BBC to transmit speeches made at meetings of professional associations, so they vied for the privilege of being aired. One wonders if Walter had any influence on this particular choice, seeing that *Time & Tide* was a periodical that Crystal contributed to.

* In those days, the BBC was not large, although it was rapidly growing. In May 1926 it had exactly 335 employees, all told. So a year earlier, at the inception of the PPB, those attending the meetings and reading the Minutes amounted to about 10% of the staff.

The following weekend, 27–28 May, she attended the National Conference of Labour Women in Birmingham.

Extracts from new plays was another vein for the BBC to explore. When *Tess of the D'Urbervilles* was adapted for the stage, Walter was given the task of arranging part of it for broadcasting and of inducing Thomas Hardy to say a few words. That must have rejoiced his heart. Then in 1926, while plans were being drawn up for a special American broadcast on 4 July, Walter suggested that Ruth Draper (1884–1956), famous for her monologues and monodramas, might be asked to perform. Ending a season in London, she was shortly to give a command performance before King George V at Windsor Castle. As Walter was personally acquainted with her,* he was entrusted with sounding her out; when she declined, he was directed to lunch with her and see if she was open to persuasion. She was not. She consistently refused to perform without a live audience, for she spontaneously modified her monologues as a function of the response she was receiving; each performance was unique. Only in the mid-1950s, shortly before she died, did she consent to make recordings for RCA.

Walter's job was not all culture and free lunches, however. In September 1925, the BBC received a request from the Homing Pigeon Union that listeners should be advised each week of the need to place corks on the ends of radio aerials to prevent injury to homing pigeons. The board accepted the principle, but thought it sufficient to issue the warning less frequently. The item was minuted for action by Walter.

In the summer of 1925, Rosalind paid another visit to England, bringing Bruguière over with her for the first time. She did not introduce him to her parents, for they would not have approved of her living with him without being married. Curt, proper as ever, was also reproachful. 'If you both lived in London,' he opined, 'You would find it very difficult to have friends.'[57] They laughed at this; their friends were far more open-minded than that. This did not prevent Rosalind, Bruguière, Cynthia and Curt from holidaying together in Germany. Cynthia was particularly taken with Bruguière, for he accepted her as an artist and encouraged her painting. When she had a son, fifteen months later, she named him Conrad Francis: the first after the novelist, and the second after Bruguière.

Rosalind found her parents discontented with Allum Cottage in Bournemouth. It was too large for just the two of them, and they wanted to move

---

* I do not know how Walter came to be acquainted with Ruth Draper; was it through Rosalind? Draper is not mentioned in Rosalind's autobiography – but she was surely an inspiration for Rosalind's later career in the field of monodrama.

away from the coast. With the money she had made as Ophelia – she was paid $175 a week – Rosalind bought them a little house in Petersfield, with a garden full of roses and buddleias and butterflies. They named it Roslyn Cottage. Curt handled the deed of sale, of course, and Walter oversaw the move. It must have raised mixed feelings in him to see Rosalind buy a house for their parents. Having spent twenty years trying to provide for his family, he will have been both grateful that she should spend her money like this, and humbly proud that she had achieved what had always been far beyond his means.

During Rosalind's two-month visit, Crystal drove down to Marseilles with a City Councillor of Glasgow, Mrs Dollon, and Morris Hillquit* to attend an important meeting of International Socialist Women on 21 August. They demanded the establishment of an international socialist advisory committee for women within the Labour and Socialist International. This led to a special conference in Brussels in December 1926 (with eighteen women representing twelve countries) at which statutes were elaborated, and in February 1927 the International Advisory Committee for Women was officially established. Crystal's report on the Marseilles conference appeared in *Equal Rights* a month later. Since she was in the south of France, she took the opportunity to met up with Max in Juan-Les-Pins. They were joined there by Scott Fitzgerald, who let Max read the manuscript of *The Great Gatsby,* which was published on 10 April the following year. One wonders if anyone mentioned Rosalind.

In July 1925, Walter prepared a 'Memorandum on programme presentation and the organization of a special department' for the director of BBC programmes, Cecil Lewis. It argued for the creation of a training school for announcers, since their voices were the means by which 'the BBC itself, its policy and ideals' were communicated to the public. Rejecting the highly individualized style of announcing practised in America, Walter proposed that announcers from London and provinces should be brought together on a regular basis 'for the purpose of studying and discussing future programmes, and the planning of new and effective ways of presentation.' This would afford 'every possible incentive and opportunity for team work' and 'provide yet another way in which to build up in the public mind a sense of the BBC's *collective personality*' (my emphasis). 'There are many occasions,' he continued, 'when the Company might properly use the microphone for

---

* Hillquit, visiting Europe, was one of just five men who addressed the conference.

announcements of its activities, and so create a much closer sense of contact and community of interest than now exists between itself and listeners everywhere.'[58]

These were groundbreaking concepts, the first formulation of the idea that an institution like the BBC might actively model how it was perceived by the public through the medium of broadcasting. It represents a natural extension of Walter's aim of shaping public opinion, as expressed in his War-against-War exhibition. Summing up his proposal, he foresaw

> the training and equipment of an efficient body of announcers, and through them to present to the general public not only the daily programmes in an attractive way, but also to present the BBC itself, its policy and ideals, as a great public service institution for entertainment, education, and inspiration.[59]

The BBC put these suggestions into practice, with the result that its public image, known and respected the world over, now occupies a unique position in the universe of mass communication. The concepts of a *corporate image* and a *corporate identity* are familiar today, yet they date only from the 1950s. Walter's ideas were again years ahead of their time.*

Part of Walter's inspiration came no doubt from his long experience of directing his sisters' stage presence and elocution, followed by organizing seminars in public speaking for members of the WPP. He saw clarity of diction and modulation of rhythm and tone as crucial to quality communication. He also shared the British assumption that how a person speaks reveals their level of education, culture, refinement, social status, and even their moral qualities. Walter had definite ideas about correct pronunciation; his family still recall that he would sound the 'h' after 'w', thereby distinguishing 'which' from 'witch' and 'whale' from 'wail'. He had also noticed that how we speak depends on context. When his sisters donned their early Victorian dresses, they took on at the same time their professional personas, with specific body language (bearing, gestures, etc.) and elocution. It is probably not by chance, then, that shortly after Walter submitted his report, Reith introduced his famous rule that announcers should wear dinner jackets while on duty in the evening. The following year, 1926, saw the institution of the BBC's Advisory Committee on Spoken English. It made recommendations to announcers on the pronunciation of words, either because they were unfamiliar, or because they had two or more current pronunciations.

---

* He even preceded the book that developed the idea of manipulating public opinion: *Propaganda* by Edward Bernays was published in 1928.

This said, we may wonder whether Walter ever broadcast. According to Cynthia's daughter Monica,

> in 1926 or 1927 he had to comment on the Lord Mayor's Show as it progressed past Bush House. [She means Savoy Hill.] He got hold of his son Jeffrey – a year or so older than me – and bore us off to a window overlooking the procession with the order to 'tell the country' what we were seeing. Jeffrey was tongue-tied but I'm delighted to be able to tell you that my journalistic career began there, since I apparently hardly stopped talking.[60]

This is highly unlikely. As we have seen, announcing and – after 1926 – commentating were carefully rehearsed and planned on the BBC. I have little doubt that Walter invited Jeffrey and Monica to *pretend* that they were commentating, and her memory transformed this into fact. The fact is, there is no record – or even a rumour – of Walter broadcasting.

On 29 September 1925, Reith issued an internal memo: 'W. G. Fuller, who has been working part time with us for some months, has been appointed to take central charge of the work of the London and Daventry stations.' As far as I can ascertain, this became effective at the end of November, allowing Walter to give the *Weekly Westminster* three months' notice. It was good timing, for the paper was declining rapidly. On the advice of Ramsay Muir, Maurice Gorham had already left it for the *Westminster Gazette*.

Director of the London (2LO) and Daventry (5XX) stations – the actual title was 'London Executive' – was a key position in the BBC, but Gorham tells us that Walter

> was not too happy in it. For one thing, it meant a lot of desk work, and that was not his forte; he was better at getting ideas than at clearing his In tray. Also he was surprised by his inaugural interview with Mr Reith. He went to it expecting to be given some direction, not to say inspiration, in his task of running the BBC's London station. What Mr Reith said to him, so he told me at the time, was to this effect:
>
> > 'Now remember, Fuller; if I come into Savoy Hill one night and find the men playing cards and drinking whisky, I shan't blame them for it. I shall blame you.'[61]

No one was discovered playing cards, or drinking whisky, on Walter's watch. In any case, it is hard to imagine Walter making the rounds of an evening to check on such matters. If he remained in the office after hours, as he often did, it was the better to do his job. This included attending the meetings of the PPB. On 6 October, it was decided, for instance, that the Armistice night programme would be organized by Mr Pitt 'in conjunction with Mr Fuller.' Fortunately for Walter and his In tray, within weeks of becoming London

Executive, he was earmarked for another, far more prestigious job: Editor of *Radio Times*.

In the earliest days of broadcasting, when stations were on the air for little more than an hour a day, and not even every day at that, registered listeners received postcards advising them of when they should tune in. Then it became more practical to put announcements in the press. The BBC provided programme lists and the newspapers printed them as news. (Some newspapers, particularly the *Daily Mail*, responded with suggestions for things to broadcast.) From 1 January 1923, for instance, the BBC's programme for the day could be found in the *Times*. Two column inches sufficed to inform readers that Children's Hour would be aired from 5 to 5.45 p.m., followed by 55 minutes of classical music starting at 6.30, for instance. But then, on 13 January, the Newspaper Proprietors' Association decided that these were *advertisements* for the BBC and should be paid for as such. Reith was not going to stand for this. While he cast about for an alternative, Gordon Selfridge included the listing for 2LO free of charge within his store's advertisements in the *Pall Mall Gazette*, a leading evening newspaper. Its sales went up. Realizing that wireless programme announcements paid for themselves in added circulation, the Association reversed its decision in February – for a period of six months.

This gave Reith time in which to plan a dedicated listings magazine for the BBC's growing audience. In this he was helped by a report in July 1923 from the research department of Metropolitan-Vickers, suggesting that there should be 'a weekly printed programme . . . of the best possible quality' in design, layout, printing, and paper, with 'photographs of personalities as well as details of broadcasts' and space for listeners' letters.[62] While Reith could have piggybacked on or taken over an existing periodical like *Wireless World, Popular Wireless Weekly*, or *The Broadcaster*, he soon decided to equip the BBC with its own 'official organ', *Radio Times*.* Reith invited tenders from printing firms, estimating the print run at 250,000 copies a week. That presupposed a company with a large spare capacity, and not unsurprisingly only one firm made an offer, George Newnes Ltd. It was the largest periodical publisher in the country; its 1923 letterhead listed no less than nineteen

---

* Reith is reputed to have chosen the title himself, with its prescient 'radio' rather than 'wireless', but a letter from Arthur Burrows, the Director of Programmes, has recently come to light showing that until the printing block of the masthead was being readied in September 1923, it was called 'Radio News'. While offering definitive advice on the somewhat fussy masthead, Burrows proposed that 'Times' was more appropriate, 'as the times of the performances form the principal feature.'[63]

titles (ending 'etc. etc.'), including the *Strand, John o'London's, Country Life,* and *Tit-Bits* (to mention only a few of its long-running titles). Newnes agreed to publish *Radio Times* on a profit-sharing basis, with a guarantee of £1000 a year for the BBC.

The first issue was due on the newsstands on 28 September 1923. Instead of seeking a new editor for this title, Newnes waited until the editor of *Tit-Bits*, Leonard Crocombe, came back from his summer holiday, and then told him to do the job. Luckily, Crocombe was a radio fan. He had written enthusiastically about broadcasting in *Tit-Bits*, he was a friend of the Director of Programmes, and he had badgered the BBC and even the Post Office until he was allowed to give a talk on 2LO in March that year. So he took up this challenge with zest and put together the first *Radio Times* in a mad rush. 'There was no time to work out an original "make-up" [i.e. page layout] or to choose types [fonts], so the printer was told that "make-up" and types were to follow the style of *John o'London's Weekly*.'[64] Issued on time, the first *Radio Times* sold out at once. Despite the cribbed design, its circulation crept up steadily, averaging half-a-million copies a week during 1924 and 750,000 in 1925, with dips in the summer and a peak at Christmas. For the festive edition, Crocombe risked a colour cover and priced it sixpence instead of tuppence. It sold out, netting both Newnes and the BBC a handsome profit.

But the BBC was often dissatisfied with *Radio Times*. Staff complained that Newnes was cutting their articles and high-handedly altering titles and headings. They also wanted more space for the texts of broadcast talks. Discussion with Newnes produced no change; in fact the BBC found its attitude unhelpful and obstructive. Recognizing that the remedy had to be drastic, Reith decided on 9 September 1925 that the BBC would publish *Radio Times* itself, and he terminated the contract with Newnes. This raised the question: should they continue with *Radio Times* unchanged, or have separate publications for each field? John Stobart wanted a *Radio Academy* to deal with educational programmes, for instance; the music staff wanted *Radio Music* and went to far as to produce a dummy issue for themselves. The executives decided to stick with *Radio Times,* and set about finding someone to edit it. This was a major appointment in British journalism. Gladstone Murray (now deputy managing director of the BBC) was of the opinion that they should consult Lord Riddell, who was the Chairman of Newnes and also on the board of the BBC. Others suggested that they should simply poach Leonard Crocombe from Newnes. After much consultation, the BBC found that it already had the right man under its very nose: Walter Fuller. So when the change took effect at the end of 1925, he became the new Editor of

Radio Times. Meanwhile, he was still coming up with ideas for the PPB: on 22 December he suggested a story in three episodes, each by a different author, and also a half-hour feature of film music – an early recognition of film music as a separate genre.

Now that each department had its own idea about what it wanted *Radio Times* to contain, and each had its own idea of how to present it, Walter's task was not going to be easy. The challenge was similar to Reith's aims for broadcasting itself: to reconcile conflicting expectations; to entertain as well as inform; to bring the best of everything to as many people as possible, always aiming to achieve the highest standards in every aspect of the enterprise. For the next six months Walter drew on all his experience in England and America to review both the appearance and contents of the BBC's flagship publication, making it more of a magazine than a bare listing of programmes. He looked at other periodicals, especially the *Saturday Evening Post*, and consulted his colleagues.* The choices he made won their approval and remained unaltered, in essence, for the next fifty years. (There was a major facelift in September 1960, by which time television had taken precedence over radio.) He recruited sub-editors to take charge of specific areas. The first was Percy Scholes, who had been appointed the BBC's music critic in 1923; as the unashamedly opinionated compiler of the *Oxford Companion to Music*, he had a long-term effect on British musical taste – and remained a lifelong admirer and supporter of Walter. Not all Walter's suggestions were so well received. According to an editorial in the *Manchester Guardian*, he 'overflowed with ideas for educational programmes.'[65] These were the responsibility of John Stobart, who was protective of his territory. When Walter proposed a separate department for religious programmes – also Stobart's responsibility – under a freelance cleric-turned-journalist, H. W. Fox, who provided *Radio Times* with 'Broadcast Pulpit' articles, 'Stobart was not in favour and did not care much for Fox's advice.'[66]

In June 1926 Walter was joined by Maurice Gorham, 'a shy, smouldering Irishman' whose memories tell us something of life at the BBC.[67] 'Walter Fuller worked in a little room on the fourth floor over the churchyard with his attractive red-haired secretary, and I shared the office with them.' On one of Gorham's first days, 'an angry woman burst into the office' in Walter's absence, 'stood over me with arms akimbo, abused me for ten minutes with-

---

* An internal memo dated 25 May reads: 'AC agrees that Mr Fuller's conception of the ideal RT towards which we are working should be a kind of humanized combination of the *Literary Digest*, the *Scientific American* and the *Ladies' Home Journal*.'

Three generations: Mr Fuller, Walter, and Jeffrey in 1927

out stopping, and flounced out again, all before I had the least idea of who she was.' As to his workload,

> I had had various assurances from Fuller, all of which he himself sincerely believed. One was that this would be a bread-and-butter job; I was to work strict office hours and then go home and do my own private writing – you couldn't work late, Fuller said, because at six o'clock the cleaners came in and began to sweep the floors. This dream vanished in the first few days.[68]

Walter worked at least as hard as Gorham. After all, if he had been in the habit of leaving the office at 5.30 each afternoon, he would not have experienced the nightly invasion of the cleaning staff.

April 1926 brought Walter's forty-fifth birthday. On this occasion he visited his parents 'with my son and heir (value of estate in British Isles, 3 shillings and four pence) in the old home in Bournemouth.' From there he reported to Cynthia and Curt, who were on holiday in Italy, that his mother (now in her seventieth year) was 'spry and hearty' while his father (approaching seventy-one) was 'equally concerned about the coal crisis and the outcome of Tuesday's meeting of the Young Helpers League.' Crystal, it would appear, had also planned to visit Italy, but had 'wilted' at the thought of the journey, so she was in the Channel Islands, with Annis (aged five-and-a-half) and her nanny, while Jeffrey (now nine) was shortly to go and stay with Riss, 'very happy at the prospect of a journey in the coach all by himself.'[69]

A month later, the coal crisis that so worried Mr Fuller escalated into the General Strike, which lasted from 6 to 12 May. As the BBC was declared an essential service, work continued there and programmes continued to go out, but there was no *Radio Times* for 14 May because the printers had been called out. This was a turning point in the history of the BBC. Today it is almost synonymous with up-to-the-minute, objective news, but until the General Strike, it broadcast almost no news. This is because the newspapers and their agencies, fearing competition from radio, provided the BBC with information only on condition that it agreed not to broadcast any before seven o'clock in the evening (by which time the newspapers had sold out). They even imposed coded sports commentaries: listeners had to buy a newspaper to learn what was meant when they heard that 'team A' was leading in a football match or the Boat Race, for instance.

All this changed with the Strike, during which the national newspapers were closed down by the TUC so that it could monopolize information through its propaganda sheet, the *British Worker*. The general public trusted that no more than they trusted the *British Gazette,* launched and edited by the Chancellor, Winston Churchill. Rumour was rife. One popular story had it that Russia was sending the Red Army to take control of the country. Recognizing 'a stupendous opportunity to show what broadcasting could do in an emergency,'[70] Reith made the news agencies suspend their restriction on the content and timing of news broadcasts for the duration of the Strike, and prepared to supply the reliable information that the nation so desperately wanted. Having no proper news team nor, for that matter, any experience of the news process, he could but improvise. He ordered his secretary, Miss Shields, to accompany Walter to 'the DCCC office at the Admiralty' where official news from the ten government centres around the country was centralized. From there Walter sent bulletins back to Savoy Hill by dedicated landline. Edited by a small team, and supplemented with information from a Reuters teleprinter, these bulletins were broadcast at three-hourly intervals throughout the day.* During the Strike, only 'one or two BBC employees went out collecting news,'[71] so the BBC's sole supplier of national news was Walter Fuller. After a few days, he was joined by Gladstone Murray, whose personal appreciation of the situation was broadcast as a 'leading article'. There was also a paternalistic editorial after the evening nine o'clock news, written by Major C. F. Atkinson (assistant director of publicity), dealing reassuringly with such subjects as transport arrangements, how to keep calm, how to behave, and so on.

Being a novelty as well as the sole source of news, the three-hourly bulletins were immensely popular. Fortunate owners of a wireless set would place it in a window, or at the door of their homes, so that people in the street could listen in. Groups gathered around the doorways of closed shops and strained to hear the measured tones of the announcer coming from the puny loudspeaker. (At home, most people used headphones, as Walter is doing in the drawing that heads this chapter.) Just as the Coronation of 1953 precipitated the acquisition of televisions, so the Strike did more than any other single event to promote the purchase of a radio receiver. And Reith's inflexible defence of the independence of the BBC established it as the sole source of trusted, up-to-date information. When the Strike was over, the press expressed the public's appreciation in terms that sound like thanks-

---

* A report in *The Times* of 19 May 1926 gives some idea of their contents. A bulletin would open with special messages, then official communications from government departments. This was followed by a summary of the general situation of the country, beginning with news from the Home Office and Civil Commissioners, then news from agencies plus what information the BBC had managed to glean by its own means. The second part consisted of a precis of the daily measures taken by Parliament, and other news from home and abroad.

giving for divine intervention. 'For our news, for the dispelling of false rumour and for the pronouncements of great public men upon the situation, we thank the Voice from the Air.'[72]

What exactly was this fount of information, 'the DCCC office at the Admiralty' to which Walter was despatched? The only document in the BBC Archives that mentions it does not spell out the name. It could refer to the office of J. C. C. Davidson, the financial secretary to the Admiralty who was appointed Deputy Chief Civil Commissioner to liaise with Reith; he also had overall editorial control of Churchill's *British Gazette*. But the document (which is carefully drafted) does not say 'the DCCC's office'.* Moreover Davidson would be unlikely to clutter his office with hundreds of messages and people to read them. It seems to have been a pre-existing office where information was routinely centralized or pooled. A long shot: in the early 1930s the letters DCCC came to stand for 'double current cable code' – a technique that made it possible to turn cable transmissions directly into wireless messages. This would not supply news, only a means of conversion. As it is, for the abbreviation to have been used during the Strike, the Admiralty would have had to develop the technique, and coin the term, at least five years before anyone else. A very long shot. Yet the Admiralty was at the forefront of information gathering.

For most of the twentieth century, the world's diplomatic communications were generally conducted by means of cyphered cable messages. At the outbreak of WWI, the British government entered into a secret agreement with the cable companies allowing its intelligence services to eavesdrop on all their messages.† A team was assembled in Room 40 of the Admiralty to decode them and, where necessary, translate them. This is how the British were able to provide the Americans with the contents of the notorious Zimmermann telegram, sent in code from the German Foreign Office to the German ambassador in Mexico, which precipitated the entry of the United States into the war. (A cover story was concocted to hide from the Americans that the British were tapping their cable and from the Germans that their codes had been broken.) In 1919, the team of code-breakers in Room 40 became the innocuous-sounding Government Code and Cipher School; during WWII it was located at Bletchley Park. Today it is called the Govern-

---

* Because his title was created for the duration of the Strike, it does not feature in the Admiralty's list of telephone numbers for 1926.

† The agreement remained secret until the late 1960s when it was revealed by an investigative journalist.

ment Communications Headquarters (GCHQ) and located at Cheltenham; it continues to monitor the communications of foreign countries, the activities of terrorists, and anything else the government might wish to know about. At the time of the General Strike, there was no doubt an office at the Admiralty which received all the news culled from intercepted messages, including the *d*ecoded *c*able *c*ompanies' *c*ommunications. If this was the DCCC office, it was the big ear that heard everything. Even if my theory is only partially correct, it would explain why the Naval Historical Branch of the Admiralty should profess complete ignorance of this office.

The intense pressure under which Walter worked during the Strike took its toll on his health. After all, the news staff at Savoy Hill worked in relays, whereas apart from Reith's secretary, Miss Shields, Walter was alone. So it should come as no surprise that six weeks later, as soon as the new *Radio Times* had been launched, he was obliged to take sick leave, suffering from almost continuous headaches caused by high blood pressure. He was away for a long time. Writing of these events fifteen years later, Richard Lambert, who edited the *Listener* from 1929 to 1939, recalled that Walter was absent 'for many months . . . ordered by his doctor to keep absolutely quiet.'[73]

That summer, Walter, Crystal and their two children joined Max and Eliena down on the Côte d'Azur, to which Max had returned after a holiday in Austria and a visit to Gurdjieff's community at the Prieuré des Basses Loges.* I do not know how long Walter stayed there; the following January, Crystal told Paul Kellogg that she had spent 'three lazy months at Antibes.' To help with Jeffrey and Annis, the Fullers took with them 'an attractive, healthy, simple-hearted creature' of nineteen or twenty, Jean Pateman.[74] Among the many Anglo-Saxon expatriates and visitors in Juan-les-Pins that summer was Yvonne Kapp, with her artist husband Edmond (always called Peter) and their infant daughter. Yvonne knew Walter from the *Weekly Westminster* days, when she had been Girl Friday to the editor of the *Sunday Herald*.† More than sixty years later (by which time she had written her masterly biography of Karl Marx's daughter Eleanor), Yvonne recalled that 'The Fullers were about to go permanently to the United States, where

---

* Max decided that Gurdjieff was a charlatan who practised mass hypnosis on his followers.

† Shortly after this meeting with the Fullers, Yvonne developed ugly spots around her mouth. A chance encounter with Dr Joan Malleson (see p.325) put her mind at rest: she was suffering from impetigo and not a venereal disease. Five or six years later, she became a friend of C.K. Ogden. When Yvonne visited Russia in 1935, Ivy Litvinov (see note on p.331) let on that she too was corresponding with Ogden. See also p.375.

Walter had been offered a job, taking with them their young English nanny.'⁷⁵ This is doubtless the impression she retained from talking with Crystal. Be that as it may, the nanny, Jean Pateman, transferred her allegiance to the Kapps and shared Yvonne's life for the rest of her days.

In addition to making *Radio Times* more of a magazine, the main change that Walter made was to replace the bare timetables with 'illustrated and annotated programme pages' – 'how well I remember the phrase,' exclaims Gorham.⁷⁶ He improved the layout, adding more information and photographs, ranging from the actors whose voices were to be heard to views of the theatre sets when extracts from stage plays were broadcast. There were also specially commissioned drawings, some of them cartoons of popular radio personalities. The budget for outside contributions was limited to £50 a week; on one memorable occasion Walter beat down a contributor who wanted fifty guineas to a mere thirty. The BBC congratulated him on his admirable vigilance, but it was no doubt at some personal cost.

He continued Crocombe's initiative of a full-colour cover for the Christmas issue. For his first, in 1926, he fought for and obtained a dramatic abstract depiction of lightning by Edward McKnight Kauffer instead of the sentimental 'kiddies-round-the-Christmas-tree' pictures of previous years. Eleven other illustrators contributed to that issue, including: Dora M. Batty, best remembered for her London Transport and Underground posters; Eric Fraser, whose name became associated with *Radio Times,* so numerous and so well loved were his contributions; Paul Nash; and *Punch* illustrator George Morrow. Newnes (who continued to print *Radio Times*) opposed the design, just as they always opposed the BBC's initiatives; they prophesied that the Christmas number would not sell. In the event, it sold better than any previous Christmas number and netted the BBC a profit of over £6000. On this occasion the BBC rewarded Walter with a bonus of £100, which 'made a new man of him for a week,' as Crystal put it to Ruth Pickering.* What's more, 'We paid half our debts in one blow.'⁷⁷ *Radio Times* rapidly became the BBC's second largest source of revenue (licences being the first), thanks to the paid advertising in its pages.

In March 1927, Walter launched the first special issue of *Radio Times*, a Beethoven Centenary Number, arranged in conjunction with Percy Scholes. It was the first issue to sell a million copies, and the BBC celebrated with a

---

* To put these figures into perspective, Gorham was paid 'an exceptional starting salary' of £400 a year.⁷⁶

dinner at which Lord Riddell, the Chairman of Newnes, made tactless comparisons with the *News of the World* (which Newnes also printed); Reith was not amused. 'There were other speeches, but Walter Fuller was not called. The BBC did not regard the Editor as being of much importance on an occasion like that,' sniffed Gorham.[79]

By November 1926, however, the BBC had recognized both Walter's usefulness and the need to spread his workload: 'Mr Fuller's pre-eminent value to the paper is in his ideas and his editorial conceptions. A distraction from this side of his work is definitely uneconomical,' declared an internal report dated 5 November and signed AC (presumably Admiral Carpendale). So that he could 'devote himself to the development of the paper' and 'concern himself with feature and editorial ideas, the artistic arrangement and literary quality of the journal,' a managing editor in the person of Eric Maschwitz* was appointed in December to work under Walter's direction.[80] Maschwitz soon 'came to know and love' his editor-in-chief.[81] He and Gorham also became firm friends,

> and we had a lot of fun; though I'm afraid our ribald attitude towards the job was a real trial to poor Fuller, who had deep convictions about the potentialities of radio. He was right, of course, but it was hard to see the distant wood from amongst the trees at Savoy Hill.[82]

Their high spirits can be illustrated with an anecdote from Gorham's memoir. The window of Walter's long narrow office on the fourth floor

> gave onto a wide cornice that ran right round the corner of the building. I forget what made me first use the cornice; I believe I was locked either into or out of my room. Anyway, I found that I had here a wonderful hold over the grey-haired lady who ordered the [printing] blocks [for illustrations in *Radio Times*]. Miss B was as tough as they make them, but she had her Achilles heel: she could not bear to see me on the cornice. So when all else failed, I would get out of my window, walk round to hers, and tap on the glass to be let in.[82]

Such diversions can have done nothing for Walter's blood pressure, or his workload. Despite the arrival of Maschwitz, the need for further staff was recognized in February 1927, when it was noted that both Fuller and Maschwitz were overworked.

One of Walter's ideas that came to fruition in the spring of 1927 was a

---

* Eric Maschwitz (1901–69) came from Outside Broadcasting, having been recruited to the BBC not long before by Lance Sieveking (see next chapter). He was married to the actress Hermione Gingold, and became a well-known script writer and lyricist.

Braille version of *Radio Times*. It was a project that he particularly cherished, for he realized what a great resource the radio could be for the blind. However, owing to the rivalry between the National Institute for the Blind (now the Royal National Institute of Blind People), and St Dunstan's, the charity for blind ex-servicemen (now called Blind Veterans UK), it was hard to negotiate. In the end, the Braille *Radio Times* was published under the auspices of the NIB.

A project that Walter did not originate but with which he was closely associated was the *Listener*. The inspiration was Richard Lambert's. Hired to develop Adult Education (which Stobart mocked as 'Addled Education') he did some lateral thinking and came up with the idea of a periodical that would bring broadcast talks in printed form to the general public.* In the early stages of this project, which he saw as a possible extension of *Radio Times*, Lambert had long talks with Walter, whom he considered

> a remarkable man, not adequately appreciated at the BBC. He was of a gentle disposition, acute intelligence and wide culture: his outlook was progressive, but he was neither pushful nor intriguing. He had edited *Radio Times* during its most difficult period – that is, ever since the day when the BBC had taken it over from George Newnes [to turn it] into a popular home journal, with reading matter apart from its programme pages. Walter Fuller was appointed to grapple with this task, and he had already made big advances when his health gave way.
>
> When I first laid before him my scheme for the new educational journal, I could see that he regarded it wistfully, with some desire to retain the new venture within the orbit of his own paper. But he realized that the obstacles were insuperable, and was too much of an altruist to obstruct another's plans for a negative reason only.[83]

Having no experience in either publishing or editing, Lambert benefitted greatly from his discussions with Walter, but they were interrupted by Walter's illness.

This time, in June 1927, hypertension caused a blood vessel to burst in the retina of his right eye. 'A doctor whom he thought could cure him,'[84] advised rest and prescribed medication.† He went to stay with Riss, who spoiled him,

---

* Reith would not agree to reviews of novels on the air; for him fiction was not 'wholesome'. He permitted such distasteful matters to be discussed in the highbrow *Listener*, however, and during the 1930s Edwin Muir established its reputation for serious literary criticism.

† His doctor seems to have been Frances Elinor Rendel (known as Ellie), the daughter of Lytton Strachey's sister Elinor. She treated all the Bloomsbury set, being Virginia

bringing him breakfast in bed. He was, however, feeling very sad, having just learned of the death of his fellow student at Owen's College, Bill Hankinson. Only a few weeks before, Bill's sister Hilda had looked him up at the BBC, with the news that Bill was thinking of spending some of his holiday with Walter. Now, as he lay in a darkened room, Walter kept thinking of him. He had been such a good friend, although he had seen very little of him as late. He knew that, had he asked, Bill would have come to see him, 'the way, in Dickens, Jo went to see Pip when Pip was ill.' Sending his condolences to Hilda, he described Bill as 'always benign – always good tempered – always patient – always unselfish. How much do I owe him – a whole flood of happy memories overwhelm me as I think of him.'[85]

To his mother he reported:
Every day I take my medicine – three times daily before meals – such nasty stuff, and Riss brings me a nice piece of ginger to take the taste away. . . . And they pile the good food on my plate, and I say when they ask me, 'just a *very* little' just as you used to do! And in the morning they weigh me, and Riss brings me a cup of malted milk at eleven – and sits and smiles at me as I drink it, and I feel the violet rays pouring in on me and doing me good – body and soul. After a week of this health-restoring treatment I shall be quite well and shall be back at work at Savoy Hill like a giant refreshed – and then, the weekend after, I'll be coming along down to see you, and show you what a fine new son you've got.[86]

The following week he wrote to Cynthia: 'Here I am safe in the arms of 'Riska – and if I die here – as I hope I shall some day, but not this time – I shall exclaim with my last breath, "O grave, where is thy victory?"' As his vision was improving, he decided he was fit for work again. 'I shall be at my desk at Savoy Hill on Monday morning, bright and early – not to fall sick again until next June – which, as you know, is my month for being ill in – and a very nice month it is too.' It was the month of Crystal's birthday, and he asked Cynthia to send her some flowers and call her on the phone. 'She'd appreciate it so much, and she'll be all alone.'[87]

It was in fact a good deal longer than that before Walter went back to work; even then he did not feel refreshed by 'all these weeks of absence and idleness.'[88] 'About a week after his return to the office,' recalled Lambert,

I met him at lunch at the National Liberal Club. At once I could see that he was not himself. 'Lambert,' said Fuller sadly, 'I feel anything but well again.

Woolf's physician from 1924 until her death. By today's standards, her prescriptions – such as eating mercury – were highly unorthodox.

My doctor tells me I ought not to be back at work. But I dare not stay away any longer – for the sake of my job.'[89]

He was driving himself too hard.

By the beginning of 1927, Crystal was desperate. It was two years since she had returned to England, and she had not managed to secure regular employment – in 'research, organizing, editorial, speaking, *anything*.' She had been 'a very hard-working girl all the fall,' playing a leading role, along with Edna Thomas and Betty Gram Swing, in organizing an English branch of the US National Woman's Party, but in January she felt 'terribly demoralized': 'Christmas, and having the children home for five weeks, and my complete failure to get a job, have undermined my character.' So she asked Paul Kellogg and Ruth Pickering to be on the look-out for work for her in New York. Because she was 'rich in health and strength now,' she felt 'simply crazy to work.' 'I want work and economic independence more than I want anything else (except, perhaps, to live with Annis, God bless her), and I cannot get it here in England.' 'Anyhow, what a fine country America is from all I hear! Walter will follow when he can – one day.'[90] She and Walter were much alike in their recurrent hope that the grass would be greener on the other side of the ocean. While anxious to leave, she was as active as ever, attending (as a member of the executive committee) the first Annual Meeting of the Open Door Council, held at Caxton Hall, Westminster on 4 April, 1927.[91]

In July, she and Walter spent a weekend with his mother, and they visited Portsdown Hill together. At long last, Crystal felt accepted by her mother-in-law, and told her that 'it is a delight to be taken a little way into your favor.'[92] She and Jeffrey and Annis finally sailed from Southampton on the *Rotterdam* on 24 August 1927. The following day Walter wrote her one of those chatty letters that she loved to receive:

Dear old Crystal – I'm missing you awfully. I've just had a lonely dinner and am now up here in our beautiful big room. The fog is coming in fast – I shan't try to get in touch with the Ciscos. I think I shall read a little & then go to bed. Let me tell you what I did after you left. You looked so sweet & beautiful up there – all the other women – the good-looking ones too – look so hard and selfish compared with the tenderness of you. – I suppose the French *tendresse* is a better word – Your beautiful face has more the look of the children's faces that were there on the ship – or were on the pier with me. Jove, how Jeffrey will love you – & be proud of you when he grows up.

I watched your ship round the lighthouse & then I made a bee line for the newspaper shop. And sat outside in one of those public seats and read yesterday's *Times* and today's *Herald* till I was as blue as a policeman's uniform and as depressed as a submarine in sight of an enemy convoy. In that heavy mood I dragged myself over to the Library & spent a pleasant hour browsing there....

The fog is heavier tonight than it has been any night during the week. I hope the Captain of your ship will keep his weather eye open very carefully all the time. I'm very sure of one thing and that is that I simply cannot get on – cannot live – without you. I know how to live about as well as I know how to swim. I feel about as happy and as comfortable and as much at home in the world as I feel in the water. My only hope and prayer is that you will have patience & love enough to stay around within call & hold me up occasionally . . . until the time comes when I feel cold and have to step ashore.

Goodnight my dear swimming master.[93]

It's the last surviving letter by Walter.

◆◇◆

During this time, Rosalind had been enjoying her career on Broadway. She never again attained the heights of *Hamlet* – it was 'like a first love, never to be repeated'[94] – but she always found work, particularly with the Provincetown Players and the Village Players. Bruguière remained her partner and in 1927 he had his first one-man show, under the auspices of the Pictorial Photographers of America, at the Art Center in New York. His ninety-four photographs and ten paintings were much admired, although no one realized at the time that by fusing abstraction with recognizable shapes he was introducing surrealism to the American continent, four years ahead of its official debut at the Wadsworth Atheneum. 'Bruguière's surrealism was not so much a part of the social revolutionary commitment, common to the European advocates, as it was an attempt to free photography from its role as a purveyor of reality.'[95]

The exhibition drew international attention and Bruguière was invited to show his works in Herwarth Walden's 'Der Sturm' gallery in Berlin, Germany. Having delivered them personally, he and Rosalind decided to visit England before returning to New York. Walter was delighted at the news. ''Twill be a joy to see you,' he wrote, 'and to hear all your good news – and tell you mine – some of it bad and some indifferent – but with you around everything will seem bright and beautiful.'[96] Rosalind found another letter from him when she arrived:

> Rosalind dearest girl – welcome back to the land of your birth – these words bring back to mind the picture of three dear girls bursting their throats with

'Come back to Erin' – you the loudest and tenderest of all – on some platform in any Middle Western town you care to name – and me knowing the show was over, and all that remained was to collect the cheque and get a taxi![97]

As usual, Rosalind made the rounds of family and friends, including Norman Angell. Back in London, she and Bruguière arranged to dine with Walter on 14 September, at the National Liberal Club. When they arrived, however,

> he was not in the hall to meet us. When I enquired for him at the desk they told me he had been taken ill and I should go up to his room at once. I waited for the lift in a circle of fear and rushing to his room I found he had had a stroke. He was lying on his bed, unable to move or speak. We looked at each other and I think he knew me. I took his unresponsing hand in mind, telling him that he would be all right, feeling what I said couldn't be true. I told him how much I loved him, but my words came back to me, as though I was speaking in an echo-chamber.
>
> It was strange to be looking down instead of up at him. When we were children, he sometimes came to kiss us goodnight, a tall figure bending over the rails of my bed, and I would wish his soft full lips would stay against my face for ever.
>
> All my life I wanted more of his love than I could or dared have.[98]

Quickly she arranged to have Walter transferred to a nearby nursing home and on the way there she found she was repeating to herself, 'I could not do without Thee.' It had been her favourite hymn when she was a child, and in her own mind, 'I had always substituted Walter for God.'

At the nursing home, she was provided with a room for the night. 'I was so frightened I didn't undress,' she writes.

> I just sat on my bed, listening for death. Very early the next morning, I was called to his room. 'Hurry,' they said. Walking almost unconsciously up the stairs I opened his door and saw a nurse putting her hand under his pyjama jacket. . . . Pushing her aside I bent down to kiss him and heard for the first time the rattle of death.[99]

Walter Fuller had stepped ashore.

11

Epilogue

We in America feel that the world is poorer without Walter Fuller.[1]
Norman Thomas

Fuller's influence was felt by all who worked with him. He spread a spirit of light-hearted gaiety, idealism, duty and good fellowship that were natural to him.[2]   Percy Scholes

How well do I remember Fuller's quick, outstretched hand, his bright nervous eye, and his puckish moments of inspiration.[3] *New Republic*

Rosalind in the sea (date not known)

THE FOLLOWING DAY, listeners to the BBC were surprised to hear Sir John Reith saying, 'We have a personal announcement to make: the Editor of *Radio Times* has just died of a cerebral haemorrhage at the early age of 46.'* He mourned 'the loss of a colleague marked by singular devotion and enthusiasm.' This was a unique occasion, for the BBC never made personal announcements, and Sir John's voice was rarely heard over the air.

Walter's death was a terrible shock for all who knew and loved him. Only a week before, his father had sent him an 'Ezyreade' – a magnifying glass for long-sighted readers – with a note saying 'I thank God every day for *you* & all that *you* are to mother and me. God bless & keep you in good health.'[4] That only Rosalind had been present at the last made it all the harder for her sisters. Dorothy complained that 'it was cruel to send a telegram when it was too late!' They all wished that he could have had his family around him.

As Mrs Fuller did not feel up to attending the funeral at Golder's Green Crematorium, Cynthia and Riss spent the day with her in Petersfield. A week later, Rosalind brought her a small wooden box containing Walter's ashes:

> Mother almost smiled as she took it. There were no tears. Putting it carefully in an oak chest that stood in the living room, she covered it with a silk scarf, tucking it round as she used to tuck us up in bed for the night.[5]

The funeral itself was organized by the BBC, and the full BBC Choir was there to sing the hymns. Gorham 'disliked the presence of a posse of BBC officials appearing as officials rather than as friends, and I was sorry to see Reith himself reading the lesson in white spats.'[6] Twenty years later, Gorham was still bitter. 'I have always believed that the BBC killed Walter Fuller.'[7]

In *Radio Times* Percy Scholes recalled how Walter 'had the charm that unlocks the hearts of both men and women – it's not a gift that we can cultivate, but was part of the essence of the man himself. Fuller had this and with it a brilliant mind, wit, and humour.' And he concluded: 'I never enter the *Radio Times* office without finding that he is still alive.'[8]

In lieu of an obituary, *Radio Times* printed an original poem (whose author remains unidentified), followed by a few words which Gorham attributed to Reith himself:

---

* Walter's death certificate lists three causes: '(a) Cerebral Haemorrhage; (b) Arterio Sclerosis; (c) Hyperpiesis [i.e. high blood pressure with no identifiable cause]; ditto Intestinal toxaemia.'

Walter Fuller

> He always loved the stars; to him
> The tiny spark, remote and dim,
> Was filled with life and superman,
> So far his speculation ran.
> O more to him the night's array
> Than all the pageantry of day;
> The far-lit citadel of space
> Than earth's supreme abiding place.
> What ecstasy of joy to him
> To seek the last horizon's rim;
> To find in some vast cave of space
> The vagrant comet's resting place.
> Where is he now? I think, maybe,
> His shallop sails the ether sea
> In happy search of some bright star
> Where ancient dreams as substance are.

To those who knew Walter Fuller, and especially to all who worked with him, the significance of these verses will be apparent. For many years to come, memories of that eager and radiant spirit will flash upon them. He loved beauty and constantly sought to serve it. His devotion and restless enthusiasm were infectious. High inspiration and far-flung imagination characterized his work; and with it all a childlike simplicity and modesty of demeanour made him beloved. The personal sorrow – especially of his immediate associates – is mitigated by the inspiration of his friendship.

For an institution like the BBC, by then a public corporation, it was a notably heart-felt tribute, indicative of the depth of affection that Walter had inspired in all who knew him.

Part of his inspiration lived on in the *Listener*. Lambert, who claimed the dubious honour of having been 'one of the last of his colleagues to exchange personal confidences' with Walter, recorded, without a trace of bitterness, that 'the vast *dossier* of memoranda' of the *Listener* project, which had been in Walter's possession when he died, 'could not be found among his papers afterwards. So a fresh start had to be made.'[9] Since Walter is reputed to have lost the marked up proofs of a complete issue of *Radio Times* on the Underground while taking them to the printer,[10] it could be that Lambert's *dossier* shared a similar fate. (High blood pressure can lead to absent-mindedness and lapses of memory.) Miss King, Walter's red-haired secretary, could not help find the *dossier* either, for on Walter's death, she handed in her notice. The *Listener* was finally launched on 16 January 1929, and lasted sixty years. There was of course much competition to succeed Walter as editor of *Radio Times*. Eric Maschwitz served as Acting Editor for six years, and then Maurice Gorham took over.

It should be added that the BBC acted handsomely by paying off all Walter's remaining debts, which must have been a relief for Crystal. It also made provision for his children, although this was apparently not paid to them for more than twenty years. In 1949, Jeffrey asked Max for 'the exact date and place of Crystal's death' which he had to supply to Curt Dehn's partner in London: 'he is trying to send us the money the BBC left us at the time of Walter's death.'[11]

Crystal herself was devastated by the news. 'I nearly died of tears and desolation at first,' she told Charles Hallinan. Early in October she had her tonsils removed and she 'nearly died of pain and anaemia' then too.[12] One of her first letters was to Rosalind:

> It's almost all I can do to live along, and not destroy myself with crying. I don't dare really write to you what I feel. I don't dare let go of myself that much. Will you understand that – and Cynthia and Riss and your mother?
>
> I think of you all the time when I'm not thinking of Walter. But I must wait to say any more.

Without consulting the Fullers, Curt had offered to send Walter's ashes to Crystal. She took it very well that they had gone to Walter's mother, who so wanted reminders of him. She was also very understanding when the Fullers took until the end of the year to send her a few mementoes of Walter. 'I'm glad you could at last send me the things. It would have been just as impossible for me' to part with them, she admitted. Among them was a crumpled handkerchief. 'It must have been in his dear hands and touching his face. I just put my face in it and cried. You don't know how many, many times I've cried in his handkerchiefs and been comforted by him!' She was thankful for her children, for they had 'so much of Walter's charm in each of them.'[13]

To Rosalind she wrote:

> I want to thank Curt for the kindness of his message. And please tell him and bless him for helping persuade me not to go back to America before I did. I might have missed that last precious time. And you – God bless you – your cable – I can't think about it. But I love you. And my arms around Cynthia – my tears with hers.
>
> Your mother – my love to her – I've longed to say something strong and comforting to her. I'm so glad we finally got to like each other. Your dear father – his sweet face now so much sadder. Riss – Dorothy – I think of them too – and love them.

> I must say that I'm all right – you mustn't worry. I have not gone to pieces. I'm going to go on getting well, and lift up my head and go on with the business of my life. Ruth [Pickering] is taking care of me down here [in Croton] for a few days – the first terrible days. She is wonderful. Max has been here too – and all the Croton people that love me and know Walter – admired and loved him. I'm in the best hands. But you know how deeply I long to be there with you, don't you.
>
> The children are well, I think. I will have them as soon as I am well enough to do it. There is nothing to be anxious about.
>
> I wonder if you will come home to America sometime – and tell me? Or will you stay and comfort your mother a while?
>
> Crystal[14]

While recovering from having her tonsils removed she also wrote to Cynthia, using the same sea metaphor as in Walter's last letter (which she had no doubt read and re-read until she knew it by heart). 'I am fighting so hard not to drown and to get my health and hold on to it, so that I'll be equal to supporting the children and making a happy home for them.'[15] There were times when she felt 'such great homesickness for England' – wanting to be with Walter's family, 'all sad and remembering together.' They were, she realized, her 'nearest and dearest. If it weren't that I can't make a living there, I should want to go right back.' Then, after 'days and days of bracing sunny air' out at Croton, injections of iron and meals of liver, she began to feel it was 'impossible to get permanently depressed' and bounced back 'from acute sorrow to my usual joy in activity; there is *so much* for me to do.'[16] The little house at Croton needed renovating from top to bottom, for she had spent less than six months there in the last five years.* As she was preparing to take a job in New York and would be away from Monday to Friday, she knew that her weekends would be 'spent in 14-hour days trying to catch up with home problems at Croton.'[17]

The job was at the *Nation*, 'promotion, not editorial', co-ordinating a celebration of the tenth anniversary of Oswald Garrison Villard's editorship,

> a sort of whirlwind campaign, resting solely on me. Oh – how I miss Walter in this job! What a rare person he was. If he could come back and I could have work & he could have work too, I think I would know just how to live with him.

---

* The letters and other documents now in the Fuller Fonds (Special Collections) at the library of the University of British Columbia, were discovered under the roof of this house more than fifty years later.

Epilogue

My trouble was, largely, that I was never well all those eleven years, never equal to life. Now I am so much stronger. I can stand up to a day now.

Working for the *Nation* brought her a welcome $100 a month – but raised fresh worries. 'Please don't tell anybody but Hazel,' she enjoined Hal:

The brothers-in-law – as trustees – are holding some money the BBC gave them for us. I need it *very much right now*, and if they think I have gone to work, God knows when they will send it. Don't tell anybody this. They know I am probably going to work in Jan. – so let that be what you tell outside the family.[18]

Her job started at the beginning of December 1927 and was to last four months. After that, she planned

to come to England in late March or early April and visit everybody – and talk about Walter. I feel I can't bear it if I don't. . . . Of course, part of the reason is to see 6 Upper Park Road again – dispose of everything, and give it up. It will break my heart to come, but it will hurt me more not to come.

I want to be there before you have all forgotten and stopped talking about him. . . .

I am after [all] *very homesick* for London. I hope to come back and live there again some day. – But, oh, Hal, the beauty of Croton all through a golden fall – and now in snow. This morning everything gleaming with ice! I wish I could commute from Croton to London.[19]

She did not know that Riss, level-headed and practical as ever, had already taken charge of clearing out the Hampstead house. 'When the end came, Father and I had to destroy all [Walter's] papers,' she confessed to Jack Odell, who was collecting material for an account of the Fuller Sisters' American tours.* They apparently made a bonfire of press cuttings, and she realized that there must have been letters and other documents among them. 'I was too blind [with tears, presumably] to see.'[21]

Rosalind was not involved in this. Her appendix had been grumbling for a while; ten days after Walter's death, it was removed in a London clinic, although she was not in a good state of mind for an operation. 'You see,' she told Norman Angell, with whom she was in regular contact,

I have no philosophy to help me with such a blow as this. He was so much more than a brother – I have always been 'in love' with him. All the memo-

---

* This account never materialized, but his intention explains how Jack and Dorothy's daughter Carol came to inherit a trunkful of family letters. At this point, Jack was composing and writing *The Plumber's Opera*, which was well received – 'a most appealing bit of nonsense . . . the essence of burlesque' – but it has now been quite forgotten.[20]

ries of my childhood and girlhood are surrounded in the brightest glow of my love and worship of him. And now I am frightened and terror stricken in my heart – I can see outside: myself trying to comfort myself.[22]

So 'when I was given the anaesthetic and everything dissolved into a brightly coloured turning wheel, I felt I shouldn't mind much if I didn't come back.'[23]

Back she came though, like 'a whirlwind.'[24] Just before going into the clinic she auditioned for a play, having decided to remain in London. 'When I opened my eyes, I saw lying on the table near my bed my first British contract, to play Nubi in *The Squall.*'[25] That gave her fresh purpose and soon she was fit enough to begin rehearsals. She was to play 'a gypsy who, during a terrible storm, begs for shelter in the home of a happy respectable family. . . . Once in the house she seduces the son, the manservant, and the husband, and when her gypsy-master comes to claim her the squall is over.'[26] It might have been written specially for Rosalind, who found it 'the sort of part in which it is easy to make a hit.'[27] It opened on 15 November at the Globe Theatre, and a review in the *Express* summed up the general impression: 'She looked like Nazimova* and acted with a fierce intensity, a sinuous grace and a wheedling persuasiveness that made her a London reputation in a night. The audience roared itself hoarse for her and will continue to do so.'[28]

During the brief weeks between Rosalind's arrival in England and Walter's death, Walter introduced Bruguière to a colleague, Lancelot de Giberne (known as Lance) Sieveking (1896–1972), whom he had occasionally lunched with that year. Arriving at the BBC in April 1926, Sieveking had started as an assistant to the Director of Education and then went into radio plays,† becoming the BBC's drama script editor throughout the 1940s. As Walter had anticipated, he and Bruguière immediately saw eye to eye; each was aspiring to arouse powerful feelings through non-representational works, just as Sieveking's lifelong friend Paul Nash was doing in art. Meeting Bruguière gave Sieveking the confidence to produce his high modernist radio play, 'The Kaleidoscope', which was broadcast on 4 September 1928. The pair then collaborated on a surrealist book, *Beyond This Point,* published in 1929, in which the text by Sieveking is interrupted by photographs by Bruguière. The images, mostly cut-paper abstracts, aim to supply the thoughts and feelings that are omitted from the text.

---

*   The celebrated American actress Alla Nazimova (1879–1945) had been offered the part but turned it down.

†   Rosalind performed in the radio adaptation of Stevenson's story 'The Bottle Imp' that Sieveking produced on 18 May 1933.

Epilogue

Oswell Blakeston (1907–85) came to interview Bruguière for *Close-Up*, and he became one of Rosalind and Bruguière's 'dearest friends, a person of great charm with a brilliant fast-moving mind, one idea coming after another as smoothly as quicksilver changes its pattern.'[29] Bruguière took many double-exposure photographs of him. They collaborated on the first abstract film to be made in England, *Light Rhythms* (1930), and also on a book, *Few Are Chosen: studies in the theatrical lighting of life's theatre* (printed by Eric Partridge at the Scholartis Press in 1931). Like *Beyond This Point* it marries fiction (nine short stories) and photographs of cut paper (which in this case hint at human forms and faces). The two books and the film were all thoroughly avant-garde.

One of Walter's *Radio Times* illustrators, Edward McKnight Kauffer, met Bruguière at this point; they too collaborated to combine photographs, text, and surreal imagery in advertisements during the 1930s. Kauffer lived at 101 Swan Court, Chelsea, with Marion Dorn, famous for her rug and carpet designs; Rosalind and Bruguière moved into the flat just below theirs, and remained there throughout the 1930s. In the evenings, when Rosalind returned home from the theatre, she would find Sieveking, Blakeston, Kauffer, Dorn, and Bruguière all deep in discussion.

Yet another person to benefit from Bruguière's presence in London in the autumn of 1927 was a young man named Cecil Beaton, who was just starting out in photography. While taking portraits of him, Bruguière shared some of his lighting techniques and showed how he shot his abstracts. This inspired Beaton to make some 'imitation Bruguière abstract photographs' which he included in the portfolio that he hawked round publishers and agents that autumn.[30] In the end, though, he stuck with portraiture. Although his approach to photography was the polar opposite of Bruguière's, he learned from him how to harmonize the relationship between sitter and background with patterned materials and painted backdrops, treating the photograph like a painting in light and shadow.

After Bruguière's death, Rosalind asked Beaton to open the retrospective exhibition of his work that she arranged to have put on during May 1949 at the Focal Press Gallery in London. He accepted, 'proud that I can have the opportunity of re-paying the kindness that your husband [*sic*] showed when I first started my career.'[31] In his published writings, however, Beaton downplayed Bruguière's influence on his photographs.

In 1927, the old friend and admirer of the Fuller Sisters, Maurice Browne of the Chicago Little Theatre, also returned to England. Cecil Lewis (who abruptly resigned from the BBC in 1926) showed him the translation he had just made of Paul Raynal's tragedy on the futility of WWI, *The Unknown Warrior*. At once, Browne decided that it had to be staged. There were only three characters: a soldier, his fiancée, and his father. Browne wanted to play the soldier; he asked Rosalind to play the fiancée, and he got Huntley Wright (1868–1941) to play the father. Launched at the Arts Theatre in February 1928, it proved such a success that it was transferred to the Little Theatre in the West End, followed by matinées at various other theatres. In a review, George Bernard Shaw declared that 'it was worth having a war to get such a play as this.' He called Rosalind 'a wonder' in a letter to Barry Jackson, encouraging him to go and see the play for himself.[32] St John Ervine, drama critic of the *Observer*, called her performance 'a most beautiful one, poignantly done, gravely done. . . . One of the finest pieces of acting I have ever seen given by a young actress.'* According to Browne, Rosalind, 'like swansdown, responded to the lightest breath, the gentlest touch of a fingertip.'[33] After the initial run, there were three private performances at Dartington Hall, plus a benefit performance; a revival at the Little Theatre in November 1930; and various reprises, especially on Armistice Day, throughout the 1930s. In October 1931, Rosalind and Maurice Browne took it to the Morosco Theater in New York for a few nights. For her, this was an important role, for it demonstrated to English theatre directors that she could handle tragedy quite as well as the more physical part of Nubi in *The Squall*.

However, she did not tour *The Unknown Warrior*† because in April 1928 she was invited to take over from Sybil Thorndike the role of Rosamond Withers in *The Stranger in the House*. Then, starting from 2 June, she played Pauli Arndt in *The Enemy*. This was the stage production of an American film (starring Lilian Gish as Pauli) about newly-weds torn apart by war that premiered in New York in December 1927. In Britain it launched at the King's Theatre, Edinburgh, briefly toured the provinces and then ran for four weeks at the Strand from 23 July 1928. With these three plays, Rosalind made a triumphant stage debut in England; she only regretted that Walter was not there to witness it.

---

* Rosalind took the opportunity of her return to England to drop nine years off her age. The IMDb and many reference books continue to give her year of birth as 1901. So she was passing for thirty when she was in reality close on forty.

† Her part was taken by an unknown actress called Catherine Lacey – and it launched her career. She is perhaps best remembered as the secretive nun who wears high-heel-shoes in Alfred Hitchcock's *The Lady Vanishes* (1938).

Epilogue

She would have been delighted if Crystal had come over that spring, but Crystal never made a return visit to England. The nephritis that had been gnawing away at her kidneys ever since the birth of Jeffrey, and possibly much longer, was causing violent fluctuations in her health. One week she would be prostrated by a complete loss of energy, accompanied by terrible headaches. The next she would be feeling better. Early in June she went to stay with Max, taking the children with her. On 8 June, she told Ruth Pickering.

> Yesterday and today have been so wonderful that I am happy even with this nasty taste in my mouth and every mouthful more than doubtful – my eyes almost useless – and a roaring in my head at night like a train puffing up hill. And it is great to be here with the children. My heart is warm and life is sweet.[34]

Her dearest wish was to 'get well and live to make a happy childhood' for Jeffrey and Annis. 'I don't care about anything else. When that is done, I think I'll be pretty tired of life and quite ready to die.'[35]

Her wish was not granted. As her condition deteriorated, Max took her out to Battle Creek Sanitarium in Michigan (where the Fuller Sisters had sung during their final tour). She was seen by her brother Peter, a doctor, but medicine could do no more for her. Remaining 'heroic – so gloriously loyal to her brave and great self' right to the end,[36] she died, with her brothers at her bedside, on 8 July 1928, just two weeks after her forty-seventh birthday.

She had outlived Walter by less than ten months. On one of her last days, she managed to pen a note to their children, now aged eleven and seven-and-a-half:

> Dear Jeff and Annis,
> I want to leave you all my love and all my joy in life.
> — Crystal — Mother
> Don't forget your darling father. He was a darling.[37]

Max, who broke off all contact with his own son when he separated from Ida Rauh at the end of 1916, had no desire to play the parent and look after the orphans. He set about finding adoptive parents for them. Over in England, Riss (who was two years younger than Crystal) would dearly have loved to take charge of them. She had no children of her own, had often looked after them already, and had a home and the means to do so.* But Max, who barely knew Riss, entrusted them to a wealthy American couple that the children

---

* Basil Ward was a prosperous doctor; on his death in November 1940, his estate was valued at £64,466 2s. 11d, a substantial sum in those days.

had scarcely seen before, Agnes and Henry Goddard Leach.* So he deprived them of what they needed most, the loving presence of their closest relatives.

What the Leaches did supply was the stability that had been sadly lacking in their lives. They had crossed the Atlantic, in one direction or the other, every two or three years. Although Jeffrey had spent more time in America than in England, his schooling had been English. Even in 1920, he had 'a pronounced English accent in his baby talk.'[38] Annis had lived longer in England than America. In both countries they had often been looked after by relatives and friends. Dorothy recorded that Annis would anxiously watch the door or peer out of the window, awaiting her mother's return, and Jeffrey would regularly ask where he would be staying the next day. Things did not improve when they returned to America with Crystal. She was either not well enough or too busy working to look after them, so in the vacations she sent them to a 'school-on-a-farm' at Poughquag, on the edge of West Mountain State Forest in New York State. On New Year's Eve, 1927, she recorded that when they returned to Croton, 'I shall have one day in which to amalgamate them with a new nurse-cook-housekeeper before I go to work [in New York] at 8.12 on Tuesday.'[39]

Jeffrey and Annis returned to England twice more, spending a month there in the summers of 1929 and 1932. For their first visit, they seem to have been accompanied on the outward trip by Max, but they were alone – entrusted to the care of the ship's captain – for the return crossing, as Max stayed a couple of weeks longer than they did. For their second visit, Agnes Leach came with them. Jeffrey made a solo visit in the summer of 1934.

Because their parents had spent so much time apart between 1922 and 1927, Jeffrey and Annis had seen Walter mainly at weekends and during holidays, so he must have become a somewhat distant figure for them.† In the June of his last year, when he was on sick leave from the BBC, he wanted to spend time with them, but Jeffrey was at a school somewhere in Bucking-

---

* Agnes Leach (1888–75) had been active in the WPP and AUAM. She helped form the Civil Liberties Bureau; she was on the board of directors of Survey Associates from 1920 through to the 1950s, and worked on fundraising with Paul Kellogg. She was also prominent in civic and educational activities in New York City. Henry Leach (1880–1970) was a leading intellect of his time, editor of the *Forum* (1923–40), and President of the American-Scandinavian Foundation (1926–47). Having no children of their own, they supported Jeffrey and Annis, and their children, for the rest of their lives.

† Although Walter's father had always been at home during Walter's childhood, apart from occasional trips to London to buy cloth, he became a more distant figure from 1911 onwards, often travelling on Young Helpers business.

Epilogue

Walter with
Annis and Jeffrey
(Petersfield, 1927)

hamshire and 'Annis is, I think, at a school in Dorset.'[40] Even fit and healthy, he would have needed to ask Crystal where to find them. He loved them no less for all that and would have been proud to learn that Jeffrey studied at Harvard, graduating in 1938 with a major in Slavic languages and history. Part of the attraction of Russian for Jeffrey probably stemmed from Max's involvement with Trotsky and Russian Communism, and partly from Max's wife Eliena, whom he found exciting to know, not unlike his mother. He paid a visit to Moscow in 1936, and his proficiency in Russian stood him in good stead in WWII.

Unlike his parents, Jeffrey was not a pacifist. In England, he had seen Dorothy's husband Jack nearly as often as his own father, and Jack entertained him with activities that little boys love, like watching steam trains, flying kites, sailing paper boats on a pond, and sleeping in a tent. He also told him how much he had enjoyed the Army, and regaled him with stories of fighting the Hun in the trenches. Drafted in January 1941, Jeffrey was commissioned as a second lieutenant in October 1942 and as *aide de camp* and interpreter (Russian and French) served Major General D. H. Connolly of the Persian Gulf Command. A liaison officer in Qazvin, Iran, he worked closely with the Russians in May 1943. After the defeat of the Japanese, he was earmarked for training in military government and civil affairs in preparation for the occupation of Japan, but in May 1945 he was seen to be of greater use to the Office of Strategic Services (OSS, the predecessor of the CIA), and worked for a year as a field operative in Berlin and Central Europe. He was discharged in June 1946 with the rank of major. He could have joined the CIA, and chose not to.

After an abortive venture into organic plant food – like some of Walter's ideas, it was too far in advance in its time – he joined the staff of the ACLU, where he succeeded in increasing both its membership and funding. After eleven years with the ACLU, he left to manage the fundraising department of a direct mail firm, where he was better paid, but he continued to edit the ACLU's newsletter, *Civil Liberties,* until 1966.* He died of an aortic aneurism on 24 February 1970, aged fifty-three. He was married and left three children, two girls and a boy.

He and Annis saw more of Rosalind than any of the other Fullers. Although she made her life in England, she would visit them (and make love with Max, of course) whenever she crossed to the States. On one occasion, in 1953, Jeffrey drove her and Annis out to Croton, where they picnicked together, refreshing old memories – vivid for Rosalind, but only vague for Walter's children. Annis returned to England only in 1966, by which time she was married with three children, two girls and a boy. Hazel Hunkins Hallinan welcomed her like a long-lost daughter.

Rosalind remained in regular contact with Max until his death in March 1969, and she continued to see – and discreetly make love with – Norman Angell for many years. After receiving the Nobel Peace Prize in 1932, he became ever more protective of his good name, but he foolishly let the cat out of bag in his autobiography, *After All* (1951). He describes how he was called to the telephone one day in the early 1930s to receive a telegram, which was read out to him by the local operator: '"Can sleep with you after the theatre Friday night. Love. Rosalind' – a message which I heard with very mixed emotions. For though I knew the Rosalind in question, those were not my relations with her – "cross my heart" as the children say.'[41] He claims that Rosalind assured him that she had written 'sup', not 'sleep'. He goes on:

> I was in the House of Commons at the time and knew Lees-Smith, the then Postmaster-General, pretty well. I told him (if not altogether seriously, then half-seriously) 'I'm going to sue you for damages. Think of my reputation among my country neighbours.'
>
> A day or two later he came to me: 'Nothing doing, my dear fellow. Reflections on a man's chastity are not actionable unless he is a clergyman. You are not a clergyman. Ergo, no action lies.[42]

Had he not made such a fuss, only the post office employee would have realized what was going on. Now we all know.†

---

* Jeffrey can have had no idea of his father's role in bringing this concept to America. The periodical might be called an anonymous monument to Walter.

† Rosalind was staying with Angell at Christmas 1934 when a reporter turned up unexpectedly to interview him and take pictures of his house. On this occasion they let nothing slip. See *Illustrated Weekly* for 29 December 1934.

Epilogue

Riss in 1938

Rosalind's career continued apace. In 1929 she acted alongside Ion Swinley in *The Unwritten Law*, one of the very first English talkies – in fact, the first made in England by an English film company with synchronized sound on the film, not on a separate disc. Ten years later, she was in the first play to be broadcast live on British television, *Rehearsal for a Drama*. In between, she acted in several films, including *Perfect Understanding* (1933), which starred Gloria Swanson and Laurence Olivier, with Miles Malleson. She regularly performed in radio plays – some two dozen of them by my count – and on the stage she acted in three or four different plays each year, with several singing roles, including a revival Edward German's 1902 comic opera, *Merrie England,* in 1934 and '35.* The Glasgow *Herald* felt that 'Miss Fuller deserves a special word for the clever waywardness of her playing in the difficult part of Jill-all-Alone,'[43] and in the opinion of *The Times* she 'showed how near akin are witchcraft and irresistible charm.'[44]

She was disappointed that her sisters had lapsed into dull domesticity.

---

* She probably did not boast of having performed in Walter's staging of *Merrie England* way back in 1911: her revised birth date would have made her only ten at the time. Rosalind was also one of those who participated in a forgotten Experimental Theatre (at 59 Finchley Road), with André Van Gyseghem, Aubrey Menon, and Nikolay Pavlovich Okhlopkov (producers) and Duncan Grant, Paul Nash and John Rowdon (decors). Francis Bruguière handled the lighting.[45]

Walter Fuller

Riss, who had let herself be trapped by Basil, had a proven talent that was lying dormant. Rosalind prodded her into making at least nine broadcasts of folksongs, ballads, and Celtic stories, accompanying herself on the harp, between December 1932 and May 1939. Some were aired in the context of Children's Hour; others at 8 p.m., a peak hour for popular culture. On the last occasion, when her 'full and feeling interpretation' of Border ballads was noticed by the *Manchester Guardian*,[46] the programme was arranged in collaboration with Joan Littlewood, who was soon afterwards banned from the BBC for her communist sympathies. Riss died at the end of 1942, and her harp was given to the BBC Northern Orchestra.

Dorothy, on the other hand, declined to be roused. In 1927, she had made drawings for the cover and endpapers of Robert and Katharine Barrett's *The Himalayan Letters of Gypsy Davy and Lady Ba* ('with decorations by the Ballad Singer'), and this led to her providing delightful illustrations, in a style reminiscent of E. H. Shepherd, for a volume of poems, *Red Shoes*, by Katharine Barrett.[47] (The Barretts had re-entered the lives of the Fuller sisters after seeing Rosalind in *Love for Love*.) But that was it. Her daughter Carol (1921–2013), however, grew up to be a children's writer; while yet a teenager she had stories accepted for Children's Hour by the BBC. She married an Australian, George Foote, and went to live in Sydney, where she continued to write and promote literature for children. Her parents joined her in the mid-fifties and spent the rest of their lives there. Thus it came about that Carol discovered, in an old trunk, the illustrated book of traditional singing games that Dorothy had made at Cornish in the summer of 1917. She had it published in 1983. Twenty-five years later, she was made a Member of the Order of Australia (AM) 'for services to children's literature as an author, scriptwriter and presenter.'

It was Francis Bruguière who encouraged Cynthia's talents, persuading her to experiment with oil paint. Following his first visit to England, she produced poster-like illustrations for six folksongs. Curt had them printed in a portfolio which was distributed through Bumpus in London and Boni in New York,* where Crystal did what she could to help with promotion. 'I think you have a future as a poster artist,' she told Cynthia,[48] but although she continued to paint, Cynthia did not explore this field any further. She

---

* *A Set of Six Folksongs and Ballads* was given lengthy and favourable notice in the Chicago *Evening Post Literary Review* of 24 August 1928 by a reviewer who fondly remembered 'the days of the Chicago Little Theatre and the recitals of folksongs by the Fuller Sisters.'

often served as a model for Bruguière alongside Rosalind, and helped him prepare the cut paper for his abstract photographs. In recognition of his influence on her art (and her love for him), she adopted the pseudonym 'Francyn'. This explains an odd little book that appeared in 1935: *Man's Moment: poems provoked by Francyn's Paintings* (with a foreword by James Agate). The poems – by Katharine Barrett, whose name does not appear in the book, any more than Cynthia's does – are printed opposite reproductions of seven of Cynthia's paintings. The contribution by London's most daunting theatre critic James Agate is less surprising when we realize that he was the best friend of Curt's cousin Fred. His foreword begins, 'I am the last person who should be asked to write about these dreadful, shocking, awful, appalling pictures and the poems they have inspired.' They filled him with dread and awe because 'though they pretend to deal with birth, they really deal with the thing in life which I most want to forget – that thing called death.'

The book was brought out by Stanley Nott, who set himself up as a publisher in 1934.* During the mid-twenties, he had divided his life between New York and Gurdjieff's community just outside Paris. One day in September 1927, a strong feeling came over him that he had to return to London, *immediately*. 'It was so compelling that I made no effort to resist it,' he writes.

> I left at once and reached London that night. It was too late to call on my dearly loved friend Walter Fuller, as I usually did when I arrived in London, so I went on to Harpenden to spend the night with my parents. When I opened *The Times* the next morning, there was an account of Fuller's sudden death, and a long obituary.[49]

Soon after this, he decided to remain in England.† Joining forces with A. R. Orage, Nott became the business manager of the *New English Weekly*, which they launched in April 1932. Under the influence of Orage, he espoused C. H. Douglas's theory of Social Credit, and he became a publisher the better to promote it.‡ This brought him into contact with another proponent of

---

* It was possibly this renewed contact with one of the Fuller sisters that prompted Nott to write his memoir of Walter for *New Democracy*, an American periodical that supported Social Credit.

† His wife Rosemary became a teacher at Beacon Hill, the school that Bertrand Russell and Dora opened in 1927. Her two years there happened to coincide with the breakdown of the Russell marriage. (See p.264.)

‡ Nott's list was not all in economics. One of his first books was *Beside the Sea: six variations* edited by 'Yvonne Cloud', the pseudonym of Yvonne Kapp. (See p.350.)

Walter Fuller

Social Credit, Ezra Pound. Thus Nott came to publish Pound's pamphlet, *Social Credit: An Impact*; his essay *Jefferson and/or Mussolini*; and, as 'The Poet of Titchfield Street', *Alfred Venison's Poems: Social Credit Themes,* all in 1935.

When WWII broke out, Rosalind was on a camping holiday in Death Valley, California, with Robert and Katharine Barrett, whom she still called Gypsy Davy and Lady Ba. A year before, she had become one of the leading ladies in Donald Wolfit's Shakespeare Company, touring in the parts of Lady Macbeth; Portia in the *Merchant of Venice;* Beatrice in *Much Ado about Nothing;* Rosalind in *As You Like It;* and Desdemona in *Othello* – five different roles on five consecutive evenings a week. In September 1939, Wolfit telegraphed that he needed her at once for a fresh tour. She flew back to New York and booked a steamer passage.† While waiting for her ship, she learned that Americans were being repatriated *en masse* from Europe, amid fears that London would shortly be reduced to rubble. It occurred to her that if Bruguière were to return home, she might not be able to go with him. An American friend of Bruguière's, Johnny Becker, offered a simple solution: he proposed to her. She accepted; they were married, and she sailed back to England with an American passport, confident that she could accompany Bruguière wherever he might go. Four years later, Becker met a woman he wanted to marry for real, so he and Rosalind divorced by mutual consent, having spent less than twenty-four hours together as a married couple.

Back in London, Rosalind and Bruguière closed their flat and Bruguière went to live with Cynthia in Middleton Cheney, where Curt had been lent a house well away from the expected bombs. While Cynthia produced anti-war paintings, Rosalind toured the provinces with Wolfit's Shakespeare Company, which returned to the Kingsway Theatre in London in the spring of 1940. Two months later, she sang in the revival of the WWI hit, *Chu Chin Chow,* which saw several productions during the early '40s. The following autumn, by which time the Blitz was well under way, she joined Wolfit in putting on 'Lunch-Time Shakespeare' at the Strand Theatre. Although the back of the theatre and the dressing rooms had been blown away by a bomb, they put on excerpts from the plays, songs, sonnets and prologues between one and two in the afternoon. They were paid only three guineas a week and the theatre lost money on it, but thousands of Londoners found solace in the

---

† Wolfit and all who knew Rosalind were struck by her courage and determination to return to England at this juncture. We can see here a reflection of the events of the summer of 1917 – only this time there was no brother Walter to dissuade her.

Epilogue

words of Shakespeare during their lunch break. (Sometimes they were obliged by air raids to remain long after the performance was over; then actors and audience would sing together to keep their spirits up.) By Christmas, six other theatres had adopted similar programmes.

During the following years, Rosalind toured many plays, returning in her free time to join Bruguière; sometimes he came to see her at one venue or another. Surviving the war by just one day, he died with Rosalind and Cynthia beside him in May 1945. Three years later it was Curt's turn, carried off by cancer. For the next seventeen years, Cynthia lived with Ilse Schutte, who had been a governess to her son Conrad before the war and who came back from Germany to help nurse Curt in his final months. Cynthia continued to exhibit her paintings, both in England and on the Continent. This brought her into contact with the novelist, poet and illustrator Mervyn Peake (b.1911), with whom she enjoyed a sporadic love affair in the 1950s. Several of the poems that she had privately printed in 1968 – the year of Peake's death – relate to this relationship. Cynthia herself died only in 1987.

Throughout the first half of the 1950s, at the same time as acting in numerous plays, Rosalind was developing a one-woman show of her own. She started by adapting 'Fraulein Else', a short story by Arthur Schnitzler, the pioneer of 'stream-of-consciousness' writing in German, for solo performance on the stage. Unlike Ruth Draper, she played only one character, but used her voice and gestures to people the stage with others. A test at the Watergate Theatre Club in London early in 1950 confirmed that she could pull it off. So she adapted short stories by Anton Chekhov, Katherine Mansfield and Guy de Maupassant and tested these at the Watergate too. Over the next four years, she added to her repertoire, and finally launched her series of monodramas, 'Hearts and Faces', in November 1954 in New York, where the Fuller Sisters had started their career as folksingers more than forty years before and where she had made her own debut as an actress in 1920. She landed a contract to tour her show throughout the United States for three consecutive winter seasons. The third was cancelled because her agent went out of business. Yet the success of her show was such that when it was put on at the Arts Theatre Club in London on two successive Mondays in October 1956, demand justified extending it to a full week of performances.

Her work was noticed by the recently formed British Council, and (after an audition before its Drama Committee in Cynthia's studio) she was invited to perform under its auspices throughout the world. It proved physically challenging: in May 1958, having toured through Iraq and the Persian Gulf, she had a mild heart attack in Baghdad. She was in hospital for five weeks there and when she got home she was advised at a London hospital to rest for two months. So she asked, was it all right to make love? 'The doctors went into a huddle as though they were going to sing in close harmony. It seemed the words 'make love' were not often heard in heart hospitals' – more especially (we might add) in the mouth of a sixty-six-year-old woman. She had two regular partners at this time, plus other lovers during her tours. 'Yes, but in moderation,' advised the doctors, glancing at her 'slight boyish figure.'[50] This amused Rosalind no end. 'Don't kiss the joy too strongly as it flies,' she quipped.[51]

Over the following twenty years, she continued to expand her repertoire, adding stories by many other authors – Charles Dickens, Fyodor Dostoyevsky, Nadine Gordimer (who approvingly attended one of her performances), Henry James, Rudyard Kipling, and Emile Zola, to name a few. She toured them, interspersed with occasional stage appearances, under a variety of titles ('A Night with Guy de Maupassant'; 'Subject to Love'; 'The Human Voice'), throughout Britain and many other countries all over the world.* Her achievement was recognized by the award of the MBE for services to the theatre in the New Year honours of 1966. Her last show during the 1970s was called 'The Snail under the Leaf: the life and works of Katherine Mansfield.' She launched it in Durban, South Africa.

In 1979 Hazel Hunkins Hallinan noticed that, having reached the age of eighty-seven, Rosalind had 'finally come to grips with the fact that she cannot play Juliet again, but she is fascinating and lively and even to an audience of one she gives a good account of herself.'[52] She died in her sleep at Cynthia's house on 15 September 1982, aged ninety, fifty-five years *to the day* after Walter's death, having proved him right: she could do whatever she wanted, if she put her mind and imagination to it, with courage and enthusiasm.†

---

* They include: South Africa (Swaziland, Basutoland) and Uganda in 1957 and 1961; Australia, New Zealand, Fiji, Mauritius and Kenya between July and December 1962; Europe (Holland, Norway, Poland, Germany) in 1963; Iran, Afghanistan, Malaysia, Australia, Trinidad, Jamaica, British Honduras, and the Bahamas between May and December 1964; South Africa in 1965; England and the Continent (Holland, Sweden, Turkey, Poland) 66 and 67; Australia, Tasmania, Manila, Hong Kong, Katmandu in 1968; England in 1969; England and the Continent in 1970; and so on throughout the 1970s.

† As Scott Fitzgerald remarked to Max Perkins, 'Before I'd finished she almost stole the story!'[53]

Epilogue

As a young man, Walter Fuller wanted to be a doctor, so that he could relieve people's suffering, but he failed to qualify because he sympathized too closely with the patient. At the time, his sympathy appeared to be a weakness; it was in fact his strength. It was what made him such a good editor: the ability to put himself in another's place made it easier for him to grasp what a writer was trying to say and reword it more clearly and elegantly.

Every human quality has its downside and Walter was to discover more drawbacks to qualities in his character. The next came soon after: when his father went bankrupt, Walter strove to keep his family afloat, and ended up in a sea of debt himself. He tried to make his sisters' fortunes, and failed: first because he charged too little for their recitals and, second, because any good cause – orphans, the blind, the sick, victims of war or, of course, peace itself – would awaken his sympathy and he would have the girls sing for free. It is hard to make money when you are as unselfish and generous as he was.

Walter's sympathy for the disadvantaged (which he inherited from his father and grandfather) was a form of altruism; it made him want to work for social improvement and write something worth reading on his life's slate.[53] And this led to his achievements. By bringing together the student councils of Britain, he laid foundations for a national association of students. Through *Comradeship*, with its Ruskinian appreciation of, and respect for, the cultural heritage of the countryside, he helped promote ecologically friendly holidays for everyone. When he took his sisters across the Atlantic to sing in the New World, he was motivated quite as much by their need for money as he was by his belief in the beneficent effect of folksongs: reconnecting the listeners with their cultural roots, 'they soften the hardest, unbend the stiffest, and make everybody lovable,'[56] as Riss put it. At the same time, in reviving folksongs, first as public entertainment and then as vehicles for anti-war protest, Walter pointed in the direction that popular music was to take in the mid-twentieth century. In fact, had he lived as long as his sisters, he would have felt perfectly at home in the 1960s, for he rehearsed that decade's protest movements fifty years in advance.

From the moment the First World War broke out, he was an instinctive pacifist, moved not by political or economic arguments (as Norman Angell was), nor even by philosophical or religious principles (like the Quakers), but rather by his anticipation of the immense suffering that it would cause. Even before the slaughter started, he sensed that a thousand *Titanics* were sinking and he felt as though he were drowning.[54] Striving to prevent the United States from despatching its conscripted citizens to the killing-fields of France, he became a peace activist. Realizing that the world can be changed (for the better, as for the worse) by changing how people perceive it, he stumbled on fundamental principles that underlie all modern propaganda (more than ten years before the first book on the subject). To defend US conscripts against their own government, he brought them from Britain the concept of *civil liberties*. And this resulted in the creation of the American Civil Liberties Union.

The small-circulation periodicals that he edited between 1917 and 1923 allowed Walter to express his ideals more fully, defending women and peace in *Four Lights* while at the same time remaining perfectly anonymous (to the point where nobody realized until now that he was its true editor); peace and conscientious objectors in the *World Tomorrow*; literature and liberal principles (formulated with wit and style) in the *Freeman*.

Back in England, where he helped numerous – but mostly still unidentified – artists and writers, Walter was headhunted by the BBC. Called in to advise on programmes, he was soon making suggestions as to how the BBC might shape its public image – at least twenty-five years before the concept gained currency. Then he was selected to edit *Radio Times*. Hardly had he come up with his redesign of the periodical when, with his sympathy for the disadvantaged as strong as ever, he introduced a Braille edition of it for the blind.

At the heart of Walter's achievements was his love for his fellow men and women, for which he was much loved in return. The *New Republic* wrote, 'deeds and achievements scatter like dust, whilst such a life leaves a permanent trace on every person it touched'[55] – but that permanence does not outlive the persons it touched. So, by recounting Walter's life in this book, I have made a more durable record of it.

Sources

In the references, documentary sources are identified by abbreviations:

ACLU Records of the American Civil Liberties Union. Subgroup 1, the Roger Baldwin years, microfilm reel 9, Vol. 73; in the Department of Rare Books and Special Collections, at Princeton University Library. See http://findingaids.princeton.edu/collections/MC001.01

ALD 'Arthur Lindsay Dakyns, 28.5.83–10.3.41, from letters to his father H. G. (Graham) Dakyns, and his sister Frances Dakyns (1877–1960), and from published source material.' Unpublished document in COC, compiled by Janine Dakyns, 1 October 1988. (There is now a copy in the Henry Graham Dakyns Papers (reference GEN MSS 698) in the Beinecke Library.)

AUAM Archives of the American Union Against Militarism Records, Swarthmore College Peace Collection. Microfilm reels 10.1 and 10.2.

Axon Papers of Dr William Edward Armytage Axon (1846–1913) in Special Collections at the John Rylands University Library in Manchester.

BRA Bertrand Russell Archives, McMaster University, Hamilton, Ontario, Canada.

BTC Rosalind Fuller papers in the University of Bristol Theatre Collection.

BWAC The BBC Written Archives Centre, Reading, England.

CEP Crystal Eastman Papers, 1889–1931; reference 82-M4, folders 197 and 198. Schlesinger Library, Radcliffe Institute, Harvard University, Cambridge, Mass.

CHA Minutes of the committee meetings of the Co-operative Holidays Association in the Greater Manchester County Record Office.

CKO Box 20 of the C. K. Ogden fonds in the William Ready Division of the Archives and Research Collections at McMaster University Library, Hamilton, Canada.

COC Carol Odell's private collection of Fuller family letters and diaries.

CSD   Cecil Sharp's Diaries, digitized and placed online by the English Folk Dance and Song Society. http://library.efdss.org/cgi-bin/sharpdiaries.cgi
DC   The Debs Collection in the Cunningham Memorial Library at Indiana State University.
Diary Walter Fuller's diaries for 1899 and 1901, in the care of Charles Young.
DNB   The *Oxford Dictionary of National Biography* online.
EWP   Edmund Wilson Papers (reference YCAL MSS 187) in the Beinecke Rare Book and Manuscript Library, New Haven, CT.
FF#   The Fuller Fonds in Special Collections at the library of the University of British Columbia, reference RBSC-ARC-1685. The number following the letters FF indicates the folder.
HHH   Hazel Hunkins-Hallinan Papers, 1864–1984; reference MC 532, folder 9.6. Schlesinger Library, Radcliffe Institute, Harvard University.
Lilly Letters from Rosalind and from Jeffrey to Max Eastman, courtesy the Lilly Library, Indiana University, Bloomington, IN.
MMC   Manchester Medical Collection, John Rylands University Library, Manchester. Biographical files, reference GB 133 MMC/2/IrvingH, item 3: 'Letter from Irving to EBL, 25 June 1929.'
MOH   the Manley Ottmer Hudson Papers in the archives of Harvard Law Library. Reference HOLLIS 601668.
OCUM   *Owens College Union Magazine*. Copies can be found in the British Library and in the John Rylands University Library, Manchester.
ODC   The First Annual Report (1926–27) of the Open Door Council (1926–1965), in the National Archives (reference GB 106 5ODC/A/01). Also in the National Woman's Party Records in the Library of Congress, Group II, Box 262.
OPS   'Origin of a Peculiar Species', memories of her family by Cynthia Dehn, née Fuller, in the Schlesinger Library, Radcliffe Institute, Harvard University, Cambridge, Mass.
PGP   Patrick Geddes Papers at Strathclyde University Archives, Scotland; reference T-GED/9/649, 750, 844, 1024 and T-GED/12/3/10.
RYC   Rebecca Young's private collection of letters.
Report *Report of the First American Conference for Democracy and Terms of Peace held at Madison Square Garden, New York City, May 30 and 31st, 1917.* Published by the Organizing Committee, People's Council of America for Democracy and Peace, [no place], 1917.
RF   Rosalind Fuller's unpublished and untitled autobiography. A copy is in COC.

SSK   The papers of S. S. Koteliansky in the Taylor Bodleian Slavonic & Modern Greek Library, University of Oxford.

WHW   The 'H. W. Willson [sic] files' in Box 67 of the Sir Norman Angell Papers in Archives and Special Collections, Ball State University Library, Muncie, Indiana. Angell kept Rosalind's letters, and also some from Dakyns to Rosalind that she forwarded to him. In the early 1980s, William H. Willson, who was writing a biography (never published) of Angell, copied some of them and made notes on others. Most of these letters were subsequently destroyed by Angell's secretary, after Angell's death. References to the MS of Willson's book, *Sir Norman Angell and the Last Illusion,* are followed by the page number of his MS, which is dated December 1989.

WPP   Archives of the Woman's Peace Party in the Swarthmore College Peace Collection. Microfilm reels 12:1–23.

Books and articles are identified by the author's name.

Anon. 'To Replace Rag-time.' *The Literary Digest,* 46, no. 12 (22 March 1913), p.641.

Addams, Jane. *Peace and Bread in Time of War.* New York: Macmillan, 1922.

———. *The Second Twenty Years at Hull House.* New York: Macmillan, 1930.

Angell, Norman. *After All.* London: Hamish Hamilton, 1951.

Ashby, Eric, and Mary Anderson. *The Rise of the Student Estate in Britain.* London: Macmillan, 1970.

Baker, Ray Stannard, *Woodrow Wilson: Life and Letters: War Leader 1917–1918.* New York: Charles Scribner's Sons, 1946.

Barker-Benfield, G. J., and Catherine Clinton. *Portraits of American Women: From Settlement to the Present.* New York: OUP, 1998.

[Barrett, Katharine]. *Man's Moment. Poems Provoked by Francyn's Paintings.* With a Foreword by James Agate. London: Stanley Nott, 1935.

Barrie, J. M. *Peter Pan, or The Boy Who Would Not Grow Up.* As produced at the Duke of York's Theatre on December 27, 1904. A Project Gutenberg of Australia eBook.

Beaton, Cecil. *Photobiography.* London: Odhams Press, [1951].

Bernays, Edward L. *Propaganda.* New York: Liveright, 1928.

Blakeston, Oswell, and Francis Bruguière. *Few Are Chosen. Studies in the Theatrical Lighting of Life's Theatre.* Privately published, London: Eric Partridge, 1931.

Boughton, Alice. 'Three Maids A-singing Go.' *Harper's Bazaar,* autumn 1913, p.36.

Briggs, Asa. *The Birth of Broadcasting.* London: OUP, 1961.
Brooks, Van Wyck. *Days of the Phoenix: the Nineteen Twenties I Remember.* New York: Dutton, 1957.
Browne, Maurice. *Recollections of Rupert Brooke.* Chicago: Alexander Greene, 1927.
———. *Too Late to Lament: an autobiography.* Bloomington: Indiana UP, 1956.
Butcher, Fanny. *Many Lives, One Love.* New York: Harper and Row, 1972.
Callaghan, John and Kevin Morgan. 'The Open Conspiracy of the Communist Party and the Case of W. N. Ewer, Communist and Anti-Communist.' *Historical Journal,* 49, no. 2 (June 2006), pp.549–564.
Chambers, John Whiteclay II. *The Eagle and the Dove: the American peace movement and United States foreign policy 1900–1922.* 2nd ed. Syracuse, New York: Syracuse UP, 1991.
Conolly, L. W. (ed.). *Bernard Shaw and Barry Jackson.* Toronto, Buffalo, London: U of Toronto P, 2002.
Cook, Blanche Wiesen (ed.). *Crystal Eastman on Women and Revolution.* New York: OUP, 1978.
Creel, George. *How We Advertised America.* New York: Harper, 1920.
Curran, Jennifer. *To Make War Unthinkable. The Woman's Peace Party of New York 1914–1919.* MA dissertation, U Newfoundland, 1997.
Currie, Tony. *The Radio Times Story.* Tiverton: Kelly Publications, 2001.
Day, Kenneth, and Ann. *History of Work and Labour Relations in the Royal Dockyards.* London: Routledge 1999.
Dell, Floyd. *Homecoming: an autobiography.* New York: Farrar & Rinehart, 1933.
Derwent, Clarence. *The Derwent Story: my first fifty years in the theatre in England and America.* New York: Henry Schuman, 1953.
Dilling, Elizabeth Kirkpatrick. *The Red Network: a 'who's who' and handbook of radicalism for patriots.* Chicago: Ayer Publishing, 1977.
Dos Passos, John. *The Best Times: an informal memoir.* London: Andre Deutsch, 1970.
Eastman, Max. *The Enjoyment of Living.* New York: Harper, 1948.
———. *Love and Revolution. My Journey through an Epoch.* New York: Random House, 1964.
Eddy, Sherwood. *With Our Soldiers in France.* New York: YMCA Press, 1917.
Ege, Arvia MacKaye, *The Power of the Impossible: the life story of Percy and Marion MacKaye.* Falmouth, ME: The Kennebec River Press, 1992.
Eliot, Valerie (ed.). *The Letters of T. S. Eliot. Volume I: 1898–1922.* London: Faber & Faber, 1988.

Endres, Kathleen L., and Therese L. Lueck (eds). *Women's Periodicals in the United States: social and political issues.* Westport, CT, & London: Greenwood Press, 1996.

Enyeart, James. *Bruguière: his photographs and his life.* New York: Knopf, 1977.

Fitzgerald, F. Scott. *Before Gatsby: the first 26 stories.* Ed. Matthew Joseph Bruccoli and Judith Baughman. Columbia: U of South Carolina P, 2001.

Fleischman, Harry. *Norman Thomas: a biography 1884–1968.* New York: Norton, 1969.

Freeberg, Ernest. *Democracy's Prisoner: Eugene V. Debs, the great war, and the right to dissent.* Cambridge, MA: Harvard UP, 2008.

Fuller, Cynthia. *The Inward Eye. Poems.* Hayward's Heath, Sussex: Breakthru Publications, 1968.

—— (illus.). *A Set of Six Folksongs and Ballads.* London: J & E Bumpus, and New York: Albert & Charles Boni, 1927. Limited to 500 copies.

Fuller, Dorothy (illus.). *English Folk Songs. [As sung by] the Fuller Sisters.* New York: H. W. Gray, n.d.

Fuller, Rosalinde. 'A Shakespeare Tour in Wartime.' *Theatre Arts,* xxiv, no. 3 (March, 1940). pp.179–181.

Fuller, Walter G. [John Wessex, pseud.]. *A Masque of the Seasons.* Songs, music and dances arranged by Oriska V. Fuller and Rosalind Fuller. Sturminster Newton: The Minster Press, 1911.

Gilbert, Alma M., and Judith B. Tankard. *A Place of Beauty: artists and gardens of the Cornish Colony.* Berkeley, CA: Ten Speed Press, 2000.

Gorham, Maurice. *Sound and Fury. Twenty-one Years in the BBC.* London: Percival Marshall, 1948.

Gosciak, Josh. *The Shadowed Country: Claude McKay and the romance of the Victorians.* New Brunswick, NJ, and London: Rutgers UP, 2006.

Goss, Madeleine. *Modern Music-makers: contemporary American composers.* New York: E. P. Dutton, 1952.

Gregory, Raymond F. *Norman Thomas: the great dissenter.* New York: Algora, 2008.

Hanley, Keith, and John K. Walton. *Constructing Cultural Tourism: John Ruskin and the tourist gaze.* Bristol, Buffalo and Toronto: Channel View Publications, 2010.

Hapgood, Hutchins. *A Victorian in the Modern World.* New York: Harcourt, Brace and Co., ca. 1939.

Harper, George McLean (ed.). *President Wilson's Addresses.* New York: Henry Holt & Co, 1918.

Harper, Ida Husted (ed.). *The History of Woman Suffrage,* Volume VI. 1900–1920. New York: the National American Woman Suffrage Association, 1922. http://www.gutenberg.org/files/30051/30051.txt

Hendy, David. 'Painting with Sound: the kaleidoscopic world of Lance Sieveking, a British radio modernist.' *Twentieth Century British History,* 24, no. 2 (September 2012), pp.169–200. DOI:10.1093/tcbh/hws021

Hickman, Miranda B. (ed.). *One Must Not Go Altogether with the Tide: the letters of Ezra Pound and Stanley Nott.* Montreal: McGill UP. 2011.

Huebsch, B. W. (comp.) *The* Freeman *Book: selections from the eight volumes of the Freeman 1920–1924.* New York: B. W. Huebsch, 1924.

Hunt, Frazier. *One American and His Attempt at an Education.* New York: Simon & Schuster, 1938.

Hurley, Joseph. 'Barrymore Takes Broadway!' In the *Variety History of Show Business.* Ed. the editors of *Variety.* New York: Harry N. Abrams, and London: Hamlyn, 1993.

Kapp, Yvonne. *Time Will Tell. Memoirs.* London: Verso, 2003.

Kipling, Rudyard. *The Letters of Rudyard Kipling.* Vol. 4 (1911–1919). Ed. Thomas Pinney. London: Macmillan, 1999.

Kirk, Elise K. *Music at the White House: a history of the American spirit.* Urbana: U of Illinois P, 1986.

Kittredge, G. L. 'Ballads and Songs'. *The Journal of American Folklore,* 30, no. 117 (July–September, 1917), pp.283–369.

Kosek, Joseph Kip. *Acts of Conscience: Christian nonviolence and modern American democracy.* New York: Columbia UP, 2011.

Kuehl, John, and Jackson Bryer, eds. *Dear Scott/Dear Max: the Fitzgerald-Perkins correspondence.* New York: Charles Scribner's Sons, 1971.

Kuhlmann, Erika. '"Women's Ways in War": the feminist pacifism of the New York City Woman's Peace Party.' *Frontiers: A Journal of Women Studies,* 28, no. 1 (1997), pp.80–100.

Lambert, Richard S. *Ariel and All his Quality: an impression of the BBC from within.* London: Gollancz, 1940.

Law, Sylvia A. 'Crystal Eastman: organizer for women's rights, peace, and civil liberties in the 1910s.' *Valparaiso University Law Review,* 28, no. 4 (1994), pp.1305–26.

Link, Arthur S. (ed.). *The Papers of Woodrow Wilson. Volume 43: June 25–August 20, 1917.* Princeton, NJ: Princeton UP, 1983.

Lissner, Will. 'Crusader for Justice: a tabloid biography of Francis Neilson.' Essays in Honor of Francis Neilson, Litt. D., on the Occasion of His

Eightieth Birthday. *American Journal of Economics and Sociology*, 6, no. 2 (January 1947), pp.139–158.

Lora, Ronald, and William Henry Longton, eds. *The Conservative Press in Twentieth-century America.* Westport, CT: Greenwood Press, 1999.

Lunn, Kenneth, and Ann Day. *History of Work and Labour Relations in the Royal Dockyards.* London: Routledge, 1999.

MacKaye, Percy. *A Substitute for War.* New York: Macmillan, 1915.

Madeira, Victor. 'Moscow's Interwar Infiltration of British Intelligence, 1919–1929.' *Historical Journal,* 46, no. 4 (December 2003), pp.915–933.

Malleson, Andrew. *Discovering the Family of Miles Malleson 1888 to 1969.* Privately published in Canada, 2012.

Maschwitz, Eric. *No Chip on My Shoulder.* London: Herbert Jenkins, 1957.

McLelland, Sarah. 'A Scot Remembered.' http://patrickgeddes.co.uk/feature_fifteen.html

Mellow, James R. *Invented Lives: F. Scott and Zelda Fitzgerald.* New York: Houghton Mifflin, 1984.

Meyers, Fern K., and James B. Atkinson. *New Hampshire's Cornish Colony.* Charleston, SC: Arcadia, 2005.

Miller, Donald L. *Lewis Mumford: a life.* New York: Grove Press, 2002.

Morrison, Michael A. *John Barrymore, Shakespearean Actor.* Cambridge: CUP, 1997.

Mountain, Penny (comp. & ed.). *Stur: The Story of Sturminster Newton.* The Sturminster Newton Museum Society, 2006.

Mumford, Lewis. *My Works and Days: a personal chronicle.* New York: Harcourt Brace Jovanovich, 1979

———. *Sketches from Life: the autobiography of Lewis Mumford. The Early Years.* New York: Dial Press, 1982.

Murphy, Paul L. *World War I, and the Origin of Civil Liberties in the United States.* New York: W. W. Norton & Co, 1979.

Neal, Mary. *The Esperance Morris Book: a manual of Morris dances, folk songs and singing games.* London: Curwen. Part 1 in 1910; part 2 in 1912.

Neilson, Francis. 'Literary Talent on *The Freeman.*' *American Journal of Economics and Sociology,* 12, no. 3 (April 1953), pp.315–24.

———. 'The Story of the *Freeman.*' A supplement to the *American Journal of Economics and Sociology,* Vol. 1 (October 1946).

Nock, Alfred Jay. *Memoirs of a Superfluous Man.* 2nd ed. New York, Harper, 1943.

Nott, C. S[tanley]. *Journey Through this World. The Second Journal of a Pupil.* New York: Samuel Weiser, 1969.

Walter Fuller

Nott, C. S[tanley]. 'Memories of Walter Fuller. I.' *New Democracy*, 3, no. 1 (15 August 1934), pp.7–8.

——. 'Memories of Walter Fuller. II.' *New Democracy*, 3, no. 3 (1 October 1934), pp.49–51.

——. *Teachings of Gurdjieff: a pupil's journal.* (1961) London: Arcana, 1990.

Novak, Frank G. (ed.). *Lewis Mumford and Patrick Geddes: the correspondence.* London: Routledge, 1995.

Odell, Carol (comp.). *The Children's Book of Old Fashioned Singing Games.* Illustrated by Dorothy Fuller. Sydney, Auckland, London, Toronto, New York: Four Winds Press, 1983.

Osborne, Charles E. *The Life of Father Dolling.* London: Edward Arnold, 1903.

Parker, John. 'The Search for Jessie Holliday.' *The Shavian*, 4, no. 9 (1974).

Paymer, Marvin E. *Sentimental Journey: intimate portraits of America's great popular songs, 1920–1945.* Darien, CT: Two Bytes, 1999.

Peterson, H. C., and Gilbert C. Fite. *Opponents of War 1917–1918.* Madison: U of Wisconsin P, 1957.

Peterson, Merrill D. *The President and His Biographer: Woodrow Wilson and Ray Stannard Baker.* Charlottesville: U of Virginia P, 2007.

Powys, Llewelyn. *The Verdict of Bridlegoose.* New York: Harcourt, Brace, 1926.

Presley, Sharon. *Suzanne La Follette: the Freewoman.* Libertarian Feminist Heritage Series. Paper 2. New York: Association of Libertarian Feminists, 1981.

Rappaport, Helen. *Encyclopedia of Women Social Reformers.* Volume 1. Santa Barbara, California: ABC-CLIO. 2001.

Russell, Bertrand, *Autobiography.* London: Routledge, 1998.

Sanders, M. L. 'Wellington House and British Propaganda during the First World War'. *The Historical Journal*, 18, no. 1 (March 1975), pp. 119–146.

Saint, Andrew. 'Ashbee, Geddes, Lethaby and the Rebuilding of Crosby Hall.' *Architectural History*, 34 (1991), pp.206–33.

Schorer, Mark. *Sinclair Lewis: an American life.* New York, London, Toronto: McGraw-Hill, 1961.

Secor, Lella. *A Diary in Letters 1915–1922.* Ed. Barbara Moench Florence. North Stratford, NH: Ayer Publishing, 1978.

Seymour-Jones, Carole. *Painted Shadow: a life of Vivienne Eliot.* London: Constable, 2001.

Sharpey-Schafer, Joyce A. *Soldier of Fortune: F. D. Millet.* Privately published: Utica, New York, 1984.

Sheridan, Clare. *My American Diary.* New York: Boni & Liveright, 1922.

Sieveking, Lance, and Francis Bruguière. *Beyond This Point*. London: Duckworth, 1929.
Spender, Dale. *There's Always Been a Women's Movement This Century*. London: Pandora Press, 1983.
Spiller, Robert E. (ed.). *The Van Wyck Brooks Lewis Mumford Letters: the record of a literary friendship, 1921–1963*. New York: Dutton, 1970.
Swanberg, W. A. *Norman Thomas: the last idealist*. New York: Scribner, 1976.
Swomley, John M. 'John Nevin Sayre: Peacemaker.' *Fellowship: the journal of the Fellowship of Reconciliation*. New York. November 1977.
Tanselle, G. Thomas. 'Unsigned and Initialed Contributions to *The Freeman*'. *Studies in Bibliography* 17 (1964), pp.153–75.
Tracey, Michael. Introduction to the microfilm edition of *BBC and the Reporting of the National Strike*. East Ardsley, Wakefield: Microform Academic Publishers, 2003.
Turner, Susan J. *A History of* The Freeman: *literary landmark of the early twenties*. New York: Columbia U P. 1963.
Van Voris, Jacqueline. *Carrie Chapman Catt: a public life*. New York: Feminist Press at the City University of New York, 1987.
van Wienen, Mark W. *Partisans and Poets: the political work of American poetry in the Great War*. Cambridge: Cambridge University Press, 1997.
—— (ed.). *Rendez-vous with Death: American Poems of the Great War*. Champaign: U of Illinois Press, 2002.
Villard, Oswald Garrison. *Fighting Years: memoirs of a liberal editor*. New York: Harcourt Brace, 1939.
Ward, Harriet. *A Man of Small Importance: my father Griffin Barry*. Debenham, Suffolk: Dormouse Books, 2003.
Whisnant, David E. *All That Is Native and Fine: the politics of culture in an American region*. Chapel Hill: U of North Carolina Press, 1995.
Whitney, Richard Merrill. *Reds in America: the present status of the revolutionary movement in the United States* (1924). Boston & Los Angeles: Western Islands Press, 1970. http://www.gutenberg.org/files/30051/30051.txt
Witt, John Fabian. 'Crystal Eastman and the Internationalist Beginnings of American Civil Liberties.' *Duke Law Journal*, 54 (2004), pp.705–63.
Wolfe, Kenneth M. *The Churches and the British Broadcasting Corporation, 1922–1956: the politics of broadcast religion*. London: SCM Press, 1984.
Woolf, Virginia, Nigel Nicolson, and Joanne Trautmann Banks. *The Letters of Virginia Woolf*. Volume 1, 1888–1912. London: Hogarth Press, 1975.
Zieger, Robert H. *America's Great War: World War I and the American experience*. Lanham, MD: Rowman & Littlefield, 2001.

Walter Fuller

Periodicals

The Advocate of Peace, issued by the American Peace Society (Washington DC). Vols 78 (1916) and 79 (1917).
Available at http://catalog.hathitrust.org/Record/000506976

Comradeship, the magazine of the Co-operative Holidays Association in connection with the National Home Reading Union. Vol. 1, no. 1 (October 1907) to Vol.5, No 3 (December 1911).

Four Lights, issued by the New York branch of the WPP, issues 1–20 (1917) and 21 (1919), in the Archives of the Woman's Peace Party in the Swarthmore College Peace Collection. Box 5, folder 13 (microfilm reel 12:3).

The Freeman, edited by Francis Neilson, A.J. Nock, and others. New York: The Freeman, Inc., 1920–24.

Votes for Women [the journal of the Women's Social and Political Union]. Ed. Emmeline and Frederick W. Pethick-Lawrence.

The New World [retitled *The World Tomorrow* from May 1918]. 'The voice of the American Fellowship of Reconciliation' published by the Fellowship Press, New York, 1918–19.

Readers' Review. A Monthly Guide to Books and Reading. Published for the Editorial Board of the National Home Reading Union and the Library Association. London: Sherrat & Hughes. 3 volumes: February 1908–August/September 1910 (whole issue 30).

The Survey. A Journal of Social Exploration. [Renamed *Survey Graphic* in 1919.] New York: Survey Associates, Inc. Vols 33–40, 1914–18.

The University Review. 'A magazine of academic and general interest.' London: Sherrat & Hughes. 7 volumes: May 1905–June 1909 (whole issue 45).

References

Introduction, pages xvii–xx

1. *New Republic*, 14 December 1927.
2. *The Nation*, and then the *New Republic*, quoted by Tanselle, p.153.
3. *The Times*, 16 September 1927.
4. Mumford, *Sketches*, pp.353–4.
5. Walter to Riss, August 1916. COC.
6. Powys, p.103.
7. *The Times*, 22 January 1968, p.7.

Editor, pages 1–28

1. Walter to Riss, 28 September 1904. COC.
2. Arthur Dakyns to Cynthia, September 1927. COC.
3. Norman Thomas to Major Atkinson of the BBC, September 1927. COC.
4. From the *Owens College Union Magazine*, Vol. XI, no. 89 (December 1903), p.351.
5. Portsmouth *Evening News*, 12 June 1959,, p.2.
6. Lunn & Day, p.111.
7. Walter to Riss, Spring 1909. COC.
8. OPS, p.12.
9. RF, p.10.
10. RF, p.1.
11. Diary, 3 January 1899.
12. Diary, 27 February 1901.
13. Walter to his sisters, undated letter in COC.
14. Diary, 15 January 1901.
15. Diary, 27 February 1901.
16. OCUM No 90 (January 1904), p.70.
17. OCUM No 87 (June 1903), p.211–12.
18. OCUM No 88 (November 1903), p.10.
19. OCUM No 88 (November 1903), p.2.
20. Walter to Riss, 27 November 1903. COC.
21. Walter to Riss, All Soul's Day i.e. 2 November 1903. COC.
22. Mr Fuller to Riss, 11 March 1904, COC.
23. OCUM No 95 (June 1904), p.240.
24. OCUM No 95 (June 1904), p.241.
25. Walter to Riss, 24 July 1904. BTC.
26. Gorham, p.27.
27. Walter to Riss, 25 November 1904. BTC.
28. OCUM January 1904, p.80.
29. Diary, 3 March 1901.
30. Walter to Riss, 28 September 1904. COC.
31. Walter to Riss, 3 April 1905. COC.
32. From an undated cutting from the *Manchester Guardian* in COC.
33. Walter to Crystal, 1 July 1924. CEP.
34. Riss to Basil Ward, 24 June 1905. COC.
35. UR 3:12 (April 1906), p.5.
36. UR 3:16 (August 1906), p.395.
37. UR 3:16 (August 1906), p.397.
38. Ashby & Anderson, p.58.
39. Letter fragment in BTC.
40. Ashby & Anderson, p.59.
41. Walter to Humbersture dated 8 May 1906, PGP.
42. Mumford to Geddes, 14 April 1920. Novak, p.69.
43. *Hampshire Telegraph*, 27 October 1906, p.5.
44. *Hampshire Telegraph*, 22 June 1907, p.3.
45. DNB.
46. June 1907, CHA.

47 *Comradeship*, 1:1, p.2.
48 CHA annual report for 1911.
49 Hanley & Walton, p.168.
50 Hanley & Walton, p.169.
51 Letter dated 9 August 1907 from A. Cawthorne to *The Library World*, Vol. 10, pp.148–9.
52 Walter to Axon, 6 April 1908. Axon.
53 Walter to Geddes, 6 June 1908. PGP.
54 Walter to Axon, 20 September 1909. Axon.
55 Walter to Geddes, 13 January [1908]. PGP.
56 Stanley Nott's autograph book, 5 March 1908.
57 OPS, p.7.
58 Rosalind to Cynthia, late June 1908. BTC.
59 Riss to Basil Ward, 20 December 1907. BTC.
60 Walter to Riss, 23 August 1908. BTC.
61 RF, p.13.
62 Walter to Riss 23 August 1908. BTC.
63 Walter to Riss 23 August 1908. BTC.
64 RF, p.14.
65 Walter to Riss 11 September 1908. BTC.
66 Riss to Curt Dehn, September 1908. BTC.
67 RF, p.14.
68 OPS, p.11.

Peter Pan, pages 29–62

1   Barrie, the opening of Act IV of *Peter Pan*.
2   Diary for 1899.
3   Walter to Rosalind, 30 March 1909. BTC.
4   Rosalind to Curt Dehn, 30 October 1908. COC.
5   Letter dated 1 January 1906 in Russell, p.187.
6   Woolf, p.372.
7   Dakyns to his father, 8 October 1908. ALD, p.5.
8   ALD, p.5.
9   Riss to Curt Dehn, September 1908. BTC.
10 RF, p.16.
11 RF, pp.16–17.
12 OPS, p.9.
13 Rosalind to Curt Dehn, 30 October 1908. COC.
14 Irving to Mr Fuller, 9 January 1909. BTC.
15 RF, p.19.
16 Walter to Riss, June 1909. COC
17 Walter to Riss, 1 July 1909. BTC.
18 Diary, 20 January 1901.
19 Diary, 22 September 1901.
20 Kipling, vol. 4, p.480; 12 January 1918.
21 Kipling, vol. 4; letter of 25 December 1917.
22 Walter to Riss, ca November 1908. COC.
23 Walter to Riss, ca. November 1908. COC.
24 Walter to Riss, 21 April 1909. BTC.
25 Walter to Riss, 31 August 1909. COC.
26 Walter to Riss, autumn 1908. COC.
27 Cf. the opening of Act IV of *Peter Pan*.
28 Walter to Riss, 31 August 1909. COC.
29 Riss to Basil Ward, 20 September 1909. COC.
30 Walter to Riss, 31 August 1909. COC.
31 Riss to Basil Ward, 22 September 1909. BTC.
32 Boughton.
33 Walter to Riss, early October 1909. BTC.
34 Walter to Riss, 27 October 1909, BTC.
35 Walter to Rosalind, 8 October 1909. BTC.
36 Walter to Cynthia, 7 October 1909. COC.
37 Walter to Riss, 17 October 1909. COC.
38 Walter to Riss, 27 October 1909. COC.
39 Walter to his parents, 1 January 1915. COC.
40 Rosalind to Cynthia, 5 October 1909. COC.
41 Walter to Rosalind, 30 October 1909. BTC.
42 Walter to Rosalind, 30 October 1909. BTC.
43 Walter to Riss, 10 November 1909. COC.
44 Walter to Rosalind, 30 October 1909. BTC.
45 Diary, 7 October 1899.
46 Walter to Rosalind, 30 October 1909. BTC.
47 Walter to Riss 22 November 1909. COC.
48 ALD, p.8.
49 Walter to Riss for her birthday, September 1910. COC.
50 ALD, p.8.
51 ALD, p.8.
52 Walter to Riss for her birthday, September 1910. COC.
53 Basil Ward to Curt Dehn, 15 March 1916. BTC.
54 Walter to Riss for her birthday, September 1910. COC.
55 Dakyns to his father, 17 May 1910. ALD, p.8.

56 ALD, p.8.
57 Dakyns to Rosalind, 13 September 1910. BTC.
58 Monica Wilson to GPW, 19 October 2007.
59 Riss to Basil Ward, 26 December 1910. BTC.
60 ALD, p.9.
61 Riss to Basil Ward, 26 December 1910. BTC.
62 Walter to Geddes, 6 October 1911. PGP.
63 Walter to Geddes, 6 October 1911. PGP.
64 *Western Gazette,* 25 December 1914, p.2.
65 Riss to Basil Ward, 15 July 1911. BTC.
66 MMC.
67 Riss to Basil Ward, 15 July 1911. BTC.
68 *Musical Times,* 1 October 1911, p.654.
69 Riss to Basil Ward, 21 September 1911. COC.

Impresario, pages 63–104

1   Walter to Patrick Geddes, October 1911. PGP.
2   Walter to Riss, 23 August 1908. COC.
3   Walter to Geddes, 6 October 1911. PGP.
4   Walter to Geddes, 6 October 1911. PGP.
5   RF, p.25.
6   Frank Sorensen to Walter, 16 September 1911. FF3.
7   Walter to Cynthia, 14 December 1911. CEP.
8   Walter to Cynthia, 14 December 1911. CEP.
9   Riss to Basil Ward, Christmas 1911. COC.
10 Rosalind to her parents, January 1912. COC.
11 Rosalind to her parents, January 1912. COC.
12 Riss to Basil Ward, January 1912. COC.
13 Vassar *Miscellany,* Volume XLIV, No 3, 17 December 1914.
14 Boughton, from a cutting in COC.
15 H.T. Parker, Boston *Transcript,* 13 July 1913.
16 Walter to his mother, February 1912. COC.
17 Walter to his father, February 1912. COC.
18 New York *Times,* 9 June 1912.
19 Rosalind to Cynthia, April 1912. COC.
20 New York *Times,* 28 October 1912.
21 Washington *Post,* 8 August 1915.
22 Walter to his parents, April 1912. COC.
23 Walter to his parents, April 1912. COC.
24 Quoted in Sharpey-Schafer, p.29.
25 Walter to his parents, April 1912. COC.
26 Walter to his parents, 1 January 1915. COC.
27 Rosalind to Curt Dehn, 23 July 1912. BTC.
28 Riss to her mother, May 1912. COC.
29 Walter to his father, March 1912. COC.
30 From an undated press cutting in COC. Felix Borowski (1872–1956) was a composer and teacher who moved from Britain to the United States in 1896 to become Director of the Chicago Musical College.
31 From an undated press cutting in COC. Arthur Guiterman (1871–1943), best known for his humorous poems, was an editor of the *Woman's Home Companion* and the *Literary Digest.*
32 Springfield *Republican,* April 1912.
33 *Harper's Weekly,* 31 January 1914, p.25.
34 Riss to her parents, May 1912. COC.
35 Springfield *Daily News,* 30 April 1914, p.5.
36 H.K. Moderwell in a Boston newspaper, probably the *Evening Transcript,* April 1912, quoted by the *Springfield Republican* on 21 December 1913.
37 Arthur Guiterman in an undated press cutting in COC.
38 H.K. Moderwell in a Boston newspaper, probably the *Evening Transcript,* April 1912, quoted by the *Springfield Republican* on 21 December 1913.
39 New York *Herald,* mid-February 1914.
40 Arthur Guiterman in an undated press cutting in COC.
41 H.K. Moderwell in a Boston newspaper, probably the *Evening Transcript,* April 1912, quoted by the *Springfield Republican* on 21 December 1913.
42 Browne, p.141.
43 Rosalind to her parents, May 1914. COC.
44 Rosalind to her parents, spring 1914. COC.
45 Arthur Guiterman in an undated press cutting in COC.
46 Given Name Frequency Project, http://www.galbithink.org/names/us200.htm.
47 Dorothy to her parents, January 1913. COC.
48 Riss to Rosalind, 10 February 1913. BTC.
49 Walter to Riss, January 1913. COC.
50 Cynthia to her parents, April 1913. COC.
51 Rosalind to Riss, spring 1913. COC.
52 Dorothy to her parents, April 1913.

Walter Fuller

53 Walter to his parents, 31 March 1913. COC.
54 Information from Elise K. Kirk.
55 Dorothy to her parents, May 1913. COC.
56 Dorothy to her parents, May 1913. COC.
57 Cynthia to her parents, May 1913. COC.
58 Dorothy to her parents, May 1913. COC.
59 Walter to Riss, May 1913. COC
60 Browne, p.140.
61 Browne, *Recollections,* p.23.
62 Browne, p.141.
63 From a press cutting dated May 1913 in COC.
64 Washington *Herald*, 13 May 1913, p.4.
65 Walter to Riss, early 1913. COC.
66 Walter to his parents, December 1913. COC.
67 Walter to his parents, December 1913. COC.
68 Hapgood, pp.310–11.
69 *Harper's Weekly,* Vol. LVIII, 31 January 1914, pages 2 (photo) and 25 (article).
70 Browne, p.140.
71 Butcher, p.49.
72 Dorothy to Riss, mid-February 1914. COC.
73 *Who Was Who in American Art*, p.787.
75 Springfield *Republican,* 30 April 1914.
75 Derwent, p.125.
76 Rosalind to Riss, April 1913. COC.
77 Cynthia to her parents, May 1914. COC.
78 Walter to Riss, spring 1913. COC.
79 Dell, p.225.
80 Letter dated 4 June 1915, quoted in Whisnant, p.113.
81 *Survey,* Vol. 39, 30 March 1918, pp.718–19.
82 Goss, p.197.
83 Anon, p.641.

Peace Activist, pages 105–136

1 Quoted by Kosec, p.32.
2 Walter to his sisters, 3 August 1914. BTC.
3 Walter to Curt Dehn, 6 August 1914. BTC.
4 Walter to Curt Dehn, 6 August 1914. BTC.
5 Walter to Curt Dehn, 28 August 1914. BTC.
6 Dated 8 January 1912, it appeared in the New York *Times* on 22 January 1912.
7 RF, p.33.
8 Walter to Riss, November 1914, COC.
9 Rosalind to her parents, ca. 26 November 1914, COC.
10 Addams, *Peace,* p.1.
11 Van Voris, p.123.
12 Van Voris, p.123.
13 *Votes for Women*, 16 October 1914, p.21.
14 New York *Times,* 15 November 1914.
15 Walter to Curt 27 November 1914. BTC.
16 Dorothy to her parents, ca. 5 Dec 1914. COC.
17 Dorothy to her parents, February 1915. COC.
18 Rosalind to her parents, ca 6 December 1914. COC.
19 Cynthia to her parents, November 1914. COC.
20 Two letters from Dorothy dated 17 January 1915, merged. COC.
21 van Wienen, *Partisans,* p.62.
22 Dorothy to Curt Dehn, 17 January 1915. COC.
23 Walter to Riss, January 1915. COC.
24 Addams, *Hull*, p.122.
25 Personal communication, 2010.
26 van Wienen, *Rendez-vous,* p.291.
27 Degen, p.58.
28 Cynthia to her parents, late February 1915. COC.
29 Colorado *Gazette Telegraph,* 20 February 1915.
30 Cynthia to her parents, 3 April 1915. COC.
31 Walter to Riss, April 1915. COC
32 Walter to Basil Ward, April 1915. COC.
33 Walter to Riss, late April 1915. COC.
34 Degen, p.58.
35 Quoted in Degen, p.61.
36 Chicago *Record-Herald*, April 13, 1915 quoted by Degen, p.74.
37 Quoted back to Curt by Walter, 8 May 1915. COC.
38 John Ruskin, *The Crown of Wild Olive*; Walter's ellipses.
39 Walter to Curt Dehn, 8 May 1915. COC.
40 Rosalind to Riss, end of January 1915. COC.
41 Walter to Riss, 10 June 1915. COC.
42 Walter to Riss, 3 July 1915. COC.
43 Walter to Riss, 3 July 1915. COC.
44 Walter to Riss, mid-July 1915. COC
45 Boston *Globe*, 26 August 1915.
46 Walter to Riss, 10 June 1915. COC.

47 Detroit *Free Press*, 22 August 1915.
48 MacKaye, pp.25 and 26.
49 Ege, p.255.
50 *Professional Geographer*, Vol. 24, No 1, February 1972, p.30.
51 Addams, *Peace*, p.4.
52 Walter to his sisters, 21 July 1915. FF1.
53 Ege, p.256.
54 Dorothy to her parents, August 1915. COC.
55 Walter to his mother, September 1915. COC.
56 Dorothy to her parents, September 1915 COC.
57 Epigram number 186, quoted by H. W. C. D. in the *Manchester Guardian* of 4 August 1916.
58 Walter to Riss, autumn 1916. COC.

Propagandist, pages 137–180

1 Bernays, pp.9, 10, & 20.
2 New York *Times*, 22 May 1912.
3 *Oregonian*, 6 March 1910.
4 Grand Forks *Herald*, 23 January 1913.
5 Eastman, *Enjoyment*, p.107.
6 Eastman, *Enjoyment*, p.39.
7 Eastman, *Enjoyment*, p.85.
8 Quoted by Cook, p.5.
9 Diary, 12 January 1901.
10 New York *Times*, 28 January 1913.
11 Eastman, *Love*, p.443.
12 Eastman, *Enjoyment*, p.341.
13 Ida Harper. From ch. 31 of Volume VI: 1900–1920.
14 O'Neill, p.123.
15 Walter to Riss, mid-September 1915. COC.
16 Walter to his father, 20 September 1915. COC.
17 Walter to Riss, September 1915. COC.
18 Walter to Riss, September 1915. COC.
19 Eastman, *Love*, p.49.
20 Walter to Riss mid-September 1915 (COC), with a few words added from a letter (FF1) to his sisters of 22 September 1915.
21 Walter to his sisters, 21 September 1915. FF1.
22 Philadelphia *Inquirer*, 21 November 1915.
23 Rosalind to Walter, 11 November. FF5.
24 Dorothy to Walter, 13 November. FF6.
25 Browne, p.141.
26 Maurice Browne to Walter, 2 November 1915. FF3.
27 Dorothy to Walter, 25 October 1915. FF6.
28 Rosalind to Walter, 8 November 1915. FF5.
29 Walter to sisters, 26 October 1915. FF1.
30 Walter to his sisters, 15 November 1915. FF1.
31 Walter to his sisters, 1 November 1915. FF1.
32 Quoted from the New York *Sun* by several newspapers, including the *Kansas City Star*, 31 October 1915.
33 Walter to his sisters, 8 November 1915. FF1.
34 Walter to his sisters, 8 November 1915. FF1.
35 FF3.
36 New York *Times*, 16 November 1915.
37 Chicago *Daily Journal*, 2 November 1915.
38 Walter to his sisters, 21 November 1915. FF1.
39 Walter to Riss, ca. 5 December 1915. COC.
40 Villard, p.281.
41 Creel, p.4.
42 Dorothy to her parents, mid-December 1915. COC.
43 Cynthia to her mother, mid-December 1915. COC.
44 Cynthia to Riss, mid-December 1915. COC.
45 Dorothy to her mother, mid-December 1915. COC.
46 New York *Times*, 29 December 1915.
47 Dell, p.189.
48 Eastman, *Love*, p.72.
49 Bernays, p.9.
50 Sanders, p.120.
51 Sanders, p.127.
52 Cynthia to her mother, 8 January 1916. COC.
53 AUAM.
54 From a press cutting in the archives of the WPP.
55 Greensboro *Daily News*, 3 February, 1916.
56 Walter to Mrs Karsten, 2 March 1916. WPP, Box 4 (mf reel 12.11).
57 Walter to Mrs Karsten, 29 February 1916. WPP, Box 4 (mf reel 12.11).
58 *Survey*, XXXVI, 1 April 1916, p.37.
59 New York *Sun*, 2 April 1916, p.12.
60 Seattle *Daily Times*, 5 April 1916, p.6.

61 *Survey*, XXXVI, 6 May 1916, p.165.
62 *Survey*, XXXVI, 6 May 1916, p.165.
63 Kansas City *Star*, 29 February 1916.
64 New York *Times*, 5 April 1916.
65 New York *Evening Call*, 17 April 1916.
66 New York *Times*, 30 May 1916.
67 New York *Evening Call*, 17 April 1916.
68 Degen, p. 167.
69 New York *Morning Telegram*, 14 May, 1916.
70 Degen, pp.166 and, p.167.
71 WPP, Box 5, folder 2 (mf reel 12.11).
72 Transcript of meeting of 8 May 1916 made by Wilson's personal stenographer, and printed in the *Papers of Woodrow Wilson*; quoted in Chambers, p.73.
73 New York *Times*, 17 March 1916.
74 Springfield *Sunday Republican*, 23 April 1916.
75 Walter to Riss, April 1916. COC.
76 Rosalind to Riss, 28 April 1916. WHW.
77 Rosalind to Riss, 28 April 1916. WHW.
78 Cynthia to her mother, April 1916. COC.
79 Rosalind to Riss, April 1916. COC.
80 Walter to his sisters, 20 May 1916. BTC.
81 *Advocate of Peace*, October 1916, p.276.
82 *Advocate of Peace*, December 1916, p.343.
83 Walter to his sisters, 19 June 1916. BTC.
84 Walter to his sisters, 19 June 1916. BTC.
85 Cook, p.250.

Husband, pages 181–212

1 From President Wilson's address, 'Labor Must Be Free', to the American Federation of Labor Convention at Buffalo, New York, 12 November 1917, quoted in George Harper, p.274.
2 *Four Lights*, no. 17, 8 September 1917, quoting the *Bulletin* of the People's Council.
3 Quoted in Grubbs, p.24.
4 Dakyns to Rosalind, May 1916. COC.
5 *Manchester Guardian*, 19 August 1916.
6 Dakyns to Rosalind, 7 June 1916. BTC.
7 Dakyns to Rosalind, 13 June 1916. BTC.
8 Dakyns to Rosalind, 18 June 1916. BTC.
9 Dakyns to Rosalind, 26 June 1916. BTC.
10 Dakyns to Rosalind, 16 August 1916. BTC.
11 Rosalind to Cynthia, 8 August 1916. BTC.
12 Dakyns to Rosalind, 13 June 1916. BTC.
13 Dorothy to Rosalind, 29 July 1916. BTC.
14 Walter to Riss, August 1916. COC.
15 Mary Breck to Walter, 7 August 1916. FF4.
16 Cynthia to Rosalind, 11 August 1916. BTC.
17 Jeannette Peabody to Walter, 5 September 1916. FF3.
18 Walter to Rosalind, 6 July 1917. BTC.
19 WPP, box 14, folder 'D' (mf reel 12.20).
20 WPP, box 4, Crystal Eastman correspondence (mf reel 12.10).
21 New York *Times*, 14 November 1916.
22 Fort Wayne *Daily News*, 22 November 1916.
23 *Oregonian*, 13 November 1916.
24 Dell, p.309.
25 Eastman, *Love*, p.70.
26 Walter to Riss, mid-October 1916. CEP.
27 Walter to his mother, 26 October 1916, COC.
28 Dorothy to her parents, mid-November 1916. COC.
29 Dorothy to Riss, early November 1916. COC.
30 Cynthia to her mother, December 1916. COC.
31 Cook, p.15.
32 Eastman, *Enjoyment*, p.563.
33 Dakyns to Cynthia, 24 December 1916. BTC.
34 Dakyns to Rosalind, 1 September 1916. BTC.
35 Dakyns to Rosalind, autumn 1916. COC.
36 Rosalind to Curt Dehn, December 1916. COC.
37 Rosalind to Angell, 7 September 1916. WHW.
38 Rosalind to Angell, August 1917. WHW.
39 Eastman, *Enjoyment*, p.563.
40 Eastman, *Enjoyment*, p.563–4.
41 Eastman, *Enjoyment*, p.578.
42 Eastman, *Enjoyment*, p.586.
43 Eastman, *Enjoyment*, pp.578–9.
44 Rosalind to Max, 3 August 1946. Lilly.
45 RF, p.46b.
46 Eastman, *Love*, pp.503–4.
47 RF, p.138.
48 Cf. Eastman, *Love*, p.29.
49 Addams, *Peace*, p.113.
50 New York *Herald*, 15 July 1917.

51 AUAM minutes, 5 January 1917.
52 Fairbanks *Daily Times,* 15 September 1916.
53 'Bells are Ringing, Sailors Singing.' *Survey,* 20 January, 1917., p.454–5.
54 'The Lady with the Lamp.' *Masses,* January 1917, p.29.
55 Walter to his sisters, 20 January 1917. FF1.
56 Cf. Eastman, *Love,* p.151.
57 From the first page of first issue of *Four Lights,* 27 January 1917.
58 The quotes and the attributions are from *Four Lights,* no. 11, 16 June 1917.
59 Van Wienen, *Partisans,* p.174.
60 Norman Thomas to Major Atkinson at the BBC, 22 October 1927. COC.
61 Endres & Lueck, p.110.
62 *Four Lights,* no. 11, 13 July 1917.
63 Endres & Lueck, p.110.
64 Walter to Riss, ca. 5 December 1915. COC.
65 12 July 1917, punctuation added. WPP, Box 5, folder 13 (mf reel 12:4).
66 WPP, box 5, folder 13 (mf reel 12:4).
67 Barker-Benfield & Clinton, p.416.
68 Rappaport, p.212.
69 *Four Lights,* no. 13, 14 July 1917.
70 *Four Lights,* no. 13, 14 July 1917.
71 Grand Forks *Herald,* 3 February 1917.
72 Rosalind to Walter, 17 January 1917. FF5.
73 Rosalind to Walter, 13 February 1917. FF5.
74 Kalamazoo *Gazette,* 28 February 1917.
75 Rosalind to Walter, 3 or 4 March 1917. FF5.
76 CSD, 28 March 1917.

Father, pages 213–236

1. Walter to his parents, January 1918. COC.
2   The opening words of Max Eastman's speech to the First American Conference for Democracy and Terms of Peace, 30–31 May 1917, in *Report.*
3   Walter to Riss, 22 February 1917. COC.
4   Cynthia to her parents, 24 April 1917. COC.
5   Dorothy to Walter, from Dr Tait Mckenzie's home in Philadelphia, 30 March 1917. FF6.
6   Dorothy to her parents, late April 1917. COC.
7   Dorothy to Riss, early April 1917; her emphasis. COC.
8   Dorothy to her parents, late April 1917. COC.
9   *Survey,* vol 37, 24 February 1917, p.612.
10 Villard, p.322.
11 Peterson & Fite, pp.6–7.
12 Boston *Globe,* 10 April 1917.
13 Villard, p.323.
14 Villard, p.324.
15 Marchand, p.255, note 80, quoting an undated letter in the Pinchot Papers, in the Library of Congress.
16 Cook, p.5.
17 *Report,* p.4.
18 New York *Tribune,* 1 June 1917.
19 *Report,* p.3.
20 Villard, p.337.
21 *Report,* p.7.
22 Murphy, pp.40–41.
23 Patterson v. Colorado, 205 US 454 (1907), cited by Murphy, p.42.
24 Murphy, p.42.
25 See Peterson & Fite, passim, and in particular chapter 18, 'The American Reign of Terror.'
26 New York *Times,* 21 April 1917.
27 Eastman, *Love.,* p.35.
28 New York *Times* of 3 July 1917.
29 Witt, p.748.
30 Springfield *Daily News,* 5 June 1916, p.12.
31 New York *Sun,* 24 June 1917
32 FF7.
33 New York *Times,* 12 September 1918, quoting Attorney General Gregory.
34 Dakyns to Riss, 22 February 1917. FF8.
35 Rosalind to Dakyns, 18 April 1917. BTC.
36 Rosalind to Dakyns, 24 May 1917. BTC.)
37 Dakyns to Rosalind, mid-June 1917. COC.)
38 Walter to Rosalind, 6 July 1917. BTC.
39 Copied by Walter to Rosalind, 7 July 1917. BTC.
40 Copied by Walter to Rosalind, 7 July 1917. BTC.
41 Walter to Rosalind, 10 July 1917. BTC.
42 Rosalind's annotation to a letter from Walter to her, 13 July 1917. BTC.
43 Dakyns to Walter, 9 August 1917. FF8.
44 Dakyns to Walter, 9 August 1917. FF8.
45 Eliot, p.187; confirmed in Seymour-Jones, p.185.

46 RF, p.49.
47 Margaret Lane to Agnes Leach, 18 June 1917. WPP box 16, folder L (mf reel 12:21).
48 Crystal to WPP members. WPP records, box 5 folder 8 (mf reel 12:11).
49 New York *Times,* 30 August 1917.

New Worlder, pages 237–280

1 George Creel, in his first memorandum to President Wilson, 1917, quoted by Peterson, p.95.
2 Samuel Gompers in a statement widely quoted in the US press on 2 and 3 January 1918.
3 NCLB pamphlet, 'The Individual and the State: the problem as presented by the sentencing of Roger N. Baldwin,' p.4. DC.
5 Eastman, *Love,* p.49.
6 From the CPI files, quoted by Peterson & Fite, p.76.
7 Adams County *Free Press,* 4 July 1917, p.4.
8 Waterloo *Evening Courier,* 4 August 1917.
9 New York *Times,* 11 August 1917, p.6.
10 New York *Times,* 18 August 1917, p.6.
11 Numerous newspapers dated 9 October 1917.
12 New York *Tribune,* 10 August 1917, p.6.
13 Eastman, *Love,* pp.53–56.
14 New York *Times,* 31 August 1917.
15 Boston *Globe,* 31 August 1917.
16 *Four Lights,* no. 17, 8 September 1917.
17 Villard, p.339.
18 Murphy, p.89.
19 Murphy, p.126.
20 Villard, pp.338–9.
21 Freeberg, pp.88 and 102.
22 *Four Lights,* No 10, 2 June 1917.
23 WPP, box 5, folder 13 (mf reel 12:3).
24 Max to President Wilson, 12 July 1917. Link, p.165.
25 Baker, p.115n.
26 Eastman, *Love,* p.62.
27 Eastman, *Love,* p.63, and also Link, pp.210–11.
28 Eastman, *Love,* p.60.
29 Dell, p.327.
30 Eastman, *Love,* p.61.
31 Congressional Records, quoted by Peterson & Fite, p.100.
32 Eastman, *Love,* p.70.
33 Thomas to Major Atkinson at the BBC, 22 October 1927. COC.
34 Eastman, *Love,* p.70.
35 Eastman, *Love,* p.195.
36 New York *Times,* 18 July 1937.
37 Both letters are in MOH
38 Dell, p.334.
39 Walter to Crystal, 12 August 1918. CEP.
40 Walter to Crystal, not dated. CEP.
41 Walter to Crystal, dated 'Friday morning'. CEP.
42 Walter to Crystal, dated 'Friday afternoon'. CEP.
43 Pub.L. 65-150, 40 Stat. 553.
44 Swanberg, p.63.
45 Fleischman, p.21.
46 Fleischman, p.69. See also Swomley, p.7.
47 Gregory, p.51.
48 Eastman, *Love,* pp.79–81.
49 Rosalind to Cynthia, no date, August/September 1917. BTC.
50 Rosalind to Angell, 21 October 1917. WHW.
51 Dakyns to Walter, 9 August 1917. FF8.
52 Eliot, p.193.
53 RF, p.51.
54 Seymour-Jones, p.208.
55 RF, p.52.
56 Dakyns to Bertrand Russell, 27 June 1918. BRA item 710.048817.
57 RF, p.56.
58 Dos Passos, p.77.
59 *World Tomorrow,* January 1919, pp.20–21.
60 *World Tomorrow,* December 1918, p.296.
61 *World Tomorrow,* December 1918, p.296.
62 *World Tomorrow,* January 1919, p.21.
63 *World Tomorrow,* January 1919, p.20.
64 Cook, p.23.
65 Cook, pp.114–8.
66 Walter to Ogden, dated by context. CKO.
67 Walter to Ogden, dated Tuesday. CKO.
68 Gosciak, p.99.
69 Gosciak, p.100.
70 Langdon-Davies to deSilver, 30 June 1919. ACLU.

71 Walter to deSilver, 5 August 1919. ACLU.
72 Walter to deSilver, 5 August 1919. ACLU.
73 Walter to deSilver, 5 August 1919. ACLU.
74 Walter to deSilver, 5 August 1919. ACLU.
75 Langdon-Davies to deSilver, 13 August 1919. ACLU.
76 Langdon-Davies to deSilver, 27 August 1919. ACLU.
77 Manus to deSilver, 4 September 1919. ACLU.
78 Lansbury to Walter, 30 July 1919. FF8.
79 RF, p.64.
80 RF, pp.64–5.
81 RF, p.65.
82 RF, p.68.
83 See Eliot, p.309 and Seymour-Jones, p.241–2.
84 RF, p.69.
85 New York *Tribune*, 18 April 1920.
86 RF, p.69.
87 National Archives, ref. CAB 24/93, pages 1–2.
88 National archives, ref. KV 2/1101.
89 Callaghan & Morgan, p.561.
90 RF, p.70.
91 RF, p.80.
92 Rosalind to Edmund Wilson, 17 September 1967. EWP.
93 RF, p.81.
94 Fitzgerald, p.131.
95 Fitzgerald, pp.148 and 151 respectively.
96 Fitzgerald, p.151.
97 Rosalind to Edmund Wilson, 17 September 1967, repeating Wilson's words to her, and he was repeating what Fitzgerald had told him. EWP.
98 Kuehl & Bryer, pp.59–60.
99 RF, p.82.
100 Mellow, p.84.
101 Law, p.1326.

Rewrite Man, pages 281–312

1 Powys, p.103.
2 Tanselle, p.154.
3 Lissner, p.155.
4 Eastman, *Love*, p.180.
5 Crystal to Cynthia, 27 September 1920. RYC.
6 Nock, p.169.
7 Neilson, *Story*, pp.28–29.
8 Nock, p.170.
9 Mumford to Geddes, 14 April 1920, in Novak, p.69.
10 Mumford, My Works, p.70.
11 Mumford, *Sketches*, p.353–4.
12 Mumford, *My Works*, p.80.
13 Spiller, p.359.
14 *Freeman*, 11 August 1920, p.506.
15 Spiller, pp.2–3.
16 Mumford, *Sketches*, p.368.
17 Nock, p.171.
18 Lora & Longton, p.313.
19 Neilson, *Story*, p.30.
20 Lora & Longton, p.312.
21 Lissner, p.155.
22 *New Republic*, 24 March 1920.
23 Information from Neilson, 'Literary Talent.'
24 Powys, pp. 103–4.
25 New York *Tribune*, 18 April 1920.
26 Paymer, p.24.
27 *Freeman*, 14 April 1920, pp.111–12.
28 Dakyns to his sister Frances, 21 June 1920. ALD, p.10.
29 Dakyns to his sister Frances, quoted but not dated in ALD.
30 Dakyns to Cynthia, September 1927. COC.
31 RF, p.73.
32 RF, p.94.
33 ALD, p.12.
34 RF, p.92.
35 'The Camera and the Scene,' March 1924, quoted in Enyeart, pp.25–26.
36 RF, p.93.
37 Brooks, p.57.
38 Turner, p.80.
39 Brooks, p.62.
40 Neilson, *Story*, p.29.
41 Nock, pp.168–70.
42 Crystal to Cynthia, 1 November 1920. RYC.
43 Neilson, *Story*, p.35.
44 *Freeman*, 1 September 1920, p.592.
45 *Freeman*, June 23 1920.
46 *Freeman*, 8 December 1920, p.307.
47 *Freeman*, 16 June 1920, p.330.

48 *Freeman,* 5 May 1920, p.186.
49 *Freeman,* 1 September 1920, p.578.
50 *Freeman,* 17 August 1921, p.531.
51 *Freeman,* 24 November 1920, pp.258–9.
52 *Freeman,* 16 June 1920, p.329.
53 *Freeman,* 1 September 1920, p.578.
54 *Freeman,* 12 October 1921, p.98.
55 *Freeman,* 4 May 1921, p.170.
56 *Freeman,* 8 September 1920, p.616–7.
57 Turner, p.169.
58 *New Republic*, 14 December 1927.
59 Novak, pp.105–6.
60 *Freeman*, 11 August 1920, p.506.
61 From a press release printed in many newspapers on 10 April 1921.
62 *New York Times*, 30 December 1910.
63 Geroid Robinson in the *Freeman*, 1 June 1921, p.269.
64 Seventy-First Congress, Third Session Part I. Volume No. 5, (December, 1930).
65 Cook, p.77.
66 Cook, p.77.
67 Cook, p.78.
68 Cook, p.81.
69 Cook, p.80.
70 Eastman, *Enjoyment,* p.15.
71 Cook, p.80.
72 Cook, p.83.
73 RF, 137.
74 Telegram from Crystal to Walter, 17 August 1920. FF8.
75 Eastman, *Enjoyment*, p.39.
76 Crystal to Cynthia, September, 1921. RYC.
77 Crystal to Cynthia, 1 November 1920. RYC.
78 Mumford, *Sketches,* p.297.
79 Quoted from http://brightlightsfilm.com/53/53charlie.php. Consulted 25 April 2013.
80 Crystal to Florence Deshon, 17 August 1920. CEP.
81 Eastman, *Love,* p.206.
82 RF, pp.78–79.
83 Eastman, *Love,* p.279.
84 Sheridan, p.71.
85 Sheridan, p.129.
86 Sheridan, p.131.
87 Sheridan, pp.129–130.
88 Crystal to Cynthia, 21 March 1922. RYC.
89 Walter to his parents, 28 March 1922. RYC.
90 Walter to Riss, December 1915. COC.
91 RF, p.100–01.
92 RF, p.103.
93 Barrymore to Michael Strange, quoted by Morrison, p.133.
94 Blanche Yurka, *Bohemian Girl,* quoted by Morrison, p.134.
95 RF, p.103.
96 Morrison, pp.129–30.
97 John Burnham, *Jelliffe: American Psychiatrist and Physician,* quoted by Morrison, p.131.
98 RF, p.100.
99 Morrison, p.131.
100 Morrison, p.131.
101 RF, p.103.
102 *New Republic,* 6 December 1922.
103 RF, p.145.
104 RF, p.103.
105 Browne, p.141.
106 RF, p.106.
107 *Hamlet,* Act 1, Sc. 2.

Radio Man, pages 313–357

1 Cook, p.28.
2 Crystal to Walter, 14 April 1922. Cook, p.28, and COC.
3 Neilson, *Story*, pp.29–35.
4 Crystal to Walter, 14 April 1922. COC.
5 Nott, Memories I, p.7.
6 Nott, Memories I, p.7.
7 Hunt, p.248.
8 Hunt, p.250.
9 Hunt, p.251.
10 Schorer, p.330. I have been unable to trace the letter that Mark Schorer quotes from.
11 Nott, Memories I, pp. 7–8.
12 Nott, Memories I, p.7.
13 This rate is based on a letter from Walter to Bertrand Russell, dated 12 April 1923. BRA.
14 Undated letter from Walter to C. K. Ogden. CKO.

References

15 Nott, Memories I, p.7.
16 Eliot, p.603.
17 *Pravda* No. 254, 10 November 1922. See http://www.marxists.org/archive/lenin/works/1922/oct/ 27.htm (consulted 6 January 2014).
18 Nott, Memories II, p.49.
19 Crystal to Walter, undated, in COC.
20 Crystal to Walter, undated, in COC.
21 Crystal to Walter, undated, in COC.
22 Crystal to Walter, 23 August 1922, RYC.
23 Crystal to Cynthia, 9 September [1922]. RYC.
24 Nott, Memories II, p.49.
25 *The Times*, 16 September 1927, p.13.
26 Gorham, p.15.
27 Gorham, p.11.
28 Gorham, p.13.
29 Walter to S.S. Koteliansky, 30 April 1925. SSK.
30 RF, p.107.
31 *New Republic*, 'Suffragists Ten Years After,' 27 June 1923.
32 Nott, *Memories* I, p.50.
33 Eastman, *Love*, p.440.
34 Walter to C.K. Ogden, undated letter. CKO.
35 Eastman, *Love*, p.440.
36 Walter to Crystal, 1 July 1924. CEP.
37 Walter to Crystal, 1 July 1924. CEP.
38 Crystal to Cynthia, not dated. RYC.
39 Walter to Crystal, 1 July 1924. CEP.
40 Crystal to Walter, 4 November 1924, RYC.
41 Crystal to Cynthia, not dated. COC.
42 Crystal to Walter, 4 November 1924, RYC.
43 Crystal to Walter, 4 November 1924, RYC.
44 Crystal to Walter, 14 December 1924, RYC.
45 *The Times*, 16 September 1927.
46 Gorham, pp.11–12.
47 Gorham, p.12.
48 Reith, in a 1925 *Memorandum*, quoted in Briggs, p.7.
49 From a speech by Reith on 16 December 1926, quoted in Briggs, p.7.
50 Lambert, p.34.
51 Gorham, p.27.
52 Gorham, p.18.
53 Gorham, p.14.
54 Lambert, p.45.
55 Gorham, pp.18–19.
56 Gorham, pp.19–20.
57 *RF*, p.126.
58 Document WAC/R34/252/Fuller in BWAC.
59 Document WAC/R34/252/Fuller in BWAC.
60 Monica Wilson to GPW, letter dated 30 September 2007.
61 Gorham, p.12.
62 Briggs, p.87.
63 http://www.colander.org/radiotimes/ consulted 10 April 2013.
64 Crocombe in *Radio Times*, quoted by Currie, p.9.
65 *Manchester Guardian*, 16 September 1927.
66 Wolfe, p. 57.
67 Maschwitz, p.52.
68 Gorham, pp.22.
69 Walter to Cynthia and Curt, 3 April 1926. COC.
70 Reith, 'Parliamentary Affairs,' *Forsan* (Winter 1963–4), quoted by Tracey, p.11.
71 Briggs, p.368.
72 Herts and Essex *Observer*, 15 May 1926.
73 Lambert, p.93.
74 Kapp, p.129.
75 Kapp, p.128.
76 Gorham, p.18.
77 Crystal to Ruth Pickering, undated letter.
78 Gorham, pp.26–27.
79 Gorham, p.25.
80 Internal memo dated 19 November 1926. BWAC.
81 Maschwitz, p.51.
82 Gorham, p.31.
83 Lambert, pp.92–93.
84 Gorham, p.26.
85 Walter to Hilda Hankinson, mid-June 1927, COC.
86 Walter to his mother, mid-July 1927, COC.
87 Walter to Cynthia, 22 or 23 June 1927. COC.
88 Walter to his parents, letter dated Thursday, RYC.
89 Lambert, pp.93–94.
90 Cook, p.33.
91 ODC.

Walter Fuller

92 Crystal to Walter's mother, 15 July [1927]. RYC.
93 Walter to Crystal, 'Thursday night' [25 August 1927]. CEP.
94 RF, p.109.
95 Enyeart, p.52.
96 Walter to Rosalind, July/August 1927. COC.
97 Walter to Rosalind, August 1927. COC.
98 RF, pp.137–8.
99 RF, p.138.

Epilogue, pages 359–380

1 Norman Thomas to Major Atkinson of the BBC, September 1927. COC.
2 *Radio Times,* 30 September 1927, quoted in Currie, p.22.
3 *New Republic,* 14 December 1927.
4 Mr Fuller to Walter, 6 September 1927. FF8.
5 RF, p.140.
6 Gorham, p.27.
7 Gorham, p.27.
8 *Radio Times,* 30 September 1927, quoted in Currie, p.22.
9 Lambert, pp.93–94.
10 Maschwitz, p.51.
11 Jeffrey to Max, 11 September 1949. Lilly.
12 Crystal to Charles Hallinan, 5 December 1927. HHH.
13 Crystal to Cynthia, New Year's Eve, 1927. RYC.
14 Crystal to Rosalind, September 1927. BTC.
15 Crystal to Cynthia, 11 October 1927, quoted by Cook p.34.
16 Crystal to Cynthia, October 1927. RYC.
17 Crystal to Charles Hallinan, 5 December 1927. HHH.
18 Crystal to Charles Hallinan, 5 December 1927. HHH.
19 Crystal to Charles Hallinan, 5 December 1927. HHH.
20 *Music Supervisors' Journal,* Vol. 16, No. 2 (December 1929), p.91.
21 Riss to Jack Odell, 28 May 1928. COC.
22 Rosalind to Norman Angell, ca. 22 September 1927. BTC.
23 RF, p.142.
24 *The Times,* 16 November 1927, p.12.
25 RF, p.142.
26 RF, p.143.
27 RF, p.144.
28 *Daily Express,* 16 November 1927.
29 RF, p.141.
30 Beaton, p.40.
31 Cecil Beaton to Rosalind, 24 April 1949. BTC.
32 Conolly, p.28.
33 Browne, p.301.
34 Cook, p.34.
35 Crystal to Cynthia, New Year's Eve, 1927. RYC.
36 Max to Hazel Hunkins Hallinan, 2 September 1928 (postmark). HHH.
37 Crystal to her children, no date. COC.
38 Crystal to Cynthia, 27 September 1920. RYC.
39 Crystal to Cynthia, New Year's Eve, 1927. RYC.
40 Walter to Cynthia, 22 or 23 June 1927. COC.
41 Angell, p.292.
42 Angell, pp.292–3.
43 *Glasgow Herald,* 5 March 1935.
44 *The Times,* 8 September 1934.
45 *The Times,* 2 November 1934.
46 *Manchester Guardian,* 13 May 1939.
47 *Red Shoes.* New York: The Woman's Press, 1930.
48 Crystal to Cynthia, August 1928. COC.
49 Nott, *Teachings,* p.120.
50 *The Times,* 22 January 1968.
51 RF, p.257.
52 Hazel Hunkins Hallinan to Joyce Fuller, 9 July 1979. HHH.
53 cf. Walter to Patrick Geddes, October 1911, quoted on page 63.
54 Walter to Curt Dehn, August 1914. See p.107.
55 *New Republic,* 14 December 1927.

Index

All Walter's signed contributions to periodicals are posted on this book's website www.TheLetterworthPress.org/WalterFuller/Documents&images.html
The *University Review* and the *Readers' Review* are indexed there too:
www.TheLetterworthPress.org/WalterFuller/Indexes/URindex.html, and
www.TheLetterworthPress.org/WalterFuller/Indexes/RRindex.html

ACLU, *see* American Civil Liberties Union
Addams, Jane, 106 (illustration), 113–14, 118–19, 126–8, 135, 147, 154, 156–7, 190, 201, 203, 210, 225–6n, 248
Albert, Prince of Wales, 262n
Allen, Mary Hope, 328
American Civil Liberties Union (ACLU), 226, 252, 271, 276, 301, 371
American Union Against Militarism (AUAM), 160, 161, 163–6, 168, 171–3, 176–7, 179, 189, 194, 201–03, 218–20, 225–7, 243, 247–8, 318, 370n
Anderson, Murray, 290–1
Angell, Pauline Knickerbocker, 227, 234, 254
Angell, Norman, 53, 109, 125, 130n, 135, 151, 153, 160, 171–2, 175, 177, 185–6, 197, 202, 208, 230; holiday with the Fuller sisters on Lake Champlain 233–4; 235–6, 260–4, 271–2, 275, 289, 297, 329, 357, 365, 372, 379
Anthony, Katharine Susan, 210, 334
Atherton, Frederick and Ellen, 89, 96
Atherton, Percy Lee, 89, 95, 102–03
AUAM, *see* American Union Against Militarism

Baker, Ray Stannard, 68, 79, 144, 150, 158, 161, 179, 246

Balch, Emily Greene, 203, 220, 222, 225n, 248
Baldwin, Roger Nash, 194, 225–7, 251, 252, 301
Barrett, Roger and Katharine (née Ellis), aka Gypsy Davie and Lady Ba, 132, 133, 135, 189, 374–6
Ba, Lady, *see* Katharine BARRETT
Barbusse, Henri, 249
Barnes, William, 57, 289
Barrie, J. M., 29, 33, 43, 272
Barry, Griffin, 101, 179, 260, 264, 274–5, 319, 329, 368
Barrymore, John, 309–12, 329
Baynes, Dr H.G., 320
Beaton, Cecil, 367
Beatty, Bessie, 332
BBC, 328–49, 351–4, 361–7, 370, 374, 379
Beethoven, Ludwig van, 37, 41, 57, 100, 117, 119–20, 130, 224, 351
Benedict, Wallace J., 141, 170, 182, 190, 192, 194
Bennett, Arnold, 162n, 270, 273
Berkman, Alexander, 227
Bernays, Edward L., 137, 162, 168, 169, 170, 253n, 341n
Berrington, Adrian, 32, 58
Berrington, Emilia (pseudonym of Rosalind FULLER), 32, 247

403

Walter Fuller

Best, Mary Agnes (aka Mollie), 71, 75, 98, 107, 109, 112, 159, 289
Billson, Joan, 325n, 350. *See also* MALLESON
Binney, Constance, 152–3, 156, 194
Binyon, Laurence, 35, 110, 112, 155
Black, Dora, *see* Dora RUSSELL
Blakeston, Oswell, 367
Boissevain, Eugen, 191, 259, 305
Boughton, Alice, 44, 64, 72, 85
Branford, Victor, 31, 285
Breck, Mary, 87n, 94, 98, 107, 112, 159, 165, 173, 187–8, 195, 196, 229, 235–6
Briggs, Harold and Lionel, 146n
Brooke, Rupert, 91, 97n
Brooks, Van Wyck, 285–6, 288, 294, 296, 299, 315
Browne, Maurice, 83–4, 86, 91, 93, 97, 118, 152–4, 289, 311, 367–8
Bruguière, Francis, 292–4, 339; exhibits in New York and Berlin 356–7; 366–7, 373–4, 376–7
Bryant, Louise, 254, 332n
Bulletin (of the People's Council), 181, 221–2, 239, 241–3
Burchenal, Elizabeth and family, 70–1, 85, 87, 93–4, 100, 155, 179
Burgess, Mrs, 88, 98, 109, 125
Burleson, Albert S. (Postmaster General), 209, 246, 258, 265
Butcher, Fanny, 97n

Cambridge Magazine, 269–70
Cannan, Gilbert, 272, 273, 289
Captain, and Captain Hook, *see* Hamilton IRVING
Carpendale, Admiral, 337, 352
Carrington, Margaret Huston, 309–10
Catt, Carrie Chapman, 113–4, 119, 217
CHA, *see* Co-operative Holidays Association
Chaplin, Charlie, 248, 306–07
Chesterton, G. K., 162n, 248, 286n
Chubb, Percival, 92–3, 118
Civil Liberties Bureau, 225–7, 251, 370; *see also* National Civil Liberties Bureau (NCLB)
Cloud, Yvonne, 375n; pseudonym of Yvonne KAPP
Co-operative Holidays Association (CHA), 19–20, 34
Committee on Public Information (CPI, aka Creel Committee), 158, 168, 203, 233, 240

Comradeship, 19–20, 22, 379
Creel Committee, *see* Committee on Public Information
Creel, George, 237, 240, 241, 245
Crocombe, Leonard, 344, 351

Daily Eagle (Brooklyn), 157n, 329
Dakyns, Arthur L., 1, 33–6, 41, 53, 55, proposes marriage to Rosalind 56; 57; his father dies 60; 110, 184–9, 195–8; 'America-or-me ultimatum' 228–35, 261–3; threatens suicide 275; 277; in New York 290–2, 320, 329
Dakyns, Henry, 33, 35, 229
Dalcroze, Emile Jacques, 45, 262
Dana, Henry Wadsworth Longfellow (aka Harry 220, 221
Dana, Edmund Trowbridge Dana III (aka Ned), 77
Darrow, Clarence, 211, 226n, 235n
Debs, Eugene, 244, 248, 253 (illustration), 258, 296
Degen, Marie Louise, 121, 125
Dehn, Conrad (son of Cynthia), 339, 377
Dehn cousins: Edward, Dickie, Frank, Fred (and his son Paul), Harold (reported killed 185), and Tom 33
Dehn, Curt, 8, 11–12, 14, 18, 23, 26–7, 31–3, 35–7, 41, 53, 55, 60, 100, 107, 109, 110, 128, 184–6, 197, 232; marries Cynthia 260; 268, 292, 339, 340, 347, 363, 374–7
Dehn, Cynthia (née Fuller), born 4; Curt Dehn determines to marry her 12; learning the piano 45; replaces Riss as the Fuller Sisters' harpist 85–6 *et seq*; seeks work in England 260; marries Curt Dehn 260; illustrates folksongs and ballads 374; adopts pseudonym Francyn 375; affair with Mervyn Peake 377; death 377
Dehn, Monica, *see* Monica WILSON
DeLamarter, Eric, 91
Dell, Floyd, 101, 161, 191n, 254
Dennett, Mary Ware, 242
Deshon, Florence, 235, 255–7, 259, 268, 279, 283, 305; affair with Charlie Chaplin 306; death 307; 309
deSilver, Albert, 189, 226n, 251–2, 271, 273, 275
Dickens, Charles, 3, 85, 109n, 170, 249, 286n, 298, 354, 378

Index

Dickinson, Lowes, 128, 273
Donnelly, Dorothy, 275
Dorn, Marion, 367
Dos Passos, John, 264, 275, 289
Dostoyevsky, Fyodor, 328, 378
Doty, Madeleine, 205, 252
Draper, Ruth, 339, 377
Dudley, Ada Chase, 242, 245

Eager Heart (play by Alice Buckton), 41, 52, 57
Eastman, Catherine Crystal (legally Crystal Fuller, Walter's wife), 59, 114, 119, 132, 136; family background 139–41; writes film scenario with Walter 144–51; marries Walter 189; birth of Jeffrey 214–16; and civil liberties 225–7; sets up *The Liberator* 249; and Equal Rights Amendment 283; birth of Annis 308–09; lives in England 325–311; in England again 335–56; death 369
Eastman, Eliena (née Krylenko), 330–1, 350, 371
Eastman, Max, 140; makes love with Rosalind 196–9; 198 (illustration); takes over Walter's office 204n; tried under the Espionage Act 246; leaves for Europe and Russia 307; marries Eliena Krylenko in Moscow 330; returns via England 331; places Crystal and Walter's children with Agnes Leach 370; describes Crystal's death 369
Eliot, T.S. and Vivien, 233, 263, 275, 285, 320, 327
Ellis, Katharine, 133. See BARRETT
Espionage Act, 178, 223, 227, 243–6, 252, 257
Evans (of *The Nation*), 34, 35
Evans, Edmund C., 226n
Evans, Edward, 248
Ewer, Norman (aka Trilby), 111, 112, 117, 120, 274–6, 289, 319, 329

Farbman, Michael, 320
Farnsworth, Prof Charles, 67, 68, 70, 72
Fellowship of Reconciliation (FoR), 124, 248, 257, 258
Filene, Edward, 89, 94, 95, 135, 253, 256
Fitzgerald, Scott, 278, 279, 340, 378n
'Five Souls' (poem by Norman Ewer), 111; set to music by Rosalind 117; 118–20, 122, 125, 144, 158, 177, 229, 274

Folies Bergère, 263, 275, 290
Ford, Ford Madox (aka Max Hueffer), 35, 162n
Ford, Henry, 61, 126, 131, 149, 153–7, 159, 160, 203
Ford Peace Ship (*Oscar II*), 156, 157, 190n
Four Lights, 181, 204–11, 224, 227, 242–5, 268, 270, 296, 334, 380
Fourteen Points (President Wilson's statement of 8 January 1918), 128, 241. *See also* Woodrow WILSON)
France, Anatole, 15, 254
Frankfurter, Felix, 276
Freeman, The, 242, 281, 284–91, 294–6, 298–302, 309, 315–19, 329, 380
Freeman, Elizabeth, 242
Freud, Sigmund, 169–170, 200, 310
Friday Club, 34–5, 110
Friedley, Durr, 71, 75–6, 99, 191
Frothingham, Frances, 119–20
Fry, Roger Eliot, 34n, 260
Fuller, Annis Diana (Walter's daughter), birth 308–09; 324–6, 330, 333–4, 347, 350, 355, 369, 370, 371–2
Fuller, Crystal, *see* Catherine Crystal EASTMAN
Fuller, Cynthia Rose, *see* Cynthia DEHN
Fuller, Dorothy Daisy, *see* Dorothy ODELL
Fuller, Elizabeth (Walter's mother), 5, 23, 27, 37, 59, 61, 267, 361
Fuller, Jeffrey (Walter's son, aka Jeff), birth 214–16; 219, 234, 250–1, 253, 255–7, 260, 267–8, 279, 291, 295, 302, 305, 324–6, 330, 334, 342, 346–7, 350, 355, 363, 369, 370–72
Fuller, Oriska Violet (aka Riss), *see* Riss WARD
Fuller, Rosalind Ivy (stage name Rosalinde Fuller), born 4; dislikes performing on stage 4; plays Beethoven 37; attends Woodbrooke 43–5, 48, 50–2; sings for Cecil Sharp 59, 61; sets 'Five Souls' to Beethoven 117–18; makes love with Max Eastman 196–9; and Prince Albert 262n; joins *Folies Bergère* 264; affair with Scott Fitzgerald 277–9; stage debut in New York 290–1; meets Francis Bruguière 292; plays Ophelia to John Barrymore's Hamlet 309–12; returns to England 356; present at Walter's death 357; career in Britain 366, 368, 375, 377; international solo career 377–8; MBE 378; death 378

405

Fuller, Walter Gladstone, studies medicine 5–10; edits OCUM and organizes students 6–10; edits UR 11, 14–17, 53; recognizes himself in Peter Pan 12–13; edits *Comradeship* 19–20; edits RR 20–22, 53–54; encourages Riss to collect folksongs 26, 50–51; falls for Rosamond Impey 40–42, 55; writes *A Masque of the Seasons* 57; *Masque* performed 58; arrives New York 66; almost dies of blood poisoning 74; directs his sisters' singing 81–84; meets Crystal Eastman 136; devises War-against-War Exhibition 146–9; marries Crystal 188–9; edits *Four Lights* 204 et seq; edits *The World Tomorrow* 248–9, 257–9, 287; meets C. K. Ogden 269–70; facilitates 'Anglo-American Tradition of Liberty' conference 271–3; edits *The Freeman* 284–90; contributes to *The Freeman* 294–9; helps found the Intercollegiate Liberal League 301–2; leaves New York 309; runs Transatlantic Literary Agency 318–21, 326; edits *Weekly Westminster* 327–9; writes for the Brooklyn *Daily Eagle* 329; works for BBC 335–42; appointed editor of *Radio Times* 345; in the General Strike 347–50; redesigns *Radio Times* 351–3; *Radio Times* in Braille 353; advises on *The Listener* 353; death 357

Fuller, Walter Henry (Walter's father), 3, 5, 7, 8, 9, 18; goes bankrupt, seeks work 22–7; 31, 37, 38, 39, 47, 52, 59, 60, 107, 172, 267, 342, 345, 346, 347, 352

Gannett, Lewis, 264n
Geddes, Sir Patrick, 15, 17, 19, 20, 22, 31–2, 40–1, 45–6, 47, 52, 57, 63, 65, 252n, 285, 293, 300
George V, King, 98, 339
George VI, King, 262n
George, Henry, 147, 284
Gilman, Charlotte Perkins, 113, 301
Goldman, Emma, 227
Gomme, Laurence and Alice, 10, 32n
Gompers, Samuel, 237, 240, 241
Gorham, Maurice, 327–8, 335, 337–8, 342, 345, 347, 351–2, 361, 363
Gosciak, Josh, 270–1
Gray, H. W. (publisher and father of Constance BINNEY), 116, 152

Gulick, Luther, 67, 70n, 75, 95n, 101, 149n
Gurdjieff, George, 326, 327, 350, 375
Guthrie, Woody, 104, 133n
Gypsy Davie, *see* Robert BARRETT

Hallinan, Charles Thomas (aka Hal), 161, 163, 166, 172, 173; witness at Crystal and Walter's wedding 189; 202, 216, 225n, 289, 318, 323, 325, 326, 330, 363, 372, 378
Hankinson, Annie, 40
Hankinson, Frederick, 40n
Hankinson, Hilda, 8, 40, 41, 42, 60, 146n, 354
Hankinson, William (aka Bill – to Walter – and Willie – to his family) 6, 8, 31, 40, 107, 110, 184, 269n, 354
Hapgood, Norman, 81, 95, 150, 154, 179
Hardy, Thomas, 26, 44, 45, 208, 270, 289, 339
Harper's Bazaar / Magazine / Weekly, 44, 72, 81, 95, 96, 144n, 293
Herendeen, Anne, 206, 319
Hillquit, Morris, 171, 220, 221, 247, 254n, 301n, 340
Hobson, J. A., 16, 20, 22, 109, 167, 273
Holliday, Jessie, 23–24, 57, 76–7
Holmes, Rev. John Haynes, 105, 161, 171, 201, 225n, 226n, 248, 258, 301
Hoover, Edgar J., 283
Hopkins, Arthur, 194, 309–11
Hudson, Manley O., 201, 233, 248, 252, 264
Hull, Professor William Isaac, 128, 144, 203, 221
Hunkins-Hallinan, Hazel, 218, 318, 325, 330, 365, 372, 378
Hunt, Frazier, 317–19, 325, 331

Impey, Rosamond, 40, 41–3, 45, 49–50, 55, 60, 146, 193, 368
Irving, Hamilton (aka Captain, short for Captain Hook), 7, 11, 14, 18, 23, 36, 38; marries Dorothy 39; abandons her 59; divorce and remarriage 60; 68, 71, 96, 186, 199
Irwin, Elisabeth, 210

'Jingo', 167, 168, 169 (illustration), 170, 178, 227
Jones, Robert Edmond (aka Bobbie), 159, 191, 195, 293, 310
Jones, Rufus M., 248
Jordan, Dr David Starr, 117, 161, 181, 205, 225n
Jung, Carl Gustav, 320

Index

Kapp, Yvonne (pseudonym: Yvonne Cloud), 350, 375n
Kauffer, Edward McKnight, 351, 367
Keller, Helen, 97n, 109n, 163
Kellogg, Paul, 141, 161, 172–3, 201–03, 225, 226n, 315–16, 350, 355, 370
Kenton, Edna, 207
Kipling, Rudyard, 40, 162n, 208, 378
Knight, Holford, 272
Koteliansky, S. S., 328
Kuhlmann, Erika, 205

Lady Ba, *see* Katharine BARRETT
La Follette, Robert, 93, 126, 217, 225n, 287, 315
La Follette, Suzanne (aka Clara), 285, 287, 315
La Follette's Magazine, 165
la Motte, Ellen, 204, 249
Lambert, Richard, 350, 353, 354, 362
Lane, Margaret, 189, 209, 245; with her husband Dan and son David 253; 254; David plays with Jeffrey 305; 307
Langdon-Davies, B. N., 130n, 262n, 271–3
Lansbury, George, 273–4
Lawrence, D. H., 58, 329
Lawrence, Frederick, *see* PETHICK-LAWRENCE
Leach, Agnes Brown, 218, 226n, 370
Lee, Ivy Ledbetter, 161
Lee, Stanley, 154, 160
Lenin, Vladimir, 16, 308, 320, 332
Lewis, Cecil, 340, 367
Lewis, Sinclair, 299, 317, 318
Liberator, The, 161, 204, 249–50, 254–7, 266, 269n, 270, 279, 283, 296, 307, 308, 318
Lippmann, Walter, 264, 301
Lochner, Louis, 127, 141, 153–4, 157, 161, 201, 219, 221, 239, 241–2
Lodge, Sir Oliver, 15, 39
Lucy Stone League, 283
Lusk Report, 223, 240, 243, 334

MacDowell Colony, 229–30, 260
MacKaye, Percy and Marion, 125, 131–3, 135, 151, 159, 179n
Magnes, Rabbi Judah, 221, 252
Malleson, Miles, 325, 350, 373. *See also* Joan BILLSON
Malone, Dudley Field, 235, 247, 254, 291, 307, 326

Mansfield, Katherine, 327, 377
Manus, Marjorie, 262, 273
Maschwitz, Eric, 352, 363
Masefield, John, ixx, 162, 163, 270, 273, 331
Massingham, Dorothy, 320
Masque of the Seasons, A, 57–8
Masses, The, 93, 137, 142, 151n, 159, 162, 169, 178, 192n, 204, 207, 216n, 230, 246–7, 249–52, 254n
McKay, Claude, 270, 320
McKenzie, Dr & Mrs Robert Tait, 99, 196
Mencken, H. L., 251, 289, 299
Merrie England (comic opera by Edward German), 59–60, 92, 373
Meynell, Francis and Vera, 331
Milholland, Inez, 139, 157, 190, 259
Miller, Hugh, 320
Millet, Josiah 78, 95, 98, 99; and his brother Francis Davis (aka Frank), 78n
Moderwell, H. K. (the pen-name of Hiram K. MOTHERWELL), 82, 84, 206, 318, 325
'Monkey Trial', 92, 211, 235n
Moore, Howard, 265
Morison, Stanley, 319
Motherwell, Hiram Kelly, 151, 178 (*see also* Moderwell)
Muck, Karl, 125, 224
Muir, Edwin, 289, 353
Muir, Ramsay, 15, 327, 342
Mumford, Lewis, 17, 285–7, 289, 299, 300, 305
Murray, Dr Francis W., 74, 80, 100
Murray, Gladstone, 337, 344, 348

Naismith, James, 67n, 196n
Nash, Paul, 351, 366, 373n
National Civil Liberties Bureau (NCLB), 251–3, 271
National Council for Civil Liberties (NCCL), 226–7, 262n, 271–4
National Home-Reading Union (NHRU), 19, 20–22, 24, 53
Neal, Mary, 51, 114, 186
Nearing, Scott, 205, 239
Neilson, Francis, 284–5, 287, 294, 295, 315
Nelles, Walter R., 226n, 252, 253
Nightingale, John, 233, 264
Nock, Albert Jay, 284–5, 287–8, 295, 299, 300, 315

407

Nott, C. Stanley, 22, 53, 55, 110, 261, 316–21, 325–27, 331, 375

O'Brien, Kate, 45–6, 320, 326
Odell, Carol, 156n, 365n
Odell, Dorothy (née Fuller), born 4; singing voice 4; marries Hamilton Irving 38–9; abandoned by Irving 59; starts illustrating folksongs and ballads 116; finds Alum Cottage with Cynthia 186; war job with RAF 261; marries Jack Odell 261; looks after Jeffrey 267–8, and Annis 332, 370; illustrates books by Barretts 374; emigrates to Australia 374; her book of illustrated children's singing games is published 374; receives the Order of Australia 374
Odell, Jack, 261, 325, 365
Ogden, C. K., 15, 268–71, 320, 328, 331, 350n
Orage, Alfred R., 284, 326, 375
Osborne, Thomas Mott, 154
Owens College, 2, 4, 5, 6, 7, 11, 49, 65, 86, 252

Palmer raids, 283
Pankhurst, Christabel, 24n, 49, 57
Parker, Dr (psychoanalyst), 228, 231, 292, 304
Parrish, Maxfield, 133, 135
Parry, Sir Hubert, 55n, 59, 188
Paton, J. B., 19, 21, 95
Paul, Alice, 217, 218, 250
Peabody, Charles and Jeannette, 89, 95, 117, 125
Peabody, Josephine, 117–18
People's Council, 181, 221–2, 225, 239–43, 248, 252
Peter Pan, 12–14, 27, 29, 33n, 35, 37, 39, 40–1, 43, 45, 47, 49, 51, 53, 55, 57, 59–61, 65–6, 97, 272
Pethick-Lawrence, Emmeline, 24n, 40n, 51, 114, 119, 127
Pethick-Lawrence, Frederick, 40n, 109, 120, 272
Pickering, Ruth, 151, 178, 259, 289, 334, 351, 355, 364, 369
Pinchot, Amos, 150, 166, 203, 218, 219, 226n, 259, 289, 334
Pound, Ezra, 375–6
Powys, John Cowper, 91
Powys, Llewellyn, 281, 289

Radio Times, 313, 338, 343–5, 347, 350–3, 361–3, 367, 380
Rae, John (aka Jack) and Helen, 68, 88, 93, 98, 100, 136, 151, 176, 187–8, 192
Rauh, Ida, 199, 301n, 369
Readers' Review (RR), 21–22, 32, 34–5, 54
Reed, John (aka Jack), 178n, 246, 249, 254, 260, 307, 332n
Reiss, Winold, 154, 164
Reith, John (later 1st Baron Reith), 335, 337–8, 341–5, 348–9, 352–3, 361, 379
Rendel, Frances Elinor (known as Ellie), 353–4
Rhys, Ernest 53, 76
Robinson, Boardman, 178–9, 207, 254, 255
Roosevelt, President Franklin and Mrs, 88n, 96, 113, 128,
Roosevelt, Theodore, 116, 201
Royde-Smith, Naomi, 327–8
RR, *see Readers' Review*
Ruskin, John, 19n, 20, 52, 128, 379
Russell, Dora (née Black), 264, 268, 375n
Russell, Lord Bertrand, 15, 33–4, 109, 184, 202, 208, 233, 262, 264, 268, 270–71, 273, 289, 319–20, 325n, 375
Russell Sage Foundation, 67n, 102, 141

Sackville, Lady Margaret, 109, 160
Sadler, Michael, 33n, 53
Sanborn, Franklin B., 76, 81n
Sassoon, Siegfried, 58, 270
Saturday Westminster, 54, 327; see also *Weekly Westminster* and *Westminster Gazette*
Sayre, Francis, 132, 258
Sayre, J. Nevin, 258, 287
Scholes, Percy, 345, 351, 359, 361
Schwimmer, Rosika, 114, 119, 127, 156
Scopes, John T., 92, 211, 235n
Seccombe, Thomas, 21, 34
Secor, Lella Faye, 157, 201, 221, 223, 239, 243, 268
Sedition Act (1798), 223; (May 1918) 257
Selfridge, Gordon, 32, 269, 343; his wife and daughter 269n
Sewall, May Wright, 122
Sharp, Cecil, 11n, 51n, 59, 61, 65n, 70, 91, 102, 107, 125, 129, 152, 212

Index

Shaw, George Bernard, 23, 115, 208, 262n, 270, 273, 342, 368
Sheepshanks, Mary, 34, 109
Shelly, Rebecca, 201, 220–1, 239, 243
Sheridan, Clare, 308
Sieveking, Lance, 352, 366–7
'silent sentinels', 217–8, 235, 250, 318
Sinclair, Upton, 226n, 247, 301n
Sowerby, Leo, 102
Spender, J. A., 327
SRC, see Student Representative Council
Steffens, Lincoln, 68, 179, 253, 264, 307
Stevens, Doris, 254, 307
Stevens, Frank, 242
Stobart, John, 344, 345, 353
Stokes, Helen Phelps, 226n, 252, 301n
Stokes, Rose Pastor, 252n, 253 (illustration)
Strachey, Lytton, 331, 353
Student Representative Council (SRC), 6–9, 11

Taft, President William H., 78, 79, 99, 130, 157, 166
Tagore, Rabindranath, 136
Tarbell, Ida, 68, 158, 161
Thomas, Ewan, 265
Thomas, Norman Mattoon, 1, 10, 170, 202n, 205, 218, 220, 225n, 226n, 239, 247–9, 258, 265, 273, 287, 300, 359
Thompson, Colonel Means, 79, 92
Tiffany, shop and family, 73, 101
Tiger Lily, see Kathleen WHEELER
Time & Tide, 326, 338
Transatlantic Literary Agency, 318–21, 325–6, 328, 331
Trotsky, Leon, 16, 308, 330, 332n, 371
Twain, Mark, 78n, 139, 208

Union of Democratic Control (UDC), 109, 119, 123, 130n, 157n, 262n, 269, 271, 273
University Review, 10, 11, 14–17, 22, 32–3, 39, 43, 53, 167, 254, 273, 327

van Wienen, Mark W., 118, 120, 205, 208n
Vaughan Williams, Ralph, 11n, 33, 55
Villard, Fanny Garrison, 113, 142, 163
Villard, Oswald Garrison, 113, 142, 143, 163, 171, 217–19, 221n, 225n, 248, 249n, 270n, 285, 364

Volk, Douglas, 68, 151, 159

Wald, Lilian, 201, 203, 218, 220
War-against-War Exhibition, 144, 146–8, 149, 154, 157, 172–3, 202, 211, 217, 284n
Ward, Basil Vernon, 9, 22, 36, 55, 71; marries Riss 80–1; and RAMC 123, 174; refuses to let Riss return to US with her sisters 188; 261, 325, 369n, 374
Ward, Riss (née Fuller), born 4; plays harp and studies at RCM 4–5; graduates 13; finds Laurel Cottage 26; attends Woodbrooke 43–5, 48, 50–2; holidays with Vaughan Williams 55; sings for Cecil Sharp 59, 61; marries Basil Ward 80; war job with RAF 261; looks after Walter's children 325, 347; cares for Walter 353–4; burns Walter's papers 365; 373 (illustration); performs on BBC radio 374; death 374
Waugh, Alec, Arthur and Evelyn, 320–1;
Weekly Westminster, 327–9, 338, 342, 350
Welby, Lady Victoria, 15
Wells, H. G., 22, 32n, 208, 331
Wessex, John (Walter's pseudonym), 58
Westminster Gazette, 54
Wendy (from *Peter Pan*), 14, 27, 29, 36, 40, 43, 66, 100, 236
Wheeler, Kathleen (aka Tiger Lily), 14, 24, 97–9, 211, 240n
White House, 79, 80, 89–92, 99, 114, 132, 156, 217, 249–50, 318
Wilkinson, Norman, 154, 164
Wilson, Monica (née Dehn; daughter of Cynthia), birth 324–5; remembers Walter 342
Wilson, President Woodrow, his wife and daughters, 67n, 79n, 89; enjoys Fuller Sisters' performance at the White House 90; sends birthday card to Cynthia 94; 114, 125, 127n, 129, 130n, 131n; at Cornish 132; discusses women's suffrage with Max 142n; 155, 156, 157, 158, 160, 163, 164, 170, 172, 173, 179, 181; hosts Fuller Sisters at Shadow Lawn 195; 202, 203, 206, 207, 208; declares war on Germany 216; 217, 218, 220, 233n, 234n, 235, 239; personally supports the American Alliance for Labour and Democracy 240; 243, 244;

409

Wilson, President Woodrow, his wife and daughters (*continued*), writes to Max 246; 247, 249n; supports women's suffrage 250; intervenes in favour of the *World Tomorrow* 258; 264, 287, 291. *See also* Fourteen Points

Winter, Ella, 264

Wise, Rabbi Stephen S. 22, 71, 143, 171, 218, 219, 234, 240, 276

Witherspoon, Fannie May, 245

Wolfit, Donald, 376

Woman's Peace Party (WPP), 119–20, 125–6, 129, 132, 146, 155–6, 158, 160, 163, 166–7, 170–2, 177, 188–9, 192n, 201–04, 207n, 209, 211, 215, 217, 219, 225–7, 234, 245, 248, 250–1, 254, 266, 269, 283, 285, 319, 341, 370n

Wood, Hollingsworth, 149, 161, 170, 201, 218, 220, 225n, 226, 239, 248, 252

Woodbrooke (Quaker college), 41, 43–5, 47, 49–52, 59, 146, 248n

Woolf, Leonard, 21, 331n

Woolf, Virginia, 21, 34, 353–4n

World Tomorrow, The, 248–9, 255, 257–9, 265–6, 268, 270, 287–8, 296, 319, 380

Young, Joy, 206

Lightning Source UK Ltd.
Milton Keynes UK
UKHW011941091221
395336UK00002B/54